The Water Works Directory And Statistics ...,
Volume 27

WATER WORKS

DIRECTORY AND

STATISTICS.

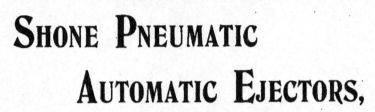

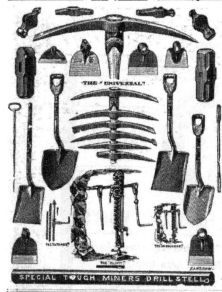

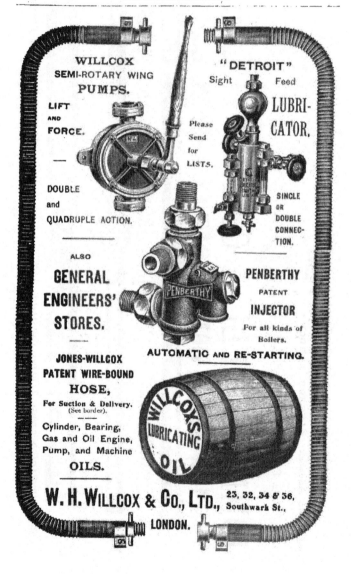

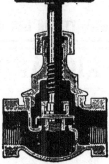

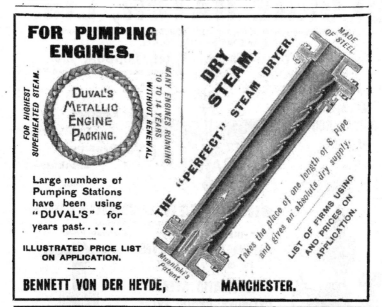

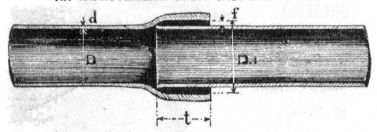

TWENTY-SEVENTH ISSUE.]

THE

WATER WORKS DIRECTORY AND STATISTICS,

1907.

INCLUDING

ALPHABETICAL INDEX OF OFFICIALS,

AND

LIST OF ASSOCIATIONS OF WATER ENGINEERS.

London:

HAZELL, WATSON AND VINEY, LD.,

52, LONG ACRE, W.C.

1907.

AWARDED GOLD MEDAL, MILAN INTERNATIONAL EXHIBITION, 1906.

REGISTERED TRADE MARK

BELDAM'S
PILOT
PACKING.

Also Manufacturers of the PATENT CORRUGATED METALLIC VALVE.

THE BELDAM PACKING & RUBBER CO.,
93 & 94, Gracechurch St., London, E.C.

TEL. No.: 192 CENTRAL.   TEL. ADD. "CORRUGATED."

HARRIS AND PEARSON,
STOURBRIDGE, ENGLAND.

Telegrams: "FIRECLAY, STOURBRIDGE."   *Telephone:* BRIERLEY HILL, No. 7.

MANUFACTURERS OF
Fire-Clay Gas Retorts.
BEST FIRE-BRICKS.
LUMPS and TILES of every description.
SPECIAL BOILER SEATING BLOCKS.
FLUE COVERS & FUEL SAVING COVERING BRICKS.
WHITE & COLOURED GLAZED BRICKS.
PORCELAIN BATHS. STAFFORDSHIRE BLUE BRICKS AND
EARTHENWARE SANITARY PIPES.
Best Retort Balls, Cast Iron Retort Mouth-Pieces, Fittings and Lids.
CAST IRON GAS AND WATER PIPES.
WROUGHT IRON AND LEAD TUBING.
LARGE STOCK ALWAYS ON HAND.   INSPECTION INVITED.

CONTENTS.

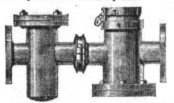

PREFACE.

WE beg to tender our hearty thanks to the Managers, Engineers, and Secretaries of the various Water Undertakings, for their kindness and courtesy in supplying the data from which we have compiled the greater portion of this, the Twenty-seventh Edition of "THE WATER WORKS DIRECTORY AND STATISTICS."

Every effort has been made to bring the volume right up to date, and to give the fullest and most reliable information obtainable.

We have the satisfaction of announcing that The Association of Water Engineers, appreciating the value of general information relative to the Water Undertakings of this Country, have given their support and assistance in the preparation of the present volume, and in presenting the work to our subscribers, we beg to call attention to the large increase in the bulk of the present issue as compared with previous issues, and to hope that the additional information now published will prove of great value.

It is also hoped that as the value of this publication becomes more generally appreciated, it will be possible to make it even more comprehensive than it is at present.

The "List of Associations" and "The Index of Officials" are again included.

THE EDITOR.

52, LONG ACRE, LONDON, W.C.,
July, 1907.

GENERAL INDEX.

WATERWORKS
FILTERS.

THE CANDY AUTOMATIC COMPRESSED AIR AND OXIDIZING SYSTEM.

Is THE MOST EFFICIENT for Removing from Water Peaty or other Discoloration, Iron, Organic Impurities in Solution and Suspension, as well as Bacteria, rendering Supplies Pure, Palatable and Sparkling.

MORE ECONOMICAL THAN SAND OR ANY OTHER FILTER.

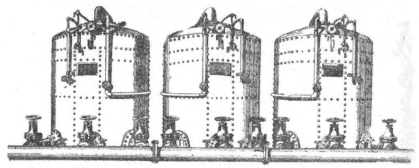

Part of a Battery of Filters at the Cardiff Corporation Waterworks for dealing with a million gallons daily.

Adopted by the Corporations of HARROGATE, MERTHYR, HASTINGS, NEWPORT, MON., CARDIFF, by the WEST GLOUCESTERSHIRE WATERWORKS COMPANY, and many other Public and Private Authorities in this Country, on the Continent, and in the Colonies, and by H.M. GOVERNMENT, WAR OFFICE DEPARTMENT.

For Particulars, Reports and Estimates, apply to—
THE OANDY FILTER COMPANY, LTD.,
5, Westminster Palace Gardens, Westminster, London, S.W.
Telegrams: "CIMOLITE, LONDON."   *Post Office Telephone*: No. 1057 VICTORIA.

GENERAL INDEX OF OFFICIALS

OF

WATER WORKS.

(*viz.*)

Fagg, J.	..	Tonbridge	Gisby, G. H.	.. Ware
Fawcett, A.	..	Cleckheaton	Glass, J. ..	.. Met. Water Board
Fawcett, J.	..	Hetton	Gledhill, J. M.	.. Filey
Fenten, M.	..	Ashton-under-Lyme	Gleig, Col. A. C.	.. Leatherhead
Fenwick, J. B.	..	East Retford	Glover, J. J.	.. Dumfries
Ferguson, J. B.	..	Duns	Glover, Alderman T.	Pontefract
Fergusson, W.	..	Barrow-in-Furness	Goldsworthy, T.	.. Newport (Mon.)
Ffrench, H. S.	..	Trowbridge	Gooch, G. ..	.. Herne Bay
Field, J. H.	..	Huddersfield	Gordon, H.	.. Bridport
Finch, W. C.	..	Chatham	Gordon, J.	.. Old Meldrum
Finlayson, M.Provost	Crieff		Gordon, W.	.. Aberdeen
Fisher, H. O.	..	Rhymney	Gothard, S. A.	.. Alcester
Fitzsimmons, G.M...	Stony Stratford		Goudie, A. H.	.. Stirling
Fitzwilliam, Earl	..	Malmesbury	Gouinon, R.	.. Menzies (W.A.)
Fooks, C. C S.	..	South Essex	Gould, R. T.	.. Glastonbury
Forbes, A. H.	..	Saffron Walden	Gowan, J. H. W.	.. Dumfries
Ford, J.	..	Duns	Grace, A. W.	.. Launceston
Forde, H. ..		Hoylake	Graham, A.	.. Mansfield
Forster, A. L.	..	Newcastle-on-Tyne	Graham, C.	.. Kendal
Forster, C. D.	..	Bedlington	Graham, W. V.	.. Epsom
Foster, C. H.	..	Chipping Ongar	Graham, W. V.	.. Sutton
Foster, E. P.	..	Wells	Grainger, A.	.. Sevenoaks
Foster, H. D.	..	Newquay	Grainger, T. B.	.. Ely
Foster, W.	..	Chesham	Grange & Wintring-	
Fowlds, W.	..	Keighley	ham	.. Gt. Grimsby
Fowle, W.	..	Northallerton	Grant, W.	.. Portsmouth
Fowler, Major	..	Louth	Gratton, J.	.. Wirksworth
Fox, C.	..	St. Albans	Gray, A. B.	.. Falkirk
Fox, C. J.	..	South Essex	Gray, B. Mac-	
Fox, D. M.	..	Santos	Gregor	.. Selby
Francis, S.	..	Clacton	Gray, C. E.	.. Hemel Hempstead
Francomb, Ald.R.W.	Warrington		Gray-Owen, J	.. Llangollen
Franey, E.	..	Banbury	Gray, W.	.. Birmingham
Frank, J.	..	Pickering	Gray, W. W.	.. Cambridge
Freeman, A. W.	..	Purleigh	Green, B. J.	.. Kidderminster
Freeman, A. W.	..	Southminster	Greenhalgh, W. W.	Wakefield
Freke, A. D. Hussey	Highworth		Greenhow, E.	.. Hetton
Frew, A.	..	Kilsyth	Greenshields, N.	.. Bedford
Friend, C. A.	..	Seville	Greenslade, G.	.. South Hants
Frost, J. K.	..	Cromer	Greenwood, E. S.	.. Thetford
Fry, H. C.	..	Clevedon	Gregson, J.	.. Padiham
			Grieves, W. H.	.. Buxton
			Griffith, F. ..	.. Leicester
			Griffith, Percy	.. Skegness
Gainsford, Ald.T.R.	Sheffield		Griffith, Percy	.. Gainsborough
Gamon, J. P.	..	Neston	Griffith, T. P.	.. Southport
Garland, F. J.	..	Frimley	Griffiths, H. L.	.. Brecon
Garner, J.	..	Glossop	Griffiths, H...	.. Kenilworth
Garry, Provost G. ..	Lochgelly		Griffiths, R. T.	.. Hay
Gavin, L.	..	Mullingar	Groves, A. ..	.. Henley-on-Thames
Gawley, W.	..	Monte Video	Guiton, P. P.	.. Jersey
Gayner, R. H.	..	Sunderland	Gunning, J. H.	.. Calne
Geer, L. S.	..	South Oxfordshire	Gutteridge, A.	.. Dunstable
Gibbon, J.	..	Haverfordwest		
Gibson, W.	..	Kilmarnock		
Gill, J.	..	Bangor		
Gill, J. C.	..	Peterborough	Haddock, J. W.	.. Pontefract
Giraud, F. F.	..	Faversham	Haldane, W.	.. Bridge of Allan

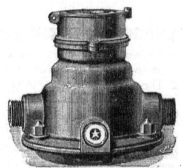

LISTS OF ASSOCIATIONS

OF

MANAGERS & ENGINEERS

OF

WATERWORKS.

ASSOCIATIONS OF WATER ENGINEERS.

ENGLAND.

Association.	Date of Foundation.	President,	Secretary's Name and Address.	No. of Members.	Date of Meetings 1907.	Place of Meetings.
The Association of Water Engineers.	1896	Robert H. Swindlehurst, M.Inst. C.E. (1903-4. Wm. Millhouse, Assoc. M. Inst. C.E. (1906-7). C. Sanity, M.I. Mech. E., (1907-8).	Percy Griffith, M. Inst. C.E., F.G.S., 54, Parliament Street, Westminster, S.W.	332	June 6, 7, and 8, and December.	Windsor
The Institution of Civil Engineers.	1818	Sir Alex. B. W. Kennedy, LL.D, F.R.S.	J. H. T. Tudsbery, D.Sc., Great George Street, S.W.	*8363	(Annual)Last Tuesday in April, 8 p.m. (Ordy.) Tuesdays, Nov. to April, 8 p.m.	Great George Street, Westminster, S.W.
Provincial Water Companies' Association.	1885	Sir Theodore Fry, Bart., Chairman. Alfred J. Alexander, Deputy Chairman.	R. L. S. Badham, 1, Victoria Street, Westminster, S.W.	—		

GERMANY.

Association.	Date of Foundation.	President,	Secretary's Name and Address.	No. of Members.	Date of Meetings 1907.	Place of Meetings.
German Association of Gas and Water Engineers.	1859	T. Nolte, General-Direktor der Neuen Gas-Aktien-Gesellschoft, Berlin.	Prof. Dr. Bunte, Karlsruhe, Baden, Germany.	1007	June annually.	Hanover, 1904. Coblenz, 1905. Bremen, 1906. Mannheim, 1907.

UNITED STATES.

Association.	Date of Foundation.	President,	Secretary's Name and Address.	No. of Members.	Date of Meetings 1907.	Place of Meetings.
American Waterworks Association.	1880	Dabney, H. Maury, C.E., 129, N. Jefferson Ave., Peoria, Ill.	J. M. Diven, 14, George Street, Charleston, S.C.	666	June, 17-22, 1907	Toronto, Ontario, Canada.
New England Waterworks Association.	1882	John C. Whitney, Newton Mass,	Willard Kent, Narragansett Pier, R.I.	700	6 meetings during the year.	Boston.
Western Society of Engineers.	1869	W. L. Abbott.	J. H. Warder, 1734-41, Monadnock Block, Chicago.	925 1/1/07	Generally 1st & 3rd Wednesdays, and 2nd Friday each month.	Chicago.

* All classes, including students.

Section I.

DIRECTORY AND STATISTICS

OF

WATER WORKS

IN

GREAT BRITAIN AND IRELAND.

1907.

ERRATA.

Alton (Hants.).   Page 10.
    For " G. Bertram Hartgee (Surveyor)," read " G. Bertram Hartfree."

Blaenavon.   Page 45.
    Add :—" Consulting Engineer, Percy Griffith, M.I.C.E., F.G.S."

Cheltenham.   Page 76.
    For " J. S. Pickering, A.M.I.C.E.," read " J. S. Pickering, M.I.C.E.'

Derwent Valley.   Page 103.
    For " Edward Sandeman," read " Edward Sandeman, M.I.C.E."

Kingston-on-Thames.   Page 187.
    For "Kingston-on-Thames (supplied by Lambeth Water Company),"
    read "Kingston-on-Thames (supplied by Metropolitan Water
    Board)."

Lincoln.   Page 200.
    For " Engineer in charge, Neil McKechnie, Barron," read " Engineer in
    charge, Neil McKechnie Barron."

Ramsgate.   Page 274.
    For " Secretary," read " Town Clerk." " F. N. Ritson," read " Johnson.'

Rhymney.   Page 278.
    For " Rhymney and Aber Valley Gas and Water Company, Ltd.," read
    " Rhymney and Aber Valley Gas and Water Company."

Skegness.   Page 306.
    For " The Earl of Scarborough," read " The Earl of Scarbrough."
    For " Percy Griffiths," read " Percy Griffith, M.I.C.E., F.G.S."
    For " Special Acts," read " Special Act."
    For " New supply," read " New works (1907) at Welton."

South-West Suburban.   Page 314.
    Add :—" Engineer, Daniel Rankine."

Sunderland and South Shields.   Page 327.
    For " Alfred B. E. Blackburn, B.S.C., etc.," read "Alfred B. E. Blackburn,
    B.Sc., etc."
    For " F. and C. Hawksley," read " T. and C. Hawksley."

Torquay.   Page 339.
    For " Samuel C. Chapman, A.M.I.C.E.," read "Samuel C. Chapman,
    M.I.C.E."

Tunbridge Wells.   Page 343.
    For " W. H. Maxwell, A.M.I.C.E.," read " W. H. Maxwell, M.I.C.E.'

Tynemouth.   Page 344.
    " F. R. Hull, M.I.C.E., is not now in charge of Font Reservoir."

Wigan.   Page 372.
    Add :—" Engineer and Manager, Thos. L. Hughes."

WATER WORKS.

PARTICULARS RECEIVED TOO LATE FOR CLASSIFICATION.

Broadstairs, Kent. Railway, S.E. & C. Distance from London, 74 miles.
Authority, Broadstairs and St. Peters Urban District Council.
Clerk to Council, L. A. Skinner.
Office, Council Office, Broadstairs.
Works established, 1859 ; purchased by local authority, 1901.
Special Act, Broadstairs and St. Peters Water and Improvement Act, 1901.
Loans, £60,604.
Interest on loan, 3¾ per cent. for 50 years.
Towns and villages in area supplied, Broadstairs, St. Peters, Reading Street, North-
down, Westwood, Northwood, Dumpton.
Annual profit on undertaking, including Capital charges, £236, after paying
instalment of principal and interest on loans.
Total population of area supplied, 7,193 ; estimated summer population, 15,000.
Average death rate, 11·96 per 1,000.
Source of supply in use, adits in the chalk, 160 ft. below surface, 2 miles from
town.
Storage in service reservoirs, 200,000 gals.
Character of water, good ; total hardness, 18° ; filtration, none.
Head on distributing mains, maximum, 50 ft., minimum, 21 ft.
Daily consumption per head of population—domestic, 28·27 gals. ; trade, 6·16 gals.
Annual supply of water, 125,000,000 gals.
Maximum day's supply, 540,000 in August.
Number of meters in use, about 260.
Length of mains, about 30 miles.
Scale of charges—domestic assessment, 1s. 3d. on £, gross estimated rental ; 5s
for every w.c. ; 6s. for bath.
Trade price per 1,000 gals., 1s. 6d. by meter.
Municipal　　　,,　　1s. 6d.　　,,

Rothwell.
Authority, Rothwell Urban District Council.
Chairman, F. Barlow.
Clerk to authority, Wm. Tozer.
Engineer, T. C. Betts.
Council Office, Market House, Rothwell.
Works constructed, 1902.
Loan, £9,650.
Population supplied, 4,000.
Average death rate (4 years), 10·78.
District of supply, Rothwell.
Sources of supply, the old Shotwell Mill, about 40 acres in extent.
Storage capacity, 200,000 gals.
Daily supply per head for all purposes, 40 gals.
Annual supply of water, 15,000,000 gals.
Character of water, 21¾° hardness.
Head on distributing mains—maximum, 150 ft. ; minimum, 18 ft.
Authorised charge by meter, 1s. per 1,000 gals.
Present average　　,,　　,,　　9d.　　,,
No. of meters, 22.
Length of rising main, 1 mile ; distributing mains, 4 miles.

I.—DIRECTORY AND STATISTICS
OF
WATER WORKS IN GREAT BRITAIN AND IRELAND.

Abbots Langley (supplied by RICKMANSWORTH).

Abbots Kerswell, (supplied by TORQUAY).

Abdy, Yorks (supplied by WATH-UPON-DEARNE).

Aberaman (supplied by Aberdare).

Aberavon, Wales. Railways, G.W., and Rhondda and Swansea Bay. Distance from London, 202 miles.
   Authority, Corporation.
   Secretary, Town Clerk.
   Engineer, James Roderick.
   Loan, £10,000.
   No Special Act for water.
   Total population of area supplied, 10,000.
   Sources of supply, springs.
   Storage capacity, 6,250,000 gals.
   Character of water, soft.
   Death rate, 17·5 per 1,000.
   Number of meters, 10.
   Assessment charge, A.
   Price per 1,000 gals.—according to consumption.

Abercanaid (supplied by MERTHYR TYDVIL).

Abercarn, Mon. Railway G.W. Distance from London, 161 miles.
   Authority, Abercarn Urban District Council.
   Chairman, Chairman of Council.
   Clerk to Council, T. S. Edwards, Solicitor.
   Total capital invested, including loans, £20,000.
   Towns and villages within the area of control, Abercarn, Newbridge, Crumlin, Cwmcarn.
   Works established, 1892.
   Total population of area of control (1901), 14,000.
   Estimated population actually supplied, 14,000.
   Source of supply, springs.
   Character of water, soft.
   Storage capacity, 3,500,000 gals.
   Daily consumption per head, 20 to 25 gals.
   Assessment charge, 1s. in £ on rateable value.

1

Abercwmboi (supplied by ABERDARE).

Aberdare, Wales. Railway, G.W. Distance from London, 177 miles.
　　Authority, District Council.
　　Chairman of Committee, Rees Llewellyn.
　　Resident Engineer, Owen Williams.
　　Clerk, Thomas Phillips, Solicitor.
　　Office, Town Hall.
　　Loan, £100,000.
　　Area supplied, 16,000 acres.
　　Towns and villages in the area of control, Aberdare, Hirwain, Llwydcoed,
　　　　Penywain, Cwmdare, Trecynon, Abernant, Aberaman, Cwmbach, Cwmaman,
　　　　Abercwmboi.
　　Works established, 1858. Special Acts, 1870, 1894.
　　Total population of area of control: 1901, 45,000; 1907, 50,000.
　　Total number of consumers, 10,000.
　　Annual supply of water for all purposes, 401,500,000 gals.
　　Maximum day consumption, 1,200,000 gals.
　　Source of supply, gathering grounds at Bwllfa, Nanthir, and Nantawel.
　　Population of drainage area, none.
　　Nature of drainage area, mountain land, sheep pasture, peaty soil on sandstone
　　　　and millstone grit.
　　Maximum annual rainfall over drainage area, 96·15 inches, 1892.
　　Minimum　　,,　　　,,　　　,,　　　,,　　41·40　　,,　　1889.
　　Average　　,,　　　,,　　　,,　　　,,　　58·29　　,,　　period 10 years.
　　The Committee have no control over the area.
　　Storage capacity—
　　　　Nantawell capacity, 78,000,000 gals.
　　　　Nanthir　　　,,　　42,000,000　,,
　　　　Bwllfa　　　　,,　　7,000,000　,,
　　　　Storage ponds ,,　　1,250,000　,,
　　Filtering area, 800 square yards, in two filter beds, and an installation of high
　　　　pressure filters, total capacity of 2,750,000 gals. per day.
　　Analysis of water—
　　　　Appearance in 2-ft. tube, faintly green, clear.
　　　　Reaction, alkaline.

Total solid matter—		
(a) volatile		—
(b) fixed		—
Appearance on ignition		—
Total hardness—	Parts per 100,000.	8.0
(a) Temporary		—
(b) Permanent		—
Chlorine		·8
Nitrogen as nitrates		Practically nil.
Saline or free ammonia		—·0010
Organic (or albuminoid) ammonia		—·0012
Poisonous metals		Nil.
Nitrites		,,
Phosphates		,,
Sulphates		

　　　　Microscopic Examination of ⎱　　Practically nil.
　　　　　　the Sediment　　　　　　⎰　　Animalculæ, rare.
　　Remarks—A moderately soft water. Chemical analysis indicates the sample to
　　　　be of a high degree of organic purity.
　　Death rate, 16·38 per 1,000.
　　Number of meters, 70.
　　Length of mains, 50 miles.
　　Scale of charges—assessment rateable value.

ABERDARE—*continued.*

Scale of charges for supply by meter, quarterly consumption—

		Gallons.		Per 1,000 Gallons, or Fraction of ditto.	
				s.	d.
Under	..	10,000	..	1	6
10,000	and under	20,000	..	1	5
20,000	"	30,000	..	1	4
30,000	"	40,000	..	1	3
40,000	"	50,000	..	1	2
50,000	"	60,000	..	1	1
60,000	"	70,000	..	1	0
70,000	"	80,000	..	0	11
80,000	"	90,000	..	0	10
90,000	"	100,000	..	0	9
100,000	"	500,000	..	0	8
500,000	"	1,000,000	..	0	7
1,000,000	and upwards	..	..	0	6

Total water rent received, £5,000.

Aberdeen. Railways, Caledonian, N.B., and G.N. of Scotland.
Authority, Town Council of the City and Royal Burgh of Aberdeen.
Chairman, the Lord Provost.
Secretary, Wm. Gordon, Town Clerk.
Engineer in charge, Wm. Dyack, M.I.C.E., Burgh Surveyor.
Office, Town House, Aberdeen.
Total capital invested, including loans, £313,366.
Profit, £20,000, sinking fund to reduce debt.
Works opened, 1866.
Special Acts, Aberdeen Police and Waterworks Act, 1862, 1867, 1881, 1885, 1893.
Total population of area of control, 1881, 105,538; 1891, 124,943; 1901, 153,497.
Estimated population actually supplied, 175,000.
Average death rate, 20·4 per 1,000, period five years.
The supply is drawn from the river Dee at Cairnton, 21 miles west from Aberdeen.
Total quantity of water drawn from river Dee, 2,372,500,000 gals.
Water available, Parliamentary powers to draw 8,000,000 gals. per diem from river Dee.
Population of drainage area of river Dee west of in-take, 11,462. Only small proportion of area under cultivation.
The Town Council, after obtaining Parliamentary powers, have laid out and manage irrigation farms (area 37 acres) for the purification of the sewage of Kincardine-O'Neil, Aboyne, Ballater, and Bræmar villages situated on the drainage area of the river above the point of in-take.
Geological data, chiefly granite and the older schistose rocks.
Character of water, soft; total hardness, 1·5° to 1·7°.
Filtration none; softening none.
Settling reservoir, Invercannie, capacity 12,000,000 gals.
Pumping stations, steam, Cults (mid service), capacity 99,000 gals. per hour.
    "   "   hydraulic, Cults (high service), capacity 12,000 gals. per hour.
Service reservoirs, Mannofield, No. 1 (low service)   "   6,000,000 gals., open.

"	"	"	" 2	"	"	12,000,000	" "
"	"	Cattofield	"	"	"	2,500,000	" "
"	"	Slopefield (mid service)	"		"	6,000,000	" "
"	"	Pitfodels (high service)			"	500,000	" "

Head on distributing mains—maximum, 220 feet; minimum, 30 feet.
Average consumption per head per day—domestic, 27·5 gals.; trade, &c., 11·5 gals.
Maximum day's consumption, 8,437,000 gals. in June, 1906.
Charges authorised, 2d. in the £ on owner; no limit on occupier.

ABERDEEN—*continued.*

    Present charges, 1¼d. in £ on owner ; 6d. on occupier.
    Price per meter, trade purposes, 7d. to 2d. per 1,000 gals.
    Number of meters, 814 trade meters, 80 Deacon meters.
    Length of distributing mains, 138 miles.

Aberdour, N.B. (supplied by DUNFERMLINE).

Aberfan, Glam. (supplied by MERTHYR TYDVIL).

Aberfeldy, Scotland. Railway, Highland.
    Authority, Aberfeldy Gas Light Company.
    Manager, James Clark.
    Secretary and Treasurer, Chas. Munro.
    Office, Union Bank Buildings.
    Town Clerk's Office, Aberfeldy.
    Share capital paid, £1,967. Dividend, 4 per cent.
    Area supplied, Aberfeldy only.
    Works established, 1854.
    Total population of area supplied, 1,500.
    Source of supply, Hill Burn.
    Character of water, soft.
    System of filtration, gravelly bed.
    Death rate, 15.333 per 1,000.
    Number of meters, about 200.
    Assessment charge, 1¼d. in the £.

Abergele, Flint (supplied by RHYL).

Abernant (supplied by ABERDARE).

Abersychan, Mon. (supplied by PONTYPOOL).

Abertillery, Mon. (G. and W.) Railway, G.W. Distance from London, 168¼ miles.
    Authority, Urban District Council.
    Works established, 1894.
    Total population of area supplied, 21,955.

Aberystwyth, Wales. Railways, Cambrian, Manchester and Milford. Distance from London, 243 miles.
    Authority, Corporation.
    Secretary, A. J. Hughes, Town Clerk.
    Engineer and Surveyor, Rees Jones.
    Cost of Works, £19,000.
    Area supplied, borough only.
    Works established, 1882. Special Acts, 1892.
    Total population of area supplied, 13,465.
    Annual supply of water, 125,000,000 gals.
    Daily consumption per head all purposes, 35 gals.
    Source of supply, Plynlimon Lake.
    Storage capacity, 55,000,000 gals.
    Character of water, soft.
    Death rate, 16·35 per 1,000.
    Number of meters, 28.
    Length of mains, 13 miles.
    Assessment charge, 2s. in £.
    Price per 1,000 gals. 6d.

Abingdon. Railway, G.W. Distance from London, 61 miles.
Authority, Corporation.
Chairman, The Mayor.
Secretary, Town Clerk.
Resident Engineer, G. Winship.
Office, Borough Buildings.
Works established, 1887. Special Act, Public Health Act, 1875.
Total population of area supplied, 6,480.
Sources of supply, wells in the coral rag, 4 miles from town.
Average death rate, 14 per 1,000.
Area supplied, town of Abingdon only.
Character of water, hard.
Storage capacity, nil.
Daily consumption per head, domestic, 5½ gals.
Number of meters, about 700.
Length of mains, about 8 miles.
Price per 1,000 gals., 1s.
Total water rent received, about £700.

Abridge (supplied by HERTS AND ESSEX).

Accrington. (G. and W.) Railways, L.Y., L.N.W., M. Distance from London, 226 miles.
Authority, Accrington District Gas and Water Board.
Chairman, D. C. Dewhurst.
Clerk to the Board, A. H. Aitken.
General Manager, Charles Harrison.
Accountant, W. B. Rhodes.
Office, St. James Street, Accrington.
Loans outstanding, £448,535.
Interest, 2¾ and 3½ per cent.
Towns and villages in area supplied—Accrington, Clayton-le-Moors, Great Harwood, Rishton, Church, Huncoat and Altham.
Works established, 1841.
Purchased by local authority, January 1st, 1895.
Special Acts—1841, 1854, 1863, 1869, 1893 ; Board's Act, 1894, 1905, 1906.
Sources of supply—gravitation and pumping station to high service reservoir.
Storage reservoirs - capacity, 550,000,000.
Filtration, sand and gravel.
Total population of area supplied, 89,000.
Annual death rate, 13·4.
Daily consumption per head, 21 gallons.
Total quantity of water supplied per annum, 511,000,000.
Charges authorised, domestic supply from £6 13s. 4d. p. cent. to £10 p. cent. on R.V.
Present rate charged,　　　 „　　 „　£5 0s. 0d.　　 „　£7 10s. „　　 „
Price charged per meter, 1s. 6d. to 6d. per 1,000 gals.
Annual loss on undertaking, including capital charges, £3,474.
Number of meters in use, 385.
Length of distributing mains, 62¼ miles.
Price per 1,000 gals., from 1s. 6d. to 6d.
Total water rent received, £21,193 16s. 3d.

Ackworth (supplied by PONTEFRACT).

Acocks Green (supplied by BIRMINGHAM).

Acomb (supplied by YORK).

Acre (supplied by Bury).

Acton Grange (supplied by Warrington).

Addingham (supplied by Bradford, Yorks).

Addlestone, Surrey (supplied by West Surrey Water Co.`.

Adel (supplied by Leeds).

Adwalton (supplied by Bradford, Yorks).

Ainsworth (supplied by Bolton).

Airdrie and **Coatbridge.** Railways, Caledonian and N.B.
Authority, Airdrie, Coatbridge and District Water Trust.
Chairman, Provost McCosh.
Clerk to Authority, John J. McMurdo.
Engineer and Manager, John Chisholm, C.E.
Office, Water Trust Buildings, Airdrie, near Glasgow.
Total capital invested, £478,296 14s. 4d.
Works established, 1846; purchased by Water Trust, 31st May, 1903.
Special Acts, 1846, 1874, 1890, 1892, 1899, 1900.
Total population of area supplied, 87,750.
Towns and villages within area of supply, Airdrie (portion of Barony parish),
Banrachnie, Boghall, Broomhouse, Baillieston, Calderbank, Caldervale, Coat-
bridge, Easterhouse, Glenboig, Hillhead, Moffat, Mount Vernon, Old and New
Monkland, Plains Glenmavis.
Source of supply—(a) Roughrigg, parish of Shotts, County of Lanark, about 6
miles S.E. of Airdrie. (b) Cowgill, parish of Lamington, County of Lanark,
8 miles from Biggar and 4 miles from Lamington Station. This gathering area
is situated S.E. of the Roughrigg area, about 33 miles distant.
Population on drainage areas, 875.
Nature of drainage areas, pasture lands.
Authority have no absolute control of drainage areas.
Quantity of water drawn, 1905-6, 1,285,990,960 gals.
Estimated quantity of water available per annum, 1,472,410,000.
Annual supply of water, domestic purposes　...　...　931,896,102 gals.
　　,,　　,,　　,,　trade (meter)　...　...　...　331,309,266　,,
　　,,　　,,　　,,　municipal purposes　...　...　21,305,592　,,
　　,,　　,,　　,,　in bulk to other authorities　...　280,000　,,
Daily consumption per head, domestic, 87·750; trade, 29·09.
Maximum day's supply, 3,750,000 gals. in June.
Analysis—

						Grains per Gallon.
Mineral matter...	...	...	...	...	...	5·04
Organic　,,　...	...	...	...	...	...	·51
Total solid matter	...	...	...	...	...	5·55
Nitrates ...	...	...	...	...	...	None.
Free ammonia ...	...	...	..	...	...	·001
Albuminoid ammonia ...	...	...	...	...	·009
Total ammonia...	...	..	...	...	...	·010
Temporary hardness	...	...	...	...	...	2·28°
Permanent　,,	...	...	...	...	...	1·53°
Total hardness ...	...	...	...	...	...	3·81°
Colour (Loch Katrine water equals 10)	...	...	10

AIRDRIE and COATBRIDGE—*continued.*

> The absence of Nitrates and the presence of only minute proportions of Free and
> Albuminoid Ammonia show that the water is free from all contamination by
> matter of the nature of sewage, and is exceedingly well adapted for drinking,
> cooking, and all household purposes, including washing.
> Filtration, sand, 3,500 square yards, for Roughrigg supply only.
> Average death rate, 14·66 per 1,000.
> Storage capacity—
> <table>
> <tr><td>Roughrigg reservoir</td><td>...</td><td>...</td><td>...</td><td>capacity</td><td>560,000,000 gals.</td></tr>
> <tr><td>Upper　　　,,　　　Cowgill</td><td>...</td><td>...</td><td></td><td>,,</td><td>230,000,000 ,,</td></tr>
> <tr><td>Lower　　　,,　　　,,</td><td>...</td><td>•••</td><td></td><td>,,</td><td>42,500,000 ,,</td></tr>
> </table>
> Service reservoirs, Old Clear Water Basin, Roughrigg　600,000 gals., open.
> 　,,　　　　,,　　New　,,　　,,　　,,　　,,　　3,000,000　,,　　,,
> Scale of charges—1/3 or 6¼ per cent. in the £ on annual value ; 25 per cent.
> extra for outside the area of supply.
> Supplied by meter from 6¼d. to 1/-, according to scale ; 25 per cent. extra
> outside area of supply.
> Number of meters in use, 400.
> Length of mains, about 125 miles.

Aismunderley (supplied by RIPON).

Albourne (supplied by BURGESS HILL).

Albrighton, Staffs. (supplied by WOLVERHAMPTON).

Alcester. Railways, M. and G.W. Distance from London, 121¼ miles.
Chairman, S. A. Gothard.
Secretary and Manager, J. H. Bomford.
Office, Swan Street.
Date of formation, 1877.
Population supplied, 11,400.
Source of supply, springs at Oversley.
Character of water, good.

Aldeburgh, Suffolk. Railway, G.E. Distance from London, 99⅓ miles.
Authority, Company.
Total population of area supplied, 2,500.
No returns supplied.

Aldenham, Herts. (supplied by COLNE VALLEY WATER CO.).

Alderley Edge (supplied by STOCKPORT).

Aldershot Camp (these works have been transferred by purchase to the ALDER-
SHOT GAS AND WATER CO.).

Aldershot. (G. and W.) Railways, L.S.W. and S.E. Distance from London, 34½
miles.
Authority, Aldershot Gas and Water Company.
Chairman, A. F. Wilson.
Secretary and General Manager, R. W. Edwards.

ALDERSHOT- -*continued.*

Office, Victoria Road.
Share Capital paid up, gas and water, £209,500.
Loan   „   „   „   £53,283.
Interest on loans—Mortgage, 3½ per cent.
　　　　　　　　Debenture, 4 per cent.
Dividend on gas and water—A, ordinary, 11½⅜ per cent.
　　　　　　　　B,   „   8½⅒ per cent.
　　　　　　　　E, F & G,   7 per cent.
　　　　　　　　C & D pref., 6 per cent.
　　　　　　　　E, F & G pref., 5 per cent.   Pref. stock, 5 per cent.
Area supplied, 4,178 acres.
Towns and villages in the area supplied—Aldershot Town, Aldershot Camp, and
　　Tongham village.
Works established, 1866.
Special Acts, 1866, 1895, and 1901 ; Provisional Orders, 1879, 1890, and 1903.
Population of area supplied, 20,000 civil, 20,000 military.
Death rate, 15 per 1,000.
Annual supply of water, 364,420,000 gals.
Source of supply, wells in chalk.
Storage capacity—Service reservoirs, ...　　...　　...　　...　　360,000 gals.
　　　　　　„　　　　„　　about to be constructed, 1,500,000 gals.
　　　　　High service tower,　　...　　...　　...　　60,000 gals.
　　　　　　　　　　　　　　　　　　　　　　1,920,000 gals

Character of water, 15° to 16° hardness—Very good, clear, and brilliant.
Average daily supply per head, Domestic, 24·5 gals.
　　„　　　„　　„　　„　　Trade   7·1　„
Charges authorised, 6 per cent. to 5 per cent. on Rack Rental or Annual Value.
　　„　　　„　　per meter, 1s. 6d. to 11d. per 1,000 gals.
No. of meters, 162.

Aldington, Worcester (supplied by EVESHAM).

Aldridge (supplied by SOUTH STAFFORDSHIRE WATERWORKS CO.).

Aldrington, Sussex (supplied by BRIGHTON).

Alexandria, Bonhill and **Jamestown,** Scotland.   Railways, Dumbarton and
Balloch Joint.
　　Authority, District Council
　　Chairman, James Shearer.
　　Secretary, A. H. Lindsay.
　　Manager, Daniel Murray.
　　Office, 124, Bridge Street.
　　Capital, £12,000.
　　Works established, 1880.
　　Total population supplied, 15,000.
　　Annual supply of water, 160,000,000 gals.
　　Sources of supply—Loch Lomond, and partly gravitation.
　　Storage capacity, 5,000,000 gals.
　　System of filtration, sand filters.
　　Character of water, good.
　　Death rate, 14 per 1,000.

ALEXANDRIA—*continued.*

Number of meters, 22.
Scale of charges—assessment charge, 1s. 2d. in the £.
Price per 1,000 gals., trade, 6d.

Alfreton, Derby. Railway, M. Distance from London, 135 miles.
Authority, Alfreton Urban District Council.
A new undertaking now in hand at a cost of £15,000.

Alkham (supplied by FOLKESTONE).

Allestree (supplied by DERBY).

Allithwaite (supplied by GRANGE OVER SANDS).

Alloa, N.B. Railways, N. B. & Caledonian. Distance from Edinburgh, 30 miles.
Authority, Alloa Town Council.
Chairman, John J. Calder.
Secretary, F. G. Ewing.
Resident Engineer, Andrew Mackie.
Office, Burgh Chambers, Alloa.
Loans outstanding, £43,788.
Interest on loan, 3 and 3¼ per cent.
Towns and villages in the area supplied—Part of Alloa and part of Clackmannan.
Works established, 1854.
Special Act, Alloa Water Act, 1891.
Total population supplied, 16,400.
Average death rate, 13·25
Sources of supply, Saline Hills.
Characteristics of water, soft ; total hardness, 6·5°.
Storage capacity, 437,500,000 gals.
System of filtration, downward, sand.
Pressure in mains, 45 lbs. per square inch maximum ; 15 lbs. minimum.
Average daily consumption per head, 48 gals.
Number of meters, 62.
Length of mains, 16 miles.
Charges authorised—6d. in £ to occupiers (fixed yearly) ; owners, public purposes
and shops, 1½d. in £.
Charges authorised by meter, 6d. to 3d. per 1,000 gals., fixed yearly.
Total water rent received, £2,533.

All Stretton, Salop.
Authority, All Stretton Waterworks Co., Ltd.
No returns supplied.

Alnwick (Rural District). Railways, G.N. and N.E. Distance from London, 309
miles.
Authority, Alnwick Rural District Council.
Office, Market Place, Alnwick.
Loan, £3,685. Interest, 3¼ per cent.
Area supplied—extensive colliery and agricultural district.
Works established, 1892. Special Acts, 1891.
Total population of area supplied, 12,519.
Daily consumption per head, domestic, 10 gals.
Sources of supply—spring at Sturton Grange.

ALNWICK (Rural District)—*continued.*

> Storage capacity, 26,000 gals.
> Character of water, good.
> Death rate, 15 per 1,000.
> Number of meters, 2.
> Length of mains, 10 miles.
> Assessment charge, 2¼d. per week per house.
> Price for 1,000 gals., 6d.

Alnwick (Urban District). Railways, G. N. and N. E. Distance from London, 300 miles.
> Authority, Alnwick Urban District Council.
> Secretary, R. Middlemas, Clerk to U.D.C., Alnwick.
> Engineer in charge, G. Wilson, C.E.
> Office, U.D.C. Offices, Green Bat, Alnwick.
> Total capital invested, including loans, £6,500 under Public Health Act.
> Interest on loan, 3½ to 4 per cent.
> Area of control, Alnwick and suburbs
> Works established, 1854. Special Acts, 1850, 1887.
> Estimated population actually supplied, 6,800.
> Daily consumption, 25 to 30 gals. per head.
> Source of supply, springs and borings flowing direct into gravitation mains.
> Filtered through sand filter-beds before entering service reservoir.
> Service reservoirs, one; capacity, 210,000 gals., covered.
> Death rate, 16·82, or deducting public institutions, 13·99.
> Character of water, 16° of hardness.
> Assessment charge, 4d. in the £ annually on £20,000 assessable value for Water Rates; rateable value, £25,000.
> Price per 1,000 gals., 6d.; taps in gardens, 2s. 6d. each.
> Number of meters in use, 15.
> Length of distributing mains, 10 miles.

Alphington (supplied by EXETER).

Alrewas (supplied by SOUTH STAFFORDSHIRE WATERWORKS Co.).

Altham (supplied by ACCRINGTON and partly by PADIHAM).

Alton, Hants. Railway, L.S.W. Distance from London, 46½ miles
> Authority, Alton Urban District Council.
> Chairman, Gerald Hall, J.P., Chairman of Council.
> Secretary, Bradley W. Trimmer, Clerk to the Council.
> Engineer in charge, G. Bertram Hartgee (Surveyor).
> Office, High Street, Alton.
> Loans, £7,914, borrowed for construction of works. These loans will be paid off in 1907.
> Interest, 3½ per cent.
> Works established, 1876.
> Total population of area supplied (1901 Census), 5,479.
> Total number of consumers, 5,000.
> Area supplied, Alton only and the Princess Louise Hospital.
> Source of supply, deep well at Windmill Hill, Alton. Top of well situated on middle chalk formation. Well 140 feet deep, boring 480 feet deep to upper greensand formation. Two large breweries have their own wells within a ¼ mile.
> Character of water, total hardness 19°.

ALTON—*continued.*

Filtering, none.
Annual supply of water, 60,000,000 gals.
Daily consumption per head, domestic and trade, 26 gals.
Storage capacity, 95,000 gals.
Number of meters in use, about 18.
Length of mains, about 6¼ miles.
Scale of charges—
    Assessment charge, 6d. in £ rateable value for domestic purposes and 4s. each
      per annum for cottages.
    Price per 1,000 gals., domestic, 6d. ; trade, 1s.
Total revenue received, £540 per annum.

Altofts (supplied by WAKEFIELD).

Altrincham (*see* NORTH CHESHIRE).

Alva, Scotland.   Railway, Alva.
Authority, Alva Town Council.
Works established, 1881.
Special Act, Burgh Gas Supply Scotland Act, 1876.
Total population of area supplied, 4,743.
Length of mains, 5 miles.

Alvaston (supplied by DERBY).

Amblecote (supplied by STOURBRIDGE).

Ambleside, Westmoreland.   Railway, L.N.W.   Distance from London, 265 miles.
Authority, Urban District Council.
Chairman, James Jackson.
Engineer, Manager and Secretary, J. T. Battersby.
Office, Church Street.
Loans outstanding, £16,313.
Interest on loan, 3 per cent.
Works established, 1866, taken over by the council, July 1st, 1898.
Total population supplied, 2,536.
Death rate, average 5 years, 10·50 per 1,000.
Area supplied, Ambleside only.
Sources of supply, Scandale Beck, green slate
Character of water, very pure and soft.
Storage capacity, 268,000 gals.
Daily consumption per head, 100 gals. for all purposes.
Maximum day's supply, 5,000,000 gals. in August.
Length of mains, 6 miles.
Scale of charges, assessment charge, 5 per cent. on rateable value, or 9d. per
    1,000 gals.
  Trade, 9d. per 1,000 gals.
  Municipal purposes, £20 per annum for flushing, watering streets, urinals, etc.
Total revenue received, £765.

Amersham, Bucks.   Railway, Metropolitan.   Distance from London, 23¾ miles.
Authority, Amersham, Beaconsfield and District Waterworks Co., Ltd.

AMERSHAM—*continued.*

Office, High Street, Amersham.
Share capital paid up, £12,000.
Loan, £3,000. Interest on ditto, 4 per cent.
Towns and villages supplied—Amersham, Beaconsfield, Chalfont St. Giles, Coleshill, part of Penn, part of Chesham Bois.
Works established, 1895.
Special Act, Water Orders Confirmation Act, 1896.
Total population of area supplied, 7,900.
Total number of consumers, 490, service.
Total quantity of water drawn, 40,000 gals. per day.
Sources of supply, artesian boring in chalk.
Service reservoir at Coleshill, capacity, 100,000 gals.
Filtering, none.
Character of water—drawn from water-bearing chalk 150 feet below surface ; very pure ; 21° hardness, 3° permanent, 18° temporary.
Number of meters in use, 23.
Length of mains, 26 miles.
Assessment charge, from 8 to 6 per cent. on rateable value.
Price per 1,000 gals., by arrangement.

Ampthill, (Beds.)
The Ampthill Rural District Council have adopted a water-supply scheme, at an estimated cost of £12,500, to supply Woburn, Woburn Sands, and Aspley Guise. *June.* 1907.

Andover, Hants. Railways, L.S.W., M. & S. W. Junction. Distance from London, 67 miles.
Authority, Corporation, 1891.
Manager, Robert Walter Knapp.
Office, Guildhall.
Works established, 1875.
Total population of area supplied, 6,509.
Annual supply of water, about 30,000,000 gals.
Sources of supply, wells in the chalk.
Storage capacity, 120,000 gals.
Character of water, softer than chalk water generally.
Filtration, none required.
Number of meters, 12.
Assessment charge, 6d. in the £.
Price per 1,000 gals., 1s. and by arrangement.

Anglesey, Hants. (supplied by GOSPORT).

Anlaby, Yorks. (supplied by HULL).

Annan, Scotland. Railways G.S.W., and Caledonian. Distance from Edinburgh, 100 miles.
Total population of area supplied, 3,476.
No returns supplied.

Anniesland (supplied by GLASGOW).

Anstruther (East and West), Fife. Railway, N.B. Distance from London, 460 miles.
Authority, Town Councils of Pittenween and East and West Anstruther.

Anstruther—*continued.*

Chairmen, Provosts of Pittenween and East Anstruther, in alternate years.
Engineer, Geo. Lockhart.
Clerk, Town Clerk of Pittenween.
Office, Town Clerk's, Pittenween.
Towns and villages in the area supplied, Pittenween, East and West Anstruther.
Works established, 1872; reconstructed, 1887; new reservoirs added, 1897.
Special Acts, none.
Total population of area supplied, 3,500.
Annual supply of water, 18,250,000 gals.
Daily consumption, 90,000 gals.
Sources of supply, streams from Kellielaw and other high ground, all surface.
Storage capacity, 7,500,000 gals.
Character of water, medium hard.
System of filtration, sand filters.
Number of meters, none.
Assessment charge, Pittenween and East Anstruther, 1s. 2d.; West Anstruther, 1s. 10d. Municipal purposes, nil.
Price for 1,000 gals.—trade purposes, not fixed; steamboats, 5s. for each filling of boiler.

Ansty (supplied by CUCKFIELD).

Ansty (supplied by LEICESTER).

Apperley (supplied by BRADFORD, Yorks.).

Appleby, Westmoreland. Railways, M. and N.E. Distance from London, 276 miles.
Authority, Corporation.
Chairman, C. W. Moordaff.
Secretary, Town Clerk, W. Hewetson.
Resident Engineer, F. T. Balmer.
Consulting Engineer, Baldwin Latham.
Office, Town Hall.
Works established, 1876-7.
Total population of area supplied, 2,500.
Average death rate, 14 per 1,000.
Source of supply, springs in Freestone Rock.
Character of water, pure, medium hardness.
Service reservoirs, 120,000 gals.
Total quantity supplied per annum, 58,800,000 gals.
Maximum supply per day, 200,000 gals. in August.
Average daily supply: Domestic, 75,000 gals.; trade, &c., 91,000.
Pressure in mains: Max., 60 lbs. per sq. in.; min., 35 lbs. per sq. in.
Charges for domestic supply, free.
Charges per meter, 2d. per 1,000 gals. above a maximum.
Annual profit, £200.
Length of supply mains, 4 miles; distributing mains, 5 miles.
A few farms supplied on route of mains.

Appleton (supplied by WARRINGTON).

Appleton-le-Moors (supplied by KIRKBY MOORSIDE).

Apsley (supplied by HEMEL HEMPSTEAD).

Arbroath, Scotland. Nolt Loan Supply. Railways, N.B. and C. Distance from Edinburgh, 58 miles.

Authority, Arbroath Town Council.
Chairman of Committee, Bailie Alexander McLaren Robertson.
Secretary, W. K. Macdonald, Town Clerk.
Manager and Resident Engineer, P. C. Smith, C.E., Burgh Surveyor.
Office, Burgh Engineer's Office, Police Chambers, Arbroath.
Consulting Engineers, Crouch & Hogg, Glasgow.
District of supply, Arbroath and St. Vigeans—Burgh Division only.
Total capital invested, including loans, £37,000, about £24,550 paid off (Nolt Loan).
Works opened, Nolt Loan Supply, 1871.
Special Acts, Arbroath Corporation Orders, 1904-5. Noran Supply.
Total population of area of control, 1881, 21,758; 1891, 22,997; 1901, 22,569; 1907, 22,518.
Estimated population actually supplied, 22,500.
Average death rate, 13·61.
Annual supply of water—

For domestic purposes	...	92,000,000 gals. = 11 gals. per head per day.
„ trade	„ ...	8,000,000 „ nearly 1 gal. „ „
„ municipal „	...	2,500,000 „ „ ¼ „ „ „

Note.—The above is all that is available—
Average day's consumption, 271,005 gals.= to 12·04 gals. per head for all purposes.
Maximum day's consumption, 356,800, on November 12th, 1906.
The source of feeder for gravel bed is not definitely known.
Rainfall seems to have no appreciable effect on the supply.
Natural rest level of water below surface, 37 feet, above O.D., 20 feet.
Level of water below surface (when pumping about 280,000 gals. per day), 53 feet.
Strata tapped by wells, gravel bed from 5 to 7 feet thick.
Locality and extent of outcrop, not clearly defined.
Pumping station, Nolt Loan Waterworks, 102,500,000 gals. per diem.
Service tanks erected on an elevated tower, 240,000 gals.
General character of water (Nolt Loan), clear, sparkling, but hard.
The water is not softened or filtered; hardness, 12·4°.
Number of meters in use, 110.
Length of distributing mains, 17½ miles.
Head on distributing mains: Max., 75 ft.; min., 10 ft.
Authorised charge per meter and present actual charge, 1s. 1½d. per 1,000 gals.
The Arbroath Corporation will shortly abandon the Nolt Loan supply for a gravitation supply now being constructed under powers conferred by the Arbroath Corporation Water Orders, 1904-5. The supply is from the River Noran, chief tributary of the South Esk. The water will be conveyed to Arbroath through 24 miles of 12-in. diameter pipes. There are two service reservoirs, with a capacity of 4,000,000 gallons each. A compensation reservoir of 66,000,000 is being constructed at Glenogil. These works will give a supply of 1,250,000 gallons per day. The estimated cost of the undertaking is £80,000, of which £61,384 has already been borrowed.

ANALYSIS OF NORAN WATER, 6-2-07.

Free Ammonia	...	...	·014 parts per 1,000
Albuminoid Ammonia	...	...	·044 „ „
Carbonate of Lime, &c.	...	...	33·000 „ „
Chlorine	... ...	...	10·000 „ „
Nitrogen as Nitrates	...	...	None.
Nitrites	... ...	...	None.
Hardness in Clarke's degrees	...	2¼ degrees.
Lead or other poisonous metals	...	None.

Ardingly, Sussex (supplied by MID-SUSSEX).

Ardleigh (supplied by TENDRING HUNDRED WATERWORKS Co.).

Ardrossan, Scotland. Railways, G. & S.W. and Caledonian. Distance from London 405 miles.

    Authority, Town Council of Burgh of Ardrossan.
    Chairman, Provost John Harvey.
    Engineer and Manager, Thos. Anderson.
    Secretary, Jas. Cook.
    Office, Burgh Chambers, Ardrossan.
    Area supplied, 8,000 acres, Ardrossan only.
    Works established, 1857. Special Act, 1886; Provisional Order, 1901.
    Total population of area supplied, 6,000,
    Annual supply of water, 147,000,000 gals.
    Daily consumption per head, domestic, 35 gals.
    Sources of supply, gathering grounds.
    Storage capacity, 129,000,000 gals.
    Character of water, hard.
    System of filtration, sand.
    Death rate, 15·55 per 1,000.
    Number of meters, 45.
    Length of mains, 42 miles.
    Assessment charge, 1s. 3d. in the £.
    Price per 1,000 gals., trade, 7d.

Ardsley, Yorks. (supplied by MORLEY).

Ardwick (supplied by MANCHESTER).

Arnold, Notts. (supplied by NOTTINGHAM).

Arthenhead, Scotland (supplied by DISTRICT OF THE MIDDLE WARD OF LANARKSHIRE).

Artington (supplied by GUILDFORD).

Arundel, Sussex. Railway, L.B.S.C. Distance from London, 58 miles.
    Total population of area supplied, 2,738.
    The town has a gratuitous water supply of 30 gals. per head per day, for domestic purposes, given by His Grace the Duke of Norfolk, E.M., K.G.

Ascot (supplied by SOUTH-WEST SUBURBAN).

Ash (supplied by FRIMLEY).

Ashbank, part of (supplied by BLAIRGOWRIE).

Ashby-de-la-Zouch, Leicestershire. Railways, M. and L.N.W. Distance from London, 118¼ miles.
    Owners, Council.
    Source of supply—Milton, Derbyshire (Swadlincote and Ashby-de-la-Zouch Joint Waterworks).
    Population supplied, 4,722.
    Office, Town Hall.

Ashchurch, Glos. (supplied by CHELTENHAM).

Asheldham (*see* SOUTHMINSTER).

Ashey, I. of W. (supplied by RYDE).

Ashford, Kent. Railways, S.E. and L.C.D. Distance from London, 54 miles.
  Authority, Ashford Urban District Council.
  Chairman of Council, Dr. Wilks, J.P.
  Chairman of Committee, George Knowles.
  Clerk, John Creery, 11, Bank Street.
  Engineer and Manager, Wm. Terrill.
  Office, 5, North Street, Ashford, Kent.
  Loans outstanding, £15,524.
  Rents received for year—receipts, £2,951 16s. 5d. ; payments, £2,322 5s., including
    interest and repayments.
  Works established 1853.
  Taken over by local authority, 1870.
  Total population of area supplied—Ashford Parish, 12,808, excluding part of
    Willesborough.
  Death rate, 10·13 per 1,000 for 1905.
  Towns and villages in the area supplied—Ashford and parts of Willesborough and
    Kingsnorth.
  Sources of supply in use, 4 wells and 1,265 feet run of adits in Kentish Ragstone
    and Greensand.
  Character of water, excellent but rather hard.
  Filtering, none. Softening, none.
  Storage reservoirs—capacity, 320,000 gals. ; adits and wells, 340,000 gals.
  Head on distributing mains—maximum, 156 ft. ; minimum, 18 ft.
  Annual supply of water for all purposes, 63,116,737 gals.
  Number of meters in use, trade only, 45.
  Length of mains, 15 miles.
  Scale of charges—domestic, 5 per cent. on rateable value ; trade, 1s. 6d. to 1s. per
    1,000 gals. according to quantity ; municipal use, 9d. per 1,000 gals.
  Total assessment charge, £196 10s.

Ashford (also supplied by SOUTH-WEST SUBURBAN).

Ashley (supplied by NORTH CHESHIRE WATER CO.).

Ashley Green (supplied by GREAT BERKHAMPSTEAD).

Ashover, Chesterfield.
  Population supplied, 2,353.
  Purchased by Chesterfield Rural District Council, 1901.

Ashton-in-Makerfield, Lancs. Railways, G.C., Garswood, and L.N.W., Brynn.
  Distance from London, 191 miles.
  Authority, Urban District Council.
  Office, Public Office, Brynn Street.
  Loan capital paid up, £39,350.
  Towns and villages in the area supplied, Garswood, Brynn, Park Lane, Dounall
    Green, and Ashton-in-Makerfield.
  Works established, 1875. Special Act, 1875.
  Total population of area supplied, 20,000.
  Daily consumption per head, domestic, 8 ; trade, 2 gals.
  Source of supply, upland surface waters, 3 miles away.
  Storage capacity, 16,000,000 gals.

Ashton-in-Makerfield—*continued.*

Received from Liverpool independently, 50,000 gals. per day.
Character of water, 7° hardness.
System of filtration, downward through sand.
Death rate, 21 per 1,000.
Number of meters, 15.
Length of mains, 25½ miles.
Price per 1,000 gals., domestic, according to rateable value ; trade, 1s.
Total water rent received, £2,350.

Ashton-on-Mersey (supplied by North Cheshire Water Co.).

Ashton-under-Lyne. Railways, L.N.W., L.Y., G.C., G.N., M. Distance from London, 190 miles.
Authority, Ashton-under-Lyne, Stalybridge and Dukinfield (District) Waterworks Joint Committee.
Chairman, Alderman Mark Fentem, J.P.
Secretary, Wm. Hy. Rothwell.
Office, Town Hall Chambers, Ashton-under-Lyne.
Engineers in charge, G. H. Hill and Sons.
Total capital expended, £792,529.
Towns and villages supplied, Ashton-under-Lyne, Stalybridge, Dukinfield, Mossley, Hurst, and surrounding districts.
Works established, 1870.
Special Acts, 1870, 1875, 1885, 1892.
Total population supplied, 140,000.
Daily consumption per head, 23 gals.
Total quantity of water drawn per annum, 882,939,000 gals.
Sources of supply in use—drainage area, Swineshaw Brook and Greenfield Brook.
Storage capacity, 783,657,000 gals.
Number of meters in use, 700.
Scale of charges —Assessment charge R. or gross annual value on P.R.
   Price per 1,000 gals., 1s. 8d. to 10d.
Total water rent received, £39,605.

Askam (supplied by Barrow-in-Furness).

Aspull, Lancs. (supplied by Bolton).

Aston-with-Aughton (supplied by Sheffield).

Aston (supplied by Birmingham).

Aston Flint (supplied by Hawarden).

Aston Manor (supplied by Birmingham).

Atherton, Lancs. (supplied by Bolton).

Attleborough, Warwicks. (supplied by Nuneaton).

Auchenairn (supplied by Glasgow).

Aughton, part of (supplied by Ormskirk).

Austonley, Yorks. (supplied by Holmfirth).

Avondale (supplied by Lanarkshire).

Awsworth (supplied by Nottingham).

Aylesbury, Bucks. Railways, L.N.W., G.W., Met., and G.C. Distance from London, 38 miles.
Authority, Chiltern Hill Spring Water Company.
Office, Church Row, Aylesbury.
Share capital paid up, £60,390.
Towns and villages in the area supplied, Aylesbury, Tring, Waddesdon, &c.
Works established, 1867. Special Acts, 1870.
Total population of area supplied, 27,000.
Total quantity of water raised per day, 500,000 gals.
Sources of supply, wells in chalk. Storage capacity, 966,000 gals.
Character of water, hardness 15° before, 4° after softening.
Death rate, 13 per 1,000, average for ten years.
Number of meters, 600.
Assessment, 1 charge, 7¼ per cent. Price per 1,000 gals., 2s. 6d. to 1s.

Ayr, N.B. Railways, M. and G.S.W. Distance from London, 392¼ miles.
Authority, Corporation.
Secretary, P. A. Thomson, Town Clerk.
Engineer, John Young.
Office, Town Buildings, Ayr.
Loan outstanding, £139,841.
Works established, 1842 and 1887. Special Acts, 1841, 1865, 1867, 1873, 1885, 1899. Purchased by Corporation, 1873.
Total population supplied, 35,000.
District of supply, parishes of Ayr, Maybole, Monkton, Prestwich and Dalrymple.
Source of supply, springs at Grange and Milson. Impounding reservoirs at Grange, Carcline and Loch Finlas.
Character of water—Loch Finlas, very soft, ·84°, brown, peaty; Carcline, hard and very clear, 11·2°.
Filtration, 6 open sand filters. No softening.
Storage capacity, Loch Finlas, 347,000,000 gals.; Carcline, 34,000,000 gals.; service reservoirs, 7,000,000 gals.
Head on distributing mains—maximum, 250 feet: minimum, 30 feet.
Annual supply of water, 821,000,000 gals.
Daily consumption per head—domestic, 56 gals.; trade, 14 gals.
Maximum daily supply, 2,500,000 gals. in July.
Average death rate, 17 per 1,000.
Scale of charges, assessment charge, 10½d. in £.
Price per 1,000 gals., 1s. 6d., up to 2,500,000 gals. Above this by scale; present average, 8d.
Number of meters, 83.
Length of supply mains, 36 miles; distributing mains, 50 miles.

Bacup, Lancs. Railway, L.Y. Distance from London, 203 miles.
Authority, Corporation.
Engineer, W. H. Elce, A.M.I.C.E.
Secretary, J. Entwistle, Town Clerk.
Office, Municipal Offices.
Loans outstanding, £216,000.

BACUP—*continued.*

Works established, 1854. Special Acts, Rossendale Waterworks Act, 1853, 1854, 1894, 1898 and 1906.
Total population of area supplied, 25,000.
Area supplied, Borough of Bacup.
Source of supply, gravitation from moorlands.
Character of water, soft.
Assessment charge—charges authorised, 7½ per cent. to 9½ per cent. on R.V.
Present charge, 5 per cent. to 7½ per cent. on R.V.
Price per 1,000 gals., 2s. to 6½d.

Badsey, Worcs. (supplied by EVESHAM).

Baguley (supplied by NORTH CHESHIRE WATER Co.).

Baildon, Yorks. Railway, M.
Authority, Baildon District Council.
Chairman, G. E. Robinson.
Secretary, J. Bentley.
Manager, J. Myers.
Works established, 1852. Special Acts, 1890.
Total population of area supplied, 6,000.
Average death rate, 13·6 per 1,000, period 1896 to 1905.
Area supplied, 1,000 acres.
Sources of supply, springs and gathering grounds.
Analytical report—

					Grains per gal.
Total solid matters	...	...	...	...	5·0
Chlorine (combined)	...	...	...	...	·7
Nitrates ...	...	...	...	...	none
Nitrogen as nitrates	...	...	...	...	none
Free ammonia ...	...	...	...	...	·0014
Albuminoid ammonia	...	...	...	...	·0021
Lead ...	...	...	...	...	none
Total hardness (Clark's scale)...	...	...	...	2·2

A very pure water, showing not the least signs of either past or present sewage contamination, It is so exceedingly soft that it will very probably act on lead. A water of this description ought either to be alkalinised with soda ash, or hardened by the addition of a little lime.
Storage capacity, 42,000,000 gals.
Daily consumption per head, domestic, 20 gals.
Number of meters, 25.
Assessment charge, 1s. 6d. in £.
Price for 1,000 gals., 1s.; over 100,000, per quarter, 9d.

Baillieston, N.B. (supplied by AIRDRIE).

Bainsford (supplied by FALKIRK).

Bakewell, Derbyshire. Railway, M. Distance from London, 152¼ miles.
Authority, Bakewell Urban Council.
Chairman, Thos. Allsop.
Manager, W. Redfearn.
Secretary, Vernon R. Cockerton.

BAKEWELL—*continued.*

Office, Bridge Street.
Loan outstanding, £1,000.　Interest, 3½ per cent.
Works established, 1875.　Special Act, 1875.
Total population supplied with water, 3,000.
Average death rate, 12·5 per 1,000.
Source of supply, springs on Fallinge Moors, 1,000 feet above sea level, and
. impounding reservoirs at The Coombs.　Head on distributing mains, maximum
210 feet, minimum 60 feet.
Storage capacity, 600,000 gals.
Character of water, clear and bright, soft and free from lead.
System of filtration, wire screens.
Total supply per annum—domestic, 33,000,000; trade, 4,000,000 gals.
Average daily supply per head, 30 gals. ; trade, 12,500 gals.
Present rate of charge, 8d. in £ on rateable value.
Authorised and present actual charge by meter, 8d. 1,000 gals.
Number of meters, 10.
No charge for municipal purposes.

Balcombe, Sussex (supplied by CUCKFIELD).

Baldingstone (supplied by BURY).

Balderton (supplied by NEWARK).

Balfron, N.B.
Authority, County Council, managed by Sub-committee Special Water Supply
District.
Clerk and Inspector, John Henry.
Works established, 1885.
Total population of area supplied, 900.
Sources of supply in use—Spittal spring, supplemented by Glasgow Corporation,
Loch Katrine supply, further supplemented by Shian spring.
Storage capacity, 37,000 at spring.　Supplementary supply taken by meter; no
storage.
Assessment charge, 10d. in the £, half on owner and occupier.

Ballingdon, Suffolk (supplied by SUDBURY).

Balloch (supplied by ALEXANDRIA).

Bally (supplied by DONCASTER).

Bamford, Lancs. (supplied by HEYWOOD).

Banbridge. *See* PORTADOWN.

Banbury, Oxon.　Railways, G.W., G.C., L.N.W.　Distance from London, 77 miles.
Authority, Banbury Water Company.
Chairman, Ed. Franey.
Manager and Secretary, W. E. Wood.
Office, 21, Marlborough Road, Banbury.
Share capital paid up, £22,000.
Loan　　,,　　　,,　　£4,900.

BANBURY—*continued.*

Dividend, 6 per cent. ordinary, 4½, 5, and 6 per cent. pref.
Area supplied, Banbury only.
Works established, 1856.
Special Act—Banbury Waterworks Act, 1865.
Total population supplied, 13,000.
Annual supply of water, 124,000,000 gals.
Daily consumption per head—domestic, 16 gals. ; trade, 10 gals.
Source of supply, River Cherwell.
Storage capacity, 250,000 gals.
Filtering, sand and gravel and Bell's patent filters.
Character of water—temporary hardness, 17° ; permanent, 8° ; total, 25°.
Number of meters in use, 85.
Length of mains, 15 miles.
Scale of charges—
　Assessment charge, 6 per cent. on rent.
　Price per 1,000 gals., 2s. 6d. to 6d.

Bandon, Co. Cork.
Sanitary and Water Authority, Rural District Council

Banff, Scotland.　Railway, G.N. of S.
Authority, Town Council of Burgh of Banff.
Office, 20, Low Street.
Area supplied, Banff only.
Special Acts, Public Health Acts.
Total population of area supplied, 3,871.
Daily consumption per head, domestic, 40 gals.
Sources of supply, spring.　Storage capacity, 119,950 gals.
Character of water, very good.　System of filtration, shingle.
Length of mains, 20 miles.
Assessment charge, 1s. 2d. in the £.
Price per 1,000 gals., trade, 1s.
Water has been introduced under statutory authority.

Bangor.　Railway L.N.W.　Distance from London, 239 miles.
Authority, Bangor Corporation.
Chairman, Councillor J. P. Williams.
Secretary, E. Smith Owen, A.S.A.A., Corporation Office, Bangor.
Engineer in charge and Manager, John Gill, A.M.I.C.E.
Office, Municipal Offices, Bangor.
Loans outstanding, £38,297.　Interest on loan, 3 per cent. ; on old loan at 4½ per
　cent.　Annuities, 4 per cent.
Annual profit, including "Capital charges," £50.
Works opened, 1847.　Purchased by local authority 1878.
Special Acts, Bangor Water and Gas Act, 1854 ; Bangor Local Board Act, 1878.
Total population of area of control, 1881, 16,574 ; 1891, 16,191 ; 1901, 17,081.
Total number of consumers, 13,085.
Average death rate, 15·8 per 1,000.
Towns and villages within the area of control, part of Bethesda—
　　　Village of Llandegai, population about　...　　...　　...　　400
　　　Mindfoedd　...　　...　　...　　...　　...　　...　　...　　140
　　　Bangor　...　　...　　...　　...　　...　　...　　...　11,700
Sources of supply—Mountain stream 1,700 feet above O. D.
　Maximum annual rainfall over drainage area, 48 inches, 1901.
　Population or cultivation on drainage area, none.　No control of drainage area
　　is necessary ; land is only used for sheep grazing.
Character of water, hardness before treatment, 1·11°, and after 1·11°.

BANGOR—*continued*.

No filtering beds, only screened through fine metallic screens.
Recent analysis of the water before filtration—total solids, 1·28 ; chlorine, 0·77 ; nitrates, 0·008 : free albuminoid ammonia, 0·001—in 100,000 parts.
Service Reservoirs, Mygwyn (No. 1) capacity 540,000 gals.
     „   „   „   (No. 2)   „   160,000   „
     „   „   Nant   „   400,000   „
Head on distributing mains—maximum, 460 feet ; minimum, 25 feet.
Average daily supply—domestic, 23 gals. ; trade, 6 gals.
Maximum day's consumption, 390,000 gals. in August.
Scale of charges—houses under £10 per year, 8s. ; above £10, 1s. 4½d. in £ ; by meter, 1s. to 7d. per 1,000 gals., according to quantity. No charge for baths and w.c.'s extra.
Number of meters in use, 172.
Length of supply mains, 7 miles ; distributing mains, 16 miles.

Bank Lane (supplied by BURY).

Bannockburn (supplied by STIRLING).

Banstead (supplied by SURREY).

Barber Green (supplied by GRANGE-OVER-SANDS).

Bardsea (supplied by ULVERSTON).

Barking (supplied by SOUTH ESSEX WATER CO.).

Barley, Lancs. (supplied by NELSON).

Barming (supplied by MAIDSTONE).

Barmouth, Merionethshire. Railways, L.N.W. and G.W. Distance from London, 247 miles.
Authority, Barmouth Urban District Council
Total population of area supplied, 2,500.
No returns supplied.

Barnes, Surrey (supplied by SOUTHWARK and VAUXHALL).

Barnet and District (G. & W.). Railways, G. N. and N. L. Distance from London, 9 miles.
Authority, Barnet and District Gas and Water Co.
Chairman, Alfred H. Baynes, F.R.A.S.
Secretary, Ernest W. Drew, F.C.A.
Engineer and Manager, T. H. Martin, A.M.I.C.E.
Office, Station Road, New Barnet, and 30, Gracechurch Street, E.C.
Share capital paid up, £322,800.—Last Dividend 7½ per cent.
Loan capital paid up, £70,740.—Rate of Interest 4 per cent.
Works established, 1872.
Special Acts for Water Supply, 1872, 1873, 1887, and 1904.
Parishes actually supplied : Arkley, Barnet Vale, Chipping Barnet, East Barnet, Enfield, Friern Barnet, Finchley, Hadley, Monken Hadley, Northaw, North Mimms, Ridge, Shenley, Riveal, South Mimms Urban, Totteridge.

BARNET AND DISTRICT—*continued.*

Total population supplied, 65,000.
Sources of supply, chalk.
Total quantity of water supplied per annum 543,493,800.
Charges authorized and actually charged, from 5 per cent to 6 per cent. on R.V
　　for domestic and trade.
Authorized charge per meter, 1s. 6d. per 1,000 gals.　Actual charge, 1s. 3d. per
　　1,000 gals.
Number of Meters 220.

Barnoldswick. (G. & W.) Railway, M. to Skipton.　Distance from London, 230
miles.
Authority, Urban District Council.
Chairman, J. M. Edmondson.
Clerk, C. Thornton, Solicitor, Nelson, Lancashire.
Water Engineer and Manager, J. W. Thompson.
Office, Gas and Water Office, Town Hall, Barnoldswick.
Total capital invested, including loans, £11,000 at 3½ per cent.
Towns and villages within area of control, Barnoldswick and Coates.
Works opened, 1891.
Total population of area of control, 1891, 4,500 ; 1901, 6,450.
Total number of consumers, 1,570.
Estimated population actually supplied, 8,000.
Annual supply of water—
　　　　　For domestic purposes ...　　...　　...　　...　30,676,400 gals.
　　　　　　„　trade　　„　...　　...　　...　　...　　1,200,000　„
Maximum day's consumption, 130,000 gals.
Total quantity of water drawn from deep wells and borings, 32,349,487 gals. per
　　annum.
Estimated total quantity of water available, 40,000,000 gals. per annum.
Sources of supply—White Moor, between Colne and Barnoldswick, Yorkshire.
　　Natural rest level of water below surface, 22 feet below O. D.
　　Level of water below surface (when pumping 120,000 gals. per day), 200 feet
　　　in driest time.
Geological data—springs in freestone or grit stone.
　　Strata tapped by wells or borings, freestone or grit stone.
Pumping station, White Moor, Foulridge, near Colne ; capacity, 120,000 gals. in
　　dry season.
　　12in. borehole, 500ft. deep.
　　80in. well, 100ft. deep.
One open service reservoir, White Moor ; capacity, 447,000 gals.
Hardness before treatment, 7° not heated.
Length of distributing mains, about 7 miles.
Pressure on distributing mains : max., 150 lbs. per sq. in. ; min., 40 lbs. per sq. in.
Authorized charge per meter 1s. 8d. per 1,000 gals.
Number of meters in use, 60.

Barnsley, Yorks.　Railways, G.N., M., G.C., L. & Y.　Distance from London, 173
miles.
Authority, The Town Council of Barnsley.
Chairman, Alderman W. E. Raley.
Secretary, H. Horsefield (Solicitor).
Engineer and Manager, J. Henry Taylor, M.I.C.E.
Office, Manor House, Barnsley.
Loans outstanding, £479,385 at 3 and 3½ per cent.
Annual loss, including capital charges after interest and sinking fund have been
　　charged, March 31st, 1906, £2,575.
Works established, 1837.

BARNSLEY—*continued.*

Special Acts, 1862, 1896 and 1900.
Total population supplied, 110,000 (estimated).
Average death rate, 20·79 per 1,000.
Towns and villages in area of supply, Barnsley, Ingberchworth, part of Hoyland-
swaine, Silkstone, Dodsworth, Gawber, rural district of Barnsley and Hems-
worth, townships of Worsborough, Ardsley, Monk Bretton, Roystone, Thurnscoe,
and Hickleton.
Area supplied, 22,000 acres.
Sources of supply—moorlands above Ingberchworth and Midhope.
Impounding reservoirs, 710,000,000 gals.
Service reservoir, 2,000,000 gals.
Filtering through sand and gravel and mountain limestone.
Character of water—soft, from the millstone grit and moors. Total hardness, 3·28°
after treatment, 3·10°.
Pressure on distributing mains—maximum, 220 lbs.; minimum, about 40 lbs. per
sq. in.
Annual supply of water, about 700,000,000 gals.
Daily consumption per head—domestic, 13 gals.; trade, 6 gals.
Scale of charges—assessment charges, 4 to 6 per cent. on rateable value.
    Trade, price per 1,000 gals.—within old limits, maximum 10d., minimum 6d.;
without old limits, maximum 10d., minimum 8d.

Barnstaple, Devon. Railways, G.W., L.S.W., and Lynton and Barnstaple. Distance
from London, 211 miles.
Authority, Barnstaple Water Co.
Chairman, C. E. Roberts Chanter.
Secretary, C. W. Parkin.
Office, Bridge Chambers, Strand, Barnstaple.
Engineers, T. and C. Hawksley.
Share capital paid up, £20,600; premiums, £7,270.
Loan, £4,900, at 3½ and 3 per cent.
Dividend, "A" 11 per cent. (including 1 per cent. on arrears of dividend), "B"
7 per cent., less income tax.
Works established, 1858. Special Acts, 1858, 1888.
Total population supplied, 14,137.
Average death rate, 16·36 per 1,000—period 1896 to 1905.
Limits of supply, Barnstaple, Pilton, Bishops Tawton, Tawstock, Goodleigh,
Landkey, and Fremington.
Source of supply, North Yeo River.
Analysis of water—

					Grains per gal.
Saline ammonia	...	...	...	...	·0003
Albuminoid ammonia	...	...	...	...	·0053
Nitrogen as nitrate	...	...	...	...	·07
Nitrites...	...	...	...	..	absent
Oxygen absorbed in 4 hours at 80 F.		...	..		·075
Chlorine as chloride ...	...	...	...	...	1·50
Total dissolved solids	...	...	...	...	9·0
Hardness	...	...	...	...	...	4·5
Poisonous metals	...	...	...	...	absent

Deposit, very slight—vegetable debris.
Colonies developed on gelatine plate, 61 per C.C.
Bacillus coli, no typical forms.
B. sporogenes enteritidis, none.
Streptococci, none.
A perfectly satisfactory domestic water, exhibiting no chemical or bacterio-
logical evidence of pollution.

BARNSTAPLE—*continued.*

Filtration, sand and gravel beds.
Storage capacity, 775,000 gals. in service reservoir.
Annual supply of water, estimated 375,000,000 gals.
Head on distributing mains—high level, 220 ft. ; low level, 115 ft.
Daily supply per head—high level (pumped), 42 gals. ; low level (gravitation), 75 gals., including waste in mains and services.
Scale of charges—
    Assessment charge—low level, 5 per cent. ; high level, 6 per cent. on R.R.
    Trade, 2s. to 6d. per 1,000 gals.
    By meter, 2s. to 6d. per 1,000 gals., average, 7½d.
Number of meters in use, 42.
Length of mains, 3½ miles ; distributing mains, 17½ miles.

Barrhead (supplied by GLASGOW).

Barrowford, Lancs. (supplied by NELSON).

Barrow-in-Furness, Lancs. Railways, M., and L.N.W Distance from London, 264½ miles.
Authority, Corporation, 1868.
Chairman, Alderman Townson.
Secretary, C. F. Preston, Town Clerk. W. W. Waite, Borough Treasurer.
Engineer and Manager, W. Fergusson.
Office, Gas and Water Works, Barrow-in-Furness.
Loans—total, £412,000 ; redeemed, £74,443.
Interest, 2½ and 5 per cent.
Total water rent received, £19,306.
Works established, 1868. Special Acts, 1869, 1872, 1873, 1875, 1881, 1892, 1901.
Total population supplied, 76,900.
Average death rate, 12·87 per 1,000.
Towns and villages in area supplied, 32,000 acres ; Barrow, Dalton, Askam, Ireleth, Marton, Lindal, Newton and Rampside.
Sources of supply, gathering ground on fells, gravitation.
Character of water, very soft ; upland, 4°.
System of filtration, sand.
Storage capacity—impounding reservoirs, 563,000,000 gals. ; service reservoirs, 13,600,000 gals.
Annual supply of water, 1,334,190,000 gals.
Daily consumption, per head, domestic, 21·8 ; trade, 20·4 gals.
Maximum day's supply, 3,960,000 gals. in September.
Scale of charges, assessment charge, 5 per cent. on annual value.
Price per 1,000 gals., 1s. to 2d. Number of meters, 230.

Barrow-upon-Soar (supplied by LEICESTER).

Barry, Glamorgan. (G. and W.) Railways, G.W. and Barry. Distance from London, 180 miles.
Authority, Barry Urban District Council.
Chairman of Water Committee, Councillor S. R. Jones (1906-7).
Clerk, T. B. Tordoff, Council Offices, Holton Road, Barry Dock.
Engineer in charge, E. W. Waite, A.M.I.C.E.
Office, Gas Works, Barry Docks.
Towns and villages within the area of control—Barry (including Barry, Barry Dock, Cadoxton and Barry Island), Sully, Wenvoe, Porthkerry, Merthyr Dovan, Dynas Powis, St. Andrews.

BARRY—*continued.*

The parish of St. Andrews Major (which includes the villages of St. Andrews and Dynas Powis) is supplied with water purchased in bulk from the Cardiff Corporation by the Barry Urban District Council.

This water being derived from a different source, the figures relating to this district are not included in the following figures.

Works established 1889.

Purchased by local authority, 1896.

Loans outstanding, £151,320.

Annual loss on undertaking, including capital charges, £4,190.

Special Acts, Barry and Cadoxton Gas and Water Company's Acts 1886, 1889 ; Barry and Cadoxton Local Board, Gas and Water Act, 1893; Barry Urban District Council's Act, 1896.

Total population of area of control, 1881, 1,239 ; 1891, 13,422 ; 1901, 27,598; 1907, 32,500.

Total number of consumers, 6,500.

Estimated population actually supplied, 32,500, including floating population (port).

Average death rate, 11·2 (1906), 12·7 (1905).

Annual supply of water (1906)—

       For domestic, trade and municipal purposes ...   263,000,000 gals.

Average daily supply (1906) per head for domestic purposes, 20 gals. ; trade. 3¼ gals.

Maximum day's supply, 1,200,000 gals. (Sept., 1906).

Estimated total quantity of water available per annum, 450,000,000 gals. (with existing works), purely speculative, but based on results obtained from an extended but temporary pumping from the sources in a dry period.

Sources of supply—deep wells or borings situated at Biglis, parish of St. Andrews Major, Glam. Latitude, 51° 21 ' 25 "; Longitude, 3° 13 ' 33 ".

Maximum annual rainfall over drainage area 40·68 inches (1886).

Minimum   „   „   25·56   „   (1887).

Average   „   „   31·43   „   (period 16 years, 1886-1901.)

The Water Authority have secured control of drainage area, to a limited extent, in the immediate neighbourhood of the wells and headings.

Natural rest level above ordnance datum, 21·87 feet (surface).

Level of water below surface (when pumping 650,000 gals. per day), 5 feet.

Overflows up to 3 inches for about four months in the year and falls to about 2 feet below, according to period of year.

Strata or formation yielding springs, carboniferous limestone—dolomitic conglomerate.

Price per 1,000 gals., from 20,000 at 1s. 6d. to 1,000,000 at 9d.

  „ for domestic supply, houses under £20 rateable value 8½ per cent. per ann.

  „   „   „   £40   „   „   8   „   „

  „   „   „   £60   „   „   7½   „   „

  „   „   „   £80   „   „   6¼   „   „

  „   „   „   £100   „   „   6   „   „

Meter Rent from 2s. 6d. per quarter for ⅜ inch to 12s. per quarter for 3 inches.

Pumping station—Biglis; capacity, 1,500,000 gals. per diem ; 2 wells, 32 feet and 40 feet deep respectively ; 1 heading, 200 yards long, 6 feet by 4 feet.

Service reservoirs, low level   ...   ... capacity, 1,000,000 gals. covered.

  „   „   high level, No. 1   ...   „   100,000 „   „

  „   „   „   No. 2   ...   „   300,000 „   „

Head on distributing mains—maximum, 200 feet ; minimum, 25 feet.

Hardness before treatment, 37 parts per 100,000, not softened.

Number of meters in use, 220.

Length of supply mains, 20 miles ; of distributing mains, 40 miles.

Recent analyses of the water—

        Date of analysis ...   .   April, 1906.

BARRY—*continued*.

Appearance in two foot tube	Very faintly green, clear
Reaction	Distinctly alkaline.
Total hardness	39·6
Temporary	25·8
Permanent	13·8
Chlorine	2·65
Nitrogen as nitrates	·52
Saline or "free" ammonia	·0016
Organic or "albuminoid" ammonia ...	·0032
Sulphates	Considerable amount.
Microscopic examination	Small amount.
of the sediment	Animalculæ rare.

(Parts per 100,000)

Remarks—A very hard water. Chemical analysis of the sample shows no evidence of contamination by sewage, animal or vegetable matter.

Barton Moss (supplied by MANCHESTER).

Barton-under-Needwood (supplied by SOUTH STAFFS. WATERWORKS Co.).

Barton-upon-Humber, Lincs. Railway, G.C. Distance from London, 174 miles.
Authority, The Barton-upon-Humber Water Company, Ltd.
Office, Whitecross House.
Share capital paid up, £15,470. Loan, £4,000 (debenture shares).
Interest on loan, 4 per cent.
Area supplied, Barton-upon-Humber only.
Works established, July, 1898.
Special Act, Barton-upon-Humber Water Order, 1897.
Total population of area supplied, 5,671 (1901).
Total quantity of water raised per annum, 8,000,000 or 9,000,000 gals.
Sources of supply, deep bore or pumps.
Storage capacity, 200,000 gals., about.
System of filtration, mechanical filters.
Character of water, spring.
Death rate, 15 per 1,000.
Number of meters, 4.
Length of mains, about 5½ miles.
Scale of charges—
  Price per 1,000 gals., domestic, from 1s. ; trade, from 9d.

Basingstoke, Hants. Railways, L.S.W. and G.W. Distance from London, 47¾ miles.
Authority, Corporation of Basingstoke.
Chairman, Ald. W. Powell, J.P.
Clerk to Authority, John A. Kingdon.
Borough Engineer, F. R. Phipps, A.M.I.C.E.
Office, Town Hall.
Loans outstanding, £22,642.
Works established, 1870, abandoned. New works, 1906. Undertaking purchased from Company, 1883.
Total population supplied, 11,000.
Average death rate, 12 per 1,000.
Towns and villages supplied : Basingstoke, Cliddesden and Basing.
Source of supply, wells and adits in the chalk at West Ham.

Level at top of well	310 O.D.
„ „ bottom of well	250 O.D.

BASINGSTOKE—*continued.*

Total number of gallons pumped in 14 days   ...   12,662,720
Average per day   904,480
The rest level of the water at starting was ...   ...   271·75 O.D.
The level of water at completion of pumping was...   259·83 ,,
One hour after completion   ...   .   268·08 ,,
24 hours   ,, ...   269·83 ,,
8 days   ,, ...   271·75 ,,
Analysis—New Well in chalk, after continuous pumping; physical properties, all good.

Colour at depth of 2 feet, colourless. Smell when heated, not noticeable. Appearance of residue after evaporation, clean and white. Turpidity, bright and clear. Suspended matter, nil.

Chemical analysis—

Expressed in parts per hundred thousand (× ·7 = grs. per gallon).

Free ammonia   ...   .   nil.
Albuminoid ammonia   ...   .   ·003
Oxygen absorbed in 15 minutes at 80° F....   ...   nil.
   ,,   ,,   after 96 hours incubation, 80° F.   trace only.
   ,,   ,,   4 hours   ...   .   ·02
Nitrogen present as nitrates and nitrites   ...   ·41
Chlorine (× 1·648 = common salt)   ...   ...   1·2
Phosphoric acid   ...   .   a trace.
Poisonous metals (lead or copper)...   ...   ...   nil.
Total solids dried at 212° F.   ...   .   30·8

Hardness by Clark's scale—total hardness, 15°; permanent hardness, 4°; removable by boiling, 11°.

Behaviour of residue on ignition, satisfactory.

Microscopical and biological examination, a few ordinary water bacteria and minute particles of mineral matter.

Bacteriological examination—MacConkey bile salt test: no acid ; no gas : number of colonies on gelatine, room temperature, 50 per c.c.

Report—An exhaustive examination has proved that this is a typical chalk water, the purest that can be obtained. It constitutes therefore a very excellent public supply.

Filtration, none ; softening, none.

Storage capacity—Service Reservoirs, low level, 315,000 gals. ; high level, 240,000 gals.

Head on distributing mains, high level—maximum 180 feet ; minimum 100 feet.
   ,, ,, ,, low ,, ,, 120 feet ; ,, 70 feet.
Total quantity supplied per annum, 145,000,000 gals.

Average daily supply, domestic, 23 gals ; trades, 13 gals.

Maximum supply per day, 500,000 gals. in July.

Present rate for domestic supply, 5 per cent. on net annual value.
   ,, ,, per meter, from 1s. 3d. to 4½d. per 1,000 gals.

Number of meters in use, 180.

Total length of supply mains, 6 miles ; distributing mains, 14 miles.

Bassaleg, Mon. (supplied by NEWPORT, Mon.).

Bath, Somerset. Railways, G.W. and M. Distance from London, 107¼ miles.
Authority, Corporation.
Secretary, Frederick Partington Waidle, Town Clerk.
Engineer in charge, Jules Dent Young, A.M.I.C.E.
Office, Guildhall.
Loan, outstanding, £115,124 ; sinking fund, £15,167.
Interest, 3 per cent.

BATH—*continued.*

Net Profit for 1906, £1,471.
Special Acts, 1846, 1851, 1870, 1903; Provisional Orders, 1875, 1876, 1887-8, 1892, 1899.
Population supplied, estimated 68,500.
Average death rate, 16·16 per 1,000.
Towns and villages in the area supplied, City of Bath, villages of Batheaston, Twerton, Weston, Charlcombe, Bathampton, Swainswick = 12,568 acres.
Daily consumption per head—domestic and public purposes, 19·32; trade, 2·72 gals.
Sources of supply, springs from oolite strata, and upper lias sands.
Character of water, 16° to 18° hardness.
Storage capacity in impounding reservoirs, 61,000,000 gals.
Number of meters, 240.
Pressure in distributing mains—maximum 120 lbs. per square inch; minimum 15 lbs. per square inches.
Total quantity supplied per annum 548,000,000.
Average daily supply per head—domestic and public, 19 gals.; trade, 2 gals.
Scale of charges—assessment charge from 2½ to 5 per cent. rateable value. Price per 1,000 gals., 8d.; charges for municipal purposes, urinals, 6d. per 1,000; street watering, £150 per annum; public fountain and drinking trough, free.

Bathgate, Scotland. Railway, N.B. Distance from London, 400 miles.
Authority, Corporation.
Secretary, W. Allan, Town Clerk.
Resident Engineer, Andrew L. Reid.
Office, 7, Mid Street.
Loans outstanding, £17,000.
Works established, 1878.
Area supplied, burgh boundaries only.
Total population of area supplied, 7,600.
Death rate, 15·9 per 1,000.
Daily consumption per head, about 30.
Sources of supply, limestone and pumping from stream into reservoir.
Storage capacity, 11,500,000 gals.
Character of water—hard, good quality.
System of filtration, sand filter beds.
Capacity of storage reservoir, 30,000,000 gals.
Average daily supply per head about 30 gals. (practically a domestic supply).
Number of meters, 3.
Length of mains, about 5½ miles.
Assessment charge, 1s. 1d. in the £ on owner and 1s. 1d. in the £ on occupier.
Price for 1,000 gals.—domestic and trade, by meter, 6d.
Length of supply mains, 6 miles.

Batley, Yorks. Railways, G.N. and L.N.W. Distance from London, 183 miles.
Authority, Batley Corporation.
Chairman of Waterworks Committee, Alderman J. W. Blackburn.
Secretary, J. H. Craik, Town Clerk.
Engineer in charge, J. C. Barrowclough.
Office, Town Hall, Batley.
Capital expenditure to April 30th, 1907, £350,000.
Loans outstanding, April 30th, 1907, £290,890.
Towns and villages within the area of control, with population of each (1901 Census)—Borough of Batley　...　..　...　...　...　30,000
　　　　　　　　Brockholes Village　...　..　...　...　...　500
Works established, 1871.
Special Acts—Batley Corporation Waterworks Act, 16 June, 1871.
　　　　　　　　　　　　　　　　　,,　16 Apl., 1878.

BATLEY—*continued.*

Total population of area of control, 1881, 27,750; 1891, 29,000; 1901, 30,500.
Total number of consumers, 30,500 for domestic purposes, and 300 for various trade purposes.
Annual supply of water (for 1906) —

For domestic purposes	...	...	...	185,000,000 gals.		
„ trade	...	...	...	...	250,000,000	„
„ municipal	...	...	...	15,000,000		„

Maximum day's consumption ... ... 1,500,000 „
Total quantity of water drawn from drainage areas and surface springs per annum (1906), 750,000,000 gals.
Estimated total quantity of water available per annum from drainage areas and surface springs, 1,000,000,000 gals.
Drainage areas and surface springs at Holmfirth, 8 miles south of Huddersfield, on the N.E. slope of the Pennine Chain.
Estimated maximum daily discharge at points of collection, 50,000,000 gals.

„	minimum	„	„	„	„	500,000 gals.
„	average	„	„	„	„	3,000,000 gals.

Maximum annual rainfall over drainage area 73·3 inches (1882).

Minimum	„	„	40·6	„	(1887).
Average	„	„	59·0	„	(period 20 years).

Population on drainage area, 50.
Nature of drainage area, chiefly moorland grazing.
Water authority have no control beyond that contained in Public Health Act and other Acts, except the portion of drainage area which the Corporation have purchased.
Geological data—
    Surface formation of drainage areas, chiefly moorland with underlying peat.
    Strata or formation yielding springs and nature of subsoil yielding water, millstone grit.
Impounding reservoirs, Yateholme Reservoir, capacity 95,500,000 gals.

„	„	Riding Wood	„	„	51,500,000	„
„	„	Ramsden	„	„	87,000,000	„
				Total	234,000,000	

Service reservoirs, Staincliffe Reservoir ... capacity 3,250,000 gals., covered.
    „   Brownhill Balancing Tank „   30,000 „   „
Number of meters in use, 350.
Length of distributing mains, 50 miles.
Average death rate per 1,000, 19·0 for last 10 years; 16·9 for 1906.
Recent analysis of the water—
    Physical character—
        Suspended matter, trace.
        Appearance of a column 2 ft. long, clear and colourless.
        Taste, normal; odour, none.
    On analysis, the sample gave the following results—
        (Grains per gallon)—
            Total solid matter, 7·56; which lost on ignition 0·56 grs.
            Chlorine, 0·80; equal to sodium chloride, 1·32 grs.
            Nitrogen in oxidised forms, trace; equal to nitric acid (anhydrous), trace.
            Poisonous metals (lead, etc.), none.
        Degrees of hardness, 3°. (Each degree of hardness represents a soap-destroying power equivalent to one grain of chalk per gallon.)
        (Parts per million)—
            Reducing power, 0·08. (Representing the oxygen absorbed by the organic and other oxidisable matters in one million parts of water.)
            Free and urcal ammonia, 0·04.
            Albuminoid ammonia, 0·12.

Batley—*continued*.

Filtration, none.
Scale of charges for domestic supply—
    Where the annual value of a house or part of a house shall not exceed
    £5 10s., rent 10s.
    From—exceeding £5 10s., but not exceeding £8 10s., rent 11s. 6d.; and
    upward to exceeding £70 but not exceeding £80, rent £2 12s.; exceeding
    £80, £3 7s. 9d. per cent. on the annual value.
    For manufacturing or trade purposes, through meter, with a minimum charge
    of 10s. per annum, at per 1,000 gals., 6d.
    Warehouses, shops, and offices—Annual value not exceeding £5, 4s. 6d. per
    annum; exceeding £90 but not exceeding £100, 16s. 11d. per annum; one
    shilling for every additional £20.
    Allowance made for houses and shops assessed together.
Outside borough—
    From rental not exceeding £3, 7s. 6d. per annum, to rental not exceeding
    £160, £8 18s. 8d. per annum.
    Water supply by meter, in addition to 10 per cent. per annum on cost of
    meter and fixing, 1s. per 1,000 gals., with a minimum charge equal to
    rental of premises supplied.
The impounding reservoirs are situate 18 miles from Batley, and the water is
    conveyed throughout in 15 inch cast iron mains, which are subject to a
    pressure of 250 lbs. per square inch at some points.
There are in Batley three separate classes of distributing mains, viz., domestic
    mains, trade or mill mains, and high level mains.

Beaconsfield (supplied by Amersham).

Bearsden (supplied by Glasgow).

Beaumaris, Anglesea. Railway, L.N.W. Distance from London, 250 miles.
    Owner, Sir R. W. Williams-Bulkeley, Bart.
    Manager and Secretary, J. E. Hughes.
    Total population of area supplied, 2,310.
    Sources of supply, mountain springs.
    Filtration, sand.
    Assessment charge, 7½ per cent.
    Price per 1,000 gals., 8d.
    Total water rent received, £500.

Beaumont (supplied by Tendring Hundred).

Beccles, Suffolk. Railway, G.E. Distance from London, 109 miles.
    Share capital, £11,100.
    Works established, 1854.
    Total population of area supplied, 6,898.
    No returns supplied.

Beddington (supplied by Sutton).

Bedfont (supplied by South-West Suburban).

Bedford. Railways, M., L.N.W. Distance from London, 50 miles.
  Authority, Corporation.
  Chairman, Councillor Jos. Miller.
  Town Clerk, Hedley Baxter.
  Engineer, N. Greensbields, A.M.I.C.E.
  Office, Town Hall.
  Area supplied, Borough of Bedford only.
  Works established, 1868.
  Total population supplied, 39,000
  Annual supply of water, 385,000,000 gals.
  Daily consumption per head, 27 gals. domestic and trade.
  Sources of supply, headings driven in limestone rock.
  Storage capacity, two days' supply.
  System of filtration, sand, &c.
  Character of water, hard.
  Death rate, 11·59 per 1,000.
  Number of meters, 500.
  Length of mains, 34 miles.
  Scale of charges, price per 1,000 gals., 1s. for all purposes.

Bedhampton (supplied by PORTSMOUTH).

Bedlington, Northumberland. Railway, N.E. Distance from London, 280 miles.
  Authority, Bedlington Urban District Council.
  Office, Council Chambers, Front Street.
  Chairman, Chairman of Council.
  Clerk to authority, C. D. Forster, 24, Grainger Street West, Newcastle-on-Tyne.
  Manager and Resident Engineer, J E. Johnston.
  Loan outstanding, £692.
  Works established, 1875.
  Total population of area supplied, 22,500 estimated.
  Death rate, average 15·95 per 1,000.
  Towns and villages in the area supplied—Choppington, Sleekburn, Guide Post,
    Cambois, Netherton, and Bedlington.
  Source of supply, River Blyth.
  Character of water, clear appearance ; colour, faintly yellow ; taste, soft ; smell,
    nil ; smell after boiling, nil ; reaction, neutral ; sediment, nil ; microscopical
    examination of sediment, nil ; total hardness, 10°.
  Filtration, sand and high-pressure filters.
  Storage capacity, service reservoir, 682,000 gals.
  Head on distributing mains—maximum, 182 feet ; minimum, 91 feet.
  Total quantity of water supplied per annum, 123,000,000 gals.
  Average daily supply—domestic, 314,200 gals. ; trade, 23,300 gals.
  Charges for domestic supply included in general district rate.
    „   by meter, 7d. per 1,000 gals.
  Number of meters, 16.

Bedlinog, Glam. (supplied by MERTHYR TYDVIL).

Bedwellty (supplied by BLACKWOOD).

Beeston, Notts. (supplied by NOTTINGHAM).

Beith, Scotland. Railways, G.B. and K., and G. and S.W. Distance from Glasgow,
  18 miles.
  Authority, Corporation.
  Chairman, Robt. Urquhart.
  Manager, Wm. Dale.
  Secretary, Samuel Kerr.
  Office, New Cross.
  Area supplied, Beith and village of Gateside.

B**mith**—*continued.*

Total population of area supplied, 5,000.
Annual supply of water, 250,000,000 gals.
Source of supply, Cuff and surrounding hills.
Storage capacity, 21,000,000 gals. (2 reservoirs).
Character of water, pure and soft.
System of filtration, sand and gravel.
Number of meters, 15.
Length of mains, 8 miles.
Assessment charge, 4s. per £ on owner or occupier.
Price for 1,000 gals. 5¼d.
Total water rent received, £204.

Belfast.
Authority, Belfast City and District Water Commissioners.
Chairman, William Kerr.
Secretary, Richard Hamilton.
Engineer, F. W. McCullough, M.I.C.E.
Office, Waterworks Office, Royal Avenue, Belfast.
Local Water Authority's total borrowing powers, £2,111,000.
Works established, 1840.
Special Acts, 1840, 1865, 1874, 1879, 1884, 1889, 1893, 1897, 1899, and 1903.
Total population supplied, 390,000.
Average death rate, 20 per 1,000.
Towns and villages in the area supplied—City of Belfast, Carrickfergus, Green-
island, Jordanstown, Whiteabbey, Dunmurry, Newtownbreda and Cregagh.
Sources of supply, catchments at Woodburn, Stonyford and Mourne. Mountain
areas, consisting of upland pastures and moorlands. Impounding reservoirs, 7
at Woodburn and 2 at Stonyford. No reservoirs yet in the Mourne Mountains
area.
Character of water, Woodburn and Stonyford waters from 7° to 8° of hardness;
Mourne water, 4°.
System of filtration, sand.
Storage capacity, impounding reservoirs, 2,486,250,000 gals.; service reservoirs,
189,000,000 gals.
Pressure on distributing mains, maximum, 130 lbs.; minimum, 20 lbs. per sq. in.
Annual supply of wa·er, 5,373,595,335 gals.
Average daily consumption per head—domestic, 24·84 gals.; trade, 13·00 gals.
Maximum day's supply, 16,500,000 gals. in August and September.
Maximum authorised rating for domestic purposes up to 1s. 8d. in £.
Current rating, domestic purposes, 1s. 4d. in £.
Public rate, 3d. in £, not assessed on dwellings.
Price per 1,000 gals., 5¼d. to 10d., according to quantity.
The new supply from the Mourne Mountains, Co. Down, by gravitation, when
fully developed, will give an additional supply of 30,000,000 gals. per day.
Number of meters, 1,200, trade.
Total length of supply and distributing mains, 375 miles.

Belhaven (supplied by Dunbar).

Bellahouston (supplied by Glasgow).

Bellshill, Scotland (supplied by District of the Middle Ward of Lanarkshire).

Belper, Derbyshire. Railway, Midland. Distance from London, 134 miles.
Authority, Urban District Council. (The works are a gift from the chairman).
Chairman, Herbert Strutt, D.L., J.P.
Clerk, Joseph Pym.
Cost, upwards of £38,000.
Sources of supply in use, springs and well.

Benenden (supplied by CRANBROOK).

Benson (supplied by SOUTH OXFORDSHIRE).

Bentley (supplied by DONCASTER).

Benwell (supplied by NEWCASTLE-UPON-TYNE).

Berkhampstead (supplied by GREAT BERKHAMPSTEAD).

Bersted, Sussex (supplied by BOGNOR).

Bervie (Royal Burgh), Scotland. Railway, N.B.
　　Authority, Bervie Town Council.
　　Chairman of Water Committee, Provost Thom.
　　Secretary, James Andrews, Burgh Treasurer, Bervie.
　　Engineer in charge, John Sim, C.E., Burgh Surveyor.
　　Area of control, Royal Burgh of Inverbervie.
　　Population (1901), 1,500.
　　Annual supply of water (year 1906)—for all purposes, 8,000,000 gals.
　　Sources of supply—Total quantity of water drawn from various surface springs
　　　at Monlgoldrum, parish of Arbutbnot, Co. Kincardine, 8,000,000 gallons per
　　　annum.
　　Strata or formation yielding springs, conglomerate and trap.
　　Length of distributing mains, 10 miles.
　　Office, 160, High Street, Montrose.

Berwick Hill (supplied by NEWCASTLE-ON-TYNE).

Berwick-upon-Tweed. Railways, N.B. and N.E.R. Distance from London, 339 miles.
　　Authority, Berwick-upon-Tweed Sanitary Authority.
　　Chairman, Alderman Geo. Alfred Harrison.
　　Secretary, William Weatherhead, Town Clerk.
　　Resident Engineer, Rob. Dickinson.
　　Office, Sanitary Authority Buildings.
　　Loans outstanding, £6,000.
　　Works established, 1855.
　　Total population of area supplied, 9,000.
　　Average death rate, 18 per 1000.
　　District of supply, Berwick and Tweedmouth.
　　Sources of supply—Springs from Fellstone rock, Carboniferous series.
　　Character of water, pure ; total hardness, 15·3°.
　　Filtration, none ; softening, none.
　　Service reservoirs, 300,000 gals.
　　Annual supply of water, 110,000,000 gals.
　　Average daily supply, per head for all purposes, 29 gals.
　　Maximum day's supply 330,000 gals. in January.
　　Assessment charge, 10d. in £ on R.V.
　　Price per 1,000 gals., 8d. ; number of meters, 80.
　　Length of supply mains, 2½ miles ; distributing mains, 5¾ miles.

Besses (supplied by BURY).

Bestwood (supplied by NOTTINGHAM).

Beswick (supplied by MANCHESTER).

Betchton. *See* CONGLETON RURAL.

Betchworth (supplied by EAST SURREY).

Bethesda, N.Wales. (G. and W.) Railway, L.N.W. Distance from London, 240 miles.
Authority, Urban District Council.
Surveyor, Inspector and Collector, H. H. Davis.
Clerk to Council, D. G. Davies, Solicitor.
Towns and villages in the area supplied, Bethesda, Gerlan, Rachub.
Works established, 1884. Special Acts, 1875, 1879, 1880, 1882, 1883.
Total population of area supplied, 5,281.
Sources of supply, tributaries of the Ogwen.
Character of water, excellent.
Death rate, 26·8 per 1,000.
Assessment charges—Houses under £5, 5s. per annum ; over £5 and under £10,
6s. per annum ; over £10, 8d. in £.
Rateable value, £9,502.

Beverley, Yorks. Railway, N.E. Distance from London, 176 miles.
Authority, The Corporation of Beverley.
Chairman, Councillor Richard Cave.
Clerk to Authority, James Willis Mills, Town Clerk.
Manager, James Wood Thirsk.
Office, 31, Lairgate, Beverley.
Loans outstanding, £21,350.
Works established, 1881 ; Special Act, Beverley Waterworks Act, 1881.
Total population of area supplied, 13,000.
Total number of consumers, 5,900.
Purchased by the Corporation, March 25th, 1907, for £20,850.
Average death rate, 16·6 per 1,000.
District of supply, Borough of Beverley only.
Sources of supply, chalk rock.
Character of water—total hardness, $19\cdot_0°$, chiefly temporary.
System of filtration, none ; softening, none.
Storage capacity, 700,000 gals.
Annual supply of water, 83,000,000 gals.
Average daily consumption per head, 26 gals. ; trade, &c., 13 gals.
Assessment charge, according to scale—

From 1/3	per quarter on Annual Rent of	£4,			
„ 3/6	„	„	··	„	£10,
„ 7/6	·,	:,	„	„	£20,
„ 9/-	„	„	„	„	£30,
To 30/-	„	„	„	„	£100,

Including one w.c.

Charges per 1,000 gallons—
Not exceeding an average for the quarter of 4,000 gals. per day, 10d.
Exceeding 4,000 and under 10,000 per day, 9d.
Exceeding 10,000 and under 30,000 per day, 8d.
Exceeding 30,000 per day, 6d.
*N.B.—Meters are provided and kept in order by the company, who will charge for the use
thereof a quarterly rent proportionate to the size.*
Number of meters, 64.
Length of mains, 11 miles.
The Corporation intend changing their source of supply to a different locality, and
Mr. Baldwin Latham has been engaged as Consulting Engineer, to advise as to
the new site.

Bewdley, Worcester. Railway, G.W. Distance from London, 137½ miles.
Authority, Town Council.
Manager, A. W. Humpherson.
Population, 2866.

Bexhill, Sussex. (G. & W.) Railway, L.B.S.C. Distance from London 71 miles.
Authority, Bexhill Water and Gas Company.
Office, Manager's office, Bexhill.
Towns and villages in the area supplied—Bexhill, Sidley, and Little Connon.
Works established, 1885.
Total population of area supplied, 12,210.
Sources of supply, wells.
Character of water, ferruginous.
System of filtration, sand.
Scale of charges—
　　Domestic, according to rental.
　　Priceper 1,000 gals., trade, 1s. 6d. to 1s.
　　Charges for municipal purposes, 1s. per 1.000.

Bicester, Oxon. Railway, L.N.W. Distance from London, 66 miles.
Authority, U.D.C.
Population supplied, 3,000.
Source of supply, deep well.
Assessment charge, 5 per cent. on R.V.

Bickerstaffe, Lancs. parts of (supplied by ORMSKIRK and SKELMERSDALE).

Bickleigh (supplied by PLYMOUTH).

Biddulph, Staffs.
Authority, U.D.C.
Population supplied, 6,300.

Bideford, Devon. Railways, L.S.W., G.W. Distance from London, 220 miles.
Authority, Corporation.
Town Clerk, W. B. Seldon.
Surveyor, R. E. L. Hookway.
Office, Broad Quay.
Population supplied, 8,754.
Daily consumption per head, 25 gals.
Source of supply in use, moorland collecting area.
Storage capacity, 24,140,000 gals.
Filtration, fine sand filters.
Character of water, soft.
Number of meters in use, 120.
Length of mains, 7 miles.
Price per 1,000 gals., 2s.
Total water rent received about £1,200.

Bidston, Cheshire (supplied by BIRKENHEAD).

Biggar, Lanark, N.B. Railway, Caledonian. Distance from London, 440 miles.
Authority, Town Council.
Engineer in charge, L. Murray Heavyside.
Clerk, Andrew Smail.
Office, Main Street.
Towns and villages in the area supplied—Biggar, Culter and District
Date of formation of Burgh, 1863.
Special Act, General Police Act, 1892.
Total population of area supplied, 2,000.
Source of supply, Kingsbeck Culter.
Character of water, very good.
Death rate, about 25 per 1,000.
Length of mains, 6 miles.
Assessment charge, 6d. per £ on rental.

Biggleswade, Beds. Railway, G.N. Distance from London, 41 miles.
Authority, Biggleswade Water Board.
Engineer, G. F. Deacon, M.I.C.E.
Works opened, February, 1907.
Source of supply, deep well into the Lower Greensand.
Length of mains, 70 miles.

Billingley (supplied by Dearne Valley).

Billington (supplied by Blackburn).

Bilston, Staffs. Railways, L.N.W. and G.W. Distance from London, 139 miles.
Authority, Bilston Urban District Council (1897).
Chairman, John William Sankey, J.P.
Clerk to Authority, John D. Wassell (Solicitor).
Resident Engineer, J. P. Wakeford, A.M.I.C.E.
Office, Town Hall, Bilston.
Consulting Engineer, Baldwin Latham, M.I.C.E., Westminster.
Loans outstanding, £55,384.
Profit (1905-6), £401 6s. 2d.
Works established 1895; Special Acts, 1893, 1896.
Total population supplied, 34,297.
Average death rate, about 17.
Area of supply, Bilston, Crosely (part), Himsley, Swindon, Leisdon, Trysull.
Source of supply, well in Red Sandstone with adits driven, situated at the Bratch,
    Wombourne, and pumped through four miles of rising mains to service reservoir.
Analysis of water, made 8th February, 1907—

	Grains per gallon.
Total solid matter dried at 212° F.	28·7
Free and saline ammonia	0·000
Albuminoid ammonia	0·000
Nitric nitrogen	0·58
Combined chlorine	1·68
Oxygen absorbed in 4 hours at 80° F.	0·000
Appearance	clear
Colour through 2 feet	very pale bluish tinge
Injurious metallic contamination	none
Hardness before boiling	19·48°
„ after „	9·20°
Temporary hardness...	10·28

Bacteriological examination—

	Organisms per cubic centimetre.
On gelatine at 20° C.	5
On agar-agar at 37° C.	2
„ „ „ „ acidified and phenolixed	1

Filtration, none; softening, none.
Storage capacity, service reservoir, 838,000 gals.
Annual supply, 291,853,000 gals.
Average daily consumption per head, domestic, 17·92 gals. per head; trade, &c.,
    5·35 gals.
Maximum day's supply, 1,120,321 gals., in September, 1906.
Assessment charge, 7 per cent. on R.V. Charge by meter.

BILSTON—*continued.*

Extract from scale—

						£	s.	d.	
5,000 gals. per quarter	...	...	...	...	0	10	0	per quarter.
10,000 ,,	,,	...	...	...	...	0	15	0	,,
20,000 ,,	,,	...	...	...	...	1	5	0	,,
30,000 ,,	,,	...	...	...	...	1	14	7	,,
50,000 ,,	,,	...	...	...	...	2	11	3	,,
100,000 ,,	,	...	...	...	...	0	0	10	per 1,000 gals.
210,000 ,,	,,	...	...	...	..	0	0	7½	,,
400,000 ,,	,,	...	...	...	...	0	0	6	,,
Over 400,000 gals.	...	...	...	...	...	0	0	5	per 1,000

No. of meters, 141.

Bilton (supplied by HARROGATE).

Bilton (supplied by Rugby).

Bimfield (supplied by WOKINGHAM).

Bingley, Yorks. Railway, M. Distance from London, 208 miles.
Authority, Bingley District Council.
Manager, Walker Crowther.
Town Clerk, Alfred Platts.
Office, Town Hall.
Loan, £11,177.
Special Act, 1881.
Total population of area supplied, 18,448.
Sources of supply—springs and Bradford Corporation supply.
Character of water, soft.
Death rate, 16·0 per 1,000.
Number of meters, 66.
Assessment charge, 5 per cent. to 7½ per cent. on the gross estimated rental.
Price for 1,000 gals., 1s. 3d.
Total water rent received, £2,969.

Binstead, Isle of Wight (supplied by RYDE).

Binstead, Surrey (partly supplied by Wey Valley).

Birkdale (see SOUTHPORT).

Birkenhead and **Claughton**, Cheshire. Railways, L.N.W. and G.W. Distance
from London, 194½ miles.
Authority, Corporation of Birkenhead, 1858.
Chairman, H. Bloor, J.P.
Water Engineer, J. W. M. Richardson, A.M.I.C.E.
Office, 52, Balls Road, Birkenhead.
Towns and villages in the area supplied, Birkenhead, Tranmere, and Bidston.
Works established, 1841. Special Acts, 1858, 1867, 1881.
Total population of area supplied, 110,547.
Annual supply of water, 1,324,006,372 gals.
Daily consumption per head, domestic, 22·75 gals.; trade, 10·40 gals.
Source of supply, wells and boreholes.
Storage capacity, 6,064,638 gals.
Death rate, 17·7 per 1,000.
Number of meters, 620.
Length of mains, 106 miles.
Assessment charge, £4 5s. 6d. per cent.
Price per 1,000 gals., when partly trade and partly domestic, 1s. 1d. less 10 per
cent.; trade, 9½d., less rebate 10 per cent.; municipal purposes, 8d. per 1,000.

Birmingham. Railways, L.N.W., M., and G.W. Distance from London, 113 miles.
　Authority, City of Birmingham Water Department.
　Chairman of Water Committee, Alderman E. Lawley Parker, J.P.
　Clerk to authority, Ebenezer Antony Lees, 44, Broad Street, Birmingham.
　Resident Engineer for Elan Supply, F. W. Macaulay, M.I.C.E., Springfield House,
　　Ludlow.
　Resident Engineer for Local Works and distribution, William Gray, A.M.I.C.E.,
　　Birmingham.
　Office, 44, Broad Street, Birmingham.
　Loans outstanding to 31st March, 1907, £7,959,429 13s. 7d.
　Annual loss on undertaking, including "Capital Charges," 31st March, 1907,
　　£84,615 18s. 11d.
　Works established, first service laid in the year 1831.
　Purchased by local authority 1st January, 1876.
　Acts of Parliament or Provisional Orders (with dates)—
　　　　Birmingham Waterworks Act, 1826
　　　　　　　　"　　　　"　　(Capital) Act, 1854
　　　　　　　　"　　　　"　　Act, 1855
　　　　　　　　"　　　　"　　"　1866
　　　　　　　　"　　　　"　　"　1870
　　　　　　　　"　　(Corporation) Water Act, 1875
　　　　　　　　"　　　　"　　　"　　"　1879
　　All the powers contained in the above Acts were confirmed under the
　　　Birmingham Corporation (Consolidation) Act, 1883
　　　　　　　　"　　　　"　　Water Act, 1892
　　　　　　　　"　　　　"　　"　　"　1896
　　　　　　　　"　　　　"　　"　　"　1902
　　　　　　　　"　　　　"　　Act, 1905
　Towns and villages within the area of control, with population of each (1901
　　Census)—City of Birmingham ...　...　...　...　...　...　522,204
　　　　　　　　Aston Manor　...　...　...　...　...　...　77,326
　　　　　　　　Erdington　...　...　...　...　...　...　15,695
　　　　　　　　Witton　...　...　...　...　...　...　...　673
　　　　　　　　Handsworth　...　...　...　...　...　...　52,921
　　　　　　　　Perry Barr　...　...　...　...　...　...　2,348
　　　　　　　　King's Norton　...　...　..　...　...　...　35,790
　　　　　　　　Northfield　.　...　...　...　...　...　20,767
　　　　　　　　Castle Bromwich　...　...　...　...　...　845
　　　　　　　　Minworth　...　...　...　..　...　...　688
　　　　　　　　Curdworth　...　...　...　...　...　...　419
　　　　　　　　Water Orton　...　...　...　...　...　...　620
　　　　　　　　Coleshill　...　...　...　...　...　..　2,593
　　　　　　　　Bickenhill　...　...　...　...　...　...　528
　　　　　　　　Sheldon　...　...　...　...　...　...　419
　　　　　　　　Yardley　...　...　...　...　...　...　33,946
　　　　　　　　Solihull (including Olton)　..　...　...　...　7,517
　　　　　　　　Elmdon　...　...　...　...　...　...　203
　　　　　　　　　　　　　　　　　　　　　　　　　　　　──────
　　　　　　　　　　　　　　　　　　　　　　　　　　　　775,502

　All the above are supplied with the exception of Sheldon and Elmdon.
　Total population of area of control, 1881, 561,537 ; 1891, 647,972 ; 1901, 775,502.
　Estimated population actually supplied—31st March, 1907—on the basis of 4·5
　　persons to each house, 800,167.
　Death rate (year ending 31st December, 1906), 16·8 per 1,000.
　Source of Supply :—The full supply is now obtained from the new works in the
　　Elan Valley, Mid Wales, from the watersheds of the Elan and Claerwen
　　tributaries of the River Wye—the local sources being retained as stand-by
　　and supplementary.
　General characteristics of water, pure and soft.

BIRMINGHAM—*continued.*

System of filtration, rough sand filtration at the source, with second fine sand
　　filtration at Frankley—*i.e.*, the Birmingham end of the aqueduct.
Softening none, ; hardness after second filtration, 3·0°.
Analysis of water:—

Total solid matter ...　...　...　...　...	6·4
Free ammonia　...　...　...　...　...	·000
Albuminoid or organic ammonia　...　...	·000
Nitrogen in nitrates　...　...　...　...	·0
Oxygen consumed in 4 hours at 27° C. ...　...	·23
Chlorine in chlorides　...　...　...　...	1·0
Hardness　...　...　...　...　...　...	3·0
Total alkalinity as CaCO₃　...　...　...	2·8
Turbidity　...　...　...　...　...　...	0
Colour :—Appearance in 2 ft. tube	
Red ...　...　...　...　...	1·0
Yellow　...　...　...　...	5·0
Blue　...　...　...　...	0

Total alkalinity as $CaCO_3$ = 2·8

Storage capacity of impounding reservoirs, 12,341,250,000 gals.
　　　　　　,,　　　　,,　　　　,,　　service reservoirs, 225,500,000 gals.
Pressure on distributing mains—Maximum, 97½ lbs. per sq. in.
Head　　　,,　　　　,,　　　　,,　　　　225 feet.
Pressure　,,　　　　,,　　　　,,　　Minimum, 8½ lbs. per sq. in.
Head　　　,,　　　　,,　　　　,,　　　　20 feet.
Total quantity of water supplied per annum (year ending March 31st, 1907),
　　7,810,000,000 gals.
Average daily supply per head—domestic, fire and waste, 13·7 gals. ; trade or
　　special, 10·08.
Maximum day's supply, 25,471,000 gals. in month of January, 1907.

EXTRACTS FROM SCALE OF CHARGES.

SCALE No. 1.—OCCUPIERS.

SCHEDULE OF ANNUAL WATER RENTS FOR DOMESTIC PURPOSES.

Weekly Rents, Occupiers paying Rates and Taxes.	NET ANNUAL VALUE.	Annual Water Rents.	Maximum Authorised Water Rents.
s.　d.		£　s.　d.	£　s.　d.
2　3	Not exceeding £5　0　0　...　...　...　...	0　6　0	0　6　0
2　9	Exceeding £5　0　0 but not exceeding £7　10　0	0　8　0	0　8　0
3　5	Ditto　　　　　　ditto　　　...　...	0　8　0	0　8　0
3　6	Exceeding £7　10　0 but not exceeding £10　0　0	0　10　0	0　10　4
4　6	Ditto　　　　　　ditto　　　...　...	0　10　0	0　10　4
4　9	Exceeding £10　0　0 but not exceeding £12　10　0	0　16　0	0　16　9
5　6	Ditto　　　　　　ditto　　　...　...	0　16　0	0　16　9
5　9	Exceeding £12　10　0 but not exceeding £15　0　0	1　4　0	1　4　0
6　9	Ditto　　　　　　ditto　　　...　...	1　4　0	1　4　0
7　0	Exceeding £15　0　0 but not exceeding £17　10　0	1　7　0	1　11　0
7　9	Ditto　　　　　　ditto　　　...　...	1　7　0	1　11　0

BIRMINGHAM—*continued.*

Weekly Rents, Occupiers paying Rates and Taxes.	NET ANNUAL VALUE.			Annual Water Rents.			Maximum Authorised Water Rents.		
s. d.				£	s.	d.	£	s.	d.
8 0	Exceeding £17 10 0 but not exceeding £20 0 0			1	10	0	1	18	0
9 0	Ditto　　　　　　　ditto　　　...　　...			1	10	0	1	18	0
9 3	Exceeding £20 0 0 but not exceeding £25 0 0			1	18	0	2	4	6
10 0	Ditto　　　　　　　ditto　　　...　　...			1	18	0	2	4	6
Annual Rents.									
£ s. d.									
30 0 0	Exceeding £20 0 0 but not exceeding £25 0 0			1	18	0	2	4	6
35 0 0	Ditto £25 0 0　　ditto　£30 0 0			2	5	0	2	9	6
40 0 0	Ditto £30 0 0　　ditto　£35 0 0			2	12	0	2	14	0
50 0 0	Ditto £35 0 0　　ditto　£40 0 0			2	17	0	2	17	0
60 0 0	Ditto £40 0 0　　ditto　£50 0 0			3	0	0	3	0	0
	Exceeding　...　...　...　...　£50 0 0			At the rate of 6 per cent. on the amount of the Net Annual Value.			At the rate of 6 per cent. on the amount of the Net Annual Value.		

SCALE No. 2.—LANDLORDS.

Weekly Rents, Landlords paying Rates and Taxes.	NET ANNUAL VALUE.			Annual Water Rents to Landlords who agree to pay whether the Houses are occupied or not.			Maximum Authorised Water Rents.		
s. d.				£	s.	d.	£	s.	d.
2 9	Not exceeding £5 0 0　...　...　...　...			0	6	0	0	6	0
3 6	Exceeding £5 0 0 but not exceeding £7 10 0			0	8	0	0	8	0
4 3	Ditto　　　　　　ditto　　　...　　...			0	8	0	0	8	0
4 6	Exceeding £7 10 0 but not exceeding £10 0 0			0	10	0	0	10	4
5 9	Ditto　　　　　　ditto　　　...　　...			0	10	0	0	10	4
6 0	Exceeding £10 0 0 but not exceeding £12 10 0			0	15	0	0	16	9
8 0	Ditto　　　　　　ditto　　　...　　...			0	16	6	0	16	9
8 3	Exceeding £12 10 0 but not exceeding £15 0 0			1	0	0	1	4	0
9 6	Ditto　　　　　　ditto　　　...　　...			1	0	0	1	4	0
9 9	Exceeding £15 0 0 but not exceeding £17 10 0			1	2	0	1	11	0
10 0	Ditto　　　　　　ditto　　　...　　...			1	2	0	1	11	0
Annual Rents.									
£ s. d.									
25 0 0	Exceeding £17 10 0 but not exceeding £20 0 0			1	4	0	1	18	0
30 0 0	Ditto £20 0 0　　ditto　£25 0 0			1	9	6	2	4	6
35 0 0	Ditto £25 0 0　　ditto　£30 0 0			1	15	6	2	9	6
40 0 0	Ditto £30 0 0　　ditto　£35 0 0			2	1	6	2	14	0
50 0 0	Ditto £35 0 0　　ditto　£40 0 0			2	7	6	2	17	0
60 0 0	Ditto £40 0 0　　ditto　£50 0 0			2	17	0	3	0	0

BIRMINGHAM—*continued.*

N.B.—Retail Shop Premises.—Where any part of the supply is used for domestic purposes, the annual water rent charges will be the sums of between 5 and 3 per cent. on the net annual value or rateable value, as the particular nature of the supply and the amount of the net annual value or rateable value exceeding £50 may determine, subject to the right of the Corporation to supply the water by meter on terms.

    Retail Shops, Offices, etc.—The annual water rent charges will be the sum of 3 per cent. on the net annual value or rateable value exceeding £50, but in no case to be less than £2 10s. a year, with a further charge for any supply other than that of an ordinary kind to retail shops, offices, etc., subject to the right of the Corporation to supply the water by meter on terms.

BATHS AS FOLLOWS:—

Houses of a net annual value not exceeding	£25	0	0	£0	6	0
Exceeding £25 0 0 but not exceeding	£50	0	0	£0	8	0
Exceeding £50 0 0				£0	10	0

    A supply of water for domestic purposes shall include a supply for one water-closet, but not for baths, or for cattle, or for horses, or washing carriages, where such horses or carriages are kept for hire, or by common carriers, or for any trade, manufacture, or business whatsoever, or for watering gardens, or for fountains, or for any ornamental purpose.

    In addition to the rates for the supply for domestic purposes, the Corporation may demand and receive, for every additional water closet beyond the first, in any house, any yearly sum not exceeding four shillings.

Supplies for other than domestic purposes by agreement.

SCALE No. 3.—METERS.

SCALE OF CHARGES FOR THE SUPPLY OF WATER BY METER FOR TRADE PURPOSES.

Payable Quarterly.

For any quantity not exceeding 10,000 Gallons, 20s. per quarter.
Exceeding 10,000, but not exceeding 15,000, 25s. per quarter.
Exceeding 15,000, but not exceeding 20,000, 30s. per quarter.

Exceeding	20,000, but not exceeding	50,000,	per quarter, at	1/7	per 1,000	gallons
Ditto	50,000,	ditto	100,000,	ditto	1/6	ditto
Ditto	100,000,	ditto	150,000,	ditto	1/5	ditto
Ditto	150,000,	ditto	200,000,	ditto	1/4	ditto
Ditto	200,000,	ditto	250,000,	ditto	1/3	ditto
Ditto	250,000,	ditto	300,000,	ditto	1/2	ditto
Ditto	300,000,	ditto	350,000,	ditto	1/1	ditto
Ditto	350,000,	ditto	450,000,	ditto	1/-	ditto
Ditto	450,000,	ditto	600,000,	ditto	-/11	ditto
Ditto	600,000,	ditto	800,000,	ditto	-/10	ditto
Ditto	800,000,	ditto	1,000,000,	ditto	-/9	ditto
Ditto	1,000,000,	ditto	1,500,000,	ditto	-/8	ditto
Ditto	1,500,000,	ditto	2,000,000,	ditto	-/7	ditto
Ditto	2,000,000, per quarter	-	-	-	-/6	ditto

MINIMUM QUARTERLY CHARGES FOR SUPPLIES OF WATER THROUGH METERS OF A LARGER SIZE THAN ORDINARY.

½	Inch £1 10s. (entitling the Consumer to 19,000 gallons per quarter).					
¾	Inch £2 5s.	ditto	ditto	29,000	ditto.	
1	Inch £4 10s.	ditto	ditto	60,000	ditto.	
1½	Inch £10	ditto	ditto	142,000	ditto.	
2	Inch £16	ditto	ditto	275,000	ditto.	

No boiler is to be supplied direct from the corporation main.

BIRMINGHAM—*continued.*

Scale of charges :—
Present average charge by meter (March 31st, 1907), 11·25d. per 1,000 gals.
Number of meters, 4,218 (March 31st, 1907).
Total length of supply mains (not including aqueduct), 139¼ miles ; total length of service mains, 599¼ miles.

Birstall, Leicester (supplied by LEICESTER).

Birstall, Yorks., near Leeds. (G. and W.) Railways, L.N.W. and G.N. Distance from London, 185 miles.
Authority, Birstall Urban District Council.
Clerk, Wm. Middlebrook, Morley, nr. Leeds.
Total capital invested, including loans, £11,550.
Area of control, Birstall Urban District.
Works established, 1864. Special Act, 1872. Provisional Order, 1887.
Total population of area of control, 1891, 6,528 ; 1901, 6,559.
Total number of consumers, 1,900.
Death rate, 19·85 per 1,000.
Annual supply of water for domestic purposes, 19,295,000 gals ; trade, 18,923,000 gals.
Water is purchased from Bradford Corporation by meter.
Service reservoir at Drighlington ; capacity, 250,000 gals., covered.
Character of water, soft.
Number of meters in use, 101.
Length of distributing mains, 11 miles.
Assessment charge, from 2s. 6d. per quarter.
Price per 1,000 gals, trade only, 2s. 6d. to 10d.
Office, Gas Works, Birstall, nr. Leeds.

Birtley (supplied by NEWCASTLE).

Bisham (supplied by GREAT MARLOW).

Bishop Auckland, Durham. Railway, N.E. Distance from London, 250 miles.
Authority, Urban District Council.
Engineer and Manager, R. Lindsay, Town Hall Buildings.
Towns and villages in the area supplied, Bishop Auckland, Southchurch and Bonchester.
Works established, 1859.
Total population of area supplied, 13,000.
Daily consumption per head—domestic and trade, 27 gals.
Total quantity of water drawn per annum, 115,000,000 gals.
Sources of supply in use, central drifts underneath gravel beds, with catchpits.
Storage capacity, 400,000 gals.
Filtration, sand after being pumped from drifts.
Character of water, very good, both tests and bacteriologically, only 40 per cub. centimetre after filtering.
Death rate, 16 per 1,000.
Number of meters in use, 12.
Length of mains, 6 miles.
Scale of charges—domestic assessment 4d. in the £.
Trade purposes, 6d. per 1,000 gals.
Total water revenue received, £1,900.

Bishopbriggs (supplied by GLASGOW).

Bishop's Castle, Salop. Railway, L.N.W. Distance from London, 180 miles.
  Authority, District Council.
  Total population of area supplied, 1,378.
  Sources of supply, mountain stream (gravitation).
  Assessment charge, 1s. in £.

Bishopston (supplied by RIPON).

Bishopstone (supplied by NEWHAVEN).

Bishop's Stortford, Herts.
  Authority, Urban District Council.
  Clerk, T. Swatheridge.
  Population, 7,000.

Bishopstrow (supplied by WARMINSTER).

Bishopthorpe (supplied by YORK).

Bisley (supplied by WOKING).

Bix (supplied by SOUTH OXFORDSHIRE).

Blackburn, Lancs. Railways, L. & Y., L.N.W. & M. Distance from London, 212
  miles.
  Authority, Corporation, 1875.
  Chairman, Edwin Hamer.
  Manager, Joseph Wilson.
  Secretary, Lewis Beard, Town Clerk.
  Engineer in charge, Wm. Stubbs, A.M.I.C.E.
  Office, Municipal Offices.
  Special Acts, 1845, 1868, 1877. Works established, 1845. Purchased by the Cor-
    poration, 1877.
  Stock, £623,119 5s. 10d. (3 per cent.).
  Loans, £34,160 ; annuities (taken at 33½ years' purchase), £230,545.
  Annual loss, including " Capital Charges," £305.
  Population supplied with water, 134,438.
  Average annual death rate, 16·4.
  Area supplied, 7,000 acres.
  Towns and villages in the area supplied—Blackburn, Cherry Tree, Wilpshire,
    Linesey, Hurst Green, Langho and Billington.
  Source of supply, Gathering ground, Forest of Bowland.
  General character of water, peaty ; 2° to 3° hardness.
  No filtration.
  Storage in service reservoirs, 400,000,000 gals.
  Head on distributing mains—maximum, 275 feet ; minimum, 45 feet.
  Length of supply mains, 20 miles ; distributing mains, 124¼ miles.
  Total quantity supplied per annum, 1,240,443,000 gals.
  Average daily supply—domestic, 1,852,000 gals. ; trade, 1,545,000 gals.
  Maximum supply per day, 3,725,000 gals., in July.
  Authorised charge (domestic), 10% on R.V. ; present actual charge, 8% on R.V.
  Price charged by meter, 2s. to 6d. per 1,000 gals. No. of meters, 725.

Black Lane (supplied by BURY).

Blackley (supplied by MANCHESTER).

Blacko (supplied by NELSON).

Blackpool, Lancs. (supplied by THE FYLDE WATERWORKS CO.).

Blackrock (supplied by DUBLIN).

Blackston, Scotland (supplied by PAISLEY).

Blackwater, Hants (supplied by FRIMLEY).

Blackwell (supplied by CARLISLE).

Blackwood, Mon. Railway, L.N.W. Distance from London, 160 miles.
  Authority, Bedwellty Urban District Council.
  Chairman, J. V. Lewis, J.P.
  Engineer and Manager, J. H. Lewis, A.M.I.C.E., Surveyor.
  Clerk, T. J. Thomas.
  Towns and villages in the area supplied—Argoed, Rock, Blackwood, Bedwellty,
    and New Tredegar in the summer.
  Works established, 1890.
  Total population supplied, 9,000.
  Sources of supply—in bulk from Tredegar Urban District Council.
  Character of water, spring.
  Death rate, 17·23 per 1,000.
  Number of meters, 37.
  Length of mains, 6 miles.
  Price for 1,000 gals.—domestic, 3¼d. ; trade, 5d.

Blaenau Festiniog (see FESTINIOG).

Blaenavon, Mon. Railways, L.N.W. and G.W.
  Authority, Urban District Council.
  Works established, 1867. Special Acts, 1871.
  Total population of area supplied, 10,869.
  Source of supply—spring.
  Character of water, 2·90° hardness.
  Death rate, 15·67 per 1,000.

Blaina (*see* NANTYGLO and BLAINA).

Blairgowrie, Scotland. Railway, Caledonian. Distance from London, 500 miles.
  Authority, Local Authority.
  Towns and villages supplied—Blairgowrie, Rosemont, part of Rattray, Oakbank,
    Bramblebank and Ashbank.
  Works established, 1870.
  Special Act, Public Health Act.
  Total population supplied, 5,000.
  Daily consumption per head—domestic and trade, 40 gals.
  Source of supply, Highland loch about 8 miles N.W. of Blairgowrie.
  Storage capacity, 275,000 gals. in tanks and 30,000 in filters.
  System of filtration, sand.
  Character of water, pure and soft.
  Death rate, 15 per 1,000.

BLAIRGOWRIE—*continued.*

    Number of meters in use, 1 Deacon meter on main, 3 on service.
    Length of mains, 10 miles.
    Scale of charges—
        Assessment, 5d. in the £, payable by owner and occupier equally.
        Price per 1,000 gallons, trade, 6d.
    Total revenue received, £627.

Blandford, Dorset. Railway, S. and D. Joint. Distance from London, 120 miles.
    Authority, Blandford Water Co., Ld.
    Chairman, W. E. Lammer.
    Manager and Secretary, Chas. E. Porter.
    Office, 3, Alexandra Street, Blandford.
    Share capital paid up, £8,200 ; loan debentures, £2,000.
    Dividend, 5 per cent. (1906); interest on loan, 4 per cent.
    Towns and villages in the area supplied, Blandford, Pimperne, Blandford St.
      Mary, Bryanstone, Langton, Charlton Marshall, Spettisley.
    Works established, 1894.
    Total population of area supplied, 3,700.
    Source of supply, deep wells in the chalk.
    Storage capacity, 150,000 gals.
    Character of water, excellent. 12° of hardness.
    Filtration, none.
    Total quantity of water supplied per annum, 25,000,000 gals.
    Average daily supply—domestic, 70,000 ; trade, 1,000.
    Length of mains, 6 miles.
    Charges authorised and actually charged, 6 per cent. on rateable value.
        „   „   per meter, 2s. 6d. per 1,000 gals., actual charge, 1s. 9d. to 9d.
    per 1,000.
    No. of meters, 8.

Blandford St. Mary (supplied by BLANDFORD).

Blantyre (supplied by LANARKSHIRE).

Blaydon-on-Tyne, Durham. Railway, N.E. Distance from London, 272 miles.
    Authority, Blaydon Urban District Council.
    Chairman, William Archer, J.P.
    Clerk, Henry Dalton, Council Offices, Blaydon-on-Tyne.
    Engineer in charge, George Symon.
    Office, Council Office, Blaydon-on-Tyne.
    Total capital invested, including loans, £15,000. Loans outstanding, £5,781.
    Works established, 1875.
    Total population of area of control—1881, 10,687 ; 1891, 13,369 ; 1901, 19,633.
    Total number of consumers, 4,500.
    Estimated population actually supplied, 22,500.
    Average death rate, 17·81 per 1,000.
    Towns and villages within the area of control—Blaydon, Winlaton, Stella, Der-
      wenthaugh, Spen, Victoria Garesfield, Barlow, Chopwell, Thornley, Rowlands
      Gill and Winlaton Mill.
    Sources of supply—Shallow wells or collecting reservoirs situated at Stella Hall
      Wood, High Wood, near Blaydon Burn Colliery.
    Well situated at Winlaton (1), Blaydon (1).
    No geological data available ; water from surface springs only.
    Estimated total quantity of water available from various sources per annum—
        From shallow wells or subsoil   ...   .   14,587,000 gals.
        „   deep wells or borings ...   .   29,560,000 „

BLAYDON-ON-TYNE—*continued.*

Total quantity of water drawn from various sources, per annum (year 1906)—

Shallow wells or subsoil	...	...	...	...	18,684,000 gals.
Deep wells or borings	...	...	...	...	22,135,000 ,,
Purchased in bulk, Weardale and Consett Co.	...	32,317,000 ,,
,, ,, Newcastle and Gateshead Co.	47,136,000 ,,

Supply of water for all purposes (1906), 120,272,000 gals. = 14·37 gals. per head per day.

Service reservoirs—		Capacity.		
Service reservoirs—	Victoria Garesfield	45,000 gals.	424·70 feet above O.D.
,, ,,	Barlow	150,000 ,,	550·84 ,, ,,
,, ,,	Stella Hall Wood	120,000 ,,	104·32 ,, ,,
,, ,,	Blaydon Bank ...	25,000 ,,	136·22 ,, ,,
,, ,,	Stella House ...	very small.	55·70 ,, ,,

Consett Water Co.'s Horsegate Reservoir, 783·20 feet.

Chopwell springs :—West spring, 698·10 feet ; tank, 685·82 feet ; east spring, 597·17 feet.

Tank near Clayton Terrace, 652·11 feet ; tank on Barlow Fell, 559·84 feet.

Wind motor tank, Winlaton, 449·00 feet : tank on Blaydon Bank, 232·52 feet ; tank (new) at High Thornley, 428·70 feet.

NOTE,—Altitudes given are those of *outlet* of reservoirs and springs and *surface* of tanks.

Filtration none.

Water is not softened—(not necessary).

Head on distributing mains, maximum, 234 ft. ; minimum, nil.

Number of meters in use, 117.

Length of distributing mains, 38·8 miles, and 5·75 Ryton and Blaydon joint mains.

Assessment charge, 2 per cent. to 5 per cent. on R.V.

Average charge by meter, 1s. per 1,000 gals.

The district is situated partly within the area that may legally be supplied by Consett Waterworks Company and partly within that of the Newcastle and Gateshead Water Company, from both of whom they purchase water in bulk, having two connections with each, at Chopwell and Horsegate and at Swalwell and Blaydon. The Council also possess five sources of supply of their own at Stella (two), Blaydon Burn (one), Blaydon Bank (one) and Winlaton (one).

Blean. Eddington, nr. Canterbury.
Authority, Blean Rural District Council.
No returns supplied.

Blyth U.D.C. (supplied by NEWCASTLE-ON-TYNE).

Bobbingworth (supplied by HERTS and ESSEX).

Boddington (supplied by CHELTENHAM).

Bodeboyddan (supplied by RHYL).

Bodmin, Cornwall. Railways, G.W., L.S.W. Distance from London, 271½ miles.
Authority, Bodmin Waterworks Co.
Chairman, John Martin H. Cardell.
Secretary, E. J. Bricknell.
Office, Fore Street, Bodmin.
Shares, capital paid up, £13,000.
Loan, £900. Interest, 4 per cent.
Dividend, 5 per cent. on pref., 5 per cent. on ordinary.
Total water rent received, £1,164.

BODMIN—*continued.*

Works established, 1866.
Special Acts, 1866, 1893.
Source of supply, Hamatethy, St. Breward.
Towns and villages supplied, Bodmin borough and parish, St. Breward parish.
Character of water, soft.
Filtration, sand.
Daily consumption per head, 40 gals.
Service reservoir, 250,000 gals.
Pressure in distributing mains—max. 110 lbs. per sq. in. ; min., 40 lbs. per sq. in.
Length of mains, 12 miles.
Total quantity supplied per annum, 100,000,000 gals.
Average daily supply per head, 36 gals.
Maximum daily supply per head, 40 gals.
Charge authorised and present actual charge, 6 to 7 per cent. on rateable value.
Average charge per meters, 1s. 2d. per 100 gals.

Bognor, Sussex. Railway, L. B. S. C. Distance from London, 66 miles.
Authority, Bognor Water Company.
Chairman, Captain E. H. Hills, R.N., J.P.
Secretary, Wilson Tickle.
Address, London Road.
Engineer and Manager, Edward Brown.
Share capital paid up—Ordinary, 10 per cent., £8,950; Ordinary, 7 per cent.,
  £6,000; Preference, 5 per cent., £20,520 ; Debenture stock, 4 per cent., £8,860.
Dividends—8¾ per cent. on Ordinary 10 per cent. shares ; 6⅛ per cent. on Ordinary
  7 per cent. shares ; 5 per cent. on Preference shares.
Works established, 1870 ; special Act, 1891.
Total population supplied, 6,180.
Annual supply of water, 60,000,000 gals.
Sources of supply, deep wells in chalk.
Storage capacity, 550,000 gals., 100 feet above sea level.
Filtering, none.
Character of water, excellent.
Death rate, 11·6 per 1,000.
Number of meters in use, 150.
Length of mains, 15 miles.
Scale of charges, assessment charge, domestic, 5, 6 & 7 per cent. on rental.
  Trade, prices per 1,000 gals., 2s. 6d., 2s., 1s. 6d. and 1s., according to quantity.
Total revenue received, £4,417 8s. 7d.

Bold (supplied by WIDNES).

Bollington.
Authority, Urban District Council.
Population, 5,000.

Bolney (supplied by MID SUSSEX).

Bolsover, Derby. Railway, G.N. Distance from London, 151 miles.
Authority, Bolsover and District Water Co., Ltd.
Population of area supplied, 6,844.

Bolton, Lancs. Railways, L.N.W. and L. and Y. Distance from London, 196 miles.
Authority, Bolton Corporation.
Chairman of Water Committee, J. T. Cooper, solicitor.
Town Clerk, Samuel Parker, Town Hall.
Engineer in charge, R. H. Swindlehurst, M.I.C.E., Town Hall.

BOLTON—*continued.*

Total capital invested, including loans, £969,539 7s. 4d.
Towns and villages within the area of control, with population of each (1901 Census)—

Bolton	168,215
Farnworth	25,927
Kearsley	9,217
Turton	12,353
Worsley (Higher Division)	8,938
Little Hulton	7,294
Clifton	2,947
Over Hulton (part of)	550
Ainsworth	1,718

Works Established, 17th June, 1824.
Purchased by local authority, 8th June, 1847.
Special Acts, Bolton Improvement Acts of 1854, 1864, 1865, 1877, 1882, respectively. Bolton Corporation Act of 1872. Local Government Board's Provisional Orders Confirmation Acts, viz. (No. 11) Act, 1888 (No. 15) Act, 1894 (No. 5) Act, 1899. Bolton Act, 1905.
Total population of area of control, 1881, 183,637; 1891, 207,823; 1901, 237,159; 1907, 259,501.
Total number of consumers, 51,801.
Estimated population actually supplied, 265,000.
Annual supply of water—

For domestic purposes ...	...	...	...	1,475,000,000 gals.
„ trade „	..	...	...	700,000,000 „
„ municipal „	...	...	...	10,000,000 „
In bulk to other Authorities	...	...	...	135,000,000 „

Maximum day's consumption ... ... 9,000,000 „ July
Total quantity of water drawn from drainage area per annum, 2,185,000,000 gals.
Estimated total quantity of water available per annum from drainage areas— 2,555,000,000 gals.
Sources of supply in use—Drainage areas situated at Belmont, Heaton, Entwistle.
Maximum annual rainfall over drainage area Belmont 81·70 inches (1877).

„	„	„	„	„	Heaton	57·10 „	„
„	„	„	„	„	Entwistle	67·70 „	„
Minimum	„	„	„	„	Belmont	38·90 „	1887
„	„	„	„	„	Heaton	24·10 „	„
„	„	„	„	„	Entwistle	31·30 „	„
Average	„	„	„	„	Belmont	56·81 „	(period 58 years)
„	„	„	„	„	Heaton	42·21 „ „ 42 „	
„	„	„	„	„	Entwistle	53·06 „ „ 33 „	

Population on drainage area, 371.
Nature and extent of cultivation of ditto—
> 1,000 acres moorland, not under cultivation; 1,356 and 904 acres rough pasture meadow under ordinary cultivation for grazing. Out of a total drainage area of 3,260 acres, 2,356 acres have been purchased by the corporation.

Surface formation of drainage areas consists of shales and grits of the "Millstone Grit" series, covered in part by glacial drift.

Storage reservoirs, Springs...	...	...	...	capacity,	134,000,000 gals.
„ „ Dingle ...	...	...	...	„	79,000,000 „
„ „ Entwistle	...	...	...	„	625,000,000 „
„ „ High Rid	...	...	...	„	135,000,000 „

Filtering area provided, 15,258 square yards in 9 filter beds.

Service reservoirs, Heaton	...	capacity,	91,000,000 gals.	16·959 acres open
„ „ Sweetloves	„	90,000,000 „	13·304 „ „
„ „ Crowthorn	„	3,500,000 „	1·223 „ „

BOLTON—*continued*.

In addition to the above, which is purely for "domestic supply," there are separate drainage areas and reservoirs for the compensation water, which are as follows—

	Drainage area.	Capacity of reservoirs.	Statutory quantity to be delivered per day of 12 hours.
Belmont ...	1,823 acres ...	468,000,000 gals. ...	15 cubic feet per second
Rumworth...	684 „ ...	95,000,000 „ ...	4 „ „
Wayoh ...	3,437 „ ...	550,000,000 „ ...	16 „ „

Character of water, soft.
Death rate, 17·4 per 1,000.
Number of meters in use, 1,353.
Length of distributing mains, 181 miles.
Meter supplies for trade purposes—
　Inside the borough, minimum charge 5s. per quarter ; 6d. per 1,000 gals. above 10,000 gals per quarter.
　Outside the borough, minimum charge 7s. 6d. per quarter ; 9d. per 1,000 gals. above 10,000 gals. per quarter.
Water charges within the Borough—

	Domestic purposes.	Shops with Houses.	Lock-up Shops.
Rent £11 ...	... £0 15 0 ...	... £0 15 0 ...	... £0 12 0
to £100 ...	... 4 0 0 ...	... 2 13 4 ...	... 1 6 8

Above £100, 4 per cent. pro rata.
Water charges outside the Borough—

Rent £11 ...	... £0 15 4 ...	... £0 15 4 ...	... £0 12 0

Above £100, 5 per cent. pro rata.

Bolton-on-Dearne (supplied by DEARNE VALLEY).

Bonchester (supplied by BISHOP AUCKLAND).

Bondgate (supplied by RIPON).

Bo'ness, Scotland. Railway, N.B. Distance from London, 420 miles.
　Authority, Town Council.
　Chairman, Provost Marshall.
　Manager, John P. Lawrie, Borough Surveyor.
　Secretary, R. J. Jamieson, Town Clerk.
　Engineers, Leslie and Reed, C.E.
　Office, Burgh Chambers.
　Loans outstanding, £47,000.
　Works first constructed 1845. From 1876 to 1900 regulated by the Borough Police (Scotland) Act, 1892, and Town Councils Act, 1900. Provisional Order, 1897.
　Total population of area supplied, 12,000.
　Average death rate, 14·5 per 1,000 in Burgh only.
　Towns and villages in the area supplied, Bo'ness, Newtown, Carriden and district, also parts of the boroughs of Linlithgow and Grangemouth.
　Sources of supply, springs from limestone and surface water collected in the Carriber and Lochcote impounding reservoirs.
　Character of water, excellent ; 15° hardness.
　Filtration, Bell's Mechanical Filters.
　Storage capacity, impounding reservoirs, 234,000,000 gals. ; service reservoir, 16,000,000 gals.
　Pressure on distributing mains—maximum, 120 lbs. ; minimum, 45 lbs. per sq. in.
　Daily consumption per head, all purposes, about 23 gals.
　Maximum (meter) supply per day 354,733 gals. in September.
　Scale of charges—assessment, 1s. in £.
　Price for 1,000 gals., 6d. and 4½d.
　Total water rent received, from £2,000 upward.
　Number of meters, 48.
　Length of mains, supply—12 miles ; distributing mains, 10 miles.

Bonhill, Scotland (*see* ALEXANDRIA).

Bonnyrigg, Scotland.
Authority, Bonnyrigg Water Company, Ltd.
Office, High Street.
Share capital paid up, £4,746.　Loan capital, £1,100.
Interest, 4 per cent.
Towns and villages in the area supplied, Bonnyrigg, Rosewell, part of
　Lasswade, &c.
Works established, 1858.
Total population of area supplied, 4,000.
Annual supply of water, 40,000,000 gals.
Sources of supply, Moorfoot Hills, Midlothian, and private spring.
System of filtration, sand and gravel.
Death rate, low.
Length of mains, 10 miles.
Assessment charge, 1s. 6d. in the £, upper district, 1s.
Price per 1,000 gals., trade, 1s. to 9d., municipal, 10d.

Boosbeck (supplied by CLEVELAND).

Bootle (supplied by LIVERPOOL).

Boston, Lincolnshire.　Railway, G.N.　Distance from London, 107¼ miles.
Authority, Boston Waterworks Company.
Chairman, Benjamin Bissill Dyer.
Secretary, Staniland & Son.
Engineer and Manager, John Shaw.
Office, 1, High Street, Boston.
Share capital paid up, £30,000.
Dividend, 9 per cent. (1906).
Annual profit, £3,300.
Works constructed, 1848; special Act, 1848.
Total population supplied, 20,000.
Average death rate, 16·7 per 1,000.
Towns and villages in the area supplied, Boston, Skirbeck, Skirbeck Quarter, New
　Bolingbroke, Revesby, Carrington, West Fen, Frithville, Silsey, Wyberton.
Sources of supply—Minningsby beck, drift gravel, sand and boulder clay.
Character of water, surface water mainly from pasture land.
Filtration through Trent sand; minimum depth, 2 feet 6 inches.
Character of water, 11° of hardness.
Storage capacity—impounding reservoirs, 80,000,000 gals.; service reservoirs,
　240,000 gals
Pressure in distributing mains—maximum, 40 lbs. per square inch; minimum,
　21 lbs. per square inch.
Annual supply of water, 110,000,000 gals.
Average daily supply per head, domestic, 15 gals.; trade, 5 gals.
Maximum day's supply, 503,000 gals. in July.
Charges authorised—domestic, 7 per cent. on annual value.
Present rate—domestic, 3½ per cent. to 7 per cent. on annual value.
Present charge per meter, 10d. to 6d. per 1,000 gals.
Number of meters in use, 60.
Length of mains—supply, 18 miles; distributing, 35 miles.

Botcherby (supplied by CARLISLE).

Bothwell (*see* DISTRICT OF THE MIDDLE WARD OF LANARKSHIRE).

Boulton (supplied by DERBY).

Bourn (supplied by St. IVES, Hunts).

Bourne, Lincs.
　Authority, Company.
　Population, 4,250.

Bourne End (supplied by Great Marlow).

Bournemouth, Hants. (G. and W.) Railway, L.S.W. Distance from London, 107¼ miles.
　Owners, Bournemouth Gas and Water Company.
　Chairman, G. C. Whiteley.
　Secretary, W. Cash, 90, Cannon Street, London, E.C.
　Engineer and General Manager, H. W. Woodall.
　Office, Bourne Valley, Bournemouth.
　Share capital paid up £526,000. Last dividend, 6, 7 and 14 per cent.
　Loan　　„　　„　„ £127,300 at 3 and 4 per cent.
　　Gas and water combined.
　Works established, 1863.
　Special Acts, Bournemouth Gas and Water Act, 1873, 1878, 1902, 1903, 1906.
　Total population of area of control, 1901, 85,920.
　Total number of consumers, 11,560.
　Estimated population actually supplied, normal, 80,000; holiday season, 100,000.
　Average death rate, 14 per 1,000.
　Sources of supply—shallow wells at Longham; deep wells or borings at Wimborne.
　District of supply, Bournemouth, Poole (part of), Holdenhurst (part), Kinson, Hampreston (part), Canford Magna (part).
　Natural rest level of water below surface (Wimbourne), 11 ft; above O.D., 59 ft.
　Level of water below surface (when pumping 2,000,000 gallons per day), 90 feet.
　Estimated total quantity of water available per annum—
　　　　Shallow wells or subsoil ... ...　728,000,000 gals.
　　　　Deep wells or borings　 ... ...　1,092,000,000　„
　Nature of subsoil yielding water, gravel.
　Strata tapped by wells or borings, chalk.
　Analysis of Bournemouth water supply, March, 1907—
　　　　　　　　　　　　　　Results expressed in parts per 100,000.

Total solid residue...	22·58
Organic carbon	·073
Organic nitrogen	·007
Ammonia, free and saline...	0
Ammonia albuminoid	·004
Nitrogen as nitrates	·074
Nitrogen as nitrites	0
Total combined nitrogen	·081
Oxygen consumed (4 hours at 80)	·031
Combined chlorine	2·05
Hardness, total (by soap tests)	14·3
Temporary	9·7
Permanent	4·6

　Remarks, clear and bright.
　Filtration, sand—8,065 yards in 5 beds.
　Storage reservoir at Alderney ... ... capacity 5,000,000 gals.
　Pumping stations, Longham ... ... „　　400,000 „ per diem
　　„　　„　Wimborne ... ... „　4,000,000 „　„
　Service reservoirs, Alderney ... ... „　1,000,000 „ covered
　　„　　... ... ... „　3,000,000 „　„
　Head on distributing mains—maximum, 115 feet; minimum, 45 feet.
　Annual supply of water for all purposes, 785,000,000 gals.
　Average day's supply for all purposes, 2,000,000 gals.
　Maximum day's consumption, 3,000,000 gals., in July.
　Assessment charge, 4¾ to 5 per cent. on rateable value.

BOURNEMOUTH—*continued.*

Price per 1,000 gals., 2s. maximum.
Number of meters in use, 1,200.
Length of supply mains, 15·2 miles; distributing mains, 93·1 miles.

Bournemouth C.C. (supplied by CHRISTCHURCH).

Bovingdon (supplied by RICKMANSWORTH).

Bowdon (supplied by NORTH CHESHIRE WATER COMPANY).

Boxley (supplied by MAIDSTONE).

Brackley, Northants. Railways, L.N.W. and G.C. Distance from London, 59¼ miles.
Authority, Corporation.
Manager, Wm. Shaw.
Works established, 1879.
Total population of area supplied, about 2,600.
Average death rate, 16·1 per 1,000.
Source of supply—Well, 179ft. 6in. deep. A new well in course of sinking to be 209ft. through limestone rock.
Character of water, 7° hardness.
Filtration, none; softening, none.
Storage capacity in service reservoirs, 220,000 gals.
Pressure of distributing mains—maximum, 90 lbs.; minimum, 15 lbs. per sq. in.
Annual supply of water, 20,000,000 gals.
Daily consumption per head, domestic, 14 gals.
Number of meters, 7.
Length of mains, 4 miles.
Assessment charge, free.
Price per 1,000 gals., 1s.

Bracknell (supplied by WOKINGHAM).

Bradfield, Essex (supplied by TENDRING HUNDRED).

Bradfield, Yorks. (supplied by SHEFFIELD).

Bradford-on-Avon, Wilts. Railway, G.W. Distance from London, 98 miles.
Authority, Bradford-on-Avon Urban District Council.
Chairman, D. K. Stothert, M.I.C.E.
Clerk to authority, James Compton.
Resident Engineer, A. S. Wootton.
Office, Town Hall.
Works established, 1876.
Annual profit, including "capital charges," £200.
Total population of area supplied, about 7,687.
　　　　　"　　　　　"　　　supplied with water, 4,700.
Average death rate, 13 per 1,000.
Area supplied, Bradford-on-Avon Urban District.
Source of supply, Avoncliff Springs from oolite beds.
Character of water, good. Hardness after treatment, 15·5°.
System of filtration, sand.
Storage capacity, 375,000 gals.
Pressure on distributing mains—maximum, 120 lbs.; minimum, 5 lbs. per sq. in.
Annual supply of water, 35,000,000 gals.
Average daily supply per head—domestic, 16 gals.; trade, &c., 5 gals.
Maximum day's supply, 120,000 gals. in June.
Assessment charge, 1s. 3d. on gross rental.
Price per 1,000 gals., 1s. 3d.
Number of meters, 102.
Length of mains—supply, 2 miles; distributing, 3 miles.

Bradford, Yorks. Railways, M., G.N., L. & Y., G.C., and N.E. Distance from London, 200 miles.

Authority, Bradford Corporation.
Chairman, Alderman Wm. Holdsworth, J.P.
City Treasurer, Geo. A. Thorpe, F.S.A.A.
Town Clerk, Frederick Stevens.
Engineer in charge, James Watson, M.I.C.E.
Office, Town Hall, Bradford.
Loans, £3,605,014; repaid, £642,733. Net debt, outstanding, £2,962,281.
Interest on loan and in sinking fund, £108,258.
Annual loss, including capital charges (1906), £9,117.
Total incomes, £175,758.
Works established—company, 1793; corporation, 1854.
Special Acts, 1784 to 1902.
Total population supplied, 450,000.
Death rate, 15·1 per 1,000 (1905).
Towns and villages in the area supplied—Addingham, Adwalton, Apperley, Bingley, Birstal, Burnsall, Calverley, Clayton, Cleckheaton, Denholme, Draughton, Drighlington, Farsley, Gildersome, Gomersal, Hunsworth, Liversedge, Morton, Pudsey, Queensbury, Shelf, Shipley, Silsden, Wilsden and Wyke.
Source of supply—springs and drainage areas in the valleys of the rivers Kidd, Wharfe, Aire and Worth.
Character of water, soft; total hardness, 2·6 to 4·9 degrees.
Filtered downward through sand.
Storage capacity—impounding reservoirs, 1,444,857,000 gals.; service reservoirs, 373,800,000 gals.
Pressure in distributing mains—maximum, 170 lbs.; minimum, 20 lbs. per sq. in.
There are three separate services—high, intermediate and low.
Total quantity of water supplied per annum, 4,745,000,000 gals.
Average daily consumption per head, in city only—domestic, 19·8; trade, 20·5 gals.
Maximum supply per day, 17,000,000 gals., occurring in dry months and frost.
Length of mains, 344 miles.
Scale of charges—domestic, rentals of £20 per annum and under, 7½ per cent., varying to 5 per cent. on rentals of £100 and upwards.
    Trade purposes, per 1,000 gals., 400,000 gals. and under, 9d.; all above 400,000 gals., 7½d.
Municipal purposes, now under consideration.
Number of meters 1,546.

Bradley, Yorks. Railway, Mid. Nearest station, Cononley, 2 miles.

Authority, Bradley Waterworks Company Ltd.
Office, Bradley Wesleyan Day-school.
Share capital paid up, £540; dividend, 5 per cent.
Works established, 1888.
Total population of area supplied, 609.
Storage capacity, 40,000 gals.
Character of water, soft.

Bradwell. *See* Congleton Rural.

Braintree and Bocking, Essex.

Authority, Urban District Council.
Total population of area supplied, about 6,000.
Daily supply of water, 130,000 gals.
Sources of supply, wells in the chalk.
Character of water—moderately soft, alkaline, and contains about 48 grains of common salt per gal.

Bramblebank, part of (supplied by BLAIRGOWRIE).

Bramley (supplied by GODALMING).

Brampton (supplied by WATH-UPON-DEARNE).

Branstone (supplied by SOUTH STAFFS. WATERWORKS CO.).

Bray, Berks (supplied by MAIDENHEAD).

Bray, Ireland (supplied by DUBLIN).

Breadsall (supplied by DERBY).

Brechin, Forfarshire, Scotland. Railway, Caledonian.
　　Authority, Brechin Town Council.
　　Chairman of Water Committee, Bailie Alexander Hampton.
　　Secretary, James Scott, Esq., Panmure Street, Brechin.
　　Burgh Surveyor and Water Engineer, Wm. Eggie.
　　Office, Municipal Buildings, Brechin, N.B.
　　Total capital invested, including loans, £20,000.
　　Works established, 1874.
　　Special Acts, Public Health (Scot.) Supplemental Act, 1872.
　　Total population of area of control, 1901, 8,941.
　　Death rate, 16 per 1,000.
　　Total number of consumers, 9,000.
　　Annual supply of water (year 1901)—
　　　　　　For domestic purposes　...　...　...　...　98,550,000 gals.
　　　　　　　„　trade　　„　　...　...　...　...　10,950,000　„
　　Maximum day's consumption, 300,000 gals.
　　Total quantity of water drawn from drainage areas, 109,500,000 gals. per annum.
　　Estimated total quantity of water available, 250,000,000 gals. per annum.
　　Source of supply—drainage area at Hill of Wirren, in Grampian Range, 12 miles
　　　　from Brechin.
　　　　Population on drainage area, none. No cultivation. Sheep grazing.
　　　　Water authority have no control of drainage area.
　　　　Service reservoir, Trinity Reservoir, open, one mile from Brechin, capacity,
　　　　　　2,000,000 gals.
　　　　Character of water, soft.
　　Number of meters in use, 50.
　　Length of distributing mains, 9 miles (exclusive of main to reservoir).
　　Assessment charge, 1s. per £ of rental.
　　Price for 1,000 gals., 6d.

Brecon, or Brecknock, Wales. Railway, M. Distance from London, 183 miles.
　　Authority, Brecon Corporation.
　　Chairman, The Mayor of Brecon.
　　Secretary, G. Hyatt Williams, Town Clerk.
　　Manager and Resident Engineer, Hugh Ll. Griffiths, M.I.A.M. & C.E., M.R.S.I.,
　　　　Borough Surveyor and Water Engineer.
　　Loan.—All loans paid off.
　　Death rate, 17·7 per 1,000.
　　Parishes within " District of Supply," St. John, St. Mary, St. David's.
　　Works established, 1866.
　　Total population of area supplied, 5,875.
　　Source of supply, mountain stream in red sandstone.
　　Character of water, 7° hardness.
　　Filtration, continuous filtration downwards through sand.
　　Storage capacity—impounding reservoir, 1,000,000 gals.; service reservoir, 200,000.
　　Pressure in distributing mains—maximum, 62 lbs. per sq. inch, minimum, 5 lbs.
　　　　per sq. inch.

BRECON, OR BRECKNOCK—*continued.*

Length of supply mains, 7½ miles ; distributing mains, 10 miles.
Total quantity supplied per annum, 100,000,000 gals.
Average daily supply—domestic, 190,000 gals., trade, 70,000 gals.
Maximum supply per day, 280,000 gals.
Scale of charges—assessment charge, 8d in the £. per annum.
Price per meter, uniform charge of 6d. per 1,000 gals.
Number of meters in use, 25.

Bredbury (supplied by STOCKPORT).

Brenkley (supplied by NEWCASTLE-ON-TYNE).

Brentwood (supplied by SOUTH ESSEX WATER Co.).

Bridgend, Glamorgan (G. and W.) Railways, G.W., M., and C. Distance from London,
183¼ miles.
Owners, Bridgend Gas and Water Company.
Chairman, Thos. George Smith.
Secretary, Engineer and Manager, J. H. Dyer, Bridgend.
Office, Company's Office, Quarella Road, Bridgend.
Total capital invested in undertaking, £39,000; loans, £9,750, expended on water-
works. Capital is not divided.
Current rate of dividend, 3 per cent., 1906. Interest on loan, 4½ per cent. and 4 per
cent.
Date of establishment, 1869 Act passed ; 1871 waterworks constructed.
Special Acts, Bridgend Gas and Water Act, 1869 (32 & 33 Vict., cb. 51) ; Gas and
Water Orders Corporation Act, 1875 (38 & 39 Vict., ch. 169).
Total population of area of control, 1891, 4,996 ; 1901, 6,062 ; 1906, 7,000. Figures
given apply to the town of Bridgend only.
Death rate, 14·40 per 1,000.
District of supply, Bridgend, Oldcastle, Newcastle, Lower Merthyrmawr.
Total quantity of water drawn from surface springs, estimated 70,000,000 gals.
per annum.
Estimated total quantity of water available from surface springs, 2,000,000
gals. every twenty-four hours.
Source of supply—Surface springs. Fynon Schwyll, about 2½ miles from the
town of Bridgend, near ruins of Ogmore Castle, marked on Ordnance Maps.
Strata or formation yielding springs, limestone.
Character of water—a clear water faintly green, in 2 ft. tube, alkaline reaction,
considerable amount of sulphates ; total hardness, 21°.
Filtration, sand.
Water is not softened.
Pumping station—Ogmore Mill Pumping Station comprises one pair of engines
and pumps, capable of 35,000 gals. per hour, two 3-throw pumps driven by water
wheels, 8,000 gals. per hour, also recently added a Tangye gas suction plant,
with pumps throwing 20,000 gals. per hour, which is used in lieu of steam with
considerable economy.
Pumping being both by steam and water the service of both varies considerably
throughout the year, owing to the varying water power derived from the stream,
subject to climatic influences.
Storage capacity—main reservoir (constructed in 1904 at Flemingsdown, 280 feet
above O.D.), before filtration, 1,250,000 gals., Service reservoirs, Brackla, 126·0
feet above O.D., 450,000 gals., open ; Newcastle, 187·3 feet above O.D., 30,000
gals., covered and one covered; reservoir of 100,000 gals.
Total quantity of water supplied per annum, 1906, estimated at 102,000,000 gals.
Assessment charge, 1s. 1½d. under £20, 5 per cent. over £20 on rack rental.
Price for the supply of water by meter for trade and other purposes subject
to a quarterly minimum rental—

BRIDGEND—*continued.*

Quarterly consumption from under 10,000 gals., 1s. 6d. per 1,000 gals., or fraction of to 1,000,000 gals. and upwards, 6d.; present average, 9d. per 1000.
Rent of meter and minimum charges per quarter—

Diameter.	Meter rent.	Minimum charge for water.	Total minimum charge.
From ⅜″ ...	2s. 6d. ...	5s. ...	7s. 6d.
To 6″ ...	40s. ...	100s. ...	140s.

N.B.—The above charges include periodical inspections, testing when required, repairs and renewals when necessary by ordinary fair wear and tear.
Maximum day's consumption, estimated 350,000 gals. in months of June, July and August.
Number of meters in use, 40.
Length of distributing mains, say seven miles.
Also supplies Southerndown, who buy in bulk through a local private company.

Bridge Hewick (supplied by Ripon).

Bridge-of-Allan, Scotland. Railways, Caledonian & N.B. Distance from Edinburgh 40 miles.
Authority, the Bridge-of-Allan Water Co.
Chairman, W. Haldane, M.D., J.P.
Surveyor, Alexander Morrison.
Secretary, R. A. Hill, S.S.C.
Office, Lilybank, Bridge-of-Allan.
Share capital paid up, £11,000.
Loans outstanding, £3,000.
Dividend, 5 per cent.
Works established, 1866.
Special Act, 1866.
Total population of area supplied, 4,000.
Sources of supply, Coxburn and Wharrie Burn.
Filtration, sand and gravel.
Character of water, pure upland water.
Assessment charge, 1s. in the £ on rental.

Bridgmary (supplied by Gosport).

Bridgnorth, Salop. Railway, G.W. Distance from London, 149 miles.
Authority, Corporation.
Population of area supplied, 5,865.
No returns supplied.

Bridgwater, Somerset. Railways, G.W. and L.S.W. & M. joint line. Distance from London, 151¾ miles.
Authority, Corporation.
Chairman, the Mayor.
Manager, F. Parr, A.M.I.C.E., Borough Surveyor.
Accountant, Chas. Chard.
Office, Town Hall.
Loan, £41,983; repaid, £7,959.
Interest on loan, between £1,000 and £1,100.
Area supplied, Bridgwater and two parishes.
Works established, 1877.
Special Acts, 1877, 1878.
Total population of area supplied, 17,000.
Sources of supply, Quantock Hills.
Storage capacity, 690,000 gals.
Filtration, sandbeds.

BRIDGWATER—*continued*.

Character of water, first class purity, 7·5°.
Death rate, 18·2 per 1,000.
Length of mains, 30 miles.
Scale of charges, assessment charge, 5 per cent. on rental.
Price per 1,000 gals., 1s. to 9d.

Bridlington, Yorks. Railway, G.N. Distance from London, 225½ miles.
Authority, Corporation of Bridlington.
Manager, W. Lee.
Office, Victoria Road, Bridlington Quay.
Works established, 1865. Special Act, 1895.
Total population of area supplied, 13,500.
Sources of supply, wells.
Storage capacity, 2,500,000 gals.
Character of water, rather hard.
Death rate, 16·84 per 1,000.
Number of meters, 12.
Scale of charges—Assessment charge, 1s. in £; w.c., 10s.; bath, 5s.
Price for 1,000 gals., 2s. to 6d.

Bridport, Dorset. Railway, G.W. Distance from London, 154½ miles.
Authority, Bridport Waterworks Co.
Chairman, Major T. J. Colfox, J.P.
Manager and Secretary, Hy. Gordon.
Office, Downes Street.
Works established, 1872. Special Act, 1872.
Total population of area supplied, 7,000.
Towns and villages in the area supplied—Bridport, West Bay, Burton, Bradstock,
    and parts of Bradpole and Bothenhampton.
Source of supply—Litton Cheney (greensand).
Character of water, excellent, medium hardness.
Storage capacity, 3,500,000 gals.
Daily consumption per head, 16 gals.
Assessment charge, 6 per cent. on gross value.
Price per 1,000 gals., 1s. 6d. and 1s.

Brierfield (supplied by NELSON).

Brierley Hill (supplied by SOUTH STAFFS. WATERWORKS Co.).

Brighouse, Yorks. Railways, G.N., L. & Y. Distance from London, 189 miles.
Authority, Brighouse Corporation.
Chairman of Water Committee, John Wood.
Secretary, James Parkinson, Town Clerk, Municipal Offices, Brighouse.
Engineer, William Andrew.
Office, Mill Lane, Brighouse, Yorkshire.
Loans outstanding, £16,745.
Works established, 1869. Rastrick Waterworks purchased 1891.
Special Act, Brighouse Corporation Act, 1895.
Total population of area of control, 1891, 20,666 ; 1901, 21,735 ; 1906, 22,250.
Death rate, 14·77 per 1,000 average.
Area of control, Brighouse, Rastrick and Hove Edge, forming borough of
    Brighouse.
Source of supply, the water supply of the borough is received from the mains of
    the Halifax Corporation in bulk ; the Rastrick supply is from springs in the
    ragstone.
Character of water, soft; filtration, none ; softening, none.
Service reservoir, Lands, Rastrick, capacity 350,000 gals., open.

BRIGHOUSE—*continued.*

Head on distributing mains—maximum, 300 feet ; minimum, 60 feet.
Annual supply of water, 180,092,000.
Average daily supply per head—Domestic, 11·26 gals. ; trade, 10·92 gals.
Maximum day's consumption, 600,000 gals. in May.
Charges authorized and charged—Domestic, 5 per cent. to 3½ per cent. on rateable value.
Price by meter, 8d. per 1,000 gals., trade purposes.
Number of meters in use, 240.
Length of distributing mains, 26 miles.

Brightlingsea, Essex. Railway, G.E. Distance from London, 62½ miles.
Authority, Urban District Council.
Clerk, W. I. Osborn.
Office, Foresters' Hall, Sydney Street, Brightlingsea.
Loans outstanding, £8,726.
Works established, 1869. Purchased by local authority, 1899.
Total population of area supplied, 4,800.
Average death rate, 13 per 1,000.
Area supplied, Brightlingsea only.
Sources of supply in use, two 15-inch boreholes in chalk, 300 feet deep.
Character of water, very pure ; total hardness, 15°.
Filtration, none ; softening, none.
Storage tank, capacity, 80,000 gals.
Average daily consumption per head, 20 gals., constant supply.
Number of meters in use, 12.
Scale of charges—Assessment charge, 7½ per cent. below £6.
Trade, price per 1,000 gals., 1s.
Total revenue received, £800.

Brighton, Hove, and Preston. Railway, L.B.S.C. Distance from London, 50½ miles
Authority, Corporation.
Chairman, Alderman Edward Lowther.
Town Clerk, Hugo Talbot.
Office, 12, Bond Street, Brighton.
Engineer in charge, James Johnston, M.I.C.E., M.I.M.E., F.G.S.
Loans outstanding, £867,738.
Towns and villages supplied, Brighton, Hove, Preston, Rottingdean, Ovingdean, Patcham, West Blatchington, Aldrington, Southwick, Kingston-by-Sea, Portslade, Portslade-by-Sea, New Shoreham, Old Shoreham, Lancing, Hangleton, Falmer, and Pyecombe.
Works established, 1834 ; purchased by Corporation, 1872.
Special Acts, 1834, 1853, 1854, 1865, 1872, 1883, 1896, 1900.
Total population supplied, 180,000, excluding visitors.
Annual supply of water, 2,302,000,000 gals.
Daily consumption per head, domestic, 27 gals., trade, 8 gals.
Sources of supply—wells in the chalk at Goldstone, Patcham, Lewes Road, Aldrington, Portslade, Falmer, and chalk springs at Shoreham.
Storage capacity, 11,500,000.
Character of water, hard.
Number of meters in use, 1,124.
Scale of charges, assessment charge, 9d in the £, portion of county district 1s. in £.
Price per 1,000 gals., 1s. 3d. to 7d.

Brinsley (supplied by NOTTINGHAM).

Bristol. Railway, G.W. Distance from London, 118½ miles.
Authority, Bristol Water Works Company.
Chairman, Henry Napier Abbott.
General Manager and Secretary, A. J. Alexander.
Resident Engineer, J. A. Macpherson, C.E.
Office, Bristol.
Share capital paid up, £444,090. Last dividend (1906), £7 15s. per cent.
7 per cent. maximum stock, £544,600 ; last dividend (1906), £5 8s. 6d. per cent.
Works established, 1846. Special Act, 1846.
Total population of area supplied, 381,469.
Area supplied, Bristol and District.
Source of supply, springs in limestone conglomerate, and deep wells in new red
    sandstone and impounding reservoirs on the river Yeo.
Character of water, hardness 18°.
Filtration, sand.
Storage capacity, impounding reservoirs, 2,400,000,000 gals.; service reservoirs,
    10,000,000 gals.
Daily consumption per head, 24 gals.
Scale of charges, according to locality and level, fixed by special Act.
Price per 1,000 gals., 1s. 6d. to 7d., and by agreement.
Number of meters, 2,000.

Brithdir (supplied by NEW TREDEGAR).

Briton Ferry (see NEATH).

Brixham, Devon. Railway, G.W. Distance from London, 222½ miles.
Authority, Urban District Council.
The Council are now bringing a new supply from Dartmoor at a cost of £40,000.
Manager, J. H. Johns.
Total population supplied, 10,000.
Price per 1,000 gals., trade, 1s. to 8d.

Broadstairs, Kent. Railway, S.E. & C. Distance from London, 74 miles.
Authority, Broadstairs and St. Peters Urban District Council.
Clerk to Council, L. A. Skinner.
Office, Council Office, Broadstairs.
Purchase money, £50,000.
Interest on loan, 3⅜ per cent. for 50 years.
Towns and villages in area supplied, Broadstairs, St. Peters, Reading Street, North-
    down, Westwood, Northwood, Dumpton.
Works established, 1859.
Purchased by local authority, 1901.
Special Act, Broadstairs and St. Peters Water and Improvement Act, 1901.
Total population of area supplied, 7,000 ; estimated summer population, 14,000.
Daily consumption per head of population—Domestic, 30 gals. ; trade, 6 gals.
Source of supply in use, the chalk, 2 miles from town.
Storage in tanks ; filtration, none.
Character of water, good.
Death rate, 8·16 per 1,000.
Number of meters in use, about 100.
Length of mains, about 30 miles.
Scale of charges—domestic assessment, 1s. 3d. on £ rental ; 5s. for every w.c.,
    6s. for bath.
    Trade price per 1,000 gals., 1s. 6d. by meter.
    Municipal   „   1s. 6d.   „
Total revenue, about £6,000.

Broadstone (supplied by Poole.

Broadwater (supplied by Worthing).

Brockhurst (supplied by Gosport).

Brockmoor (supplied by South Staffs. Waterworks Co.).

Brocton (supplied by Stafford).

Bromley (N.E. of the parish of) (supplied by Newcastle-on-Tyne).

Brompton, Kent (*See* Chatham).

Brompton, Yorks. (supplied by Northallerton).

Brompton, Scarboro' (supplied by Wath-upon-Dearne).

Bromsgrove (supplied by East Worcestershire).

Brookhouses (supplied by Cheadle).

Broseley (supplied by Much Wenlock).

Brotton (supplied by Cleveland Water Co.).

Broughton, Flint. (supplied by Hawarden).

Broughton, Lancs. (supplied by Manchester).

Broughty Ferry (supplied by Dundee).

Brownsover (supplied at Rugby).

Bryanstone (supplied by Blandford).

Brymbo, Denbigh.   Railway, A.W., via Wrexham.   Distance from London, 199 miles.
    Authority, The Brymbo Water Co.
    Total population supplied, 4,213.

Brynmawr, Mon. Railway, G.W. Distance from London, 175 miles.
Authority, Urban District Council.
Manager and Resident Engineer, H. B. Jones.
Office, Market Chambers, Beaufort Street.
Loans outstanding, £4,656. Borrowed in 1903 for new distributing mains.
Works constructed, 1859.
Total population supplied, 7,500.
Source of supply—Impounding reservoirs on upland surface, gathering ground
　with clay subsoil.
Character of water—Moderately soft, very palatable, sometimes after heavy rain
　slightly discoloured by peat. Total hardnes, 8·06 degrees.
Filtration, sand.
Storeage capacity—Impounding reservoirs, 18,000,000 gals.; service reservoirs,
　86,000 gals.
Head on distributing mains—Max., 337·98 feet; min., 202·38 feet.
Total annual supply of water, 55,000,000 gals.
Average daily supply per head (domestic only), 20 gals.
Maximum day's supply, 165,000, in August.
Length of supply mains, 1¼ miles; distributing mains, 7 miles.

Buchanhaven (supplied by PETERHEAD).

Buckhurst Hill (supplied by EAST LONDON).

Buckingham. Railway, L.N.W. Distance from London 61 miles.
Authority, Corporation.
Total population of area supplied, 3,151.

Buckley (supplied by HAWARDEN).

Bude and Stratton, Cornwall. Railway, L.S.W. Distance from London, 226 miles.
Authority, Urban District Council of Stratton and Bude.
Works opened May 21st, 1903.
Source of supply—The Council has purchased the whole of the Bude Canal
　Company's undertaking.

Bullbrook (supplied by WOKINGHAM).

Burbage (supplied by BUXTON).

Burford and Upton, Oxford. Railway, G.W. Distance from London, 72 miles.
Authority, Company. Works established, 1875.
Total population supplied, 1,600.
Annual supply of water, 12,755,000 gals.
Source of supply, limestone.
Assessment charge, 1s. in £, on gross estimated rental.
Price per 1,000 gals., 9d., 8d., and 7d.

Burgess Hill, Sussex. Railway, L.B.S.C. Distance from London, 42 miles.
Authority, Burgess Hill Water Company.
Chairman, William Wood, sen., The Knoll, Hurstpierpoint.

BURGESS HILL—*continued.*

Engineer and Secretary, Simeon Henry Norman.
Office, London Road, Burgess Hill.
Share capital paid up, £37,016.   Loan, £8,925.
Dividend, 7¼ and 5¼ per cent. per annum.
Town and villages in the area supplied, Burgess Hill, Hurstpierpoint, Ditchling
   Keymer, Hassocks, Clayton and Albourne.
Works established, 1870.   Special Acts, 1886 and 1901.
Total population supplied, 11,500.
Annual supply of water, 52,000,000 gals.
Daily consumption, 15 gals. domestic.
Sources of supply, Southdown Hills.
Number of meters, 198.
Scale of charges, assessment charge, rateable value.
   Price per 1,000 gals.—Municipal purposes, 1s. 3d. ; trade purposes, 2s.
Total water rent received, £4,866 (one year to March 31st, 1907).

Burghmair, N. B. (supplied by PERTH).

Burnage supplied by (MANCHESTER).

Burnham, Essex.   Railway, G.E.   Distance from London, 43¼ miles.
Authority, Urban District Council.
Population of area supplied, 2 918.
Source of supply—wells in gravel, subsoil, and well bored to Thanet bed ; good
   supply.

Burnley, Lancs.   Railway, L. & Y.N.   Distance from London, 214½ miles.
Authority, Corporation.
Engineer in charge, W. Williamson.
Secretary, Hy. Clark.
Office, 54, Yorkshire Street.
Loan outstanding, £184,488.
Annual profit including "Capital charges" £3,331.
Area supplied, 4,000 acres.
Works established, 1846.   Special Acts, 1846, 1854, 1871, 1883, 1889
Total population of area supplied, 104,000.
Annual supply of water, 932,000,000 gals.
Daily consumption per head—Domestic, 21·3 ; trade, 4.97.
Source of supply, gathering grounds.
Storage capacity—Impounding reservoirs, 400,000,000 gals. ; service reservoirs,
   26,000,000 gals.
Head on distributing mains, maximum, 500 feet ; minimum, 184 feet.
Character of water, soft, 3° ; system of filtration, sand.
Death rate, 19 per 1,000.
Number of meters, 580.
Scale of charges—
   Assessment, 5 per cent. on gross R.V.
   Price per 1,000 gals., 8d.

Burnsall, Yorks. (supplied by BRADFORD).

Burntisland, Scotland.   Railway, N.B.
Authority, Burntisland Town Council.
Chairman of Water Committee, Provost John C. Wallace.
Clerk, Thomas A. Wallace, Town Clerk, Burntisland.
Engineer in charge, J. Alexander Waddell, Burgh Surveyor.
Office, Town Hall.
Loans outstanding, £18,046.

Burntisland—*continued.*

Works established, 1877.   Special Act, Burntisland Burgh Act, 1876.
Total population of area of control, 1881, 4,096 ; 1891, 4,692 ; 1901, 4,726 ; 1906,
   estimated population actually supplied, 6,000 holiday season, 5,000 normal.
Average death rate, 12·5 per 1,000.
Area of control, Burntisland, and district.
Maximum day's consumption, 350,000 gals. holiday season, 300,000 gals. normal
Total quantity of water drawn from drainage areas, 109,500,000 gals. per annum.
Estimated total quantity of water available, 150,000,000 gals. per annum.
Sources of supply—area drained by the Dour Burn, in the parishes of Burnt-
   island and Aberdour.
Estimated maximum daily discharge at points of collection, 30,000,000 gals.
   „   average   „   „   „   „   „   761,000 „
Maximum annual rainfall over drainage area, 39·9 inches.
Minimum   „   „   „   „   25·2   „
Average   „   „   „   „   32·8   „   (period 4 years).
Population on drainage area, about 100.
Nature of area, mostly woods and arable land, part cultivated.
Water authority has no control of drainage area.
Surface formation of drainage areas, hilly surface overlying trap rock, with
   limestone cropping out.
Storage reservoir, Cullaloe Reservoir, capacity, 122,000,000 gals.
Filtering area, 1,308 square yards in two ordinary sand filter-beds.
Service reservoir, Kilmundy Reservoir, 1 mile from town, capacity, 350,000 gals.,
   open.
Analysis of sample of water after filtration, 7th April, 1906.   One million parts
   of this water yield—

Free ammonia	·022
Albuminoid ammonia...	·128
Carbonate of lime, etc.	145·96
Chlorine...	18·00
Nitrogen as nitrates	1·28
Nitrites	None
Hardness, in Clark's degrees	10¼ degrees
Lead or other poisonous metals	None

Average daily supply of water—domestic   ...   220,000 gals.
                              trade   ...   80,000 „
Assessment charge, 6d. per £ for domestic supply,
Price by meter, 9d. per 1,000 gallons.
Number of meters in use, 14.
Length of distributing mains, about 4 miles.
Compensation water to the extent of 350,000 gals. per day has to be given
   from the storage reservoir.

Burntwood (supplied by South Staffordshire Waterworks Co.).

Burradon (supplied by Newcastle-on-Tyne).

Burslem (supplied by Staffordshire Potteries Water Co.).

Burton (supplied by Christchurch).

Burton-in-Lonsdale, Yorks.   (Authority, Burton-in-Lonsdale Waterworks
   Co., Ltd.).   No returns supplied.

Burton Joyce (supplied by Nottingham).

Burton-on-Trent (supplied by South Staffordshire Waterworks Co.).

Burtonwood (supplied by WARRINGTON).

Burwash (suppled by TICEHURST),

Bury, Lancs. Railway, L. & Y. Distance from London, 195 miles.
Authority, Bury and District Joint Water Board.
Chairman, Alderman John Parks, J.P.
Clerk, John Haslam.
Manager, R. B. Rigby, Parsons Lane, Bury.
Engineer, Joshua Cartwright, C.E.
Office, Parsons Lane, Bury.
Share capital paid up, £195,326.
Loan　　 ,,　　　 ,,　　 £611,464.
Interest on Loans, £20,245. Dividend on Annuities, £16,776.
Annuities as per Act, 1872. Works established, 1872. Special Acts, 1838, 1853,
　　1858, 1872, 1885, 1889, 1899, 1900, 1903.
Total population supplied, 158,155.
District of supply ; Bury, Haslingden, Rawtenstall, Radcliffe, Ramsbottom, Little
　　Lever, Whitefield, Tottington, Outwood, Prestolee, Ringley, Unsworth.
Sources of supply, springs and gathering grounds at Haslingden and Rawtenstall.
Storage capacity, impounding reservoirs, 796,075,000; service reservoirs, 51,500,000.
Character of water, soft. Filtration, sand.
Average Death rate, 17·04 per 1,000 (Bury).
Number of meters, 1,302.
Annual supply of Water for trade purposes, 303,392,210 gals.
Assessment charge A—domestic, 10 per cent. to 6¾ per cent. on annual rack rent.
Price per 1,000 gals., trade as per scale, 2s. 3d. to 6½d.
Municipal sanitary purposes, 6d. per 1,000 gals.
Total water rent received, £55,667.

Bury St. Edmunds, Suffolk. Railway, G.E. Distance from London, 87¼ miles.
Authority, Corporation.
Chairman, Alderman Jaggard.
Secretary, A. P. Wheeler, town clerk.
Engineer and Manager, Walter D. Harding.
Office, Town Hall, Bury St. Edmunds.
Loans outstanding, £7,950 at 3%.
Works established, 1864, by the Corporation.
Total population supplied, 16,255.
Death rate, 15·8 per 1,000, average for 10 years.
Area supplied, Bury St. Edmunds only.
Sources of supply, wells in the chalk.
Character of water, of the highest organic purity, free from metals, and
　　excellent drinking water.
Filtration, none.
Storage reservoirs—capacity, one, 500,000 gals. ; one, 70,000 gals.
Head on mains—maximum, 119·6 ft. ; minimum, 57·5 ft.
Total annual supply of water, 107,550,000 gals.
Average daily consumption, 200,000 gals.
Maximum daily supply, 508,535 gals., in August.
Scale of charges—assessment charge, 3% to 4% per annum on R.V.
　　Per 1,000 gals., domestic and trade, 1s. up to 300,000 gals. per annum ; 10d. fo
　　every additional 1,000 ; present average, 11d.
Number of meters in use, 15.
Length of supply mains, 14 miles ; distributing mains, 13½ miles.

Busby, Scotland. Railway, Caledonian. Distance from London, 400 miles.
Authority, Busby Water Company.
Office, 192, St. Vincent Street, Glasgow.
Share capital paid up, £20,000. Loans, capital paid up, £2,100.

BUSBY—*continued.*

Towns and villages supplied — Busby, Sheddens, Clarkstow, Giffnock, and
Netherlee.
Works established, 1875. Special Acts, 1875 and 1882.
Total population of area supplied, 4,000.
Day's consumption per head, domestic and trade, between 50 and 60 gals.
Sources of supply, Highflat Burn, gravitation.
Storage capacity, 52,186,700 gals.
System of filtration, downwards through sand,
Number of meters, 24.
Length of mains, 11¾ miles.
Assessment charge, 1s. 6d. in the £.
Price per 1,000 gals., trade, 7⅛d.
Total revenue received, £1,435 10s. 6d.

Busham (supplied by PAIGNTON).

Bushey, Herts. (supplied by COLNE VALLEY WATER Co.).

Bushbury, Staffs. (supplied by WOLVERHAMPTON).

Buxton, Derbyshire.   Railways, L.N.W. and M.   Distance from London, 163 miles.
Authority, Buxton Urban District Council.
Chairman, Frederick Rowland, J.P.
Clerk, Jonah Tayler.
Manager, W. H. Grieves.
Office, Town Hall, Buxton.
Engineers for new works, G. H. Hill and Sons.
Loan outstanding, £119,843 at 3¾ per cent. (average.)
Purchased by local authority, 1874.
Special Acts, Buxton District Council Water Act, 1902.
Death rate, 9·4 per 1,000.
Towns and villages in the area supplied—Buxton, Burbage, Ladmanslow, part
of Fairfield, and part of Hartington (upper quarter).
Sources of supply, springs from Axe Edge and Coombs Moss—millstone grit—by
gravitation.
Character of water, upland surface water from moorlands, excellent.
System of filtration, none required. Bell's high-pressure filters for new reservoir.
Storage capacity, in impounding reservoirs on Stanley Moor, Burbage, Lightwood,
and Hogsham, 25,000,000 gals.   Will shortly be increased by 80,000,000 gals.
Head on distributing mains—maximum, 200 feet.
Total quantity of water supplied per annum, 219,000,000 gals.
Daily consumption per head, domestic, 40 gals.; trade, 15 gals.
Scale of charges—1s 6d. in £ on poor rate, including 1 w.c.; additional w.c., 5s.;
baths, 10s. per annum.
Trade and municipal, per 1,000 gals., 1s.   Fire extinguishing purposes free.
Number of meters, 64.
Length of mains, approximately 23 miles.
Total water rent received, £7,663.

Byfleet, Surrey (supplied by WEST SURREY WATER Co.).

Cadeby (supplied by HINCKLEY).

Caerleon, Mon. (supplied by NEWPORT).

Cakemore (supplied by SOUTH STAFFS WATERWORKS Co.).

Calderbank, N.B.(supplied by AIRDRIE).

Caldervale (supplied by AIRDRIE).

Caldy, Cheshire (supplied by Hoylake).

Callington, Cornwall. Railways, G.W. and L.S.W. Distance from London, 214 miles.
Authority, Callington Waterworks Co., Ltd.
Chairman, Dr. H. Davies, J.P.
Secretary, George Parsons.
Resident Engineer, William A. Murch.
Office, Callington.
Share capital paid up, £1,000; dividend, 4 per cent.
Loan   „   „   £1,000 ; interest, 4   „
Population supplied, 1,900.
District of supply, Callington and Stokechinsland.

Calne, Wilts. Railway G.W. Distance from London, 99 miles.
Owners, Calne Waterworks Company, Ld.
Chairman, T. E. Redman Cattlefield House.
Secretary, Bertram Spackman, The Green, Calne.
Manager and Resident Engineer, J. H. Gunning, Mill Street, Calne.
Consulting Engineer, W. B. Bryan.
Office, Patford Street, Calne.
Total capital invested including loans, £6,092.
Dividend, 9 per cent.
Works established, 1883.   Special Act, 1882.
Total population supplied—Calne, 4,000; Calne Without part, 1,000.
District of supply—Calne, Blashland, partly, Calstone, partly.
Source of supply—Calstone Springs at rise of river Marden.   Gravitation.
Recent analyses of the water—clean and colourless.   1,000,000 parts of water
  yield—

Chlorine	...	...	...	...	1·0
Free ammonia	...	...	...	...	.0
Nitrogen or nitrates	...	...	..	...	·015

  "Highest degree of organic purity."
Service reservoir at Calstone, capacity, 2,000 gallons, covered.
Head on distributing mains, 90 feet.
Average daily consumption per head, 25 gals.
Maximum day's consumption, 72,000 gals.
Number of meters in use, 25.
Length of distributing mains, 3 miles.
Assessment charge, 1s. 6d. per £ on rateable value.
Price per 1,000 gallons, 10s. for 5,000, varying for larger quantity.

Calverley, Yorks. Railway, M. Distance from London, 206¾ miles.
Authority, District Council.
Office, Calverley.
Total population of area supplied, 2,853.
Annual supply of water, 6,066,000 gals.
Source of supply, water purchased in bulk from the Bradford Corporation.
Character of water, good, soft.
Assessment, A.
Price per 1,000 gals., 1s. 6d.

Calverton End (supplied by Stony Stratford).

Camberley, Surrey (supplied by Frimley).

Cambois (supplied by Bedlington).

Camborne, Cornwall. Railway, G.W. Distance from London, 307¾ miles.
Authority, Camborne Water Company.
Share capital paid up, £14,400.
Loan „ „ £6,900.
Dividends, A, £9 ; B, £6 6s. per cent.
Area supplied, Camborne, Illogan, and Crowan parishes.
Works established, 1867. Special Acts, 1867 and 1890.
Total population supplied, 20,000.
Daily consumption per head, 20 gals.
Source of supply, springs in granite formation, Crowan.
Storage capacity, 31,000,000 gals.
Character of water, excellent.
Death rate, 18 per 1,000.
Number of meters, 15.
Assessment charge, 6 per cent. on rateable value above £5.
Price per 1,000 gals., 5s. to 4½d.
Total water rent received, £2,422.

Cambridge. Railways, G. E., G.N. Distance from London, 55¾ miles.
Authority, Company.
Chairman, F. Whitting, M.A.
Engineer, Manager and Secretary, W. W. Gray, A.M.I.C.E.
Office, 4, Benet Street.
Share capital, paid up, £118,500 ; loan, £24,000 ; dividend, 10 and 7 per cent.
Towns and villages supplied, Cambridge Town and District of Chesterton,
    Villages of Cherryhinton, Fulbourn, Great Shelford, Histon, Impington,
    Trumpington, and Grantchester.
Works established, 1853.
Special Acts, 1853, 1855, 1866, 1871, 1886.
Total population supplied, 56,000.
Source of supply in use—chalk and lower green sand.
Storage capacity, 1,000,000 gals.
Number of meters in use, 675.
Scale of charges, assessment charge, 4¼ and 5 per cent. on annual value.

Cambuslang (supplied by LANARKSHIRE).

Cambusnethan (supplied by LANARKSHIRE).

Camelon (supplied by FALKIRK).

Campbeltown.
Authority, Corporation.
Loans, £9,450.
Works established, 1876.
Total population of area supplied, 8,000.
Daily consumption per head, 32 gals.
Sources of supply in use, Lochrnan and Crosshills.
Storage capacity, 57,000,000.
Assessment charge, 6d. in the £.

Can House (supplied by DONCASTER).

Cannock, Staffs. Population, 23,992 (supplied by South Staffs. Waterworks Co.).

Canongate (supplied by Alnwick Rural).

Canterbury, Kent. (G. and W.) Railways, L.C. and S.E. Distance from London, 61¾ miles.
　Authority, Canterbury Gas and Water Co.
　Secretary and General Manager, James Burch.
　Engineer, Thomas Buckley.
　Office, Castle Street.
　Share capital paid up, £64,500.
　Loan　　　,,　　　,,　　£6,500.
　Dividend, 8 per cent.
　Towns and villages in the area supplied—Canterbury, Harbledown, Hackington, Sturry, Westbere.
　Works established, 1824. Special Acts, 1824, 1866, 1873, 1890.
　Total population supplied, 26,000.
　Annual supply of water, 234,005,893 gals.
　Sources of supply—bore-holes in chalk.
　Character of water, hard, softened by Dr. Clark's process before delivery to consumers.
　Length of mains, 28¼ miles.
　Assessment charge, rateable value.
　Price per 1,000 gals., various.

Cantley, part of (supplied by Doncaster).

Canwick (supplied by Lincoln).

Capel-le-Ferne (supplied by Folkestone).

Cardiff. Railway, G.W. and local lines. Distance from London, 163 miles.
　Authority, Council of the County Borough of Cardiff (Cardiff Corporation Waterworks).
　Chairman, Alderman David Jones, J.P.
　Clerk, J. L. Wheatley, Solicitor, Town Clerk.
　Engineer and Manager, C. H. Priestley, M.I.C.E.
　Office, Town Hall, Cardiff.
　Total capital invested, including loans, £1,295,993.
　Towns and villages within the area of control, with population of each (1901 Census) — County Borough of Cardiff... ... ...　164,315
　　　　Penarth Urban District (including Penarth, Cogan
　　　　　and Llandough) ... ...　13,792
　　　　Llandaff and Dynas Powis Rural District, including
　　　　　Llandaff ... ...　5,777
　　　　Whitchurch ... ...　4,862
　　　　Llanishen ... ...　1,212
　　　　Lisvane ... ...　242
　　　　St. Andrew's ... ...　1,632
　Supply in bulk to a number of other districts.
　Works established, 1850.
　Purchased by local authority, 1879.
　Special Acts, Waterworks Company's Acts, 1850, 1853, 1860 and 1878, Cardiff Corporation Acts of 1879, 1884 and 1894, Provisional Order, 1902,

CARDIFF—*continued*.

Total population of area of control, 1881, 90,000 ; 1891, 140,000 ; 1901, 190,000.
Total number of consumers, about 31,000.
Estimated population actually supplied, 218,000.
Annual supply of water (1906)—

For domestic purposes	... .		1,109,400,000 gals.
„ trade „	... ...	}	951,500,000 „
„ municipal „	... .	
In bulk to other authorities	... ...	
Maximum day's consumption (in July, 1906)			7,010,000 „

Total quantity of water drawn per annum—from drainage areas, 3,155,000,000 gals.
Source of supply—the whole of the water used at present is from a drainage area of 4,000 acres of moorland and pasture situate at the foot of the Brecon Beacons, in Breconshire, 35 miles distant from Cardiff.
Average daily supply per head—domestic, 14·14 gals. ; trade, &c., 12·12 gals.
Surface formation of drainage areas, old red sandstone.

Storage reservoirs,	Beacons, Breconshire	... ...	capacity,	345,000,000 gals.
„ „	Cantreff, „	... ...	„	322,000,000 „
„ „	Llanishen, Glamorganshire	...	„	317,000,000 „
„ „	Lisvane, „	... ...	„	80,000,000 „

Filtering area provided, low level zone 10,000 square yards in 6 filter beds, sand.
„ „ high „ 1,670 „ 5 „
Mechanical filters (Candy system).
Pumping stations and capacity per day of each—

Ely, in reserve ...	... ...	capacity,	1,000,000 gals. per day.
Cogan, for high level supply to Penarth		„	600,000 „ „

Service reservoirs,	Rhubina	... ...	capacity,	2,860,000 gals.,	3 covered, 1 open
„ „	Heath	... ...	„	3,000,000 „	2 „
„ „	Penhill	... ...	„	2,000,000 „	1 open.
„ „	Penylan	... ...	„	3,000,000 „	1 „
„ „	Cogan	... ...	„	2,000,000 „	1 „
„ „	Llandough	...	„	600,000 „	1 „
„ „	Leckwith ...	...	„	2,000,000 „	1 „

Average death rate, 14·2 per 1,000.
Character of water, pure soft moorland water, 3° to 4° hardness.
Number of meters in use, 1,800.
Head on distributing mains—maximum, 290 feet ; minimum, about 10 feet.
Length of distributing mains—about 225 miles (including trunk and distributing mains—trunk mains are sometimes tapped for supply).

Scale of charges—		£	s.	d.
Dwelling houses ... { from £5 rateable value water rental		0	6	0
to £100 „ „		5	0	0
Shops and dwellings { from £30 „ „		1	10	0
combined ... { to £1,000 „ „		21	5	0
Warehouses, lock-up { from £20 „ „		0	10	0
shops and offices { to £1,000 „ „		8	0	0

For all places outside the borough (except Penarth), 25 per cent. extra.
Trade purposes, from under 10,000 gallons 1s. 6d. per 1,000, to 1,000,000 and upwards 6d. per 1,000.
Meter rents, 1 inch, 5s. per quarter ; minimum charge for water, 15s. ; quantity allowed per minimum, 10,000 gals. ; other sizes in proportion.

Cardigan, Wales. Railway, G.W. Distance from London, 279 miles.
Authority, Corporation of Cardigan.
Chairman, The Mayor.
Town Clerk, D. Morgan Jones, Town Clerk's Office.
Area of control, Cardigan.
Special Act, Market Act, 1857.

CARDIGAN—_continued._

Total population of area of control,.1881, 3,500 ; 1891, 3,550 ; 1901, 3,600.
Total number of consumers, 2,300.
Daily supply, 55,000 gals.
Storage reservoir, capacity, 30,000 gals.

Cardonald (supplied by GLASGOW).

Carleton, near Skipton, Yorks.
Authority, Carleton Waterworks Company.
No returns supplied.

Carleton, Pontefract (partly supplied by PONTEFRACT CORPORATION).

Carlinhow, Yorks. (supplied by CLEVELAND).

Carlisle (G. and W.) Railways, L.N.W., M., N.E., M. and C., Cal., G. and S.W., and
N.B. Distance from London, 299¼ miles.
Authority, Corporation.
Chairman, Geo. Coulthard.
Town Clerk, A. H. Collingwood.
Engineer and Manager, H. C. Marks, M.I.C.E. Deputy Engineer, Thos. P.
Collinge, A.M.I.C.E.
Office, 36, Fisher Street, Carlisle.
Capital expended, £237,060.
Loans owing (March, 1906), £163,871.
Special Acts, Carlisle Corporation Acts, 1887, 1898, and 1906.
Old works purchased 1865, present works commenced 1904, water turned on 1906.
Total population supplied, 53,000 (1906).
Death rate, 16·7 per 1,000 (1906).
Towns and villages in the area supplied, City of Carlisle, Parishes of Stanwix
and Belle Vue, Townships of Scotby, Botcherby, Harraby, Upperby, Blackwell,
and Kingstown.
Source of supply, springs at Geltsdale, impounding reservoirs at Castle Carrick.
Character of water, total hardness, 6·7° ; temporary, 2·5° ; permanent, 4·2° ;
excellent water, suitable for drinking and domestic use.
System of filtration, sand, seven beds covering 5,250 square yards ; no softening.
Storage in impounding reservoirs, 170,000,000 gals. ; service reservoirs, 5,000,000.
Head on distributing mains—maximum, 205 feet ; minimum, 135 feet.
Total quantity supplied per annum, 505,445,503 gals.
Average daily supply per head—domestic 17·06 gals. ; trade, &c., 9·06 gals.
Maximum day's supply, 1,912,321 gals., in July, 1905.
Scale of charges—
Assessment charge, fixed charge according to rentals, 5 per cent. to 7 per cent.
on same.
Price per 1,000 gals., trade, 10d. to 6d., according to quantity.
Municipal, by agreement.
Number of meters, 190.
Annual profit, including " Capital Charges," £7,556 ; net loan charges, £1,076 18s.
Length of supply mains, 13¼ miles ; distributing mains, 65 miles.

Carlton (supplied by NOTTINGHAM).

Carluke, Scotland. Railway, C. & N.B. Distance from Edinburgh, 30 miles.
Authority, Local Authority.
Population supplied, 4,000.
No returns supplied.

Carmarthen, Wales. Railway, G.W. Distance from London, 238½ miles.
Authority, Corporation.
Town Clerk, R. M. Thomas.
A new water supply has lately been laid on at a cost of £42,000.
Population supplied, 9,935.
No returns supplied.

Carnarvon, Wales. Railway L.N.W. Distance from London, 247½ miles.
Authority, Carnarvon Corporation.
Chairman of Sanitary and Water Committee, Councillor M. E. Nee.
Secretary, Albert Holden, Borough Accountant, Carnarvon.
Engineer in charge, Edward Hall, Borough Surveyor and Water Engineer, Carnarvon.
Office, Guildhall, Carnarvon.
Total capital invested, including loans, cost of works, £26,578 ; loans outstanding, £8,651.
Area of control, Town of Carnarvon and parish of Llanbeblig.
Works established 1865.
Special Act, the Carnarvon Waterworks Act, 1865.
Death rate, 18·9 per 1,000.
Total population of area of control at present supplied, 1881, 10,258 ; 1891, 9,804 ; 1901, 9,760.
Estimated population actually supplied, 9,500. On market, fair, and other special days the population is increased from 25 to over 100 per cent.
The L. & N.W. Rly. Co. are supplied at the rate of about 1,000,000 gals per month.
Maximum day's consumption, about 317,000 for all purposes from, say 6 a.m. to 6 p.m. ; this gives a supply of about 30 gals. per head for town and trade purposes during such hours under normal conditions.
The rate of night consumption would be at least 75 per cent. less.
Source of supply—drainage area situated at Bettws Gartnon parish, in the County of Carnarvon, see 1, Ordnance Street, 119.
　　The water supplied to Carnarvon is abstracted from the River Gwyrfai, which has its source in " Llyn-y-Gader," and passes through " Llyn Quellyn " towards Carnarvon, both lakes being situate at the head of the valley lying between the " Llanberis " and " Nantlle " vales. The intake is at " Nant Mill," situate about half a mile below Quellyn Lake, in the direction of and distant about 7 miles from Carnarvon. Several rivulets, including the overflows of some small lakes on the western slopes of Snowdon, discharge into Quellyn Lake, the drainage area of which is about 8 square miles, or 5,120 acres, including the land draining into the portion of river above intake.
Maximum annual rainfall over drainage area. No record available. See particulars of rainfall at Carnarvon.

Year 1899	Total No. of days 153	Total No. of inches rainfall 45·95
,, 1900	,, ,, 171	,, ,, ,, 49·25
,, 1901	,, ,, 169	,, ,, ,, 47·96
,, 1902	,, ,, 170	,, ,, ,, 36·2
,, 1903	,, ,, 188	,, ,, ,, 63·26
,, 1904	,, ,, 183	,, ,, ,, 44·19
,, 1905	,, ,, 180	,, ,, ,, 41·19
,, 1906	,, ,, 200	,, ,, ,, 52·67

Population on drainage area about 200.
Nature, mainly sheep pasture land, craggy and stony in places.
Arrangements have been made between the town council and two district councils concerned for the proper scavenging of the village of Rhyd-ddu, situate on the banks of the river Gwyrfai, to the satisfaction of the Local Government Board.
Surface formation of drainage area, agricultural and peaty soil overlying slate and granite rocks.
Service reservoirs, Yspytty reservoir, capacity, 3,000,000 gals., open.
　　,,　　,,　　Segontium　,,　　　,,　　170,000　,,　covered.

CARNARVON—*continued.*

Number of meters in use, ten. No "recording" or "water detecting meters" in use.

Analysis of water taken from the town mains, July, 1899—

Total solid matter in solution	3·00
Loss on ignition	0·64
Phosphoric acid	S.t.
Chlorine	0·88
Nitrogen as nitrates and nitrites	0·026
Oxygen required to oxidise organic matter in 3 hours ...	0·046
Oxygen required to oxidise organic matter in 15 minutes	0·042
Free ammonia	0·0005
Albuminoid ammonia	0·0035
Total hardness	0·32
Permanent hardness	„
Temporary „	„

In parts per 100,000 of water.

Scale of charges—

Premises assessed under £4 5s. (ann. rateable value) minimum charge 6s. 2d.

„   „ £4 5s. to £8   „   „   1s. 6d. in the £ less 30 per cent.

„   „ £8 and upwards   „   „   1s. 6d.   „   „   10   „

Lock up shops, minimum charge, 8s. 8d. per annum.

„   „   when rateable value greater than that to which 8s. 8d. per ann. applies.—Charge 6d. in the £ on rateable value.

Water supplied by meter, 6d. per 1,000 gals.

Meter rent, 3s. per quarter for 1 inch.

Other sizes proportionately as cases require.

Carnforth. Railways, L. N. W., M. and F. Distance from London, 235½ miles.
  Authority, Carnforth District Waterworks Company.
  Share capital paid up, £13,500.
  Dividend, 7½ per cent.
  Towns and villages supplied, Carnforth and Warton.
  Works established, 1877. Special Act, 1877.
  Total population supplied, 3,000.
  Sources of supply, 300 acres watershed.
  Storage capacity, 75,000,000 gals.
  Filtering, animal charcoal under pressure.
  Character of water, good.
  Number of meters in use, 10.

Carnoustie, Scotland. For statistics, see DUNDEE.

Carnoyle (supplied by GLASGOW).

Carr, Lancs. (supplied by NELSON).

Carrickfergus (supplied by DUBLIN).

Carridor (supplied by BO'NESS).

Carrington, Lancs. (supplied by MANCHESTER).

Carrington, Lincs. (supplied by BOSTON).

Carshalton, Surrey (supplied by Sutton).

Castle Bromwich (supplied by Birmingham).

Castle Church, Staffs. (supplied by Stafford).

Castleford (supplied by Wakefield).

Castleton, Derbyshire.
Authority, Castleton Waterworks Company, Ltd.
Population supplied, 541.

Castleton, Lancs. (supplied by Heywood).

Catcliffe (supplied by Sheffield).

Caterham (supplied by East Surrey Waterworks).

Cathcart (supplied by Glasgow).

Catrine, Scotland.   Railway, G.S.W.   Distance from Edinburgh, 39 miles.
Authority, County Council.
Office, Catrine.
Area supplied, Quoad Sacra Parish of Catrine.
Works established, 1878.   Special Acts, under Public Health Act.
Total population supplied, 2,340.
Daily consumption per head, about 9 gals.
Sources of supply, springs.
Storage capacity, tank holding about 21,600 gals.
Character of water, hard.
Death rate, 17·3 per 1,000.
Assessment charge, 9d. in the £ on proprietor and tenant equally.

Caughall (supplied by Chester).

Causewayhead (supplied by Stirling).

Caversham, Berks. (supplied by Reading).

Cayton, Yorks. (supplied by Scarborough).

Cefn Coed (supplied by Merthyr Tydvil).

Cefn, Rhosymedre, and Acrefair, N. Wales.   Railway, G.W.   Distance from
London, 194¾ miles.
Authority, Cefn, Acrefair, and Rhosymedre Water Company.
Chairman, E. Lloyd Edwards.
Secretary, Geo. W. Spurring.
Engineer, Fredk. Storr.
Office, Trefynant, nr. Ruabon.
Also supplies Cefn Bychan and Trevorissa.
Works established, 1866.
Total population supplied, about 8,000.
Sources of supply, mountain springs and river.
Character of water, very good.
Price per 1,000 gals., per scale, as Act.

Ceres (supplied by Cupar).

Chadderton, Lancs. (supplied by Oldham and Heywood).

Chaddesdon (supplied by Derby).

Chalfont St. Giles (supplied by Amersham).

Chalfont St. Peter's (supplied by Rickmansworth).

Chalvey, Bucks (supplied by SLOUGH).

Chapel Brampton (supplied by NORTHAMPTON).

Chapel-en-le-Frith, Derbyshire. Railway, M. Distance from London, 167 miles.
Authority, Chapel-en-le-Frith Waterworks Co., Ltd.
Population supplied, 4,647.
No returns supplied.

Chapelizod (supplied by DUBLIN).

Chapelfield (supplied by BURY).

Chard, Somerset. Railways, G.W. and L.S.W. Distance from London, 142 miles.
Authority, Chard Corporation.
Chairman, J. Hawker.
Engineer and Manager, S. G. Rogers, C.E., M.R.San.I.
Office, Fore Street.
Total population supplied, 4,437.
The town supply is a very old one, and no reliable statistics are available. The
council are considering a new scheme.

Charlecombe, Somerset (supplied by BATH).

Charlestown, N.B. (supplied by DUNFERMLINE).

Charlton, Berks (supplied by WANTAGE).

Charlton Kings (supplied by CHELTENHAM).

Charlton Marshall (supplied by BLANDFORD).

Chatham and District, Kent. Railways L.C.D. & S.E. Distance from London
30 miles.
Authority—Brompton, Chatham, Gillingham and Rochester Waterworks Com-
pany.
Chairman, John S. Benton, J.P.
Secretary and Manager, Godfrey G. Catt.
Engineer (Resident), W. Coles Finch.
Office, Railway Street, Chatham.
Consulting Engineers, J. Taylor, Sons & Co.
Share capital, including premiums, £163,365.
Loan, £14,750. Dividend, 10 per cent. "A," 7 per cent. "B."
Towns and villages in the area supplied—Chatham, Rochester, Old and New
Brompton, Gillingham.
Works established—1856 ; special Acts, 1860, 1868, 1898 and 1905.
Annual supply of water, 750,000,000 gals.
Daily consumption per head, 15 gals.
Sources of supply—Wells and adits in chalk formation, and boring to lower green
sand.
Storage capacity, 9,500,000 gals.
Character of water, rather hard.
Death rate, 16 per 1,000.
Number of meters in use, 493.
Length of mains, 75 miles.
Scale of charges—Domestic, assessment charge A.
Trade 2s. to 9d. per 1,000 gals., less 5 per cent. discount.
Municipal purposes, 7d. per 1,000 gals., less 5 per cent. discount.
Total revenue received, £27,325

Cheadle, Staffs. Railway, North Staffs. (three miles distant). Distance from London,
146 miles.
Authority, Cheadle (Staffs.) Waterworks Company.
Office, High Street.
Towns and villages in the area supplied, Cheadle (Staffs.), Brookhouses and
Woodhead.

CHEADLE—*continued*.

Works established, 1854.
Total population supplied, 4,000.
Source of supply, natural spring in sand rock pumped up to high level.
Character of water, good water for a town supply.
System of filtration, none needed.
Length of mains, about 3 miles.

Cheam, Surrey (supplied by SUTTON).

Cheetham (supplied by MANCHESTER).

Checkendon (supplied by SOUTH OXFORDSHIRE).

Chelmsford, Essex. Railway, G.E. Distance from London, 29¾ miles.
Authority, Town Council.
Area supplied, Chelmsford and Widford.
Total population supplied, 12,580.
Sources of supply, wells and springs.
Character of water—hard, some soft.
Assessment—domestic, 7d. in £ on rateable value.
Price for 1,000 gals.—trade, 1s. 6d.

Chelmsford Rural District Council—

Supplies—
 Great Waltham from spring. Ingatestone from springs filtered through polarite. Loan sanctioned for sinking deep well.
 Great Baddow and Springfield, from gravel spring, 70,000 gals. per day. Deep boring proposed.
 Little Baddow, Danbury, Woodham Ferris, Runwell and East Hanningfield, spring on Danbury Common. R.D.C. have decided to purchase another large spring.
 Length of mains, 20 miles.
 An extensive scheme is just being completed for supplying the following parishes—Woodham Mortimer, Hazeleigh, Purleigh, Stow Maries, Cold Norton, North Fambridge, Latchington and Althorne, from springs at Woodham Walter. Total cost, about £12,000.

Chelsea Water Company (*see* METROPOLITAN WATER BOARD).

Cheltenham, Gloucester. Railways, M., G.W. and M. and S.W.J. Distance from London, 121 miles.
Authority, Cheltenham Corporation.
Chairman, H. Waghorne.
Town Clerk, R. O. Seacome.
Engineer in charge, J S. Pickering, A.M.I.C.E.
Office, Municipal Offices, Cheltenham.
Capital invested, including loans, £359,820.
Towns and villages within the area of control—Cheltenham, Tewkesbury, Charlton Kings, Leckhampton, Prestbury, Staverton, Swindon, Boddington, Ash Church, Tristlington, Stoke Orchard, Uckington, Elmstone Hardwick, Deerhurst, Deerhurst Walton, Walton Cardiff, Evington, The Leigh, Norton, Down, Hatherley, Badgeworth, Shardington-up-Hallurley.
Works established, 1824.
Purchased by Local Authority, 1878.
Special Acts—1824, 1839, 1847, 1858, 1865, 1878, 1881.
Death rate, 14 per 1,000 in the borough.
Total population of area of control, approximately, 1881, 55,000; 1901, 60,000,
Total number of consumers, ordinary, 12,100.
Meters, trade, 340.
Estimated population actually supplied, 50,000, exclusive of Tewkesbury.

CHELTENHAM—*continued.*

Annual supply of water—

Trade	69,317,000 gals.
Municipal	Not metered.
In bulk to other authorities	22,507,000 gals.

Maximum day's consumption, 1,397,000, exclusive of supply in bulk to Tewkesbury.

Sources of supply—Drainage areas situated at Dowdeswell.

Surface springs situated at parish of Charlton Kings.

Shallow wells or collecting reservoirs situated at Cheltenham.

River Severn at Tewkesbury.

Maximum annual rainfall over drainage area 38·21 inches (1882).

Minimum   „   „   19·51   „   (1892).

Average   „   „   27·84   „   (period 21 years).

Population on drainage area, about 100.

Nature of ditto—almost exclusively grass and woodland.

The water authority have no control of drainage area except the construction of drainage system to convey the drainage from all houses in the area to a point below the reservoir, and the ordinary P. H. A. powers.

Surface formation of drainage areas—Oolitic, resting upon lower lias.

Nature of subsoil yielding water, sand bed upon lias clay.

Storage reservoirs, Dowdeswell ...	..	capacity,	100,023,701 gals.
„ „ Hewletts No. 1 ...		„	70,400 „
„ „ „ „ 2 ...		„	1,911,360 „
„ „ „ „ 3 ...		„	14,800,178 „
„ „ „ „ 4 ...		„	15,659,925 „
„ „ Leckhampton ...		„	1,756,004 „

No service reservoirs used, supplies drawn direct from storage.

Filtering area provided—2,155 square yards in seven filter-beds at Dowdeswell.

„   „   1,320   „   four   „   Tewkesbury.

Pumping stations and capacity per hour—

Tewkesbury (River Severn), capacity, 30,000 gallons, also available for Tewkesbury. There is other plant=20,000 gallons. Sandford Mead, capacity, 25,000 gallons.

Water is not softened.

Number of meters in use, 340.

Length of distributing mains, 96 miles.

The only special arrangements are : Automatic valve to relieve main (13 miles) if a valve is shut whilst pumping. Automatic valve to shut off steam and open vacuum in case of serious leakage, fracturing main, etc.; made by James Simpson & Co., Pimlico, London. Sand washers by J. Tylor and Co., London.

Scale of charges—5 per cent. on gross annual value.

Fitted baths, 10s. each per annum.

Horses 10s. 6d. each per annum.

Carriages : 4-wheel, 21s.; additional carriages, 10s. 6d. each.

„   2-wheel, 10s. 6d. each.

Greenhouses : 5s. per 100 super feet to   500 feet.

„   4s.   „   from 500 to 1,000   „

„   3s.   „   over 1,000   „

Gardens, without hose, 4d. per perch.

Garden hose, 10s. 6d. in addition to above.*

Laundries, 10s. per annum for each woman employed, the first free.

Supplies by meter, 1s. 3d. per 1,000 gals.

Trade supplies by agreement.

Street watering, no charge.

Electric lighting generating station, 6d. per 1,000 gals

* The Corporation reserve to themselves the right in any particular case, or cases to require the consumer to pay for water to be measured by meter at a rate to be agreed upon.

Chepping Wycombe, Bucks. Railway, G.W. Distance from London, 34¼ miles.
Authority, Corporation of Chepping Wycombe.
Chairman of Water Committee, Alderman C. W. Beacon, J.P.
Mayor, Arthur Vernon, J.P., C.C.
Borough Surveyor and Waterworks Engineer, T. J. Rushbrooke, High Wycombe.
Total capital invested, including loans, £45,000.
Works established 1875. Purchased by local authority September, 1900.
Special Act, The High Wycombe Water Order, 1874.
Total population of area of control, 22,500 (1906).
Total number of consumers, 2,450.
Estimated population actually supplied, 11,650.
Area of control, Tylers Green, Loudwater and Hazlemere, in addition to the
  borough of Chepping Wycombe.
Source of supply—Deep wells or borings situated at High Wycombe.
  Natural rest level of water below surface, 8 feet, below ordnance datum
    224 feet.
  Level of water below surface (when pumping 500,000 gallons per day) 9·9 feet.
  Nature of subsoil yielding water, chalk.
  Pumping station, Chepping Wycombe Waterworks, capacity 1,000,000 gals. per
    day (24 hours).
Result of analysis expressed in parts per 100,000, October 4, 1897.

Total solid impurity	28·36
Organic carbon	·007
,, nitrogen	·003
Ammonia	0
Nitrogen as nitrates and nitrites	·302
Total combined nitrogen	·305
Chlorine	1·3
Hardness, temporary	19·7
,, permanent	3·0

Remarks—Clear.
Service reservoirs, high level ... ... capacity, 131,120 gals., covered.
   ,,   ,,   low level ... ...   ,,   119,837 ,,   ,,
Maximum day's consumption, 500,000 gals.
Number of meters in use, 77.
Gross assessment charges, less 10 per cent. Price per 1,000 gals., 1s. to 2s.

Chepstow, Mon. Railway, G.W. Distance from London, 141 miles.
Authority, Chepstow Water Company.
Chairman, F. W. T. Brain. A.M.I.C.E.
Engineer and Secretary, H. Swinney.
Office, 27, Bridge Street, Chepstow.
Works established, 1843. Special Act, 1843.
Total population supplied, 3,250.
Average death rate, 13 per 1,000.
Towns and villages supplied—Chepstow, S. Arvans, Pwl Megric and part of
  Tidenham.
Sources of supply, borings and springs in old red sandstone.
Character of water, most excellent, soft, but not so soft as to affect lead; total
  hardness, 4·3°.
Filtration, none.
Storage capacity, service reservoir, 1,200,000.
Average daily consumption per head for all purposes, 30 gals.
Scale of charges—

By meter according to scale	...	from	5,000 per quarter	£0	7	6
,,	,,	,,	,,	20,000	,,	1	3	4
,,	,,	,,	,,	40,000	,,	2	0	0
,,	,,	,,	,,	50,000	,,	2	10	0
,,	,,	,,	,,	100,000	,,	4	11	8

CHEPSTOW—*continued.*

By meter according to scale	...	from	200,000 per quarter	£8	6	8
,,	,,	,,	,, 300,000 ,,	12	1	8
,,	,,	,,	,, 400,000 ,,	add 8d. per 1,000
,,	,,	,,	,, 500,000 ,,	,, 7d. ,,
,,	,,	,,	over 500.000 ,,	,, 6d. ,,

Special rates for various purposes.　　　And intermediate prices.
Meter rents according to scale, from 2s. 6d. per quarter for ⅝-in. meters to 15s. per quarter for 3-in. meters.
Municipal purposes at fixed rates and by meter.
Length of mains, 13,588 yards.

Cherryhinton (supplied by CAMBRIDGE).

Cherry Tree (supplied by BLACKBURN).

Chertsey, Surrey (supplied by WEST SURREY WATER COMPANY)

Chesham, Bucks. Railway, Metropolitan. Distance from London, 25¾ miles.
Authority, Chesham Urban District Council.
Chairman, H. G. Rose, J.P. Chesham.
Clerk to authority, J. Gibbon How, Solicitor, Chesham.
Manager, W. Foster.
Engineer, Percy C. Dormer.
Office, Urban District Council offices.
Works established, 1882.
Total population supplied, 9,000.
Average death rate, 9·5 per 1,000.
Area of supply, urban district of Chesham.
Sources of supply, bore hole in chalk, 240 ft. deep.
Filtration, none.　Character of water, excellent.
Service reservoir, 335,000 gals.
Head on distributing mains—maximum, 275 ft.; minimum, 100 ft.
Annual supply of water, 75,000,000 gals.
Average daily consumption per head, 16 gals., domestic ; trade, &c., 7 gals.
Scale of charges, assessment charge, 5 per cent. on rateable value.
Price per 1,000 gals., trade 1s., domestic 1s., municipal purposes 1s.
Number of meters, 38.
Length of mains—supply main, 1 mile ; distributing mains, 14 miles.

Chesham Bois (partly supplied by AMERSHAM).

Cheshunt, Herts. Railways, G.E. and M. Distance from London, 14¼ miles.
Authority, Urban District Council.
Population supplied, 12,288.
Water supplied to the Council in bulk by the Metropolitan Water Board.

Chester. Railways, L.N.W., G.W., G.C. Distance from London, 179 miles.
Authority. Chester Waterworks Company.
Chairman, F. E. Roberts, J.P.
Engineer, George Crowe.
Secretary, William S. Moss.　Office, 15, Newgate Street.
Share capital paid up, £72,000.　Loan capital paid up, £15,000.
Interest on loan, 3 to 4 per cent.　Dividend, 6, 7 and 7½ per cent.
Works established, 1826 ; Special Acts, 1857 and 1874.

CHESTER—*continued.*

Total population of area supplied, 53,000.
Average death rate, 17·9 per 1,000.
Towns and villages in the area supplied, Chester, Christleton, Rowton, Littleton, Hoole, Hoole village, Newton, Upton, Caughall, Moston, Mollington, Blacon, Saltney, and Boughton Heath.
Source of supply, River Dee. Storage capacity, 3,000,000 gals.
Character of water, 8° hardness. System of filtration, sand.
Head on distributing mains, maximum, 154 feet ; minimum, 49 feet.
Annual supply of water, 685,000,000 gals.
Average daily consumption per head—domestic, 24·4 gals. ; trade, 11 gals.
Maximum day's supply, 3,022,504 gals., December, 1901.
Scale of charges, assessment, 5 to 7 per cent. rental. Baths and w.c's. extra.
Price per 1,000 gals., trade, 1s. 6d. to 8½d.
Number of meters, 300. Length of mains, 55 miles.

Chesterfield Railway, M. Distance from London, 146 miles.
Authority, Chesterfield Gas and Water Board.
Works established, 1825. Special Acts, 1825, 1855, 1865, 1871, 1876.
Total population supplied, 40,000.
Source of supply, moorland and springs.
No returns supplied.

Chester-le-Street (supplied by the WEARDALE AND CONSETT WATER CO.).

Chesterton (supplied by the STAFFORDSHIRE POTTERIES WATER CO.).

Chesterton, District of (supplied by CAMBRIDGE).

Chichester, Sussex. Railway, L.B.S.C. Distance from London, 69 miles.
Owners, the Mayor, Aldermen, and Citizens of the City of Chichester.
Chairman, the Mayor.
Office, Lion Street (for City Surveyor).
Towns and villages in the area supplied, City of Chichester and Fishbourne, Shopwyke, the Broyle, &c.
Works established, 1872. Special Acts, Company's Act, 1872 ; Corporation's Act, 1897.
Total population supplied, 14,000.
Annual supply of water, 175,000,000 gals.
Daily consumption per head, domestic, 35 gals. ; trade, 62,000 gals. per day.
Source of supply, springs from chalk.
Storage capacity, 200,000 gals.
Character of water, a typical chalk water of the highest quality and purity, and only moderately hard.
Death rate, average for last 10 years, 16 per 1,000.
Length of mains, about 21 miles.
Scale of charges—assessment charge, where rateable value does not exceed £5, 2d. per week ; not exceeding £30, 7½ per cent. on rateable value ; exceeding £30, 6 per cent. on rateable value.
Price per 1,000 gals., 1s. 6d. under 100,000 ; 1s. 3d. over 100,000 and under 200,000 ; 1s. over 200,000 per quarter ; larger quantities by agreement.
Municipal purposes, 10d. per 1,000.
Total water rent received, about £4,496.

Chigwell (supplied by EAST LONDON WATER CO).

Chilton, Suffolk (supplied by SUDBURY).

Childwickham (supplied by EVESHAM).

Chiltern Hills, Bucks.
Authority, Chiltern Hills Spring Water Company.
See AYLESBURY.

Chilvers Coton, Warwick (supplied by NUNEATON).

Chingford (supplied by EAST LONDON WATER Co.).

Chipping Norton, Oxon. Railway, G.W. Distance from London, 89¼ miles.
Authority, Corporation.
Chairman, Alderman A. A. Webb, J.P.
Town Clerk, T. Mace.
Engineer, Thos. Coombes, jun.
Town Clerk's Office, Chipping Norton.
Area supplied, Chipping Norton borough.
Works established, 1878.
Total population supplied, 3,780.
Annual supply of water, 36,500,000 gals.
Daily consumption per head, 20 gals.
Maximum day's supply, 110,000 gals. in January.
Sources of supply, springs from Glyme, near Chipping Norton.
Storage capacity, 967,000 gals.
Character of water, good (lime). Filtration, none; softening, none.
Number of meters, 7.
Length of supply mains, 3 miles; distributing mains, about 5 miles.
Average charge by meter, 1s. 2d. per 1,000 gals.

Chipping Ongar.
Authority, The Ongar Water Company, Ld.
Chairman, H. E. Jones.
Secretary, C. H. Foster.
Manager, J. C. Price.
Consulting Engineer, F. H. Jones.
Office, High Street, Ongar.
Share capital paid up, £3,000; last dividend, 5 per cent.
Formation of company and works constructed, 1898.
Population supplied with water, about 1,500.
District of supply—Chipping Ongar, Shelley, High Ongar and Greenslea.
Source of supply, springs.
Price per 1,000 gals., 2s. 6d.

Chipstead (supplied by EAST SURREY WATER Co.).

Chirnside, Berwickshire, N.B.
Authority, Chirnside Waterworks Company.
Population supplied, 854.
No returns supplied.

Choppington, Northumberland (supplied by BEDLINGTON).

Chorley, Cheshire (supplied by STOCKPORT).

Chorley, Lancs. (supplied by LIVERPOOL).

Chorlton (supplied by MANCHESTER).

Christchurch, Hants. Railway, L.S.W. Distance from London, 104 miles.
Authority, West Hampshire Water Co.
Chairman, John King, J.P., C.C.
Manager, Secretary and Resident Engineer, S. Newlyn.

(81)

Christchurch—*continued.*

Consulting Engineer, R. St. George Moore, M.I.C.E.
Office, 16, Stour Road.
Share capital paid up, £59,270.   Dividend, 2¼ per cent., 1906.
Debenture stock, £9,460 at 4 per cent.
Works established, 1894.   Special Acts, 1893, 1902.
Total population supplied, about 12,000, in district over 20,000.
Average death rate, 14·2.
Sources of supply—River Avon.   Borings are in progress, and have reached a
    depth of 620 feet, but with no result to date.
Towns and villages in the area supplied. Christchurch, Mudeford, Southbourne,
    Ward, Jumpers, Iford, Burton, Highcliffe Milton, and New Milton, Bourne-
    mouth C.C., Hordle, Milford, Keyhaven, Everton and Pennington.
Character of water, first rate, aerated and doubly filtered, sand and polarite.
Service Reservoirs and Water Towers 400,000 gals.
Pressure in distributing mains, 66 lbs. constant.
Total quantity of water supplied per annum, 78,000,000 gals.
Average daily supply per head, domestic, about 18 gals.
Scale of charges—assessment charge, 5 per cent. to 6 per cent. on R.V. ; baths,
    10s. 6d. per annum extra ; more than one w.c. 7s. 6d. each per annum.
Authorised charge per meter, up to 50,000 gals. per quarter, 2s. per 1,000 ; above
    that quantity 1s. 6d. per 1,000; trade, 1s.; municipal purposes, 1s.
Length of mains, supply and distributing combined, 70 miles.
Number of meters, 62.

Christchurch, Mon. (supplied by Newport).

Christleton (supplied by Chester).

Chudleigh Knighton (supplied by Torquay).

Church, Lancs. (supplied by Accrington).

Church Stretton, Salop. Railways, L.N.W. and G.W. joint.   Distance from
    London, 153 miles.
Authority, Church Stretton Waterworks Co.
Office, 18, Adam Street, Adelphi, London, W.C.
Share capital paid up, £8,000.
Loan   „   „   £2,000.
Further capital being issued up to £12,000.
Interest, 4 per cent.   Dividend, 4 per cent. (1900).
Towns and villages in the area supplied— Church Stretton, Little Stretton, and
    district within the parish of Church Stretton.
Special Act, Church Stretton Water Act, 1899.
Total population of area supplied, 2,500, increasing rapidly.
Source of supply, springs in hills, absolutely pure.
Storage capacity, 15,000,000 gals., when new reservoir is completed.
Assessment charge—7 per cent. on rateable value for domestic supply.

Churwell, Yorks. (supplied by Morley).

Cinderford, Glos. Railway, G.W.   Distance from London, 128 miles.
Population supplied, 3,002.
No returns supplied.

Cirencester, Glos. Railways, G.W., M., & S.W.J.   Distance from London, 96 miles.
Authority, Urban District Council.

CIRENCESTER—*continued*.

> Clerk, Robert Ellett.
> Surveyor, Thos. Hibbert.
> Total population supplied, 7,536.
> No returns supplied.

Clackmannan (supplied by ALLOA).

Clacton-on-Sea, Essex. (G. and W.) Railway, G.E. Distance from London, 71 miles.
> Authority, Clacton Urban District Council.
> Engineer, Sydney Francis.
> Office, Town Hall.
> Loan capital paid up, £46,000.
> Area supplied, Clacton-on-Sea and Great Clacton.
> Purchased by local authority, June 24th, 1899.
> Special Acts, 1876, 1885, 1898.
> Total population supplied, 8,000.
> Daily consumption per head, 22 gals.
> Source of supply, wells in gravel and chalk.
> System of filtration, sand.
> Death rate, 12·08 per 1,000.
> Price per 1,000 gals., domestic and trade, 2s. 3d, to 1s. 6d.

Clarkston, N.B. (supplied by BUSBY).

Claughton. *See* BIRKENHEAD.

Clay Cross, Derbyshire. Railway, M. Distance from London, 142 miles.
> Population supplied, 8,583.
> No returns supplied.

Clayton (supplied by BRADFORD, Yorks).

Clayton, Lancs. (supplied by MANCHESTER).

Clayton, Sussex (supplied by BURGESS HILL).

Clayton-le-Moors, Lancs. (supplied by ACCRINGTON).

Cleator Moor, Cumberland. Railways, L.N.W., and Fur. Joint. Distance from London, 300 miles.
> Authority, Urban District Council.
> Clerk, Henry Rothery.
> Engineer, Robert Robertson.
> Offices, Public Offices, Cleator Moor.
> Loan, £18,898.
> Area supplied, 2,946 acres.
> Works established, 1864. Special Act, 1881.
> Total population supplied, 9,500.
> Annual supply of water, 150,000,000 gals.
> Sources of supply, springs and mountain streams.
> Storage capacity, 44,000,000 gals.
> Character of water—hardness very slight.
> Death rate, 15·21 per 1,000.
> Number of meters, 47.
> Scale of charges—assessment charge A.
> Price for 1,000 gals., 10d. to 1d.

Cleckheaton, Yorks.　Railways, G.N., L. & Y., and L.N.W.　Distance from London
195 miles.
　　Authority, District Council.
　　Chairman, Abraham Fawcett.
　　Secretary, John H. Linfield, Clerk to Council.
　　Engineer and Manager, Geo. H. Niven.
　　Office, Town Hall.
　　Loan, £17,000, all repaid.
　　Annual profit, £142.
　　Works established, 1865.
　　Total population supplied, 13,000.
　　Average death rate, 15·07 per 1,000.
　　Towns and villages supplied, Cleckheaton, and parts of Hunsworth and Gomersal.
　　Area supplied, 1,850 acres.
　　Source of supply—water is obtained from the works of the Bradford Corporation
　　　in bulk.
　　Total annual supply, 93,938,000 gals.
　　Number of meters, 260.
　　Scale of charges—
　　　Assessment charge, rateable value.
　　　Price per 1,000 gals., trade, 11d.
　　Authorized charge by meter, 11d. per 1,000 gallons.
　　Total water rent received, £4,557 14s. 9d.

Cleethorpes, Lincs. (supplied by Great Grimsby Waterworks Co., Ld.).

Clent (supplied by Stourbridge).

Clevedon, Somerset.　Railway, G.W.　Distance from London, 134 miles.
　　Owners, Clevedon Waterworks Company, Ltd.
　　Chairman, E. Button, J.P.
　　Secretary, H. C. Fry, 12, Bellevue Road, Clevedon.
　　Engineer in charge, Jos. H. Pye.
　　Total capital, £40,000 ; not all called up.
　　Dividend, 4½ per cent. ordinary, 4½ per cent. preference.
　　Area of control—Clevedon　...　　...　　...　population 5,898 (1901)
　　　　　　　　　　　Walton in Gordano　　...　　　,,　　　731 (1901)
　　Works established, 1865.
　　Death rate, 13 per 1,000.
　　Source of supply, spring ; assessment charge, gross annual value.
　　Price per 1,000 gallons, 1s. 3d.

Cleveland Water Co.　See Saltburn-by-the-Sea.

Clewer, Berks. (supplied by Windsor).

Cliddesden (supplied by Basingstoke).

Clifton, Lancs. (supplied by Bolton).

Clifton (Brighouse), Yorks. (supplied by Halifax).

Clifton, Middlethorpe (supplied by York).

Clitheroe, Lancs. Railway, L. & Y. Distance from London, 220 miles.
  Authority, Corporation, 1877.
  Chairman, Councillor J. Sagar.
  Secretary, J. W. Mitchell.
  Office, Church Street, Clitheroe.
  Engineer and manager, Arthur R. Bleazard.
  Loan capital, £53,253.
  Area supplied, 2,381 acres.
  Towns and villages supplied, West Bradford and Grindleton.
  Works established, 1854. Special Act, 1878.
  Total population of area supplied, 13,000.
  Daily consumption per head, domestic and trade, 23 gals.
  Sources of supply, springs and brook.
  Storage capacity, 12,500,000 gals.
  Character of water, soft, 5° hardness.
  System of filtration, brook water through coke : spring not filtered.
  Death rate, 15·2 per 1,000.
  Number of meters in use, 59.
  Scale of charges—
    Assessment charge, 7¼ per cent. under and 6 per cent. over £20.
    Price per 1,000 gals., 1s. per qr. up to 100,000 gals., above that quantity, 3d. per
      1,000 gals.
  Total water rent received, £3,250.

Clontarf (supplied by DUBLIN).

Cloughfold (supplied by BURY).

Cloughton, Yorks. Railway, G.N. Distance from London, 233 miles.
  Authority, Cloughton Water Co., Ld.
  Population supplied, 571.
  No returns supplied.

Coalbrookdale (supplied by MUCH WENLOCK).

Coalport (supplied by MUCH WENLOCK).

Coalville, Leicestershire.
  Chairman, R. Blower.
  Resident Engineer and Manager, L. L. Baldwin.
  Clerk to authority, Thos. Jesson.
  Office, Council Chambers, Coalville.
  As works have not yet been completed for twelve months, a full year's returns are
      not available.
  Supplies Coalville, Whitwick, and Hugglescote.
  Population supplied, about 9,000.
  Works constructed, 1905.
  Source of supply, borings to red sandstone measures.
  Character of water, an excellent domestic water—total hardness, 17° ; after treat-
      ment, 9°.

Coatbridge. *See* AIRDRIE.

Cockermouth. *See* WORKINGTON.

Cockington, Devon. (supplied by TORQUAY).

Coddington, Notts. (supplied by NEWARK).

Cogan (supplied by CARDIFF).

Colchester, Essex. Railway, G.E. Distance from London, 51¾ miles.
    Authority, Corporation.
    Chairman, Alderman Watts, J.P.
    Superintendent, Chas. E. Bland.
    Office, Town Hall.
    Loans outstanding, £95,652.
    Works established, 1880. Special Act, 1879.
    Total population supplied, about 43,000.
    Average death rate, 13·2 per 1000.
    Area supplied, Borough of Colchester and part of Stanway Rural District.
    Sources of supply, well, with boring to the chalk, and springs from the gravel beds.
    Character of water, hardness, 12·1.
    Storage capacity, 220,000 gals.
    Annual supply of water, 282,867,750 gals.
    Average day's consumption per head for all purposes, 17 gals., under a constant supply.
    Scale of charges—
        Assessment charge, 5 per cent. on rack rent or annual value. No additional charge for extra w.c.'s, nor for garden watering by hand.
        Price per 1,000 gals., trade, 1s. 2d. to 7d.
    Number of meters in use, 185 ; number of hydrants, 418.
    Length of mains, 48 miles.
    Total water rent received, £13,244.

Coleshill (supplied by BIRMINGHAM).

Coleshill, Bucks. (supplied by AMERSHAM).

Colnbrook, Bucks. (supplied by SLOUGH).

Colne Lancs. Railway, M., L. & Y. Distance from London, 219 miles.
    Authority, Colne Corporation.
    Area supplied, 5,330 acres.
    Works established, Colne Water Co., 1806. Special Acts, 1881, 1897.
    Total population supplied, 22,000.
    Daily consumption per head, 16 gals.
    Source of supply, gravitation.
    Storage capacity, service reservoir, 4,500,000 gals. ; compensation, 89,000,000 gals.
    Character of water, soft.
    Death rate, 12·8 per 1,000.
    Scale of charges—
        Assessment charge, 6 to 10 per cent. on rateable value.
        Price per 1,000 gals., 1s. 3d.

Colne Valley. Railway, L.N.W. Distance from London, 16 miles.
    Authority, Colne Valley Water Company.
    Chairman, Charles E. Keyser.
    Secretary and General Manager, W. Verini.
    Engineer in charge, John Blackburn.
    Office, New Bushey, Watford.
    Consulting Engineers, Taylor, Sons & Santo Crimp.

COLNE VALLEY—*continued.*

Share capital paid up, £250,000.
Debenture stock, £65,000.
Premium, £71,618.   Dividends, 9½ and 7 per cent. on the 10 and 7 per cent. shares respectively.
Area supplied, about 76 square miles.
Works established, 1873.
Total population supplied, 82,000.
Annual supply of water, 900,000,000 gals.
Daily consumption per head—domestic, 24 gals.
Sources of supply—wells in chalk.
Storage capacity, 7,000,000 gals.
Character of water—Hard, but softened to about 5° by Clark's process.
Number of meters, 1,000.
Scale of charges—Assessment charge, rack rent.
   Price per 1,000 gals., 1s. 4d. to 7d.
Total water rent received, £38,000.

Coley (supplied by HALIFAX).

Colon (supplied by NEWQUAY).

Colwall (partly supplied by MALVERN).

Colwick (supplied by NOTTINGHAM).

Colwyn Bay and Colwyn. Railway, L.N.W. Distance from London, 220 miles.
   Authority, Colwyn Bay and Colwyn Urban District Council.
   Engineer and Surveyor, William Jones, A.M.I.C.E.
   Office, Council Office, Colwyn Bay.
   Total population supplied, 12,000 ; in summer, 24,000.
   Sources of supply—Cowlyd Lake.
   System of filtration, strainers.
   Character of water, soft.
   Death rate, 11·1 per thousand. Residents only, 9·1 per 1,000.
   Length of mains, 19½ miles.
   Scale of charges—Price per 1,000 gals., trade, 1s.; no charge for domestic purposes.

Compton (partly supplied by GODALMING).

Congleton, Cheshire. Railways, L.N.W, and N.S.R. Distance from London, 157¼ miles.
   Authority, Corporation.
   Office, Town Hall.
   Works established, 1881. Special Act, Public Health Act, 1875.
   Total population supplied, 10,800.
   Average death rate, 17·2 per 1,000.
   Area supplied, borough of Congleton.
   Sources of supply, springs in millstone grit. Character of water, good.
   Annual supply of water, 54,726,269 gals. Daily consumption per head, 16 gals.
   Scale of charges—Assessment charge, 5 per cent. ; cottages, 2s. per quarter.
   Price per 1,000 gals., 10d.
   Length of mains, 9 miles.
   Congleton Rural District Council for the supply of townships of Bradwall, Elton and Betchton is supplied with water by the Sandbach District Council.

Connah's Quay, Flint (G. and W.) Railways, L.N.W., W.M., and C. Quay. Distance from London, 188½ miles.
   Owners, Connah's Quay Gas and Water Co., Ld.

CONNAH'S QUAY—*continued.*

Total capital invested, including loans, £9,600.
Dividend, 7½ per cent.
Area of control, Connah's Quay, including the townships of Wepre, Golftyn, and Kelsterton.
Works established 1877.
Special Act, chapter xcii., an Act for Confirming Certain Provisional Orders, 1876.
Estimated population actually supplied, 4,000.
Source of supply—wells and springs.
Character of water, hard.
System of filtration, sand and gravel.
Storage capacity, 100,000.
Length of mains, 2½ miles.

Connington (supplied by ST. IVES, HUNTS.).

Cononley, Yorks. Railway, M. Distance from London, 216 miles.
Authority, Cononley Water Co., Ltd.
Chairman, Peter Nelson.
Secretary, C. Walker
Manager and Resident Engineer, Peter Nelson, Main Street.
Office, Spring Bank, Cononley.
Share capital paid up, £1,240. Dividend, about 4 per cent.
Annual profit, including "Capital Charges," £50.
Works established, 1888.
Total population supplied, 900.
Area supplied, part of Cononley.
Sources of supply—springs, and from an old tunnel.
Character of water, both soft and hard.
System of filtration, none.
Average daily consumption per head, domestic, 16 gals.
Storage reservoir, capacity, 250,000 gals.
Length of mains, 1¾ miles.
Total water rent received, £80 per annum.

Consett. The Consett Company has been amalgamated with the Weardale and Shildon Waterworks Company by Act, 1902, and is known as the Weardale and Consett Water Company.

Conway, Wales. Railway, L.N.W. Distance from London, 225 miles.
Authority, Corporation.
Chairman, Councillor John Williams.
Secretary, T. E. Parry.
Engineer, F. A. Delamotte.
Office, Town Hall.
Towns and villages in the area supplied, Conway, Tywyn, and Deganway.
Works established, 1871. Purchased by local authority, 1880.
Total population supplied, 4,660.
Source of supply, Cowlyd Lake.
Storage capacity, practically unlimited.
Character of water, soft.
Death rate, 18·5 per 1,000.
Number of meters, 6.
Length of mains, 16 miles.
Scale of charges—
    Assessment charge, A.
    Price per 1,000 gals., 9d., trade.

Cookham and Cookham Green (supplied by MAIDENHEAD).

Coopersale (supplied by IIERTS. AND ESSEX WATER Co.).

Copt Hewick (supplied by RIPON).

Cork, Ireland. Railway, G.S.W. Distance from Dublin, 165¼ miles.
Authority, Corporation.
Chairman, the Mayor (ex officio).
Office, Municipal Buildings, Albert Quay, Cork.
Area supplied, City of Cork and suburbs within radius of 3 miles.
Special Act, Cork Bridge and Waterworks Act, 1856.
Annual supply of water, about 2,000,000,000 gals.
Daily consumption per head, about 53 gals.
Source of supply, River Lee.
Character of water, good.
System of filtration, through river bank into tunnel and settling basin.
Scale of charges, assessment charge, public water rate, 3d. in £ on annual
    valuation, and domestic rate of 6d. in £.
Price per 1,000 gals., from 2d. up according to consumption.

Corkerhill (supplied by GLASGOW).

Cornard, Suffolk (supplied by SUDBURY).

Corsham, Wilts. Railway, G.W. Distance from London, 98¼ miles.
Authority, Corsham Waterworks Company.
Chairman, Jacob Selman.
Secretary, Lewin Spackman.
Consulting Engineer, A. E. Adams, C.E.
Office, High Street, Corsham.
Share capital paid up, £6,000; last dividend, 5 per cent.
Loan   „   „   £1,500, at 4 per cent.
Works established, 1889. Special Act, 1889.
Total population supplied, 3,500.
Average death rate, 12 per 1,000.
Area supplied, Lacock and Corsham.
Source of supply, Loxwell springs, from the sand at Bowden Hill.
Springs supply, 76,000 gals. per day, average.
Character of water, soft.
Filtration, none; softening, none.
Storage capacity, 30,000 gals.
Daily consumption per head, 10 gals.
Scale of charges—assessment charge, 5 per cent. to 8 per cent. in £ on rateable
    value.
Price per 1,000 gals., from 1s. 9d. downwards.
Number of meters, 40.
Length of mains, 10 miles.

Corwen, Wales. Railways, G.W. and L.N.W. Distance from London, 200 miles.
Owner, Private Company.
Office, Dee View.
Works established, 1870.
Total population supplied, 2,764.
Source of supply, Berwyn Mountains.

Coseley (supplied by SOUTH STAFFS. WATERWORKS CO.)

Cosham (supplied by PORTSMOUTH).

Cottenham, Cambs. (G. and W). Railway, G.E., Oakington Station. Distance from London, 52 miles.
    Authority, the New Cottenham Gas and Water Company, Ltd.
    Chairman, Thomas Ivatt.
    Manager and Secretary, A. C. Harradine.
    Office, High Street, Cottenham.
    Total population supplied, 2,550.
    Length of mains, 4 miles.
    Scale of charges, municipal purposes, £165 per annum.

Cottingham, Yorks (supplied by HULL).

Cottingley.
    Authority, Cottingley Waterworks Co., Ltd.
    Population supplied, 800.
    No returns supplied.

Coulsdon (supplied by EAST SURREY WATERWORKS CO.).

Coupar Angus, Scotland. Railway, Cal. Distance from London, 500 miles.
    Population supplied, 2,106.
    No returns supplied.

Cove, Hants (supplied by FRIMLEY).

Coventry, Warwick. Railway, L.N.W. Distance from London, 94 miles.
    Authority, Coventry Corporation.
    Chairman, Alderman F. Bird.
    Town Clerk, Geo. Sutton.
    Water Engineer, J. E. Swindlehurst.
    Office, St. Mary's Hall, Coventry.
    Loans outstanding, £114,270.
    Annual profit, including "capital charges," £4,000.
    Works established, 1842. Special Acts, 1842, 1888.
    Total population supplied, 87,000.
    Average death rate, 14·82 per 1,000.
    District of supply, the parishes of St. Michael, the Holy Trinity and St. John the Baptist in the City of Coventry, and parts of parishes of Foleshill and Stoke.
    Sources of supply, Artesian wells in new red sandstone.
    Character of water, good. Total hardness, 28·5°.
    Storage capacity, 3,000,000 gals.
    Annual supply of water, 703,000,000 gals.
    Daily consumption per head. Domestic, 19 gals ; trade, 4 gals.
    Maximum day's supply, 2,689,349 gals. in September.
    Assessment charge, 3¼ per cent. to 6 per cent. on R.V.
    Price per 1,000 gals., 8d. to 1s. ; trade, according to consumption.
    Number of meters, 406.
    Length of mains, 65 miles.
    Total water rent received, £18,231.

Cowes, Isle of Wight. Railway, L.S.W. Distance from London, 87 miles.
　Authority, Cowes Urban District Council.
　Surveyor and Water Engineer, John W. Webster.
　Office, High Street, Cowes.
　Total capital invested, £49,650.
　Loans outstanding, £22,400.
　Works established, 1845 ; purchased by the Council, 1859.
　Area supplied, Cowes Urban District.
　Population of area of control, 1881, 6,300 ; 1891, 7,690 ; 1901, 8,654.
　Total population supplied, 10,000 ; including visitors and shipping, 20,000.
　Average death rate (10 years), 11·62 per 1,000.
　Sources of supply—Deep well and catchment area at Broadfield, boring carried
　　down to 173 feet.
　Character of water—Deep well from analysis, good quality, total hardness, 14·5° ;
　　removed by ebullition, 12·5°. Catchment area, most excellent quality, total
　　hardness, 9·0° ; removed by ebullition, 4·0°.
　Filtration, none ; softening, none.
　Storage capacity, service reservoirs, 16,000,000 gals.
　Pressure on distributing mains—maximum, 70 lbs. ; minimum, 30 lbs. per sq. in.
　Total quantity of water drawn per annum from drainage area, 18,250,000 gals.
　　　　　　　,,　　　　　　　,,　　　　　　,,　　　　deep wells　73,750,000　,,
　Estimated quantity available per annum—
　　From drainage areas　　...　　...　　...　　... (average)　16,000,000　,,
　　　,,　deep wells　...　　...　　...　　...　　...　　...　150,000,000　,,
　Estimated maximum daily discharge at points of collection　400,000　,,
　　　,,　　minimum　　,,　　　,,　　　,,　　　,,　　5,000　,,
　　　,,　　average　　,,　　　,,　　　,,　　　,,　　50,000　,,
　Maximum annual rainfall over drainage area　37·84 in. in 1894.
　Minimum　　　,,　　　,,　　　,,　　　,,　　22·60　,,　,,　1887.
　Average　　　,,　　　,,　　　,,　　　,,　　28·68　,,　,,　period 20 years,
　　　　　　　　　　　　　　　　　　　　　　　　　　　　　　1878-1897.

　Population on drainage area, nil.
　Nature and extent of cultivation, very small ; portion under cultivation.
　The Council have no control over drainage area.
　Natural rest level of water—below surface, 158 feet ; above O.D., 9 feet.
　Level of water below surface when pumping 400,000 gals. per day, 270 ft.
　Surface formation of drainage areas, compact gravel and clay.
　Strata or formation yielding springs, sand and gravel.
　Nature of subsoil yielding water, sand and gravel.
　Strata tapped by wells or borings, upper Bagshot series.
　Locality and extent of outcrop of same, surface level 167 ft. above O.D.
　Annual supply of water, 92,000,000 gals.
　Daily consumption per head, 20 gals.
　Maximum day's supply, 270,000 gals. in August.
　Scale of charges—Assessment charge, 2d. in £ per annum on rateable value.
　Price per 1,000 gals, 8d.
　Number of meters—20 trade purposes only.
　Length of mains, distributing 13 miles.

Cowley (supplied by RICKMANSWORTH).

Cowling, Yorks. Railway, M. Kildwick Station, 3 miles distant. Distance from
　London, 200 miles.
　Owners, Cowling Water Co., Ld.
　Chairman, William Rushton.
　Manager, Edward Smith.
　Secretary, Ben Snowden, Fold Lane, Cowling, nr. Keighley.

COWLING—*continued.*

Share capital paid up, £2,365.
Loan capital paid up, £660 at 3 per cent.
Dividend, 5 per cent.
Area of control, township of Cowling only.
Works established, 1884.
Constructed by the Company under the Companies Acts.
Total population of area of control, 1881, 1,915 ; 1891, 1,928 ; 1901, 1,950.
Total number of consumers, 430.
Estimated population actually supplied, 1,500.
Annual supply for domestic purposes, 20,000,000 gals.
Maximum day's consumption, 50,000 gals.
Total quantity drawn from surface springs, 20,000,000 gals. per annum.
Natural rest level of water below surface, 15 feet.
Service reservoir at Redshaw, capacity, 400,000 gals., open.
Character of water, very good analytical report for domestic use.
Length of distributing mains, two and a half miles.
Water is for domestic use only.
Charges based upon gross rental of property.
Price 1s. per 1,000 gals. when used for business purposes.

Cowpen, U.D.C. (supplied by NEWCASTLE-ON-TYNE).

Cradley (supplied by SOUTH STAFFORDSHIRE WATERWORKS CO.).

Cranbrook, Kent. Railway, S.E. Distance from London, 48 miles.
Authority, Cranbrook District Water Company.
Offices, Cranbrook.
Towns and villages in the area supplied, Cranbrook, Sissinghurst, Hawkhurst, Goudhurst, Benenden, Tenterden. St. Michaels, Bolvenden.
Total population supplied, 17,000.

Cranford (supplied by SOUTH WEST SUBURBAN).

Cranleigh, Surrey. Railways, L.B.S.C. and L.S.W. Distance from London, 48 miles.
Authority, Cranleigh Water Company, Ld.
Chairman, W. Welch.
Secretary, H. J. Hayman.
Share capital paid up, £7,000 ; dividend, 8 per cent.
Works established, 1886.
Total population supplied, 2,400.
Character of water, total hardness, 3·5°.
Storage capacity, 540,000 gals.
Number of meters, 10.
Scale of charges—assessment charge, 1s. 6d. in £.
Price per 1,000 gals., 2s. 6d. to 1s.
Total water rent received, £782.

Crawley, Sussex. Railway, L.B.S.C. Distance, 30 miles.
Authority, Crawley Water Company.
Population supplied, 3,824.

Crawshawbooth (supplied by BURY).

Cray's Pond (supplied by SOUTH OXFORDSHIRE).

Crediton, Devon.　Railway, L.S.W.　Distance from London, 179 miles.
  Authority, Urban District Council.
  Manager, Thos. Jones, Surveyor.
  Secretary, John Symes, Clerk.
  Office, Masonic Hall.
  Loan outstanding, £7,000.
  Works established, 1892.
  Total population supplied, 3,970.
  Average death rate, 14·2 per 1,000.
  Area supplied, Crediton only.
  Source of supply, Clannaborough gathering ground.
  Character of water, exceptionally pure.
  Storage capacity, 240,000 gals.
  Daily consumption per head, 20 gals,
  Scale of charges —assessment charge, 10d., under £20; 9d. above £20.
  Price per 1,000 gals., 8d. to 100,000 gals., 6d. above.
  Number of meters, 18.
  Length of mains, 14 miles.

Crewe, Cheshire.　Railways, L.N.W., G.W. and North Staff.　Distance from London
  158 miles.
  Authority, L.N.W. Ry. Co.
  Total population supplied, 42,075.
  The L.N.W. Ry. Co. under Parliamentary powers supply the Corporation of
  Crewe from their works about 10 miles distant, but the works exist primarily
  for railway purposes.

Crewkerne, Somerset. (G. and W.) Railway, L.S.W.　Distance from London
  131¼ miles.
  Chairman, John Tompsett.
  Engineer and Secretary, John Nicholls.
  Office, Gas Works.
  Share capital paid up, £8,000.
  Dividend, 6 per cent.
  Works established, 1883.
  Total population supplied, 5,000.
  Sources of supply, springs in green sand.
  Character of water, very good, inclined to hardness.
  Storage capacity, 400,000 gals.
  Scale of charges—
    Assessment charge, 5 per cent. on rental, less 25 per cent. prompt cash.
    Price per 1,000 gals., 2s. 6d. to 6d.
  Number of meters, 20.
  Total water rent received, £790.

Crickhowell, S. Wales.　Railways, L N.W. and G.W., to Abergavenny, 6 miles away.
  Distance from London, 140 miles.
  Authority, District Council.
  Office, District Council Board Room, Standard Street.
  Loan capital paid up, £3,100.
  Works established, 1890.
  Total population of area supplied, 800.
  Quantity of water drawn, 17 gals. per minute at midsummer.
  Sources of supply, from near Table Mountain.　Storage capacity, 108,000 gals.
  Character of water, first class spring water; no filtering required.

CRICKHOWELL—*continued.*

  Death rate, 19 per 1,000.
  Length of mains, 2½ miles.
  Scale of charges—assessment charge, 1s. 6d. in the £.
  Extra w.c., 5s.; fixed baths, 5s.; horses and cows, 5s. each; churches, etc., 5s.
    per annum; building, 5s. per cent. on total cost of building, etc., etc.
  Total water rent received, £230 per annum.

Cricklade, Wilts. Railway, M. & S.W.J. Distance from London, 108 miles.
  Authority, Cricklade and Wootton Bassett Rural District Council.
  Clerk to Council, H. Bevir.
  Engineer, F. Redman, 34, Wood Street, Swindon.
  Works constructed, 1905.
  Source of supply, gravel.
  System of filtration, sand.
  Service reservoir, 60,000 gals.
  Total population in area of supply, 1,700.

Crieff, Perthshire. Railway, Caledonian. Distance from London, 440 miles.
  Authority, Burgh Local Authority.
  Chairman, Provost M. Finlayson.
  Town Clerk, C. E. Colville.
  Office, 14, Comrie Street.
  Works established, 1864.
  Total population supplied, 5,209.
  Sources of supply—Loch Turret (six miles away).
  Storage capacity, practically unlimited.
  Character of water, excellent.
  Scale of charges—assessment charge, 7½d. in the £.

Croft, Lancs. (supplied by WARRINGTON).

Cromer, Norfolk. Railways, G.E. and M. and G.N. Joint. Distance from London,
  138¾ miles.
  Authority, Urban District Council.
  Clerk, J. K. Frost.
  Council Office, Town Hall.
  Consulting Engineer, J. C. Mellis, M.I.C.E.
  Towns and villages in the area supplied—Cromer, Overstrand and Runton.
  Works established, 1875.
  Taken over by local authority, 1st October, 1902, under Cromer Water Act.
  Total population supplied, about 4,800.

Crompton (supplied by OLDHAM).

Crondall (supplied by FRIMLEY).

Cronton (supplied by WIDNES).

Crook (supplied by WEARDALE & CONSETT WATER CO.).

Crookham (supplied by FRIMLEY).

Crookston, Scotland (supplied by PAISLEY).

Crossbank (supplied by OLDHAM).

Crosshills, Yorks. Railway, M. Distance from London, 220 miles.
Authority, Crosshills Water Company, Ltd.
Chairman, R. B. Ackroyd.
Secretary, Walter Thornton, Sutton Mill.
Manager and Resident Engineer, W. Clapham.
Office, 9, Keighley Road, Crosshills, Keighley, Yorks.
Share capital paid up, £1,730. Dividend, 5 per cent.
Loan 　 „ 　 „ 　 £1,730, 4 per cent.
Works established, 1854-5. Registered as Limited Company, 1893.
Total population supplied, 2,400.
Sources of supply—All from natural springs (no collected water).
Character of water, good, no filtration or softening required; temporary hardness, 3½° to 4°.
Storage capacity, impounding reservoirs, about 3,000,000 gals.
Average daily consumption per head, 10 gals.
Maximum day's supply, 25,000 gals.
Scale of charges, price per 1,000 gals., up to 5,000, 2s. 6d.; 10,000, 2s. 3d.; 20,000, 2s.; 50,000, 1s. 9d.; 100,000, 1s. 3d.; 150,000, 1s.
Number of meters registering, 9; Deacon's waste water, 2.
Length of mains, 3 to 4 miles.

Crosslie, Scotland (supplied by PAISLEY).

Crowborough, Sussex. Railway, L.B.S.C.
Authority, Crowborough District Water Co.
Chairman, W. S. Hounson, J.P.
Secretary, Edward J. Carter,
Manager and Resident Engineer, J. Middleton,
Consulting Engineer, E. Brough Taylor.
Office, Crowborough.
Share capital paid up, £45,000. Dividend, Dec., 1906, 4¼ per cent.
Loan 　 „ 　 „ 　 £7,500, at 4 per cent.
Annual profit. including " capital charges," £975 13s. 9d.
Works established, 1898.
Total population supplied, 9,000.
Number of supplies, December 31st, 1905, 1,049; December 31st, 1905, 1,156.
Area of supply, Crowborough, Rotherfield, Mayfield, Wadham, Withyham (part), Bunted (part).
Character of water—Colour, none; smell, none; sediment, none.
Chemical analysis afforded the following—

Total solids ...	...	...	...	...	7·4 grains per gal.
Solids after ignition ...	...	...	...	...	5·6 　 „ 　 „
Chlorine ...	...	...	...	...	1·6 　 „ 　 „
Ammonia (free)	...	...	...	...	·010 parts per million.
Ammonia (albuminoid)	...	...	...		·030 　 „ 　 „
Oxygen taken from permanganate in ¼ hour		...			None.
Oxygen taken from permanganate in 4 hours		..			Trace.
Nitrogen as nitrates and nitrites ...		...		...	None.
Nitrites	...	...	...	...	None.
Hardness (total) ...	...	...	...	...	2·6° Clark,
Hardness after boiling	...	...	...	...	2·0° Clark
Phosphates ...	...	...	...	...	.. None.
Metallic impurity ...	...	...	...	.,.	None.

Bacteriological examination—The organisms per cubic centimetre which grew on gelatine at 22° C. and which were visible to the naked eye in three days, numbered two.

CROWBOROUGH—*continued.*

Special tests were carried out for Typhoid bacilli and Coli communis with entirely negative results.

The above combined chemical and bacteriological examinations shows the water is very pure and quite suitable for drinking purposes and domestic use.

Present rate of charge, 7 per cent. on R. V.

Authorized charge by meter, 2s. 6d. per 1,000.

Crowmarsh (supplied by SOUTH OXFORDSHIRE).

Crown Hill, Devon. (supplied by PLYMOUTH).

Crowthorne (supplied by FRIMLEY).

Croydon, Surrey.　Railways, L.B.S.C. & L.S.W.

Authority, Croydon Corporation.

Chairman, Ald. F. W. M. King, J.P.

Town Clerk, F. O. Lloyd, Town Hall.

Engineer in charge, Geo. F. Carter, M.I.C.E.

Office, Town Hall.

Total capital invested, including loans, £447,000 (loans outstanding, £380,821).

Annual profit—receipts balanced expenses in 1906.

Works established, December, 1851.

Special Acts, Croydon Corporation Acts, 1884 and 1895.

Total population of area of control, 1881, 79,615; 1891, 102,697; 1901, 133,895; 1906, 155,000.

Average death rate, 12·7 (1906).

Area of supply, county borough of Croydon, village of Addington, and Croydon Mental Hospital.

Sources of supply (year 1905)—from Metropolitan Water Board, 450,000,000 gals.; deep wells and borings at Croydon and Addington in the chalk, 1,380,000,000 gallons.

Character of water—Analysis, 2nd November, 1906—

Appearance, clear and bright.

Odour at 100° Fahr., none.

Total solids—grains per gallon, 23·9.

　　”　　”　　appearance on ignition, no blackening.

Phosphoric acid, no trace.

Hardness—total degrees, 17·2.

　　”　　permanent degrees, 4·2.

Ammonia, free—grains per gallon, 0·0011.

　　”　　albuminoid—grains per gallon, ·0024.

Chlorine, grains per gallon, ·91.

Oxygen absorbed from permanganate at 80° Fahr.—

In 15 minutes, grains per gallon —

In 4 hours,　　”　　　　”　　·0024.

Organic elements, parts per 100,000—

Carbon　.:.　·040.

Nitrogen　...　·011.

Total　　...　·051.

Nitrogen as nitrates, &c.—grains per gallon, ·310.

Cultivation on gelatine plates, colonies per C.C., 10.

Micro-filter, m.m. per litre, very slight trace.

Pathogenic organisms, coli-like organisms in 100 C.C.; no streptococci.

Microscopical examination, few fibres and little débris.

Remarks—There is a slight rise in the organic constituents; but no importance can be attached to this in view of the very low number of bacteria, viz. :—

CROYDON—*continued.*

only 10 per C.C. and the absence of even B. coli-like organisms in less than 100 C.C. A searching microscopical examination failed to detect anything more than a few fibres and indefinite particles with some mineral débris. The water is therefore of the highest quality.

Estimated minimum daily discharge at points of collection, 5,250,000 gals.

Maximum annual rainfall over drainage area, 40·39 inches in 1903.

| Minimum | „ | „ | „ | „ | 19·89 | „ | in 1898. |
| Average | „ | „ | „ | „ | 25·34 | „ | period 11 years. |

The Authority have no control over drainage area.

Pumping stations, Surrey Street Wells, daily capacity, 2,250,000 gals.

	Waddon	„	„	1,250,000	„
	Addington	„	„	1,000,000	„
	Stroud Green	„	„	750,000	„
Service reservoirs,	Park Hill	„	„	950,000	„
	Addington	„	„	5,000,000	„

Head on distributing mains—maximum, 250 ft.; minimum, 60 ft.

Filtration, none; softening, none.

Annual supply, 1,830,000,000 gals.

Average daily supply per head—domestic, 25 gals.; trade, &c., 7 gals.

Maximum day's supply, 6,750,000 gals. in September.

Scale of charges—Domestic:

Houses not exceeding £12 per ann., 4d. in the £ on R. V. (occupiers), and a further charge of 2s. 6d. per house per half year.

Houses exceeding £12 per ann. 4d. in the £ on R. V. (occupiers), and a further charge of 4s. per house per half year,

Trade and special purposes—

Gardens, 1s. per 1,000, min. 10s. per ann., and 6s. per ann. for hire and repair of
Fountains, 1s.   „   10s.   „   6s.   „   „   [meter
Caretakers, 10s. per half-year.

Trades, 25 per cent. more than domestic charge, or by meter.

Slaughter houses (private), not to exceed 45s. per ann.

Water by meter—The charge for water supplied by meter will be 1s. per 1,000 gals,, with a minimum charge of 20s. per half-year, except when used for garden hose or fountains, when the minimum charge will be 10s. per year as above.

Livery stable keepers—Livery stable keepers and cab proprietors, 5s. per stall per annum.

Cowkeepers—Cowkeepers, 2s. 6d. each cow per annum.

Tanks in fields, steam boilers and gas engines by special agreement only.

Brewers, &c.—Brewers, mineral water manufacturers, brickmakers, dyers, and railway companies (by meter only, to be provided by the consumer and approved by the Council) at the above meter rate.

Builders—The charge to builders for water for building purposes, 2s. 3d. per room.

Present average charge per meter, 1s, per 1,000 gals.

Number of meters, 2,000.

Crumlin, Mon. (supplied by ABERCARN).

Crumpsall (supplied by MANCHESTER).

Cuckfield. Railway, L.B.S.C. Distance from London, 38 miles.
Authority, Cuckfield Rural District Council.
Chairman, J. J. Lister, J.P.
Clerk to Authority, C. H. Waugh.
Manager and Engineer, Francis Martin, C.E.
Office, Council Buildings, Haywards Heath.
Loan, £78,280.
Works established, 1888. Special Acts, 1890.
Purchased by local authority, 1898.

(97)

CUCKFIELD—*continued.*

    Total population supplied, 14,000.
    Average death rate, 10·7 per 1,000.
    Towns and villages in the area supplied—Haywards Heath, Cuckfield, Balcombe.,
        Ardingly, Lindfield, Bolney, Warminglid, Ansty, Slangham, Staplefield,
        Handcross.
    Sources of supply—wells in sandstone, Balcombe Forest.
    Character of water, 6·0° hardnesss.
    System of filtration, Leighton Buzzard sand.
    Storage capacity, 600,000 gals.
    Annual supply of water, 73,000,000 gals.
    Average daily consumption per head, 14 gals.
    Scale of charges—assessment charge, 5½ to 7 per cent.
      Price per 1,000 gals. Domestic, 2s.; trade, 1s. 6d.; municipal purposes, 2s.
    Number of meters, 150.
    Length of mains, 78 miles.
    Total water rent received, £5,400.

Cuddington (supplied by SUTTON).

Cuerdley (supplied by WIDNES).

Culcheth (supplied by WARRINGTON).

Culross, N.B. (supplied by DUNFERMLINE).

Culter, Lanark. (supplied by BIGGAR).

Cults (supplied by CUPAR).

Cupar, Scotland. Railway, N.B. Distance from London, 424 miles.
    Authority, Town Council of the Royal Burgh of Cupar, Fife.
    Convener, W. Lauderdale Brown.
    Clerk, J. L. Anderson.
    Manager, John Kirkcaldy.
    Engineers, Bruce & Proudfoot.
    Offices, 67, Crossgate, Cupar; and Kirk Wynd, Kirkcaldy.
    Loans outstanding, £16,950 at 3 per cent.
    Works established, 1874. Special Acts, 1874.
    Total population supplied, Burgh, 4,898 ; Landward, 1,120.
    Consumption per day, 276,000 gals.
    Average death rate, 14·82 per 1,000.
    Area supplied, parishes of Cupar, Moniment (part of), Kettle, Cults, Ceres.
    Sources of supply—Impounding reservoirs on streams and Clatto gathering ground,
        820 acres in extent.
    Character of water, moderately soft, about 8° of hardness.
    System of filtration, sand and gravel beds 4 ft. deep.
    Storage capacity—Impounding reservoirs, 60,000,000 gals.; service reservoirs,
        275,000 gals.
    Head on distributing mains—Max., 300 ft.; min., 220 ft.
    Annual supply of water, 72,918,000 gals.
    Average daily consumption per head—domestic, 30 gals.; trade, &c., 15 gals.
    Charges authorized—Domestic, £12 10s. per cent. to £15 0s. per cent. on R.V.
    Present rate of charge   „   £2 10s.   „   £2 18s. 4d.   „   R.V.
    Authorized charge by meter, inside burgh, 8d.; outside, 10d. per 1,000.
    Present average, 9d. per 1,000.
    Number of meters, 12,
    Length of mains—Supply, 8 miles; distributing, 5 miles.

Cwmaman (supplied by ABERDARE).

Cwmbach (supplied by ABERDARE).

Cwmcarn, Mon. (supplied by ABERCARN).

Cwmdare (supplied by ABERDARE).

Cwmsyflog (supplied by NEW TREDEGAR).

Dagenham (supplied by SOUTH ESSEX WATER Co.).

Dalkeith, Scotland.　Railway, N.B.　Distance from Edinburgh, 6 miles.
　　Authority, Commissioners of Police, 1878.
　　Special Act, General Police Act.
　　Total population supplied, 6,953.
　　Assessment charge, 1s. 1d. per £.
　　Price per 1,000 gals., 9d.

Dalkey (supplied by DUBLIN).

Dalry, Scotland.
　　Authority, Local Authority.
　　Population supplied, 4,500.
　　No returns supplied.

Dalserf (supplied by DISTRICT OF THE MIDDLE WARD OF LANARKSHIRE).

Dalton, Lancs. (supplied by BARROW-IN-FURNESS).

Dalziel (supplied by DISTRICT OF THE MIDDLE WARD OF LANARKSHIRE).

Danbury, Essex.
　　Authority, Chelmsford Rural District Council.
　　Office, High St., Chelmsford.
　　Towns and villages in the area supplied, Danbury, Little Baddow, Woodham Ferris,
　　　　Street, Rettendon, East Hanningfield, part of parish of Sandon.
　　Works established, 1891.
　　Total population of area supplied, about 4,000.
　　Sources of supply, springs.

Daresbury (supplied by WARRINGTON).

Darfield (supplied by DEARNE VALLEY).

Darington, Kent (supplied by FAVERSHAM).

Darlaston (supplied by SOUTH STAFFS. WATERWORKS CO.).

Darley Abbey (supplied by DERBY).

Darlington, Durham.　Railway. N.E.　Distance from London, 232 miles.
　　Authority, Corporation.
　　Secretary, J. W. Armitage, Borough Accountant.
　　Engineer and Surveyor, Geo. Winter.
　　Loan capital, £104,290. .

777834

Darlington—continued.

    Area supplied, borough and suburbs.
    Works established, 1854. Special Acts, 1861, 1872.
    Total population supplied, 46,000.
    Annual supply of water, 685,000,000 gals.
    Daily consumption per head, domestic, 21.
    Sources of supply, River Tees.
    Storage capacity, 7,500,000 gals.
    Character of water, 6° Clark's scale.
    Death rate, 15 per 1,000.
    Number of meters, 200.
    Scale of charges, assessment charge.   Annual rateable value, 4½ to 7 per cent.
        Price per 1,000 gals., 1s. to 4d.
    Total water rent received, £13,482.

Darras Hall (supplied by Newcastle-on-Tyne).

Dartmouth, Devon. Railway, G.W. Distance from London, 229½ miles.
    Authority, Urban District Council.
    Chairman, J. Brown (Mayor).
    Secretary, Sydney J. Pope, Town Clerk.
    Engineer, Manager and Inspector, J. H. Wallis, R.C.P.
    Consulting engineer, J. W. Joyce, Surveyor.
    Office, Victoria Road.
    Total population supplied, 6,500,
    Average death rate, 11 per 1,000.
    Area of supply, Dartmouth.
    Source of supply—springs from Guttery Meadow, 249 ft. above O.D.; Crosby
        Meadow, 190 ft. above O.D.; Townstall, 350 ft. above O.D.; Lapthorne, 300 ft.
        above O.D.; Bozomzeale, 225 ft. above O.D.
    Estimated average daily discharge, 90,000 gals.
    Nature of drainage area, pasture land, leased from the Raleigh Estate and other
        owners.
    Geological data, Shale.
    Service reservoirs—Guttery Meadows, 230,000 gals.
                        Coombe   96,000 „
                        Crosby Meadow   49,000 „
                        Townstall   36,450 „
                                        ─────────
                    (All covered)   411,450 gals.
    The Council are now awaiting the sanction of the Local Government Board for a
        proposed pumping scheme from Old Mill, 1½ miles from the town, and 30 ft.
        above O.D., to a high level reservoir, 481 ft. above O.D., at Long Cross, 350,000
        gals. capacity, for the purpose of supplying the "Britannia," R.N. College,
        and for augmenting the present supply. The possible pumping power to be
        electric motors of 30 h.p.
    Character of water, medium.
    System of filtration, sand, 184 square yards in two beds.
    Storage capacity, service reservoirs, 411,000 gals.
    Head on distributing mains—maximum, 187 ft.; minimum, 24 ft.
    Annual supply, 58,500,000.
    Maximum day's supply, 165,000 gals. in August.
    Average daily consumption per head—domestic and trades, about 28 gals.
    Scale of charges—
        Assessment charge, 1s. in the £ on £10 and over; cottage rate, 8s. 8d. per
            annum.
        Authorized price per 1,000 gals.—domestic and trade, 1s. 6d.; present actual
            charge, 1s. per 1,000 gals.
    Total water rent received, average £900 per annum.

Darton, Yorks. (supplied by PENISTONE).

Darwen, Lancs. Railway, M., L. and Y. Distance from London, 206 miles.
Authority, Corporation, 1872.
Chairman, Councillor Cooper.
Secretary, J. H. Ellison.
Engineer and Manager, R. W. Smith-Saville, A.M.I.C.E.
Office, Corporation Offices.
Loan, £60,269 ; interest on loan, 3¼ per cent.
Area supplied within the borough and Eccleshill (waterside).
Works established, 1847. Special Acts, 1847, 1855, 1873, 1879, 1887, 1899.
Total population supplied, 40,000.
Used per annum (exclusive of compensation), 201,000,000 gals.
Daily consumption per head—domestic, 11 gals ; trade, 3½ gals.
Sources of supply—gathering grounds (upland surface).
Storage capacity, 200,000,000 gals.
System of filtration, downward, through gravel and stone.
Character of water, soft.
Death rate, ·14 per 1,000 (1906).
Number of meters, 182. Length of mains, 34 miles.
Scale of charges—assessment charge, 8 per cent. on rateable value.
Price per 1,000 gals., 2s. to 1s. graduated scale.
Total water rent received, £11,070.

Datchet, Bucks (supplied by SLOUGH).

Daventry, Northamptonshire. Railway, L.N.W. Distance from London, 74 miles.
Authority, Daventry Waterworks Company, Ltd.
Office, Waterhouse.
Share capital paid up, £1,540. Dividend, 10 per cent.
Works established, 1716.
Total population supplied, 4,000.
Sources of supply, springs. Character of water, soft.

Davyhulme (supplied by MANCHESTER).

Deal and Walmer, Kent. Railways, S.E. and L.C.D. Distance from London, 88 miles.
Authority, Corporation of Borough of Deal and U.D.C. of Walmer jointly.
Chairman of Joint Board, E. H Hinds.
Clerks to Authorities, A. C. Brown (Deal), F. W. Hardman (Walmer).
Resident Engineer, J. F. Cullen.
Office, 23, Queen Street, Deal.
Loans outstanding, £46,000 (Deal), £24,000 (Walmer).
Works established, 1840; dissolved, 1898; purchased, 1897. Special Act, 1897.
Total population of area supplied, 18,600 (largely increased in summer).
Average death rate, 15·8 per 1,000.
District of supply, Deal, Walmer, Sholden, Ringwold, and part of Mongeham Ripple. Area about 3,100 acres.
Source of supply, wells in the chalk.
Character of water, pure, slightly hard.
Storage capacity, 850,000 gals.
Daily consumption per head, domestic, 18 gals. ; trade, 6 gals.
Annual supply of water, 172,206,000 gals.
Maximum day's supply, 674,000 gals. in August.
Assessment charge, 5 to 8 per cent., rateable value.
Number of meters, 120.
Length of mains, 30 miles.
Price per 1,000 gals., average 10d.

Deans Hill, Herts. (supplied by Watford).

Deans Hill (supplied by Stafford).

Dearne Valley, Yorks. Railways, G.C. and M. (Wombwell station). Distance from London, 168 miles.
  Authority, Dearne Valley Waterworks Company.
  Chairman, Walter John Sykes.
  Secretary, John Robinson.
  Office, Park Street, Wombwell.
  Engineers, J. & T. Mitchell, Barnsley.
  Works established, 1884. Special Act, 1880.
  Total population supplied, 47,000.
  Towns and villages in the area supplied—Wombwell, Darfield, Hoyland Nether, Bolton-on-Dearne, Houghton Magna, Houghton Parva, Killingley, Goldthorpe.
  Source of supply—deep well and Sheffield supply.
  System of filtration—sand.
  Character of water, pure and hard.
  Storage capacity, service reservoir, 400,000 gals.
  Average daily consumption per head, 10·5 gals., domestic.
  Scale of charges, assessment charge, 6 per cent. on rack rental.
    Price per 1,000 gals., trade, first 50,000 1s., over 50,000, 10¼d.

Deganway (supplied by Conway).

Denbigh, Wales. Railway, L.N.W. Distance from London, 208¼ miles.
  Authority, Denbigh Water Company.
  Office, Vale Street.
  Share capital paid up, £14,000.
  Loan　　　　,,　　　£3,000.
  Works established, 1863.
  Total population supplied, 6,579.
  Annual supply of water, 10,000,000 to 15,000,000 gals., depending on season as to rainfall.
  Sources of supply, hill, watershed and well.
  Storage capacity, 5,000,000 gals.
  Character of water, soft.
  Number of meters, 22.
  Scale of charges, assessment charge, 7 per cent. on rateable value.
    Price per 1,000 gals., 1s. 6d., trade purposes.

Denham (supplied by Rickmansworth).

Denholme (supplied by Bradford, Yorks.).

Denny, Stirlingshire.
  Authority, Corporation.
  Office, Gasworks, Denny.
  Towns and villages in the area supplied, Denny and Dunipace.
  Total population supplied, about 5,000.
  Storage capacity, 22,000,000 gals.
  Assessment charge, 9d. in £.
  Price per 1,000 gals., 4d., with discount for large consumers.
  Number of meters, 5.
  Part of Denny is supplied by Falkirk.

Denton, Lancs. (supplied by Manchester).

Denton, Sussex (supplied by NEWHAVEN).

Denton, Yorks. (supplied by ILKLEY).

Derby. Railways, M., L.N.W., G.N. Distance from London, 128¾ miles.
Authority, Derby Corporation.
Chairman, Sir H. H. Bemrose, J.P.
Secretary, G. Trevelyan Lee, Town Clerk.
Engineer and Manager, John Ward, M.I.C.E.
Consulting Engineers, T. & C. Hawksley, Westminster.
Office, Babington Lane.
Loans outstanding, £494,344.
Loss on undertaking, including capital charges, £24,600, *less* £18,000 Sinking
Fund and interest on loans, &c.=£6,600.
Works established 1848.
Purchased by local authority, 1880, at a cost of £364,000.
Special Acts, 1848, 1868, 1873, 1879, 1890.
Total population supplied, 125,410.
Average death rate, 14·3 per 1,000, borough only.
Parishes within "District of Supply"—(those actually supplied are printed in
caps.):—BOROUGH OF DERBY, ALVASTON AND BOULTON, NORMAN-
TON, Sinfin Moor (part), ALLESTREE, BREADSALL, Chaddesdon, DARLEY
ABBEY, Little Eaton, Littleover, Mackworth, MARKEATON, Mickleover,
Spondon.
Sources of supply—filter tunnels in gravel strata alongside river, about 18 feet
below surface.
Character of water, hard; total hardness, 22°.
System of filtration, sand beds.
Storage capacity, in 4 impounding reservoirs, 3,798,000 gals.; service reservoirs,
1,601,000 gals.
Pressure on distributing mains—maximum, 100 lbs. per square inch; minimum,
45 lbs. per square inch.
Annual supply of water, 1,047,122,575 gals. to March, 1906.
Average daily consumption per head. Domestic, 14·52 gals.; trade, 8·44 gals.
Maximum day's supply, 4,958,656 gals. in March.
Number of meters, 821.
Length of mains, 95¼ miles.
Scale of charges—assessment charge, from 5 to 3 per cent. per annum on rateable
value.
Price per 1,000 gals, trade, 1s. to 6d., domestic, according to rental; municipal
purposes, 4½d.

Derwent Valley Water Board.
Constituent authorities, Derwent Valley Water Board, and the Corporations of
Derby, Leicester, Nottingham, Sheffield.
Chairman, Alderman T. R. Gainsford.
Clerk and Solicitor, O. B. Steward.
Chief Engineer, Edward Sandeman.
Office, Bamford *via* Sheffield.
Date of formation of Water Board, Acts of Parliament, 1899, 1901, and 1904;
construction of works commenced, 1901.
The Board will supply water to Sheffield, Derby, Nottingham and Leicester, and
to the County of Derby.
The Board is an entirely independent supply, and is not in any way connected with
the Sheffield water supply.
Five masonry dams are projected to impound about 10,000 million gallons. Two
of these dams are now being constructed. The ultimate daily supply will be
about 33 million gals. The area of the watershed is nearly 32,000 acres, and
has an average rainfall of 48 inches.
The Board are constructing about 50 miles of main aqueduct, and a large covered
service reservoir will be commenced very shortly at Ambergate.

DERWENT VALLEY WATER BOARD—*continued.*

The drainage area is mostly uninhabited, and consists of grouse moors and mountain pastures.

Surface formation of drainage areas, Yoredale shales, sandstones and grits; strata almost horizontal. The grits occur chiefly on the highest grounds.

Storage reservoir, Howden reservoir　　…　　…　　… 1,940,000,000 gals.
　　　　,,　　　,,　　Derwent …　　…　　…　　… 2,000,000,000　,,
　　　　(These are the only two storage reservoirs at present.)

Service reservoir—Ambergate service reservoir, part now being built for first instalment, will contain about 30,000,000 gals.

Filtering area, 27,000 square yards of filter beds are now being made.

Natural hardness of water, 2° to 4°.

Devizes, Wilts. Railway, G.W. Distance from London, 86 miles.
Authority, District Council.
Town Clerk, J. T. Jackson.
Total population supplied, 6,542 inside Borough and probably another 500 outside.

Devonport, Devon. Railways, G.W. and L.S.W. Distance from London, 229¼ miles.
Authority, Devonport Corporation.
Chairman, Alderman Blackall.
Clerk to Authority, Town Clerk.
Engineer, F. W. Lillicrap.
Office, Municipal Buildings, 31, Ker Street.
Loans outstanding, £282,383.
Works established, 1793; transferred to Corporation, June 30th, 1906.
Special Acts, 1793, 1876, 1889, 1893, 1897, 1902.
Total population supplied, 70,000.
Average death rate, 13·1 per 1,000.
Sources of supply, rivers West Dart, Cowsic, and Blackabrook.
Character of water, 1·5° of hardness.
System of filtration, sand.
Storage capacity, 27,000,000 gals.
Head on distributing mains, maximum, 230 feet; minimum, 46 feet.
Annual supply of water, 819,348,000 gals.
Daily consumption per head—domestic, 19·45 gals.; trade, 12·61 gals.
Maximum day's supply, 2,800,000 gals. in August.
Assessment charge, annual rateable rental or value.
Price per 1,000 gals., 8d. to 3d.; present average 4d. for quantities over 500,000 gals.
Number of meters, 475.
Length of mains, 21 miles.

Dewsbury and Heckmondwike. Railways, G.N., L.N.W., and L. and Y. Distance from London, 185 miles.
Authority, Corporation of Dewsbury three-fourths, and Urban District Council of Heckmondwike one-fourth.
Chairman, S. Wood, Heckmondwike.
Clerk, H. Ellis.
Consulting Engineers, G. H. Hill & Son, Manchester.
Water Engineer, H. Dearden, A.M.I.C.E., A.R.I.B.A., Borough Surveyor.
Office, Town Hall, Dewsbury.
Capital, £411,587.
Towns and villages in the area supplied, Dewsbury, Heckmondwike, Batley (part), Ossett, Ravensthorpe, Soothill Nether, Skelmanthrope, Flockton.
Works established, 1876. Special Acts, 1876, 1890.
Annual supply of water, 900,000,000 gals. (to all the towns).
Daily consumption per head (Dewsbury only), domestic and sanitary, 27·54; trade, 17·02 gals..
Sources of supply, lofty hills in the parish of Penistone.

DEWSBURY AND HECKMONDWIKE—*continued.*

Storage capacity, 722,046,358 gals.
Filtration, none.
Character of water, 2½° to 3° hardness.
Death rate, Heckmondwike, 18·63 per 1,000.
　　　　　" 　　Dewsbury, 18·78　　　"
Number of meters, upwards of 200.
Length of mains, from the waterworks to Dewsbury, 21 miles.
Scale of charges—assessment charge, gross estimated rental.
　Price per 1,000 gals., trade, 6d. ; no charge for municipal purposes.

Didsbury (supplied by MANCHESTER).

Dinas Powis (supplied by CARDIFF).

Dinnington (supplied by NEWCASTLE-ON-TYNE).

District of the Middle Ward of Lanarkshire.　Railways, Caledonian and N.B.
Authority, County Council of Lanarkshire.
Chairman, Colin Dunlop.
Secretary, W. E. Whyte.
Manager, W. L. Balmer.
Engineers, Leslie & Reid, Edinburgh.
Office, Middle Ward of Lanarkshire District Offices, Hamilton.
Works established, 1881.　Special Acts, 1878, 1881, 1892, 1895, 1896, 1902.
Total population of area supplied, 140,000.
Average death rate, 15·3 per 1,000.
Parishes in the area supplied—Bothwell, Blantyre, Cambuslang, Dalserf, Stone-
　house, Avondale, Hamilton, East Kilbride, Cambusnethan, Dalziel, Sholto,
　Glassford, New Monkland.
Sources of supply, springs and streams from Glengavel water shed.
Character of water, soft ; total hardness, 3·2°.
System of filtration, sand (gravitation) ; no softening.
Storage capacity in impounding reservoirs on Glengavel, Logan and Loch
　Fennock streams, 596,000,000 gals. ;　service reservoirs, 12,250,000 gals.
Head on distributing mains—maximum 800 feet ; minimum, 40 feet.
Total quantity of water supplied per annum, 1,824,000,000.
Average daily consumption per head, domestic, 28·5 gals. ; trade, 5·5 gals.
Maximum supply per day 4,750,000 gals.
Assessment charge, domestic, 11d. in £.
　Price per 1,000 gals., trade and municipal purposes, 6d.
Number of meters, 600.
Length of mains, supply and distributing, 300 miles.

Ditchling, Sussex (supplied by BURGESS HILL).

Ditton (supplied by WIDNES).

Dolgelly, Wales.　Railways, G.W., L.N.W.　Distance from London, 242 miles.
Authority, Dolgelly Water Company, Ltd.
Chairman, E. W. Evans.
Secretary, R. Guthrie Jones.
Manager, E. E. Jones.
Office, Bank Buildings, Dolgelly.
Share capital paid up, £4,200.　Issued and paid up, £3,800 (value £10 each).
Last dividend, 5 per cent.
Works established, 1877.
Total population supplied, 4,000.
Source of supply, impounding reservoirs on Lyn Cynwch.
District of supply, Dolgelly and Brithdir.

Doncaster, Yorks. Railway, G.N. Distance from London, 156¼ miles.
Authority, Doncaster Corporation.
Chairman, Councillor R. Robinson, J.P.
Clerk to Authority, R. A. H. Tovey, Town Clerk.
Resident Engineer, F. Oscar Kirby, M.Sc., A.M.I.C.E.
Office, Mansion House, Doncaster.
Total capital invested, including loans, £170,000, plus new works in course of
  construction, £160,000=£330,000.
Loans outstanding, £275,804 6s 9d. (31st March, 1906).
Annual loss on undertaking, deficit for year ending Mar. 31st, 1905, £1,199 12s. 9d.
                              „   „   „   „   „   1906, £3,660 1s. 6d.
Works established, Thrybergh and Firsby, 1880 ; Langsett and Underbank, 1896,
  Special Act, Doncaster Corporation Waterworks Act, 1873, Provisional Order,
  1879, Doncaster Corporation Waterworks Acts, 1880, 1883, Sheffield Corporation
  Water Act, 1896, Doncaster Water Act, 1904.
Total population of area of control, 1881, 32,107 ; 1891, 40,888 ; 1901, 54,188.
Towns and villages within area of control, with population of each, 1901 census—

Doncaster (Borough of)	28,933
Conisborough	8,546
Warmsworth	387
Balby ⎫ Hexthorpe U.D.C. ⎬	6,781
Denaby	2,670
Bentley ⎫ Arksey ⎬	2,403
Kirk Sandall	577
Wheatley U.D.C.	3,579
Carr House ⎫ Elmfield ⎬	149
Loversall	161
Armthorpe, Sprotborough and Cantley	—

Total population supplied, 44,440 (estimated 1st March, 1907).
Death rate, 15·20 in 1906 (average 15 years, ending 1905 = 17·75 per 1,000).
Sources of supply—Drainage area situated at Thrybergh, Firsby, Langsett and
  Underbank.
Maximum annual rainfall over Thrybergh and Firsby drainage area,
                                        31·89 inches (1895).
Minimum   „   „   17·19 „   (1885).
Average   „   „   25·41 „   (period 21 years).
Population on drainage area, 507. Nature of ditto—chiefly pasture.
Water authority has secured control of drainage area. By arrangement with land-
  owners possible sources of pollution have been diverted at cost of corporation.
Character of water—Thrybergh, 12° ; and Langsett, 3·1° of hardness.
Assessment charge, 6 per cent. to 10 per cent. on gross estimated rental.
Water is not softened.
Number of meters in use, 110.
Length of distributing mains, 37 miles.
System of filtration, sand; area provided, 1,568 square yards in four filter beds.
Service reservoirs, Warmsworth, capacity, 1,141,000 gals. (covered) ; a second
  reservoir contemplated.
Storage reservoirs, Thrybergh Reservoir ... ... capacity, 254,592,113 gals.
      „   „   Firsby, No. 1 „   ... ...   „   20,000,000 „
      „   „   „   No. 2 „   ... ...   „   20,000,000 „
Warmsworth Service Reservoir, 1,141,000 gals.
The Corporation have also in conjunction with Sheffield and Rotherham a share
  in reservoirs at Langsett and Underbank.
Head on distributing main, maximum, 73 ft. ; minimum, 46 ft.
Annual supply of water 344,478,800 gals., year ending December 31st, 1906.
Maximum day's consumption—average in July, 1906, 1,059,484 gals. per day.
      „   „   „   Maximum, July 27, 1906, 1,406,000 gals.

DONCASTER—*continued.*

Average daily supply per head—domestic, 21·02 gals.; trade, &c., 0·73 gals. (year ending December 31st, 1906).

Estimated total quantity of water available per annum, 1,500,000 gals., inclusive of 1,000,000 gals. from joint reservoir at Langsett and Underbank.

Authorised charge per meter, 8d. to 1s. 3d. per 1,000 gals.

Present average charge per meter, 11¼d.   „   „   „

Charges for municipal purposes, £100 per annum.

Length of mains—supply, 13¼ miles; distributing, 43 miles.

Dorchester, Dorset. Railways, L.S.W. and G.W.   Distance from London, 135¼ miles.

Authority, Corporation.

Town Clerk, A. G. Symonds.

Engineer and Manager, G. J. Hunt, C.E.

Offices, Guildhall Chambers, 11, South Street.

Works established, 1856.

Total population supplied, 10,000.

Annual supply of water, 127,750,000 gals.

Daily consumption per head, domestic, 30 gals., trade, 5 gals.

Sources of supply, deep well in chalk.

Storage capacity, 400,000 gals.   Filtration, none.

Character of water, 15° hardness.

Death rate, 12·7 per 1,000 (1902).

Number of meters, 80.   Length of mains, 10½ miles.

Scale of charges—assessment charge, 8d. in the £.

Price per 1,000 gals., trade, 1s. to 6d.

No charge for municipal purposes.

Total water rent received, £1,948, year ending, March 31st, 1902.

Dore (supplied by SHEFFIELD).

Dorking, Surrey. Railways, S.E. & L.B.S.C. Distance from London, 26 miles.

Authority, Dorking Water Co.

Chairman, Robert Barclay.

Secretary, W. J. Down.

Engineer and Manager, James Dawes, 15, Church Street.

Office, 72, High Street.

Capital, Share, paid up, £38,140 ; last dividend, 7½ per cent.

Debenture stock, £5,750 at 5 per cent.

Mortgages, £4,000 at 4 per cent.

Works established, 1869. Special Acts, 1869 and 1900.

Total population supplied, 14,423.

Average death rate, Dorking Urban, 14 per 1,000 ; other parishes, 12·2 per 1,000.

Area supplied, Urban and Rural District of Dorking, Capel and Ockley.

Sources of supply—Station Road and Tower Hill wells, and Westcott Rookery and Redlands gathering grounds.

Character of water, soft from the green sand, 3° hardness.

System of filtration, polarite, sand filters and Fisher plates.

Storage capacity, 700,000 gals.

Head on distributing mains-- maximum, 270ft.; minimum, 26ft.

Annual supply of water, 103,000,000 gals.

Daily consumption per head, domestic, 22 to 23 gals.

Number of meters, 163.

DORKING—*continued.*

Scale of charges—
　　Assessment charge, 6 per cent. over £20 annual value ; 7½ per cent. £20 and
　　under.
　　Price per 1.000 gals., 2s. 6d. to 1s. ; Municipal purposes, 1s.
　Length of mains, 48 miles.

Douglas, Isle of Man.　Railway, L.N.W.
　Authority, Corporation.
　Chairman of Water Committee, Councillor R. D. Cown.
　Resident Engineer, J. Caugherty.
　Secretary, Alexander Robertson.
　Consulting Engineers, G. H. Hill & Sons.
　Office, Town Hall, Douglas.
　Works established, 1890.
　Special Acts, Douglas (West Baldwin) Water Act.
　Interest on loan, 3 and 3½%.
　Total population supplied, 25,000.
　District of supply, town of Douglas and parishes of Couchan.
　Source of supply, impounding reservoirs on rivers, and Bradon.
　Character of water, good ; filtration, none ; softening, none.
　Storage in impounding, which are also service reservoirs, 378,000,000 gals.
　Service reservoirs, 35,000 gals.
　Authorized charges—domestic, 8% ; present rate, 7·3% on R.V.
　Average charge per meter, 2s. per 1,000 gals.
　Scale of charges—assessment charge, domestic, 6 per cent. on net value ; outlying
　　districts, 8 per cent.
　　Charges for municipal purposes, 2d. in £ on all property within borough.

Dove Holes, Stockport, Derbyshire.
　Authority, Dove Holes Water Company, Ltd.
　No returns supplied.

Dover.　Railway, S.E. and C.R.　Distance from London, 76¼ miles.
　Authority, Dover Corporation.
　Chairman, the Mayor.
　Secretary, the Town Clerk.
　Manager and Resident Engineer, W. C. Hawke, C.E.
　Office, Maison Dieu House, Biggin Street, Dover.
　Total capital invested, including loans, £65,000.
　Area of control, Borough of Dover only.
　Works established, 1855.
　Total population of area of control—1881, 30,270 ; 1891, 33,300 ; 1901, 41,782 ;
　　1906, 43,000.
　Total number of consumers, 8,000.
　Estimated population actually supplied, 46,000 holiday ; 42,000 normal.
　Annual supply of water (1906)—
　　　　　For domestic purposes...　　...　　...　　348,277,000 gals.
　　　　　　„　trade　　„　　...　　...　　...　　78,000,000　„　*
　　　　　　„　municipal　„　　...　　...　　...　　20,000,000　„
　Maximum week's consumption, 9,795,064, July, 1906.
　Total quantity of water drawn from deep well at Connaught Road in the
　　chalk 200 ft. deep with 1,000 ft. of adits, 432,507,611 gals. per annum.

---

　　* By meter.　There are other trade supplies to butchers, fishmongers, &c., several trades paying
a double rate, and not by quantity ; these are included under " domestic " supplies.

DOVER—*continued.*

　　Estimated total quantity of water available, 600,000,000 gals. from present works, but if other wells were sunk in the watershed probably the quantity could be doubled or trebled.

　　Character of water, 18·6° hardness.

　　Filtration, none ; softening, none.

　　Maximum annual rainfall over drainage area, 34·78 inches (1896).

　　Minimum　　　„　　　　　„　　　　„　　19·45　　„　　(1901).

　　Average　　　„　　　　　„　　　　„　　25·98　　„　　(period 6 years).
　　　　　　　　　　　　　　　　　　　　　　　　　　　　(1896 to 1901).

　　Nature of ditto, arable and pasture.

　　Water authority have no control of drainage area.

　　Natural rest level of water below surface, 194 feet ; above ordnance datum 17 feet.

　　Level of water below surface (when pumping 1,250,000 gals. per day), 215 feet at end of the day.

　　A full well shows 24 feet on the gauge, and 3 feet at the end of the day when pumping ceases.

　　Strata tapped by wells or borings, chalk.

Wells, borings, headings, &c.—Three wells, 6 feet diam., 200 feet deep, all close together and connected by short adits.　One large adit, 200 yards, by 6 feet high and 4 feet wide.

Pumping stations, Waterworks, Connaught Road, Dover.

　　　　　　A engine, capacity, 984,000 gals. per diem.

　　　　　　B　　„　　　„　　984,000　„　　„

　　　　　　C　　„　　　„　1,728,000　„　　„

Service reservoirs, at Connaught Road—

　　　　　　High reservoir, capacity, 500,000 gals., covered.

　　　　　　Low　　„　　　„　1,000,000　„

　　Average death rate, 14·7 (last 10 years) per 1,000.

　　Number of meters in use, 150.

　　Length of distributing mains, 40 miles.

　　Water is not filtered.

　　Assessment charge, 3d. in the £.

　　Price per 1,000 gals., 6d.

　　The lowest water rate in England.

　　The water is obtained from the chalk in the Dover watershed, the greatest feeders to which are the catchment areas of the Dour, Alkham, and Lydden valleys.

Dovercourt (supplied by TENDRING HUNDRED WATERWORKS CO.).

Dowlais, Glam. (supplied by MERTHYR TYDVIL).

Downfield (supplied by DUNDEE).

Draughton (supplied by BRADFORD, Yorks.).

Drayton, Hants. (supplied by PORTSMOUTH).

Drayton, Herts. (supplied by RICKMANSWORTH).

Driffield, Yorks.　Railway, N.E.　Distance from London, 195 miles.

　　Authority, Driffield Water Co.

　　Office, Exchange Street.

　　Total population supplied, 5,703.

Drighlington (supplied by BRADFORD, Yorks.).

Dringhouses (supplied by YORK).

Drogheda. Railway, G.N. of Ireland. Distance from Dublin, 32 miles.
Authority, Drogheda Corporation Waterworks Committee.
Chairman, the Mayor (ex officio).
Office, St. James House, Drogheda.
Total capital invested, including loans, £25,337.
Area of control, Drogheda Urban District.
Works established, 1864.
Taken over by local authority, August, 1898.
Special Acts—Drogheda Corporation Act, 1896 (59 and 60 Vic. c 210), L.G.B.
   Provisional Order 1899 (62 and 63 Vic. c 131).
Total population of area of control—1881, 12,297; 1891, 11,873; 1901, 12,690.
Total number of consumers, 1,000.
Estimated population actually supplied, 13,000.
Annual supply of water (1901)—

For domestic purposes	58,400,000 gals.
„ trade „	13,605,100 „
„ municipal „	4,791,000 „

Average day's consumption, 200,000 gals.
Total quantity of water drawn per annum (1901)—
   From drainage areas ... ... 80,000,000 gals.
Estimated total quantity of water available per annum—
   From drainage areas ... ... 200,000,000 „
Sources of supply, drainage areas situated at Tobernasolais and Slate Hill.
   Maximum annual rainfall over drainage area—
      25·67 inches (1901), no gauge prior to 1901.
   Population on drainage area under 50. Nature of ditto, mostly grass land.
   Water authority has no control of drainage area.
Storage reservoir, Killineer, capacity, 17,000,000 gals.
New storage reservoir at "Barnattin," with a capacity of about 60,000,000 gals.,
   will be completed in July next.
Filtering area provided, 145,800 square feet in 3 filter-beds.
Service reservoir, Rosehall, capacity, 5,000,000 gals., open.
Character of water, soft; good water much in request for boilers, as it leaves no
   incrustation.
Number of meters in use average 100.
Length of distributing mains, about 8 miles.
Assessment charge, 1s. 6d. in £, Poor Law valuation.
Scale of charges—Domestic purposes, 1s. 6d. in £ on Poor Law valuation.
                    Trade   „   from 1s. 6d. to 5d. per 1,000 gals.

Droitwich. Railway, G.W. and Mid. joint. Distance from London, 126 miles.
Authority—East Worcestershire Waterworks Company, Ltd., own the works and
   sell to the Droitwich Corporation in virtue of the Act of Parliament. The
   Droitwich Corporation are owners of the storage and distribution works in
   the borough.
Chairman, Councillor T. Willis.
Secretary, S. J. Tombs, Town Clerk.
Engineer in charge, Henry Hulse, C.E.
Office of Town Council, Droitwich.
Loans outstanding, £4,560.
Works established, East Worcestershire Waterworks Act, 1877.
Total population supplied, 4,163.
Average death rate, 15·2.
Area supplied, Borough, and a few properties outside boundary.
Sources of supply—Burcot springs, Lickey Hill.

DROITWICH—*continued.*

Character of water, good, no filtration.
Storage capacity, service reservoir, 175,000 gals.
Pressure on distributing mains—max., 70 lbs. per sq. in. ; min., 35 lbs. per sq. in.
Annual supply of water—38,000,000 gals. supplied to Corporation for all purposes.
Daily consumption per head—domestic, 18·25 gals. ; trade, 6·7 gals.
Maximum day's supply, 142,000, August 22nd, 1906.
Scale of charges—domestic assessment, 1s. 6d. in £ ; municipal, 1s. 6d. in £ on R.V.
    Trade, price per 1,000 gals., 1s. 6d. up to 200,000 gals. per quarter, after that,
    1s. per 1,000.
Number of meters in use, 66.
Length of distributing mains, 10 miles.

Droylsden (supplied by MANCHESTER).

Drumcondra (supplied by DUBLIN).

Dublin, Ireland.   Railways, L.N.W., M., etc.
    Authority, Corporation of Dublin.
    Engineer, Spencer Harty.
    Office, City Hall.
    Waterworks loan outstanding to date, £595,500.
    Works established, 1861.   Special Acts, 1863, 1865, 1870, 1874, 1885, 1893, 1897.
    Population now supplied with water, 380,000.
    Average annual death rate, in City of Dublin, 24·1 per 1,000.
    Towns and villages in the area supplied, Bray, Killiney, Dalkey, Kingstown,
        Blackrock, Pembroke, Kilmainham, Drumcondra, Clontarf, Chapelizod.
    Source of supply, River Vartry, which supplies the impounding reservoir at
        Roundwood.
    General characteristics of water, pure and soft.
    System of filtration, downward through sand.
    Storage in impounding reservoir, 2,400,000,000 gals.
        „   „   service reservoir, 160,000,000 gals.
    Total quantity of water, supplied per annum, 4,748,000,000 gals.
    Average daily supply per head, 37 gals. per day for all purposes (23-24 being for
        domestic purposes).
    Average daily supply, 13,000,000 gals.
    Charges authorized (domestic supply), maximum 1s. 3d. in the £ on the valuation.
    Present rate of charge, 5¼d. in the £ on the valuation.
    Present charge by meter, 6d. per 1,000 gals.
    Total length of supply mains, 43 miles ; distributing mains, 200 miles.

Dudley (supplied by SOUTH STAFFS. WATERWORKS Co.).

Dukinfield (supplied by ASHTON-UNDER-LYNE).

Dumbarton, Scotland.   Railways, N.B. and Caledonian.   Distance from London,
420 miles.
    Authority, Corporation.
    Office, Municipal Buildings.
    Engineers, Babtie & Bain, C.E.
    Loan, £65,000.
    Area supplied, 1,259 acres.
    Works established, 1857.   Special Acts, 1857, 1869, 1883.
    Total population supplied, 21,000.

DUMBARTON—*continued.*

    Annual supply of water, 237,250,000 gals.
    Daily consumption per head, 38·4 gals.
    Sources of supply, springs and drainage area.
    Storage capacity, 339,039,850 gals.
    Character of water, 1·5° hardness.
    Death rate, 13·9 per 1,000.
    Number of meters, 44.
    Scale of charges, assessment charge, public 6d., domestic 1¼d.
      Price per 1,000 gals., 3d.

Dumfries and Maxwelltown, Scotland.   Railways, G. and S.W. and Caledonian
    Authority, Dumfries and Maxwelltown Waterworks Commissioners.
    Chairman, Joseph J. Glover, Provost.
    Clerk, James R. W. Gowan, 135, Irish Street, Dumfries.
    Manager and Engineer, Nigel B. Wilson, Water Works Office, 19, Loreburn
      Street, Dumfries.
    Total capital invested, including loans, £46,214 14s. 6½d.
    Loans outstanding, £7,750.
    Works established, 1850.
    Special Acts, Dumfries and Maxwelltown Waterworks Acts, 1850 and 1897.
    Total population of area of control (1901), 18,883.
    Total number of consumers, 4,759.
    Estimated population actually supplied, 21,617.
    Average death rate in Dumfries, 19·16 ; in Maxwelltown, 13·85 per 1,000.
    Towns and villages within the area of control, with population of each (1901.

Census) – Dumfries ...	...	...	...	...	...	13,094
Maxwelltown	...	...	...	...	...	5,789
Suburbs ...	...	...	...	...	...	3,000 (estimated).

    Sources of supply in use—drainage areas of 3,500 acres., and surface springs
      draining into Lochrutton.
      Population on drainage area, 500.
      Nature of ditto—partly arable, partly pastoral.
    Estimated total quantity of water available per annum from drainage areas and
      surface springs, 800,000,000 gals.
    Character of water, peaty ; containing quantity of suspended matter.
    Analysis of water after filtration in February, 1907—

						Grains per gallon.
Free ammonia	...	...	...	...	...	0·0042
Albuminoid ammonia	...	...	...	...	...	·0098
Chlorine	...	...	...	...	...	1·05
Nitrates	...	...	...	...	...	Trace
Volatile matter	...	...	...	...	...	1·88
Mineral ,,	...	...	...	...	...	8·92
Total solids	...	...	...	...	...	10·80
Hardness ...	...	...	...	...	...	6·2 degrees

    Filtration—6 sand beds, area 3,100 square yards, and 1 12-foot Mather and
      Platt's gravity filter feeding to 2 sand beds of 570 square yards each ; no
      softening.
    Storage in impounding reservoirs, 144,000,000 gals., viz. :—natural loch of 125
      acres area T.W.L. Surface of water, 305·20 O.D.
    Service reservoirs, clear water, at filters, Lochfoot, capacity, 318,278 gals.,
      covered.
    Head on distributing mains—maximum, 189 ft. ; minimum, 92·28 ft.
    Average daily supply per head—domestic, 39·45 gals., including street watering
      and flushing sewers ; trade, &c., 2·85 gals., not including flushing sewers.
    Total annual supply of water measured by 2 bulk meters of Deacon type on mains
      at works, 333,906,000 gals.

Dumfries and Maxwelltown—*continued*.

Maximum day's consumption, 1,042,000 gals. in July, 1906.

Scale of charges, assessment charge, public rate, 1d.; domestic, within compulsory limits, 3d.; beyond compulsory limit, 8d.

Supply by meter, per 1,000 gals., 5d., the Commissioners supplying the meter at an annual rent of 10 per cent. on cost, the consumer to pay the expense of putting in and removing the meter. In the event of any irregularity in the working of a meter, the consumer is charged on an average of the six previous half years. Minimum charge per meter, £1.

Number of meters in use, 51.

Length of distributing mains, 23 miles; supply mains, 5 miles each of 12 in. dia. and 8 in. dia.

Dumpton (supplied by Broadstairs).

Dunbar, Scotland. Railway, N.B. Distance from London, 361 miles.

Authority, Corporation.

Convener, Bailie Low.

Engineer, A. S. Paterson.

Clerk, Robert White.

Office, Town Clerk's.

Loan, £5,618 7s. 7d. Interest, 4 per cent.

Towns and villages in the area supplied—Dunbar, Belhaven and Roxburgh Terrace, and farms on line of main pipe on route.

Works extended, 1874.

Total population of area supplied, 5,000.

Daily consumption per head, domestic, 18 gals. average.

Source of supply, springs.

Storage capacity, 900,000 gals.

System of filtration, sand.

Character of water—

		Tank 1	Tank 2
Total solid residue		8·32	11·52
Consisting of ⎱ Volatile residue		2·88	3·20
and ⎰ Saline residue		5·44	8·32
containing ⎰ Chlorine		1·36	1·38
Phosphoric Acid		none	none
Nitrates		traces	traces
Nitrites		none	none
Iron		traces	traces
Saline ammonia		·0016	·0016
Albuminoid ammonia		·0024	·0024

While there is a slight variation in the saline residue of these waters, they are in all other respects practically identical.

Water entirely free from the slightest suggestion of pollution.

No trace either of phosphoric acid or of nitrites, while the nitrate and iron reactions are similar to what we find in our purest water supplies.

The bacteriological examination is entirely satisfactory.

These waters must be regarded as being conspicuously pure, and excellently suited to all household uses.

Death rate, 15·059 per 1,000.

Number of meters, 24.

Length of mains, 14 miles.

Assessment charge, 8d. in the £.

Price per 1,000 gals., trade, 1s. 3d.

Total revenue received, £1,254 14s. 9d.

Dundalk, Co. Louth, Ireland. Railway, G.N. Distance from Dublin, 54½ miles.
Authority, Town Commissioners.
Office, Town Hall.
Works established, 1884.
Cost of construction, £35,000.
Total population supplied, 16,000.
Sources of supply, gravitation, conveyed from mountain 7 miles from Dundalk.
Storage capacity, reservoir, 3,500,000 gals., in addition to 300,000 gals. dry weather
  yield in streams per day.
The mains from service reservoir are now found, owing to increased demand, to
  be too small, and the commissioners have under consideration the advisability
  of laying in another main a distance of about 2½ miles.

Dundee. Railways, L. N. W. and Caledonian.
Authority, Dundee Water Commissioners.
Chairman, Lord Provost Longair.
Secretary, Wm. H. Blyth Martin, Town Clerk, Town House.
Resident Engineer and General Manager, George Baxter, A.M.I.C.E., Municipal
  Buildings, 93, Commercial Street, Dundee.
Loans outstanding to date, £813,762, including purchase of Company's under-
  taking, viz., perpetual annuities to shareholders.
Towns and villages within the area of control—
  Dundee, Broughty Ferry, Monifieth, Panbride, Liff and Benvie, Mains and
  Strathmartine, Forgan, Ferry-Port-on-Craig, Carnoustie, and Balmerino.
Works established, 1845. Purchased by local authority, 1869.
Special Acts, Dundee Water Acts, 1869, 1905.
Total population of area of control, 202,000.
Estimated population supplied, 202,000.
Average death rate, 14·57 per 1,000.
Sources of supply—drainage areas situated at Lintrathen and Monikie.
  (Lintrathen, 8 miles W. of Kirriemuir and 6 miles N. of Alyth.
  Monikie, 9 miles E. of Dundee and 5 miles N. of Carnoustie.)
Estimated maximum daily discharge at points of collection,

			293,631,604 gals.	⎫
„	minimum	„ „	21,693,075 „	⎬ 1901.
„	average	„ „	31,969,108 „	⎭

Maximum annual rainfall over drainage area 49·20 inches (1877).
Minimum   „   „   24·95 „ (1887).
Average   „   „   35·09 „ (period 27 years).
Population on drainage area, 550.
Nature and extent of cultivation of ditto—
        Lintrathen, 28¼ square miles, 4 per cent. cultivated.
        Monikie, 5½ square miles, 30 per cent. cultivated.
Water authority has no control of drainage area.
Character of water, 2° to 5° of hardness.
Filtration, sand for Monikie supply, 3,000,000 gals. per day.

Storage reservoirs,	Lintrathen	... ...	⎫
„	„	Clatto	
„	„	North Reservoir (Monikie)	
„	„	South „ „ ...	⎬ 2,273,648,957 gals.
„	„	Clear Water Basin „ ...	
„	„	Crombie	⎭
Service	„	Stobsmuir	⎫
„	„	Lawton	⎬ 97,770,058 gals.
„	„	Wormit	⎭

Head on distributing mains—maximum, 248 ft.; minimum, 30 ft.
Annual supply of water, 3,989,833,615 gals.
Estimated total quantity of water available per annum—
        From drainage areas   ...   .   11,680,000,000 gals.

DUNDEE—*continued.*

　　Average daily supply per head for all purposes, 54 gals.
　　Maximum day's supply, 13,537,646 gals., in July.
　　Charges authorised—domestic, 10% on R.V.
　　Present charge—domestic, 3¼% to 5¼% on R.V.
　　Present charge, per meter—trade, 6d. to 8d. per 1,000; minimum, £2 10s.
　　Number of meters in use, 750.
　　Length of supply mains, 59½ miles; distributing mains, 253 miles.

Dunfermline. Railways, L.N.W., M., G.N., and N.B.
　　Authority, Dunfermline Corporation.
　　Chairman, the Provost of the Burgh, J. Currie Macbeth, J.P.
　　Secretary, William Simpson, Esq., Solicitor and Town Clerk, Corporation
　　　　Buildings.
　　Engineer in charge, Andrew W. Bell, A.M.I.C.E., F.S.I., F.R.G.S., &c., City &
　　　　Waterworks Engineer, and Manager.
　　Office, Corporation Buildings.
　　Total capital invested, including loans, £89,090.
　　Interest on loans, 3, 4¼, and 4¾ per cent.
　　Works established, 1878.
　　Special Act, the Dunfermline Water Act 1876. No Provisional Order.
　　Total population of area of control—1881, 17,085; 1891, 22,357; 1901, 25,250;
　　　　1907, 27,000.
　　Estimated population actually supplied, 33,720.
　　Average death rate, 13·5 per 1,000.
　　Towns, villages and districts supplied within the area of control, with popula-
　　　　tion of each (1901 Census). (Area of control, Dunfermline only. All others
　　　　supplied by agreement.)—

Dunfermline ...	...	...	...	...	...	27,000
Culross ...	...	...	...	...	...	400
Inverkeithing	...	...	...	...	...	1,920
Limekilns ...	...	...	...	...	...	700
Charlestown ...	...	...	...	...	...	750
Rural district	...	...	...	...	...	1,000
North Queensferry ...	...	...	...	...	...	750
Aberdour ...	...	...	...	...	...	1,000
Other districts	...	...	...	...	...	200

　　Sources of supply in use, drainage area situated at Glen Sherup, off Glendevon,
　　　　Perthshire, on Ochil Hills. Surface springs, Glassiebarns, 3 miles W.N.W. of
　　　　Dunfermline.
　　Estimated maximum daily discharge at points of collection,
　　　　　　　　　　　　　　　　　　　　5,000,000 gals.
　　　　,,　　　minimum　　　,,　　　,,　　　,,　1,000,000 ,,
　　　　,,　　　average　　　,,　　　,,　　　about 3,000,000 ,,
　　Maximum annual rainfall over drainage area, 74·28 inches (1894).
　　Minimum　　　,,　　　,,　　　,,　　54·33　,,　(1895).
　　Average　　　,,　　　,,　　　,,　　64·01　,,　(period 10 years,
　　　　　　　　　　　　　　　　　　　　　　　　1892—1901).
　　Population on drainage area, none. Cultivation of ditto, none.
　　Water authority has absolute control.
　　The drainage area is on the Ochil Hills, and the reservoir is at a level of 900
　　　　feet above the sea. The water is very clear and is not filtered. It is brought
　　　　by gravitation a distance of 17 miles to Glassiebarns service cistern (within
　　　　3 miles of the city), and from it service pipes carry to all parts of the district.
　　　　In addition to this there is a reservoir for storm water close to the service
　　　　cistern and takes its overflow.
　　Characteristics of water, soft and pure.

DUNFERMLINE—*continued.*

Recent analyses of the water, which is not filtered—
Grains per imperial gallon—

Saline matter	...	...	...	...	...	2·96
Organic and volatile matter	...	...	...	..		0·32
Total solid matter	...	...	..	..	...	3·28
Nitrates and nitrites	...	...	...	...	..	none
Chlorine	...	...	...	...	...	0·54
Chloride of sodium	..	...	...	..	...	0·88

Parts per million—

Saline ammonia	...	...	...	...	...	0·06
Albuminoid ammonia	...	...	...	...	...	0·03

Filtration, none ; softening, none.
Storage reservoirs, Glen Sherup　...　...　capacity, 153,000,000 gals
　　　　　”　　　Craigluscar (at Glassiebarns)　　”　　41,000,000　,,
　　　　　”　　　Total effective capacity　...　　...　194,000,000　,,
Service reservoirs at Glassiebarns　...　...　capacity, 25,000 gals., covered.
Pressure on distributing mains—max., 150 lbs. per sq. in. ; min., 30 lbs. per sq. in.
Annual supply of water—

For domestic purposes	...	...	...	311,000,000 gals.
,, trade	,.	...	...	165,600,000 ,,
,, municipal	,,	...	...	5,000,000 ,,
In bulk to other authorities	...	...	90,000,000 ,,

Total quantity of water drawn per annum (1906)—

From drainage area	...	...	...	516,000,000 gals.
,, surface springs	...	...	...	30,000 ,,

Estimated total quantity of water available per annum—

From drainage area	...	...	...	1,000,000,000 gals.
,, surface springs	...	...	...	30,000 ,,

Average daily supply per head—domestic, 31·55 gals. ; trade, 13·76 gals. (1906).
Assessment charge—public rate, 1d. ; domestic rate, 1s. 1d. in £.
Charges for municipal purposes, nominal, about £20.
Supplies by meter—
Minimum charge, £2 per annum within Burgh.
　　,,　　”　　£4　　,,　　outside　　,,

For the first 1,000,000 gals.	...	6d. per 1,000 gals.
,, second 1,000,000 ,,	..	5d. ,, ,,
For all above 2,000,000 ,,	...	4d. ,, ,,

(Each million gals. of the total consumpt being charged according to these
respective rates.)
Meter rent, 10 per cent. per annum on cost.
Number of meters in use, 100.
Length of distributing mains, about 20 miles within area of control.

Dunham Massey (supplied by NORTH CHESHIRE WATER CO.).

Dunhcoed, Borough of (otherwise LAUNCESTON, which see.)

Dunipace (supplied by DENNY and FALKIRK).

Dunmurry (supplied by DUBLIN).

Dunnottar (supplied by STONEHAVEN).

Dunoon, Scotland.
Authority, The Dunoon Town Council.
Secretary, J. Vabrose, Town Clerk.
Resident Engineer, James Andrew.
Office, Burgh Buildings, Dunoon.

DUNOON—*continued*.

　　Loan outstanding, £21,000.
　　Works established, 1868.
　　Population supplied—minimum, 7,500 ; maximum, 30,000.
　　Source of supply, impounding reservoirs on bed of Balgie Burn.
　　Character of water, very soft; and in summer and autumn, very turbid.
　　Total hardness, 2°.
　　Filtration, twelve Bell's patent mechanical filters, each 8 feet diameter.
　　Storage capacity—impounding reservoirs, 90,000,000; service reservoirs, 6,000,000
　　　　gals.
　　Head on distributing mains—maximum, 180 feet ; minimum, 75 feet.
　　Annual supply, 335,000,000 gals.
　　Average daily supply per head, 32 gals.
　　Maximum　　,,　　,,　1,200,000 gals. in July.
　　Length of supply mains, 4 miles ; distributing mains, 12 miles.

Duns, Berwickshire.
　　Authority, Duns Water Company, Ld.
　　Chairman, John Ferguson.
　　Secretary, John Ford.
　　Office, Royal Bank Buildings, Duns.
　　Share capital paid up, £2,500; last dividend, 5 per cent.　Loan capital paid up,
　　　　£1,752 at 3¼ per cent.
　　Works constructed, 1858.
　　Population supplied with water, 2,200.
　　Sources of supply, springs and impounding reservoir at Hardens.
　　Filtration, Wilson's patent automatic filter.
　　Storage capacity, impounding reservoir, 4,000,000 gals. ; service reservoir,
　　　　120,000 gals.
　　Assessment charge, 1s. 2d. in £ on rental.
　　Length of supply mains, 2 miles ; distributing mains, 4 miles.

Dunstable, Beds. (G. & W.)　Railways, L.N.W. and G.N.　Distance from London,
　　33 miles.
　　Authority, Dunstable Gas and Water Company.
　　Secretary, A. Gutteridge.
　　Manager, W. Allwood.
　　Engineer, A. F. Phillips, M.I.C.E.
　　Office, High Street, N. Dunstable.
　　Share capital paid up, £13,800; dividends, 6¼, 4¾ and 3¼ per cent.
　　Loan, £2,500 at 4 per cent.
　　Towns and villages in the area supplied, Dunstable and Upper Houghton Regis.
　　Works established, 1871.
　　Annual supply of water, 48,000,000 gals.
　　Sources of supply, deep well in chalk.
　　Character of water, slightly hard; filtration, none.
　　Death rate, 14·39 per 1,000.
　　Number of meters, 15.
　　Price per 1,000 gals., municipal purposes, 1s. ; domestic, 2s. ; trade, 1s.

Durham (City of).　Railways, G.N. and M.　Distance from London 256 miles.
　　Population supplied, 14,641.
　　Supplied by Weardale and Consett Water Co.

Earby, near Leeds, Yorks.　Railway, M.　Distance from London, about 260 miles.
　　Authority, Earby Water Company, Ltd.
　　Office, Wesleyan school (class-room).
　　Share capital paid up, £1,875; dividend, 5 per cent.
　　Towns and villages in the area supplied, Earby, *via* Colne.

EARBY—*continued.*

Works established, June, 1891.
Total population supplied, about 3,400.
Sources of supply, springs from sandstone grit.
Storage capacity, 70,000 gals. The company contemplate making a new reservoir in the near future.
Character of water, soft ; system of filtration, none.
Scale of charges—assessment charge, £50. Domestic, 2d. per tap per week.
Price per 1,000 gals.—trade, 1s. 3d.

Earsdon, U.D.C. (supplied by NEWCASTLE-ON-TYNE).

Easington Lane, Durham. *See* HETTON.

East Blatchington (supplied by NEWHAVEN).

East Brook (supplied by CARDIFF).

Eastbourne, Sussex. Railway, L.B. and S.C. Distance from London, 65 miles.
Authority, Eastbourne Water Co.
Chairman, the Duke of Devonshire.
Secretary, F. Alfred Currey.
General Manager, A. J. Howard.
Engineer, Frank Stileman.
Area supplied, 12,000 acres.
Works established, 1859. Special Acts, 1875, 1881, 1889, 1896 and 1897.
Total population supplied, 55,000.
Daily consumption per head, 29 gals.
Sources of supply, deep wells in chalk.
Death rate, 10·69 per 1,000.
Number of meters, 500.
Scale of charges— assessment charge, annual value.
Price per 1,000 gals., 1s. to 7d.

East Clandon (supplied by WOKING).

East Dereham, Norfolk. Railways, G.E. and M. Distance from London, 122 miles.
Authority, Local Authority.
Population supplied, 5,545.
No returns supplied.

Eastergate, Sussex (supplied by BOGNOR).

Easterhouse, N.B. (supplied by AIRDRIE).

East Farleigh (supplied by MAIDSTONE).

East Grinstead, Sussex. (G. & W.) Railway, L.B.S.C. Distance from London, 30 miles.
Authority, East Grinstead Gas and Water Company.
Manager, R. G. Payne.
Share capital paid up, £37,814 ; dividends, £9 and £6 6s. per cent.
Loan capital paid up, £8,053 at 4 per cent.
Works established, 1878. Special Acts, 1878, 1892.
Total population supplied, 6,094.
Number of meters, 60.
Scale of charges, assessment charge, A.
Price per 1,000 gals., 1s. 6d. to 1s.

East Ham (supplied by East London).

East Horsley (supplied by Woking).

East Hunts. *See* St. Ives.

East Kent District Water Company.
Chairman, Colonel T. J. Holland, C.B., D.L.
Manager and Secretary, F. L. Ball.
Office, High Street, Snodland, Kent.
Share capital paid up, £36,000 ; last dividend, 4½ per cent.
Loan capital paid up, £7,450 at 4½ per cent.
District of supply, St. Margaret's-at-Cliffe, Kearsney, Eythorne, Temple Ewell, East Langdon, West Cliffe, Coldred, Ripple, Kingsdown, Studdal, Shepherds-well, River, Whitfield, Martin, Guston, Oxney, Ringwould, Sutton, Tilmanstone.
Source of supply, wells in chalk, 250 feet.
Analysis—

	Parts per 100,000.
Ammonia, free	·0005
,, albuminoid	none
Oxygen absorbed, in 15 minutes	·011
,, ,, 4 hours	·022
Total solid residue	33·20
Chlorine	2·60
Nitrogen, as nitrates and nitrites	·503
Temporary hardness	18·0
Permanent hardness	5·6
Total hardness	23·6

Remarks : Clear, palatable, and free from poisonous metals.
Annual supply of water, 32,000,000 gals.
Assessment charge, 7½ per cent. to 5 per cent. on R.V.
Price per 1,000 gals., 1s. to 2s. scale.

East Kilbride (supplied by District of the Middle Ward of Lanarkshire).

East Loftus, Yorks. (supplied by Cleveland).

East London Waterworks. *See* Metropolitan Water Board.

East Retford. *See* Retford.

East Surrey Water Company. Redhill, Surrey. Railways, S.E. and L.B.S.C.
Works at Kenley and Purley.
Chairman, Peter Riddock.
Engineer, Manager and Secretary, A. E. Cornewall-Walker, A.M.I.C.E., F.C.I.S.
Office, Redhill, Surrey.
Share capital paid up, £367,522 ; last dividends, 10, 7 and 5 per cent.
Loan capital, £172,409 ; interest, 4 per cent.
Towns and villages within the area of control—26 parishes, including Betch-worth, Caterham, Chipstead, Coulsdon, Godstone, Horley, Kenley, Lingfield, Merstham, Nutfield, Purley, Redhill, Reigate, Sanderstead, Walton and Warlingham.
Area of district, 160 square miles.
Original works established, 1862.
Special Acts, Caterham Spring Co.'s Water Act and Order, 1862, 1873 and 1881 ; East Surrey Water Acts or Orders, 1885, 1894, 1896 and 1900.

EAST SURREY WATER COMPANY—*continued.*

Total population of area of control, 1881, 46,000; 1891, 60,500; 1901, 80,000; 1906, 83,000.
Total number of customers, 14,850.
Estimated population actually supplied, 81,000.
Annual supply of water (1906-7)—for all purposes, 764,000,000 gals.
Maximum day's consumption, 19,000,000 gals.
Total quantity of water drawn per annum—
     Deep wells or borings   764,000,000
Estimated total quantity of water available per annum—
     Deep wells or borings, very large; beyond present estimate.
Sources of supply in use—deep wells or borings situated at Kenley and Purley.
Natural rest level of water below surface, 30 to 60 feet; above Ordnance datum, 150 to 180 feet.
Level of water below surface when pumping, 50 to 80 feet.
Strata tapped by wells or borings, chalk formation.
Pumping stations, Kenley and Purley.
Service reservoirs, Caterham, Merstham, Reigate, and Sanderstead, capacity, 5,500,000 gals., covered.
Hardness before treatment 18°, and after 4°; water softened by " Clark's " process, pure and soft.
Number of meters in use, 650.
Length of distributing mains, 400 miles.
Results of analysis, expressed in parts per 100,000—

	Kenley supply.	Purley supply.
Total solid matters	11·72	10·40
Organic carbon	·021	·025
Organic nitrogen...	·005	·005
Ammonia	—	—
Nitrogen as nitrates and nitrites ...	·465	·546
Total combined nitrogen	·470	·551
Chlorine	1·7	1·3
Hardness—		
Temporary	0·2	
Permanent	4·4	
Total	4·6	4·9
Remarks	Clear	Clear

Death rate of district, 14 per 1,000.
Assessment charge on annual value—Water meter, 1s. to 2s. 6d. per 1,000 gals.; present rate of charge, 2s. Pressures throughout the district generally high.
Flush allowed for w.c.'s, 2 gals.

Eastwood, Notts. (supplied by NOTTINGHAM).

East Worcestershire. Railway, M. Distance from London, 120 miles.
Authority, East Worcestershire Water Company.
Chairman, Earl of Plymouth.
Secretary, P. W. Walker.
Manager, W. J. Shinner, Bromsgrove.
Office, 18, Waterloo Street, Birmingham.
Share capital paid up, £73,250.
Debenture stock, £8,000.
Dividend, 5 per cent.
Works established, 1877.
Special Acts, 1877 and 1902.
Total population supplied, 32,000.
Annual supply of water pumped, 378,254,000 gals.
Sources of supply, well and boring in new red sandstone.

EAST WORCESTERSHIRE—*continued*.

    Storage capacity, 575,000 gals.
    Character of water, soft, hardness 4·2° on Clark's scale.
    Number of meters, 124.
    Scale of charges—
      Assessment charge, 5 and 6 per cent. on gross rateable value.
      Price per 1,000 gals., 1s. 6d., 1s., 10d., 9d., 8d.
    Total water rent received, £10,278.

Ebbw Vale, Mon. Railway, G.W. Distance from London, 172¼ miles.
    Authority, Urban District Council.
    Chairman, Thomas Morgan.
    Clerk to authority, T. Hughes, Solicitor.
    Resident Engineer of new waterworks, H. L. Pearson.
    Surveyor, T. J. Thomas, A.M.I.C.E.
    Consulting Engineer, G. F. Deacon.
    Office, Council Office, Ebbw Vale.
    Works established, 1875.
    Total population supplied, 40,000.
    Average death rate, 16 per 1,000.
    Towns and villages in the area supplied, Ebbw Vale, Nantyglo, Blaina, Sirhow, and Dukestown.
    Sources of supply, catchment area.
    System of filtration, sand.
    Storage capacity—impounding reservoirs, 71,000,000 gals.; service reservoir, 120,000 gals.
    Annual supply of water, 215,000,000 gals.
    Daily consumption per head—domestic, 20 gals.; trade, 2 gals.
    Maximum day's supply, 750,000 gals.
    Scale of charges—cottages, 2d. per week, 5 per cent. above £10; by meter, 6d. to 1s. 6d. according to scale.
    Length of mains, 30 miles.

Eccles, Lancs. (supplied by MANCHESTER).

Ecclesfield (supplied by ROTHERHAM AND SHEFFIELD).

Eccleshill, Yorks. (supplied by BRADFORD).

Eccleshill, Waterside (supplied by DARWEN).

Eccleston, Lancs. (supplied by ST. HELENS).

Eddington, near Canterbury. *See* Blean.

Edenfield (supplied by BURY).

Edingley, Notts. (supplied by NEWARK).

Edgware, Middlesex (supplied by COLNE VALLEY WATER CO.).

Edinburgh and Leith. Railways, G.N., L.N.W. and M. Distance from London, 400 miles.
    Authority, Corporation, 1870.

EDINBURGH AND LEITH—*continued.*

Chairman, Lord Provost of Edinburgh.
Secretary, Wm. Boyd, W.S.
Engineer, W. A. Tait.
Treasurer, Wm. Anderson.
Office, City Chambers.
Share capital paid up, £414,000, annuities still unredeemed.
Loan　　„　　„　£1,600,261 (including £414,000 annuities).
Works established, 1819, transferred to Corporation, 1869.
Special Act, 1819.
Total population supplied, 435,500.
Delivered per day, 16,990,500 gals.
Daily consumption per head, domestic, 40·45 gals.
Sources of supply—Pentland and Moorfoot Hills, gravitation.
Number of meters, 1,100.
Length of mains, 80 miles.
Scale of charges—
　Assessment charge, 5d.
　Price per 1,000 gals. 6d.

Egham (supplied by SOUTH WEST SUBURBAN).

Egremont (supplied by WALLASEY).

Elderslie (supplied by PAISLEY).

Elgin, Scotland. Railways, Highland, and G.N. of S. Distance from London, 577 miles.
Authority, Elgin Town Council.
Chairman, Francis Davie.
Secretary, Hugh Stewart, Town Clerk.
Manager, Acton A. Turriff, Burgh Surveyor.
Office, City Chambers.
Loan outstanding, £9,360.
Works taken over by local authority, 1875, working under general Acts.
Total population supplied, 8,500.
Death rate, 16 per 1,000.
Area supplied, Elgin.
Sources of supply—springs at Easterton and Blackhills.
Character of water, pure and wholesome spring water, 3° to 4° of hardness.
Storage in service reservoir, 80,000 gals.
Head on distributing mains—maximum, 123 ft.; minimum, 50 ft.
Daily consumption per head, 42 gals.
Number of meters, 30.
Scale of charges—
　Assessment charge, 6d. in the £ within, and 9d. in the £ outside the Burgh on rental value.
　Price per 1,000 gals., 6d. within borough and 10d. outside.

Elland (supplied by HALIFAX).

Elliot Town (supplied by NEW TREDEGAR).

Ellon (Aberdeenshire).
Authority, Ellon Town Council.
Chairman, John Rae, Provost.
Secretary, A. J. Raeburn, Town Clerk.
Resident Engineer, John Baxter.

ELLON—*continued.*

Office, 44, Market Street, Ellon.
Works established, 1875.
Total population supplied, 1,500.
Source of supply, springs at Harewell and Ardgrain, Ellon.
Character of water, excellent.
Storage, impounding reservoirs at Auchterellon, 40,000.
Pressure on distributing mains, 40 lbs. per square inch.
Total annual supply, 22,000,000
Average daily supply per head, 40 gals.
Length of mains—supply, 3¼ miles ; distributing, 3 miles.

Elmfield (supplied by DONCASTER).

Elstead (partly supplied by GODALMING).

Elstree, Herts. (supplied by COLNE VALLEY WATER Co.).

Elton (supplied by BURY).

Elton. *See* CONGLETON RURAL.

Ely, Cambridge. Railway, G.E. Distance from London, 70¼ miles.
Authority, Ely Urban District Council.
Chairman, T. B. Granger, J.P.
Surveyor and Engineer, W. McKelvie, A.M.I.C.E.
Office, City Surveyor's Office, Waterside.
Towns and villages supplied, Ely, Stuntney Hamlet (supplied by meter).
Special Act, under the Public Health Act, 1848.
Total population supplied, 9,778.
Annual supply of water, 71,300,000 gals.
Daily consumption per head, 20 gals., for all purposes.
Source of supply, Isleham.
Storage capacity, 350,000 gals.
Character of water, from the chalk.
Death rate, 11 to 12 per 1,000.
Number of meters, 45.
Length of distributing mains, 12 miles ; rising main, 13 miles.
Scale of charges—
　　Assessment charge　　...　　...　　10d. in the £.
　　Price per 1,000 gals.　　...　　...　　7d. any quantity.
Total water rent received, about £430.
　　　,,　　rate　　　　　　£460.
　　　　　　　　　　　　　————
　　　　　　　　　　　　　£890

Ely, Glam. (supplied by CARDIFF).

Embsay, Yorks. *See* SKIPTON.

Emmbrook, Berks. (supplied by WOKINGHAM).

Emsworth (supplied by PORTSMOUTH).

Enfield (supplied by BARNET)

Epping, Essex (supplied by HERTS AND ESSEX).

Epsom, Surrey. Railways, L.B.S.C. and L.S.W. Distance from London, 14 miles.
Authority, Urban District Council.
Chairman, W. G. Langlands, J.P.
Secretary of Water Committee, G. J. Bean.
Clerk to Council, E. G. Wilson.
Manager and Resident Engineer, W. Young.
Consulting Engineer, W. V. Graham.
Office, East Street, Epsom.
Works established, 1853. Special Act, 1853.
Loans outstanding, £18,000.
Total population of area supplied, 16,000.
Average death rate, 11·3 per 1,000.
District of supply, Epsom Urban district.
Sources of supply—wells in chalk 400 ft. deep, and adits.
Character of water, high degree of purity, and of excellent hygienic quality.
Bacteriological examinations of the water are made monthly.
Storage capacity, 930,700 gals.
Pressure on distributing mains—maximum, 125 lbs. ; minimum, 50 lbs. per sq. in.
Constant supply since 1900.
Scale of charges—assessment charge, 10d. in the £ on R.V.
Price per 1,000 gals., 10 l. to 1s.

Erdington (supplied by BIRMINGHAM).

Erskine (supplied by PAISLEY).

Essington, part of (supplied by SOUTH STAFFS. WATERWORKS Co.).

Estrop, Hants. (supplied by BASINGSTOKE).

Etchingham (supplied by TICEHURST).

Eton (supplied by WINDSOR).

Everton (supplied by CHRISTCHURCH).

Evesham, Worcester. Railways, G. W. & M. Distance from London, 106¾ miles.
Authority, Evesham Town Council.
Chairman, Alderman Hughes.
Secretary, the Town Clerk.
Engineer and Manager, Robert C. Mawson, Borough Surveyor.
Office, Town Hall.
Loan, £13,450.
Towns and villages in the area supplied, Evesham Town, Childwickham, Hampton
    Wickhamford, Badsey, Aldington and part of Norton and Lenchwick villages.
Works established, 1883.
Total population supplied, 10,000.
Annual supply of water, 100,000,000 gals. (no pumping).
Daily consumption per head, domestic, 17, trade, 4 gals.
Sources of supply, Cotswold Hills, upper lias sands, gravitation.
Character of water, total solids, 17 grains per gal., permanent hardness, 4·2.
Death rate, 14·4 per 1,000 (average 10 years).
Number of meters, 73.
Length of mains, 20 miles.
Scale of charge—
    Assessment charge, 1s. in the £ on net rateable value
    Price per 1,000 gals., 1s. to 6d. according to quantity.
Total water rent received, £2,071.

Ewell (supplied by Sutton).

Ewloe (supplied by Hawarden).

Ewood Bridge (supplied by Bury).

Exeter, Devon. Railways, G.W., 194 miles, and L.S.W., 171 miles from London.
Authority, Corporation, 1878.
Chairman, Councillor W. Wreford.
Secretary, H. Lloyd Parry, Town Clerk.
Water Superintendent, Alex. Kneel.
Engineer, Thomas Moulding, A.M.I.C.E., City Engineer and Surveyor.
Office, Municipal Office, Exeter.
Loans outstanding, £158,000.
Annual loss, including " Capital Charges," £1,621 (1906) ; £1,500 (1905).
Works established, 1833. Special Acts, 1878. Works purchased by Corporation,
    1878.
Total population supplied, estimated 61,000.
Average death rate, 1903, 1904, 1905, Exeter, 15·5 per 1,000.
Source of supply, river Exe.
Towns and villages in the area supplied—Exeter, Heavitree, Pinhoe, Alphington,
    Wonford and Whipton.
Area supplied, 3,620 acres.
Character of water, soft river water ; total hardness, 4·3° ; permanent, 1·4°.
System of filtration, sand downwards.
Storage capacity, service reservoirs, 6,100,000 gals.
Head on distributing mains—maximum, 180 feet ; minimum, 40 feet.
Annual supply of water, 720,000,000 gals.
Daily consumption per head—domestic, 25 gals. ; trade, 5 gals.
Maximum day's supply, 2,500,000 gals., in August.
Scale of charges—assessment charge, 5 per cent. on rateable value.
Price per 1,000 gals., domestic, 1s., 8d., and 4d. ; trade, 1s. 6d. to 6d. ; baths, 4d.
No charge for municipal purposes.
Number of meters, 120.
Length of mains—supply, 13 miles ; distributing, 60 miles.

Exmouth. Railway, L.S.W. Distance from London, 182 miles.
Authority, Exmouth Urban District Council.
Chairman, Thomas Abell.
Secretary, H. C. Adams, Public Hall Chambers, Exmouth.
Engineer and Surveyor, Samuel Hutton.
Consulting Engineer, G. R. Strachan, 9, Victoria Street, S.W.
Total capital invested, including loans, £82,777.
Annual loss, £800 taken from rates to pay interest on loans.
Works established, 1836.
Purchased by local authority 9th May, 1902.
Special Acts, 1864, 1880, 1892, 1900.
Total population of area of control—1891, 8,000 (approx.) ; 1901, 11,261.
Total number of consumers, 11,350 normal, 15,000 in season.
Average death rate, 13·5 per 1,000.
Source of supply—Drainage areas situated at East Budleigh and Bicton Common,
    725 acres, 400 feet above Ordnance datum ; uncultivated and without any
    population.
Area of control, Exmouth, Withcombe, Littleham and East Budleigh.
Surface formation of drainage area—surface layer of gravel and sand.
Estimated minimum daily discharge at points of collection, 220,000 gals.
Average annual rainfall over drainage area, 35 inches (period 30 years).
Water authority has no control of drainage area.

Exmouth—*continued.*

Character of water, very pure and soft; total hardness, 1·2°.

Filtering area provided, 3,819 square yards in 4 filter-beds—sand.

Storage reservoirs, Squabmoor, capacity, 12,500,000 gals.; Service reservoir, 157,000 gals., covered; proposed do., 184,000 gals.

Head on distributing mains—max., 180 ft.; min., 50 ft.

Total quantity of water drawn per annum from drainage areas, 114,852,000 gals.

Annual supply of water (1906)—

Domestic	...	...	...	...	...	95,000,000 gals.
Trade	...	...	...	...	...	3,729,000 „
Municipal	...	...	...	...	...	2,000,000 „

Average daily consumption per head, 23 gals. (based on normal population) (20½ gals., allowing for visitors); trade, 1½ gals.

Maximum day's supply, 327,000 gals., in July, 1906.

Assessment charge, 8s. 8d. per ann. under £5; 1s. 3d. in £ up to £20, 1s. 2d. in £ over £20 rental.

Average charge per meter, 1s. per 1,000 gals.

Number of meters, 45.

Length of supply mains, 8¼ miles; distributing mains, about 20 miles.

Failsworth (supplied by Oldham).

Fairfield, Derbyshire (supplied by Buxton).

Falkirk and Larbert. Railways, N.B. and Caledonian.

Authority, Falkirk and Larbert Water Trust.

Chairman, Provost of Falkirk.

Secretary, A. Balfour Gray, Burgh Chambers, Falkirk.

Engineer, Charles Massie, Water Trust Offices, Falkirk.

Consulting Engineer, W. R. Copland, Glasgow (for new scheme under 1901 Bill).

Total capital invested in, including loans, £204,569.

Works established, 1888.

Special Acts, Falkirk and District Water Acts, 1888, 1896, 1900.

Total population of area of control, 48,000.

Estimated population actually supplied, 51,800.

Average death rate, 14 per 1,000.

Towns and villages within the area of control, parts of Falkirk, Larbert, Grangemouth, Kilsyth, Denny, and Dunipace.

Sources of supply—drainage areas are situated at or near Carron Bridge, being in parish of Kilsyth and distant about 6 miles from Denny and 12 from Falkirk.

Character of water, soft, free from moss and discolouration.

Filtering area provided, 2,300 square yards in 6 filter beds—sand.

Storage reservoirs, Faughlin   ...   ...   capacity 31,257,000 gals.

Service reservoirs, 266,000,000 gals.

Pressure on distributing mains—max., 90 lbs.; min., 40 lbs. per sq. in.

Annual supply of water, 996,590,640 gals.

Estimated total quantity of water available per annum—

From drainage areas ..   ..   550,000,000 gals.

Daily discharge at points of collection, variable, entirely dependent on rainfall

Water authority have only water rights over drainage area.

Surface formation of drainage areas, little moss, gravel and rock; all upland pasture land.

Average daily supply per head, 42 gals.

Maximum day's consumption, about 2,494,000 gals. in January; average about 2,200,000 gals.

Assessment charge, 1s. 2d. to 1s. 4d. in the £ rental dwelling houses; 7d. to 8d. in the £ on rental of shops or works.

FALKIRK and LARBERT—*continued.*

Price per meter, 4½d. per 1,000 gals.
Number of meters in use, 100.
Length of supply mains, 22 miles; distributing mains, 95 miles.
Duplication of existing works is in progress, authorized by Act of 1900.

Falmer, Sussex (supplied by BRIGHTON).

Falmouth, Cornwall.   Railway, G.W.   Distance from London, 306½ miles.
Authority, Falmouth Waterworks Company.
Chairman, W. S. Cuff.
Secretary, J. M. Hamilton.
Manager, Alfred Cox.   Office, Suffolk House, Laurence Pountney Hill, E.C.
Share capital paid up, £42,994.
Interest, 5 per cent. consolidated pref. and ordinary stock.
Loan capital (debenture stock) paid up, £8,750.
Dividends paid regularly on pref. stock; dividend paid on ordinary, 2 per cent.
Towns and villages in the area supplied, Falmouth and Penryn.
Works established, 1847.
Special Acts, 1847, 1862, 1877 and 1891.
Total population supplied, 15,000.
Sources of supply, springs and watershed.
System of filtration, sand.
Character of water, especially filtered and well fitted for drinking and all domestic
    purposes.
Death rate, 17·1 per 1,000.
Total water rent received, £4,299.

Far Coton (supplied by NORTHAMPTON).

Fareham, Hants.   Railway, L.S.W.   Distance from London, 84½ miles.
Authority, Urban District Council.
Clerk to the Urban District Council, Leonard Warner.
Engineer, Surveyor to Urban District Council.
Total population supplied, 8,246.
Scale of charges—assessment charge, 6d. in £.
Price per 1,000 gals., 6d.
Total water rent received and rates, £635 per annum.

Farnborough, Hants.   *See* FRIMLEY.

Farndon, Notts. (supplied by NEWARK).

Farnham, Surrey.   Railway, L.S.W.   Distance from London, 37½ miles.
Authority, Farnham Water Co., Ltd.
Office, Town Hall.
Works established, 1836.
Special Act, Farnham Water Order, 1886; Frimley and Farnham Water Act, 1898.
Total population supplied, 12,376.
Source of supply, pumping from green sand and springs.
Price per 1,000 gals., 1s. 6d. to 6d. minimum.

Farnham Rural District and part of Farnham Parish (supplied by WEY
    VALLEY WATER CO.).

Farnham Royal, Bucks. (partly supplied by SLOUGH).

Farnsfield, Notts. (supplied by NEWARK).

Farnworth, Lancs. (supplied by BOLTON).

Farsley, Yorks.
Authority, Farsley Urban District Council.
Office, Town Street, Farsley.
Works established, 1866.
Total population supplied, 5,800,
Daily consumption per head, domestic, 19 gals.
Source of supply, purchased in bulk from Bradford City Council, who deliver it at boundary at 9d. per 1,000 gals.
Character of water, good.
Assessment charges, 3s. 6d. to 33s. per quarter, according to rateable value.
Price per 1,000 gals., 1s. 6d.

Faversham, Kent. Railway, L.C.D. Distance from London, 51¾ miles.
Owners, Faversham Water Company.
Chairman, J. A. Anderson.
Secretary, F. F. Giraud.
Resident Engineer and Manager, A. H. Settatree.
Office, 50, Preston Street, Faversham.
Works established, 1864.
Special Acts—the Faversham Water Order, 1889, the Faversham Water Act, 1901.
Total population of area of control, 15,530.
Estimated population actually supplied, 13,900.
Average death rate, 13·1 per 1,000.
Towns and villages within the area of control—Faversham, North and South Preston, Ospringe, Davington and Oare.
Source of supply in use—deep wells, borings, and headings in the chalk, situated at Ospringe and South Preston Without. Plot Nos. 217, 218, 219, and 36.
Average annual rainfall over drainage area, 25·87 inches (period 4 years).
The Water Authority are now treating for control of drainage area.
Natural rest level of water below surface, 90 feet; above ordnance datum. 140 feet.
Level of water below surface (when pumping 480,000 gals. per day), 130 feet.
Geological data—
    Surface formation of drainage area, brick, earth and Thanet sand.
    Strata tapped by wells or borings, chalk.
Pumping station, Copton   ...   ...   capacity, 484,000 gals. per day.
Character of water, good—20·9° before boiling, 2·8° after (permanent).
Service reservoirs at Copton—
    One ...   .   capacity, 235,000 gals., covered.
    Two ...   .   „   535,000   „   „
Annual supply of water (1906)—
    For all purposes ...   .   102,400,000 gals.
Maximum day's consumption, 302,000 gals. in December, 1906.
Total quantity of water drawn per annum (1906)—
    From deep wells, borings, and headings,   102,400,000 gals.
The Works consist of two Cornish boilers and two horizontal tandem compound surface condensing engines, with pumps of ram and bucket type, estimated to raise 330 gals. per minute each. The No. 2 engine is arranged for coupling a 7-inch ordinary 3-throw pump, in this way raising 500 gals. per minute. There is also a 7-inch 3-throw pump worked by windmill, to raise 170 gals. per minute, connected and worked by oil engine when required, and not sufficient wind.

FAVERSHAM—*continued.*

    Average day's supply—domestic, 18·24 gals.; trade, 1·88 gals.
    Assessment charge, 6 to 8 per cent. on R.V.
    Price per 1,000 gals.—authorised, 1s. 6d.; present average, 1s.
    Length of supply mains, 26 miles; distributing mains about 25 miles.

Fazlington (supplied by PORTSMOUTH).

Fearby (supplied by MASHAM).

Fearnhead, Lancs. (supplied by WARRINGTON).

Featherstone (supplied by WAKEFIELD).

Felinfoel (supplied by LLANELLY).

Felpham, Sussex (supplied by BOGNOR).

Feltham (supplied by SOUTH WEST SUBURBAN).

Fenham (supplied by NEWCASTLE-ON-TYNE).

Fenstanton (supplied by ST. IVES, HUNTS).

Fenton (supplied by STAFFORDSHIRE POTTERIES WATER CO.).

Ferniegair, Scotland (supplied by DISTRICT OF THE MIDDLE WARD OF LANARKSHIRE).

Festiniog, Wales. Railway, G.W. Distance from London, 244¼ miles.
    Authority, Urban District Council.
    Engineer, W. E. Alltwen Williams, A.M.I.C.E.
    Office, Public Offices, Blaenau Festiniog.
    Interest on loan, 3¼ and 3¾ per cent.
    Area supplied Festiniog and Blaenau Festiniog.
    Works established, 1876.
    Total population supplied, 11,500.
    Daily consumption per head, domestic, 20 gals.
    Sources of supply, Lake of Morwynion, 1,300 feet above sea level.
    Character of water, soft and peaty.
    System of filtration, coke breeze and copper wire gauze.
    Death rate, 15·70 per 1,000.
    Scale of charges, assessment charge, water rental of 2s. per quarter.
    Price per 1,000 gals., trade, 9d.

Fetteresso (supplied by STONEHAVEN).

Fifield (supplied by MAIDENHEAD).

Filey, Yorks. Railway, N.E. Distance from London, 233¼ miles.
    Authority, Filey Urban District Council.
    Chairman of Water Committee, Nicholas Maley, Esq.
    Secretary, Thomas Johnstone, Council Offices, Filey.
    Resident Engineer, J. M. Gledhill.
    Consulting Engineer, Henry Tobey, Malton.
    Office, Council Office, Filey.
    Total capital invested, including loans, £35,250.
    Works established, 1856. Purchased by local authority, 1898.

FILEY—*continued.*

Special Acts, Company's Acts, Filey Waterworks Act, 1856, and Filey Water and
  Gas Act, 1891 ; Council's Act, Filey Water and Gas Act, 1898.
Total population of area of control, 3,400.
Total number of consumers, 1,050.
Estimated population actually supplied, 5,000 holiday season, 3,000 normal.
Average death rate, 10 per 1,000.
Towns and villages within the area of control, Filey, Gristhorpe, and Libberston.
Source of supply—drainage areas situated at Hunmanby, East Riding, Yorks. ;
  deep wells or borings situated at Filey, East Riding, Yorks.
Natural rest level of water below surface 60 feet, above Ordnance datum 60 feet.
Level of water below surface (when pumping 80,000 gals. per day), 72 feet.
Geological data—surface formation of drainage areas, Speeton clay ; strata tapped
  by wells or borings, calcareous grit.
Estimated total quantity of water available per annum—
    From drainage areas ...   .   20,000,000 gals.
      „   deep wells or borings   25,000,000   „
Character of water, clear and bright ; total hardness, 11°.
Filtering area provided, 60 square yards in two filter-beds ; polarite. Softening,
  none.
Pumping station, Filey, capacity, 80,000 gals. per day,
Storage in impounding reservoir, Hunmanby, capacity, 5,500,000 gals.
Service reservoirs, Hunmanby, capacity, 18,000 gals.
Annual supply of water (1906), 41,000,000 gals.
Maximum day's consumption, 150,000 gals. in August, holiday season.
Assessment charge, rate 2s. in £. Premises under £5 rateable 8s. 8d. per annum ;
  one w.c. free, remainder 7s. 6d. each ; baths, 10s. each per annum.
Price per 1,000 gals., 2s. to 1s. 2d., according to quantity.
Number of meters in use, 20.
Length of supply mains, 3 miles ; distributing mains 7 miles.

Finchley (supplied by BARNET).

Fishguard. *See* NORTH PEMBROKE.

Fivemiletown, Co. Tyrone.
  Authority, Board of Guardians, Clogher Union.

Fleetwood, Lancs. (supplied by FYLDE WATERWORKS CO.).

Fletton (supplied by PETERBOROUGH).

Flint, Wales. (G. & W.) Railway, L.N.W. Distance from London, 192 miles.
  Chairman, C. E. Dyson.
  General Manager and Secretary, Hugh Owen.
  Works Manager, J. Morris.
  Office, Mumforth Street.
  Share capital paid up, £7,000. Loan capital paid up, £1,300.
  Dividend, 5 per cent.
  Works established, 1852 ; special Acts, 1876.
  Total population supplied, 4,624.
  Source of supply, stream and spring.
  Scale of charges, assessment charge A.

Flixton (supplied by MANCHESTER).

Flockton, Yorks. (supplied by DEWSBURY).

Fofany Storage Reservoirs, Co. Down, Ireland.
  Manager, George Mitchell, Kilcoo Post Office.

Folkestone. Railway, S.E. Distance from London, 70 miles.
Authority, Folkestone Waterworks Co.
Chairman, George Spurgen, J.P.
Secretary, Frederick Kelly.
Engineer in charge, Henry Turner.
Office, 63, Guildhall Street.
Total capital invested—

Share Capital, including premiums, £147,608.		
Debenture Stock	„　„	£26,013.
Preference Stock	„　„	£54,917.

£228,998.

Last Dividends, 9 per cent. on ordinary, and £6 6s. 0d. per cent. on new ordinary
shares; 4 per cent. perpetual debenture stock; 4 per cent. preference stock.
Interest on debenture and preference stocks has been paid regularly in full.
Works established, 1848. Special Acts, 1848, 1855, 1858, 1864, 1871, 1888, 1898.
Total population of area supplied 50,000, exclusive of season visitors and troops
quartered for annual training at Shorncliffe Camp.
Towns and villages in the area supplied—Folkestone, Cheriton, Shorncliffe Camp,
part of Sandgate, Alkham, Capel-le-Ferne, Hawkinge, and Lydden, with power
to supply outside the statutory area; the Borough of Hythe is supplied under
this power.
Sources of supply—adits driven in chalk at foot of downs on same level as springs
emerge; adits driven in green sand formation from bottom of wells at Shearway
Works, and in chalk at Standen Works.
Total quantity of water drawn per annum (1906), from—

Surface springs and adits	...	...	...	86,632,000 gals.
Deep wells	„	(Shearway)		62,974,000 „
„	„	(Standen)		305,295.000 „
Estimated daily discharge at points of collection				2,940,000 „
„ minimum „	„	„	„	858,000 „
„ average „	„	„	„	1,240,000 „

Character of water—
Water analysis, from chalk well.—N.B.—All numerical results expressed in grains
per gallon—

Description or No. of sample	...	...	...	"From Standen."
Appearance ...	..	...	...	...	clear.
Colour	...	...	...	...	Green-blue.
Smell...	...	...	...	...	None.
Chlorine in chlorides			...	1·82.
Phosphoric acid in phosphates	...	...	...	None.
Nitrogen in nitrates	...	..	...	0·14
Ammonia ...	...	...	...	...	0·0004.
Albuminoid ammonia	...	...	...	0·0011.
Oxygen absorbed in 15 minutes ...	...	...	Trace only.
Oxygen absorbed in 4 hours	...	...	...	0·016.
Hardness before boiling (total) ...	...	...	18·9.
Hardness after boiling (permanent)	...	...	3·1.
Total solid matter	...	...	...	...	...	22·89
Microscopical examination of deposit ...	...	Slight and unimportant.

The above results are satisfactory throughout and indicate water organically
pure and free from sewage percolation.
The microscopical examination calls for no adverse remarks.
Water analysis, lower green sand.—N.B.—All numerical results expressed in
grains per gallon.

Description or No. of sample	...	...	...	From No. 5 well.
Appearance	..	..	..	...	Clear.
Colour	..	...	...	...	...	Green-blue,
Smell	...	..	...	...	..	...	None.

FOLKESTONE—*continued.*

Chlorine in chlorides	2·52.
Phosphoric acid in phosphates	None.
Nitrogen in nitrates	0·12.
Ammonia	·0031.
Albuminoid ammonia	·0028.
Oxygen absorbed in 15 minutes	Trace only.
Oxygen absorbed in 4 hours	·042.
Hardness before boiling (total)	23·1.
Hardness after boiling (permanent)	5·4.
Total solid matter	32·76.
Microscopical examination of deposit	Slight and unimportant.

The above results are very satisfactory in every respect, and indicate water of
great organic purity.

Filtration, none ; softening, none.

Storage capacity—The Hart Reservoir ...	12,000,000 gals.	
„ Spurgen „ ...	6,000,000	„
„ Bateman „ ...	2,000,000	„
Pumping stations and capacity per 24 hours—		
Shearway	600,000	„
Standen	2,200,000	„
Upper (used for pumping from reservoir to service tank	420,000	„
Service reservoir—high service tank (covered)	630,000	„
camp supply tank) „	120,000	„

Head on distributing mains—maximum, 280 ft. ; minimum, 90 ft.
Average daily supply per head—domestic, 20 gals. ; trade, &c., 4 gals.
Maximum supply per day, 1,500,000 gals. in August.
Assessment charge, 7 per cent. on rateable value.
No charge for first w.c., and no charge for baths.
Authorised charge by meter, 1s. 6d. per 1,000 gals.
No. of meters, 142.
Length of distributing mains, 45 miles.

Forfar, Scotland. Railways, N.B. & C. Distance from Edinburgh, 90 miles.
Authority, Corporation.
Population supplied, 13,000.
No returns supplied.

Forres, Scotland. Railway, H. Distance from Edinburgh, 170 miles.
Authority, Forres Town Council.
Chairman, Provost Lawrence.
Town clerk, Robt. Urquhart, Junr.
Resident Engineer, John Rankine.
Office, 4, Gordon Street.
Loans outstanding, £17,200.
Works established, 1845. Purchased by Town Council, 1898. Special Act, 1898.
Population supplied with water, 6,000.
Average death rate, 18·4 per 1,000.
District of supply—Rafford, Dallas, Forres, Kinloss.
Source of supply, springs.
Character of water, good ; filtering, none ; softening, none ; total hardness, 5°.
Storage—impounding reservoirs, 100,000,000 gals. ; service reservoirs, 160,000 gals.
Total quantity of water supplied per annum, 91,250,000 gals.
Average daily supply per head, 32 gals.
Maximum day's supply, 290,000 gals. in July and August.
Assessment charge, 5 per cent. in the £.

FORRES—*continued.*

    Price by meter, 6d. per 1,000 gals.
    No. of meters, 4.
    Length of supply mains, 9 miles; distributing mains, 15 miles.

Forrest Green (supplied by MAIDENHEAD).

Forton, Hants. (supplied by GOSPORT).

Foryd (supplied by RHYL).

Fountains (supplied by RIPON).

Frankby, Cheshire (supplied by HOYLAKE).

Frant (supplied by TUNBRIDGE WELLS).

Fraserburgh, Scotland. Railway, G.N.S.
    Authority, Burgh Commissioners.
    Total population supplied, 7,360.
    Water supplied by Town Council under Act of Parliament.
    Scale of charges—assessment charge, 3d. in the £ on owners and occupiers, as
    per valuation roll. (March 5th, 1903.)

Frensham (supplied by WEY VALLEY WATER Co.).

Frimley and Farnborough. Railway, L.S.W. Distance from London, 33 miles.
    Owners, Frimley and Farnborough District Water Company.
    Chairman, Arthur C. Pain, Esq., M.I.C.E., C.C., J.P. for Surrey.
    Secretary and General Manager, Frederick J. Garland, Waterworks House,
      Frimley Green.
    Consulting engineer, A. R. Nunn, 17, Victoria Street, Westminster, S.W.
    Total capital invested, including loans, £108,880, including £16,829 premiums
      on shares sold by auction and upon debentures sold by tender.
    Dividend, 7%.
    Towns and villages within the area of control—Camberley, Yorktown, Frimley,
      Frimley Green, Ash and Normandy, in Surrey; Farnborough, Cove, Blackwater,
      Hawley, Yateley, Minley, Fleet, Crookham, Crondall, Winchfield and Odiham,
      in Hampshire; Wellington College, Sandhurst and Crowthorne, in Berkshire.
    Works established, 1896. Special Acts—Frimley and Farnborough District
      Water Act, 1893, Wey Valley, Frimley and Farnham Water Act, 1898, Frimley
      and Farnborough District Water Order, 1901 and 1904.
    Total number of consumers, 4,937, at December 31st, 1906.
    Estimated population actually supplied, 26,000, including the Barracks at Deep
      Cut, Blackdown and Ewshot.
    Annual supply of water (1906)—

For domestic purposes ...	...	...	185,000,000 gals.
„ trade „	...	...	... 60,000,000 „ *
„ municipal „	...	...	... 5,000,000 „
In bulk to other authorities	...	(average)	18,000,000 „ †

---

  * Including 25,666,000 gals. supplied to Blackdown, Ewshot and Deep Cut Barracks, and
5,171,000 gals. to Wellington College.
  † To Wey Valley Water Company.

FRIMLEY AND FARNBOROUGH—*continued.*

Average days' consumption, 734,246 gals.
Total quantity of water drawn per annum (1906)—

From surface springs	96,516,356 gals.	
„ deep wells or borings	183,832,000 „	

Sources of supply in use—surface springs situated at Frimley, Well at Itchell Crondall, near Farnham.
Itchell well—natural rest level of water, level with surface; above Ordnance datum, 262 feet.
Level of water below surface (when pumping 500,000 gals. per day), 45 feet.
Strata or formation yielding springs—chalk at Itchell Well, Bagshot sand at Frimley.
Water at Frimley is drawn from the Bagshot sand, and is 3½° of hardness.
Water at Itchell is drawn from wells and borings of a total depth of 300 feet. The water is about 21° of hardness, softening plant on the "Haines" system reducing hardness to 8°.
Capacity of engines at pumping stations—Sturt Lane, Frimley Green, Surrey, 1,000,000 gals. per day; Mill Lane, Itchell, Crondall, Farnham, Surrey, 1,960,000 gals. per day.
Service reservoirs—

Frith Hill (open) ...	capacity, 400,000 gals., 368 feet above O.D.			
„ (covered)	„	750,000	„	„ „
Heathy Hill, Hale (covered) „	300,000	„	„	„
„ „ „ „	613,000	„	610 feet	„
„ „ „ „	613,000	„	„	„

Assessment from 9 to 6 per cent. poor rate on assessment.
Price by meter per 1,000 gals., 2s. to 1s.
Number of meters in use, 322.
Length of distributing mains, 147 miles.

Frinton-on-Sea (supplied by the TENDRING HUNDRED WATERWORKS Co.).

Frithville (supplied by BOSTON).

Frodsham, Cheshire. Railways, L.N.W. and G.W. Joint.
Authority, Rural District Council of Runcorn.
Office, 71, High Street, Runcorn.
Towns and villages in the area supplied—Frodsham and Frodsham Lordship.
Works established, 1894, extended to Frodsham Lordship, 1900.
Total population supplied, 4,131.
Sources of supply, well with bore hole 300 feet deep.
Storage capacity, 175,000 gals.
Character of water, first class, rather hard.
Death rate, 13·2 per 1,000.
Assessment, 2d. per week on cottage up to £7 rateable value, and 7½ per cent. over £7.

Frome, Somerset. Railway, G.W. Distance from London, 106¾ miles.
Authority, Urban District Council.
Chairman, E. R. Trotman, J.P.
Clerk, H. E. Amies, solicitor.
Engineer and Manager, Fred. W. Jones.
Office, Public Office, Christchurch Street, Frome.
Loan outstanding, £5,717.
Works established, 1879.
Total population supplied, 12,000.

FROME—*continued*.

Death rate, 13·34 per 1,000 in 1906.
Source of supply, wells limestone rock at Egford.
Character of water, 25° hardness; excellent; the hardness is chiefly temporary.
Filtration, none necessary.
Storage capacity, 1,000,000 gals. in service reservoir.
Pressure in distributing mains—maximum, 90 lbs. per square inch; minimum, 20 lbs. per square inch.
Annual supply of water, 124,500,000 gals.
Daily consumption per head—domestic, 20·5 gals.; trade, &c., 7·5 gals.
Maximum day's supply, 492,000 gals. in August.
Scale of charges—
  Assessment charge, 1s. 2d. in the £ on R.V.
  Price per 1,000 gals., 1s. 3d. to 6d.
Number of meters, 100.
Length of mains, 16 miles.

Fulbourne, Cambs. (supplied by CAMBRIDGE).

Fulford (supplied by YORK).

Fulmer (supplied by RICKMANSWORTH).

Furnace (supplied by LLANELLY).

Fylde, Lancs. Railways, L.N.W. and L. & Y. Distance from London, 217½ miles
Authority, Fylde Water Board.
Chairman, Alderman John Bickerstaffe.
Superintendent and accountant, C. Arthur.
Engineer, W. Wearing.
Office, Blackpool, Lancashire.
Share capital, 2¾ per cent. stock paid up, £614,849.
Loan, £422,152.
Towns and villages in the area supplied—Blackpool, Fleetwood, Lytham, St. Annes, Kirkham, Poulton-le-Fylde, Garstang, and about 25 more townships.
Works established, 1861. Special Acts, 1897, 1899.
Total population supplied, 120,000.
Sources of supply, Grizedale Brook, millstone grit.
Character of water, soft.
Number of meters, 609.
Scale of charges, assessment charge, rateable value.
  Price per 1,000 gals., 1s. 6d. to 6d.

Galashiels, Scotland. Railways, M. and N.B. Distance from London, 364 miles.
Authority, Corporation of Burgh of Galashiels.
Secretary, Town Clerk.
Works established, 1876. Special Act, 1876.
Total population supplied, 13,595.
Annual supply of water, 365,000,000 gals.
Daily consumption per head, 40 gals.
Sources of supply—river Caddon.
Character of water, soft.
Death rate, 15 per 1,000.
Number of meters, 38.
Scale of charges—assessment charge, 1s. in the £.
  Price per 1,000 gals., 6d.

Gainsborough, Lincs. Railways, G.N. and G.E. Joint and G.C. Distance from London, 140 miles.

    Authority, Urban District Council.
    Chairman of Committee, Thomas Lobley.
    Engineer and Surveyor, Sam. W. Parker.
    Clerk, Decimus M. Robbs.
    Office, 6, Lord Street.
    Consulting Engineer, Percy Griffith, M.I.C.E., M.I.M.E., F.G.S., 54, Parliament Street, S.W.
    Loans outstanding, £23,820.
    Works established, 1866 ; taken over by Council, 1871.
    Towns and villages in the area supplied, Gainsborough and Morton.
    Total population of area supplied, 20,000.
    Average death rate, 12·1 per 1,000.
    District of supply, U.D. of Gainsborough and parish of Morton.
    Sources of supply, two boreholes—No. 1. 1,351 ft. deep; No. 2, 1,515 ft. deep to new red sandstone water-bearing strata 720 ft. below surface, and River Trent , as supplementary supply.
    Character of water, good, but hard, 23°.
    System of filtration, sand for river water, which is only used for trade purposes ; softening, none.
    Storage capacity, 1,667,152 gals.
    Service reservoirs, two at surface level, one in tower.
    Head on distributing mains—maximum, 110 ft. ; minimum, 96 ft.
    Annual supply af water, 258,670,000 gals.
    Average daily supply per head—domestic ... ... 23 gals.
                       trade, well water $5 \left.\right\}$ $10\frac{1}{4}$,,
                       river, ,, ,, $5\frac{1}{4}$
    Maximum day's supply, 657,000 gals. during summer.
    Assessment, 3 per cent. on R.V.
    Price per 1,000 gals., 6d.

Garlinge (supplied by Margate).

Garstang, Lancs. (supplied by Fylde Waterworks Co.).

Garston (supplied by Rickmansworth).

Garw, Glam. Railway, G.W.
    Authority, Garw Water Co.
    Secretary and Manager, A. J. Lawrence
    Office, Pontycymmer, Glamorgan.

Gateshead. *See* Newcastle-on-Tyne.

Gaywood (supplied by Lynn).

Gedling (supplied by Nottingham).

Gerlan (supplied by Bethesda).

Gifford (supplied by South Oxfordshire).

Gigg (supplied by Bury).

Gildersome, Yorks. (supplied by Bradford).

Gillingham (supplied by Brompton).

Glan Conway (supplied by Llandudno).

Glasgow, Scotland. Railways, L.N.W., M., G.N. Distance from London, 401¼ miles.
Authority, City of Glasgow Corporation Water Department.
Chairman, the Lord Provost.
Secretary, Adam Whitson Myles.
Treasurer, Robert Wilson.
Engineer, John Robertson Sutherland.
Office, 45, John Street.
*Cost of works, £4,066,058.
Loan capital, £2,787,599.
Interest on loans and annuities payable, £98,226.
Area supplied, about 16 miles north to south, and 12 miles east to west, or 87
　　square miles.
Towns and villages supplied—Glasgow, Govan, Partick, Milngavie, Rutherglen,
　　Renfrew, Barrhead, Pollokshaws, Nitshill, Thornliebank, Cathcart, Cardonald,
　　Shettleston, Tollcross, Mount Vernon, Carmyle, Millerston, Auchenairn, Bishop-
　　briggs, Lambhill, Anniesland, Yoker, Scotstounhill, Scotstoun, Bearsden, Strath-
　　blane, Stepps Road, Linthouse, Bellahouston, Jordanhill and Corkerhill.
Works established, 1859 ; duplication of works, 1885.
Special Acts, 1855, 1885, 1892.
Total population of area supplied, 1,125,666.
Supply of water per day, 64,985,613 gals.
Daily consumption per head, domestic, 35 gals.; trade, 21 gals.
Sources of supply—Loch Katrine and Gorbals, Barrhead.
Storage capacity, 10,750,000,000 gals.
Character of water, 1° of hardness.
System of filtration—Loch Katrine, water not filtered ; Gorbals, water through
　　sand.
Death rate, 17·2 per 1,000.
Number of meters, 4,392.
Length of mains, 648 miles.
Scale of charges—
　　Assessment charge rated on full annual value, 5d. in the £ within, and 10d. in
　　　the £ beyond municipal boundary.
　　Price for 1,000 gals. —domestic unlimited supply ; trade purposes, warehouses,
　　　&c., according to appliances ; factories by meter, 4d. per 1,0000 gals.
　　Municipal purposes, rate of 1d. in £ payable by the owner, levied on all property
　　　within municipal boundary.
Total water rent received, £255,237.

Glassford (supplied by DISTRICT OF THE MIDDLE WARD OF LANARKSHIRE).

Glasshoughton (supplied by WAKEFIELD).

Glastonbury, Somerset. Railway, Somerset and Dorset Joint Line. Distance from
London, 132½ miles.
Authority, Glastonbury Corporation.
Town Clerk, R. T. Gould.
Engineer, Geo. Alves (Surveyor).
Office, Town Clerk's Office, Glastonbury.
Town and villages in the area supplied, the Borough and West Pennard, and
　　partly North Wootton and Pilton.
Special Act, 1899.
Total population supplied, 4,250.
Daily consumption per head, domestic, 15 gals.
Source of supply, springs. Storage capacity, 5,350,000 gals.
Character of water, good. Filtration, none required.
Death rate, 12·6 per 1,000.
Number of meters, 75.

---

* The difference between this amount and the loan capital is debt extinguished through the
sinking fund.

GLASTONBURY—*continued.*

    Length of mains and distributing mains, about 15 miles.
      Assessment charge on rental, from 1s. 7½d. per quarter for houses rated at £5
      to 7s. 6d. on £50, and pro rata.
      Price per 1,000 gals. from first 10,000, 1s. per 1,000 gals. to 400,000 at 6d. per
      1,000 gals. inside district, 50 per cent. extra outside.

Glenboig, N.B. (supplied by AIRDRIE).

Glengarnock (supplied by KILBIRNIE).

Glen Parva (supplied by LEICESTER).

Glossop, Derbyshire. Railways, M. and G.N. Distance from London, 190 miles.
    Authority, Corporation, 1880.
    Chairman, Ed. Partington.
    Secretary, Theodore Walter Ellison.
    Manager, John Garner.
    Office, Manchester.
    Works established, 1853 ; Special Act, 1865.
    Population supplied, 15,000.
    District of supply, Glossop, Whitfield, Dinting.
    Source of supply, springs from the hills and gathering ground and impounding
      reservoir.
    Filtration, none ; softening, none.
    Storage in impounding reservoir, 56,000,000 gals.
    Head on distributing mains—maximum, 280 feet ; minimum, 30 feet.
    Annual supply of water, 138,700,000 gals.
    Average day's supply, 25 gals. per head for all purposes.
    Maximum day's supply, 380,000 gals.
    Authorised charge by meter, 8d., 10d. and 1s. per 1,000 gals. Present average
      charge, 8d.
    No. of meters, 58.
    Length of supply mains, 2½ miles. Distributing mains, 8 miles.

Gloucester. Railways, G.W. and M. Distance from London, 114 miles.
    Authority, Corporation of Gloucester.
    Chairman, S. Sitken (The Mayor).
    Secretary, G. S. S. Blakeway, Town Clerk, Guildhall, Gloucester.
    Engineer in Charge, R. Read, A.M.I.C.E., City Surveyor. (Wm. Fox, M.I.C.E.,
      for 1894 Act ; J. F. Bateman, M.I.C.E., for 1855 Act).
    Total capital invested, including loans, £150,000. Loans outstanding, £92,413.
    Works established, 1855, Witcombe ; 1894, Newent.
    Special Acts, Acts of Parliament, G.W.W., 1855, 1894.
    Total population of area of control, about 60,000.
    Population actually supplied, 56,000.
    Death rate, 13·7 per 1,000 (1906).
    Area of control—City of Gloucester.
    Sources of supply in use—drainage areas situated at Witcombe, 5 miles east of
      Gloucester, 1,500 acres on inferior oolite ; deep wells situated at Newent, 11
      miles west of city, in red sandstone, 170 feet deep.
    Maximum annual rainfall over drainage area, 42·37 inches (1872)
    Minimum   ,,   ,,   ,,   20·37 ,,   (1892)
    Average   ,,   ,,   ,,   30·00 ,,   (period 40 years)
    Population on drainage area, about 20.
    Nature of   ,,   ,,   all pasture and woodland.
    Water authority diverted the drainage by arrangement with land owners.
    Natural rest level of water below surface, 3 feet ; above ordnance datum, 100 feet
      at Newent.

GLOUCESTER—*continued.*

Level of water below surface (when pumping 600,000 gals. per day), 50 feet.
Geological data—
    Surface formation of drainage areas, grass and woodland, Witcombe.
    Strata or formation yielding springs, inferior oolite, Witcombe.
    Strata tapped by wells or borings, Keuper and Bunter beds, new red sandstone.
    Locality and extent of outcrop of same, about 12 square miles between two
       parallel faults at Oxenhall, 11 miles west of city, near Newent.
The top water level of the Witcombe reservoirs is 290 feet above ordnance datum ;
    the water gravitates 5 miles through a 12-inch main to the city, which lies
    between 40 feet and 80 feet above ordnance datum.
The top water level of the Upleadon reservoirs is 250 feet above ordnance datum
    the water gravitates 8 miles through a 14-inch main to the city.
Storage reservoirs—No. 1   ...   .   capacity, 60,000,000 gals.
                No. 2   ...   .   „   30,000,000 „
                No. 3   ...   .   „   30,000,000 „
Robinswood reservoir   ...   .   10,000,000 „
                                                130,000,000 „
Filters, 10 Bell Bros.' mechanical filters, rated at 1,500,000 gals. per day.
Pumping stations, Newent pumping station ; capacity, 600,000 gals. per day of
    10 hours.
Two compound vertical engines by Messrs. Summers & Scott, of Gloucester.
Service Reservoirs—
        Two at Upleadon, 3 miles from
        pump and 8 miles from city—1. capacity, 600,000 gals., covered
           „   „   2.   „   1,200,000   „   „
                                    1,800,000
Character of water, from Witcombe, 13° hardness ; after boiling, 4° ; from
    Newent, total hardness, 21° ; permanent, 12°.
Head on distributing mains—maximum, 195 feet ; minimum, 135 feet.
Annual supply of water (1906)—
        For domestic purposes   ...   . 15 gals.) 20 gals.
        „ trade   „   ...   .   3 „   } per head
        „ municipal „   ...   .   2 „   ) per day.
Maximum day's consumption, 1,100,000 gals.
Total quantity of water drawn per annum (1906)—
        From drainage areas ...   . 200,000,000 gals.
        „   deep wells or borings ...   . 200,000,000 „
Estimated total quantity of water available per annum—
        From drainage areas ...   . 330,000,000 gals.
        „   deep wells or borings ...   . 365,000,000 „
Maximum days' supply, 1,365,714 gals. (September, 1906).
Charges authorized, from 5 to 6 per cent. on gross rental.
Present rate of charge, 10d. in the city, and 1s. 2d. outside.
Price per 1,000 gals., 10d. in city ; 1s. 2d. outside city.
Number of meters in use, 750.
Length of supply mains, 16 miles ; distributing mains, 45 miles.

Glusburn, Yorks. (supplied by CROSSHILLS).

Godalming, Surrey. Railway, L. & S.W. Distance from London, 34 miles.
    Authority, The Godalming Corporation.
    Chairman, Councillor John Wright.
    Clerk, T. Percival Whately, Town Clerk, High Street, Godalming.
    Engineer in charge, J. Herbert Norris, Borough Surveyor and Water Manager,
       Municipal Offices, Godalming.
    Total capital invested, including loans, £86,408.

GODALMING—*continued.*

Annual loss on undertaking, including "capital charges," £739.
Works established, 1880. Purchased by local authority, 1900.
Special Act, Godalming Corporation Water Act, 1899.
Total population of area of control, 17,400 (approx.).
Total number of consumers, 2,500.
Estimated population actually supplied, 12,650.
Death rate, 10 per 1,000.
Towns and villages within the area of control, with population of each (1901 Census)—

Godalming (Borough)	...	...	...	...	...	8,748	
„ (Rural)	...	...	...	...	...	1,787	
Bramley	...	...	...	...	...	1,915	(approx.)
Compton, part	...	...	...	...	...	500	„
Elstead „	...	...	...	...	...	500	„
Hambledon „	...	...	...	...	...	600	„
Witley „	...	...	...	...	...	3,000	„
Peperharow „	...	...	...	...	...	150	„
Shalford „	...	...	...	...	...	200	„

Sources of supply in use—surface springs situated at Catteshall Lane, Godalming.
Shallow wells or collecting reservoirs situated at Peperharow Road, Godalming, and Borough Road, Godalming.
Geological data—strata or formation yielding springs, lower greensand.*
Nature of subsoil yielding water, river drift and gravel.*
Strata tapped by wells or borings, lower greensand.*
Locality and extent of outcrop of same—the lower greensand occupies the south-western corner of Surrey, below Godalming, and a narrow slip stretches west to east across the county.
Character of water—hardness before treatment, 14°.
Water is not filtered.
Recent Analysis—the sample contained and yielded in grains per gallon—

Total solid matter ...	...	...	...	...	...	21·70
Loss on ignition	...	...	...	...	...	1·82
Combined chlorine...	...	...	...	...	...	1·52
Equal to common salt	...	...	...	...	...	2·51
Nitrogen as nitrates	...	...	...	...	...	0·47
Nitrites	...	...	...	...	...	None
Ammonia	...	...	...	...	...	0·003
Albuminoid or organic ammonia	...	...	...	0·004
Oxygen required to oxidise the organic matter	...	0·029

Hardness in degrees—
Temporary ... ... 9° ⎫
Permanent ... ... 5° ⎭ 14°

Pumping station, Borough Road, Godalming, capacity, 1,000,000 gals. per day.
Service reservoirs, Frith Hill ... ... capacity, 411,000 gals., covered.
„ „ Tower ... ... „ 21,000 „ „
„ „ Munstead ... ... „ 200,000 „ „
„ „ Tower ... ... „ 40,000 „ „
Number of meters in use, 64.
Head on distributing mains—maximum, 400 ft.; minimum, 45 ft.
Annual supply of water, 150,000,000 gals.
Estimated total quantity of water available per annum—
From surface springs, shallow wells or subsoil, 280,000,000 gals.
Average daily supply per head—domestic, 27½ gals.; trade, 5 gals.
Maximum day's consumption, 608,000 gals. in June.

---

* There is no doubt some of the water comes from the chalk which overlies the lower green sand.

GODALMING—*continued.*

Scale of charges—domestic rate, calculated on rateable value for Poor Rate—
Houses not exceeding £5 nett rateable value, 8s. 8d. per annum.
    ,,   exceeding   £10   ,,   ,,   16s.   ,,
    ,,   ,,   £10 and not exceeding £20, 7½ per cent. per annum on the
                nett rateable value.
    ,,   ,,   £20, 7 per cent. per annum on the nett rateable value.
Meter supply—for all water used up to 100,000 gals. per quarter, at 2s. per 1,000
gals. ; over 100,000 but not exceeding 200,000 gals., at 1s. 9d. per 1,000 gals. ;
over 200,000 gallons, at 1s. 6d. per 1,000 gals. ; larger quantities down to 1s. 3d.
and 1s. per 1,000 gals.
Number of meters, 80.
Length of supply and pumping mains, 4 miles ; distributing mains, 40 miles.

Godstone (supplied by EAST SURREY WATERWORKS).

Golborne, Lancs.
Authority, Urban District Council.
Population, 7,000.

Goldcliffe (supplied by NEWPORT, Mon.).

Gomersal, Leeds, Yorks.
Authority, Urban District Council.
Chairman, Benjamin Rhodes Bateman.
Clerk to authority, Henry Ashwell Cadman.
Manager, George Sykes.
Office, Hill Top.
Population supplied, 3,580.
Also partly supplied by Cleckheaton.
No returns supplied.

Goodmanham, Yorks. (supplied by MARKET WEIGHTON).

Goole and District. (G. & W.) Railways, G.N., and N.E. Distance from London,
168 miles.
Authority, Goole Urban District Council.
Office, Doyle Street Gasworks, Goole.
Supplies Old Goole and Goole.
Works established, 1881. Special Act, 1899, New Waterworks.
Total population supplied, 17,500.
Daily consumption per head, 24·79 gals.
Sources of supply—2 wells and borehole at Rawcliffe Bridge.
    New waterworks at Pollington are being constructed for the supply of Goole,
    Pollington, Gowdall, Snaith, and Rawcliffe. Water, 10° hardness.
Character of water, 38° hardness.
Death rate, 18·5 per 1,000.
Length of mains, 15 miles.
Scale of charges—assessment charge, 5 per cent. on gross rental.
Price for 1,000 gals.—domestic and trade, 1s., or 5 per cent. on gross estimated
rental ; municipal purposes, 12½ per cent. discount.

Gorebridge, Midlothian, N.B.
Authority, Gorebridge Waterworks Co., Ltd.
Population supplied, 1,363.
No returns supplied.

Goring and Streatley. *See* South Oxfordshire Water and Gas Co.

Gorton (supplied by Manchester).

Gosforth (supplied by Newcastle-on-Tyne).

Gosport, Hants. Railway, L.S.W. Distance from London, 86¼ miles.
Authority, Gosport Waterworks Company, incorporated 1858.
Chairman, William E. Churcher.
Secretary, Manager and Resident Engineer, Edward T. Hildred, A.M.I.C.E.
Office, 1, High Street, Gosport.
Share capital paid up, £98,500 ; last dividends, 5 and 3½ per cent.
Loan   „   „   „   £27,060 ; rates of interest, 4, 3½ and 3 per cent.
Works established, 1858-1861. New Soberton Scheme, 1905-1907.
Special Acts, Gosport Water Act, 1858 ; Gosport Water Orders, 1872, 1883, 1897 ;
    Gosport Water Act, 1904.
Total population supplied, 30,500.
Average death rate, 14·7 per 1,000.
Towns and villages in the "district of supply," Alverstoke (which includes
    Gosport, Anglesey, Elson, Hardway, Forton, Brockhurst, and Bridgemary),
    Rowner, Crofton, Wickham, Shedfield and Swanmore.
Source of supply, well and headings in the chalk situated at Mislingford, in the
    parish of Soberton, Hants.
Character of water, typical chalk water, of the highest organic purity. The
    hardness is moderate, and there is no excess of saline matter. Bacteriologically,
    the water gives no indication of the presence of any polluting matter. It is
    the purest obtainable, and exceedingly well adapted for all purposes of a public
    supply.
Analysis :—

PHYSICAL EXAMINATION.

Turbidity : Clean and bright. Colour : Bluish tint. Odour : None.

CHEMICAL EXAMINATION.

Determinations.	Results in Grains per Gallon.	Parts per 100,000.
Total solid matter dried at 180° C.	21·7	31·0
Chlorine	1·4	2·0
Equivalent to chlorides (60% Cl.)	2·3	3·3
Nitric nitrogen	0·19	0·27
Equivalent to nitrates (17% N.)	1·14	1·6
Nitrites	Absent	
Hardness : Permanent 3·5, temporary 11·20 ...	14·70	21°
Lead, copper, zinc, iron	Absent	
Free ammonia	0·0001	0·0002
Organic ammonia	0·0000	0·0000
Oxygen absorbed at 98 F. in 3 hours	0·0000	0·0000

Filtration, none ; softening, none.
Storage capacity—service reservoirs, 2,400,000 gals.
Mean head on distributing mains, 55 ft. ; this can and will be increased to 75ft.
Annual supply of water, 257,000,000=23·1 gals. per head per day for all
    purposes. Average day's supply—domestic, 238,000,000 gals. (includes
    53,500,000 gals. meter supply to naval and military establishments. Trade,
    12,000,000 gals., District Council, 7,000,000 gals.
Maximum day's supply, 800,000 gallons in August.
Scale of charges—assessment charge from 5½ to 6 per cent. on gross rental by
    meter ; sliding scale, 1s. 6d. to 1s. per 1,000 gallons.

(142)

GOSPORT—*continued.*

Number of meters, 109.
Annual net profit, £5,261 for 1906.
The above returns ignore the old works and sources, as they will shortly be abandoned.

Goudhurst (supplied by CRANBROOK).

Govan (supplied by GLASGOW).

Gowdall (supplied by GOOLE).

Granbey (supplied by RIPON).

Grand Junction Waterworks. *See* METROPOLITAN WATER BOARD.

Grange, Lancs. (supplied by GRANGE-OVER-SANDS).

Grangemouth (supplied by FALKIRK).

Grange-over-Sands. Railway, Furness, Distance from London, 250 miles.
Authority, Grange-over-Sands Urban District Council.
Engineer, Thomas Huddleston.
Council Office, Grange-over-Sands.
Loans outstanding, March 31st, 1907, £3,087 12s.
Works established, 1879.
Total population supplied, 5,600 (estimated).
Death rate, 12 per 1,000.
Towns and villages in the area supplied, Grange, Kents Bank, Arnside, Lindale-in-Cartmel, Newton-in-Cartmel, Allithwaite, Barber Green.
Sources of supply, gathering ground, moorland.
Character of water, good, soft and pure ; total hardness, 3·64 in 100,000 degrees.
System of filtration, sand and polarite.
Softening, none.
Storage capacity, 21,000,000 gals. in impounding reservoir.
Head on distributing mains—maximum, 460 feet ; minimum, 23 feet.
Annual supply, 40,880,000 gals.
Average daily consumption per head, 20 gals.
Maximum supply per day, 130,000 gals. in August.
Scale of charges—assessment charge, £150 part only ; price per 1,000 gals., 8d.
Length of mains, 12 miles.
Number of meters, 43.
Total water rent received, £1,170.

Grantchester (supplied by CAMBRIDGE).

Grantham, Lincolnshire. Railway, G.N. Distance from London, 105¼ miles.
Chairman, John G. Thompson.
Engineer and Secretary, Henry Preston, F.G.S.
Share capital paid up, £40,000.
Loan   „   £8,750.
Dividend, 10 per cent.
Works established, 1848. Special Act, 1873.
Total population supplied, 19,000.
Annual supply of water, 200,000,000 gals.
Source of supply, springs.
Character of water, 14° hardness.
Death rate, 17 per 1,000.
Number of meters, 120.
Scale of charges—assessment charge A.
Price per 1,000 gals. 1s. 3d.

Grappenhall, Lancs. (supplied by WARRINGTON).

Grassington, Yorks.
Authority, Grassington Waterworks Co. Ltd.
Chairman, John Chapman.
Secretary, Wm. Harker.
Water Manager, Jos. Longstaff.
Office, Town Hall.
Share capital paid up, £1,000.   Last dividend, 5 per cent.
Works constructed, 1887.
Population supplied with water, 500.

Gravesend, Kent.   Railways, S.E. and L.C.D.   Distance from London, 24 miles.
Authority, Gravesend and Milton Waterworks Company.
Chairman, M. A. Troughton, J.P.
Secretary, W. H. Troughton, Solicitor, Gravesend.
General Manager, Arthur King.
Waterworks office, Berkley Crescent, Gravesend.
Works established, 1833.
Towns and villages within the area of control—Gravesend, Milton and Northfleet.
Source of supply, deep wells in chalk.
Character of water, "Admirable drinking water"—Dr. Dupré.
Price per 1,000 gals., 2s. 6d. to 9d.

Grays (supplied by SOUTH ESSEX WATER Co. from chalk quarries north of the town).
Character of water, very hard and of high organic purity.

Greasboro' (supplied by ROTHERHAM).

Greasby, Cheshire (supplied by HOYLAKE).

Greasley (supplied by NOTTINGHAM).

Greaston (supplied by ROTHERHAM).

Great Barr (supplied by SOUTH STAFFS. WATERWORKS Co.)

Great Berkhampstead, Herts.   Railway, L. & N.W.   Distance from London, 28
. miles.
Authority, Great Berkhampstead Waterworks Company.
Chairman, Geo. Chilton.
Secretary, M. Ballam.
Manager, W. G. Howard.
Engineer, A. F. Phillips, M.I.C.E.
Office, 166, High Street.
Share capital paid up, £43,000.
Loan   „   £4,250.
Interest on loan, 4½ per cent.
Dividend, maximum of 4 per cent. ordinary stock, 4 per cent. on preference stock.
Works established, 1864.   Special Acts, 1900.
Total population supplied, 9,000.
Towns and villages in the area supplied, Berkhampstead, Northchurch, Pottenend,
    Ashley Green, Latimer.
Sources of supply, tube wells.
Character of water, hard and chalky.
Quantity of water raised, about 300,000 gals. per day.

GREAT BERKHAMPSTEAD—*continued.*

Storage capacity, 450,000 gals.
Daily consumption per head—domestic, 15 gals.; trade, 30 gals.
Scale of charges—assessment charge, 1s. 6d. in the £; ⅓ extra if from high level.
Price per 1,000 gals., trade, 1s. 6d.; municipal purposes, by agreement (4½d. per
load for roads); domestic, nil.
Number of meters, 58.
Length of mains, about 50 miles.
Total water rent received, £3,641 for 1906.

Great Grimsby, Lincs. Railways, G.C. and G.N. Distance from London, 155 miles.
Authority, Great Grimsby Waterworks Co., Ltd.
Chairman, W. Bennett.
Secretaries, Grange and Wintringham.
Engineer and Manager, Henry Hewins,
Office, Town Hall Square.
Share capital paid up, £100,000.
Dividend, 10 per cent.
Towns and villages in the area supplied—Grimsby and Cleethorpes, &c.
Works established, 1864.
Total population supplied, 90,000.
Annual supply of water, 1,231,000,000 gals.
Daily consumption per head—domestic, 20 gals.; trade, 7 gals.
Source of supply, artesian boring.
Storage capacity, 350,000 gals.
Character of water, medium hard, quality excellent, no filtering.
Death rate, 13·050 per 1,000.
Number of meters, 427.
Price per 1,000 gals., 1s. to 4d., according to quantity.

Great Harwood (supplied by ACCRINGTON).

Great Holland (supplied by TENDRING HUNDRED WATERWORKS Co.).

Great Marlow. Railway, G.W. Distance from London, 36 miles.
Authority, Great Marlow Water Co., Ltd.
Office, Beaufort Cottage, Marlow.
Towns and villages in the area supplied—Marlow, Little Marlow, Bourne End,
Wooburn, Bisham.
Works established, 1884; reconstructed 1889. Special Act, 1889.
Total population supplied, 5,000, out of estimated 9,000 in district.
Daily consumption per head, 22 gals.
Source of supply—chalk, 130 feet below sea level.
Character of water, hard, with carbonate of lime.
System of filtration, none.
Length of mains, 12 miles.
Scale of charges—assessment charge, rateable value.
Price per 1,000 gals., 2s.

Great Neston, Cheshire (supplied by BIRKENHEAD).

(145)

Great Sankey (supplied by WARRINGTON).

Great Shelford (supplied by CAMBRIDGE).

Great Yarmouth, Norfolk. Railway, G.E. Distance from London, 121 miles.
Authority, Company.
Chairman, R. H. Inglis Palgrave.
Engineer and Manager, Joseph Hawksley.
Secretary, T. A. Rising.
Consulting Engineers, T. & C. Hawksley.
Share capital paid up, including preference, £242,500.
Loan   ,,   ,,   £53,500.
Dividend, 4 per cent. ordinary ; interest on loan, 4 per cent.
Works established, 1853. Special Acts, 1853, 1857, 1869, 1880, 1899.
Population supplied, estimated 55,000.

Greenford (supplied by RICKMANSWORTH).

Greenisland (supplied by DUBLIN).

Green Mount (supplied by BURY).

Greenock. Railways, Caledonian and G. and S.W. Distance from London, 422¼ miles.
Authority, Corporation of Greenock.
Office, Municipal Buildings.
Loan capital, £446,498.
Works established, 1825.
Special Acts, 1825, 1845, 1865, 1869, 1875, 1901.
Total population supplied, 68,756.
Sources of supply, gathering grounds from trap rock.
Storage capacity, 4,212,500,000 gals.
Character of water, soft.
Death rate, 19·8 per 1,000.
Number of meters, 228.
Scale of charges—assessment charge, 6d. in the £ of rental value.
Price per 1,000 gals., 3¾d. first 6,000,000 (per quarter), 1d. per 1,000 above that
    quantity.

Greetland (supplied by HALIFAX).

Greetwell (supplied by LINCOLN).

Greyshott (supplied by WEY VALLEY).

Grindleton, Lancs. (supplied by CLITHEROE).

Gristhorpe, Yorks. (supplied by FILEY).

(146)

Groby (supplied by Leicester).

Grosmont, Yorks. (supplied by Whitby).

Grove, Berks. (supplied by Wantage).

Guernsey.
Authority, Guernsey Water Company, Ld.
Chairman, William J. Davey.
Secretary, Ernest D. Davey, A.C.A.
Offices, 28, Victoria Street, Westminster, London, S.W., and Guernsey.
Consulting Engineer, E. M. Eaton, C.E.
Share capital paid up, £35,700. Div., nil.
Loan   „   „   £30,000 at 4 per cent. ; £14,575 at 4½ per cent.
Works established, 1895 ; new works completed, 1897. Formation of new company, October, 1906.
Total population supplied, 7,000 ; population of island, 40,000.
Area supplied, the whole island.
Sources of supply—wells and drifts in granite formation for pure water supply, and large storage quarries for a separate glass-house supply.
Storage capacity, 50,000,000 gals. of rain water for horticultural purposes, in addition to reservoir for domestic use.
Character of water, exceptionally good and wholesome.
Filtration, none.
Annual supply, about 40,000,000 gals. from pure supply.
     „   „   „   20,000,000   „   „   glass-house supply.
Average daily supply per head—domestic, 15 gals.
Maximum day's supply, 500,000 gals. in August.
Authorised and present charge, 5 per cent. on R.V.
     „   charge by meter, 1s. 6d. per 1,000 gals.; present average charge, 1s. 2d.
No. of meters, 750.
Length of mains, about 50 miles.

Guildford, Surrey.   Railways, S.E., L.B. S.C., L.S.W.   Distance from London, 28 miles.
Authority, Town Council of the Borough of Guildford.
Chairman, Alderman F. F. Smallpeice, J.P.
Town Clerk, F. S. Miller.
Borough Engineer and Surveyor, C. G. Mason, A.M.I.C.E.
Office, Tuns Gate, Guildford.
Total capital invested, £42,082. Loans outstanding, £13,067.
Annual profit, including " capital charges," £3,000.
Works established, 1707. Totally acquired by Council, 1865. Special Act, 1886.
Total population supplied, 21,000. Number of services, 4,535.
Average death rate, 12·3 per 1,000.
District of supply, Guildford, Shalford, Arlington, and part of Stoke.
Source of supply—8 ft. well 36 ft. deep, and a 15½ ft. well with borehole 329 ft. deep.

GUILDFORD—*continued.*

Section of 15½ in. borehole at the Guildford Waterworks—

	Feet.	Inches.
Made ground	6	6
Dark sand	1	0
Clean sharp sand	4	0
Sand and ballast	6	0
Ballast sand and chalk	7	0
Chalk and flints	21	0
„ with less flints	39	0
Gray chalk	1	6
Chalk and flints, in layers, (10 ft. cement joint) ...	29	0
„ „ with gray layers	23	0
White chalk...	49	6
Chalk marl	4	6
Gray chalk	59	0
„ „ marl	5	0
White chalk...	4	0
Gray „	28	0
White rock chalk	24	0
Rock chalk with flints	6	0
Melbourne rock	11	0
	329	0

Annual supply of water, from shallow well, 248,000,000 gals.
" " " " deep boring, little used at present.
" estimated supply available, from shallow well, 313,900,000 gals.
" " " " " deep boring, 237,250,000 „
Natural rest level of water—below surface, 10 ft. ; above O.D., 97·40 ft.
Level of water when pumping 918,000 gals. per day, 32 ft. ; above O.D., 75·40 ft.
Surface formation of drainage area, arable and pasture land.
Strata yielding springs, chalk.
Authority has no control over drainage area.
Character of water, clear and sparkling; total hardness, 15° (Clark).
Filtration, none ; softening, none.
Storage capacity—service reservoir, Porlay Hill,   450,000 gals., covered.
" " " " Semaphore Road, 600,000 „ „
" " " " Albury Road, 100,000 „ „
Pumping station, Millhead, capacity 1,000,000 gals. per day.
Head on distributing mains—maximum, 280 ft. ; minimum, 46 ft.
Average daily supply per head—domestic, 21·3 gals. ; trade, 11 gals.
Maximum day's supply, 918,000 gals. in July.
Annual supply—domestic, ... 148,333,000 gals.
                 trade, ... 12,720,000 „
                 municipal, ... 23,000,000 „
                 in bulk to Railway Co. 48,352,000 „
Charges authorised and charged—domestic, 5 to 7½ per cent. on R.V.
" by meter per 1,000 gals.—1s. in borough ; 1s. 6d. outside.
Number of meters, 82.
Length of mains, 38 miles.

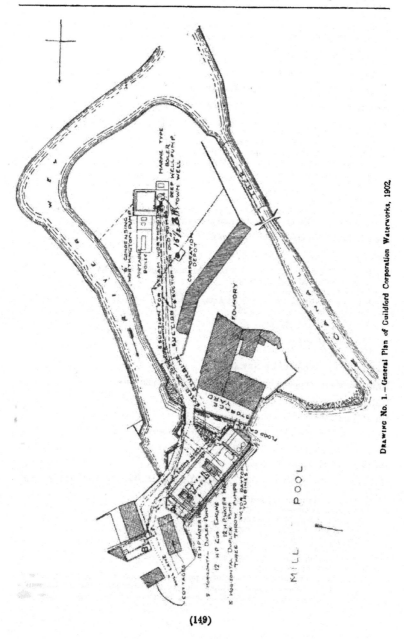

DʀAWɪɴɢ No. 1. — General Plan of Guildford Corporation Waterworks, 1902.

Guiseley, Yorks. Railway, M. Distance from London, 205 miles.
　　Authority, Guiseley Waterworks Co., Ltd.
　　Population supplied, 4,558.
　　No returns supplied.

Gwendale (supplied by RIPON).

Gwernaffield, Flint. (supplied by HAWARDEN).

Hackington, Kent (supplied by CANTERBURY).

Haddington, Scotland. Railway, N.B. Distance from London, 388 miles.
　　Authority, Corporation.
　　Total population supplied, 4,000.
　　Daily consumption per head, about 30 gals.
　　Sources of supply—springs, Lammermoor Hills, etc., gravitation.
　　Storage capacity, none.
　　Character of water, good, pure, free from lime.
　　System of filtration, none.
　　Scale of charges—
　　　　Assessment charge, 6d. in the £ on owners and occupiers, one half each.
　　　　Price per 1,000 gals., 8½d. for manufacturing purposes.

Hafod, Denbigh (supplied by RUABON).

Hagley (supplied by STOURBRIDGE).

Hailsham, Sussex. Railway, L.B.S.C. Distance from London, 64 miles.
　　Share capital paid up, £16,000.
　　Dividend, 4¼ per cent.
　　Works established, 1884; Special Acts, 1885.
　　Total population supplied, 3,369.
　　Source of supply, lands.
　　Storage capacity, 150,000 gals.
　　Character of water, 8° hardness.
　　Office, 13, North Street.

Halam, Notts. (supplied by NEWARK).

Hale, Cheshire (supplied by NORTH CHESHIRE WATER CO.).

Hale, Lancs. (supplied by WIDNES).

Hale Bank (supplied by WIDNES).

Halesowen (supplied by SOUTH STAFFS. WATERWORKS CO.).

Hale Wood (supplied by WIDNES).

Halfway (supplied by LLANELLY).

Halifax, Yorks. Railways, G.N., L. and Y., M., L.N.W. Distance from London,
194 miles.
　　Authority, Halifax Corporation.
　　Chairman, M. Crossley.
　　Town Clerk, Keighley Walton.
　　Engineer, Richard James Hartley, C.E.
　　Office, Gibbet Hill.
　　Loans outstanding, £940,099.
　　Annual loss on undertaking, £14,351.
　　Works incorporated, 1848.
　　Local authorities within district of supply:—Brighouse, Clifton, Coley, Elland,
　　　　Greetland, Hebden Bridge, Hipperholme, Luddenden Foot, Morley, Mytholm-
　　　　royd, Norwood Green, Soothill (Upper), Southowram, Sowerby Bridge, and
　　　　Thornhill.

HALIFAX—*continued.*

　　Total population supplied, 108,000 in the borough ; 120,000, approximate, outside.
　　Sources of supply—moorland water and springs.
　　Character of water, soft, acid, peaty, 2° to 3° hardness.
　　Filtration, practically none ; softening, none.
　　Storage in impounding reservoirs, 1,286,474,000 gals. ; in service reservoirs, 59,458,000 gals.
　　Head on distributing mains—maximum, 240 lbs. per sq. in.
　　Total quantity of water supplied per annum, 1,760,211,000 gals.
　　Daily consumption per head in the borough, domestic, 15 gals. ; trade, 12 gals.
　　Maximum day's supply, 10,577,000 gals. in July, 1906.
　　Scale of charges, from 8¼ per cent. to 4 per cent. according to scale ; outside borough, 50 per cent. extra.
　　Price per 1,000 gals., 8d. to 6d., by scale.
　　Number of meters, 1,000.
　　Length of distributing mains (approx.), 150 miles.

Hallow (supplied by WORCESTER).

Halstead, Essex.
　　Authority, Urban District Council.
　　Chairman, R. L. Hughes, J.P.
　　Secretary, R. R. Morton.
　　Resident Engineer, W. A. Nicholson.
　　Office, Head Street, Halstead.
　　Total outlay, £12,150.
　　Loans outstanding, £3,644.
　　Annual profit, including capital charges, £215.
　　Works established, 1862 ; additions, 1889 to 1901.
　　Average death rate, 16·4 per 1,000.
　　Area of supply—Halstead Urban District.
　　Sources of supply,·deep well in chalk, 250 ft.
　　Character of water, rather hard, but very pure.　Calcareous.
　　Storage capacity—tanks, 135,000 gals.
　　Pressure on distributing mains—maximum, 65 lbs. ; minimum, 8 lbs. per sq. in.
　　Annual supply of water, 58,500,000 gals.
　　Daily consumption per head—24 gals., all purposes.
　　Assessment charge, 5 per cent. on rental value.
　　Price per 1,000 gals. by meter, 1s.
　　Number of meters, 20.
　　Length of supply mains, ½ mile ; distributing, 6¼ miles.

Halton (supplied by LEEDS).

Halton. *See* RUNCORN.

Hambledon, Surrey (partly supplied by GODALMING).

Hamilton, Scotland.　Railways, N. B. and Caledonian.　Distance from London, 400 miles.
　　Authority, Hamilton Town Council.
　　Chairman of Council, Provost Keith.
　　Chairman of Water Committee, Bailie Smellie.
　　Secretaries, W. Pollock and P. M. Kirkpatrick (joint Town Clerks).
　　Engineer and Manager, W. H. Purdie.
　　Consulting Engineer, W. Robertson Copland, 144, West Regent Street, Glasgow.
　　Office, Burgh Buildings.
　　Loans outstanding, £127,705.
　　Works established, 1857.　Special Acts, 1875, 1878, 1888, 1898 1903.
　　Total population supplied, 37,000.

HAMILTON—*continued*.

    Average death rate, 15·24 per 1,000.
    Area supplied, 1,236 acres, Hamilton only.
    Sources of supply—drainage area (gathering grounds).
    Character of water, a good potable water from peaty ground ; total hardness, 2·3°.
    System of filtration, downward (sand, gravel, road metal), and 1 mechanical filter.
    Storage capacity in impounding reservoir, 315,038,000 gals.
    Pressure on distributing mains—maximum, 90 lbs.; minimum, 40 lbs. per sq. in.
    Annual supply of water, 803,000,000 gals.
    Daily consumption per head—domestic, 53 gals.; trade, 8 gals.
    Scale of charges—assessment charge, domestic rate, 2d. in £ on rental; public
      rate, 6d. in £ on rental.
      Price per 1,000 gals., trade, 6d.
    Total water rent received, £5,262.
    Number of meters, 158.
    Length of mains—supply, 18 miles ; distributing, 20 miles.

Hammerwick (supplied by SOUTH STAFFS. WATERWORKS Co.).

Hampden, Wilts. (supplied by HIGHWORTH).

Hampton, Middlesex (supplied by GRAND JUNCTION WATERWORKS Co.).

Hampton, Worcester (supplied by EVESHAM).

Handcross (supplied by CUCKFIELD).

Handsworth, Staffs. (supplied by BIRMINGHAM).

Handsworth, Yorks. (supplied by SHEFFIELD).

Hangleton (supplied by BRIGHTON).

Hanley (supplied by STAFFORDSHIRE POTTERIES WATERWORKS Co.).

Hanworth (supplied by SOUTH WEST SUBURBAN).

Harbledown, Kent (supplied by CANTERBURY).

Harborne (supplied by BIRMINGHAM).

Hardway, Hants. (supplied by GOSPORT).

Harefield, Middlesex (supplied by RICKMANSWORTH).

Harlington, Middlesex (supplied by RICKMANSWORTH).

Harlow (supplied by HERTS AND ESSEX WATERWORKS Co.).

Harpenden, Herts. Railways, M. and G.N. Branch. Distance from London, 25
miles.
    Authority, The Harpenden Water Co., Ld.
    Chairman, John R. Brown.
    Engineer, Wm. R. Phillips.
    Secretary, Alfred J. Lake.
    Office, Castle Street, Luton.
    Share capital paid up, £11,500.
    Loan   ,,   £2,250.

HARPENDEN—*continued.*

Total water rent received, £2,110.
Dividend, 10 per cent. A, 6 per cent. B, 5 per cent. C.
Works established, 1896. Special Act, Provisional Order.
Total population supplied, 5,100.
Sources of supply, deep wells in chalk.
Character of water, excellent.
Storage capacity, 170,000 gals.
Annual supply of water, 38,500,000 gals.
Daily consumption per head—domestic, 17·5 gals.; trade, 2·7 gals.
Maximum day's supply, 150,000 gals.
Assessment charge, poor rate assessment, £800.
Price per 1,000 gals., 1s.
Number of meters, 21.
Length of mains, 11 miles.

Harpurhey (supplied by MANCHESTER).

Harraby (supplied by CARLISLE).

Harrogate, Yorks. Railway, N.E. Distance from London, 200 miles.
Authority, Harrogate Corporation.
Chairman, Alderman W. H. Milner, J.P.
Town Clerk, J. Turner Taylor.
Engineer in charge Fred. J. Dixon, F.G.S., A.M.I.C.E.
Office, 14, Albert Street, Harrogate.
Loans outstanding, £727,476 19s. 6d.
Gross receipts for 1906, £24,506.
Works established, 1846. Purchased by local authority, May, 1898.
Special Acts, Harrogate Water Works Acts, 1846, 1849; Harrogate Water Order,
1880; Harrogate Water Works Act, 1897; Harrogate Corporation Water Works
Transfer Act, 1897; Harrogate Water Act, 1901; Harrogate Water Act, 1903;
and 1904.
Estimated population actually supplied—Harrogate, 42,205; in the season, 52,200;
Knaresborough Urban, 5,500. Total 57,700.
Average death rate, 12·1 per 1,000.
Towns and villages within the area of control, Harrogate, Knaresborough Urban;
also parishes of Pannal, Bilton, Starbeck, Scriven, and Knaresborough.
Source of supply, drainage areas and impounding reservoirs on clays and shales,
resting on the millstone grit series, situated on the Oak Beck, a tributary of the
River Nidd, West Riding of York; also on the Pott Beck, tributary of River
Burn, North Riding of York.
Total quantity of water drawn per annum—
From drainage areas and surface springs, 451,000,000 gallons.
Estimated total quantity of water available per day—
　　　　From drainage areas ...　　...　　...　　...　　1,576,931 gals.
　　　　　,,　surface springs ...　　...　　...　　...　　15,000　,,
Estimated maximum daily discharge at points of collection ... 25,000,000 gals.
　　,,　　minimum　　,,　　　　,,　　　,,　　...　100,000　,,
　　,,　　average　　　,,　　　　,,　　　,,　　...　1,576,931　,,
Average annual rainfall over drainage area, 28·58 inches (period 11 years),
calculated 30 years' mean, 30·20 inches.
Population on drainage areas, 50.
Nature and extent of cultivation of ditto, moor and rough pasture, 400 acres
under cultivation. No arable.
The Water authority have not secured any control of drainage area, but
Corporation thoroughly drain all farm buildings and keep tanks cleaned out
under agreement with owner.

HARROGATE—*continued.*

Surface formation of drainage areas, clays and shale, resting on millstone grit series.

Filtration, sand, and by Candy's automatic compressed air and oxidizing filters.

Softening, none.

				Watershed in acres.
Storage reservoirs, Scargill	capacity, 200,000,000 gals.	1,100
,, ,, Upper Beaver Dyke	,, 30,000,000 ,,	} 1,260
,, ,, Lower Beaver Dyke	,, 118,000,000 ,,	
,, ,, Ten Acres	,, 35,000,000 ,,	410
,, ,, Roundhills ...	,, 575,000,000 ,,	3,000
Service reservoirs, No. 1, Irongate Bridge	capacity, 3,000,000 gals., uncovered.	
,, ,, No. 2, ,, ,,	,, 4,000,000 ,, ,,	
,, ,, No. 3, ,, ,,	,, 7,000,000 ,, ,,	
,, ,, Harlow Hill ,,	,, 14,000,000 ,, ,,	

Analyses of water, September 24th, 1906 : Scargill, taken out of Harlow Hill service reservoir; Beaver Dyke and Ten Acres, taken out of Irongate Bridge service reservoirs.

The sample contains in grains per gallon (parts per 70,000), after filtration—

	*Scargill.	‡Beaver, &c.
Chlorides equal to common salt	1·84	1·84
Calcium sulphate	4·55	4·08
Alkaline and calcium magnesium carbonates, &c.	trace	0·09
Volatile and organic matter	0·05	1·80
Total dissolved solids	6·44	7·81
Chlorine ... ,,..	1·12	1·12
Ammonia	0·008	0·002
Organic ammonia	0·003	0·007
Oxygen required to oxidise organic matter in 4 hours	0·003	0·148
Hardness before boiling, ...	2·7°	3·1°
,, after ,, ...	2·5°	3·0°

Colour, blue.

Sediment, very minute, principally peaty matter.

Microscopic examination does not show the presence of animalculæ.

Head on distributing mains—maximum, 245·4 feet ; minimum, 54·4 feet.

Annual supply of water, 569,776,795 gals.

In bulk to other authorities, included in domestic, as not metered.

Average daily supply per head, domestic, 23·4 gals. ; trade, 8·3 gals.

Maximum day's consumption, holiday season, 2,058,180 gals. (August.)

Scale of charges for domestic purposes—

Where the rateable value of premises does not exceed £7 10 ... £8 10 0 {per cent. per ann.

,,	,,	,,	,,	,,	12	0 ... 10 per cent.
,,	,,	,,	,,	,,	30	0 ... 8 ,,
,,	,,	,,	,,	,,	60	0 ... 7 ,,
,,	,,	,,	,,	,,	120	0 ... 6 ,,

Where the rateable value exceeds £120, the rate of £5 10 0 per ann. on such rateable value.

Meter price domestic and trade ...	under 100,000, 1s. per 1,000 gals.
,, ,, ,, ...	,, 300,000, 11d. ,,
,, ,, ,, ...	,, 500,000, 10d. ,,
,, ,, ,, ...	over 500,000 9d. ,,
,, municipal purposes	7½d. ,,

Number of meters in use, 150.

Length of supply mains, 16½ miles ; distributing mains, 71¾ miles.

---

* In its present state this water is of good quality and well suited for a town supply.

‡ In its present state this water is of good quality and well suited for a public supply. The total dissolved solids and hardness are rather less than in the Harlow Hill water.

Hartlepools, The, Durham. (G. & W.). Railways, L.N.W., G.N., N.E. Distance from London, 247 miles.
　　Authority, Hartlepool Gas and Water Co.
　　Engineer and Manager, Thos. Bower, M.I.C.E.
　　Secretary, W. Scott.
　　Office and Works, West Hartlepool.
　　Date of formation, 1845; Special Acts, 1846, 1849, 1855, 1867, 1874, 1878, 1898, 1900.
　　Capital paid up (Gas and Water)—
　　　　5 per cent. maximum ordinary stock, £672,000.
　　　　Loan capital paid up, £105,150.
　　　　Dividends, 5, 5, and 5 per cent.
　　　　Interest on loans, 3, 3¼, 3½ and 3¾ per cent.
　　Total population supplied, 86,000.

Hartlip (supplied by Rainham).

Harwich (supplied by Tendring Hundred Waterworks Co.).

Hasbury (supplied by South Staffs. Waterworks Co.).

Haslingden, Lancs. (supplied by Bury).

Hassocks, Sussex (supplied by Burgess Hill).

Hastings, Sussex. Railways, S.E. & L.B.S.C. Distance from London, 62 miles.
　　Authority, Corporation.
　　Chairman, Alderman Tree.
　　Secretary, B. F. Meadows, Town Clerk.
　　Engineer, P. H. Palmer, M.I.C.E.
　　Debt, £210,000.
　　Works established, 1832.
　　Total population supplied, 75,000.
　　Death rate, 14·20 per 1,000.
　　Area supplied, 4,769 acres.
　　Source of supply, deep wells entirely.
　　Character of water, very soft.
　　Annual supply of water, 560,000,000 gals.
　　Daily consumption per head, 18 gals.
　　Scale of charges—assessment charge, 1s. 4d. in the £.
　　Price per 1,000 gals., 2s.
　　Number of meters, 274.

Haswell Durham. (G. & W.) Railways, G.N. and N.E.
　　E. M. Clay, Lessee.
　　Population supplied, 6,276.
　　No returns supplied.

Hatton (supplied by Warrington).

Havant (supplied by Portsmouth).

Haverfordwest, Pembroke. (G. & W.) Railway, G.W. Distance from London, 264¾ miles.
　　Authority, Corporation.
　　Chairman, James Reynolds (Mayor).
　　Secretary, F. J. Warren, F.S.A.A., Incorporated Accountant.
　　Engineer and Manager, J. Gibbon.
　　Office, Borough Accountant's Offices,
　　Loan, £17,980; repaid, £13,448.
　　Interest on loan, 4½ per cent., 3¾ per cent.
　　Area supplied, Haverfordwest only.

HAVERFORDWEST—*continued*.

Works established, 1868.
Annual supply of water, 36,500,000 gals., estimated.
Daily consumption per head—domestic and trade, 16¾ gals.
Sources of supply, gravitation and pumping.
Storage capacity, 268,000 gals.
System of filtration, none.
Character of water, excellent.
Average death rate, 18·46 per 1,000.
Length of mains, 5 miles.
Scale of charges—assessment charge, 1s. in the £ on net annual value for domestic purposes; 1s. 6d. net for trade.
Municipal purposes; £5 per year charged to general district fund for flushing sewers.

Haverhill, Suffolk.
Authority, Urban District Council.
No returns supplied.

Hawarden, Flintshire. Railways, L.N.W., G.C., and W.M. and C. Distance from London, 186 miles.
Authority, Hawarden and District Waterworks Co.
Chairman, James Tomkinson, M.P.
Secretary, E. Andrews, 27, Eastgate Row, N., Chester.
Engineer, William Simmons, at the Works, Buckley, N. Chester.
Office, 27, Eastgate Row, N. Chester.
Share capital paid up, £36,730. Debenture bonds, £7,500.
Dividend, 3½ per cent.
Works established, 1886; Special Act, Hawarden and District Waterworks Act, 1883.
Total population of area supplied, 17,500.
Towns and villages in the area supplied, Hawarden, Ewloe, Buckley, Sandy-croft, Queensferry, Shotton, Aston, Mancott, Northop Hall, Broughton, Pantymwyn and Gwernaffield.
Source of supply, impounding reservoir; storage at Cilcain.
Storage reservoir, 14,000 gals.; service reservoir, 2,000 gals.
Character of water, 2½° hardness.
Filtration, none; softening, none.
Average daily supply per head, 15¼ gals.
Authorised charge by meter, 1s. 6d. per 1,000 for first 50,000, and 1s. after.
Number of meter, 20.

Hawick. Railway, N.B. Distance from Edinburgh, 50 miles.
Authority, the Town Council of the Burgh of Hawick.
Chairman, John Melrose, Provost.
Secretary, Robert Purdon, Town Clerk, Hawick.
Engineer in charge, Charles Brown, Burgh Surveyor.
Office, Municipal Buildings, Hawick.
Total capital invested, including loans, £32,200.
Works established—Allan Supply, 1868; Dodburn Supply, 1881.
Total population of area of control—1881, 16,184; 1891, 19,204; 1901, 18,000.
Supply of water (1906)—
　　For domestic, trade, and municipal purposes, 1,384,953 gals. per 24 hours.
Average daily supply per head, domestic, 40 gals.; trade and special purposes 36·94 gals.
Towns and villages within the area of control, with population (1901 Census)—Burgh of Hawick and outskirts in county. Population, 18,000.
Sources of supply in use—drainage areas situated at (1) Allan Water, at Lochburn Plantation; (2) from Dodburn, to the west of Acreknowe Farm.

HAWICK—*continued.*

 Population on drainage area, about 20.
 Nature of ditto, hill pasture.
 Water authority have no control of drainage area.
 Storage reservoirs, Acreknowe　...　...　capacity 80,000,000 gals.
  ,,　　　,,　　Allan　...　...　..　　,,　　1,000,000　,,
 Service　,,　　Loanhead　...　...　,,　　　523,000　,,　covered.
 Charges authorised, 6d. per 1,000 gals.
 Number of meters in use, 44.
 Length of supply mains, 8 miles ; distributing mains, 25½ miles.

Hawkhurst (supplied by CRANBROOK).

Hawkinge (supplied by FOLKESTONE).

Hawkshaw Lane (supplied by BURY).

Hawley, Hants. (supplied by FRIMLEY).

Hawn (supplied by SOUTH STAFFS. WATERWORKS CO.).

Haworth (supplied by KEIGHLEY).

Hawthorne Hill (supplied by MAIDENHEAD).

Hay, Brecknock, S. Wales. Railway, M. Distance from London, 164¼ miles.
 Authority, Hay Urban District Council.
 Chairman, James Evans.
 Secretary, R. T. Griffiths, Hay.
 Engineer in charge, David Morgan, Surveyor, 19, Castle Street, Hay.
 Consulting Engineer, J. Linacre.
 Total capital invested, including loans, £3,800.
 Towns and villages within the area of control, with population of each (1901
  census)—Hay, 1,680 ; Cusop, 150.
 Works established, 1862. Purchased by local authority, 1895.
 Total population of area of control—1881, 1,930 ; 1891, 1,920 ; 1901 1,830.
 Estimated population actually supplied, 1,750.
 Sources of supply in use—drainage areas situated at Hay Common.
  Surface springs situated at Llangwathan.
   Estimated maximum daily discharge at points
        of collection ...　...　70,000 gals.
   ,,　　minimum　　　　,,　　　,,　　32,000　,,
   ,,　　average　　　　,,　　　,,　　50,000　,,
 Population on drainage area, 30.
 Nature of ditto, mostly pasture.
 Water authority have no control of drainage area.
 Character of water—spring, rather hard.
 Filtering area provided, 450 square yards in one filter-bed.
 Storage reservoirs, Hay Common, capacity, 385,000 gals.
 Annual supply of water—
   For domestic purposes　...　...　...　...　11,680,000 gals.
   ,,　trade　　,,　　...　...　...　...　500,000　,,
   ,,　municipal　,,　　...　...　...　...　500,000　,,
 Daily consumption per head, 16 gallons.
 Total quantity of water drawn per annum—
   From drainage areas　...　...　...　...　1,000,000 gals.
   ,,　surface springs　...　...　...　...　11,680,000　,,

HAY—*continued.*

Scale of charges for domestic supply—
Houses assessed at not exceeding £6 per annum, 8s. 8d.
             ,,   ,,   £10   ,,   10s.
           ,,   at over £10 per annum 1s. 2d. in £ (annual Poor Rate).
Charge per meter from 5,000 at 1s. 3d. per 1,000 gals.
           ,,   to   70,000 at 11d.
           ,,   above 100,000 at 10¼d. per 1,000 gals.
Length of distributing mains, 3 miles.

Hayes, Middlesex (supplied by RICKMANSWORTH).

Hayfield, Derbyshire. Railway, M. Distance from London, 175½ miles.
Authority, Hayfield Gaslight and Waterworks Co., Ld.
Office, Hayfield, *via* Stockport.
Manager and Secretary, Wm. Whitehead.

Haylands, Isle of Wight (supplied by RYDE).

Hayle, Cornwall. Railway, G.W. Distance from London, 313 miles.
Authority, Hayle Urban District Council.
Chairman, Frank Harvey.
Clerk to Authority, Edward Boase.
Resident Engineer, Z. W. Chinn.
Office, Local Government Office, Hayle.
Works established, 1868.
Population supplied, about 1,600.
District of supply—parts of St. Erith and Phillack, called Hayle Urban District.
Source of supply—Spring in winter, supplemented by windmill in dry summer
    months pumping from disused mine.
Storage capacity in service reservoirs, 165,000 gals.
Head on distributing mains—max., 105 ft.; min., 90 ft.
Assessment rate, 6d. per cent on rateable value.
Charge per meter, 6d. per 1,000 gals. to factory and shops; outside district, 1s.
    per 1,000 gals.

Haywards Heath (supplied by CUCKFIELD).

Healey (supplied by MASHAM).

Heamoor (supplied by MADRON).

Heathfield (supplied by TICEHURST).

Heatley (supplied by LYMM).

Heaton Park (supplied by BURY).

Heavitree (supplied by EXETER).

Hebden Bridge, Yorks. Railway, G.N. Distance from London, 200 miles.
Authority, Urban District Council.
Engineer, Surveyor and Manager, Tom Waddingham.
Office, Council Offices.
Population supplied, 7,600.
Source of supply, Halifax mains in bulk.

Hebburn (supplied by SUNDERLAND).

Heckmondwike. *See* DEWSBURY.

Heckwick (supplied by WARRINGTON).

Heddon-on-the-Wall (supplied by Newcastle-on-Tyne).

Hedfield (supplied by Ripon).

Helensburgh, Scotland. Railway, N.B. Distance from Edinburgh, 67 miles.
Authority, Helensburgh Town Council.
Convener, D. S. MacLachlan.
Clerks to Authority, Geo. and J. B. MacLachlan, Joint Town Clerks.
Engineer and Manager, J. R. Wilson, C.E.
Office, Municipal Buildings.
Works established, 1868; added to in 1874, 1888 and 1904,
Total population supplied, 8,500.
Area supplied, Helensburgh and 12 small villas outside of burgh.
Sources of supply—small stream and springs 4½ miles from Helensburgh.
Character of water, pure and clear, same as Loch Katrine.
System of filtration—two small sand filters, filter only ⅛th day's supply.
Storage capacity, 83,100,000 gals.
Head on distributing mains, max., 300 ft.
Annual supply of water (1906)—173,419,408 gals.
Average daily supply per head, domestic only, 55·48 gals.
Scale of charges—assessment charge, 5d. in the £ on rental.
　Charge for municipal purposes, 1d. in the £ on rental.
　Price per 1,000 gals., trade, 5d.
Number of meters, 20.
Length of mains—supply, 6 miles; distributing, 12 miles.
Total water rent received, £1,500 for year.

Helmshore (supplied by Bury).

Helmsley, Yorks. Railway, N.E. Distance from London, 219 miles.
Owner, Earl Feversham, Duncombe Park, Helmsley.
Engineer and manager, Robert Sturdy.
Office, Church Street.
Towns and villages in the area supplied, Helmsley and Duncombe Park.
Works established, 1859.
Total population supplied, 1,572.
Source of supply, springs.
Storage capacity, 160,000 gals., 6in. bore gravitation pipe from reservoir.
Character of water, medium hardness.
Number of meters, 1.
Length of mains, 2 miles.

Helston, Cornwall. Railway, G.W. Distance from London, 318 miles.
Authority, Helston Porthleven Water Co.
Population supplied, 3,198.
No returns supplied.

Hemel Hempstead. Railways, L.N.W. and M. Distance from London, 24 miles.
Authority, Hemel Hempstead Corporation.
Chairman of Committee, C. E. Gray.
Clerk and Collector, A. D. Keen.
Engineer (Resident), G. Carter.
Engineer (Consulting), A. F. Phillips, C.E.
Office, Marlowes.
Total capital invested, including loans, £52,563 2s. 6d.
Towns and villages in the area supplied—Hemel Hempstead, Leverstock Green,
　and Apsley.
Works established, 1866.
Special Acts, Provisional Order, 1896; Purchase Act, 1900.
Purchased by local authority, June, 1901.

HEMEL HEMPSTEAD—*continued.*

Total population supplied, 14,000.
Annual supply of water, 120,000,000 gals. (estimated)
Daily consumption per head for all purposes, domestic, trade, and municipal, about 23 gals.
Estimated total quantity of water available per annum, not known.
Source of supply, well.
Character of water, good, rather chalky.
Death rate, 15 per 1,000
Pumping station, Marlowes.
Service reservoirs—three (storage and service reservoirs are the same, each one answering both purposes).
Number of meters in use, 27.
Length of distributing mains, about 30 miles.
Scale of charges, assessment charge, domestic, 6 per cent. on R.V.
Price per 1.000 gals.—domestic and trade, and general purposes, 1s. per gal.

Hendon Middlesex (supplied by COLNE VALLEY and WEST MIDDLESEX WATER Cos.).

Henley-on-Thames. Railway, G.W. Distance from London, 35¾ miles.
Authority, Henley-on-Thames Water Company, Ltd.
Chairman, Archibald Brakspear.
Secretary, Alex. Groves, 19, Reading Road, Henley.
Engineer in charge, George Potter.
Consulting engineer, Wm. Matthews.

Total capital invested—A shares	...	...	...	£20,000
B ,,	...	...	...	3,000
Premiums ...	...	...	...	1,701
4 per cent. debenture stock	...	...	...	6,000
				£30,701

Dividend, 6 per cent. A, £4 4s. per cent.
Interest on debentures, 4 per cent.
Works established, 1881.
Special Acts, Henley-on-Thames Water Orders, 1881, 1901.
Total population of area of control, 1881, 5,700 ; 1891, 5,760 ; 1901, 6,980 ; 1907, 6,500.
Total number of consumers, 1,810 (*i.e.*, connections to houses, cottages and meters).
Estimated population actually supplied, 6,500.
Source of supply in use, borings to the chalk 240 feet deep (8 inch diam.) situated at Henley within the borough.
Water authority have no control of drainage area.
Natural rest level of water below surface, 25ft. ; above Ordnance datum, 121ft. ; Bench mark is 147·4.
Level of water below surface (when pumping 238,000 gals. per day), 27ft.
Death rate, 13 per 1,000.
Pumping station, Henley, capacity, 600,000 gals. per day.
Towns and villages within the area of control—Henley-on-Thames, part of Shiplake, and Remenham.
Character of water—hardness before treatment, 22° ; and after, 8°.
Recent analysis—
  Copy of analysis. Drawn from main after being softened—

Total solid matter	...	...	...	10·500 grains per gal.
Loss at red heat	...	...	...	0·960 ,,
Chlorine	...	...	...	0·994 ,,
Sulphuric acid ...	...	...	...	traces
Carb. of lime...	...	...	...	9·300 grains per gal.

HENLEY-ON-THAMES—*continued.*

Ammonia (free)...	...	...	...	none
„ (albuminoid)		...	...	none
Nitrates ...	..	...	...	none
Nitrites ...	...	...	...	none
Hardness	...	...	...	8° Clark's scale.
„ permanent	...	...	...	4° „

No vegetable matter; colour, clear pale yellow; no smell.
Filtering, after softening (Clark's process), filtered through filter cloth, Adkin's process.
Service reservoirs—one, at Badgemore, ¾ mile from works, 168ft. above works; capacity, 246,000 gals., covered.
Head on mains—maximum, 200 feet; minimun, 25 feet.
Annual supply of water (1906)—

For domestic purposes	...	...	...	85,436,000 gals.
„ trade „	...	...	...	2,994,000 „
„ municipal „	...	...	...	3,270,000 „
Maximum day's consumption ...	...	...	...	450,000 „

Total quantity of water drawn per annum (1906)—
　　From deep borings　...　...　...　...　91,700,000 gals.
Estimated total quantity of water available per annum—
　　From deep borings　...　...　...　...　220,000,000 gals.
Pumping machinery—
　2 high pressure Cornish boilers, 15 × 5.
　1 triple expansion Worthington pump.
　2 double acting low-lift pumps.
　2 12-horse single engines.
Assessment charge, 5 and 7 per cent. on rateable value.
Price per 1,000 gals.—domestic, 2s. to 1s.; trade, 1s.; municipal purposes, 10d.
Number of meters in use, 50.
Length of distributing mains, 11 miles.

Hereford. (G. & W.) Railways, G.W., M., L.N.W.　Distance from London, 144¼ miles.
　Authority, Corporation, 1854.
　Office, Town Hall.
　Loan, £13,550.
　Area supplied, 4,680 acres.
　Works established, 1854.　Special Act, 1854.
　Total population supplied, 21,382.
　Annual supply of water, 300,000,000 gals.
　Daily consumption per head, 33 gals.
　Source of supply, River Wye.
　Storage capacity, 4,000,000 gals.
　Character of water, excellent, soft, 6°.
　System of filtration, sand and gravity filters (Nathan & Platt's).
　Average death rate, 15·3 per 1,000.
　Length of mains, 18 miles.
　Scale of charges, assessment charge, 1s. in the £.
　Price per 1,000 gals., 9d. to 6d.

Herne, Kent (supplied by HERNE BAY).

Herne Bay, Kent.　Railway, S.E. & C.R.　Distance from London, 62¾ miles.
　Chairman, A. Telford Simpson, J.P., M.I.C.E.
　Secretary, Walter Colbrook, F.C.I.S.
　Manager and Collector, Geo. J. Lavel.
　Engineer, G. Gooch, A.M.I.C.E.

HERNE BAY—*continued.*

    Office, 38, Parliament Street, London, S.W.
    Share capital paid up, £43,816.   Borrowing powers, £7,950.
    Dividend, 6 per cent. preference, 5½ per cent. ordinary.
    Towns and villages in the area supplied, Herne Ray, Herne, Reculver and Hoath.
    Works established, 1867.   Special Acts, 1867, 1871, 1883, 1888, 1899, and 1906.
    Total population supplied—resident, 10,700; summer, 29,000.
    Sources of supply, wells in chalk.
    Character of water, excellent.
    Scale of charges, assessment R. R.

Herston (supplied by SWANAGE).

Hertford.   Railways, G.N. and G.E.   Distance from London, 24¼ miles.
    Authority, Corporation.
    Chairman, Councillor Ekins,
    Secretary, T. J. Sworder, Town Clerk.
    Inspector, S. Rushden.
    Manager and Engineer, J. H. Jevons, A.M.I.C.E.
    Office, Borough Surveyor's Office.
    Works established, 1862.
    Total population supplied, 9,322.
    Death rate, 15·3 per 1,000.
    Source of supply, wells in the chalk.
    Character of water, hard.
    Storage capacity, 320,000 gals.
    Annual supply of water, 94,000,000 gals.
    Daily consumption per head, 27 gals.
    Scale of charges, assessment charge, 1s. in the £ on rateable value.
    Price per 1,000 gals., domestic, 1s.; trade, 6d., with a minimum charge of 30s.
       per half year for trade purposes, and 75 per cent. per annum on the rateable
       value for domestic purposes.
    Number of meters, 50.
    Length of mains, about 12 miles.
    Total water rent received, £2,250.

Herts and Essex.   Railway, G.E.
    Authority, Herts and Essex Waterworks Co., Ltd.
    Secretary and Manager, William Jones.
    Office, Harlow, Essex.
    Capital expended, £60,000.
    Works established, 1883.   Special Acts, 1879, 1885.
    Population supplied, about 13,000.
    Sources of supply—deep wells into the chalk formation in the parish of
       Sawbridgeworth.
    Parishes supplied—Sawbridgeworth, Harlow, Netteswell, Latton, North Weald,
       Bobbingworth, Coopersale, Epping, Theydon Bois, Theydon Garnon, Lamborne,
       High Ongar, and Chipping Ongar.

Hesketh-with-Becconsall (supplied by PRESTON).

Hessle (supplied by HULL).

Hetton and Easington, Durham.   Railway, N.E.   Distance from London, 270
    miles.
    Authority, Hetton-le-Hole and Easington Lane Water Company, Ltd.

Hetton and Easington—continued.

Chairman, John Fawcett.
Secretary, E. Greenhow.
Engineer, Geo. Thompson.
Office, Hetton-le-Hole.
Share capital paid up, £2,700.
Dividend, 2s. per share per annum, equals 11⅛ per cent. on 18s. called up.
Towns and villages in the area supplied—Hetton-le-Hole, Hetton Down, Easington Lane.
Works established, 1863.
Total population supplied, 16,000.
Annual supply of water, 66,000,000 gals.
Daily consumption per head, 10 gals.
Sources of supply, limestone feeders.
Storage capacity, 750,000 gals.
Character of water, hard.
Scale of charges, 1s. 2d. per 1,000 gals.
Total water rent received, about £1,200 a year.

Hetton-le-Hole, co. Durham. *See* Hetton and Easington.

Heworth (supplied by York).

Hexham, Northumberland.
Authority, Urban District Council.
Population, 7,000.
Assessment for water rate, £32,685.

Hexthorpe (supplied by Doncaster).

Heytesbury, Wilts. Railway, G.W. Distance from London, 109 miles.
Authority, Heytesbury Water Co., Ltd.
Works established, 1892.
Total population supplied, 1,000.
Sources of supply—deep wells through chalk.
Character of water, hard.

Heywood and Middleton. Railway, L. & Y. Distance from London, 206 miles.
Authority, Heywood and Middleton Water Board, 1898, late Corporation of Heywood, 1877.
Clerk, Town Clerk, Heywood.
Engineer, James Diggle.
Offices, Heywood and Middleton.
Capital expended, £500,952.
Towns and villages in the area supplied—Heywood, Middleton, Norden, Bamford, Castleton, Chadderton (part of).
Works established, 1846. Special Acts, 1846, 1855, 1866, 1877, 1883, 1889, 1898.
Total population supplied, 56,000.
Daily consumption per head, 20 gals.
Source of supply, Nayden catchment area.
Storage capacity, 320,000,000 gals.
Character of water, very soft.
System of filtration, sand.
Death rate, 18 per 1,000.
Scale of charges, assessment charge, within Heywood borough, 7½ to 10 per cent. on gross value; beyond borough, 7½ to 12½ per cent.
Price per 1,000 gals., 2s. 3d. to 6d.
The above water undertaking is now the property of Heywood and Middleton jointly. The town councils appoint six representatives from each, and the chairman is alternately appointed from the two sets. The other authorities in supply area are not represented.

High Callerton (supplied by NEWCASTLE-ON-TYNE).

Higham Ferrers and Rushden, Northants. Railway, L.N.W. Distance from
London, 63 miles.
Authority, Higham Ferrers and Rushden Water Board.
Chairman, Geo. Denton, C.C.
Clerk to authority, Geo. S. Mason, Solicitor, Rushden, Northants.
Resident Engineer, W. B. Madin.
Offices, Council Buildings, Rushden.
Consulting Engineer, Reginald E. Middleton, M.I.C.E., 17, Victoria Street,
London, S.W.
Loans outstanding, £99,523 (February, 1907).
Works established, Rushden, 1893 ; new works opened, July, 1906.
Special Acts—Higham Ferrers Water Act, 1900, Higham Ferrers and Rushden
Water Board Act, 1902.
Total population of area of control—1881, 5,125; 1891, 9,253; 1901, 14,999.
Average death rate, 10 per 1,000,
District of supply—Higham Ferrers, Rushden, Wymington. The Board have also
special powers to supply certain districts within the Wellingborough and Bed-
ford Rural District Councils' areas and the urban district of Raunds.
Source of supply—drainage area situated at from about 2 miles S.E. of Sywell,
Northamptonshire, to 2 miles N.E. of the same place, 1,747 acres in all.
Estimated average daily discharge at points of collection, 550,000 gals.
Average annual rainfall over drainage area, 25 inches (period 30 years).
Nature and extent of cultivation of ditto, pasture, arable and woodland.
Control of drainage area—by Act of 1902 Board may hold lands, &c., for
prevention of pollution, and construct necessary drains, &c., and may make
bye-laws for securing purity of water.
Surface formation of drainage areas—upper estuarine clays, lower estuarine
series and Northampton sand overlying upper lias clay.
Estimated total quantity of water available per annum—
　　　　From drainage areas　　...　　...　　...　　200,750,000 gals.
Pumping station, Sywell, for lifting water from filter-beds to service reservoir at
Rushden, 10½ miles ; capacity, 550,000 gals. per day.
Character of water, good drinking water and of an exceptional degree of bacterial
purity, 15·7° hardness.
Filtering sand and gravel area provided, 2,016 square yards in 3 filter-beds.
Storage reservoir, Sywell, capacity, 235,000,000 gals.
Service reservoirs—one, 826,436 gals., and one, 262,500 gals.
Head on distributing mains—maximum, 150 ft. ; minimum, 65 ft.
Total quantity of water supplied from July 2nd to December 31st, 1906,
39,000,000 gals.
Average daily supply per head—domestic, 14¾ gals. ; trade, 1¼ gals.
Maximum day's supply, 312,000 gals. in September.
Scale of charges—
　　Rateable value, not exceeding £6　　...　　...　　...　　2s. 2d. per quarter.
　　　　　　　　　　　　"　　£8　　...　　...　　...　　2s. 6d. „　　„
　　　　　　　　　　　　"　　£10　　...　　...　　...　　3s.　　„　　„
　　Exceeding £10, 7½ per cent. per annum on rental value.
Price by meter, 1s. 6d. per 1,000 gals.
No. of meters, 84.
Length of supply mains, 10¾ miles. Distributing mains, 20 miles.

Higham and Hundred of Hoo, Kent (supplied by the MID KENT WATER CO.).

Highbridge, Somerset. Railway. G.W. Distance from London, 145 miles.
Authority, Urban District Council.
Population supplied, 2,234.
No returns supplied.

Highcliffe (supplied by CHRISTCHURCH).

Highway (supplied by REDRUTH).

Highworth, Wilts.　Railway, G.W.　Distance from London, 83¾ miles.
Authority, Highworth Rural District Council.
Chairman, A. D. Hussey Freke.
Clerk, J. P. Kirby, Victoria Street, Swindon.
Engineer, F. Redman, Wood Street, Swindon.
Works constructed 1904.
Source of supply, well 105 feet to calcareous grit.
Service reservoir, 34,000 gallons.
Total population in area supplied, 2,000, including Hampden and Upper Inglesham.

High Wych (supplied by HERTS AND ESSEX WATERWORKS Co.).

High Wycombe.　*See* CHEPPING WYCOMBE.

Hildenborough (supplied by TONBRIDGE).

Hill (supplied by SOUTH STAFFS. WATERWORKS Co.).

Hillhead, N.B. (supplied by AIRDRIE).

Hillingdon, Middlesex (supplied by RICKMANSWORTH).

Hinckley, Leicester.　Railway, L.N.W. and M.　Distance from London, 100 miles.
Authority, Hinckley Urban District Council.
Chairman of Water Committee, Bailey Ridgway.
Clerk, A. S. Atkins, Council Offices, Hinckley.
Waterworks Engineer, E. H. Crump, A.M.I.C.E., Council Offices, Hinckley.
Total capital invested, including loans, £47,200.
Towns and villlages within the area of control, Hinckley, Swepstone and Snare-
　　stone.　Market Bosworth, Stapleton, Newton, Odstone and Cadeby are also
　　supplied by arrangement with consumers.
Works established, 1890.
Special Act, Hinckley Local Board Water Act, 1888.
Total number of consumers, 3,500.
Estimated population actually supplied, 12,000.
Annual supply of water (1906)—
　　　For domestic purposes　...　...　...　...　50,773,000 gals.
　　　 ,, trade　　 ,,　　...　...　...　...　20,577,000 ,,
　　　 ,, municipal　 ,,　　...　...　...　...　1,500,000 ,,
Maximum day's consumption, 230,000 gals.
Total quantity of water drawn per annum (1906)—
　　　From deep wells or borings　...　...　...　72,850,000 gals.
Estimated total quantity of water available per annum—
　　　From deep well　...　...　...　...　90,000,000 gals. (at present).
Sources of supply in use—deep well situated at Snarestone, 13 miles NN.W. of
　　Hinckley.
Natural rest level of water below surface, 65 feet, above Ordnance datum, 255 feet.
Level of water below surface (when pumping 180,000 gals. per day), 145 feet.
Pumping station, Snarestone, actual pumping capacity per day, 240,000 gals.
Service reservoirs, reservoir at Hinckley, capacity, 450,000 gals., covered.
　　　 ,,　　　 ,,　　 Tower at Hinckley, capacity, 50,000 gals., covered.
Character of water, hard, no filtration.
Number of meters in use, 120.
Length of distributing mains, 26 miles.
Scale of charges—
　　Within Hinckley Urban District, for domestic purposes, including one w.c. and
　　　one bath, 7½ per cent. on rateable value of houses rated over £8 per half year,
　　　and 3d. per week for each house rated at £8, and under.

HINCKLEY—*continued.*

> Outside Hinckley Urban District (with exception of Snareston, Swepston, and Newton Burgoland), domestic or trade purposes, by meter, 2s. per 1,000 gal.s
> In parishes of Snareston, Swepston, and Newton Burgoland, domestic, half charge of that of Hinckley ; trade, 2s. per 1,000 gals.
> For all trade purposes in Hinckley Urban District, 9d. to 1s. 3d. per 1,000 gals., according to scale.
> Death rate, 16 per 1,000.

Hinderton (supplied by NESTON).

Hindley, Lancs. *See* LEIGH.

Hipperholme (supplied by HALIFAX).

Hirwain (supplied by ABERDARE).

Histon (supplied by CAMBRIDGE).

Hitchin, Herts. Railway, G.N. Distance from London, 32 miles.
Authority, District Council.
Works established, 1854.
Total population supplied, 10,072.
Annual supply of water, 30,000,000 gals.
Sources of supply, springs in chalk. Character of water, medium hard.
Scale of charges, assessment charge, 9d. to 6d. in the £.
Price per 1,000 gals., 9d.

Hoath, Kent (supplied by HERNE BAY).

Hoddesdon, Herts. Railway, G.E Distance from London, 25 miles.
Authority, Hoddesdon Waterworks Co., Ltd.
Population supplied, 4,711.
No returns supplied.

Holcombe Brook (supplied by BURY).

Hollinbush (supplied by FALKIRK).

Holmfirth, Yorks. Railway, L. and Y. Distance from London, 184 miles.
Authority, Holmfirth Urban District Council.
Chairman, Jonathan Roberts.
Clerk to Holmfirth U.D.C., H. Lomax.
Manager, Geo. Bray.
Office, Urban District Council Office.
Consulting Engineer, Jas. Barrowclough.
Loans outstanding, £6,019.
Annual profit, including " capital charges," £72.
Date of formation, 1876.
Total population supplied, 6,500.
Average death rate, 13·58 per 1,000.
District of supply, Austonley, Cartworth, Upperthong, Woodale.
Sources of supply—springs from freestone rock.
Character of water, medium soft.
Storage capacity, 4,800,000 gals.
Number of meters, 25.
Scale of charges—assessment charge, 10 per cent. on rateable value.
Price per 1,000 gals., 1s.
Daily consumption per head, 8 gals.

Holt, Norfolk. Railway, G.N. Distance from London, 155 miles.
Population supplied, 1,750.
No returns supplied.

Holyhead, Anglesea. Railway, L.N.W. Distance from London, 263¼ miles.
Authority, Holyhead Waterworks Company.
Area supplied, Holyhead only.
Works established, 1866.
Special Acts—Holyhead Waterworks Act, 1866 ; Holyhead Water Order, 1885,
1895.
Total poulation supplied, 10,000.
Sources of supply, springs.

Holyport (supplied by Maidenhead).

Holywell, Cheshire.
Authority, Urban District Council.
Source of supply, Birkenhead Corporation mains.

Honiton, Devon. Railway, L.S.W. Distance from London, 154¼ miles.
Authority, the Corporation of Honiton.
Chairman, the Mayor.
Clerk, E. W. Hellier, Town Clerk.
Office, High Street.
Borough Surveyor, A. E. Hayter.
Consulting Engineers, Beesley, Son & Nicholls.
Loans, £11,600 ; repaid, £4,480.
Area supplied, Honiton only.
Works established, 1875.
Total population of area supplied—1881, 3,349 ; 1891, 3,216 ; 1901, 3271.
Total number of houses supplied, 425.
Day's consumption per head, about 20 gals.
Storage capacity, 1,500,000 gals.
Death rate, 11·1 per 1,000.
Scale of charges—assessment 10d. in the £ domestic on R. V.
                        „   1s. 3d. in the £ trade   „
Total revenue received, £420.

Hoole and **Hoole Village** (supplied by Chester).

Hordle (supplied by Christchurch).

Horley (supplied by East Surrey Waterworks Co.).

Horncastle, Lincolnshire. Railway, G.N. Distance from London 130 miles.
Authority, Horncastle Water Co.
Population supplied, 4,038.
No returns supplied.

Horninglow (supplied by South Staffs. Water Co.).

Horsell (supplied by Woking).

Horsforth, Yorks. Railways, M. & N.E. Distance from London, 201 miles.
Authority, Urban District Council.
Clerk and Surveyor, R. R. Jones.
Engineer, E. J. Silcock.
Office, High Street.
Works established, 1864. Special Acts, 1865 and 1885.
Total population supplied, 7,785.
Daily consumption per head—domestic, 16 to 18 gals.
Sources of supply, springs and rainfall.
Storage capacity, 44,000,000 gals.

HORSFORTH—*continued.*

Character of water, 8° hardness.
System of filtration, sand.
A boring, 12 inches diameter and 500 feet deep, yielding 200,000 gallons per day, was opened in April, 1907.
Death rate, 17·6 per 1,000.
Scale of charges, assessment charge, 7½ and 10 per cent. on gross rental.
Price per 1,000 gals., trade, 2s. and 1s. 4d.
The Horsforth Urban District Council by compulsory purchase acquired this undertaking for the sum of £41,969.

Horton (supplied by RICKMANSWORTH).

Horton Grange (supplied by NEWCASTLE-ON-TYNE).

Horwich Lancs. Railway, L. & Y. Distance from London, 206 miles.
Authority, Urban District Council.
Total population supplied, 15,084.
1907, Works only nearing completion; present supply of water purchased through meter.

Houghton Magna and **Houghton Parva,** Yorks. (supplied by DEARNE VALLEY WATER Co.).

Houghton with Middleton (supplied by WARRINGTON).

Houghton-le-Spring, Durham.
Authority, Urban District Council.
Population, 9,003.

Hove, Sussex. *See* BRIGHTON.

Howdon, Township of (supplied by NEWCASTLE-ON-TYNE).

Howick (supplied by PRESTON).

Howwood, Scotland (supplied by PAISLEY).

Hoylake and West Kirby (G. and W.). Railways, L.N.W. and G.W., and Wirral. Distance from London, 200 miles.
Authority, Hoylake and West Kirby Gas and Water Co., Ltd.
Chairman, William Henry Forde.
Manager and Secretary, Arthur George Readdy.
Office, Quadrant, Hoylake.
Share capital paid up (Water), £45,495.
Dividends—A, 10 per cent.; B, 7 per cent.
Loan, £12,500.
Interest on loan, 4 and 3½ per cent.
Annual profit, including "capital charges," £4,696.
Works established, 1877.
Special Acts, 1878, 1887, 1890, 1893, 1897, 1899, 1900, 1906.
Total population supplied (estimated), 18,000.
Towns and villages in the area supplied—Hoylake, West Kirby, Caldy, Frankby, Greasby, Meole, Moreton.
Sources of supply—wells and borings in the sandstone rock on Grange Hills, West Kirby.
Character of water analysis, expressed in parts per 100,000 :—

Mark and denomination of the sample.	... Tap in Hoylake
Total solid matter in solution	29·6
Oxygen required to oxidise, in 15 minutes...	·008
,, ,, ,, ,, 3 hours ...	·006
Ammonia	·001

HOYLAKE AND WEST KIRBY—continued.

    Ammonia from organic matter　...　...　·004
        (By distillation with alkaline permanganate)
    Nitrogen as nitrates　...　...　...　...　·415
    Combined Chlorine　...　...　...　...　6·1
    Temporary hardness　...　...　...　...　5·72
    Permanent　　,,　...　...　...　...　9·14
    Total　　　,,　...　...　...　...　14·86
No organisms; alkaline reaction; excellent for domestic use.
Filtration, none; softening, none.
Capacity of service reservoir, 4,000,000 gals.
Head on distributing mains—maximum, 85 lbs. per square inch; minimum,
    70 lbs. per square inch.
Annual supply of water, 242,160,000 gals.
Maximum days' supply, 1,200,000 gals., June, 1906.
Scale of charges—assessment charge, 7 to 5 per cent. on gross rentals.
Price per 1,000 gals., 1s. 6d. to 1s.

Hoyland Nether and **Hoyland Parva** (supplied by DEARNE VALLEY WATER Co.).

Huby (supplied by LEEDS).

Hucknall Huthwaite, Notts.　Railway, M.　Distance from London, 133 miles.
Authority, Hucknall Huthwaite Urban District Council.
Chairman, John Thompson.
Secretary, G. H. Hibbert, Clerk, Mansfield, Notts.
Engineer in charge, Godfrey Bostock, Surveyor and Water Engineer, Sutton Road,
    Hucknall Huthwaite.
Loans outstanding, £2,500.
Works established, 1887.
Total population of area of control, 1891, 3,022; 1901, 4,076; 1907, 4,500.
Total number of consumers, 770.
Estimated population actually supplied, 4,050.
Area of control, with population (1901 Census)—Hucknall Huthwaite only, 4,076.
Water brought in bulk from the Sutton and Ashfield Urban District Council at
    8d. per 1,000 gals.
Annual supply of water—
    For domestic purposes　...　...　...　...　13,270,000 gals.
    ,,　trade　　　,,　...　...　...　...　209,000　,,
Average day's consumption, 35,714 gals.
Scale of charges—domestic, according to rateable value; trade, 1s. per 1,000 gals.
Number of meters in use, 3.
Length of distributing mains, 4¼ miles.

Hucknall Torkard, Notts.　Railways, G.N., M., and G.C.　Distance from London,
133 miles.
Authority, Hucknall Torkard Urban District Council.
Chairman. Thomas Metcalf.
Clerk to Authority, Parker Woodward.
Engineer and Manager, W. Swann.
Office, Wotnall Road, Hucknall Torkard.
Works established, 1868.
Loans outstanding, £3,669.
Total population supplied, 16,500.
Death rate, 13·81 per 1,000.
Sources of supply, two wells 125 ft. deep. New red sandstone, Bunter pebble bed.
Analysis of water, numerical results expressed in grains—
    Silica　...　...　...　...　...　...　...　0·35
    Calcium Carbonate　...　...　...　...　...　2·45
    Magnesium　,,　...　...　...　...　...　0·50
    Calcium Sulphate　...　...　...　...　...　1·43

HUCKNALL TORKARD—*continued.*

Magnesium Sulphate ...	...	...	...	...	1·54
„ Nitrate ...	...	...	...	...	2·24
Sodium „ ...	...	...	...	...	0·37
Sodium Chloride ...	...	...	...	...	1·54
Total dissolved solids ...		...	...	...	10·42

Storage capacity, service reservoir, 500,000 gals.
Head on distributing mains—max., 62 lbs. per sq. in.; min., 45 lbs. per sq. in.
Annual supply of water—domestic, 67,363,000 gals.; trade, &c., 13,537,000 gals.
Daily consumption per head, 13·4 gals, all purposes.
Maximum supply per day, 240,000 gals,
Scale of charges—assessment charge, 5 per cent. on rateable value; price per 1,000 gals., trade 10d. maximum, 6d. minimum.
Number of meters, 32.
Length of mains—supply 6 (8 in.), distributing 9¼ miles.
Total water revenue received, £2,500.

Huddersfield, Yorks. Railways, G.N. and G.C. Distance from London, 190 miles.
Authority, Corporation.
Chairman, Alderman Alfred Walker, J.P.
Town Clerk, J. H. Field.
Manager, J. W. Schofield.
Engineers, G. H. Hill & Sons.
Office, Town Hall.
Loans outstanding, £1,665,379.
Works established, 1869.
Special Acts, 1869, 1871, 1876, 1880, 1882, 1890, 1894, 1896, 1902.
Total population of area supplied, 152,000.
Towns and villages in the area supplied, County Borough of Huddersfield and 20 townships and parts of townships outside borough.
Sources of supply in use, gravitation and impounding reservoirs.
Character of water, soft.
System of filtration—through sand, by gravitation.
Storage capacity—impounding reservoirs, 1,642,513,000 gals.
        service   „   7,068,120 „
Total quantity of water drawn per annum, 1,435,000,000 gals., exclusive of compensation to streams, &c.
Daily consumption per head, domestic, 16 gals.; trade, 10 gals.
Scale of charges—assessment charge, 6¼ to 10 per cent. on actual rent paid or gross annual value.
Charges for municipal purposes by meter, 4d. per 1,000 gals.
Price per 1,000 gals.—domestic, by scale; trade, 7d. inside borough, 8¾d. outside borough by meter.
Number of meters, 840.
Length of mains, 298 miles.
Total revenue received, £57,995 (1906).

Hull, East York. Railways, N.E., H. and B., M., G.C., and L.N.W. Distance from London, 181 miles.
Authority, Kingston-upon-Hull Corporation.
Chairman, Alderman W. G. Wharram.
Secretary, E. Laverack, Town Clerk.
Engineer, F. J. Bancroft, B.Sc., A.M.I.C.E., M.I.M.E., Town Hall.
Office, Town Hall, Hull.
Total capital invested, including loans, £500,999. Loans outstanding, £312,000.
Works established—Stoneferry, 1845; Springhead, 1864; Cottingham, 1890.
Special Acts—1843, 1872, 1875, 1879, 1882, 1883, 1884, 1893, 1897 (Consolidation Act), 1901, 1903.

HULL—*continued.*

Total population of area of control—1881, 150,924; 1891, 200,044; 1901, 246,435.

Total number of inhabited houses, 52,181.

Estimated population actually supplied, 267,500 (1906), including suburban districts.

Death rate, 19·2 per 1,000.

Towns and villages within the area of control, with population of each (1901 Census)—

Hull	240,259
Anlaby	1,004
Willerby	1,030
Kirkella	388
Hessle	3,754
	246,435

Sources of supply in use—

Deep wells, in the middle chalk, at Springhead and Cottingham.

Maximum annual rainfall over drainage area, 36·73 inches (1872).

Minimum　　　　　„　　　　„　　　17·57　„　(1887).

Average　　　　　„　　　　„　　　27·02　„　(30 years—1870—1899).

Drainage area—the Corporation may make bye-laws for securing the purity of the water which they are authorised to take, and such bye-laws shall be in force within a radius of half a mile from the waterworks pumping station at Cottingham.

Level of water below surface (when pumping 11,295,000 gals. per day), 29 feet at Springhead; 34 feet at Cottingham.

Strata or formation yielding springs, middle chalk.

Pumping stations—

Springhead .. .. capacity, 5,250,000 gals. per day.

Cottingham ... ... „　　7,250,000　„　　„

Area of control equal to 16,377 acres.

Character of water—16½° temporary hardness. Water is not softened.

Analysis of the water—

	Grains per gal.		Parts per 1,000,000.	
	Total solid residue.	Chlorine.	Free ammonia.	Albuminoid. ammonia.
Cottingham, ...	22·5	1·34	·0182	·0202
Springhead, ...	22·5	1·34	·0152	·017

Analysis of total solid residue—

Silica...	·60	grains per gal.
Oxide of iron and alumina	·50	„
Carbonate of lime	14·38	„
Sulphate of lime	3·16	„
Carbonate of magnesia	1·58	„
Chloride of sodium	2·28	„
	22·50	

Filtration, none; softening, none.

Storage capacity—

Service reservoir at Kirkella, capacity 500,000 gals.

„　　„　at Kildgate (nr. Cottingham, in course of construction), 10,000,000 gals.

Annual supply of water (1906)—

For domestic purposes	2,593,167,000	gals.
„ trade „	818,501,000	„
„ municipal, street watering and sanitary purposes	55,000,000	„
In bulk to other authorities...	23,401,000	„
	3,490,069,000	„

HULL—*continued.*

Maximum day's consumption, 11,795,000, August, 1906.
Scale of charges—
Assessment charge, 6·25 per cent. to 3·7 per cent. on gross annual value.
Trade purposes, 6d. per 1,000 gals.
Number of meters in use, 1,215.
Length of distributing mains, 250 miles.

Hulme (supplied by MANCHESTER).

Huncoat (supplied by ACCRINGTON).

Hundred of Hoo, Kent. *See* HIGHAM.

Hunmanby, Yorks. (supplied by FILEY).

Hunstanton, Norfolk. Railway, G.E. Distance from London, 112¼ miles.
Authority Urban District Council of New Hunstanton.
Population supplied, 1,725.
No returns supplied.

Hunsworth (supplied by BRADFORD, Yorks., and partly by CLECKHEATON).

Huntingdon. Railway, G.N. Distance from London, 58¾ miles.
Authority, Corporation.
Population supplied, 4,346.
No returns supplied.

Huntington (supplied by YORK and the SOUTH STAFFS. WATERWORKS Co.).

Huntly, Scotland. Railway, G.N. of Scotland.
Authority, Huntly Town Council.
Chairman, John Rhind.
Secretary, J. R. McMath, Town Clerk,
Manager, John Allan, Burgh Surveyor.
Office, 9, The Square, Huntly.
Works established, 1867.
Total population supplied, 4,500.
Death rate, 17·6 per 1,000.
Source of supply, deep underground springs on Moorland.
Character of water, soft clear water of excellent quality.
Filtration, none required.
Storage capacity, 230,000 gals. in service reservoir.
Pressure on distributing mains—maximum, 60 lbs. per sq. in.; minimum, 38 lbs.
per square in.
Annual supply of water, between 60,000,000 and 70,000,000.
Average daily supply per head—domestic, 25 gals.; trade, &c., 5 gals.
Maximum day's supply, 150,000 gals. in August.
Price per 1,000 gals.. average, 6d.
Number of meters, 2.
Length of supply mains, 5 miles; distributing mains, 6 miles.

Hunton Bridge (supplied by RICKMANSWORTH).

Hurst Green, Lancs. (supplied by BLACKBURN).

Hurst Green, Sussex (supplied by TICEHURST).

Hurtwood, Surrey.
Authority, Hurtwood Water Company, Ltd.
Source of supply, well.
Supply commenced January 1, 1905.
Supplies Holmbury St. Mary and Peaslake.

Hurstpierpoint, Sussex (supplied by Burgess Hill).

Hutton-i'-th'-Hay (supplied by Kendal).

Hutton Lane (supplied by Preston).

Hutton-le-Hole (supplied by Kirkby Moorside).

Hyde, Cheshire. Railways, G.C., G.N., Sheffield and M. Distance from London, 181¼ miles.
  Authority, Hyde Corporation.
  Chairman, Councillor S. Welsh.
  Clerk, Thos. Brownson, Solicitor, Town Clerk.
  Engineer, Joseph Mitchell, Borough Surveyor.
  Office, Town Hall.
  Loans outstanding, £11,485.
  Special Acts—Hyde Local Board (Waterworks) Act, 1870.
  Total population supplied, 33,000.
  Average death rate, 17·5 per 1,000.
  District of supply—Hyde, Newton, and Godley, townships in Hyde Borough and part of Bredbury Urban District.
  Length of mains, 34¼ miles.

Hylton (supplied by Sunderland).

Hythe, Kent. Railway, S.E. Distance from London, 66¾ miles.
  Authority, Corporation.
  Town Clerk, Geo. S. Wilkes.
  Engineer and Manager, Chris Jones, C.E.
  Office, 54, High Street.
  Towns and villages in the area supplied, Hythe and Saltwood.
  Works established, 1874; special Acts, 1874.
  Total population supplied, 6,500 winter, 15,000 summer.
  Annual supply of water, 30,000,000 gals.
  Daily consumption, per head, 15 gals.
  Sources of supply, well to lower green sand.
  Storage capacity, 600,000 gals.
  Character of water, very good. Filtration, none required.
  Death rate, 12·6 per 1,000.
  Scale of charges—assessment charge, 6 per cent. on gross rental.
  Price per 1,000 gals., 1s.
  Total water rent received, £2,200.

Iford, Hants. (supplied by Christchurch).

Ilford, Essex (supplied by East London and South Essex Water Co.).

Ilfracombe, Devon. Railways, L.S.W. and G.W. Distance from London, 225 miles.
  Authority, Ilfracombe Urban District Council.
  Clerk to the Council, R. M. Rowe.
  Engineer and Manager, O. M. Prouse.
  Office, Town Hall.
  Area supplied, Ilfracombe and district.
  Special Act, 1900.

ILFRACOMBE—*continued.*

Total population supplied, 8,630.
Daily consumption per head, no record.
Source of supply, a new supply was laid on from the River Bray, Exmoor, at a cost of £55,000 in 1904.
Storage capacity, 53,051,450 gals.
System of filtration, gravel and carbon.
Character of water, good.
Death rate, 11·3 per 1,000.
Scale of charges—
　Assessment charge, sliding scale.
　Price per 1,000 gals., mixed, trade and domestic in one building, 1s. ; trade, by arrangement or by meter, 2s. 6d. to 2s.

Ilkeston, Derbyshire.　Railways, M. and G.N.　Distance from London, 126 miles.
Authority, Ilkeston & Heanor Water Board.
Office, Town Hall.
Towns and villages in the area supplied, Ilkeston and Heanor.
Works established, 1854.
Total population supplied, 32,000.
Daily consumption per head, about 25 gals.
Source of supply, Meerbrook Sough.
Storage capacity, 3,200,000 gals.
Character of water, 15° hardness.
Death rate, 17·7 per 1,000.
Scale of charges—assessment charge A.
Price for 1,000 gals., 1s. 6d. and 9d.

Ilkley, Yorks.　Railways, N.E. and M.　Distance from London, 211 miles.
Authority, Ilkley Urban District Council.
Chairman, J. A. Middlebrook, J.P.
Secretary, Frank Hall, Clerk to Council.
Manager, T. H. Smith.
Office, Council Office, Ilkley,
Loans, £39,350, of which £10,881 has been repaid.
Interest 3¼ to 4½ per cent. on outstanding loans.
Annual profit (1906), £2,716.
Works established 1852 ; acquired by Local Authority, 1871.
Special Acts, Ilkley Local Board Acts, 1871 and 1893.
Total population supplied, 8,500, estimated summer population, 12,000.
Average death rate (10 years), 11·18, including visitors ; 9·71, residents only.
Area supplied, Township of Ilkley, Nesfield-with-Langbar, Middleton, and Denton.
Sources of supply—springs.
Character of water, soft ; total hardness, 2·8°, Clark's scale.
Filtration, none ; softening, none.
Storage in service reservoirs, 8,562,000 gals.
Daily consumption per head, 30 gals.
Authorized charges (domestic supply), 10 per cent. on annual value.
Present rate of　,,　　　,,　　,,　　5　,,　　　,,　　,,
Price per 1,000 gals., trade, 8d.
Number of meters, 30.

Ince-in-Makerfield, Lancs.
　　Authority, Urban District Council.
　　　　to Council, B. Howgate.
　　　　Manchester.
　　　　　　supplied, 23,500 (estimated).
　　　　　　pply, wells in red sandstone at Golborne **and part from the**
　　　　　　ins.

Impington (supplied by Cambridge).

Inchinnan, Scotland (supplied by Paisley).

Inkerman, Scotland (supplied by Paisley).

Inveresk (supplied by Musselburgh).

Inverkeithing, Scotland. Railway, N.B. Distance from London, 400 miles.
Authority, the Town Council of the Burgh.
Chairman, James Sim, Provost.
Secretary, John R. Menzies, Town Clerk.
Manager, John Livingston.
Office, Town Hall.
Loans outstanding, £229.
Works established, 1868. Special Act, 1862.
Total population supplied, 2,123.
Average death rate, 14 per 1,000.
Area of supply, Inverkeithing only.
Source of supply, Dunfermline Burgh Works at Glensherup.
Character of water, good.
Daily consumption per head, 29 gals.
Scale of charges—assessment charge, 6d. in £ on R.V.
Price per 1,000 gals., 8d. to 6d.

Inverness, Scotland. Railways, L. & N.W. M., and Highland. Distance from
London, 600 miles.
Authority, Burgh of Inverness.
Chairman, Arthur Dougal Ross, Provost.
Secretary, Kenneth Macdonald, Town Clerk.
Treasurer, Roderick Paterson, Town Chamberlain, Town House, Inverness.
Engineer in charge, Ewen Macdonald, Water Manager, Inverness.
Office, Town House, Inverness.
Total capital invested, £65,545.
Works established, 1826.
Purchased by local authority, 1875.
Special Acts, Inverness Water and Gas Act, 1875, and Provisional Orders dated
23rd May, 1879, 31st May, 1892, and June 5th, 1905.
Total population of area of control, 1881, 21,000; 1891, 23,000; 1901, 25,000.
Total number of ratepayers, 5,500.
Estimated population actually supplied, 25,000.
Area of control, with population (1901 Census)—Inverness and suburbs, 25,000.
Sources of supply in use—drainage areas situated at Loch Ashie.
    Average annual rainfall over drainage area, 25·86 inches (period 3 years).
    Nature and extent of drainage area, moor and pasture lands.
    Water authority have no control of drainage area.
Surface formation of drainage areas, hill and moor lands.
Character of water, soft; hardness before treatment 2°.
System of filtration, gravel and copper screen.
Storage reservoir, capacity 7,195,137 gals.
Annual supply of water—

For domestic purposes	..	..	...	400,000,000 gals.
„ trade „	...	..	..	90 000,000 „
„ municipal „	..	...	...	10,000,000 „

INVERNESS—*continued.*

Total quantity of water drawn per annum—from drainage areas, 500,000,000 gals.
Maximum day's consumption, 1,500,000 gals.
Scale of charges—Assessment, 5¼d. in the £ of rental; trade, 6d. per 1,000 gals.
Number of meters in use, 27.
Length of distributing mains, 30 miles.

Inverurie, Scotland.　Railway, G.N. of S.　Distance from London, 539 miles.
Authority, Town Council.
Secretary, H. G. L. Mollinson, Town Clerk.
Manager, Andrew Crockett.
Office, Town House.
Works established, 1873.
Total population supplied, 4,400.
Average death rate, 14 per 1,000.
Source of supply, springs.
Character of water, very good.
Filtration, none.
Storage capacity in service reservoir, 320,000 gals.
Daily consumption per head—domestic, 25.
Head on distributing mains—maximum, 90 feet ; minimum, 45 feet.
Scale of charges, price per 1,000 gals., 6d., trade purposes.
Number of meters, 4.
Length of distributing mains, 4 miles, 1¾ to reservoir, 5 miles collecting.

Ipplepen (supplied by PAIGNTON).

Ipswich, Suffolk.　Railway, G.E.　Distance from London, 69¼ miles.
Authority, Corporation, 1892.
Chairman, The Mayor.
Clerk to Authority, Will. Bantoft, Town Clerk.
Engineer and Manager, C. W. S. Oldham.
Offices, Waterworks Street.
Capital invested, £276,964.
Loans outstanding, £250,226.
Works established, 1857.　Special Acts, 1857, 1892.
Total population of area of control—1881, 50,546 ; 1891, 57,081 ; 1901,66,622 ;
　1907, 73,000.
Average death rate, 14·9 per 1,000.
Area supplied, municipal and parliamentary borough, including villages of
　Whitton and Westerfield.
Sources of supply—drainage areas situated at Holy Wells Park (S.), Brooke's
　Hall (N.W.), Spring Road (E.), Christchurch Park (N.).　Estimated annual
　supply from these areas 70,000,000 gals.　Deep wells at St. Clement's, Ipswich,
　yielding 442,050,620 gals. per annum (1905-6).
Wells and borings, No. 1, 140 ft. into chalk; No. 2, 436 ft. through chalk.
　Springs from red crag and gravel.
Strata yielding springs, gravel and red crag resting on London clay.
Strata tapped by wells and borings, gravel and upper chalk.
Natural rest level of water below surface, 10 ft. above O.D.　Level of water
　below surface when pumping 2,000,000 gals. per day, 8 ft. below O.D.
The maximum weekly consumption of water, exclusive of gravitation sources.
　has risen from 6½ million gals. in 1893 to 12½ million gals. in 1906.　The
　maximum quantity of water available per week is 14,000,000 (exclusive of
　gravitation sources), so that a further source of supply will shortly be required
　to meet the maximum summer consumption.
Character of water, good.　Total hardness, 21°.　Water not softened.

IPSWICH—*continued.*

Filtration, none.

Storage capacity—

Park Road, high service, covered reservoirs ... { No. 1. 500,000 gals.
„ 2. 1,000,000 „
„ 3. 4,500,000 .,

Spring Road, low service, covered „ ... ... 500,000 „

Pumping station, Waterworks Street, 2,000,000 gals. per day.

Annual supply of water (1905-6)—domestic ... 429,193,850 gals.
trade ... 116,692,570 „
municipal 18,164,200 „

Average daily consumption per head—domestic, 16·6 ; trade and special, 5·2 gals.

Maximum day's supply, 2,445,000 gals. in July.

Scale of charges—assessment charge, 5 per cent. on R.V., above £21.

Price per 1,000 gals., 1s. 3d. to 6d.

Number of meters, 770.

Length of mains, 80 miles.

Total water rent received, £15,011.

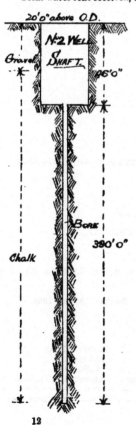

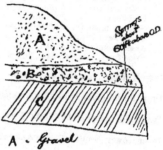

A = Gravel
B = Red crag
C = London clay.

Irlam (supplied by Manchester).

Ireleth (supplied by Barrow-in-Furness).

Ironbridge (supplied by Much Wenlock).

Irton, Yorks. (supplied by Scarborough).

Irvine. Railways, G. & S.W. and C.
　Authority, Corporation, 1881.
　Engineers, J. and A. Leslie and Reed, Edinburgh.
　Loan capital, £100,000.
　Towns and villages in the area supplied—Irvine, Saltcoats, Stevenston, and
　　Kilwinning.
　Works established, 1878. Special Acts, 1876 and 1881.
　Total population of area supplied, 25,622.
　Daily supply of water, 1,500,000 gals.
　Daily consumption per head, about 40 gals.
　Source of supply, Munnoch Burn.
　Catchment area, 1,300 acres.
　Storage capacity, 225,000,000 gals.
　Character of water, soft.
　Assessment charge, 10½d. in £.
　Price for 1,000 gals., 8½d., 7d., 5d., 4d.

Irwell Vale (supplied by Bury).

Iver, Bucks. (supplied by Rickmansworth).

Jackfield (supplied by Much Wenlock).

Jamestown, Scotland. *See* Alexandria.

Jarrow-on-Tyne (supplied by Sunderland and South Shields Water Co.).

Jericho (supplied by Bury).

Jersey, Channel Islands.
　Authority, The Jersey New Waterworks Company, Ltd.
　Chairman, Peter P. Guiton.
　Engineer, Manager and Secretary, A. J. Jenkins, A.M.I.C.E.
　Office, 27, Broad Street, Jersey.
　Total capital invested, including loans, £57,073.
　Dividend, 6 per cent.
　Towns and villages within the area of control, St. Helier, 27,975 (1901 Census),
　　St. Aubins, 4,000 (approx.).
　Works established, 1869. Present company, 1882.
　Special Act, Act of States of Jersey, Jersey Water Works Company, 1865.
　Total population of area of control (1901), 31,975.
　Total number of consumers, 2,500.
　Estimated population actually supplied, 20,000.
　Annual supply of water (1906)—

For domestic purposes	...	...	...	80,000,000 gals.
„ trade „	...	...	...	10,000,000 „
„ municipal „	...	...	...	5,000,000 „

　Maximum day's consumption,* 250,000 gals., normal. Summer, 418,000 gals.

*In summer the consumption is very largely increased by the lavish use of water for gardens.

JERSEY—continued.

Total quantity of water drawn per annum (1906)—
　　From drainage areas ...　...　...　...　95,000,000 gals.
Estimated total quantity of water available per annum—
　　From drainage areas ...　...　...　...　300,000,000 gals.
Sources of supply—drainage area situated at parishes of St. John's and St.
　　Lawrence, Jersey, and consists of table land, highest point, 420 feet, inter-
　　sected with deep, narrow valleys, and is in the centre of the island, with a fall
　　towards the south.
Estimated maximum daily discharge at points of collection,　5,000,000 gals.
　　„　　minimum　　　„　　　„　　　　100,000　„
　　„　　average　　　„　　　„　　　　800,000　„
Maximum annual rainfall over drainage area, 41·65 inches (1882).
Minimum　　　„　　　　„　　26·54　„　(1887).
Average　　　„　　　　„　　30·30　„　(period of 29 years,
　　　　　　　　　　　　　　　　　1878—1906 inclusive.)
Population on drainage area, 450 (about).
Nature and extent of cultivation of ditto, nearly whole area cultivated, chiefly
　　potatoes ; very little pasture.
Control of drainage area—mills on stream belong with one exception to company.
　　(English Acts re pollution of streams do not apply in Jersey.)
Surface formation of drainage areas, granite overlaid by a schist.
Strata or formation yielding springs, schist.
Storage reservoirs, Vicart　　...　...　...　...　capacity, 1,000,000 gals.
　　„　　　„　　Millbrook　...　...　...　...　„　13,000,000　„
Filtering area provided, 2,180 square yards in five filter-beds.
Pumping station, Millbrook　...　...　capacity, 1,000,000 gals., 24 hours day.
Service reservoirs, Millbrook　...　...　„　370,000　„ covered.
Number of meters in use, 250.
Length of distributing mains, 28 miles.
Average analysis of the water, 1906, after filtration. The results of the analysis
　　are stated in grains per gallon—
　　　　Total dissolved solid matter　...　...　...　...　22·97
　　　　Chlorine in chlorides　...　...　...　...　...　5·23
　　　　Ammonia, free and saline　...　...　...　...　·0015
　　　　Ammonia, albuminoid　...　...　...　...　...　·0052
　　　　Nitrogen in nitrates　...　...　...　...　...　·2327
　　　　Nitrogen in nitrites　...　...　...　...　...　nil
　　　　Oxygen required to oxidise organic matter (in 3 hours)　·0406
Prior to filtration water contains, average, 2,000 bacteria per c.c. After filtration
　　about 6 per c.c.
The water has about 5° of hardness.
Scale of charges—
　　Domestic purposes, when the rent of premises does not exceed :—
　　Houses under £50 per annum, 1s. 3d. in the £ per annum.
　　For excess beyond £50　...　1s.　　　„　　　　　„
　　　„　extra water closets, each per annum, 5s.
　　　„　fixed baths　　　　„　　„　5s.
　　　„　lavatories　　　　„　　„　5s.
　　For the supply in the house of a closet solely, 20s.
　　　„　the supply of one closet in a house occupied by more than one family, for
　　　　each family per annum, 10s.

	s.	d.	
4,000 gals. (minimum charge) per quarter	8	0	
Up to 30,000 gals.	2	0	per 1,000 gals.
From 30,000 to 50,000 gals.	1	9 „	„
„ 50,000 to 75,000 „	1	6 „	„
„ 75,000 to 100,000 „	1	3 „	„
„ 100,000 and upwards	1	0 „	,

The company manufacture ice.

Johnstone, Renfrewshire (supplied by PAISLEY).

Jordanhill (supplied by GLASGOW).

Jordanstown (supplied by DUBLIN).

Jumpers, Hants. (supplied by CHRISTCHURCH).

Kearsley (supplied by BOLTON).

Keighley, Yorks. Railways, G.N., and M. Distance from London, 205 miles.
Authority, Corporation of Keighley.
Chairman of Water Committee, Alderman B. S. Brigg, J.P.
Town Clerk, William Bagshaw, Esq., Town Hall, Keighley.
Engineer in charge, W. Fowlds, A.M.I.C.E., and J. Smith, Superintendent,
Office, Town Hall.
Total capital invested, including loans, £250,000. Loans outstanding (June 30th,
1906), £204,289 18s. 8d.
Works established, 1816, by a company.
Purchased by local authority, October 22nd, 1867.
Special Acts—Keighley Waterworks Act, 1816, Keighley Waterworks and Improve-
ment Acts, 1867 and 1872, Keighley Waterworks Extension and Improvement
Act, 1869, Keighley Corporation Acts, 1891 and 1898.
Total population of area of control—1881, 41,458 ; 1891, 48,857 ; 1901, 56,044.
Estimated population actually supplied, 40,000.
Average death rate, 17·38 (1896 to 1905 inclusive).
Towns and villages within the area of control, with population of each (1901
    Census) – Keighley   41,564
               Oakworth and Stanbury...   4,261
               Haworth   7,492
               Oxenhope   2,727
Sources of supply in use—
    Drainage areas situated at ... longitude 2° 3′ West, latitude 53° 50′
    Surface springs ... ... ,, 1° 56′ ,, ,, 53° 52′
Maximum annual rainfall over drainage area, 56·44 inches (1895).
Minimum ,, ,, ,,   43·68 ,,   (1899).
Average ,, ,, ,,   48·30 ,,   (period 10 years).
Nature and extent of cultivation of drainage area, 143 acres of meadow and
rough pasturing. Population, nil.
The water authority have acquired the freehold of 524 acres of moorland and
obtained the power to make bye-laws for prevention of nuisances and pollution
of the water.
Surface formation of drainage areas, millstone grit.
Analysis of filtered water, expressed in grains per gal.
    Appearance in 2 feet tube ... ... Slightly turbid.
    Chlorine in chlorides ... ... 0·9.
    Nitrogen as nitrates ... ... None.
    Ammonia, free ... ... 0·01456.
    Ammonia, albuminoid ... ... 0·00637.
    Reaction ... ... Faintly alkaline.
    Lead ... ... None.
    Oxygen absorbed in 3 minutes ... ... 0·030.
    Oxygen absorbed in 4 hours ... ... 0·121.
    Hardness (total) calculated as calcium carbonate 2·20.
    Hardness (permanent) ... ... 1·70.
    Hardness (temporary) ... ... 0·50.
    Total solid matter dried at 212° Fah. ... ... 5·32.

KEIGHLEY—*continued*.

Analysis of unfiltered water, expressed in grains per gal.

Appearance in 2 feet tube	Slightly turbid.
Chlorine in chlorides	0·95
Nitrogen as nitrates	None.
Ammonia, free	0·03234.
Ammonia, albuminoid	0·00826.
Reaction	Acid.
Oxygen absorbed in 3 minutes	0·002.
,, ,, 4 hours	0·064.
Hardness (total) calculated as calcium carbonate	2·70.
Hardness (permanent)	2·70.
Hardness (temporary)	0·00.
Total solid matter dried at 212° Fah.	7·63.
Lead	None.

The unfiltered water, owing to the peaty acids it contains, has a solvent action on the lead service pipes. This is removed to a great extent by filtration through sandstone and limestone, but to make quite certain that the water shall be alkaline, 5 lbs. of ammonia alkaline (sodium carbonate) are added daily to the water supply of about 1,300,000 gals.

Filtering area provided, 16,100 square yards in 4 filter-beds.

Storage reservoir, Watersheddles ... capacity, 150,000,000 gals.

Service reservoirs, Black Hill... ... capacity, 2,500,000 gals., open.
,, ,, Highfield ... ... ,, 10,000,000 ,, ,,
,, ,, Calversyke ... ,, 500,000 ,, ,,

Pressure on distributing mains—max., 220 lbs. per sq. in.; min., 150 lbs. per sq. in.

Annual supply of water—

For domestic and all unmetered purposes	447,000,000 gals.
,, trade purposes, sold by meter ...	50,500,000 ,,
In bulk to other authorities	12,000,000 ,,

Total quantity of water drawn per annum—

From drainage areas	474,500,000 gals.
,, surface springs	35,000,000 ,,

Average daily supply for all purposes, 1,350,000 gals.

Scale of charges for domestic purposes—

From annual rack rent or value per annum up to £5, 7s. 6d. per annum; up to £100, £5 10s.; over £100, 5 per cent.

Water for water-closets included in the above charges in respect of dwellings paying water rents exceeding 13s.; every additional water-closet, 5s.; every bath, 10s.

Price by meter—

From under 200,000 gals. per quarter ...	8d. per 1,000.
To ,, 3,000,000 ,, ,, ...	6½d. ,,
Over 3,000,000 ,, ,, ...	6d. ,,

Number of meters in use, 237.

Keith, Scotland. Railways, G.N. of S. and Highland Ry. Co.

The Superiors are, The Countess Dow. of Seafield and the Duke of Fife.

Office, Town and County Bank, Keith.

Area supplied, Keith only.

Works established, 1889.

Total population supplied, 6,000.

Source of supply, Ballach Hill.

Character of water, excellent.

Death rate, 15·79 per 1,000.

Scale of charges, assessment charge, 2d., owners and occupiers.

Price per 1,000 gals., 6d.

Kelso, Scotland. Railway, N.B. & N.E. Distance from London, 354 miles.
Authority, Town Council.
Chairman, Provost T. D. Crichton-Smith (Solicitor).
Secretary, Town Clerk.
Manager, J. Hume, Burgh Surveyor.
Office, Town Hall.
Loans outstanding, £670.
Works established, 1864.
Total population supplied, 4,175.
Average death rate, 16 per 1,000.
Sources of supply, river for flushing, spring for drinking.
Character of water—river, fair ; spring, good ; total hardness, 16°.
Filtration, river through sand.
Storage capacity in service reservoirs, 1,000,000 gals.
Head on distributing mains—maximum, 90 feet ; minimum, 60 feet.
Annual supply of water, 60,000,000 gals.
Daily consumption per head, 40 gals. of river water, 5 of spring.
Price per meter—average, 4d. per 1,000 gals.
Number of meters in use, 1 (laundry).
Length of mains, 10,000 yards.
Scale of charges, assessment, 8d. in the £ on R.V.

Kendal, Westmoreland. (G. & W.) Railway, L.N.W. Distance from London,
251¼ miles.
Authority, Corporation.
Town Clerk, J. Bolton.
Secretary, Chris. Graham, Borough Treasurer.
Engineer and Manager, W. Thomson.
Offices, Gasworks and Town Hall.
Towns and villages in the area supplied—Kendal, Scalthwarterigg, and Hutton-i'-
th'-Hay.
Works established, 1846.
Special Acts, Kendal Corporation Gas and Water Act, 1894.
Total population supplied, 14,183.
Daily consumption per head, 25 gals.
Sources of supply, gravitation.
Storage capacity, 138,000,000 gals.
Filtration, none.
Character of water, soft.
Death rate, 16·01 per 1,000.
Number of meters, 80.
Length of mains, 26 miles.
Scale of charges—Assessment charge, 1s. 4d. in £ dwelling houses, 9d. houses
and shops, 4d. shops and offices.
　Price per 1,000 gals.—trade, 1s. to 6d.
Total water rent received, £3,650.

Kenilworth, Warwickshire. Railway, L.N.W. Distance from London, 99 miles.
Authority, Kenilworth Waterworks Company, Ltd.
Office, Rosemary Hill.
Area supplied, Kenilworth and 2 houses in Leek (Wootton).
Works established, 1883.
Special Act, Kenilworth Water Order, 1882.
Total population supplied, 4,544.
Sources of supply (1) springs on common, (2) bore-hole.
Character of water good.

KENILWORTH—*continued*.

    Number of meters, 55.
    Scale of charges—
        Price per 1,000 gals., domestic and trade, 1s. 6d., 1s. 2d., 10d., municipal purposes, 6d.

Kenley (supplied by East Surrey Waterworks Co.).

Kennington, Kent (supplied by Ashford).

Kent Bank (supplied by Grange-over-Sands).

Kent Water Co. *See* Metropolitan Water Board.

Kenyon (supplied by Warrington).

Keswick, Cumberland. Railway, Cockermouth, Keswick and Penrith. Distance from London, 300 miles.
    Authority, Urban District Council.
    Secretary, J. Broatch.
    Engineer and Manager, W. Hodgson.
    Office, Town Hall.
    Loan capital, £23,000.
    Interest, 3¼ to 3½ per cent.
    Area supplied, Keswick, Portinscale, in the rural district supplied from Urban Council's mains.
    Works established, 1856.
    Total population supplied, 5,500.
    Daily consumption per head, 30 gals.
    Sources of supply, springs and streams on Skiddaw.
    Storage capacity, 380,000 gals.
    Filtration, none required.
    Character of water, soft.
    Number of meters, 3.
    Scale of charges—assessment charge, 1s. to 2s. in the £.
    Price per 1,000 gals., 1s. to 6d. No charge for municipal purposes.
    Total water rent received, £1,100.

Kettering, Northampton. Railway, M. Distance from London, 72 miles.
    Authority, Urban District Council.
    Clerk, John Bond.
    Engineer and Surveyor, T. R. Smith.
    Office, Market Place.
    Interest on loan, 3½ per cent.
    Area supplied, Kettering and Weekley.
    Works established, 1871. Special Acts, Provisional Orders, 1872, 1889, 1901.
    Total population supplied, 32,000, estimated.
    Annual supply of water, 217,600,000 gals.
    Daily consumption per head, domestic, 21·01 gals.; trade, 9·89 gals.
    Source of supply, wells and gathering grounds, about 1,800 acres.

Kettering—*continued.*

Storage capacity, storage reservoir, 160,000,000 gals.; service reservoir, 800,000 gals.
Character of water, wells about 28°; gathering, 13° hardness.
System of filtration, sand.
Number of meters, 496.
Length of mains, 29 miles.
Scale of charges—assessment charge, £2,479.
Price per 1000 gals., domestic, 2s.; trade, under 25,000 per quarter, 2s.; from 25,000 to 100,000 per quarter, 1s. 6d.; over 100,000, 1s. 3d.; municipal purposes, 1s.

Kettle (supplied by Cupar).

Keymer, Sussex (supplied by Burgess Hill).

Kidderminster, Worcestershire. Railways, G.W., L.N.W. Distance from London, 24 miles.
Authority, Kidderminster Urban District Council.
Chairman, Alderman E. Parry.
Surveyor, Andrew James.
Managing Engineer, B. J. Green.
Office, Town Hall.
Loan capital paid up, £57,574 7s. 6d. Interest on loan, £1,201 1s. 5d.
Towns supplied—Stourport, 4 miles distant, is supplied by meter at 6d. per 1,000 gals.
Works established, 1873. Special Act, Public Health Act.
Total population of area supplied, about 30,000.
Daily consumption per head, domestic, 27.
Total quantity of water raised per annum (1906)—322,000,000 gals., including 14,869,000 gals. to Stourport.
Source of supply, artesian wells.
Storage capacity, 1,971,000 gals., service reservoir, covered.
Filtration, none.
Character of water, very good, hardness before boiling 9·95, after boiling 7·11.
Death rate, 15·14 per 1,000.
Number of meters, 150.
Length of mains, 28 miles.
Scale of charges—
Assessment charge, 5 per cent. on rateable value, 7½ per cent. outside municipal area.
Water for municipal purposes, free.
Price per 1,000 gals., trade, 8d. to 5d. according to quantity.

Kidmore (supplied by South Oxfordshire).

Kidsgrove, Staffs. (supplied by Staffordshire Potteries).

Kidwelly, Carmarthen. Railway, G.W.
Authority, Kidwelly Urban District Council.
Town Clerk, D. C. Edwards.
Area supplied, Kidwelly only.
Works established, 1885.
Total population of area supplied, 2,285.

Kilbarchan, Scotland (supplied by Paisley).

Kilbirnie, Scotland. Railway, L. & A., G. & S.W.
Authority, Ayrshire County Council, Northern District Committee.
Chairman, James Allan.
Secretary, David Whiteford.
Manager, Andrew Kay.
Office, Parish Council Chambers.
Towns and villages in the area supplied, Kilbirnie and Glengarnock.
Works established, 1884; extended, 1894.
Total population supplied, 8,000.
Daily consumption per head—domestic, 25 gals.
Sources of supply, Pundeavan Burn and Small Burn (tributaries of River Garnock).
Storage capacity, 8,000,000 gals.
System of filtration, sand, and Bell's mechanical filters.
Character of water, good.
Number of meters, 23.
Scale of charges—assessment charge, 1s. 6d. in £.
Price per 1,000 gals., domestic, 6d. to 2½d., according to quantity.
An additional storage reservoir to hold 51,000,000 gals. is in course of construction on Pundeavan Burn, and will be completed by the end of 1907.

Killiney (supplied by Dublin).

Kilmacolm, Scotland.
Authority, Renfrewshire County Council, Lower Road.
Clerk to authority, W. McClure.
Resident Engineer, R. Blackwood.
Engineer for the county, James Murray, C.E.
Office, County Buildings, Paisley.
Works established, 1878; extensive additions since.
Total population supplied, 3,000.
Area of supply, Kilmacolm.
Sources of supply, gathering grounds, and impounding reservoirs on moorland streams.
Character of water, pure and wholesome, 2° hardness.
Filtration, sand.
Storage capacity, 12,000,000 gals.
Head on distributing mains —maximum, 230 ft.
Average daily supply per head—domestic, 60 gals.
Scale of charges, assessment charge, 1s. 2d. in £.
Price per 1,000 gals., 6d.
Length of mains, 15 miles.
Kilmacolm is partly supplied by Port Glasgow.

Kilmainham (supplied by Dublin).

Kilmarnock, Scotland. Railway, G.S.W. Distance from Edinburgh, 60 miles.
Authority, Kilmarnock Corporation.
Chairman, William Gibson.
Secretary, William Middlemas, Town Clerk.
Manager and Engineer in charge, Robert Blackwood, Burgh Surveyor, Market Bridge, Kilmarnock.
Total capital invested, including loans, £184,386; interest 2¾, 3, and 3½ per cent.
Works established, 1846. Purchased by local authority, 1892.
Special Acts, Kilmarnock Water Company's Acts, 1846, 1866, 1875; Kilmarnock Water Acts, 1892, 1896.
Estimated population actually supplied, 40,000.
Average death rate, 14 per 1,000.

KILMARNOCK—continued.

Towns and villages within the area of control, with population of each (1901 Census)—

Kilmarnock and Riccarton	35,000
Dreghorn	
Fenwick and Kilmaurs	3,000

Sources of supply in use—drainage areas situated at parish of Fenwick. Impounding reservoirs on Balgray Burn and Dunton Burn.

Nature of drainage area, partly pasture, partly cultivated.

Average annual rainfall over drainage area, 42·45 inches (10 years).

Character of water, 4½° hardness.

Analysis of water, 25th January, 1907, expressed in grains per gallon :—

	North Craig Water.		Craigendunton Water.
Total solid matter in solution ...	8·26	...	4·48
Chlorine	0·91	...	·84
=Chloride of Sodium	1·49	...	1·38
Nitric Acid	—	...	—
=Nitrate of Soda	—	...	—
Free or Saline Ammonia	—	...	—
Albuminoid or Organic Ammonia ...	·0112	...	·0098
Oxygen required to oxidise Organic Matter	·50	...	·84
Colour (Loch Katrine= 10)	20·	...	50

Filtering area provided, 5,100 square yards in 9 filter-beds—sand and gravel.

Storage reservoirs, North Craig	...	...	capacity 60,000,000 gals.
,, ,, Gainford	...	...	,, 3,000,000 ,,
,, ,, Burnfoot	...	...	,, 80,000,000 ,,
,, ,, Dunton	...	...	,, 130,000,000 ,,

Head on distributing mains during day—max., 170 ft. ; min., 55 ft.

Annual supply of water—

For all purposes, except meters...	550,000,000 gals.
,, trade purposes, by meter	100,000,000 ,,

Average day's supply per head for all purposes except by meter, 40 gals ; by meter, 8 gals.

Maximum day's consumption, 1,500,000 gals.

Assessment charge, 1s. in the £ ; public rate, 1d.

Price per 1,000 gals., 8d. to 5½d.

Number of meters in use, 136.

Length of distributing mains—supply, 17 miles ; distributing, 25 miles.

Kilsyth, Scotland. Railway, N.B., &c.

Authority, Town Council.

Chairman, Provost John Stark.

Secretary and Town Clerk, R. M. Lennox, Solicitor.

Engineer, Alex. Frew, C.E., Glasgow.

Office, Town Clerk's, Kilsyth.

Loans outstanding, £15,093.

Works established, 1877.

Total population supplied, 8,000.

Sources of supply, springs, bores, and reservoir on Kilsyth Hills.

Character of water, good, slightly hard.

Storage in impounding reservoirs, 25,000,000 gals.

Scale of charges—assessment charge, 1s. in £ on rental.

Price per 1,000 gals. 6d. and 1s.

Kilsyth is partly supplied by Falkirk.

Kilton Thorp, Yorks. (supplied by CLEVELAND).

Kilwinning (supplied by Irvine).

Kimberley (supplied by Nottingham).

Kingarish (supplied by Rothesay).

Kingsbridge, Devon. Railway, G.W. Distance from London, 242 miles.
  Population supplied, 3,025.

Kingsbury, Middlesex (supplied by Colne Valley Water Co.).

Kingsheath (supplied by Birmingham).

Kingkerswell (supplied by Torquay).

King's Langley.
  Authority, Rickmansworth and Uxbridge Valley Water Co. (which see).

King's Lynn, Norfolk. Railways, G.E. and M. Distance from London, 97 miles.
  Authority, King's Lynn Corporation.
  Chairman, Councillor Geo. Bristow, J.P.
  Clerk to Authority, J. W. Woolstencroft, Solicitor.
  Borough Surveyor and Water Engineer, J. N. Webb.
  Office, Town Hall, King's Lynn.
  Loans outstanding, £24,368.
  Works established, 1897 ; extended, 1906.
  Special Acts, P.O.. 1894.
  Total population supplied, 21,288.
  Average death rate, 14·96 per 1,000.
  Sources of supply, headings in chalk.
  Total hardness, 14°.
  Filtration, none ; softening, none.
  Storage in service reservoirs, 1,000,000 gals.
  Head on distributing mains—maximum, 173·4 feet.
  Annual supply of water, 250,000,000 gals.
  Average daily supply per head for all purposes, 32·41 gals.
  Maximum day's supply, 850,000 gals. in August.
  Assessment charge—3d. in £ on R.V. per annum ; by meter, 7d. per 1,000.
  Number of meters, 160.
  Length of mains—supply, 8 miles ; distributing, 25 miles.

Kingsnorth, Kent (supplied by Ashford).

King's Norton (supplied by Birmingham).

Kingsthorpe (supplied by Northampton).

Kingston-by-Sea (supplied by Tendring Hundred Waterworks Co.).

Kingston-on-Thames (supplied by Lambeth Water Co.).

Kingston-upon-Hull. *See* Hull.

Kingstown (supplied by Carlisle).

Kingstown (supplied by Dublin).

Kingswinford (supplied by South Staffs. Waterworks Co.).

Kington, Herefordshire. Railway, G.W. Distance from London, 170½ miles.
Authority, Kington Water Co., Ltd.
Population supplied, 1,953.
No returns supplied.

Kinningpark (supplied by Glasgow).

Kinross, Scotland.
Authority, Corporation.
No returns supplied.

Kirby Lawford, Essex (supplied by Tendring Hundred).

Kirby-le-Soken (supplied by Tendring Hundred).

Kirkby Moorside (Yorks). Railway, N.E. Distance from London, 220 miles.
Authority, Kirkby Moorside Rural District Council.
Chairman, Thos. Coverdale, J.P.
Clerk, R. Jennings, Jun.
Office, Kirkby Moorside.
Towns and villages in the area supplied—Kirkby Moorside, Nunnington,
    Stonegrave, Newton, Laysthorpe, Nawton, Hutton-le-Hole, Lastingham,
    Spaunton, and Appleton-le-Moors.
Works established, 1898.
Sources of supply, springs.
Storage capacity, 80,000 gals.
Filtration, none.
Character of water, soft.
Number of meters, 8.
Length of mains, 15 miles.
Scale of charges—assessment charge. By special expenses rate.

Kirkcaldy, Scotland.
Authority, Kirkcaldy and Dysart Water Commission.
Clerk, Alex. Beveridge, Solicitor.
Manager, Robt. Ritchie.
Office, Sands Road, Kirkcaldy.
Works established, 1867.
Special Acts, 1867, 1881, 1896.
Total population supplied, 44,352.
Character of water, moderately hard.
System of filtration, sand and quartz (Reeve's patent).
Storage capacity—impounding reservoirs, 667,715,284 gals. ; service reservoirs,
    6,500,000 gals.
Pressure on distributing mains—maximum, 115 lbs. per square inch ; minimum,
    70 lbs. per square inch.
Average daily supply per head, domestic, 33¼ gals. ; trade,   ; total,
    475,757 gals.
Assessment charge—8½d. in £ on rental ; public, 2d. in £ on rental.
Price by meter, 6¼d. per 1,000 gals.
Number of meters, 148.
Length of mains—supply, 24 miles ; distributing, 42 miles.

Kirkham, Lancs. (supplied by Fylde Waterworks Co.).

Kirkintilloch and Lenzie.
Authorities, Town Councils.
Secretary, David Patrick.
Engineer, William Miller.
Works established, 1874.
Total population supplied, 12,000.
Sources of supply, springs.
Storage capacity, 80,000,000 gals.
Scale of charges, assessment charge, 10d.
Price per 1,000 gals., 6¼d , or £2 12s. 6d. per 100,000 gals.

Kirkmanshulme (supplied by Manchester).

Kirkwall, Orkney.
Authority, Town Council of Kirkwall.
Chairman, John Sclater, Provost.
Town Clerk, W. J. Heddle.
Engineer, Malcolm Heddle.
Office, Municipal Buildings.
Works established 1878, under the Public Health Act, 1869, and General Police
   (Scotland) Act, 1862.
Total population supplied, 4,000.
Daily consumption per head, 17 gals. (when available).
Sources of supply—Papdale (springs).
Storage capacity, four service tanks holding altogether 2,300,000 gals.
Character of water, good for culinary purposes, hard for washing.
Length of mains, 5½ miles.
Scale of charges—assessment charge, 1s. 1d. per £ rental.

Kirriemuir, Scotland.
Authority, Town Council.
Chairman Provost Savege.
Secretary, James S. Bruce.
Office, Burgh Surveyor's Office.
Loans outstanding, £4,700.
Works established, 1877.
Total population supplied, 4,500.
Area of supply, Kirriemuir only.
Source of supply, springs from hill land.
Filtration, none ; softening, none.
Storage—impounding reservoir, 1,400,000 gals. ; service reservoir, 132,000 gals.
Head on distributing mains—maximum, 180 feet ; minimum, 36 feet.
Annual supply, 70,000,000 gals.
Maximum day's supply, 227,000 gals. in July.
Assessment charge—6¼d. in £ on R.V.
Length of mains—supply, 6¾ miles ; distributing, 7 miles.

Knapwell (supplied by St. Ives, Hunts.).

Knaresborough, Yorks.   Railway, N.E.   Distance from London, 204 miles.
Authority, Harrogate Corporation.
Chairman, Alderman W. H. Milner.
Clerk to Authority, J. Turner Taylor.
Engineer in charge, Fred. Dixon, F.G.S., A.M.I.C.E.
Office, 14, Albert Street, Harrogate.
Loans outstanding, £7,079.
Works established, 1764 ; purchased by Corporation, 1903. Special Acts, 1764,
   1902.
Total population of area supplied, 5,500.
Average death rate, 14·9 per 1,000.
District of supply—Knaresborough and Scriven-with-Tentergate.

KNARESBOROUGH—*continued.*

Source of supply, Harrogate Corporation.
Character of water—filtration softening; storage, &c., same as Harrogate.
Service tank, 212,500 gals.
Head on distributing mains—maximum, 276 feet; minimum, 57 feet.
Annual supply of water, 54,078,000 gals.
Average daily consumption per head, domestic, 25·8 gals.; trade, 1·12 gals.
Maximum supply per day, 162,000 gals. in August.
Average price per 1,000 gals., domestic and trade, 1s.
Assessment charges—5½ per cent. to 10 per cent. on R.V.
Number of meters, 8.
Length of mains, 9 miles.

Knaresborough, Outer (supplied by HARROGATE).

Knottingley (supplied by PONTEFRACT).

Knutsford, Cheshire. (G. & W.) Railway, L.N.W. Distance from London, 180 miles.
Authority, Knutsford Light and Water Company, Knutsford.
Chairman, H. T. Silvester.
Secretary, W. S. Inman, Manchester Road.
Engineer in charge, Thos. Thomas, Manager Gasworks.
Consulting Engineers, Taton & Fox.
Office, Church Hill, Knutsford.
Works established, 1863. Special Act, 1879.
Total number of consumers, 698.
Estimated population actually supplied, 4,840.
Total capital invested, including loans, £21,135.
Dividend, 7 per cent.
Area of control, Knutsford, population, 5,000 (1901 Census).
Source of supply, brook.
Character of water, total hardness, 18°.
Filtering area provided, 511 square yards in 2 filter-beds, sand and gravel.
Service reservoir, 1; capacity, 105,000 gals., open.
Pumping station, Booth Mills.
Annual supply for all purposes, 18,842,600 gals.
Maximum day's consumption, 130,000 gals.
Scale of charges—Assessment charge, 1s. in the £ on R.V.
Number of meters in use, 18.
Length of distributing mains, about 8 miles; supply, 1 mile.
Average price per 1,000 gals., 9d.

Lacock, Wilts. (supplied by CORSHAM).

Ladybank (supplied by PORT GLASGOW).

Laindon, Essex. Railway, L.T. & S. Distance from London, 22¼ miles.
Authority, The Laindon & District Gas Light, Coke and Water Co., Ltd.
Chairman, W. B. Martin.
Secretary, H. Percy Davies.
Resident Engineer, W. J. Harrill.
Office, 99, Cannon Street, London, E.C.
Share capital paid up, £4,500.
Loan　　　,,　　　,,　　£2,000 at 5 per cent.
Company formed April 28th, 1906. Special Act, 1906.
Public supply expected to be available in June, 1907.
District of supply, Laindon, Laindon Hills, Lee Chapel, and Little Burstead.
Source of supply—springs, Laindon Hills.

Laleham (supplied by SOUTH WEST SUBURBAN).

Lambeth Water Company   (see METROPOLITAN WATER BOARD).

Lambhill (supplied by GLASGOW).

Lamesley (Township of), Durham (supplied by NEWCASTLE-ON-TYNE).

Lampeter, Cardigan. Railway, G.W. Distance from London, 260 miles.
Authority, Lampeter Town Council.
Chairman Water Committee, T. Richards.
Town Clerk, J. E. Lloyd, Bryn Road, Lampeter.
Surveyor and Inspector, R. John, Lampeter.
Consulting Engineer, M. W. Davies, A.M.I.C.E., Swansea.
Total capital invested, including loans, £1,600 and £1,700.
Area of control, Lampeter town. Population, 1,732 (1901 Census).
Works established, 1883 and 1900.
Total population of area of control, 1891, 1,569 ; 1901, 1,722.
Total number of consumers, 320.
Estimated population actually supplied, 1,600.
Maximum day's consumption, College terms, 30,000 gals. ; normal, 29,000 gals.
Total quantity of water drawn per annum (1901)—
   From drainage areas or surface springs   ...   20,170,000 gals.
Estimated maximum daily discharge at points of collection, 91,000 gals.
  ,, minimum ,, ,, ,, ,, 25,000 ,,
  ,, average ,, ,, ,, ,, 58,000 ,,
Reservoirs— supply being ample, storage unnecessary.
Service reservoirs—Troedyrhiw ...   . capacity, 40,000 gals.
     ,, Isaf ...   ...   ,, 750 ,,
Length of distributing mains, 3¾ miles and 1¾ in town.
Scale of charges—
  Domestic, charge by rate.
  Building purposes according to area.
  Per horse kept   ...   . 2 0 per annum.
  ,, head of cattle and ponies   ...   . 1 0 ,,   ,,
  4-wheeled carriage, for washing purposes   ... 2 0 ,,   ,,
  2-wheeled   ,,   ,,   ,,   ... 1 0 ,,   ,,

Lanark. Railways, L.N.W. and Caledonian. Distance from London, 377 miles.
Authority, the Town Council of Lanark.
Chairman, John Keith.
Secretaries, W. & J. Annan, Town Clerks, Lanark.
Engineer in charge, Robert Tweedale, Burgh Surveyor.
Office, Hope Street, Lanark.
Total capital invested, including loans, £13,480 ; loans outstanding, £4,301.
Towns and villages within area of control, Lanark Burgh, 5084 (1901 Census)
  and Suburbs, about 1,000.
Works established, 1882. Provisional Order, 1880.
Population of area of control, Burgh only, 1891, 4,579 ; 1901, 5,084.
Total number of consumers   ...   .   1,400, holiday.
  ,, ,, ...   1,200, normal.
Estimated population actually supplied   ...   ...   7,000, holiday.
      ...   ...   6,000, normal.
Average death rate, 18·24 per 1,000.
Sources of supply in use—drainage areas situated at Tinto Hill, in parish of
  Carmichael.
Population of drainage area, nil.
Character of water, soft ; total hardness, 1·60°.
Surface formation of drainage areas, hill pasture.
Strata of formation yielding springs, red whinstone rock.

LANARK—*continued.*

Total quantity of water drawn per annum—
  From drainage areas   ...   .   102,200,000 gals.
Estimated total quantity of water available per annum—
  From drainage areas   ...   .   200,000,000 gals.
Estimated maximum daily discharge at points of collection ...   1,000,000 gals.
  ,,   minimum   ,,   ,,   ,,   ...   120,000 ,,
  ,,   average   ,,   ,,   ,,   ...   400,000 ,.
Storage reservoirs, Lochlyoch reservoir   ...   ...   capacity, 18,000,000 gals.
Service reservoirs, High level reservoir   .   ...   capacity, 60,000 gals.
  ,,   ,,   Low level ,, ...   ,,   132,000 ,,
Annual supply of water—
  For domestic purposes   ...   .   95,700,000 gals.
  ,,   trade   ,, ...   6,000,000 ,,
  ,,   municipal ,, ...   500,000 ,,
Maximum day's consumption ...   .   280,000, holidays,—July.
  ,,   ,, ...   250,000, normal.
Filtering, Reeve's patent filter.
Price per 1,000 gals., 8d. in Burgh, 1s. outside.
Number of meters in use, 50.
Length of distributing mains, 6 miles.

Lanarkshire. *See* DISTRICT OF THE MIDDLE WARD OF LANARKSHIRE.

Lancaster. Railways, L.N.W. and M. Distance from London, 230 miles.
  Authority, Corporation.
  Chairman, Alderman W. Huntington.
  Secretary, W. Clough, Borough Accountant.
  Engineer and Manager, J. C. Mount.
  Office, Town Hall.
  Loan capital, £144,963.
  Area of supply, Lancaster and adjacent townships.
  Works established, 1852.
  Special Acts, 1852, 1855, 1864, 1876, 1880.
  Total population supplied, 60,000,
  Annual supply of water, 730,000,000 gals.
  Source of supply, springs, north side of Wyre Valley.
  Storage capacity, 150,000,000 gals.
  Character of water, soft, ·09 Clark's scale.
  Death rate, 12·55 per 1,000.
  Number of meters, 250.
  Scale of charges, assessment charge, annual value.
  Price per 1,000 gals., 1s., 9d., and 6d.
  Total water rent received, £16,850.

Lancing, Sussex (supplied by BRIGHTON).

Langho (supplied by BLACKBURN).

Langley, Bucks. (supplied by SLOUGH).

Langton (supplied by BLANDFORD).

Lannochside, Scotland (supplied by DISTRICT OF THE MIDDLE WARD OF LANARK-SHIRE).

Larbert (supplied by Falkirk).

Largs, Scotland.
Population supplied, 3,187.
No returns supplied.

Larkhall, Scotland (supplied by District of the Middle Ward of Lanark-shire).

Lastingham (supplied by Kirkby Moorside).

Latchford, Lancs. (supplied by Warrington).

Lathom (partly supplied by Skelmersdale).

Latimer (supplied by Great Berkhampstead).

Latton (supplied by Herts and Essex Water Co.).

Launceston, Cornwall. Railways, G.W. and L.S.W. Distance from London, L.S.W. 223½ miles; G.W., 280 miles; by road, 213 miles.
Owners, Mayor, Aldermen, and Burgesses of the Borough of Dunheved (otherwise Launceston), acting as Urban Sanitary Authority.
Chairman, The Mayor.
Secretary, Claude H. Peter, Town Clerk.
Surveyor, A. W. Grace.
Office, Town Clerk's Office.
Loan, £10,900. Repaid £2,935.
Interest on loan, £270 15s. 7d.
Works established, 1894.
Annual supply of water, 73,000,000 gals.
Sources of supply—moorland stream at Carne Down, in the parish of Altarnun.
Storage capacity, about 400,000 gals. in service reservoir.
Character of water, soft.
System of filtration, coarse and fine sand, upward filtration.
Death rate, 17·8 per 1,000.
Number of meters, 10.
Scale of charges—assessment charge, 9d. in £ dwelling houses, 6d. offices and lock-up shops. Trade by arrangement.
Total water rent received, £590 5s. 8d.

Lavernock (supplied by Cardiff).

Lawford (supplied by Tendring Hundred Waterworks Co.).

Laysthorpe, Yorks. (supplied by Kirkby Moorside.)

Leamington. Railways, G.W. and L.N.W. Distance from London, 97½ miles.
Authority, Corporation, 1880.
Secretary, Leonard Rawlinson, Town Clerk.

13   (193)

LEAMINGTON—*continued.*

Engineer, W. de Normanville, A.M.I.C.E.
Office, Town Hall.
Total cost, £54,114.　Loans outstanding, £16,120.
Annual profit, £600 to £800.
Works established, original company, 1840.　This was entirely given up in 1880, a new supply being obtained from a well by the Corporation.　A second well was sunk in 1900, and new pumping station erected.
Special Act, 1896.
Total population supplied, 29,000.
Average death rate, 14·3 per 1,000.
Area supplied, 2,760 acres.
Sources of supply, 2 wells and 900 feet of headings in new red sandstone.　The wells and pumping stations are 1¼ miles apart.
Character of water, exceptionally pure ; hardness, one well 16°, and the other 26°.
Filtration none ; softening, none.
Service reservoirs, 1,100,000 gals.
Head on distributing mains—maximum, 128 feet ; mimimum, 44 feet.
Annual supply of water, 246,370,000 gals.
Daily consumption per head, domestic, 23 gals. ; trade and special 2·02.
Maximum day's supply, 933,000 gals., January ; cause, frost.
Length of mains—supply, 2 miles ; distributing, 32 miles.
Scale of charges—
　Assessment charge (authorised), 4 per cent. on R.V. ; present charge, 3¾ per cent.
　Price per 1,000 gals., 8d., trade purposes ; no sliding scale.
Number of meters, 240.

Leasingham (supplied by Sʟᴇᴀғᴏʀᴅ).

Leatherhead, Surrey.　Railways, L.B.S.C., and L.S.W.　Distance from London 19½ miles.
Authority, Leatherhead and District Waterworks Co.
Chairman, Colonel A. C. Gleig.
Secretary, J. Young.
Engineer, F. S. Cripps.
Population supplied, 5,000.
Source of supply, borings into chalk.

Leathley (supplied by Lᴇᴇᴅs).

Leavesden (supplied by Rɪᴄᴋᴍᴀɴsᴡᴏʀᴛʜ).

Leckhampton (supplied by Cʜᴇʟᴛᴇɴʜᴀᴍ).

Leeds.　Railways, G.N., M., L.N.W., N.E., G.C., L. & Y.　Distance from London, 186 miles.
Authority, Corporation, 1852.
Chairman, Councillor F. Ogden.
Engineer in charge, Chas. Geo. Henzell.
Office, Municipal Buildings.
Loan outstanding, March 31st, 1907, £2,590,158.
Interest, average about 3½ per cent.
Towns and villages in the area supplied, Rothwell, Oulton and Woodlesford, Seacroft, Halton, Whitkirk, Roundhay, Shadwell, Adel, Pool, Leathley and Huby.
Works established, 1852.
Special Acts, 1847, 1852, 1856, 1862, 1867, 1874, 1877, 1889, 1893, 1896, 1897, 1901, 1904, 1905.

LEEDS—*continued.*

Total population of area supplied, 463,452.
Annual supply of water, by gravitation, 5,870,057,119 gals.
Daily consumption per head—domestic, 21·8 ; trade, 12·1 gals.
Sources of supply, Washburn watershed.
Storage capacity, 3,985,900,000 gals.
Character of water, total hardness, Clarke's degree, 3·3° before boiling ; permanent, 3·0° after boiling.
System of filtration, sand and gravel.
Death rate, 15·6 per 1,000.
Number of meters, 1,500.
Length of mains in district of supply, 480 miles.
Assessment charge, 5 to 7½ per cent. rental.
Price per 1,000 gals., trade, 6d.
Total water rent received, £150,089, year ended March 31st, 1907.

Leek, Staffs. Railway, North Staffs. Distance from London, 157 miles.
Authority, Urban District Council.
Chairman, Thomas Mason.
Engineer and Surveyor, W. E. Beacham.
Secretary, Clerk to Urban District Council.
Office, Town Hall.
Works purchased by the U.D. Council, 1857.
Annual profit, including "Capital Charges," about £2,000.
Special Act, 1855.
No outstanding debts.
Total population of area supplied, 15,484, Leek only.
Source of supply, springs from millstone grit at Upper Hulme, 3½ miles from town.
Character of water, very good, suited for domestic use, total hardness, 3·8°.
System of filtration, none ; softening, none.
Storage service reservoirs, 2,000,000 gals.
Head on distributing mains—maximum, 120 ft.; minimum, 39 ft.
Annual supply of water, 164,250,000 gals.
Average daily supply per head—domestic, 25 gals. ; trade, &c., 15 gals.
Maximum day's supply, 600,000 gals., October to June.
Scale of charges—assessment, 8d. in £ on rateable value.
Price per 1,000 gals., trade, 6d.
Length of mains—supply, 3¼ miles; distributing, 27 miles.
Number of meters, about 60.

Lees (supplied by OLDHAM).

Leicester. Railways, M., L.N.W., G.N., G.C. Distance from London, 97½ miles.
Authority, Leicester Corporation Waterworks.
Chairman, Ald. Sir Ed. Wood, J.P., Mayor.
Town Clerk, E. V. Hiley, Town Hall, Leicester.
Engineer and Manager, Frederick Griffiths, M.I.C.E.
Waterworks Office, Bowlinggreen Street.
Total capital authorised including loan, £1,524,012 12s. 0d.
Works established, by Act, 1847. Purchased by local authority, 1878.
Total population of area of control, 1881, 151,728 ; 1891, 208,061.
Towns and villages within the area of control, with population of each (1901 Census)—Leicester, Barrow-upon-Soar, Quorn, Montsorrel, Rothley, Birstall, Syston, Sileby, Thurmaston, Wigston, Glen Parva, Oadby, Anstey, Newtown Linford, Groby.
Character of water, soft.

Leicester—*continued.*

Total drainage area, 10,760 acres.
Filtering area provided, 20,366 square yards in 21 filter-beds, sand.
Pumping stations, Thornton, by gravitation ... capacity, 1,500,000 gals. per day.
    „   „   Bradgate, pumping ...   ...   „   2,500,000 „   „
    „   „   Switbland   ...   .   „   2,500,000 „   „
Storage in impounding reservoirs, Thornton ...   capacity, 333,000,000 gals.
    „   „   „   Bradgate   ...   „   556,000,000 „
    „   „   „   Swithland ...   „   490,000,000 „
Service reservoirs, New Parks   ...   .   „   2,000,000 „
    „   „   Gilroes   ...   .   „   2,000,000 „
    „   „   Hallgates   ...   .   ·,   2,000,000 „
    „   „   Oadby ...   .   „   1,000,000 „
Pressure on distributing mains—maximum, 112 lbs.; minimum, 5 lbs.
Annual supply of water (1906)—
     For domestic purposes   ...   .   1,074,542,262 gals.
     „   trade   „   ...   .   450,345,433 „
     „   municipal   „   ...   .   57,661,985 „
Average daily supply per head—domestic, 10·89 gals.; trade, &c., 5·14 gals.
Maximum day's supply, 6,298,728 gals. in December.
Assessment charge, 6¼ per cent. to 4½ per cent. on R.V.
Charges by meter, 3d. to 6d., according to scale.
Total length of mains, about 300 miles.
Number of meters in use, 1,231.

Leigh (supplied by Tonbridge.)

Leigh-on-Sea, Essex.
Authority, Urban District Council.
Supply of water, 10,000 gals. per hour.
Source of supply, deep well, 600 feet.
Character of water pure and soft.

Leigh and Hindley, Lancs. Railway, L.N.W. Distance from London, 194 miles.
Authority, Leigh and Hindley Joint Water Committee.
Capital expenditure, £48,554.
Population supplied—Leigh, 40,000; Hindley, 23,504.
Source of supply, water bought in bulk from the Liverpool Corporation.

Leighton (supplied by Neston).

Leith. *See* Edinburgh.

Lenchwick, Worcester (supplied by Evesham).

Lenzie, Scotland. *See* Kirkintilloch.

Leominster, Hereford. Railways, G.W. and L.N.W. Distance from London, 156¼ miles.
Authority, Corporation.
Manager at works, J. W. Chadwick.
Engineer, James Budd, C.E., A.S.I.
Town Clerk, W. T. Sale.
Office, Town Clerk's Office.
Area supplied, Leominster only.
Total population supplied, 5,826.
Annual supply of water, 60,000,000 gals.
Sources of supply, springs.
Storage capacity, 400,000 gals.

LEOMINSTER—*continued.*

　　Character of water, hard.
　　Average day's supply—domestic, 24 gals. ; trade, etc., 2,000,000 gals. per annum.
　　Maximum day's supply, 200,000 gals.
　　Head on distributing mains—max., 224 ft. ; min., 56 ft.
　　Number of meters, 30.
　　Length of mains, 6¼ miles.
　　Total water rent received, about £770.

Leslie, Scotland.
　　Authority, Leslie Waterworks Co.
　　Population supplied, 3,421.
　　No returns supplied.

Leven, Scotland.
　　Authority, Corporation.
　　Population supplied, 6,000.
　　No returns supplied.

Levenshulme (supplied by MANCHESTER).

Leverstock Green (supplied by HEMEL HEMPSTEAD).

Lewes, Sussex. Railway, L.B.S.C. Distance from London, 50 miles.
　　Authority, Lewes Waterworks Company.
　　Chairman, Francis Verrall, Chairman of Directors.
　　Secretary, John Miles, 173, High Street, Lewes.
　　Engineer and Manager, Albert Wells, 26, Western Road, Lewes.
　　Total capital invested, £26,900.
　　Dividend, 5, 7, and 10 per cent.
　　Works established, 1833.
　　Special Acts—Lewes Waterworks Acts, 1833, and 1868.
　　Total number of consumers, 2,515.
　　Estimated population actually supplied, 12,575.
　　Average death rate, 11·46 per 1,000.
　　Area of control, Lewes, Population, 11,670 (1901 Census) ; 1906, estimated, 13,000.
　　Source of supply in use, well at Southover, Lewes.
　　Strata tapped by well, chalk.
　　Natural rest level of water below surface, 5 feet ; above Ordnance datum, 17 feet.
　　Level of water below surface (when pumping 500,000 gals. per day), 16 feet.
　　Recent analysis of the water—
　　Analysis, July 23rd, 1904—colour, quite clear and bright ; smell, none ; sediment. none.
　　　　Chemical analysis afforded the following—

Total solids	20·04	grains per gal.
Solids after ignition	12·40	„
Chlorine	2·00	„
Ammonia (free)	·012	per 1,000,000
Ammonia (albuminoid)	·026	„
Oxygen taken from permanganate in quarter hour	none	
Oxygen taken from permanganate in four hours	trace	
Nitrogen as nitrates and nitrites	·20	
Nitrites	none	
Hardness (total)	9·30° Clark	
Hardness after boiling	2·60°	
Phosphates	none	
Metallic impurity	none	

LEWES—*continued.*

Bacteriological examination.—The organisms per cubic centimeter which grew on nutrient gelatine in three days, and were visible to the naked eye, were 75, all of which were quite satisfactory. Special examination was made for Typhoid bacilli and coli communis, but with entirely negative results.

The above combined examinations show the water to be very good and quite safe for drinking purposes, there being no evidence whatever of organic contamination.

Total hardness, 3° temporary, 3° permanent.

Service reservoirs—1 on Kingston Hill　...　capacity, 327,000 gals., covered.

„	1 in High Street	...	„	322,000	„ „
„	1 on Race Hill	...	„	284,000	„ „

Annual supply of water (1906)—

For domestic purposes and unmetered trade		109,420,000 gals.
„ trade „	... ...	34,654,000 „
„ municipal „	... ...	5,926,000 „

Total quantity of water drawn per annum (1906), from well, 150,000,000 gals.

Estimated total quantity of water available, not known.

Maximum day's consumption . .　...　...　...　...　500,000 gals.

Assessment charges—　　　　　　　　　　per ann. compound rate

Houses not exceeding £6, rack rent or poor rate value 8s.	...	6s. 6d.
„ £10, „	„	12s.	...	9s. 6d.
„ £15 „	„	16s.	...	13s. 0d.
„ £20 „	„	20s.		
„ and upward to £100 „	„	100s.		
Exceeding £100 „	„	6 per cent.		

Special charges for malthouses, slaughterhouses, bakers, horses, cattle, etc.

Steam engines, 12s. for each horse power.

Price per 1,000 gals., 1s. to 6d., according to quantity.

Number of meters in use, 93.

Lewynpia (supplied by YSTRAD).

Leyland, Lancs. Railway, L.N.W. Distance from London, 205 miles.

Authority, Urban District Council.

Clerk to Authority, J. J. Johnson.

Resident Engineer, M. H. Wilkinson.

Consulting Engineer, Wm. Wrennall, C.E.

Office, Public Hall Buildings, Towngate.

Loans outstanding, £2,341.

Works established, 1881.

Population supplied, 7,000.

Average death rate, 13 per 1,000.

Area supplied, No. 1 District of Leyland only.

Source of supply, borehole 500 feet deep in millstone ; grti at Clayton-le-Wood.

Character of water—clear, alkaline, no bacteria or other organisms. Total hardness, 24·42° ; temporary, 15·28° ; permanent, 9·14°. Of excellent quality, entirely free from contamination.

Filtration, none ; softening, none.

Storage capacity, service reservoirs, 330,000 gals.

Head on distributing mains—max., 250 ft. ; min., 150 ft.

Annual supply, 63,875,000 gals.

Average daily supply per her head—domestic, 19 gals ; trade, 6 gals.

Maximum day's supply, 185,000 gals. in August.

Assessment charge—rateable value £10 and under, 13s. per annum.

„　　　„　£11 (not exceeding), 16s. per annum.

And 1s. per ann. extra per ann. for each extra £ over that amount.

Price by meter, 9d. to 1s. per 1,000 gals.

Number of meters, 29.

Total length of mains, 12 miles.

Leyton (supplied by EAST LONDON WATERWORKS Co.).

Liberton, Scotland.
　Authority, Liberton Waterworks Co.
　Population supplied, 379.
　No returns supplied.

Lichfield (City and County), Staffordshire. Railway, L.N.W. Distance from London, 118 miles.
　Authority, Lichfield Conduit Lands.
　Chairman of Trustees, Herbert M. Morgan.
　Warden, Alan E. Chinn, The Close, Lichfield.
　Surveyor and Water Engineer, Charles Evans.
　The water supply of Lichfield is a charity managed by a board of trustees appointed under a scheme formulated by the Charity Commissioners.
　Area of control, city and county of Lichfield.
　Population, 7,902 (1901 Census).
　Works established, water springs left by charity, 1301.
　Total population of area of control—1881, 8,349; 1891, 7,864; 1901, 7,902.
　Annual rainfall (year 1906), 26·06. Lat. 52° north, long. 1·58° west, height above sea level, 271·18.
　Annual supply of water (1901)—
　　　　For domestic purposes and municipal　...　45,767,350 gals.
　　　　　" 　trade　　" 　...　...　...　...　21,447,400　"
　Maximum day's consumption, 194,657 gals.
　Total quantity of water drawn per annum (1901)—
　　　　Surface springs　...　...　...　...　...　9,611,545 gals.
　　　　Wells　...　...　...　...　...　57,549,648　"
　Sources of supply in use—surface springs situated at Aldershaw. Wells at Walsall Road, Lichfield.
　Strata or formation yielding springs, red sandstone and marl.
　Strata tapped by wells or borings, red sandstone and marl.
　Pumping stations, Walsall Road, Lichfield, capacity, 142,443 gals. per day (December, 1901).
　Service reservoir, Beacon Street, Lichfield, capacity, 350,937 gals., covered.
　Number of meters in use, 135.
　Length of distributing mains, 14 miles.
　Recent analysis (March 4th, 1907)—

Total solid matter dried at 212° Fah. ...	23·8	grains per gal.
Free and saline ammonia	0·0028	"
Albuminoid ammonia	0·0021	"
Nitric nitrogen	0·55	"
Combined chlorine	1·68	"
Oxygen absorbed in 4 hours at 80° Fah.	0·021	"
Appearance	Clear.	
Colour through 2 feet	Very pale bluish green tinge.	
Hardness before boiling	15·06°	
" 　after　 " 　...	6·80°	
Temporary hardness	8·26°	

　This water is organically clean, and of suitable quality for drinking and domestic purposes.

Lichfield St. Michael's (supplied by SOUTH STAFFS. WATERWORKS Co.).

Limefield (supplied by BURY).

Limekilns, N.B. (supplied by DUNFERMLINE).

Limerick, Ireland.
　Authority, Corporation.
　Engineer, B. E. F. Sheehy.
　Office, 57, George Street, Limerick.
　Total population supplied 38,000.

Limpsfield, Surrey. Railway, L.B.S.C. Distance from London, 21 miles.
Authority, Limpsfield and Oxted Water Co., Ltd.
Population supplied, 1,469.
No returns supplied.

Linby (supplied by NOTTINGHAM).

Lincoln. Railways, M., G.N., G.E., G.C., L.D., and E.C. Distance from London
130 miles.
Authority, the Lincoln Corporation.
Chairman, The Mayor.
Secretary, W. T. Page, Junr., Deputy Town Clerk, Bank Street, Lincoln.
Engineer in charge, Neil McKechnie, Barron.
Office, Corporation Offices, Lincoln.
Total capital invested, including loans, £143,263.
Works established, 1847. Purchased by local authority, 1871.
Special Acts, Lincoln Waterworks, 1846, 1856, 1871.
Total population of area of control, 1881, 40,492; 1891, 45,324; 1901, 53,384.
Estimated population actually supplied (1906), 58,000.
Death rate, 16·4 per 1,000.
Towns and villages within the area of control, with population of each (1901
  Census), Lincoln, 48,784; Skillingthorpe, 660; Boultham, 610; Bracebridge,
  2,967; Canwick, 270; Greetwell, 93.
Sources of supply in use—drainage areas situated at Witham watershed; shallow
  wells or collecting reservoirs situated at Hartsholme and Boultham ballast pits.
The new well and bore to the new red sandstone has just been completed
  (March, 1907). Well, 12 ft. dia., 400 ft. deep, and 9 ft. dia. to a depth of
  1,502 ft. 33in. bore-hole to a depth of 1,700 ft.; and a 24 in. dia. to a total
  depth of 2,200 ft. The yield pumping from a depth of 200 ft. was 600,000
  gals. per day, but the water is unfit for domestic purposes, owing to excess of
  mineral salts.
Total quantity of water drawn per annum (31st March, 1907)—
  Drainage area at Witham and Hartsholme ...   ...   52,155,000 gals.
  Shallow wells, ballast pits   101,220,000   „
Estimated total quantity of water available per annum—

	730,000,000	Minimum.	Witham.
Drainage area	2,190,000,000	Maximum.	Hartsholme.
	116,000,000	Minimum.	„
Shallow wells	133,000,000	Maximum.	Ballast pits.
	92,000.000	Minimum.	„

Nature of drainage area, all agricultural land. Water authority have no control
  of drainage area.
Surface formation of drainage areas, alluvial, resting on the lias for storage
  reservoirs; oolite for the River Witham.
Estimated maximum daily discharge at points of collection, 30,481,876 gals.
  „   minimum   „   „   „   „   2,383,716 „
Maximum annual rainfall over drainage area, 29·53 inches (1903)
Minimum   „   „   „   „   „   18·14   „   (1893)
Average   „   „   „   „   „   23·59   „   (period 15 years)
Character of water—total hardness, 19°; no softening done.
Filtering area provided, 5,092 square yards in seven filter-beds. Two additional
  filter-beds are being made, each having an area of 720 square yards.
Pumping stations—Boultham, capacity, 2,500,000 gals. per day.
                Ballast Pit, capacity, 2,000,000   „   per day.
                    from source to filters only).
Storage reservoirs, Hartsholme Lake (impounding), 20,000,000 gals. for use when
  the river is in flood. The supply is mainly drawn from the river without
  storage.

LINCOLN—*continued.*

    Service reservoirs—Westgate   ...   ... capacity, 750,000 gals., open.
                  Cross Cliff Hill (now disused) „ 1,500,000 „   „
    Annual supply of water (March 31st, 1907)—
        For domestic purposes...   ...   . 497,250,000 gals.
        „ trade   „   ...   . 101,125,000 „
        „ municipal   „   ...   . 25,090,000 „
    Maximum day's consumption, 2,056,400 gals.
    Number of meters in use, 203.
    Length of distributing mains, 56 miles.
    Scale of charges—assessment charge, 1s. in the £.
    Price per 1,000 gals., 9d.

Lindal (supplied by BARROW-IN-FURNESS).

Lindrick (supplied by RIPON).

Lindfield, Sussex (supplied by MID-SUSSEX).

Linesey (supplied by BLACKBURN).

Linford (supplied by LEICESTER).

Lingdale, Yorks. (supplied by CLEVELAND).

Lingfield, Surrey (supplied by EAST SURREY WATERWORKS Co.).

Linlithgow, Scotland.　Railway, N.B.　Distance from Edinburgh, 16 miles.
    Authority, Linlithgow Town Council.
    Chairman, W. Braithwaite.
    Secretary, John Thom.
    Manager, James Bamberry.
    Engineer, John A. Warren, C.E., Glasgow.
    Office, 132, High Street.
    Works established, 1891.
    Special Act, Linlithgow Water Act, 1889.
    Total population supplied, 4,279.
    Source of supply, drainage.
    Storage capacity, 14,000,000 gals.
    System of filtration, filter tanks.
    Character of water, good, moderately hard.
    Death rate, 14 per 1,000.
    Number of meters, 17.
    Length of mains, 5 miles.
    Scale of charges—
      Assessment charge, 1s. 2d. per £ on rental, payable half by owner and half by
        tenant.
      Price per 1,000 gals., trade, 6d.
    Total water rent received, £300.

Linthouse (supplied by GLASGOW).

Linton, Yorks.
    Authority, The Wetherby District Water Co.
    Population supplied, 256.

Linwood, Scotland (supplied by PAISLEY).

Liscard (supplied by WALLASEY).

Liskeard, Cornwall.   Railway, G.W.   Distance from London, 260¾ miles.
  Authority, Liskeard Town Council.
  Chairman, the Mayor.
  Town Clerk, H. Lyde Caunter.
  Office, Town Clerk's Office.
  Works established, 1860.   Special Act, Liskeard Corporation Act, 1898.
  Total population supplied, 4,011.
  Sources of supply, moorland.
  Character of water, soft.
  Number of meters, 10.
  Scale of charges—assessment, domestic, 6s. 6d. to £4 10s. per annum ; trade by
    meter, and according to rateable value.
  Total water rent received, £959.

Little Callerton (supplied by NEWCASTLE-ON-TYNE).

Little Clacton (supplied by TENDRING HUNDRED WATERWORKS Co.).

Little Common (supplied by BEXHILL).

Little Eaton (supplied by DERBY).

Littleham (supplied by EXMOUTH).

Littlehampton, Sussex.   Railway, L.B.S.C.   Distance from London, 62 miles.
  Authority, Urban District Council.
  Office, Town Offices.
  Area supplied, Urban District of Littlehampton.
  Works established, 1883.
  Total population of area supplied, 7,363.
  Annual supply of water, 40,000,000 gals.
  Daily consumption per head, 22¼ gals.
  Source of supply, deep boring in chalk.
  Length of mains, 11 miles.
  Scale of charges—assessment, 1s. in £ per annum.
  Price per 1,000 gals. 1s.

Little Hulton (supplied by BOLTON).

Little Lever (supplied by BURY).

Little Marlow (supplied by GREAT MARLOW).

Little Neston, Cheshire (supplied by NESTON, BIRKENHEAD).

Littleover (supplied by DERBY).

Littlestone, Kent.
  Authority, The Littlestone and District Water Company.
  No returns supplied.

Little Stretton.   Works taken over by CHURCH STRETTON WATERWORKS Co.

Littleton (supplied by CHESTER).

Littlewich (supplied by MAIDENHEAD).

Liverpool. Railways, L.N.W., M., L. & Y. Distance from London, 201 miles.
Authority, Liverpool Corporation.
Chairman, Ald. W. J. Burgess, J.P.
Town Clerk, E. R. Pickmere, M.A.
Chief Engineer, Joseph Parry, M.I.C.E.
Office, Municipal Offices, Liverpool.
Works established, 1857; Vyrnwy Works, 1888.
Special Acts. The principal are 1847 and 1880; there are many others.
Total population supplied, within limits of compulsory supply and in and around
Chorley, 906,768.
Average death rate, 19·2 per 1,000, city only.
Towns and villages in the area supplied—Liverpool, Bootle and out townships,
including Garston and Prescot, and also various townships on the lines of
aqueduct; also Chorley.
Sources of supply, Lake Vyrnwy, Rivington Reservoir, and local wells.
Character of water, unexceptionable.
Analysis of water, expressed in parts per 100,000—
Date when taken, Year 1905.
(Average of 12 Analyses).

Source of Sample ...	Rivington.	Vyrnwy.	Dudlow Lane.	Green Lane.	(Average of 11 Analyses) Windsor.
Total solid matter in solution	10·65 ...	5·19 ...	19·15 ...	34·22 ...	41·07
Oxygen required to oxidise, in 15 mins.	·029 ...	·089 ...	·000 ...	·000 ...	·000
Do. in 3 hours ...	·060 ...	·163 ...	·001 ...	·001 ...	·000
Ammonia	·003 ...	·002 ...	·000 ..	·000 ...	·000
Ammonia from Organic matter, by distillation with alkaline permanganate	·007 ...	·006 ...	·000 ...	·000 ...	·000
Nitrogen as Nitrates	·009 ...	·000 ...	·639 ...	·568 ...	·882
Combined Chlorine..	1·58 ...	·88 ...	3·00 ...	3·37 ...	4·45
Hardness	4·40 ...	1·99 ...	8·88 ...	21·05 ...	26·97

Filtration, sand. No softening.
Head on distributing mains—maximum, 110 lbs.; minimum, 25 lbs. per sq. inch.
Storage capacity, Lake Vyrnwy, about 12,000,000,000 gals ; Rivington reservoirs,
about 4,107,000,000 gals.; service reservoirs, 31,497,000 gals.
Annual supply of water, in and around city and Chorley, 10,007,646,000 gals.
Average daily supply per head—Domestic (city only) 17·50 gals.
Trade (city only), 12·96.
Maximum day's supply, 38,406,000 gals., in January.
Scale of charges—assessment charge (domestic supplies) 5 per cent. in the £, on
assessment within the city of Liverpool, 6¼ per cent. in the £, on assessment,
outside the city limits.
Number of meters, about 2,213.
Price per 1,000 gals., trade, 6d., within city, and 9d. outside the city.
Length of supply and distributing mains, 846 miles.

Liversedge (supplied by Bradford, Yorks.).

Livesey (supplied by Blackburn).

Llanberis, Carnarvon (G. & W.). Railway, L.N.W. Distance from London, 25
miles.
Authority, Llanberis Water and Gas Co.
Works established, 1895; Special Act, 1895.
Population supplied, 2,818.
No returns supplied.

Llandaff, Glam. (supplied by CARDIFF).

Llandegai (supplied by BANGOR).

Llandevaad (supplied by NEWPORT, Mon.).

Llandough (supplied by CARDIFF).

Llandovery, Carmarthenshire. Railways, L.N.W., G.W. Distance from London, 228 miles.
 Authority, Corporation.
 Population supplied, 1,809.
 No returns supplied.

Llandudno. Railways, L.N.W., G.W. Distance from London, 227 miles.
 Authority, Llandudno Urban District Council.
 Secretary, A. Conolly.
 Engineer and manager, E. Paley Stephenson, A.M.I.C.E.
 Loan capital paid up, £92,423, including annuities capitalised.
 Interest on loan, 3, 3¾, 4, 4½, 7 per cent.
 Area supplied, Llandudno and Glan Conway.
 Works established, 1854. Special Acts, 1854, 1876, 1879, and 1897.
 Total population supplied, 9,500 residents, 20,000 visiting.
 Daily consumption per head, about 30 gals.
 Sources of supply—Llyndulyn and Melynllyn Lakes, 14 miles distant.
 Storage capacity, 139,000,000 gals.
 System of filtration, none.
 Character of water, soft, and well adapted for domestic purposes.
 Death rate, 11·5 per 1,000.
 Number of meters, 94.
 Scale of charges—assessment charge, 7 per cent. on 2s. 3d. of gross rent.
 Price per 1,000 gals., trade, 1s. 6d.
 Total water rent received, £8,419.

Llandullas, Flint (supplied by RHYL).

Llanelly. Railways, G.W., L.N.W., L. & M., R.P. & G. Distance from London, 214 miles.
 Authority, Llanelly Urban District Council.
 Clerk, Henry W. Spowart.
 Engineer in charge, George Watkeys, Borough Engineer.
 Office, Town Hall.
 Towns and villages within the area of control, with population of each (1901 Census)—

Llanelly	25,617
Llwynhendy	2,200
Furnace (part)	100
Felinfoal „	100

 Works established—Tretseddod Reservoir, 1853; Cwmlliedi Reservoir, 1878 Upper Lliedi Reservoir, 1902.
 Special Acts—Llanelly Local Board Waterworks Acts, 1865 and 1891.
 Total population of area of control—1881, 19,655 ; 1891, 23,805 ; 1901, 25,617.
 Total number of consumers, 6,000.

LLANELLY—*continued.*

Estimated population actually supplied, 28,000.
Annual supply of water—

For domestic purposes	306,600,000 gals.
„ trade „	409,648,270 „
„ municipal „	14,000,000 „
In bulk to other authorities	4,978,000 „

Maximum day's consumption, 2,500,000 gals.
Total quantity of water drawn per annum—
　　From drainage areas ... ... 735,226,270 gals.
Estimated total quantity of water available per annum—
　　From drainage areas ... ... 2,000,000,000 gals.
Sources of supply in use—
　Drainage areas situated at 1½ to 6 miles north of Llanelly.
Estimated maximum daily discharge at points of collection, 45 to 50,000,000 gals.
　　„　　minimum　　　　　„　　　　　„　　400,000 gals.
　　„　　average　　　　　„　　　　　„　　5,500,000 „
Maximum annual rainfall over drainage area, 61·37 inches (1894).
Mininium　　　„　　　　　„　　34·97 „　(1887).
Average　　　„　　　　　„　　46·32 „　(20 years).
Population on drainage area, 500.
Extent of cultivation of ditto, 5 per cent.
The water authority has no control of drainage area.
Storage reservoirs—

Tretseddod ... ... capacity,	8,000,000 gals.
Cwmlliedi ... ... „	220,000,000 „
Upper Lliedi ... ... „	200,000,000 „

Filtering area provided, none.
Death rate 15·9 per 1,000.
Character of water, 1·75° Clark's scale.
Number of meters in use, 120.
Length of distributing mains 20 miles.
Scale of charges—Assessment charge, 1s. in £.
Trade, price per 1,000 gals., maximum, 6d. ; minimum, 1½d.

Llanfairfechan, Wales. Railway, L.N.W. Distance from London, 232 miles.
　Authority, Urban District Council.
　Engineer and Manager, Thos. Hughes.
　Secretary, W. H. Ellis, Solicitor.
　Office, Council Offices.
　Works established, 1872. Special Act, 1884. Works bought from the Water
　　Company for £10,500, at the rate of 2¾ per cent. annuity system, to pay off in
　　25 years.
　Total population of area supplied, estimated 2,938.
　Daily consumption per head, 30 gals.
　Source of supply, Glansais River, in the mountains.
　Storage capacity, 2,500,000 gals.
　Character of water, good for domestic purposes.
　System of filtration, gravel.
　Death rate, 13 per 1,000.
　Length of mains, 5½ miles.
　Scale of charges, assessment, 1s. 6d. in £.
　Price per 1,000 gals., domestic and trade, 1s. ; municipal purposes free.
　Total water rent received, about £600.

Llangollen, Wales. Railway, GW. Distance from London, 202 miles.
　Authority, Urban District Council.
　Clerk to authority, E. Ffoulkes Jones.

LLANGOLLEN—*continued.*
  Manager and Engineer, J. Gray-Owen, C.E.
  Office, Town Hall, Llangollen.
  Works established, 1866.
  Total population supplied, 3,304.
  Death rate, 16 per 1,000.
  Sources of supply, springs, open brook.
  Character of water, excellent, soft.
  Storage capacity in service reservoirs, 325,000 gals.
  Daily consumption per head, 30 gals.
  Scale of charges, assessment charge, average 1s. in £.
  Price per 1,000 gals., 1s.
  Number of meters, 36.
  Length of mains, 2 miles.

Llanidloes, Montgomery.
  Authority, Town Council.
  Population 4,000 (estimated).
  Source of supply, storage reservoirs.
  Water for domestic purposes free.

Llanishen, Glam. (supplied by CARDIFF).

Llanllwchaiarn (supplied by NEWTOWN).

Llantwit-Howe (supplied by NEATH).

Llanvaches (supplied by NEWPORT, Mon.).

Llwydcoed (supplied by ABERDARE).

Llwynhendy (supplied by LLANELLY).

Llwynypia (supplied by YSTRAD).

Lochgelly, Scotland. Railways, N.B. and N.E. Distance from London, 420 miles.
  Authority, Town Council.
  Chairman, Provost George Garry.
  Secretary, Robt. Small, Town Clerk.
  Manager, Alex. Robb.
  Engineers, Buchanan and Bennett, C.E., Hill Street, Edinburgh.
  Office, Burgh Office.
  Loans, £23,500. Interest on loans, £665.
  Area supplied, Lochgelly Police Burgh.
  Works established, 1881. Special Act, 1878.
  Total population supplied, 7,500.
  Daily supply of water, 100,000 gals.
  Daily consumption, 20 gals.
  Sources of supply, gathering grounds, 611 acres.
  Storage capacity, 24,000,000 gals.
  Character of water, soft.
  Death rate, 14 per 1,000.
  Number of meters, 16.
  Length of mains, 10 miles.
  Assessment charge, 2s. 6d. in the £.
  Price per 1,000 gals., 9d.
  Total water rent received, £2,021.

Loftus, Yorks. (supplied by CLEVELAND).

Looe, Cornwall.
  Authority, Urban District Council.
  Population 2,500.

London (*see* Metropolitan Water Board).

Londonderry.
   Authority, Corporation.
   No returns supplied.

Long Benton, Township (supplied by Newcastle-on-Tyne).

Longbridge (supplied by Birmingham).

Longridge (supplied by Preston).

Longstowe, Hunts. (supplied by St. Ives).

Longton (supplied by Staffordshire Potteries Water Co. and Preston).

Lossiemouth, Scotland.
   Authority, Company,
   Population supplied, 3,486.
   No returns supplied.

Lostwithiel, Cornwall. Railway, G.W. Distance from London, 277½ miles.
   Authority, Corporation.
   Loan, £2,500; repaid, £406.
   Sources of supply, gravitation, constant.
   No charge for domestic purposes

Loughborough, Leicester. Railways, M., L.N.W., G.C. Distance from London, 110 miles.
   Authority, Corporation, 1868.
   Chairman, James Cartwright.
   Secretary, Harry Parkins, Town Clerk.
   Engineer and Manager, A. H. Walker, A.M.I.C.E.
   Office, Town Hall.
   Loans outstanding (March, 1906), £127,630.
   Annual loss (March, 1906), £898 2s.
   Special Act, 1869, 1899 and 1905.
   Works established, 1869. Blackbrook Works, 1887.
   Total population supplied, about 23,000.
   Death rate, 13·5 per 1,000.
   Towns and villages in "district of supply" supplied—Loughborough, Nanpanton, Shepshed, and Prestwold. Not yet supplied—Thorpacre, Garendon, Hathern, Long Whatton, Belton, Cotes, Stanford, Normanton, Sutton Bonnington, East Leake.
   Sources of supply, impounding reservoirs at Woodbrook and Blackbrook.
   Character of water, fairly soft; temporary hardness, very low; high purity.
   System of filtration, sand.
   Storage capacity, 530,000,000 gals.
   Annual supply of water, 214,000,000 gals.
   Average daily supply per head—domestic, 12·11 gals.; trade, 14·66 gals.
   Maximum day's supply, 920,000 gals., July, 1906.
   Charges authorised, 7¼ per cent. on rental value.
   Present charge, 4¼ per cent. on rental value.
   Price per 1,000 gals., 6d. to 9d.
   Length of supply mains, 5 miles; distributing mains, 33 miles.
   Number of meters, 140.

Loughton (supplied by Preston).

Loughton (supplied by Metropolitan Water Board).

Louth, Lincs. Railway, G.N. Distance from London, 141½ miles.
Authority, Louth Water Company.
Chairman, Major Fowler.
Secretary, F. C. Chard.
Manager and Resident Engineer, Amos Hodgson.
Office, Council House, Upgate.
Share capital paid up, £20,000, last dividend 3 per cent.
Loan   „   „   £2,525 at 4 per cent.
Works established, 1871. Special Act, 1871.
Total population of area supplied, 9,518.
Area supplied, 300 acres.
Annual supply of water, 48,238,000 gals.
Daily consumption per head, 16 gals.
Source of supply, wells and gathering grounds.
Storage capacity, 1,079,948 gals.
Character of water, good, but hard, 12° Clark's scale.
Death rate, 17·63 per 1,000.
Scale of charges—annual value on 7 per cent. to £30 ; 6 per cent. above £30.
Price per 1,000 gals., 1s. 6d. to 1s.

Loveclough (supplied by Bury).

Lower Bebington, Cheshire (supplied by Birkenhead).

Lower Halston (supplied by Rainham).

Lowestoft, Suffolk. Railways, G.E., M. and G.N. Distance from London, 117 miles.
Authority, Lowestoft Water and Gas Company.
Chairman, Chas. S. Orde.
Manager, J. Hawksley, C.E.
Secretary, Chambers E. Allerton.
Office, 137, London Road, Lowestoft.
Date of formation, 1853. Special Acts, 1857, 1863, 1877, 1897, 1899.
Share capital paid up, £262,875.
Debenture stock, £59,800 at 4 per cent.
Dividends—7½ per cent., 5¼ per cent. and 4 per cent., gas and water combined.
Total number of services, 3,571.
Total population, 38,166, including Urban District.

Luddenden Foot (supplied by Halifax).

Ludlow, Salop. Railways, L.N.W. and G.W. Distance from London, about 162 miles.
Authority, Mayor, Aldermen and Burgesses of Borough of Ludlow.
Chairman, Chairman of Sanitary Committee.
Town Clerk, J. H. Williams.
Office, Guildhall.
Total capital invested, including loans, £8,300.
Area of control—Ludlow Borough was extended last year to enclose villages.
Population, 6,328 (1901 Census).
Works established, 1875, present works, 1880.
Purchased by local authority, 1890.
Total population of area of control, 1891, 6,500 ; 1901, 6,500.
Estimated population actually supplied, 6,300.
Annual supply of water—

For domestic purposes	...	...	...	...	40,000,000 gals., estimated.
„ trade „	...	...	...	...	300,000 „
„ municipal „	...	...	...	...	250,000 „

LUDLOW—*continued*.

Maximum day's consumption, 110,000 gals.
Total quantity of water drawn per annum—
　From drainage areas　...　...　...　...　50,000,000 gals.
Sources of supply in use—
　Drainage area situated at Shropshire ...　...　...　lxxviii. 7.
　　　,,　　　　,,　　　　,,　...　...　...　lxxviii. 10.
Estimated maximum daily discharge at points of collection　...　200,000 gals.
　,,　　minimum　　,,　　　,,　　　,,　　..　140,000　,,
　,,　　average　　,,　　　,,　　　,,　　...　180,000　,,
Water authority have no control of drainage area. The gathering grounds are on
　Lord Windsor's estate and by his permission.
Surface formation of drainage areas, gravel, woods and pasture.
Nature of subsoil yielding water, loamy gravel.
Locality, bounded by hills on one side and river on other.
Storage, one reservoir, service and storage　...　...　capacity, 240,000 gals.
Filterings, none.
Pumping stations, one ...　...　...　...　capacity, 300,000 gals. per day.
Length of distributing mains, 5 miles.
Scale of charges, assessment A.
No meters in use.
Ludlow stands over a gravel basin, and water which flows into the sump under
　engine-house is pronounced pure but hard. Ludlow has been supplied from
　springs from time immemorial. These works were superseded by 8 h.-p.
　turbine, 8 h.-p. gas engine, gravitation main and reservoirs, etc., in 1880.

Luton. Railways, M. and G.N. Distance from London, 30¼ miles.
Authority, The Luton Water Company.
Chairman, Robt. Smith Tomson.
Secretary, J. G. Meadows.
Engineer in charge, W. R. Phillips.
Office, Crescent Road.
Share capital paid up, £135,668 ; last dividend, 4 per cent.
Loan　　,,　　　,,　　£11,197.
Works established, 1868. Special Act, 1865, Provisional Order, 1880, Act, 1897.
Total population of area supplied, 42,400.
Average death rate, 15·8 per 1,000.
Area supplied, Luton parish.
Sources of supply, 3 wells and deep boring in chalk.
Storage capacity, 3,800,000 gals.
Character of water, very pure.
Filtration, none ; softening, none.
Annual supply of water, 411,372,115 gals.
Daily consumption per head—domestic, 21 gals. ; trade, 7·17 gals.
Maximum day's supply, 1,250,000 gals.
Scale of charges, assessment, 4 to 6 per cent. on annual value.
Price per 1,000 gals., 1s. to 6d.
Length of mains, 47 miles.

Lydd, Kent (supplied by LITTLESTONE) and wells owned by Corporation.

Lydden (supplied by FOLKESTONE).

Lye (supplied by STOURBRIDGE).

Lyme Regis, Dorset. Railways, L.S.W. and G.W. Distance from London, 144¼
miles.
Authority, Corporation.
Town Clerk, M. C. Preston.
Manager, The Water Bailiff.

14　　　　　　　　　　(209)

Lyme Regis—*continued.*

Office, Lyme Regis.
Area supplied, Lyme Regis only.
Source of supply, springs.
Character of water, best possible.
Length of mains, over 4 miles.
Total water rent received, £338.

Lymington, Hants. Railway, L. & S.W. Distance from London, 98 miles.
Authority, Town Council of the Borough of Lymington, acting as the Urban District Council.
Secretary, J. D. Rawlins, Town Clerk, 38, High Street, Lymington.
Engineer and Manager, W. Broomfield.
Total capital invested, including loans, £11,000.
Area of control, Borough of Lymington; population, 4,165 (1901 Census).
Total number of consumers, 987.
Works established, 1883.
Annual supply of water—

For domestic purposes	...	...	...	24,500,000 gals.
„ trade „	...	...	...	2,000,000 „
„ municipal „	...	...	...	2,000,000 „

Maximum day's consumption gals., 90,000.
Total quantity of water drawn per annum—

From surface springs... ... ... 28,500,000 gals.

Quantity of water available, unknown.
Sources of supply — surface springs and collecting reservoir, lat. 50° 46', long. 1° 33'.
Estimated minimum daily discharge at points of collection, 95,000 gals.
Water authority have no control of drainage area.
Strata or formation yielding springs, gravel; nature of subsoil yielding water, gravel.
Collecting reservoir, Ampress, capacity, 75,000 gals.
Pumping station, Ampress, capacity, 200,000 gals. per day.
Service reservoir, wrought-iron tank on brick tower, capacity, 75,000 gals. covered.
Death rate, 16·36 per 1,000.
Number of meters in use, 10.
Assessment charges—domestic, 6d. in the £ half-yearly on general district rate.
Trade, 1s. 6d. per 1,000 gals., or by arrangement; shipping, 1s. per ton, cattle, 1s. 6d. each.
Analyses of water by Jenner Institute—

Parts per 100,000.

Suspended matter	...	...	...	...	...	...
Dissolved solids	...	...	...	...	...	20·6
Chlorine	...	...	...	...	...	4·1
Alkalinity expressed as calcium carbonate			...	...	3·5
Free and saline ammonia	...	...	...	...	...	·001
Albuminoid ammonia	...	...	...	...	...	·004
Nitrogen as nitrites	...	...	...	...	...	None
Nitrogen as nitrates	...	...	...	...	...	0·29

Oxygen absorbed from permanganate at 80° F.—

(a) 15 minutes	...	...	...	...	...	
(b) 4 hours	...	...	...	...	...	·009
Lead	...	...	...	...	...	None
Hardness	...	...	...	...	...	6·5

The existing pumping plant consists of 2 Cornish boilers and 2 sets of compound duplex direct-acting steam pumps; but the Council have passed plans and estimates providing for the removal of the existing machinery and substituting oil engines and treble plunger pumps in duplicate.

Lymm, Cheshire. Railway, L.N.W. Distance from London, 187 miles.
Authority, Company.
Special Act, 1874.
Population supplied, 4,707.
Area supplied, Lymm and Heatley.
Source of supply, artesian wells and borings.
Storage capacity, 156,000 gals.
Assessment charge—under £30, 7 per cent.; over £30, 6 per cent.

Lynmouth (supplied by Lynton).

Lynn, Norfolk. *See* King's Lynn.

Lynton, Devon. Railways, L.S.W., G.W. and Lynton and Barnstaple Light Railway.
Distance from London, 225 miles.
Authority, Lynton Water Company, Ltd.
Chairman, W. L. Richards.
Secretary, C. J. Collins.
Manager, Walter Yeo.
Office, Southcliffe Villa.
Share capital paid up, £2,000. Debentures, £3,200 at 4 per cent.
Dividend, 8 per cent.
Annual profit, £300.
Works established, 1866.
Total population supplied, 1,800.
Death rate, 10·28 per 1,000.
Towns and villages in the area supplied—Lynton, Lynmouth, The Tors.
Source of supply, river.
Character of water, 2·91 soft.
Filtration, Candy's Polarite, assisted by sand.
Storage in service reservoir, 50,000 gals.
Pressure on distributing mains, 30 lbs. to 70 lbs. per sq. in.
Scale of charges—assessment charge, 1s. 6d. in the £ on rateable value up to £50,
　　and 1s. over £50.
　　Price per 1,000 gals. trade, 1s.

Lytham (supplied by Fylde).

Macclesfield. Railways, L.N.W. and North Staff. Distance from London, 166 miles.
Authority, Corporation.
Chairman, Alderman Thorpe, J.P.
Resident Engineer, Chas. W. Stubbs.
Office, Town Hall.
Loans, March 31st, 1906, £81,096, repaid; £20,487.
Interest, 3½ per cent.
Annual profit, including capital charges, £1,265 (March 31st, 1906).
Works established, 1826. Special Acts, 1849 and 1882.
Special Acts, 1849 and 1852.
Total population supplied, about 35,000.
Death rate, 18 per 1,000.
Towns and villages in the area supplied, Macclesfield, Sutton, Hurdsfield, Upton
　　Prestbury, and Tytherington.
Sources of supply, springs and streams. Impounding reservoirs four miles from
　　town.
Character of water, rain gathered.
Filtration, sand. Softening, none.
Storage capacity, 204,000,000 gals.

Macclesfield—*continued.*

Head on mains—maximum, 156 ft.; minimum, 10 ft.
Number of meters, 178.
Scale of charges—assessment charge, 1s. 4¾d. to 1s. assessment of property.
  Price per 1,000 gals., 6d.
Total water rent received, £7,300.

Macduff, Banffshire. Railway, G.N. of S. Distance from London, 573 miles.
Authority, Town Council.
Loan, £3,163.
Works established, 1883.
Total population supplied, 3,722.
Sources of supply—spring at Longmanhill.
Assessment charge, 8d. in £.
Price per 1,000 gals., 8d.

Mackworth (supplied by Derby).

Madeley (supplied by Much Wenlock).

Madron, Cornwall.
Authority, Madron Urban District Council.
Secretary, Ambrose Taylor, Madron.
Consulting Engineer, Frank Latham, M.I.C.E., Municipal Office, Penzance.
Total capital invested, including loans, £3,600.
Towns and villages within area of control, Heamoor, population 1,300; Tolcarne,
  population, 600. (1901 Census.)
Works established, 1901.
Total number of consumers, about 2,000.
Total quantity of water drawn per annum—
  From shallow wells or subsoil, 100,000,000 gals.
Estimated total quantity of water available per annum—
  From shallow wells or subsoil, 150,000,000 gals.
Source of supply—shallow wells and collecting reservoirs situated at Boskinning
  for Heamoor, Trereife for Tolcarne.
  Annual rainfall over drainage area, same as at Penzance.
The water is obtained by gravitation, which at its lowest is 12 feet 6 inches below
  surface.
  Surface formation of drainage areas, moorland.
  Strata or formation yielding springs, Elvans.
  Nature of subsoil yielding water, Rab over granite
  Storage reservoirs, Tolcarne ...   .   150,000 gals.
     „   „   Heamoor ...   .   200,000 ,

Magrapaik, Yorks. (supplied by Cleveland).

Maidenhead, Berks. Railway, G.W. Distance from London, 26 miles
Authority, Maidenhead Waterworks Company.
Chairman, R. Silver, J.P.
Secretary, Charles A. Vardy.
Engineer in charge, A. Smith.
Office, Clevedon Chambers, Queen Street.
Share capital paid up, about £40,000.
5 per cent. debentures, £5,000; 4 per cent. debentures, £2,000.
Dividend, 10 and 7 per cent.
Works established, 1876. Special Act, 1875.
Total population of area supplied, 15,000.
Average death rate, 14 per 1,000.

MAIDENHEAD—*continued.*

Towns and villages in the area supplied, Maidenhead, Cookham, Bray, Cookham Dean, Pinkney's Green, Littlewich, Burchett's Green, Waltham St. Lawrence, Holyport, Hawthorn Hill, Fifield, Forrest Green, Oakley Green and Taplow (part of), White Waltham and Sholter's Brook.
Source of supply, well in chalk.
Character of water, good ; hardness, 19°.
System of filtration, none.
Storage capacity in service reservoir, 1,250,000 gals.
Annual supply of water, 250,000,000 gals.
Average daily supply per head, about 25 gals.
Scale of charges—assessment, 1s. in £ on rental generally.
Price per 1,000 gals., domestic, 6d. ; trade, 1s.

Maidstone, Kent. Railways, L.C.D. and S.E. Distance from London, 35 miles.
Authority, Maidstone Waterworks Co.
Chairman, H. W. Tyrwhitt-Drake.
Secretary, C. E. Roper.
Engineer and Manager, W. J. Ware.
Offices, Pudding Lane.
Share capital paid up, £115,038. Loan, £23,410.
Interest, 3 and 4 per cent. Dividends, £7 10s. and £5 5s.
Works established, 1860.
Special Acts, 1860, 1863, 1885, Orders, 1873, 1879, 1896, 1899, 1906.
Death rate, 14·36 per 1,000.
Towns and villages in the area supplied, Maidstone, Barming, East and West Farleigh, Boxley, and Loose.
Sources of supply—chalk and lower green sand.
Character of water, 16° total hardness, 5° permanent.
Storage capacity, 1,000,000 gals.
Annual supply of water, 280,000,000 gals.
Number of meters, 300.
Scale of charges—assessment charge, sliding scale on rental value.
Price per 1,000 gals., trade, 2s. 6d. and 6d.
Municipal purposes, meter.

Maldon, Essex. Railway, G.E. Distance from London, 37 miles.
Authority, Maldon Corporation.
Chairman of Water Committee of Town Council, W. H. Sadd.
Borough and Water Engineer, T. R. Swales, C.E.
Accountant and Collector, S. C. Spurgeon.
Office, 29, High Street, Maldon.
Area supplied, Borough of Maldon only.
Works established, 1862. Special Acts, 1898.
Total population of area supplied, 5,600.
Annual supply of water, 50,000,000 gals.
Water raised per day, 100,000 gals.
Daily consumption per head, all purposes, 20 gals.
Source of supply — two wells and borings to top bed of sand, Woolwich and Reading beds, and one well and boring to Thanet sands.
Storage capacity, 80,000 gals.
Head on distributing mains—maximum, 150 ft.; minimum, 50 ft.
Character of water, soft, and of exceptional purity. Total hardness, 3·5°; permanent hardness, 0°.
Number of meters, 16.
Length of mains, 9 miles.
Scale of charges—assessment charge, average, 1s. 2d. in £.
Price per 1,000 gals., 2s. to 1s. 6d.
Total water rent received, about £1,300 per annum.

Maldon Rural supplies SOUTHMINSTER, and works are nearing completion for supplying 7 parishes.

Malmesbury, Wilts. Railway, G.W. Distance from London, 94¼ miles.
Authority, Malmesbury Town Council.
Chairman of Committee, Mr. Alderman Joseph Moore.
Secretary, Town Clerk.
Loan capital, £7,000.
Interest, 3¼ per cent.
Area supplied, all the municipal borough, and a portion outside.
Works established, 1864. Purchased by Local Authority, Feb. 1st, 1902.
Total population of area supplied, about 2,854 in borough, 500 outside.
Total number of consumers, 468.
Daily supply of water, 35,000 gals.
Sources of supply, chalk hills (deep oolite).
Storage capacity, 27,000 gals.
Character of water, very hard.
System of filtration, none.
Death rate, 14 per 1,000.
Number of meters, 12.
Length of mains, not known.
Scale of charges—assessment, under £20, 1s. 10d. in £, over £20, 1s. 6d.
Price for 1,000 gals., 6s. to 1s. 6d., according to quantity.
Total water rent received, £708.

Malpas, Mon. (supplied by NEWPORT).

Malton, Yorks. Railway, N.E. Distance from London, 212 miles.
Authority, Urban District Council, who are lessees for the unexpired term of 58 years, from April 6th, 1907.
Owner, Earl Fitzwilliam.
Chairman, Henry Tobey, J.P.
Engineer and Manager, Robt. Richardson, C.E.
Clerk to Urban District Council, G. S. Cattle.
Office, Town Hall, Malton.
Loan, £678 6s. 8d.
Interest, £26 15s.
Principal redeemed during 1905-6, £144 13s. 4d.
Works established, 1854. Special Act, Public Health Act, 1848.
Death rate, 17·23 per 1,000.
Area supplied, Malton only.
Source of supply, Lady Well. Depth, 14 feet; diameter, 8 feet.
Character of water, good, about 14° hardness. No filtration necessary.
Storage capacity, 240,000 gals., in covered reservoir.
Annual supply of water, 67,806,845 gals. to December, 1906.
Daily consumption per head—domestic, 35 gals.; trade, 3 gals.
Number of meters in use, 23.
Length of mains, 9 miles 246 yards.
Scale of charges—assessment charge, domestic, 6d. in £ for years 1906-7.
Water by meter—trade purposes, 8d. per 1,000 gals. up to 50,000 gals., and 6d. beyond.
Total revenue received, £627 16s. 4½d. for the year.

Malvern, Worcestershire. Railway, G.W. Distance from London, 127¾ miles.
Authority, Malvern Urban District Council.
Chairman of Water Committee, Colonel E. L. Twynam, R.E.
Clerk to authority, H. L. Whatley.

MALVERN—*continued*.

Engineer, Wm. Osborne Thorpe.

Office, Council Office, Malvern.

Towns and villages in the area supplied—Malvern, Malvern Link, Malvern Wells, Poolbrooke, West Malvern, The Wyche, Upper Well, and Colwall.

Total capital invested, £117,477.

Loans outstanding, £105,930.

Works established, 1891.

Special Acts, 1891, 1895, and 1898.

Total population supplied, Winter 17,800, Summer 20,000.

Average death rate, 8·8 per 1,000.

Sources of supply—

Drainage areas situated at Malvern Hills, North of Wyche Cutting, also slopes of British Camp Hill.

Collecting reservoirs at British Camp, North Malvern, The Wyche, and Waysladd.

Deep wells or borings at Bromsberrow Heath, Glos., two 200 ft. deep; Malvern Links Gas Works, two 950 ft. deep.

Geographical data—surface formation of drainage areas: Diorite (Malvern Hills) strata tapped by borings, new red sandstone, Glos. and Worcs. Locality and extent of outcrop, Bromsberrow, 12 sq. miles.

15 in. boring (Malvern Link) 130 ft. O.D.

2 ft.	0 in.	surface soil.
124 „	9 „	red marl.
4 „	0 „	blue shale.
17 „	9 „	red mottled with blue marl and gypsum.
2 „	0 „	blue arenaceous shale and gypsum.
34 „	6 „	red and blue mottle marl with gypsum.
2 „	0 „	blue arenaceous shale and gypsum.
81 „	0 „	mottled marl.
2 „	0 „	blue shale.
14 „	0 „	mottled marl.
7 „	0 „	compact blue shale.
99 „	0 „	marl and gypsum.
2 „	6 „	blue shale.
17 „	6 „	„ marl.
2 „	0 „	compact blue shale.
18 „	6 „	red and blue marl.
2 „	0 „	blue shale.
182 „	0 „	red and blue marl with layers of arenaceous shale and much gypsum.
90 „	0 „	red and blue marl, with layers of arenaceous shale, but no gypsum.
36 „	0 „	red sandstone.
16 „	0 „	„ marl, very compact.
193 „	0 „	„ sandstone with water.

Total 949 „ 6 „

Natural rest level of water below surface, 33 ft. above O.D. 130·30.

Maximum annual rainfall over drainage areas, 37·64 in. (1903).

Minimum „ „ „ „ „ 18·73 „ (1893).

Average „ „ „ „ „ 26·26 „ (20 years).

No population above drains on the drainage area.

Nature of drainage areas, sheep pasture, gorse and bracken. Common rights on areas can only be exercised to the grazing of a limited number of sheep and cutting gorse and bracken.

Estimated total quantity of water available per annum from drainage areas, 50,000,000 to 160,000,000 gals., according to rainfall.

MALVERN—*continued.*

Estimated from borings, 328,500,000 = the total capacity of pumping plant. The available quantity is greater.

Total quantity of water drawn in 1906—drainage areas, 53,683,000 gals.
 boring, 47,972,000 gals.

Character of water, soft and pure, requiring little or no filtration ; total hardness, 3 to 6½°.

Storage reservoirs, Camp, Malvern Hills, 51,000,000 gals.

Service reservoirs—Camp ... ... 200,000 gals.
 North Malvern ... ... 750,000 „
 The Wyche Malvern Wells 750,000 „
 The Upper Wyche ... 250,000 „
 Waysladd West Malvern 100,000 „

System of filtration, sand ; softening, none.

Pumping stations—Bromsberrow Heath, Glos., capacity 810,000 gals. per day.
 Malvern Link ... ... „ 150,000 „ „ „

Filtering area, 1,200 sq. yards in 3 beds.

Pressure on distributing mains—maximum, 210 lbs. ; minimum, 15 lbs. per sq. ft.

Annual supply of water (1906)—domestic, 83,060,000 gals.
 municipal, 28,605,000 „ including Council's gas works, electricity works, destructor, street watering, and flushing.

Average daily consumption, per head—domestic, 13 gals. ; trade, 5 gals.

Maximum day's supply, 410,000 gals. in August.

Scale of charges—
 Price per 1,000 gals., domestic, 1s. 8d. ; trade, 10d. to 1s. 8d. ; municipal purposes, £2,700 charged to General District Rate.

Number of meters, 1,806.

Length of mains—supply, 14 miles ; distributing, 75 miles.

Malvern Link (supplied by MALVERN).

Malvern Wells (supplied by MALVERN).

Manchester. Railways, L.N.W., G.N., M., and G.C. Distance from London, 183¼ miles.

Chairman, Alderman Sir Brodie T. Leech.

Secretary, Wm. Blackstock.

Resident Engineer, Joseph Haynes, C.E.

Financial Superintendent, Alfred Neill.

Office, Town Hall.

Works purchased by the Corporation, 1847. Special Acts, 1847, 1848, 1854, 1858, 1860, 1863, 1865, 1867, 1869, 1872, 1875, 1879, and 1882.

Total population supplied, 1,200,000.

Death rate, 18·99.

Townships and district, which are supplied with water—
 The City of Manchester, which comprises the following, viz.—Ardwick, Beswick, Blackley, Bradford, Burnage, Cheetham, Chorlton-cum-Hardy, Chorlton-upon-Medlock, Clayton, Crumpsall, Didsbury, Harpurhey, Hulme, Kirkmanshulme, Manchester, Moss Side, Moston, Newton Heath, Openshaw, Rusholme, West Gorton, and Withington.

Townships and districts beyond the limits of the City—
 Barton Moss, Broughton, Carrington, Davyhulme, Denton, Droylsden, Eccles, Flixton, Gorton, Irlam, Levenshulme, Partington, Pendlebury, Pendleton, Prestwich, Stretford, Swinton, Urmston, Worsley.

Area supplied extends 11 miles west and 8 miles east of the Town Hall, and covers about 90 square miles, supplying city of Manchester and 24 outside districts, beside supplying Salford and other places in bulk.

Drainage ground—valley of Longdendale, 18 miles east of Manchester, in the counties of Cheshire and Derbyshire—an elevated portion of the Pennine chain

MANCHESTER—*continued.*

of hills, about 19,300 acres, varying from 486 feet to over 2,060 feet above ordnance datum, the geological formation being the lower strata of the coal measures, below the coal," millstone grit " forming the cap of the hills.

Thirlmere drainage ground, area, 11,000 statute acres ; distance from Manchester, 96 miles ; altitude, between 533 and 3,117 feet above ordnance datum.

Estimated supply, 25,000,000 gals. per day, in addition to compensation water to River Etherow.

The supply is entirely by gravitation, no pumping being necessary, and, except in dry seasons, the water supplied consists largely of *spring water* collected direct on drainage ground or taken from the storage reservoirs at Arnfield, Hollingworth, Rhodes Wood and the service reservoirs.

Average Rainfall over the watershed 45·89 inches per annum.

Character of water—excellent quality softness and purity, flowing off the ground through soft, porous rock, and absorbing a quantity of ordinary air and carbonic acid, giving it the sparkling brilliancy and taste of spring water with the softness of rain water. It is almost unrivalled for bleaching, dyeing, washing, and general household purposes. Total hardness, 2°.

Strainers—water passes from service reservoirs through copper wire gauze strainers, 30 strands to the inch, no filtration being required.

The principal reservoirs are situated on the River Etherow, which, below the works at Tintwistle, runs through Broadbottom and Compstall to Stockport, receiving the Goyt and some small streams, ultimately forming the Mersey.

Collecting and storage reservoirs at Longdendale—

Name of Reservoir.	Area.	Capacity.	Depth.	Height of Top Water Level above Ordnance Datum.	
	Acres.	Gals.	Feet.	Feet.	In.
Woodhead ...	135 ...	1,181,000,000 ...	71 ...	782	0
Torside ...	160 ...	1,474,000,000 ...	84 ...	651	3
Rhodes Wood ...	54 ...	500,000,000 ...	68 ...	574	6
Vale House ...	63 ...	343,000,000 ...	40 ...	503	0
Bottoms ...	50 ...	407,000,000 ...	48 ...	486	0
Arnfield ...	39 ...	209,000,000 ...	52 ...	540	3
Hollingworth	13 ...	73,000,000 ...	52 ...	554	0
Service reservoirs, supplied from the storage reservoirs—					
Godley	15 ...	61,000,000 ...	21 ...	478	0
Denton, No. 1 ...	7 ...	30,000,000 ...	20 ...	321	6
Denton, No. 2 ...	6 ...	23,000,000 ...	20 ...	321	6
Audenshaw, No. 1	80 ...	528,000,000 ...	27½ ...	340	0
Audenshaw, No. 2	69 ...	371,000,000 ...	22½ ...	323	0
Audenshaw, No. 3	102 ...	542,000,000 ...	22½ ...	323	0
Gorton, Upper ...	34 ...	123,000,000 ...	26 ...	259	0
Gorton, Lower	23 ...	100,000,000 ...	29 ...	244	0
Prestwich, No. 1*	4½ ...	20,000,000 ...	22 ...	352	3
Prestwich, No. 2*	4½ ...	21,000,000 ...	24 ...	352	3
Total	859	6,006,000,000			

The Manchester Royal Exchange is 121·7 feet above Ordnance Datum.

Lake Thirlmere, Cumberland—this lake will yield, when the whole of the works are completed, 50,000,000 gals. per day for 160 days, even if no rain fall during that period. The water is brought to the reservoirs at Prestwich by tunnels, cut-and-cover aqueduct and cast iron pipes, 48", 40", and 36" diameter, a distance of nearly 96 miles, and augments the supply from Longdendale.

The combined storage of Longdendale and Thirlmere is equal to 140 days' supply.

---

* Supplied from Thirlmere.

MANCHESTER—*continued.*

    Head on distributing mains varies from 130 ft. to 30 ft.

    Daily supply of water, 37,000,000 gals.

    Daily consumption per head—domestic, 17 gals. ; trade, 14 gals.

    Maximum day's supply 44,773,799 gals. in September, 1906.

    Scale of charges within the City—

        Public water rate, 2d. in £ on the poor rate assessment *on all property*, payable by the owner.

        Domestic water rate, 8d. in £ on the poor rate assessment *on all Dwelling Houses.* Minimum annual charge for internal supply, 5s.

    No dwelling house is charged less than 5s. each per annum if internally, or 4s., if externally supplied with water.

    The domestic water rate on houses assessed at £10 and under, and all houses assessed above that amount, the rent of which is payable at any shorter period than three months is charged to the owner, who is allowed a discount of 20 per cent., provided there are not less than *three* in number and payment is made, whether the same shall be occupied or unoccupied, on or before the 31st October.

    Shops in connection with dwelling houses are charged the domestic rate upon the whole premises, unless under special circumstances.

    Dwelling houses, 1s. in the £ on the net annual value. No house is charged less than 8s. per ann. Houses the rent of which is payable at any shorter period than three months are charged to the owner, who is allowed a discount of 20 per cent., provided there are not less than *three* in number and payment is made, whether the same shall be occupied or unoccupied, on or before the 31st August

    In cases where two or more houses are supplied by one service pipe from the main, the water rental is charged to the owner of the property, whether weekly or quarterly.

    Baths in weekly houses within and beyond the limits of the City are charged 5s. each per annum in addition to the supply for domestic purposes, a discount of 20 per cent. being allowed if paid for in advance.

    Tubes for watering gardens, greenhouses, and for similar purposes, 10s. per annum for the first 800 square yards or under, and 5s. for each extra 800 or part thereof.

    Tubes for washing windows or flags, 3d. in the pound on the poor's-rate assessment. If for washing both windows and flags, 3d. in the pound on the rent of the premises. Maximum charge, 20s.; minimum, 5s. per annum.

    Price per 1,000 gals., by meter—

        Extract from scale of charges—

	Inside the City.				Outside the City.	
1,000 gals. per quarter ...	£0	2	0	1,000 gals. per quarter...	£0 2 0
10,000 ,, ,, ...	0	18	8	10,000 ,, ,, ...	0 18 8
100,000 ,, ,, ...	6	9	0	100,000 ,, ,, ...	6 9 0
500,000 ,, ,, ...	20	17	0	500,000 ,, ,, ...	20 17 1
1,000,000 ,, ,, ...	30	19	8	1,000,000 ,, ,, ...	30 19 8
3,000,000 ,, ,, ...	60	13	6	1,722,000 ,, ,, ...	43 1 0½

All quantities above this charged at the rate of 4·85d. per 1,000 gals.   All quantities above this 6d. per 1,000 gals.

    Mains from service reservoirs to city are 36, 30, 28, and 24 inches diameter.

    Length of iron piping laid in streets over 904 miles.

     ,, ,, lead   ,,   ,,   260 ,,

    Number of meters, 6,808.

    Number of hydrants for fire and cleansing purposes, 15,838.

      ,,   valves ,, regulating supply of water, 6,626.

Manchester Road (supplied by BURY).

Mancott (supplied by HAWARDEN).

Manningtree, Essex (supplied by THE TENDRING HUNDRED WATERWORKS CO.).

Mansfield, Notts. (G. & W.) Railways, M. & G.C. Distance from London, 142 miles.
Authority, Corporation.
Chairman, Alderman J. E. Alcock.
Secretary, J. H. White, Town Clerk.
Engineer and Manager, Arthur Graham.
Office, Lime Tree Place.
Works established, 1870.
Total population supplied, 30,000.
Death rate, 20 per 1,000.
Towns and villages in the area supplied—Mansfield, Pleasley, Tibshelf, Mansfield,
　Woodhouse and Newton.
Source of supply, pumping from wells.
Character of water, 7° hardness.
Annual supply of water, 210,000,000 gals.
Daily consumption per head, 17 gals.
Storage capacity, 1,040,000 gals.
Number of meters, 65.
Length of mains, 20 miles.
Price per 1,000 gals., 1s. to 6d.

Mansfield Woodhouse, Notts. (supplied by MANSFIELD).

Marfleet, Yorks. (supplied by HULL).

Margam, Glam.
Authority, Urban District Council.
Population, 9,000.

Margate, Kent. Railways, S.E. and L.C.D. Distance from London, 74 miles.
Authority, Corporation of Margate.
Chairman, Sydney Shea, Councillor.
Manager, Resident Engineer and Secretary, F. Stanley, C.E.
Office, 18, Cecil Square.
Loans outstanding, £189,862.
Annual profit, including capital charges, £500.
Works established 1853. Purchased by Corporation, 1879. Special Acts, 1853,
　1900, 1902.
Total population supplied, 36,000.
Death rate, 12·8 per 1,000, residents only.
Towns and villages in the area supplied—Northdown and Garlinge, Wingham,
　Nonington, Chittenden, Knowlton, Womenswold, Bekesbourne, Adisham,
　Bishopsbourne, Bridge,Wickhambreux, Ickham, Monkton, Preston, Stourmouth,
　Elmstone, Dulebourne.
Source of supply, deep wells in chalk, and impounding reservoirs at Uffington,
　Wingham, Flote, Margate, Woodlands, Bridge.
Character of water, brilliant and remarkably pure ; hardness before boiling, 18·8° ;
　after boiling, 2·3°.
Filtration, none.
Storage capacity, 1,335,000 gals.
Pressure on distributing mains—maximum, 70 lbs. ; minimum, 15 lbs. per sq. in.
Annual supply of water, 382,481,655 gals.
Average daily supply per head—domestic, $26\frac{3}{10}$ gals.
Maximum day's supply, 1,444,000 gals. in August.
Scale of charges, assessment charge, 1s. 4d. in the £ on rack rent value.
Price per 1,000 gals., trade, from 1s. 6d. to 8d.
Municipal purposes, £542.
Number of meters, 276.
Length of mains, 95 miles.

Markeaton (supplied by DERBY).

Market Bosworth (supplied by HINCKLEY).

Market Harborough, Leicestershire.   Railway, Midland.   Distance from London, 81¼ miles.
    Authority, Urban District Council.
    Population, 8,600 (estimated).

Market Rasen, Lincs.   Railway, G.C.   Distance from London, 145 miles.
    Authority, Market Rasen Water Company.
    Office, 2 Mill Street.
    Share capital paid up, £7,670.   Dividend, 6 per cent.
    Towns and villages in the area supplied, Market Rasen and parts of Middle Rasen and Tealby.
    Works established, 1875.   Special Act, 1876.
    Total population supplied, about 3,000.
    Sources of supply, springs in chalk hills.
    Character of water, fairly soft.
    Number of meters, 8.
    Length of mains, 6 miles.
    Scale of charges, assessment charge, 1s. 2d. and 1s. 6d. in £ per annum.
    Price per 1,000 gals., 1s, 3d.

Market Weighton, Yorks, Railway, N.E.   Distance from London, 190 miles.
    Authority, the Market Weighton Water Company, Ltd.
    Towns and villages within the area of control—

Market Weighton	...	...	...	...	1,780 (1901 Census).
Goodmanham	...	...	...	...	251 ,,

    Works established, 1884.
    Provisional Order, 1884.
    Total population of area of control, 2,031.
    Annual supply of water—

For domestic purposes	...	...	...	...	9,619,000 gals.
In bulk to other authorities	...	...	...	...	5,753,000 ,,

    Maximum day's consumption, 42,400 gals.
    Natural rest level of water below surface, 30 feet.
    Level of water below surface (when pumping), 36 feet.
    Storage reservoirs...   ...   .   capacity 150,000 gals.
    Number of meters in use, 4.
    Assessment charge on rateable value.

Markinch, Scotland.   Railway, N.B.   Distance from London, 500 miles.
    Taken over by the Markinch Burgh Police Commissioners, November, 1906, and the Company wound up.
    Area supplied, Markinch only.
    Works established, 1860.
    Total population supplied, 1,500.
    Daily consumption per head, 30 gals.
    Source of supply, springs.
    Character of water, soft.
    Number of meters, 4.
    Scale of charges—assessment charge, rateable value 9d. and 4½d. per £ for dry goods shops.
    Total water rent received, £209 per annum.

Marlborough, Wilts.   Railway, G.W., M. and S.W. Junction Ry.   Distance from London, 75¾ miles.
    Authority, Town Council.
    Office, Marlborough.
    Area supplied, Marlborough and Preshute Within.

MARLBOROUGH—*continued*

  Total population supplied, 3,800.
  Daily consumption per head, about 20 gals.
  Source of supply, well.
  Storage capacity, 120,000 gals.
  Character of water, excellent,
  Death rate, 11·15 per 1,000.
  Number of meters, 25.
  Scale of charges—assessment charge ; the expenses are paid out of General District
      Rate.
    Price per 1,000 gals., for commercial purposes, at present 1s.
    Total water rent received, commercial purposes only, about £76.

Marske, Yorks. (supplied by CLEVELAND).

Martock, Somerset. Railway, G.W. Distance from London, 140½ miles.
  Authority, Martock Water Supply with Yeovil Rural District Council.
  Clerk to Martock P.C., A. W. Philpott.
  Clerk to Yeovil R.D.C., J. E. Rodber.
  Inspector and Manager, W. H. Collings, Martock.
  Office, Martock.
  Works established, 1889.
  Population supplied, 2,155.
  District of supply, Martock and Coat.
  Source of supply, springs from Rixon Common, under Ham Hill, Stoke-sub-Ham.
  Character of water, hard.
  Filtration, none ; softening, none.
  Storage capacity—impounding reservoir, low level, 40,000 gals ; high level,
      100,000 gals.
  Daily supply per head—min., 15 gals. ; max., 20 to 30 gals. when spring is high.
  Charge by meter, 9d. per 1,000 gals.
  Number of meters, 13.
  Length of mains—supply, 2½ miles ; distributing, 3 miles.

Marton (supplied by BARROW-IN-FURNESS).

Maryport Cumberland. Railways, L.N.W., M. Distance from London, 316 miles.
  Authority, Urban District Council.
  Clerk to Council, F. Kelly.
  Resident Engineer, Ralph Stockoe.
  Office, Town Hall.
  Loans outstanding, £13,200.
  Works established, 1869. Special Acts, 1866.
  Total population supplied, 30,000.
  Average death rate, 15·32 per 1,000.
  District of supply—Maryport, Netherhall, Ellenborough, Ewanrigg, Flimby,
      Dearham, Dooenby. Papcastle.
  Source of supply—River Derwent, Cockermouth.
  Character of water, good ; total hardness, 1·5°.
  Filtration—sand and gravel.
  Storage capacity—impounding reservoirs, 850,000 gals. ; service reservoir,
      360,000 gals.
  Annual supply of water, 158,000 000 gals.
  Average daily supply per head, 20 gals.
  Assessment charge, 12¼ per cent. on R.V.
  Average charge per meter, 4½d. per 1,000 gals.
  Total length of mains, 23½ miles.

Masham, Yorks. Railway, N.E.
　Authority, Masham Urban District Council.
　Manager and Engineer, W. Clark, Stanhope House, Masham, R.S.O.
　Works established, 1896.
　Total population of area supplied, 1,955.
　Towns and villages in the area supplied, Healey, Fearby, and Masham.
　Source of supply, gravitation.
　Scale of charges—
　　Domestic supply, approximately 1s. 6d. in the £ on the
　　　rateable value of the house supplied.

	s.	d.
Water closet, for each beyond the first, which is free	5	0
Stable yard and stable, attached to private residence	7	6
Slaughter-house	5	0

　Supply for any other purpose by arrangement with the Council.
　Length of mains, 8 miles.

Mason (supplied by Newcastle-on-Tyne).

Matlock, Derby. Railway, M. Distance from London, 144 miles.
　Authority, Urban District Council, July 18th, 1898.
　Clerk, M. A. Sleigh.
　Engineer, James Diggle.
　Office, Town Hall.
　Area supplied, 6 miles.
　Works established, 1860. Special Acts, 1860, 1898.
　Total population supplied, 7,000.
　Sources of supply, springs.
　Character of water, very soft.
　Death rate, 10·1 per annum.
　Number of meters, 1.
　Length of mains, about 16 miles.
　Scale of charges—assessment charge, 1s. 1d. to 2s. in £.
　Price per 1,000 gals., 2s.
　Total water rent received, £1,680 yearly.

Matlock Bath. Railway, M. Distance from London, 142 miles.
　Authority, District Council, 1882.
　Chairman, J. E. Lawton.
　Manager, J. Walker.
　Engineer, W. Jaffrey.
　Office, Council Chambers.
　Loans outstanding, £5,000.
　Interest on loan, 3½ and 3¾ per cent.
　Annual profit, including "Capital Charges," £100.
　Works established, 1863 (private company); purchased by Council, 1881.
　Special Act, 1863.
　Total population supplied, 1,820.
　Average death rate, 12·47 per 1,000.
　Towns and villages in the area supplied, Matlock Bath, Scarthin Nick.
　Sources of supply, springs in gritstone strata.
　Character of water, 1·4° hardness
　Filtration, none required.
　Storage capacity, in service reservoir, 270,000 gals.
　Head on distributing mains—maximum, 450 feet; minimum, 170 feet.
　Annual supply of water, 25,000,000 gals.
　Daily consumption per head, 28 gals. ·
　Maximum day's supply, 600,000 gals., in August.
　Scale of charge—assessment charge, 7½ per cent. under £20, 6 per cent. over £20;
　Price per 1,000 gals., trade, 2s. to 9d., as per quantity used; domestic, 2s.;
　　municipal purposes free.
　Number of meters, 30.

Matlock Bath—*continued.*
> Length of mains—supply, 5 miles; distributing, 16 miles.
> Total water rent received, £600.

Maxwelltown, N.B. *See* Dumfries.

Melling (supplied by St. Helen's).

Mellor (supplied by Blackburn).

Melrose, N.B. Railway, M. Distance from London, 365 miles.
> Authority, Town Council.
> Engineers, Belfrage and Carfrae, C.E.
> Town Clerk, Ralph Dunn.
> Population supplied, 2,195.
> No returns supplied.

Melton Mowbray, Leicester.
> Authority, Urban District Council.
> Population, 7,500.

Menston, Leeds.
> Authority, Wharfedale Rural District Council, taken over from the Menston
> Waterworks Co., Ltd.
> Chairman, Philip Padgelt.
> Clerk, E. C. Newstead, Otley.
> Clerk to Committee, Robert Davey.
> Engineer, E. J. Silcock, 10, Park Row, Leeds.
> Works established, 1875.
> Special Acts, 1899; Transfer Bill, 1900.
> Total population of area supplied, 1,400.
> Area of supply, Martock.
> Source of supply, springs at Moor Lane Top and Beestone.
> Filtration, none.
> Storage in reservoir, 2,000,000 galls.
> Assessment charge, 8 to 5 per cent. on gross rental.
> Price by meter, 1s. 3d. per 1,000 gals.
> No. of meters, 5.

Meolse, Cheshire (supplied by Hoylake).

Merrow (supplied by Woking).

Merstham (supplied by East Surrey Waterworks Co.).

Merthyr Dowlais, Glam. *See* Dowlais (supplied by Merthyr Tydvil).

Merthyr Tydfil, Wales. Railways, G.W., L.N.W., T.V.R., R.R., B. and M.R.
Distance from London, 184 miles.
> Authority, Merthyr Tydfil Borough Council.
> Chairman, Mayor F. Sydney Simons.
> Engineer and Manager, T. Fletcher Harvey, A.M.I.C.E.
> Town Clerk, T. Aneuryn Rees.
> Office, Town Hall, Merthyr Tydfil.
> Loans acquired, £318,766; now owing, £193,763.
> Annual loss on undertaking, including capital charges, £5,000.
> Works established, 1858. Special Acts, 1858, 1865, 1876, 1895, 1903.
> Total population of area supplied, 92,000.
> Average death rate, 22·64 per 1,000, period 10 years.
> Towns and villages in the area supplied, Merthyr, Dowlais, Abercanaid, Troe-
> dyrhiw, Aberfan, Treharris, Cefn, Pontsticill, Trelewis Bedlinog and Caerphilly.
> Sources of supply in use, springs from the Breconshire Beacons and impounding
> reservoir at foot of Beacons.

MERTHYR TYDFIL—*continued.*

Character of water, excellent, very soft, never above 4° hardness.
System of filtration, sand and Candy's filters.
Storage capacity, 345,000,000, 75,000,000, and 346,000,000 gals. Total, 766,000,000 gallons.
Pressure on mains—maximum, 14lbs. ; minimum, 10lbs. per sq. in.
Total supply of water per annum, 1,025,650,000 gals.
Daily consumption per head, domestic, 27 gals. ; trade, 5,000,000 gals. per day.
Maximum day's supply, 2,878,000 gals. in September, 1906.
Scale of charges—
Assessment charge, 8 per cent. to 7 per cent. on rateable value for domestic purposes.
Trade, 1s. 6d. to 6d. per 1,000 gals.
Sanitary purposes, £1,100 per annum (sewer flushing and street washing).
Total revenue received, £15,151 13s. 5d.
Number of meters, 80.
Length of trunk mains, about 56 miles.   Distributing mains, 60 miles.

Merthyr Vale (supplied by MERTHYR TYDVIL).

Methley (supplied by WAKEFIELD).

Metropolitan Water Board—
The first election of the Water Board took place early in 1903, under regulations issued by the Local Government Board, and the members then elected held office till June, 1907.   The second Board elected in June, 1907, will hold office until 1910.
Chairman, Sir R. Melvill Beachcroft.
Vice-Chairman, Mr. E. B. Barnard.
Clerk, Mr. A. B. Pilling.
Comptroller, Mr. F. E. Harris.
Chief Engineer, Mr. W. B. Bryan, M.Inst.C.E.
Director of Water Examinations, A. C. Houston, M.B., D.Sc., Chemical and Bacteriological Laboratories, 20, Nottingham Place, W. (Telephone No. 843 Paddington).
Central Offices—Savoy Court. Strand, W.C. (Telegrams—Water Board London ; Telephone Nos. 4315-9 Gerarrd).
District Offices :—Kent—Brookmill Road, Depford, S.E. (Telephone Nos. 178 and 188 Deptford) ; New River and East London—173, Rosebery Avenue, E.C. (Telephone No. Holborn 5791 and 5792) ; Southwark and Vauxhall and Lambeth —30, Southwark Bridge Road, S.E. (Telephone No. 385-6 Hop.)
Receiving Offices :—City—6, Broad Street Place, E.C. (Telephone No. 2714 London Wall) ; Chelsea—41, Commercial Road, Pimlico, S.W. (Telephone Nos. 54 and 55 Westminster) ; Grand Junction—Campden Hill Road, Notting Hill, W. (Telephone No. 109 Kensington) ; Lambeth—Brixton Hill, S.W. (Telephone No. 7 Brixton) ; West Middlesex—19, Marylebone Road, N.W. (Telephone No. 1088 Paddington).
Engineering Districts :—Eastern District—Lee Bridge, Clapton, N.E. (Telephone No. 232 Dalston) ; Kent District—Brookmill Road, Deptford, S.E. (Telephone Nos. 178 and 188 Deptford) ; New River District—173, Rosebery Avenue, E.C. (Telephone Nos. Holborn, 5791 and 5792) ; Southern District—Southwark Bridge Road, S.E., Southwark and Vauxhall and Lambeth (Telephone No. 385-6 Hop.) ; Staines Reservoirs—Stanwell New Road (Telephone No. 23 Staines ; Western District—41, Commercial Road, Pimlico, S.W. (Chelsea, Grand Junction, and West Middlesex) (Telephone Nos. 54 and 55 Westminster).

METROPOLITAN WATER BOARD—*continued.*

On June 24th, 1904, the undertakings of the Companies, with the exception of the New River Company, passed to and vested in the Water Board, who also took over all the debts and liabilities of the Companies, including their debenture stock. The appointed day in regard to the New River Company was postponed until July 25th, 1904, by the Local Government Board.

A Court of Arbitration to decide the amount of the purchase money and various other questions arising between the Water Board and the Companies, was appointed by the Act, and consisted of the Rt. Hon. Sir Edward Fry, Sir Hugh Owen, G.C.B., and Sir John Wolfe Barry, K.C.B. The Court commenced their sittings for hearing the Claims of the Water Companies in October, 1903. The Companies claimed sums amounting to about £60,000,000, including the debenture stocks transferred.

The awards to the several companies were—

East London		£3,900,000
New River		5,967,123
Grand Junction		3,349,500
West Middlesex		3,524,000
Lambeth...		4,301,000
Southwark and Vauxhall		3,603,000
Chelsea		3,305,700
Kent		2,712,000
Staines Reservoirs Joint Committee		———
		£30,662,323

The Arbitration Committee of the Board reported, Dec. 9th, 1904, that the total of the award in cash payable to the Companies under the awards of the Court of Arbitration would amount to £30,662,323, representing, on the respective bases on which the stock had been issued, £33,564,281 in 3 per cent. water stock.

The Capital Debt of the Board on March 31st, 1906, was :—

Metropolitan Water (A) Stock		£6,060,165
,, ,, (B) ,, ...		34,118,849
Redeemable Debenture Stocks		7,217,838
Mortgage Loans		37,500
		£47,434,352

The Finance Committee estimated the revenue for the year ending March 31st, 1907, at £2,814,510; and the expenditure at £2,765,017.

The total quantity of water supplied in—

    1906-7 was 82,125,249,347 gals.

    1905-6 ,, 79,572,570,244 ,,

    1904-5 ,, 80,201,618,919 ,,

The average daily supply in—

    1906-7 was 225,000,683 gals.

    1905-6 ,, 218,007,041 ,,

    1904-5 ,, 219,730,463 ,,

The average estimated population supplied in—

    1906-7 it was 6,851,045 gallons.

    1905-6 ,, 6,747,196

The supply per head per day in—

    1906-7 was 32·84 gals.

    1905-6 ,, 32·31 ,,

The estimated quantity of water for domestic purposes is 80 per cent., and for all purposes except domestic, 20 per cent.

Metropolitan Water Board—*continued.*

The Metropolis Water Act, 1902, constituted a Water Board, called the "Metropolitan Water Board," for the purpose of purchasing and carrying on the undertakings of the eight Metropolitan water companies—viz., The New River, East London, Southwark and Vauxhall, West Middlesex, Lambeth, Chelsea, Grand Junction and Kent.

The Water Board consists of 66 members appointed by the county councils and other authorities within the water area, as follows : London County Council, 14 ; City of London, 2 ; Westminster, 2 ; the other Metropolitan boroughs (27), 1 each ; West Ham, 2 ; the county councils of Essex, Herts, Kent, Middlesex and Surrey, 1 each ; the urban districts of East Ham (now a borough), Leyton, and Walthamstow, 1 each ; the combined urban districts of Buckhurst Hill, Chingford, Loughton, Waltham Holy Cross, Wanstead and Woodford, 1 ; the combined urban districts of Beckenham, Bromley, Chislehurst, Penge, Bexley, Dartford, Erith, and Footscray, 1 ; the urban districts of Tottenham and Willesden, 1 each ; the borough of Ealing and the urban districts of Acton and Chiswick, 1 ; the urban districts of Brentford, Hampton, Hampton Wick, Hanwell, Heston and Isleworth, Sunbury, Teddington, and Twickenham, 1 ; the urban districts of Edmonton, Enfield and Southgate, 1 ; the urban districts of Hornsey and Wood Green, 1 ; the boroughs of Kingston and Wimbledon, and the urban districts of East and West Molesey, Esher and the Dittons, Ham, Surbiton, Barnes, the Maldens and Coombe, 1 ; the Thames Conservators and the Lea Conservancy Board, 1 each. The chairman and vice-chairman are elected by the Water Board, either from the members, or from outside the Board, and are unpaid.

Sources of supply—

Eastern District ; rivers Thames and Lea, and Wells in the Lea Valley.

Kent District ; deep wells, 19 in the chalk and one in the lower greensand.

New River District ; river Lea, the Chadwell spring, 18 Wells in the Lea Valley, and the Thames.

Southern District ; mainly from the Thames, with wells at Selhurst, Streatham, and Honor Oak.

Western District ; Thames only.

Mexborough and District, Yorks. Railways, G.C. and G.N. Distance from London, 164 miles.

Authority, Mexborough and District Water Co., Ltd.

Office, 58, Market Street.

Area supplied, two square miles Mexborough and District.

Works established, 1879. Special Acts, incorporated under the Companies Acts 1862 and 1867, secured by Board of Trade.

Total population of area supplied, 10,417.

Annual supply of water, 58,238,000 gals.

Daily consumption per head, domestic, 15 gals. ; trade, 3,000,000 gals. per annum.

Source of supply, wells.

Storage capacity, 310,000 gals.

Character of water, good.

System of filtration, filter beds.

Death rate, 19 per 1,000.

Scale of charges—assessment, rack rent.

Price per 1,000 gals., 1s.

Mickleover (supplied by Derby).

Middlesbrough (supplied by Tees Valley Water Board).

Middle Rasen (supplied by Market Rasen).

Middlethorpe (supplied by York).

Middleton, Lancs. *See* Heywood.

Middleton, Yorks. (supplied by Ilkley).

Middlewich, Cheshire. Railway, L.N.W. Distance from London, 166 miles.
Authority, Urban District Council.
Works opened April, 1907.
Estimated cost, £14,300.
Source of supply, two bore-holes, yielding 400,000 gals. every 24 hours.

Mid-Cheshire,

Mid-Kent. Railways, S.E., L.C.D. Distance from London, 36 miles.
Mid-Kent Water Company.
Chairman, Col. B. T. L. Thompson.
Manager and Secretary, F. L. Ball.
Office, Snodland, Kent.
Capital paid up, £118,000.
Works established, 1889.
Special Acts, 1888, 1890, 1895, 1898, 1900 and 1901.
Total population supplied, 1891, 19,250 ; 1907, 59,000.
Average death rate, 15·7 per 1,000.
Area supplied, 22,200 acres.
Sources of supply, boring into lower Green sand, at Halling and Charing, 375 feet
deep.
Analysis of water, March, 1907—

	Parts per 100,000.
Ammonia, Free	·0004
„ Albuminoid	·0016
Oxygen absorbed, in 15 minutes ...	None
„ „ 4 hours ...	·010
Total solid residue	24·80
Chlorine	1·8
Nitrogen, as nitrates and nitrites ...	Trace
Temporary hardness	12·0
Permanent hardness	5·2
Total hardness	17·2

The water is clear, palatable, and free from poisonous metals.
Pumping stations—Halling, capacity, 1,500,000 gals. per day.
           Charing   „   600,000   „   „   „
Service reservoirs—Halling, 3 covered, capacity 1,600,000 gals.
           Mereworth   250,000   „
           Wrotham   320,000   „
           Charing, covered...   ...   265,0000   „
Annual supply of water, domestic, 250,000,000 gals. ; in bulk to other authorities,
50,000,000 gals.
Daily consumption per head, 16·5 gals.
Maximum day's supply, 1,500,000 gals. in July.
Scale of charges—assessment charge, 6 and 7½ per cent. on rateable value.
Price per 1,000 gals., 1s. 6d. and 1s.
Number of meters, 217.

Midsomer Norton, Som. Railway, L.S.W. Distance from London, 135¼ miles.
Authority, Midsomer Norton Urban District Council.
Office, Market Hall.
District Engineer and Surveyor, W. F. Bird.
Population supplied, 6,000.

Mid Sussex. *See* CUCKFIELD.

Milford, Staffs. (supplied by STAFFORD).

Milford, Surrey (supplied by GODALMING).

Milford Haven, l'embroke. Railway, G.W.
Distance from London, 270½ miles.
Authority, Urban District Council.
Population supplied, 5,101.

Milford Keyhaven (supplied by CHRISTCHURCH).

Millerston (supplied by GLASGOW).

Millom (G. & W.). Railways, L.N.W. and Furness. Distance from London, 274 miles.
Authority, Urban District Council.
Office, Council Offices.
Loans—Water, £5,220 ; Gas, £4,256 ; total £9,476 ; March 31, 1907.
Area supplied—Millom, Haverigg and The Hill.
Works established, 1875. Special Acts, 1875 and 1894.
Total population supplied, 10,462 (census 1901).
Daily consumption per head, 25 gals. allowed for.
Source of supply, gathering grounds.
Storage capacity, 28,000,000 gals.
Character of water, soft.
Death rate, 10·18 per 1,000 in 1906.
Scale of charges—
    Assessment charges, shops, 3¾ per cent. per annum ; dwellings, 5 per cent.
    lock-up shops, 2½ per cent.
    Price per 1,000 gals., graduated scale for trade purposes.
Total water rent received, domestic and trade, £2,063 (1906-7).

Milngavie (supplied by GLASGOW).

Milnrow (supplied by ROCHDALE).

Milton, Kent (supplied by GRAVESEND).

Milton, Somerset (supplied by WESTON-SUPER-MARE).

Milton-next-Sittingbourne.
Authority, Urban District Council.
Chairman, F. Littlewood, J.P.
Clerk, John Dixon, M.A.
Office, Town Hall.
Loans outstanding, £7,700.
Works established, 1904.
Population supplied, 8,000.
Average death rate, 12·8 per 1,000.
District of supply, Milton-next-Sittingbourne.
Source of supply, wells in upper chalk.
Character of water, of a clear blue colour, no smell, pure organically, and free
    from sewage percolation.
Total hardness, 18·6°.

MILTON-NEXT-SITTINGBOURNE—*continued.*

Filtration, none; softening, none.
Storage capacity in service reservoirs, 575,000 gals.
Annual supply, 48,000,000 gals.
Average daily supply—domestic, 14·1 gals.; trade, 2·4 gals.
Assessment charge, about 5 per cent. on rental value.
Charge by meter—1s. 6d. per 1,000 gals.
No. of meters—31 trade and 5 Deacon waste water meters.
Length of mains—supply, 6 miles; distributing, 12 miles.

Minehead, Somerset. Railway, G.W. Distance from London, 183¼ miles.
Authority, Company.
Office, 6a, Park Street.
Area supplied, Minehead Urban District.
Works established, 1869. Special Acts, none.
Total population of area supplied, 2,700.
Source of supply, springs.
Storage capacity, 200,000 gals.
Number of meters, 13.
Assessment charge, £110 10s.
Price per 1,000 gals., 1s. 3d.

Minffordd (supplied by BANGOR).

Minley, Hants. (supplied by FRIMLEY).

Minster (supplied by RAMSGATE and THE SHEPPY LIGHTING & WATER Co., Edward Street, Sheerness).

Minworth (supplied by BIRMINGHAM).

Missenden (supplied by (RICKMANSWORTH).

Mistley, Essex (supplied by TENDRING HUNDRED).

Mitcheldean, Glos. Railway, G.W. Distance from London, 128 miles.
Authority, Mitcheldean Waterworks, Ltd.
Population supplied, 730.
No returns supplied.

Moffat, N.B. (supplied by AIRDRIE).

Mold, Wales (G. and W.) Railway, L.N.W. Distance from London, 182 miles
Authority, Mold Gas and Water Co.
Works established, 1840. Special Act, 1867.
Share capital paid up, £12,000.
Population supplied, about 11,660.
Source of supply, springs.
Assessment charge, R.B.
Price per 1,000 gals., 1s. 8d..

Mollington (supplied by CHESTER).

Mongewell (supplied by SOUTH OXFORDSHIRE).

Monifieth (supplied by DUNDEE).

Moniment, part of (supplied by CUPAR).

Monk Hesleden (supplied by WINGATE).

Monkseaton (supplied by TYNEMOUTH).

Monmouth. Railway, G.W. Distance from London, 145 miles.
Authority, Monmouth Gas and Waterworks Company, Ltd.
Office, Gas and Waterworks, May Hill, Monmouth.
Total capital invested, £14,000, for gas and water.
Dividend, 10, 4, and 7 per cent.
Area of control, Monmouth.
Population, 5,095 (1901 Census).
Works established, 1840.
Provisional Order, 1873.
Total population of area of control—(1901), 5,095.
Annual supply of water—
  For all purposes, 75,000,000 gals.
Total quantity of water drawn per annum (1901)—

From deep springs	...	...	...	57,000,000 gals.
„ River Wye	...	...	...	18,000,000 „
	Total ...	...	...	75,000,000 gals.

Quantity of water available from River Wye, unlimited.
Surface formation of drainage areas—the springs rise in the Buckholt Valley, out of the old red sandstone, and then run by gravitation into Monmouth, and furnish the greater portion of the supply.
System of filtration, sand.
Pumping station pumps at Gas and Waterworks, May Hill, Monmouth, for supply from River Wye ; capacity, 120,000 gals. per day of 12 hours.
Service reservoir and filter beds on May Hill; capacity, about 3 days' supply open.
Death rate, 16·8 per 1,000.
Number of meters in use, 20.
Length of distributing mains, 4 miles.
Analysis—
  Sir E. Frankland analysed the spring water in 1898, and made the following remarks on same :—"These waters possess an extremely high degree of organic purity, and are of most excellent quality for dietetic and all domestic purposes. Any town might consider itself fortunate in being supplied with these waters."
Assessment charge, 6 to 7 per cent. on rack rental.
Price per 1,000 gallons, 1s. 6d. to 6d.

Montgomery. Railway, Cambrian. Distance from London, 169 miles.
Authority, Corporation.
Chairman, the Mayor.
Surveyor, W. P. Hole.
Inspector, R. Tomley.
Town Clerk, C. S. Pryce.
Works established, 1885.
Total population supplied, 1,034.
Sources of supply, gravitation, Town Hill.
Storage capacity, 40,000 gals.
Death rate, 21 per 1,000.
Length of mains, ¾ of a mile.

Montrose, Scotland. Railway, Caledonian & N.B. Distance from London, 488 miles.
  Authority, Town Council.
  Convener of Committee, H. Hall.
  Treasurer, John R. Mitchell.
  Town Clerk, D. C. Wills.
  Engineer, S. L. Christie, Burgh Surveyor.
  Office, Town Hall.
  Loans outstanding, £7,600 at 3½ per cent.
  Works established, 1857.
  Total population supplied, 14,500.
  Average death rate, 18 per 1,000.
  Area supplied, Burgh and Hillside.
  Sources of supply, Haughs of Kinnaber, adits in alluvial strata adjacent to River,
      North Esk.
  Character of water, soft. Total hardness, 3½°. Filtration, none.
  Storage capacity, 330,000 gals.
  Head on distributing mains, maximum 140 ft., minimum 120 ft.
  Annual supply of water, 245,000,000 gals.
  Daily consumption per head, domestic and trade, 46·4 gals.
  Maximum day's supply, 650,000 gals. in July.
  Scale of charges, assessment charge, 2d. in £ on rental.
  Price per 1,000 gals., 4d.
  Number of meters, 85.

Montrose, Scotland. (Glenskenno gravitation supply.)
  Population, officials, office, as above.
  Works established, 1741.
  Annual supply of water, 40,000,000 gals.
  Daily consumption per head, 46·4 gals.
  Sources of supply—springs.
  Storage capacity, 46,000 gals.
  Character of water, 7° hardness.
  Number of meters, 5.
  Scale of charges—assessment charge, 2d. in £ on rental.
  Price per 1,000 gals., 4d.

Moore, Lancs. (supplied by Warrington).

Moorpark, Scotland (supplied by Paisley).

Morden (supplied by Sutton).

Morecambe (supplied by Lancaster).

Moreton, Cheshire (supplied by Hoylake).

Morganstown, Glam. (supplied by Cardiff).

Morley, Yorks (supplied by Halifax).

Morpeth, Northumberland. Railway, N.E. and N.B. Distance from London,
  288¼ miles.
  Authority, Town Council.
  Town Clerk, F. Burnard.
  Engineer, J. Davison, Borough Surveyor.
  Office, Corporation Offices.

MORPETH—*continued*.

　　Loans outstanding, £6,312 (March 31st, 1906).
　　Works extended, 1897.
　　Total population supplied, 6,500.
　　Source of supply—two boreholes, one adjacent to reservoirs, the other in the town,
　　　　from which the water is forced into mains; this latter is kept as a stand-by.
　　　　Spring at Alley Banks, where small reservoir has been formed. Two impound-
　　　　ing reservoirs on small stream at Nanwell.
　　Average death rate, 17 per 1,000.
　　Character of water, excellent.
　　System of filtration, sand and gravel beds. Water from reservoir only filtered.
　　Storage capacity—impounding reservoirs, 12,750,000 gals.: service reservoir,
　　　　300,000 gals.
　　Head on distributing mains—max., 90 lbs.; min., 60 lbs. per sq. in.
　　Annual supply of water, 69,000,000 gals.
　　Average daily consumption per head, 29 gals., all purposes.
　　Assessment charge included in general district rate.
　　Price per 1,000 gals., 4 houses only, supplied outside of borough at 9d.

Morton, Lancs. (supplied by BARROW-IN-FURNESS).

Morton, Yorks. (supplied by BRADFORD).

Morton, Lincs. (supplied by GAINSBOROUGH).

Moseley (supplied by BIRMINGHAM).

Mossend, Scotland (supplied by DISTRICT OF THE MIDDLE WARD OF LANARKSHIRE).

Mossley Hurst (supplied by ASHTON-UNDER-LYNE).

Moss Pitt (supplied by STAFFORD).

Moss Side (supplied by MANCHESTER).

Moston (supplied by CHESTER).

Moston (supplied by MANCHESTER).

Motherwell. Railway, Caledonian. Distance from London, 388 miles.
　　Authority, Town Council of Burgh of Motherwell.
　　Chairman, William Purdie.
　　Secretary, James Burns.
　　Engineer, James McCallum.
　　Office, Town Hall.
　　Loan outstanding, £41,600.
　　Works established, 1877. Special Act, Motherwell Water Supply Confirmation
　　　　Act, 1889.
　　Total population supplied, 35,000.
　　Average death rate, 16·5 per 1,000.
　　Area supplied, Burgh of Motherwell only.
　　Sources of supply—impounding reservoirs on Coldstream and Springfield Burns,
　　　　Carluke; capacity, 108,000,000 gals.
　　Character of water, 6° hardness.
　　System of filtration, sand.
　　Storage reservoirs, 400,000 gals.
　　Head on distributing mains—max., 150 ft.; min., 70 ft.
　　Daily consumption per head, 50 gals.

MOTHERWELL—*continued.*

Scale of charges—assessment charge, 2s. in £.
Price per 1,000 gals., 6d., trade and domestic.
Number of meters, 50.
Length of mains—supply, 23 miles; distributing, 50 miles.
The new supply from Coulter Water, near Biggar, hoped to be completed at end of year (1907), is not included in the above returns.

Mountain Ash, Glam. Railway, G. W. and T. V. Distance from London, 200 miles.
Authority, Urban District Council.
Chairman, W. S. Davies.
Clerk, H. P. Linton.
Manager, W. G. Thomas.
Office, Town Hall.
Towns and villages in the area supplied—Mountain Ash, Penrhiwceibr, Abercynon, Ynysybwl.
Works established, 1887.
Special Acts, 1886, 1891, 1900.
Total population supplied, 40,000.
Daily consumption per head, 20 gals.
Source of supply, springs and upland collection.
Storage capacity, 16,000,000 gals.
System of filtration, downward through sand.
Character of water, soft.
Average death rate, 16·15 per 1,000.
Number of meters, 11.
Scale of charges—assessment charge, rateable value.
　Price per 1,000 gals., trade, 1s. 6d.

Mountsorrell (supplied by LEICESTER).

Mount Vernon (supplied by GLASGOW).

Much Wenlock, Salop. Railway, G.W. Distance from London, 163 miles.
Authority, Corporation.
Office, Much Wenlock.
Towns and villages in the area supplied, Much Wenlock, Broseley, Jackfield, Coalport, Shifnal, Ironbridge, Coalbrookdale and Madeley.
Works established, 1900.
Total population supplied, 20,000.
Length of mains, 20 miles.
Madeley and Ironbridge are not supplied through Much Wenlock, as there are two schemes, one for Much Wenlock and another for the other portions of the borough.

Mudeford, Hants. (supplied by CHRISTCHURCH).

Mullingar.
Authority, Rural District Council.
Chairman, Thos. J. Shaw.
Clerk to Authority, Laurence Gavin.
Manager, Michael Scally.
Consulting Engineer, C. Mullvauny, C.E., Athlone.
Office, Waterworks.
Works established, 1901; special Acts, 1896.
Total population supplied, 5,000.
Loans outstanding, £8,796 (Sept. 30th, 1906).

MULLINGAR—*continued.*

Annual loss, including "Capital Charges," £200.
District of supply, Mullingar only.
Source of supply, Loch Oust, a large lake near the town.
Analysis of Water—

Total solids 7·700 including—

Albuminoid ammonia	...	...	...	...	0,014
Saline	...	...	...	...	·005
Nitrous acid	...	...	...	...	None
Nitric acid	...	...	...	...	Trace
Chlorine	...	...	...	...	·994
Sulphuric acid	...	...	...	...	None
Phosphoric acid	...	...	...	...	None
Hardness	...	...	...	...	4°
Colour	...	...	...	...	Light yellow
Suspended particles	...	...	...	Very few
Turbidity	...	...	...	...	None
Sediment	...	..	...	...	Trace

Filtration, none ; softening, none.
Storage capacity in service reservoirs, 200,000 gals.
Head on distributing mains, average 60 lbs. per square inch.
Daily supply of water, 90,000 gals.
Assessment charges—Domestic, 9d. in £ on R.V.
　By meter, 1s. per 1,000 gals.　Number of meters, 7.

Musselburgh, Edinburgh.　Railway, N.B.　Distance from London, 400 miles.
Authority, Town Council.
Manager and Engineer, Geo. Landale.
Clerk to authority, John Richardson, solicitor.
Office, Municipal Buildings.
Works established 1874, Special Act 1871.
Total population supplied, 13,690.
Average death rate, 18·49 per 1,000.
Area supplied—Musselburgh and Inveresk.
Source of supply, Edinburgh Water Trust.
Head on distributing mains, max. 350 ft., min. 75 ft.
Annual supply, 165,149,000 gals.
Average daily supply per head, 36 gals. for all purposes.
Maximum day's supply—510,000 gals. in Aug. and Sept.
Scale of charges—

Assessment charge	...	...	...	...	1s. 3d. in £ on R.V.
Price per 1,000 gals.	...	...	...	..	Trade, 1s.

Number of meters, 44.
Length of supply mains, 3 miles ; distributing mains, 9½ miles.

Murton (supplied by SUNDERLAND).

Mytholmroyd (supplied by HALIFAX).

Nackerty, Scotland (supplied by DISTRICT OF MIDDLE WARD OF LANARKSHIRE).

Nairn, Scotland.　Railways, Highland, G.N., L.N.W., M.
Authority, Police Commissioners.
Population supplied, 4,000.
No returns supplied.

Nanpanton (supplied by Loughborough).

Nantwich, Cheshire. Railways, L.N.W. and G.W. Distance from London, 165 miles.
    Authority, Nantwich Urban District Council.
    Surveyor and Waterworks Engineer, W. F. Newey.
    Office, Urban District Council Office.
    Works established, 1854.
    Total population of area supplied, 8,000.
    Average death rate, 16·6.
    Sources of supply, mere and reservoir.
    Character of water, from a peaty source; hardness, 12·0° Clark.
    Filtration, sand.
    Storage impounding reservoir, 12,000,000 gals.; service reservoir, 160,000 gals.
    Head on distributing mains (average), 100 ft.
    Annual supply of water, about 50,000,000 gals.
    Scale of charges—

Annual R.V., not exceeding	£4	...	1s. 1d. per quarter.
„　　　„　　　„　　　„	£5	...	1s. 3d. „
„　　　„　　　„　　　„	£10	...	2s. 6d. „
„　　　„　　　„　　　„	£15	...	3s. 9d. „
„　　　„　　　„　　　„	£20	...	4s. 9d. „
„　　　„　　　„　　　„	£30	...	6s. 0d. „
„　　　„　　　„　　　„	£50	...	10s. 0d. „
„　　　„　　　„　　　„	£100	...	15s. 0d. „
„　　　„　　　„　　　„	£200	...	20s. 0d. „

    Price per 1,000 gals., 1s., and 10d., over 20,000 gals. per quarter.
    No. of meters, 26.
    Length of supply mains, 5½ miles; distributing mains, 7 miles.

Nantyglo and Blaina, Mon. Railway, G.W. Distance from London, 170 miles.
    Authority, Urban District Council.
    Clerk. H. J. C. Shepard.
    Surveyor, W. J. Davies.
    Office, Blaina.
    Total population of area supplied, 13,491.
    Annual supply of water, domestic and municipal, 49,328,000 gals.; trade, 2,842,000 gals.
    Daily consumption per head, 10 gals.
    Source of supply, Breconshire mountain (joint with the Ebbw Vale Urban District Council), the reservoir the property of Ebbw Vale Urban District Council.
    Character of water, soft. System of filtration, gravel. Number of meters, 20
    Length of mains, 16 miles.
    Scale of charges—assessment, 5 per cent. on rateable value. Houses not exceeding £10, 2d. per week; horses, 6s.; cows, 4s.; carriages, 4s. each per annum.

Quarterly consumption.		Per 1,000 gals. or fraction of ditto. s. d.	Quarterly consumption.		Per 1,000 gals. or fraction of ditto. s. d.
Under 10,000 gals....		1　9	60,000 and under 70,000 gals. ...		1　0
10,000 and under 15,000	„　...	1　6	70,000　„　80,000	„　...	0 11
15,000　„　20,000	„　..	1　5	80,000　„　90,000	„　...	0 10
20,000　„　30,000	„　...	1　4	90,000　„　100,000	„　...	0　9
30,000　„　40,000	„　...	1　3	100,000　„　500,000	„　...	0　8
40,000　„　50,000	„　...	1　2	500,000　„　1,000,000	„　...	0　7
50,000　„　60,000	„　...	1　1			

Nash (supplied by Newport, Mon. .

Nawton (supplied by Kirkby Moorside).

Neath, Glam. (G. & W.). Railways, G. W., Rhondda and Swansea Bay, Neath and Brecon. Distance from London, 196 miles.
　Authority, Neath Town Council.
　Clerk to Water Committee, Town Clerk.
　Engineer and Surveyor, D. M. Jenkins, A.M.I.C.E.
　Office of Manager, 130, London Road.
　Towns and villages in the area supplied—Neath, Briton Ferry, and part of Llantwit Lower.
　Special Acts—Neath Corporation Water Act, 1894; Gas Act, 1874.
　Total population of area supplied, about 22,000.
　Daily consumption per head, 25 gals.
　Sources of supply in use—mountain stream and springs (gravitation).
　Character of water, soft and good. Storage capacity, 42,000,000.
　Death rate, 17·7 per 1,000.
　Number of meters, 41.
　Scale of charges—assessment charge, gross estimated rental.
　　Price per 1,000 gals., 1s. 6d. to 6d.
　Total water rent received, £2,912.

Nelson, Lancs. Railways, L. & Y., G.N. and M. Distance from London, 217 miles.
　Authority, Nelson Corporation.
　Town Clerk, J. H. Baldwick.
　Engineer and Manager, James Hartley.
　Office, Town Hall, Nelson.
　Consulting Engineers, Messrs. Jno. Newton, Son & Bayley.
　Towns and villages within the area of control, with population of each (1901)

Census)—Nelson	...	...	...	...	...	...	32,816
Brierfield	...	...	...	...	...	...	7,288
Barrowford	...	...	...	...	...	...	4,958
Wheatley Lane	...	...	...	...	...	...	834
Reedley Hallows	...	...	...	...	...	...	658
Barley	...	...	...	...	...	...	287
Blacko	...	...	...	...	...	...	485
							47,326

　Works established, 1866.
　Special Acts, Nelson Water and Gas Act, 1866; Nelson Local Board Act, 1879; Nelson Improvement Act, 1886; Nelson Local Board Act, 1888.
　Total population of area of control, 1881, 19,223; 1891, 33,476; 1901, 47,326.
　Total number of consumers, 12,378.
　Estimated population actually supplied, 46,500.
　Annual supply of water—

For domestic purposes	...	..	...	237,615,000 gals.
„ trade and municipal	...	...	...	118,807,000 „
In bulk to other authorities...	...	...	3,071,000 „

　Maximum day's consumption, 1,100,000.
　Total quantity of water drawn per annum—
　　From drainage areas and surface springs　...　359,493,500 gals.
　Estimated total quantity of water available per annum—
　　From drainage areas and surface springs, 695,325,000 gals., when the authorised scheme is completed.
　Sources of supply—two drainage areas, one of 400 acres, 4 miles east of town on borders of Yorkshire, and the other of 1,100 acres, 4 miles west of town on Pendle Hill. In both cases surface springs exist, but these being for the most part in the reservoirs are not separately gauged.
　Estimated maximum daily discharge at points of collection, no data. Floods up to recognised estimate for north of England.

NELSON—*continued.*

Minimum daily discharge at points of collection, 270,000 gals.
Annual rainfall over drainage area, record not long enough to give satisfactory record.
Population on drainage area, about 10.
Cultivation of ditto, none.
Water authority have no control of drainage area.
Geological data as follows—lower coal measures and millstone grit on the east water shed and Yoredale shale and grit on the west. The millstone and Yoredale grit yields small springs.

		Storage reservoirs, Coldwell ...	...	...	...	capacity, 80,000,000 gals.
„	„	Upper Ogden (being constructed)			„	50,000,000 „
„	„	Middle Ogden (not yet constructed)			„	30,000,000 „
„	„	Lower Ogden (tenders obtained)			„	160,000,000 „

Completed scheme 320,000,000

Filtering area provided, 1,250 square yards in 2 filter-beds, also 3 gravity filters, 8 feet diameter.
Water is not softened.
Service reservoirs, Wades House, 1 mile south-east of town, capacity, 2,000,000 gals., open
Death rate, 12·3 per 1,000.
Number of meters in use, 356.
Length of distributing mains, 50 miles.
Scale of charges—
　Assessment charge when rateable value does not exceed £8 per annum, 13s. per annum; up to £30, 1s. per annum extra for every additional £ of rateable value; above £30 per annum, 10d. for every additional £ of rateable value. Subject to a discount of 1d. in the 1s. if paid during current quarter.
Lock-up premises, half above rates, with minimum of 13s. per annum.
Price per 1,000 gallons as per scale, from 1,000 gals. for 2s. to 1,500,000 gals. for £39 11s. 8d.

Nesfield with Langbar (supplied by ILKLEY).

Neston and **Parkgate**, Cheshire. Railway, L.N.W., G.W., and G.C. Distance from London, 191 miles.
Authority, Urban District Council.
Clerk, J. P. Gamon.
Surveyor, Charles E. Senior.
Office, Town Hall, Neston.
Towns and villages in the area supplied, Neston, Parkgate, Little Neston, Leighton and Hinderton.
Annual supply of water, about 40,000,000 gals.
Daily consumption per head, about 30 gals., domestic.
Sources of supply, artesian well, sunk in red sandstone at Little Neston.
Storage capacity, reservoir, 190,000, and tower for higher district, 37,270 gals.
System of filtration, none.
Character of water, hard.
Death rate, 12·4 per 1000.
Number of meters, 20 trade, 4 main.
Length of mains, 20 miles.
Scale of charges—assessment, 1s. in £. Price per 1,000 gals., trade 1s. 6d. and also by special arrangement.
Total water rent received, about £850.

Netherfield (supplied by NOTTINGHAM).

Nether Heworth (Township of), Durham (supplied by Newcastle-on-Tyne).

Netherlee, N.B. (supplied by Busby).

Netherton, Northumberland (supplied by Bedlington).

Netteswell (supplied by Herts and Essex Water Co.).

Nevin, Carnarvon.
    Storage capacity, 5,400 gals.
    Daily supply per head, 21 gals.
    Population supplied, 1,600.

Newark, Notts. Railways, G.N. & M. Distance from London, 120 miles.
    Authority, Corporation.
    Office, Carter Gate.
    Special Acts, Newark Corporation Act, 1891 and 1897.
    Total population supplied, 25,000.
    Average death rate, 15·7 per 1,000.
    Towns and villages in the area supplied—Newark, Farndon, Balderton, Codding-
       ton, Farnsfield, Edingley, Halam, Southwell, Upton, Hawton and Winthorpe.
    Source of supply, red sandstone.
    Price per 1,000 gals., 2s. to 6d., according to quantity used.

New Bilton (supplied by Rugby).

Newbold (supplied by Rugby).

New Bolingbroke, Lincs. (supplied by Boston).

New Bridge, Mon. *See* Abercarn.

New Brighton, Cheshire (supplied by Wallasey).

New Brighton, Hants. (supplied by Portsmouth).

Newbold (supplied by Rugby).

New Brompton, Kent (supplied by Brompton).

Newburgh, Fife. Railway, N.B. Distance from London, 400 miles.
    Authority, Town Council of Newburgh.
    Chairman, Alexander Edwards.
    Secretary, A. M. Sneddon.
    Engineer, James Webster Patton.
    Works established, 1877.
    Total population supplied, 2,392.
    Source of supply, Loch Mill.
    Character of water, soft.
    Assessment charge, 1s. 6½d. in the £.

Newburn, Throckley (supplied by Newcastle-on-Tyne).

Newbury, Berks. Railway, G.W. Distance from London, 53 miles.
Authority, Newbury District Water Co., Ltd.
Office, Market Place.
Area supplied, Newbury and Suburbs.
Works established, 1875. Special Acts, Gas and Water Orders Confirmation Act,
39 & 40 Vict.
Total population of area supplied, 15,000.
Source of supply, chalk springs.
Character of water, hard.
Death rate, 14 per 1,000.
Scale of charge—assessment charge, 5 per cent. on rack rent.
Price per 1,000 gals., 1s. to 8d.

Newby (supplied by SCALBY).

Newcastle-on-Tyne and **Gateshead.** Railways, G.N. & N.E. Distance from
London, 272 miles.
Authority, Newcastle and Gateshead Water Co.
Chairman, W. D. Cruddas, J.P.
Secretary and General Manager, George Smith.
Engineer, Alfred L. Forster.
Office, Pilgrim Street, Newcastle.
Share capital paid up, £3,605,368.
Works established, 1845. Special Acts, 1845, 1863, 1870, 1876, 1877, 1888, 1889,
1890, 1894, 1902 and 1904.
Total population of area supplied, 525,000.
Towns and villages in the area supplied—the boroughs of Newcastle, Gateshead,
and Wallsend; the parishes of Newburn and Ovingham in Northumberland;
the parishes of Winlaton and Ryton, in Durham; the townships of Gosforth,
Long Benton, and Howden, in Northumberland; Nether Heworth, Lamesley,
Whickham and Birtley, in the county of Durham. The urban districts of Blyth,
Cowpen, Earsdon, and Seghill. The parishes or townships of Burradon, Berwick
Hill, Brenkley, Darras Hall, Dinnington, High Callerton, Horton Grange, Little
Callerton, Mason, Ponteland and Prestwick; parish of Stannington, as lies to
the south of the River Blyth; parish of Heddon-on-the-Wall, as lies to the
south of the main highway leading from Newcastle to Carlisle; and the north-
eastern part of the parish of Bromley, as comprises the places known as
Stocksfield, Ridley Mill, Old Ridley, and Painshawfield. Tynemouth Rural
Sanitary Authority, and Tynemouth Corporation.
Sources of supply, drainage of pastoral districts, &c.
Character of water—hardness, 7° to 14° before boiling.
System of filtration, sand.
Storage capacity—impounding reservoirs, 5,366,000,000 gals.; service reservoirs,
18,000,000 gals.
Head on distributing mains—max., 200 ft.; min., 50 ft.
Annual supply of water, 6,697,000,000 gals.
Average daily consumption per head—domestic, 18·22 gals; trade, 16·73 gals.
Maximum day's supply, 22,565,000 gals. in December, 1906.
Scale of charges—
Assessment charge, gross rental.
Price per 1,000 gals., domestic and trade, 1s. 2d. to 5½d.
Number of meters, 2,591.

Newcastle-under-Lyme (supplied by STAFFORDSHIRE POTTERIES WATER CO.).

Newchurch (supplied by BURY).

Newhaven and Seaford. Railway, L.B.S.C. Distance from London, 56 miles.
Authority, Newhaven and Seaford Water Company.
Chairman, R. Lambe.
Manager, Engineer and Secretary, John T. Bickford.
Share capital paid up, £38,525.
Loan   „   £7,500.
Dividends, 5½ per cent. on £30,000, and £3 17s. per cent. on £8,610.
Interest on loans, 4 per cent. on £4,500, and 3 per cent. on £6,000.
Towns and villages in the area supplied—Newhaven, Denton, Bishopstone,
Piddinghoe, East Blatchington, and Seaford.
Works established, 1881. Special Act, 1898.
Total population supplied, 12,000.
Sources of supply, chalk, pumping.
Filtration, none; softening, none.
Storage, none.
Annual supply of water, about 84,000,000 gals., an abnormal increase in 1905-6.
Number of meters, 77.
Scale of charges—
Assessment charge, not exceeding £20, 8 per cent. per annum; over £20, 7 per
cent. per annum.
Price per 1,000 gals., trade and municipal purposes, 1s. 6d.
Total water rent received, £4,335.

Newhill, Yorks. (supplied by Wath-upon-Dearne).

New Hunstanton (see Hunstanton).

Newington (supplied by Rainham).

Newmains, Scotland (supplied by Wishaw).

Newmarket, Cambs. Railway, G.E. Distance from London, 69½ miles.
Authority, Newmarket Waterworks Co., Ld.
Chairman, B. Chinnell.
Secretary, A. H. Ruston.
Resident Engineer, C. H. H. Adams.
Office, High Street, Newmarket.
Share capital paid up, Original ... £20,000.
New   ... £15,000.
Premiums £3,460.
Four per cent. First Mortgage Debentures, £1,000.
Dividend, 10 per cent. old, 7 per cent. new.
Total population supplied, 12,000.
Average death rate, 9·5 per 1,000.
Source of supply, well 100 ft. deep.

Analysis of water—	Grains per gal.
Total solid matter	20·00
Chlorides	1·30
Equal to chloride of sodium	2·14
Nitrates (expressed as nitrogen)	·25
Ammonia (free)	·0007
Ammonia (albuminoid)	·0014
Oxygen, absorbed by organic matter in 15 minutes, at 140° F....	·0112

Appearance in 2-ft. tube, clear, pale blue.
Smell, when heated to 100° F., none.

NEWMARKET—*continued.*

Metals, none.
Microscopic examination, no deposit.
Remarks—
Total solid matter, chlorides, and nitrates are low and quite satisfactory.
Free and albuminoid ammonia and oxygen absorbed are all very low and
show the absence of organic matter.
The water is unpolluted, and quite fit for drinking purposes.
Filtration, none ; softening, none.
Service reservoirs, 265,000 gals.
Pressure on distributing mains—maximum, 110 lbs. ; minimum, 5 lbs. per sq. in.
Annual supply of water, 130,000,000 gals.
Maximum day's supply, 550,000 gals., during race meetings.
Assessment charge, 6 per cent. on rental value.
Price per 1,000 gals., 1s. 6d.
No. of meters, 369.

New Marske, Yorks. (supplied by CLEVELAND).

New Mills (Stockport, Cheshire). Railway, M. Distance from London, 173 miles.
Population supplied, 7,773.
No returns supplied.

New Monkland (supplied by DISTRICT OF THE MIDDLE WARD OF LANARK-
SHIRE).

Newnham and Newnham Murren (supplied by SOUTH OXFORDSHIRE).

Newport, Devon. (supplied by BARNSTAPLE).

Newport, Isle of Wight   Railway, L.S.W.   Distance from London, 88 miles.
Authority, Corporation of Newport, Isle of Wight.
Secretary, T. Ross Pratt, Town Clerk, 19, Quay Street, Newport.
Engineer, John W. Way.
Purchased by local authority, 1879.
Maximum day's consumption, 750,000 gals.
Pumping station—Carisbrooke, capacity, 47,200 gals.
Service reservoirs—
One   ...   .   capacity, 800,000 gals.
One   ...   .   „   200,000 „
Scale of charges—
Assessment charges, under £8 rateable value, 1s. per quarter; over £8, 1s.
per quarter.
From under 30,000 gals.   ...   ...   1s. 5d. per 1,000 gals.
To over 1,000,000 gals. ...   .   0s. 7d. „   „   „

Newport (Mon.).   Railways, G.W. and L.N.W.
Authority, Newport Corporation.
Chairman, T. Goldsworthy, J.P.
Manager, Charles Cullum.
Engineer, R. H. Haynes, Borough Engineer.
Office, Town Hall, Newport.
Total capital expenditure on undertaking, £607,064.
Annual loss on undertaking, including " capital charges," £6,017.
Works established, 1847.
Purchased by local authority, July, 1888.
Special Acts, Newport and Pillgwenlly Waterworks Act, 1854 ; Newport and
Pillgwenlly Extension Act, 1872 ; Newport and Pillgwenlly Orders, 1881 and
1883 ; Newport Waterworks Act, 1887 ; Newport (Mon.) Corporation Water
Act, 1888 ; Newport Corporation Act, 1897 ; Newport Corporation Act, 1902.

NEWPORT (MON.).—*continued.*

Estimated population actually supplied with water, 83,400.

Average death rate, 17·2 per 1,000 in county borough.

Towns and villages within area of control, with population of each (1901 Census)—

Newport	67,279
Caerleon	1,481
Christchurch	957
Malpas	495
Rogerstone	2,883
Bassaleg and Rhiwderin	1,112
St. Woollos	275
Penhow	249
Nash and St. Brides	294
Goldcliffe	253
Llanvaches	572
Llandevaud and Llangstone	157

Source of supply in use—the drainage areas, situated in the parishes of Henllys and Bettws, have an altitude ranging from 200 to 1,250 feet above Ordnance datum. The total drainage areas amount to 2,125 acres.

Maximum annual rainfall over drainage area, 60·93 inches (1894).
Minimum   ,,   ,,   ,,   34·12 ,,   (1892).
Average   ,,   ,,   ,,   46·60 ,,   (past 10 years).
Population on drainage area, about 150.

Nature of drainage area, mountain pasture and farm land with small area of arable.

Surface formation of drainage areas, old red sandstone.

Character of water—clear, bright ; no marked characteristics.

Recent analyses—
Newport Corporation Water, expressed in parts per 100,000—

Ynys-y-fro water (March, 1907) ...

,,	,,	,,	total solids	16·5
,,	,,	,,	albuminoid ammonia	·007
,,	,,	,,	free ammonia	·0012
,,	,,	,,	nitrogen as nitrates and nitrites	·046
,,	,,	,,	chlorine as chloride	1·2
,,	,,	,,	oxygen absorbed in 4 hours	·051
,,	,,	,,	hardness	12·5°

No filtration.

Pant-yr-eos water (March, 1907) ...

,,	,,	,,	total solids	15·5
,,	,,	,,	albuminoid ammonia	·007
,,	,,	,,	free ammonia	·0008
,,	,,	,,	nitrogen as nitrates and nitrites	·048
,,	,,	,,	oxygen absorbed in 4 hours	·064
,,	,,	,,	chlorine as chloride	1·2
,,	,,	,,	hardness	12°

Chemically of good qualities, but contains much suspended matter. No filtration.

Wentwood water (March, 1907) ...

,,	,,	,,	total solids	10·0
,,	,,	,,	albuminoid ammonia	·007
,,	,,	,,	free ammonia	·0008
,,	,,	,,	nitrogen as nitrates and nitrites	·058
,,	,,	,,	oxygen absorbed in 4 hours	·032
,,	,,	,,	chlorine as chlorides	1·25
,,	,,	,,	hardness	6·5°

Filtered.

Filtration—Wentwood reservoirs, Pressure Polarite filters.
     ,,   Pant-yr-eos   ,,   ,,   filters in construction.
Water is not softened.

Impounding reservoirs at Wentwood, Henllys, and Bettws, Mon. Storage in impounding reservoirs, 665,000,000 gals.

NEWPORT (MON.).—*continued.*

Storage reservoirs, Pant-yr-eos ... ... capacity, 145,000,000 gals.
    „   „   Yniy-y-fro ... ...   „   84,000,000   „
    „   „   Yniy-y-fro (subsiding)   „   36,000,000   „
Service reservoirs, Stow Hill ... ...   „   60,000   „   covered.
Head on distributing mains—max., 370 ft.; min., 60 ft.
Annual supply of water—for all purposes, 823,000,000 gals.
Average daily supply—domestic, 13 gals. ; trade, &c., 13¼ gals.
Maximum day's consumption, 2,976,000 gals. in August.
Scale of charges—
Domestic purposes, within the borough 5 per cent. per annum upon the poor rate
assessment. In the parishes of St. Woollos, Christchurch, and Malpas, where
the houses supplied are not more than 80 feet above the coping of the walls
of the Newport Old Dock, 5 per cent. per annum ; where the elevation is
more than 80 feet, 6 per cent. per annum. At all other places and parishes
in the district, 6 per cent. per annum upon the gross annual value, according to the poor rate assessments No house to be charged less than 8s. 8d.
per annum. Water-closets at premises rated above £14, 10s. per annum
for one, for each beyond one, 6s. per annum. Water-closets at houses
rated at £14 and under, 6s. per annum each. Baths, private and
capable of containing not more than 60 gals., 10s. per annum for one.
For each beyond one, 6s. per annum.
Trade, quarterly consumption—

Under 10,000 gals.	...	...	...	...	1s. 6d.	per 1,000 gals. (or frac.)
„	10,000	„	and under	20,000 gals.	1s. 5d.	„
„	20,000	„	„	30,000	„	1s. 4d.	„
„	30,000	„	„	40,000	„	·1s. 3d.	„
„	40,000	„	„	50,000	„	1s. 2d.	„
„	50,000	„	„	60,000	„	1s. 1d.	„
„	60,000	„	„	80,000	„	1s. 0d.	„
„	80,000	„	„	100,000	„	0s. 11d.	„
„	100,000	„	„	175,000	„	0s. 10d.	„
„	175,000	„	„	250,000	„	0s. 9d.	„
„	250,000	„	„	500,000	„	0s. 8d.	„
„	500,000	„	„	750,000	„	0s. 7d.	„
„	750,000	„	„	1,000,000	„	0s. 6d.	„
„	1,000,000	„	„	1,500,000	„	0s. 5d.	„
„	1,500,000	„	„	3,000,000	„	0s. 4d.	„
„	3,000,000	„	and upwards	...	0s. 3d.	„

Number of meters in use, 396.
Length of distributing and supply mains, 118 miles.

Newport (Salop). Railway, L.N.W. Distance from London, 145 miles.
Authority, Urban District Council.
Loan capital, £4,696.
Population supplied, 3,241.
Assessment charge, 10d. in £ on rateable value.
Price per, 1,000 gals., by meter, 6d.

Newport Pagnell, Bucks.
Authority, Urban District Council.
Population, 4,000.

Newquay, Cornwall. Railway, G.W. Distance from London, 297 miles.
Authority, Newquay and District Water Company.
Chairman, H. D. Foster.
Secretary and Manager, George G. Bullmore.
Consulting Engineer, G. R. Strachan, C.E.
Office, Newquay.

Newquay—*continued.*

Share capital paid up, £20,000 ; last dividend, 4 per cent.
Loan capital paid up, £5,000 ; last dividend, 5 per cent.
Works established, 1883. Special Act, 1882.
The Company are promoting a Bill (1907) to extend their limits of supply, to authorise the construction of new works and the raising of money.
Total population supplied, 3,800 normal ; 8,000 in summer.
Death rate (1905), 12·2 per 1,000.
District of supply, Newquay, St. Columb Major and St. Columb Minor, Colon.
Source of supply—Well at Mount Wise (pumping station) ; adit at Indian Queens (gravitation) ; impounding reservois at Quuintri Downs.
Character of water—gravitation supply, soft, 1⅜° hardness ; pumped supply, hard, 9° hardness.
Filtration, sand, but water is so pure that filtration is not necessary. Softening, none.
Storage impounding reservoirs, 7,500,000 gals. ; service reservoir, 200,000 gals.
Average daily supply per head, 26 gals. all purposes.
Maximum day's supply 175,000 gals. in August.
Assessment charge, 7½ per cent. on gross estimated rental for all houses over £20 per annum.
Charge by meter, 1s. 6d. per 1,000 gals.
Length of mains, 12 miles.

New River Company. *See* Metropolitan Water Board.

Newsby (supplied by Ripon).

New Shoreham, Sussex (supplied by Brighton).

Newton (supplied by Barrow-in-Furness).

Newton (supplied by Chester).

Newton, Yorks. (supplied by Kirkby Moorside).

Newton Abbot, Devon. (supplied by Torquay).

Newton Burgoland (supplied by Hinckley).

Newton Heath (supplied by Manchester.

Newton-in-Makerfield, Lancs. Railway, L.N.W. Distance from London, 190 miles.
Authority, Newton-in-Makerfield Urban District Council.
Chairman, C. B. F. Borron, C.C.
Clerk to Authority, C. Cole.
Engineer, R. T. Surtees.
Office, Town Hall, Earlestown.
Loans outstanding, £27,628.
Annual profit, including capital charges, £573.
Works established, 1874 ; special Acts, 1855.
Population supplied, 19,153.
Average annual death rate, 13·47 per 1,000.
District of supply, Urban District of Newton-in-Makerfield.

Newton-in-Makerfield—*continued.*

Source of supply, wells in red sandstone, 200 feet deep.
Character of water, 9¼° hardness.
Filtration, none; softening, none.
Storage capacity—service reservoirs, 550,000 gals.; headings reservoir, 700,000 gals.
Pressure on distributing mains—maximum, 83 lbs.; minimum, 20 lbs.
Annual supply of water, 194,462,506 gals.
Average daily supply per head, 12·5 gals.
Assessment charges, 5 per cent. on R.V.
Charge by meter—

Not exceeding 7,000 gals....	...	...	10s., per quarter.
7,000 to 50,000 gals. ...	...	...	1s. 4d. per 1,000.
50,000 gals. and upward ...	...	...	1s. per 1,000.

Number of meters, 60.
Total length of mains, about 13 miles.

Newtown, Montgomery. Railways, L.N.W. and Cambrian. Distance from London, 195 miles.
Authority, Newtown and Llanllwchaiarn Urban District Council.
Engineer and Manager, E. Clement Jones.
Works established, 1875.
Compulsorily acquired from old Co., June, 1899.
Special Act, Newtown Water Act, 1898.
Total population of area supplied, 6,500.
Daily consumption, domestic, 120,000 gals., trade, 30,000 gals,
Sources of supply—gravitation (reservoir situate at Mochdra).
Storage capacity, 13,000,000 gals.
System of filtration, nil.
Character of water, upland surface water.
Number of meters, 20.
Length of mains, 4¼ miles (duplicate 6-inch and 7-inch).
Scale of charges—assessment charge, on rateable value.
Price per 1,000 gals., trade, 2s. to 1s. 9d.; municipal purposes, £100.
Total water rent received, £1,600.

Newtown (supplied by Leicester).

Newtown Village, N.B. (supplied by Bo'ness).

New Tredegar, Mon. (G. & W.) Railways, B. and M. and Rhy. Distance from London, 168 miles.
Authority, New Tredegar Gas and Water Company, Ld.
Chairman, Alderman N. Philips, J.P.
Manager, Engineer and Secretary, D. Walter Davies.
Office, Gas and Water Offices.
Towns and villages in the area supplied—New Tredegar, Elliot Town, Cwmsyfiog, Brithdir, Tirphil.
Works established, 1873.
Special Act, 1878.
Total population supplied, 10,000.
New Tredegar has a supplemental supply from the Blackwood mains during the summer months.

Nitshill (supplied by Glasgow).

Noctorum, Cheshire (supplied by Birkenhead).

Norden, Lancs. (supplied by Heywood).

Normandy, Surrey (supplied by Frimley).

Normanton, Yorks. (supplied by Wakefield).

Northallerton, Yorks. Railway, N.E. Distance from London, 222 miles.
Authority, Urban District Council.
Chairman, John Weighell.
Clerk, W. Fowle.
Engineer and Manager, Wm. Watson.
Loan, £18,500.
Towns and villages in the area supplied, Northallerton, Brompton, Romanby, Thimbleby.
Works established, 1892.
Special Act, Northallerton Waterworks Act, 1891.
Total population supplied, 5,000.
Daily consumption per head, 15 gals.
Sources of supply, 5 springs from Hambleton Hills.
Storage capacity, 250,000 gals.
Character of water, freestone.
Death rate, 14 3 per 1,000.
Number of meters, 34.
Length of mains, 20 miles.
Scale of charges—
Assessment charge, 4s. 6d. for first £5 of rateable value, and 1s. 6d. for every additional £5.
Price per 1,000 gals., Northallerton, 6d.; Brompton, 1s.; Thimbleby and Romanby, 1s. 6d.

Northam, Devon.
Authority, Urban District Council.
Population, 5,300.

Northampton, Railways, L.N.W., M. Distance from London, 65¾ miles.
Authority, Corporation (taken over from a private company, in 1884).
Town Clerk, Herbert Hankinson.
Engineer and Manager, Frank Tomlinson.
Office, Town Hall.
Towns and villages in the area supplied—Northampton, Kingsthorpe, St. James End, Far Caton, Chapel Brampton.
Total population of area supplied, 120,000.
Daily consumption per head—domestic, 12·7 gals.; trade, 3·1 gals.
Sources of supply, surface catchment and deep wells.
Storage capacity, 400,000,000 gals.
Number of meters, 1,021.
Character of water, 50·0°, wells; 9·0°, surface.
System of filtration, sand and gravel.
Price per 1,000 gals., 1s. 6d.

North Bierley, Yorks. (supplied by Bradford).

North Bute (supplied by Rothesay).

North Cheshire.
Authority, The North Cheshire Water Company.
Towns and villages within the area of control—Altrincham, Ashton-on-Mersey, Baguley, Bowdon, Hale, Dunham Massey, Sale, Ashley, Northenden, and Northern Etchells.

NORTH CHESHIRE—*continued.*

Works established, 1858.
Special Acts, North Cheshire Water Acts, 1864 and 1877.
Total number of consumers, 12,000.
Estimated population actually supplied, 60,000.
Annual supply of water—
      For domestic purposes   ...   . 288,000,000 gals.
        „ trade and municipal purposes ...   ...   34,000,000 „
Maximum day's consumption, 1,300,000 gals.
Source of supply—the whole of the water supplied by the Company is obtained,
   in bulk, through meters, from the Manchester Corporation.
   Character of water, soft.
   Service reservoirs, Bowdon reservoir ...   . 1,000,000 gals., open.
     „   „   Bowdon tank, for highest houses ...   100,000 „   „
Number of meters in use, 350.
Length of distributing mains, 100 miles.
Scale of charges—assessment charge R. R., subject to a 10 per cent. discount if
   paid before a certain date.
Price per 1,000 gals., 2s. to 1s. 6d.

North Country (supplied by REDRUTH).

Northdown (supplied by BROADSTAIRS).

Northenden (supplied by NORTH CHESHIRE WATER Co.).

Northern Etchells (supplied by NORTH CHESHIRE WATER Co.).

Northfield (supplied by BIRMINGHAM).

Northfleet, Kent. (supplied by GRAVESEND).

Northolt, Herts. (supplied by RICKMANSWORTH).

Northorp Hall, Flint. (supplied by HAWARDEN).

North Pembroke Water and Gas Co. Railway, G.W.R. to Fishguard.
Special Act, Fishguard Water and Gas Act, 1899.
North Pembrokeshire Water and Gas Act, 1900.

North Queensferry, N.B. (supplied by DUNFERMLINE).

North Shields (*see* TYNEMOUTH).

North Skelton, Yorks. (supplied by CLEVELAND).

North Stainley (supplied by RIPON).

North Stoke (supplied by SOUTH OXFORDSHIRE).

North Tawton, Devon. Railway, L.S.W. Distance from London, 190¾ miles.
Authority, Urban District Council. The works were transferred from the North
   Tawton Water Co. under Public Health Act.
Total population of area supplied, 1,737.

North Warwickshire.
Authority, North Warwickshire Water Co.
Engineers, Joseph Quick & Son, M.I.C.E., Great George Street, Westminster.
Office, Foleshill, near Coventry.

North Weald (supplied by Herts. and Essex Waterworks Co.).

Northwich, Cheshire. Railways. C.L. and L.N.W. Distance from London 172 miles.
Authority, Urban District Council.
Chairman, W. Bailey, J.P.
Clerk to the Council, J. A. Cowley.
Engineer, John Brooke.
Office, Council Office.
Loan, £70,000.
Interest, 3¼ per cent.
Area supplied, Northwich and parishes adjoining.
Special Act, 1885.
Total population supplied, 20,000.
Annual supply of water, 146,000,000 gals.
Daily consumption per head, 20 gals.
Sources of supply, springs, Cote Brook (domestic) and Wade Brook (trade).
Storage capacity, 6 days' supply.
Filtration, none.
Character of water, excellent.
Average death rate, 12·8 per 1,000.
Length of mains, 25 miles.
Scale of charges—assessment charge, 6d. in the £.
Price per 1,000 gals., trade, 9d.
Total water rate received, £4,600.

Northwood (supplied by Broadstairs).

North Wootton, part of (supplied by Glastonbury).

Norton, Worcester (supplied by Evesham).

Norton, Yorks. (supplied by Sheffield).

Norton-in-the-Moors (supplied by Staffordshire Potteries Water Co.).

Norton Canes (supplied.by South Staffs. Waterworks Co.).

Norwich, Norfolk. Railway, G.E. Distance from London, 114 miles.
Authority, Company.
Works established, 1850. Special Act, 1850.
Population supplied, 111,728.
No returns supplied.

Norwood Green (supplied by Halifax).

Nottingham. Railways, G.N., G.C. and M. Distance from London, 123 miles.
Authority, Corporation of Nottingham.
Chairman, Alderman J. Jelley, J.P.
Secretary, Sir S. G. Johnson, Town Clerk, Guildhall, Nottingham.
Water Engineer, F. W. Davies, St. Peters' Churchside, Nottingham.

NOTTINGHAM—*continued.*

Consulting Engineer, W. B. Bryan, Elmstead Wood, Chislehurst.
City Accountant, John E. Bryan, St. Peter's Square, Nottingham.
Total capital invested, including loans, £1,174,762, at Lady Day, 1906.
Works established, 1707. Purchased by local authority, 1880.
Act of Parliament, 9 Vict. 1845.
Total population of area of control—1881, 250,000 ; 1891, 300,000 ; 1901, 350,000.
Estimated population actually supplied, 340,000, at Lady Day, 1907.
Death rate, 16 per 1,000.
Towns and villages within "District of Supply," Arnold, Awsworth, Beeston,
Bestwood Park, Bilborough (part of), Brinsley, Burton Joyce, Carlton, Colwick,
Eastwood, Gedling, Greasley, Kimberley, Linby, City of Nottingham, Nuthall,
Papplewick, Radcliffe-on-Trent, Stoke Bardolph, West Bridgeford, South
Wilford, Wollaton. An area of 75½ square miles.
Towns and villages outside Water District, supplied by agreement—Bilsthorpe,
Boughton, Bulcote, Cossall, Holme Pierrepont, Kirton, Ollerton, Perlethorpe,
Rufford, Strelley, Thoresby Park (part of Edwinstowe parish).
Sources of supply—deep wells in new red sandstone.
Character of water, 10° of hardness.
Storage capacity, 14,000,000 gals.
Annual supply (year to Lady Day, 1907)—2,744,877,463 gals.
Average daily supply per head, domestic, 11·48 gallons ; trade and special
purposes, 10·62 gallons.
Scale of charges—
Assessment charge, 3 and 5½ per cent. per annum on rental.
Price per 1,000 gals., 10d. to 6d.
Meters in use, 3,666.
Distributing mains, 389 miles.

Nuneaton, Warwickshire. Railways, L.N.W., Main Line, and M., Birmingham and
Leicester. Distance from London, 96 miles.
Authority, Nuneaton Corporation.
Chairman, F. J. Johnson, J.P.
Clerk to authority, F. S. Clay.
Engineer and Surveyor, F. C. Cook.
Office, Council Office, Nuneaton.
Loan outstanding, £69,373,
Interest, 2¾, 3, and 3½ per cent.
Annual profit (net profit, 1906), £1,290 9s. 4d.
Works established, 1882. Special Act, East Warwickshire Waterworks Act,
1882. Purchased by local authority by Act of 1897.
Total population of area supplied, 28,763.
Towns and villages in the area supplied—Nuneaton, Chilvers Coton, Attle-
borough, Stockingford, Chapel End, and Galley Common.
Death rate, 12·93 per 1,000 (1906).
Source of supply—deep wells in the permian, varying from 120 to 200 yards deep.
Character of water, good water for town purposes, slightly impregnated with iron.
System of filtration, sand ; softening, none.
Storage capacity, in service reservoirs, 1,350,000 gals.
Pressure on mains—maximum, 90 lbs. ; minimum, 25 lbs. per sq. inch.
Annual supply of water, about 181,296,500 gals.
Daily consumption per head—domestic, 12·52 gals. ; trade, 5·13 gals.
Maximum day's supply, 658,000 gals., in September.
Scale of charges—assessment, 5 to 6½ per cent. on gross rental, less 10 per cent.
Price per 1,000 gals. by meter, 8d. to 1s., less 10 per cent.
Number of meters, 111.
Length of supply mains, 1½ miles ; distributing mains, 32 miles.

Nunnington, Yorks. (supplied by KIRKBY MOORSIDE).

Nutfield (supplied by East Surrey Waterworks Co.).

Nuttall (supplied by Nottingham).

Nuttall Lane (supplied by Bury).

Oadby (supplied by Leicester).

Oakbank, part of (supplied by Blairgowrie).

Oaken, Staffs. (supplied by Wolverhampton)

Oakley Green (supplied by Maidenhead).

Oakworth (supplied by Keighley).

Oare, Kent (supplied by Faversham).

Ockenden, North and South (supplied by South Essex Water Co.).

Ockham (supplied by Woking).

Odiham, Hants. (supplied by Frimley).

Odstone (supplied by Hinckley).

Ogley Hay (supplied by South Staffs. Waterworks Co.).

Okehampton. Railway, L.S.W. Distance from London, 198 miles.
  Authority, Corporation.
  Town Clerk, J. J. Newcombe.
  Borough Surveyor, Fras. J. Worden.
  Office, Town Hall.
  Area supplied—the borough, and a number of houses outside at assessment
    charge.
  Total population supplied, 2,600.
  Annual supply of water, about 36,500,000 gals.
  Daily consumption per head, 50 gals., all purposes.
  Sources of supply, hillside springs and upland water (Dartmoor).
  Storage capacity, service reservoir, 130,000 gals. ; at dam, 200,000 gals.
  System of filtration, sand.
  Death rate, 12 per 1,000.
  Number of meters, 1 for detecting waste.
  Length of mains, about 4 miles.
  Scale of charges—
    Assessment charge, 1s. in the £.
    Price per 1,000 gals., trade, 3d.
  Total water rent received, about £400.

Oldbury (supplied by South Staffordshire Waterworks Co.).

Old Brompton, Kent (supplied by Brompton).

Oldham and District. Railways, L.N.W., L. & Y., and G.C. Distance from London, 188½ miles.
　Authority, Corporation, 1853.
　General Superintendent, Arthur Andrew.
　Engineer, C. J. Batley, A.M.I.C.E.
　Office, Greaves Street.
　Loan, £934,974; redeemed, £242,680.
　Interest on Loan, 2 and 4 per cent.
　Area supplied, 15,384 acres.
　Towns and villages in the area supplied, Oldham, Chadderton, Royton, Crompton, Lees, Springhead, Failsworth, and Crossbank.
　Works established, 1826. Special Acts, 1826, 1855, 1865, 1870, 1875, 1880, 1886.
　Total population supplied, 223,000.
　Daily consumption per head, 22 to 23 gals. for all purposes.
　Source of supply, gathering grounds at source of the rivers Medlock, Roach and Tame.
　Storage capacity, 1,976,000,000 gals.
　Character of water, soft.
　System of filtration, none.
　Number of meters, 1,409.
　Scale of charges—assessment charge, gross value, 7½ per cent. in borough, and 8½ per cent. outside.
　Price per 1,000 gals., 2s. to 6d. trade; municipal purposes, free.
　Total water rent received, about £60,720.

Old Meldrum, Aberdeenshire. Railway, G.N. of S. Distance from London, 560 miles.
　Authority, Town Council.
　Chairman, Provost Shand.
　Secretary, John Gordon, Town Clerk.
　Manager, James Henderson.
　Area supplied, Old Meldrum only.
　Total population supplied, 1,197 for Burgh.
　Sources of supply, Pearcock Spring and Blairs Springs.
　Character of water, hard.

Old Shoreham, Sussex (supplied by Brighton).

Old Swinford (supplied by Stourbridge).

Old Windsor (supplied by South West Suburban).

Olton (supplied by Birmingham).

Openshaw (supplied by Manchester.)

Openshaw Fold (supplied by Bury).

Ordsall (supplied by Retford).

Ormesby, Yorks. (supplied by Stockton).

Ormskirk, Lancs. Railway, L. & Y. Distance from London, 203 miles.
　Authority, Urban District Council.
　Chairman, C. F. Ellis.

ORMSKIRK—*continued*.

Clerk to Authority, Fred C. Hill.
Engineer, Hugh W. Chadwick, Surveyor to Council.
Office, Urban District Council Offices.
Works established 1852.
Total population supplied, 7,200.
Character of water, exceptionally good and very soft.
Average death rate, 16·17 per 1,000.
Analysis.—Results expressed in parts per 100,000. Mark and denomination of
the sample—deep well in sandstone.

Total solid matter in solution	15·260
Oxygen required to oxidise { In 15 minutes	·001
{ In 3 hours	·002
Ammonia	·003
Ammonia from organic matter by distillation with akaline permanganate	·003
Nitrogen as nitrates	·196
Combined chlorine	2·300

Clear; colourless; very faintly acid reaction; free from organisms. Very good
quality for domestic use.
Quantitative mineral analysis—

Total solids	15·26
Loss on ignition	3·84
Ferric oxide	·02
Alumina	·11
Lime	2·24
Magnesia	·99
Alkalies	·17
Silica	2·18
Sulphuric acid	1·41
Chlorine	2·30
Nitric acid	·78
Carbon dioxide	1·74

No higher metals.
Area supplied, Ormskirk, and part of Aughton and Bickerstaffe.
Filtration, none.
Source of supply, wells in sandstone.
Storage capacity, distributing tank, 100,000 gals., less than one day's supply.
Annual supply of water, 63,500,000 gals.
Daily consumption per head, domestic, 20 gals.
Maximum day's supply, 227,000 gals. in July.
Scale of charges, assessment charge, 5 per cent. in £ domestic purposes.
Price per 1,000 gals., trade, 1s., with sliding scale for large consumers.
Number of meters, 25.
Length of mains, about 7 miles; largest main, 8". smallest, 3".
Total water rent received, about £1,650 per annum.

Orsett (supplied by SOUTH ESSEX WATER CO.).

Osmaston (supplied by DERBY).

Osmotherley (supplied by ULVERSTON).

Ospringe, Kent (supplied by FAVERSHAM).

Ossett, Yorks. Railway, G. N. Distance from London, 178 miles.
Authority, Corporation.
Office, Borough Offices.
Loan capital, £27,500.

Ossett—*continued*.

Works established, 1876. Special Act, 1875.
Total population supplied, 14,140.
Daily consumption per head, 12 to 18 gals.
Sources of supply, bought in bulk from Dewsbury and Heckmondwike Water Board.
Storage capacity, service reservoir, 1 week's supply.
Character of water, good, soft.
Length of mains, 19 to 20 miles.
Price per 1,000 gals., 9d., trade purposes.

Oswaldtwistle (supplied by BLACKBURN).

Oswestry. Railways, Cambrian and G.W. Distance from London, 191 miles.
Authority, Corporation of Oswestry.
Chairman of Water Committee, Alderman Whitfield, J.P.
Clerks, S. Pryce Parry, M.A., Town Clerk; J. W. Thomas, Finance Clerk.
Engineer in charge, G. William Lacey, C.E.
Office, Guildhall, Oswestry.
Total capital invested, including loans, £41,000. Loans outstanding, £23,000.
Works established, 1866; new impounding reservoir constructed 1890-4.
Special Acts, Water and Sewage, 1865; Water and Markets, 1885.
Total population of area of control, 1881, 7,850; 1891, 8,500; 1901, 9,800; 1907, 10,000.
Estimated population actually supplied, 9,900.
Average death rate, 15 per 1,000.
Area of control, borough of Oswestry and a small population outside the boundary.
Source of supply—drainage areas situated at 5½ miles W.N.W. of Oswestry, county of Denbigh.
Maximum annual rainfall over drainage area, 60·13 inches (1903).
Minimum ,, ,, ,, ,, ,, 34·67 ,, (1906).
Average ,, ,, ,, ,, ,, 39·90 ,, (period 8 years).
No population on drainage area.
Nature of drainage area, small portion arable, but chiefly hill pasture. The Corporation purchased in 1904 the farm of 250 acres on which the impounding reservoir is situated, and which comprises a large part of the watershed.
Surface formation of drainage areas, lower silurian. The beds consist in a great measure of dark shaly and slaty rocks, which are interstratified with a series of igneous intrusive sheets.
Storage reservoir, Penygwely reservoir, capacity, 25,000,000 gals.
Service reservoirs—

Mount Reservoir, No. 1	...	capacity,	1,400,000 gals.,	open.
,, ,, ,, 2	...	,,	1,400,000 ,,	,,
,, ,, ,, 3	...	,,	3,200,000 ,,	,,

Character of water, soft; hardness total, 3·5°; permanent, 3·3°.
Pressure on distributing mains—maximum, 90lbs.; minimum, 25lbs. per sq. in.
Annual supply of water (1906), 102,000,000 gals.
For domestic purposes ... ... 58,000,000 gals.=16 gals. per head per day.
,, trade and municipal purposes 44,000,000 ,, =12½, , ,, ,,
Maximum day's consumption, 361,000 gals. in July.
Scale of charges—
Domestic, rateable value up to £15, sliding scale 6s. to 11s. per annum; over £15, 9d. in the £.
Trade and municipal, 10d. to 7d. per 1,000 gals.; minimum, 15s. per annum.
Schools, 8d. per 1,000 gals.
Domestic—outside borough, 2s. per 1,000 gals.; minimum, 30s. per annum.
Number of meters in use, 125.
Length of supply mains, 5; distributing mains, 8 miles.

Otley, Yorks.
>Authority, Urban District Council.
>Population, 9,300.

Ottery St. Mary, Devon.
>Population supplied, 3,855.
>No returns supplied.

Oulton and Woodlesford (supplied by LEEDS).

Outwood (supplied by BURY).

Overstrand (supplied by CROMER).

Ovingdean, Sussex (supplied by BRIGHTON).

Ovingham (supplied by NEWCASTLE).

Oxenhope (supplied by KEIGHLEY).

Oxford. Railways, G.W. and L.N.W. Distance from London 63¾ miles.
>Authority, Corporation.
>Chairman, Councillor S. Hutchings.
>Secretary, R. Bacon, Town Clerk.
>Engineer, W. H. White, M.I.C.E.
>Office, Town Hall, St. Aldate's.
>Works established, 1610.
>Special Acts, 1875, 1885.
>Total population supplied, 55,000.
>Area supplied, 4,676 acres (within the city). Certain outside parishes, of a total area of 8,177 acres, are also included in the area of supply, and these are now partly supplied with city water.
>Sources of supply—from River Thames 4 miles above Oxford, and auxiliary supplies from lake supplied by springs in gravel.
>Character of water, about 16° hardness.
>Storage capacity—covered service reservoir holding 1,250,000 gals., and open reservoir containing 25,000,000 gals.
>Annual supply of water, 496,000,000 gals.
>Daily consumption per head, 24 gals.
>Scale of charges—average assessment charge within the city about 3½ per cent. on the rental value, outside city, 6 per cent.
>Price per 1,000 gals. average 10d. ; outside city, 1s. 3d. per 1,000.
>Number of meters, 800.
>Average death rate 13·47 per 1,000.

Oxted, Surrey. *See* LIMPSFIELD.

Oystermouth, Glam.
>Authority, Oystermouth and District Waterworks Co., Ltd.
>Population supplied, 4,483.
>No returns supplied.

Padgate, Lancs. (supplied by WARRINGTON).

Padiham, Lancs. Railway, L. & Y. Distance from London, 228 miles.
>Authority, District Council of Padiham.
>Chairman, Councillor Roberts.
>Clerk, J. C. Waddington.

PADIHAM—*continued.*

> Engineer and Manager, Jno. Gregson.
> Office, Town Hall.
> Towns and villages in the area supplied—Padiham, part of Burnley Corporation and Altham township.
> Purchased by local authority, 1874.
> Total population supplied, 16,100.
> Daily consumption per head, 15 gals.
> Source of supply, Pendle Hill. Storage capacity, 125,000,000 gals.
> Character of water, from millstone grit, soft and very good.
> Death rate, 15 per 1,000.
> Number of meters, 54. Length of mains, 14½ miles.

Padstow, Cornwall.
> Authority, Urban District Council.
> Population, 1,600.

Paignton, Devon. Railway, G.W. Distance from London, 217¼ miles.
> Authority, Paignton Urban District Council.
> Manager, J. Crathorn.
> Clerk, James R. Mill.
> Office, Town Hall.
> Works established, 1867. Special Acts, 1867, 1900.
> Daily consumption per head, all purposes, 28 gals.
> Sources of supply, springs. Impounding reservoirs on Holme, Dartmoor.
> Storage capacity, impounding reservoirs, 200,000,000 gals. ; service, 11,000,000 gals.
> Character of water, very good, but rather hard. System of filtration, sand.
> Average death rate, 13·1 per 1,000.
> Number of meters, 11.
> Assessment, gross value, £59,924 ; rateable value, £51,926.
> Price per 1,000 gals., trade, 1s.
> Total water rent received, £4,500.
> The Council are now completing a new system of waterworks, having a good supply of pure, soft water from Holme, Dartmoor ; and have entered into agreements to supply the neighbouring towns of Teignmouth, Busham, and Ipplepen with water.

Paisley. Railways, L.N.W. and M. Distance from London, 407 miles.
> Authority, Corporation as Water Commissioners.
> Chairman, the Provost.
> Secretary, Francis Martin, Town Clerk.
> Engineer in charge, James Lee, C.E.
> Office, 13, Gilmour Street, Paisley.
> Works established, 1834. Purchased by corporation, 1854.
> Special Acts, 1835, 1854, 1866, 1876, 1881, 1897.
> Loans outstanding, £559,117.
> Population supplied with water (1907), 120,000.
> Total population of area of control— 1881, 70,000 ; 1891, 83,000 ; 1901, 101,000.
> Average death rate, 15·5 per 1,000.
> Towns and villages within the area of control—Paisley, Johnstone, Elderslie, Howwood, Kilbarchan, Houston, Linwood, Crookston, Moorpark, Blackston, Inchinnan, and Erskine.
> Character of water, upland and moorland surface water; 3° hardness after treatment.
> Filtering area provided, 10,200 square yards in 17 sand filter-beds.
> Average rainfall over drainage area, 52·36 inches (1906-7).
> Water authority have only a partial control of drainage area.
> Surface formation of drainage areas, moorland.

PAISLEY—*continued.*

Storage reservoirs, Camphill by Dalry　...　capacity, 750,000,000 gals.
　　　　　,,　　Rowbank by Howwood　　　,,　　487,500,000　,,
　　　　　,,　　Stanely, Paisley　　　...　　,,　　225,264,000　,,
　　　　　,,　　Glenburn　,,　　　...　　,,　　79,000,000　,,
　　　　　,,　　Harelaw　　,,　　　...　　,,　　89,000,000　,,
Annual supply of water—
　　For domestic and other purposes　　...　　1,662,995,325 gals.
　　　,, trade　　　,,　　　...　　...　　1,214,134,000　,,
Average supply per day, 7,882,546 gals.
　,, daily supply, per head—domestic, 40 gals. ; trade, 34½ gals.
Number of meters in use, 430.　Length of distributing mains, 40 miles.
Water analysis—Results stated as parts per 100·000.

	I.	II.
Total solids ...	9	8
Chlorine ...	1·4	1·4
Free ammonia ...	0·00	0·00
Albuminoid ammonia ...	0·01	0·018
Nitrites ...	0·0	0·0
Nitrogen as nitrates and nitrites ...	0·008	0·012
Oxygen absorbed by organic matter ...	0·37	0·23
Total hardness in degrees ...	5	6

No. 1 is the high level supply water.
No. 2　,,　low　,,　　,,　　,,
Scale of charges, assessment charges, 9d. in the £, domestic rate ; public rate,
　1d. in the £.
Supplies by meter—
　For any quantity not exceeding 150,000 gals., £2 16s. 3d.
　All above the first 150,000 gals., per annum　...　...　4¼d. per 1,000 gals.
　For hospitals, poor-houses and prison　...　...　...　3d.　　,,
　For house of refuge, reformatory, and industrial school　1¼d.　　,,
　A minimum charge of £2 16s. 3d. is made in every case where the water is laid
　　on premises with meter without regard to the quantity used, and is pay-
　　able at the end of the first quarter.
　A meter charge of 10 per cent. per annum on the cost of meters included in
　　the account for the first quarter.
Note.—Consumers outside the compulsory area are charged 25 per cent.
　　additional.　The area includes Paisley, Johnstone and Elderslee.

Palterton (supplied by BOLSOVER).

Pannal (supplied by HARROGATE).

Pantymwyn (supplied by HAWARDEN).

Papcastle, Cumberland.　Railway, L.N.W.　Distance from London, 300 miles.
　Authority, Papcastle Waterworks Company, Ltd.
　Office, Goat, Cockermouth.
　Share capital, £500.
　Area supplied, Papcastle, Goat, and Belle Vue.
　Works established, 1869.　Total population of area supplied, 870.
　Annual supply of water, 3,000,000 to 4,000,000 gals.
　Source of supply, gravitation.　Character of water, good.
　Number of meters, 2.
　Scale of charges—assessment charge, A.　Price for 1,000 gals., 4d. and 6d.

Papplewick (supplied by NOTTINGHAM).

Par, Cornwall. Railway, G.W. Distance from London, 276 miles.
Authority, Par Waterworks Co.
Office, Woodlands, Tywardreath, near Par Station.
Population supplied, 1,634.

Parkeston, Essex (supplied by TENDRING HUNDRED).

Parkgate (*see* NESTON).

Partick (supplied by GLASGOW).

Partington (supplied by MANCHESTER).

Patcham, Sussex (supplied by BRIGHTON).

Pedmore (supplied by STOURBRIDGE).

Peebles, Scotland. Railways, L.N.W. and M. Distance from London, 395 miles.
Authority, Town Council.
Chairman, Provost Ballantyne.
Secretary, Town Clerk.
Resident Engineer, S. Cowan.
Office, Town Hall.
Works established, 1850.
Total population supplied, 5,266.
Source of supply, springs from Meldon and Manor Waters.
Character of water, excellent ; hard.
Storage in impounding reservoirs, 400,000 gals.
Pressure in distributing mains, 35lbs. to 75lbs. per sq. in.
Price per meter, 8d. per 1,000 gals.
Lengths of mains—supply, 12 miles ; distributing, 6 miles.

Pelsall (supplied by SOUTH STAFFS. WATERWORKS Co.).

Pembroke. Railway, G.W. Distance from London, 272 miles.
Authority, Corporation.
Secretary, Town Clerk. Office, Town Clerk's.
The water supply for Pembroke Dock, which forms the main portion of the
    borough of Pembroke, is obtained from the pumping station at Milton, about
    five miles away. The town of Pembroke, which comprises the older portion, is
    supplied from several old reservoirs.
Total number of consumers, 15,853.
Source of supply, wells in the limestone. Character of water, excellent.

Pembroke, Ireland (supplied by DUBLIN).

Pembury (supplied by TUNBRIDGE WELLS).

Penarth, Glam. (supplied by CARDIFF).

Pendlebury (supplied by MANCHESTER).

Pendleton (supplied by MANCHESTER).

Penhow, Mon. (supplied by NEWPORT).

Penicuik, N.B. Railway, N.B.
Authority, Penicuik Town Council.
Chairman, Provost Andrew Garvin Wilson.
Town Clerk, Charles Henry Jones, 1, The Square, Penicuik, N.B.
Works established, 1864. Purchased by local authority, 1881.
Special Acts—authorised and carried out under the Police and Improvement (Scotland) Act, 1862.
Total population of area of control—1881, 3,505; 1891, 3,500; 1901, 3,320.
Total number of consumers, 4,075.
Average death rate, 11·23 per 1,000.
Area of control, Penicuik Burgh and Kirkhill village.
Sources of supply—surface springs, Silverburn and Saltersyke, Parish of Penicuik.
Estimated maximum daily discharge at points of collection,

				256,000 gals. (winter).
,,	minimum	,,	,,	,,	141,000 ,, (summer).
,,	average	,,	,,	,,	198,500 ,,

Strata or formation yielding springs, Whinstone rock at foot of Pentland Hills, with subsoil of reddish loam.
Filtration, none; softening, none.
Service reservoir, High Park Cistern, capacity, 12,000 gals., covered.
Water runs to High Park Cistern by gravitation, and is distributed from thence to Penicuik. Length of pipe from springs to service reservoir, 3 miles.
Annual supply of water about 80,000,000 gals.
Average day's supply for all purposes, 253,120 gals.
Maximum day's consumption, 374,000 gals. in November, 1906.
Length of supply mains, 3¼ miles; distributing mains, 2¼ miles.
Charges authorised up to 4s. in the £ for water and sewage assessment.
Present charge, 3d. in the £.
,, ,, by meter, 1s. 2d. per 1,000 gals. No. of meters, 1.

Penistone, Yorks. Railway, G.C. Distance from London, 176 miles.
Authority, Urban District Council.
Chairman, Dr. A. C. J. Wilson, J.P.
Secretary, Chas. Hodgkinson, Clerk to Urban District Council.
Loan capital, £17,776.
Towns and villages in the area supplied, Penistone and Darton = 4,000 acres.
Works established, 1869.
Total population of area supplied, 12,000.
Annual supply of water, 75,000,000 gals.
Daily consumption per head, 16 gals.
Storage capacity, 300,000 gals.
Character of water, 13·3° hardness.
Death rate, 14·5 per 1,000.
Number of meters, 18.
Scale of charges—assessment on yearly rental for domestic purposes.
Price per 1,000 gals., 1s. to 8½d.
Total water rent received, about £1,150 per annum for domestic purposes only.

Penketh, Lancs. (supplied by Warrington).

Penn, Staffs. (supplied by Wolverhampton).

Penn, Bucks., part of (supplied by Amersham).

Pennington (supplied by Ulverston).

Pennington (supplied by Christchurch).

Penrith, Cumberland. L.N.W. Distance from London, 281¼ miles.
Authority, Penrith Urban District Council.

PENRITH— *continued.*

Chairman, Henry Winter, J.P.
Secretary, Geo. Wainwright.
Manager, J. J. Knewstubb.
Office, Town Hall.
Works established, 1852. Special Acts, general Acts.
Total population supplied, 9,182.
Annual supply of water, 120,000,000 gals.
Daily consumption per head, 30 gals
Sources of supply—river Esmont, 5 miles below outflow of Ullswater Lake.
Storage capacity, 354,000 gals. Character of water, good.
Death rate. 15 per 1,000.
Number of meters, 40. Length of mains, 15 miles 7 furlongs.
Scale of charges—assessment charge, 6d. in £.
Price per 1,000 gals., 8d. under 100,000, 7d. under 500,000, 6d. under 1,000,000.
5d. above 1,000,000.
Total water rent received, £1,600.

Penryn, Cornwall (supplied by FALMOUTH).

Pensarn, Flint. (supplied by RHYL).

Pensnett (supplied by SOUTH STAFFS. WATERWORKS CO.).

Pentre (supplied by YSTRAD & RUABON).

Penwortham (supplied by PRESTON).

Penycae (supplied by RUABON).

Penygraig (supplied by YSTRAD).

Penywain (supplied by ABERDARE).

Penzance, Cornwall. Railway, G. W. Distance from London, 326 miles.
Authority, Penzance Corporation.
Secretary, T. H. Cornish, Town Clerk, Penzance.
Engineer in charge, Frank Latham, M.I.C.E., M.S.E. M.S.I. (also advising new scheme).
Total capital invested, including loans, £22,000.
Towns and villages within the area of control—borough of Penzance, villages of Chyandour and Wherry Town.
Works established, 1851.
Total population of area of control—1881, 12,409 ; 1891, 12,432 ; 1901 13,136.
Estimated population actually supplied—15,000 holiday season.
         ”   ”   13,136 normal.
Annual supply of water—
     For domestic purposes ...   .   75,000,000 gals.
        ” trade   ”   ...   .   5,000,000 ,,
        ” municipal (docks markets, etc.) ...   ...   10,000,000 ,,
Maximum day's consumption—400,000, holiday season.
                          380,000, normal.
Total quantity of water drawn per annum—
     From drainage areas   ...   .   75,000,000 gals.
       ” shallow wells or subsoil ...   .   15,000,000 ,,

PENZANCE—*continued.*

Estimated total quantity of water available per annum—
    From drainage areas   ...   .   75,000,000 gals.
      „   shallow wells or subsoil ...   75,000,000 „   (1902)
Sources of supply in use—drainage areas situated at—from Lanyon to
    Boscathnoe.
New pumping station at Polteggan, 220 Ordnance datum.
Estimated maximum daily discharge at points of collection, 500,000 gals.
      „   minimum   „   „   90,000 „
      „   average   „   „   320,000 „
Maximum annual rainfall over drainage area, 59·12 inches (1882).
Minimum   „   „   29·80 „   (1887).
Average   „   „   43·0 „   (period 35 years).
Population on drainage area, very small.
Nature and extent of cultivation of ditto—chiefly moorland, close piped through
    cultivated lands.
New well supply adits incomplete.
Natural rest level of water below surface, 12 feet, above Ordnance datum, 220
    feet.
Level of water below surface (when pumping 200,000 gals. per day) 12·6 feet
    (incoming water).
Geological data as follows—
    Surface formation of drainage areas, rab overlying the granite from 1 to 15
      in depth.
    Strata or formation yielding springs, elvans principally.
    Nature of subsoil yielding water. At new works it is alluvium, clay, slate, etc.
    Strata tapped by wells or borings, elvans are tapped by adits.
    Locality and extent of outcrop of same, elvan 5 miles in length against country
      alluvium ½ square mile, 50 feet in depth.
Storage reservoirs—Boscathnoe No. 1 ...   ...   capacity, 2,000,000 gals.
      „   „   No. 2 ...   ...   „   10,000,000 „
Pumping stations—Polteggan (new supply adits incomplete), capacity, 300,000
    gals. per day when finished.
Service reservoirs—new service reservoir at Polteggan incomplete, capacity,
    120,000 gals., covered.
Death rate, 15 per 1,000.
Character of water, soft and pure
Number of meters in use—9 Deacon meters on town mains to detect waste.
Length of mains, 15 miles.
Pressure reducing valves in low districts.
Scale of charges—domestic, rateable value equal to about 8d. in the £ per annum.
    Trade purposes, 6d. per 1,000 gals.
Ample water is gathered from the streams for the winter supply, but during the
    summer months there is very little water available on the surface and for some
    years past the supply to the town has been intermittent. Last year the
    engineer commenced a permanent new scheme for supplementing the summer's
    supply from a well; this although incomplete has been used with excellent
    results.

Peperharow (partly supplied by GODALMING).

Perivale (supplied by RICKMANSWORTH and UXBRIDGE).

Perry Bar (supplied by BIRMINGHAM).

Perth, Scotland. Railways, Caledonian and N.B.
    Authority, Perth Town Council.
    Chairman, Lord Provost Cuthbert.
    Secretary, Robt. Keay (City Chamberlain).
    Office, Waterworks, Mars hall Place, Perth.

PERTH—*continued*.

Engineer in charge, Alex. Davidson, Pines, Glasgow Road, Perth.
Works established, 1832.   Special Acts, 1832, 1877.
Total population of area of control—1891, 28,000; 1901, 35,000.
Estimated population actually supplied, 37,404.
Average death rate, 15·5 per 1,000.
Towns and villages within area of control, Perth, Burghmuir, Scone.
Source of supply—the water is all pumped from 2 tunnels on islands in the
    centre of the River Tay.   One tunnel 350 ft. in length and 4 ft. 4 in. diameter;
    one tunnel 270 ft. in length and 4 ft. 4 in. diameter. One 18-in. and two 12-in.
    pipes laid under bed of river conveys the water from the tunnel to works.
Analysis of water taken from 4 reservoirs (bacteriological examination)—
    No. 1—Total number of organisms per cubic centimetre—190.
        Bacillus coli communis—absent in 20 cubic centimetres, but present in 50 c.c.
        Bacillus typhosus not found.
    No. 2—Total number of organisms per c.c.—140.
        Bacillus coli communis—absent in 20 c.c., but present in 50 c.c.
        Bacillus typhosus not found.
    No. 3—Total number of organisms per c.c.—225.
        Bacillus colis communis was absent in 10 but present in 20 c.c.
        Bacillus typhosus not found.
The water may be regarded as perfectly satisfactory for all dietic purposes, and
    easily passed the latest bacteriological standard for potable waters.

	1	2	3	4
Nitrates	None	None	None	None
Free ammonia	·002	·002	·002	·002
Albuminoid ammonia	·006	·007	·008	·009
Mineral matter	4·86	4·75	4·82	4·90
Organic „	·28	·30	·30	·29
Temporary hardness	1·85	1·80	1·80	1·85
Permanent „	1·98	1·97	2·04	2·05
Colour (Loch Katrine = 10)	6	7	9	9

The waters are quite free from every trace of contamination and are equal to the
    Loch Katrine water as supplied to the City of Glasgow.   Waters as pure as
    these are rarely, if ever, met with.   It is a soft water, and very suitable for
    washing.
Filtration, natural gravel bank in centre of river.
Service reservoirs, Wellshill, covered, capacity, 428,760 gals.   ... 80 feet high.
    „   „   Viewlands „   „   814,450 „   ... 200   „
    „   „   Burghmuir, open   „   622,950 „   ... 320   „
    „   „   „   „   „   2,000,000 „   ... 320   „
    „   „   Muirhall, „   „   2,000,000 „   ... 400   „
Annual supply of water—
        For domestic purposes   ...   ...   466,000,000 gals.
        „   trade   „   ...   ...   184,000,000 „
        „   municipal   „   ...   ...   70,000,000 „
Maximum day's consumption, 2,160,000 gals.
Number of meters in use, 180.
Scale of charges—
    Domestic—Within compulsory water limits, 3d. in the £ on annual value of
            premises.
        „   Without compulsory water limits, 5d. in the £ on annual value of
            premises.
    Public water rate—Within compulsory water limits, 1d. in the £ on annual value
            of premises.
        General charges—Private tap   ...   under £10 ... 2s. 6d.
            „   „   „   ...   above £10 ... 3s. 6d.
Price per 1,000 gals. 5d. ; minimum, 10s. per annum.
Two beam engines and 2 triple-expansion engines = 340 horse-power.

Peterborough. Railways M., G.N., G.E. and L. & N.W. Distance from London, 76¼ miles.

Authority, City of Peterborough Corporation.

Mayor, J. Batton, J.P.

Town Clerk, W. Mellows.

Engineer in charge, John C. Gill, A.M.I.C.E.

Offices, Municipal Offices, Peterborough.

Total capital invested, including loans, £120,000. Loans outstanding, £85,000.

Works established, 1879. Special Acts, none.

Total population of area of supply, 36,444.

Total number of consumers, 9,000.

Estimated population actually supplied, 34,000.

Average death rate, 14·43 per 1,000.

Towns and villages within the area of supply, with population of each (1901 Census)—

Peterborough	30,870
Walton	556
Werrington	724
Stanground	1,461
Paston	88
Fletton	1,833
Woodstone	1,309
Dogsthorpe	200
Orton Longueville	247

Sources of supply in use—Deep wells and borings situated at Wilsthorpe, Lincolnshire, and Etton, Northamptonshire.

Character of water, first-class purity; hardness before treatment, 22·7°; Etton, 14·0°.

Maximum annual rainfall at pumping station, 33·37 inches (1906).

Minimum   „   „   14·73   „   (1893).

Average   „   „   20·56   „   (period 20 years).

Natural rest level of water below surface—Water overflows above Ordnance datum, 50 feet.

Level of water below surface (when pumping 1,250,000 gals. per day), 7½ feet.

Strata tapped by wells or borings, oolite.

Water is pumped direct from well and not filtered.

Pumping station, Braceborough Spa, capacity, 1,855,000 gals.; Etton, 1,500,000 gals. per day.

Service reservoir, Thurlby, Lincolnshire, capacity, 1,000,000 gals., covered.

Annual supply of water (1906)—

For domestic purposes and trade	365,500,000 gals.
„ municipal „	150,000,000 „
In bulk to other authorities	30,500,000 „

Maximum day's consumption, 2,100,000 gals.

Total quantity of water drawn per annum—

From deep wells or borings	546,000,000 gals.

Estimated total quantity of water available per annum—From deep wells or borings, practically unlimited.

Number of meters in use, 650.

Length of distributing mains, 40 miles.

Scale of charges—Assessment charge, 2d. in the £ plus 5d.

Price per meter, not exceeding 1,000 gals. per day, 1s. per 1,000 gals.

Over 1,000 and	„	2,500	„	9d. „
„ 2,500 „ „	„	5,000	„	6d. „

Special arrangement for larger quantities.

Peterhead, Scotland. Railways G.N., L.N.W., and M. Distance from London, 576 miles.

Authority, Town Council of the Burgh.

PETERHEAD—*continued.*

Chairman, William H. Leask, Provost.
Clerk to authority David Martin (Town Clerk), 77, Broad Street.
Burgh Surveyor and Water Engineer, James Dickie.
Office, Town House, Peterhead.
Total capital invested, including loans, £25,627 ; loans outstanding, £12,755.
Works established, 1820 and 1876.
Total population of area of control, 1881, 10,922 ; 1891, 13,944 ; 1901, 13,674.
Total number of consumers, 4,000.
Estimated population actually supplied, winter months, 12,000; summer months, 18,000.
Average death rate, 19·569 per 1,000, 1902-1906.
Area of control, burgh of Peterhead and rural district.
Sources of supply in use—surface springs at Cairncatta and Wellington valleys.
　　The water authority have no control of drainage area further than right to enter and make repairs when necessary.
Service reservoir, Forehill (open) ; Grange (open) = 3,000,000 gals.
The water is delivered to the town without filtration of any kind.　The Wellington section contains a quantity of iron, but Cairncatta is almost faultless as a domestic water supply.　Total hardness, 5°.
Annual supply of water (estimated)—

For domestic purposes	...	...	...	...	125,000,000 gals.
„ trade „	...	...	...	...	2,052,400 „
„ municipal „	...	...	...	...	300,000 ,
In bulk to other authorities (to harbour)				...	396,400 „

Average day's supply per head—domestic, 15 gals. ; trade, 10 gals.
Maximum day's consumption, 544,320 gals. in December.
Scale of charges—assessment charge, 4½d. on owners and 4½d. on occupiers in the £.
Price per 1,000 gals., trade, 5d.
Number of meters, 9.
Length of supply mains, 12 miles ; distributing mains, 13 miles.

Pickering, Yorks (G. and W.).　Railway, N.E.　Distance from London, 220 miles
Authority, the Pickering Gas and Water Company, Ltd.
Chairman, John Frank.
Secretary, H. M. Dawson.
Office, Hungate, Pickering.
Consulting Engineer, H. Tobey.
Share capital paid up, £10,000 ; Gas and Water loan, £750.
Dividend, 10 per cent.　Interest on loan, 4 per cent.
Area of control, Pickering only.
Works established, 1876.　Special Act, 1877.
Total population of area of control, 1891, 4,000 ; 1901, 4,000.
Total number of consumers, 415.
Estimated population actually supplied, 3,500.
Annual supply of water—For domestic purposes, 18,000,000 gals.
Source of supply, springs in red rock.
Estimated total quantity of water available per annum, 200,000,000 gals.
Sources of supply in use—surface spring, Field Head, Pickering.
Natural rest level of water below surface, 2 feet.
Level of water below surface (when pumping 50,000 gals. per day), 2 feet,
Storage reservoirs, capacity, 100,000 gals.
Pumping station—Field Head, capacity, 50,000 gals. per day ; 120 gals. for each consumer.
Service reservoir, Whitby Road, Pickering, covered.
Character of water, hard ; no filtration.
Number of meters in use, 5.
Length of distributing mains, 2¾ miles.

PICKERING—*continued*.

Assessment on R.R. on value from 8s. 8d. on a £4 house to £5 7s. 6d. for a £100 house; baths, 10s. extra.
Price per 1,000 gals., for municipal purposes, 1s. per 1,000 gals.

Piddinghoe (supplied by NEWHAVEN).

Pigslee (supplied by BURY).

Pilsall (supplied by SOUTH STAFFS. WATERWORKS Co.).

Pilton (supplied by BARNSTAPLE and partly by GLASTONBURY).

Pimperne (supplied by BLANDFORD).

Pinhoe (supplied by EXETER).

Pinkneys Green (supplied by MAIDENHEAD).

Pirbright (supplied by WOKING).

Pittenween. *See* ANSTRUTHER.

Pleasington (supplied by BLACKBURN).

Pleasley, Notts. (supplied by MANSFIELD).

Plymouth, Devon. Railways, G.W. and L.S.W. Distance from London, 246¾ miles.
Authority, Corporation of Plymouth.
Chairman of Committee, C. H. Tozer, C C.
Secretary, J. H. Ellis, Town Clerk.
Engineer in charge, Frank Howarth, A.M.I.C.E.
Office, Municipal Buildings, Plymouth.
Loans outstanding, £328,756.
Works established, 1585.
Special Acts, Plymouth Water Acts, 1585 (1825, Geo. IV.), 1867, 1887, 1893.
Total population of area of control, 1881, 95,991 ; 1891, 108,293 ; 1901, 136,568
Estimated population actually supplied—Administrative area, 126,071; in bulk, 19,115. Total, 145,186 (1905-6).
Average death rate, 18·74 per 1,000 within borough.
Towns and villages within the area of control, with population of each (1901 Census)—

Mecavy	261 (parish)
Bickleigh	296 „
Stonehouse	15,108 (urban district)
Tamerton Foliott	1,102 (parish)
St. Budeaux	6,291 (old parish)
Egg Buckland	1,285 (parish)
Pennycross	2,193 (old parish)
Buckland Monachorum	1,717 (parish)
Sheepstor	95 (parish)
Walkhampton	584 (parish)
Plymouth	107,636
Devonport, by consent	69,674

Source of supply, River Meavy, and drainage areas.
Estimated total quantity of water available per annum from drainage areas situated at Dartmoor, 4,015,000,000 gals.
Estimated maximum daily discharge at points of collection,
239,108,565 gals. (greatest observed flood)

PLYMOUTH—*continued.*

Estimated minimum (1901) daily discharge at points of collection, 3,707,000 gals.
  ,, average   ,,   ,,   ,, 11,000,000 ,,
Maximum annual rainfall over drainage area 64·22 inches (1894)
Minimum ,,   ,,   44·90 ,, (1892)
Average   ,,   ,,   51·48 ,, (period 10 years)
Population on drainage area, 59.
Nature and extent of cultivation of ditto, 1,136 acres rough pasture, 4,224 acres moorland.
The corporation own about 220 acres of land draining into storage reservoir.
Surface formation of drainage areas, mostly moorland, a little rough pasture and arable.
Strata or formation yielding springs, granite.
Character of water, very soft, without acid; 1·5° of hardness.
Analysis of a sample of Plymouth water taken at Laboratory tap, Municipal Buildings. Number of sample, 5,976; date of collection, 20th February, 1907; physical characters, pale greenish yellow in colour, not quite clear, no smell.

	Parts per 100,000
Saline ammonia	·000
Albuminoid ammonia	·004
Oxygen absorbed from permanganate in one hour at 80°F.	·087
Total solid matters	4·900
Volatile ,, ...	2·500
Fixed ,, ...	2·400
Appearance on ignition—The residue charred.	
Total hardness ⎫	
Temporary ⎬ equal to grains of carbonate of lime	·790
Permanent ⎭	
Chlorine...	1·100
Nitrogen as Nitrates	·000
,, as nitrites	·000
Poisonous metals	·000
Microscopical examination of the sediment ...	negative
Water bacteria	86 per C.C.
Bacteriological examination—bacillus coli ...	0 ,, ,,

Remarks—The condition of the water remains unchanged.
Date of Examination, 20th February, 1907.
Filtration none; softening, none.
Storage reservoir, Burrator ... ... capacity, 657,000,000 gals.
Service ,, Roborough ... ... ,, 1,000,000 ,, open
 ,, ,, Crown Hill ... ... ,, 1,100,000 ,, ,,
 ,, ,, Hartley ... ... ,, 7,130,000 ,, ,,
 ,, ,, Drake's Place ... ... ,, 3,600,000 ,, ,,
Head on distributing mains—maximum, 280 feet; minimum, 34 feet.
Annual supply of water, 2,034,510,000 gals. (1905-6).
Average daily supply per head—domestic, 25·64 gals.; trade, &c., 10·56 gals (excluding bulk).
Maximum day's consumption, 6,526,000 gals., in August.
Schedule of charges (within the borough). Domestic consumption—

When the yearly rent or value does not exceed ... ... ⎫	£5	4s.
Exceeding £5 and not exceeding	7	6s.
,, 7 ,, ,,	10	8s.
,, 10 ,, ,,	12	10s.
,, 12 ,, ,,	15	12s.
,, 15 ,, ,,	20	14s.
,, 20 ,, ,,	25	16s.
,, 25 ,, ,,	30	20s.

PLYMOUTH—*continued.*

Exceeding £30 and not exceeding 40	...	..	...	24s.
„ 40 „ „ 50	...	...	...	28s.
„ 50 „ „ 60	...	...	...	32s.
„ 60 „ „ 80	...	...	...	36s.
„ 80				40s.

Price per 1,000 gals.—within borough, 3½d.; outside borough, 6d.
Number of meters in use, 1,000.
Length of trunk, 15 miles; distributing mains, 113 miles.

Plympton, Devon. Railway, G.W. Distance from London 242 miles.
Authority, Plympton Rural District Council.
Engineer, F. A. Clark.
District of supply, Plympton St. Mary, Plympton St. Maurice, and Plymstock.
Population estimated 6,000.

Plymstock (supplied by PLYMPTON).

Pocklington, Yorks. Railway, N.E.R. Distance from London, 198 miles.
Authority, Pocklington Water Company, Ltd.
Chairman, W. O. Trotter, M.D.
Solicitor, H. B. Broomhead.
Office Beverley.
Share capital paid up, £3,640.
Loan capital paid up, £600 (4 per cent. debentures).
Interest, 4 per cent., dividend, 2½ per cent.
Area supplied, Pocklington only.
Works established, 1889. Special Acts, Prov. Orders, 1889 and 1893.
Total population supplied, 2,463.
Annual supply of water, 12,500,000 gals.
Sources of supply, gravitation from springs at Givendale.
Storage capacity, 120,000 gals.
System of filtration, none.
Character of water, calcareous, though highly pure.
Number of meters, 6.
Length of mains, about 4 miles.
Scale of charges—assessment charge, 6 per cent. on rateable value.
Price per 1,000 gals., 1s. for all purposes.
Total water rent received, £290 18s. 4d. (1906-7).

Pollington (supplied by GOOLE).

Pollockshaw (supplied by GLASGOW).

Ponkey (supplied by RUABON).

Ponsheill (supplied by MERTHYR TYDVIL).

Pontefract, Yorks. Railways, G.N., M., N.E. and L. and Y. Distance from London, 175 miles.
Authority, Corporation.
Chairman, Alderman T. Glover.
Clerk, J. W. Haddock.
Engineer and Manager, John E. Pickard, C.E.
Offices, Municipal Offices, Pontefract.
Towns and villages in the area supplied, Pontefract Borough, Ackworth, Knottingley, Roall, Wentbridge, and parts of Carlton and Smeaton.
Total population supplied, about 20,000.
Sources of supply, wells at Roall Waterworks, 9 miles away.
Number of meters, upwards of 50.

Pontefract Rural District is partly supplied by WAKEFIELD.

Ponteland (supplied by NEWCASTLE-ON-TYNE).

Pontypool, Mon. (G. and W.) Railway, G.W. Distance from London, 160 miles.
Authority, Pontypool Gas and Water Co.
Chairman, A. A. Williams.
Manager and Secretary, T. B. Pearson.
Office, Clarence Street.
Share capital paid up, £70,000. Last dividends, 7½ and 5¼ per cent.
Loan   „   £15,000, at 4 per cent.
Works established, 1850.
Special Acts, 1873 and 1890.
Total population supplied, about 33,000
Towns and villages in the area supplied, Pontypool, Abersychan, Griffithstown.
    Pontnewynydd, Garndiffaith, Varteg, Cwmavon, Sebastopol and New Inn.
Sources of supply, wells and borings in old red sandstone and springs in old red
    sandstone and carboniferous limestone.
Characteristics, clear and bright, agreeable and pleasant to drink, average hard-
    ness, about 8½°.
Filtration, sand.
Storage and service capacity, 15,000,000 gals.
Average daily supply per head—domestic, 13 gals. ; trade, &c., 1 gal.
Scale of charges, assessment charge, 5 to 8 per cent. on gross rental.
Price per 1,000 gals., 2s. to 6d.
Number of meters, 85.
Length of mains, 40 miles.

Pontypridd, Glam. Railway, Taff Vale. Distance from London, 169 miles.
Authority, Pontypridd Waterworks Company.
Chairman, Benjamin Jones.
Secretary, Morgan Morgan.
Engineer and Manager, Wm. Jones.
Office, 28, Gelliwastad Road.
Share capital paid up, £230,000. Debenture stock, £37,000.
Dividend, 5, 6, and 9 per cent.
Total water rent received, £16,000 per ann.
Works established, 1864. Special Acts, 1864, 1875, 1883, 1892, 1894.
Total population supplied, 120,000.
Death rate, 14 per 1,000.
Towns and villages in the area supplied—Rhondda Valley, Pontypridd, Taffs
    Well, and Llantintfardre.
Sources of supply—Rhondda Fach river and other sources.
Character of water, soft.
Storage capacity, 229,000,000 gals.
Daily consumption per head, 25 gals.
Number of meters, 300.
Scale of charges—assessment charge, 5, 6, and 7½ per cent. on rateable value.
    Price per 1,000 gals., 1s. 6d. to 6d.

Pool (supplied by LEEDS).

Poole, Dorset. Railway, L.S.W. Distance from London 113½ miles.
Authority, Poole Water Co., in process of transfer to the Poole Corporation (Mar.,
    1907).
Chairman, Right Honourable Lord Wimborne.
Secretary, H. F. J. Barnes.
Engineer in charge, H. F. J. Barnes.
Consulting Engineer for Corporation, Wm. Matthews, M.I.C.E.
Office, Towngate Street.

POOLE—*continued.*

Works established, 1858.　Purchased by Corporation, 1907.
Special Acts, 1859, Provisional Orders, 1881, 1887, 1893, 1906.
Total capital invested in undertaking, £72,600.
Dividends, 9¼ per cent. and 6½ per cent. per ann.
Population of area of control, 1881, 17,162 ; 1891, 24,149 ; 1901, 30,834.
Total population of area supplied, about 29,355.
Total Number of services, 6,277.
Average death rate, 14·35 per 1,000.
Towns and villages in the area supplied—Borough of Poole and parts of parishes
　　of Kinson and Canford Magna, including Broadstone, parts of parishes of
　　Corfe Mullen and Lytchett Minster, added under Poole Corporation Act, 1906.
Source of supply, springs from Bagshot Beds, and impounding reservoirs on moor-
　　lands.
The existing sources are about to be abandoned (1907), the Corporation having
　　adopted a scheme for the supply of the district from a well and headings in
　　the chalk at Corfe Mullen.
Character of water, clear and bright, soft, slightly acid and ferruginous ; total
　　hardness, 2·6°.
System of filtration, aeration and sand filters, after treatment with Paris white
　　and alumina ferric.
Estimated maximum daily discharge at point of collection, 1,914,000 gals.
　　　　,,　　minimum　,,　　　,,　　　,, ,,　　,,　　　216,256　,,
　　　　,,　　average　　,,　　　,,　　　,, ,,　　,,　　　1,137,000　,,
Maximum annual rainfall over drainage area, 40·5 in. (1903).
Minimum　　,,　　　,,　　　,,　　　,,　　,,　　21·2　,,　(1887).
Average　　,,　　,,　　　,,　　　,,　　,,　　31·0　,,　(period 23 years).
Storage capacity—Waterloo reservoir, 17,000,000 gals.
　　　　　　　　Lilliput　　　,,　　7,467,000　,,
　　　　　　　　　　,,　　　　,,　　1,510,500　,,
Service reservoirs—Broadstone, capacity 307,800 gals., covered.
　　　　　　　　Parkstone　　,,　　198,750　,,　　,,
　　　　　　　　　　,,　　　,,　　253,750　,,　　,,
　　　　　　　Broadstone Tower　62,0000　,,　　,,
　　　　　　　Parkstone　　,,　　62,000　,,　　,,
Head on distributing mains—maximum, 300 ft. ; minimum, 50 ft.
Annual supply of water—Domestic, 141,190,200 gals.
　　　　　　　　　　　　Trade, 17,880,900 gals.
　　　　　　　　　　　　Municipal, 11,379,900 gals.
Total quantity of water drawn per annum, 170,451,000 gals.
Average daily consumption per head—domestic, 13·17 gals. ; trade, 2·74 gals.
Scale of charges—
　　Assessment charge, 7 per cent. on gross rental value.
Price per 1,000 gals., 2s. 6d. to 1s. ; average, 1s. 8d.
Number of meters, 441.
Length of mains, about 69·8 miles.

Portadown and Banbridge.

Authority, Portadown and Banbridge Joint Waterworks Board.
Chairman, Charles Johnston, J.P.
Secretary, William Wilson.
Address, Town Hall, Portadown.
Total capital invested, including loans, estimated cost of scheme, £72,000.
Interest on loans, 4 per cent.
Works commenced, 1904.　Special Acts, 1902, 1903.
Towns and villages in the area on pipe line, Rathfriland, Banbridge, Gilford,
　　Tandrager, Portadown.
Engineers in charge, R. H. Dorman and J. H. H. Swiney.

PORTADOWN and BANBRIDGE—*continued.*

Source of supply, mountain catchment; area, Moyad and Cock Mountain, commons in the Mourne Mountains.
Character of water, 2·5° hardness.
Filtration, none; softening, none.
Storage capacity, impounding reservoirs, 75,000,000 gals.
Service reservoirs, 4,000,000 gals.
Pressure on distributing mains—maximum, 125 lbs.; minimum, 45 lbs.
Price per 1,000 gals., 9d. and 10d.
Length of supply mains, 26 miles; distributing mains, 16 miles.
This scheme will not be completed for two years (1907).

Port Glasgow. Railway, Caledonian.
Authority, Corporation, 1865.
Chairman, Walter M. Campbell, Provost.
Secretary, Andrew Paton, Town Clerk.
Water Superintendent, James Murray.
Office, Anderson Street.
Towns and villages in the area supplied, Port Glasgow, Langbank, and part of Kilmalcolm.
Works established, 1867.   Special Act, 1865.   Total population supplied, 18,000.
Daily consumption per head, domestic, 40 gals.; trade, 13 gals.
Sources of supply, 2 reservoirs in Kilmalcolm and 1 in Port Glasgow.
Storage capacity, 175,077,162 gals.
System of filtration, downward through sand.   Character of water, soft.
Average death rate, 19 per 1,000.
Number of meters, 47.   Length of mains, 12¼ miles.
Scale of charges—Assessment charge, 10d. in £.
    Price, trade, £3 5s. per 100,000 gals.
Total water rates received, £4,043.

Porthcawl, Glam. Railway, G.W. Distance from London, 194 miles.
Authority, Urban District Council.
Chairman, J. Elias, J.P.
Clerk, E. T. David.
Engineer in charge, R. W. Jones, A.I.S.E.
Office, Council Office.
Waterworks loan, £8,500.
Works established, 1907. Special Acts, none.
Area supplied, urban district.
Total number of consumers, normal, 2,500; in summer, about 5,000.
Average death rate, 9 per 1,000.
Source of supply, upland surface. Storage capacity, 1,500,000 gals.
Character of water, soft; total hardness, 6°.
System of filtration, none.
Head on distributing mains—maximum, 400ft.
Annual supply of water, no account kept.
Daily consumption per head, domestic, 15 gals.
Maximum day's supply, 30,000 gals.
Assessment charge 10 per cent. on R.V.
Price per 1,000 gals., 1s. 6d. for small quantities.
Number of meters, 4.   Length of mains, about 8 miles.

Portinscale (supplied by KESWICK).

Portishead, Somerset. Railway, G.W. Distance from London, 130 miles.
Authority, Portishead District Water Company.
Chairman, H. C. A. Day, Bristol.

PORTISHEAD—*continued.*

    Secretary, F. A. Jenkins.
    Manager, John Curtis.
    Office, Exchange Buildings, Bristol.
    Share capital, ordinary stock (Act 1875), £25,190; preference stock (Act 1883),
       £11,052. Debentures (Acts 1875 and 1883), less capitalised value of rent charge
       (Act 1875), £9,355. Sundry loans, £5,088.
    Works established, 1874. Special Acts, 1875, 1883, 1907.
    Towns and villages in the area supplied, Portishead, Pill and Portbury.
    Total population of area supplied, 5,000.
    Total water rent received for six months (Dec. 31st, 1906), £998 10s. 9d.

Portland, Dorset. Railways, L.S.W. and G.W. Distance from London, 147 miles.
    Population, 15,199.
    Authority, Portland Urban District Council.
    Chairman, William Edwards.
    Clerk to authority, T. Howard Bowen.
    Accountant, J. Greenwood Comben.
    Resident Engineer, R. Stevenson Henshaw.
    Consulting Engineer, Baldwin Latham,
    Council Office, New Road, Portland.
    Loan outstanding, £37,572 6s. 2d.
    Works constructed, 1899.
    Population supplied with water, 11,000.
    Average death rate, 11·4.
    District of supply, Portland and part of Upwey.
    Source of supply, well, 163 feet deep in middle chalk; additional well to be
      sunk in Portland sand—both in Upwey.
    Character of water, very high degree of organic purity. Total hardness, 13·71°;
      temporary, 12·25°.
    Storage in service reservoirs, 1,064,800 gals.
    Head on distributing mains—maximum, 528 feet; minimum, 45 feet.
    Annual supply of water, 11,302,000 gals.
    Average daily supply per head—domestic, 21·48 gals; trade, 6·79 gals.
    Maximum day's supply, 362,700 gals., in May.
    Assessment included in General District Rate.
    Authorised charge by meter, 9d. to 1s. 3d. per 1,000 gals.
    Number of meters, 91.
    Length of supply mains, 9 miles; distributing mains, 12 miles.

Portobello (supplied by EDINBURGH),

Portslade (supplied by BRIGHTON).

Portsmouth, Hants. Railways, L.S.W., and L.B.S.C. Distance from London,
    85 miles.
    Authority, Borough of Portsmouth Waterworks Company.
    Chairman, William Grant, J.P.
    Secretary, J. L. Wilkinson, F.C.I.S.
    Chief Resident Engineer, Herbert Ashley, M.I.C.E., M.I.M.E.
    Office, Commercial Road, Portsmouth.
    Consulting Engineers, Joseph Quick & Son, M.I.C.E.
    Share capital paid up, £517,630.
    Loan, do., £172,237.
    Dividend, 10, 7, and 5 per cent., full statutory.
    Interest on loans varying from 4 per cent. to 3 per cent.
    Works established, 1857.

PORTSMOUTH—*continued.*

Special Acts and Orders, 1857, 1861, 1868, 1872, 1873, 1879, 1888, 1890, 1896, 1898, 1902, 1906.
Total population of area supplied, about 210,000.
Towns and villages in the area supplied, Borough of Portsmouth and villages of Cosham, Wymering, Farlington, Drayton, Bedhampton, Havant, Warblington, Emsworth, New Brighton, Purbrook, Waterloo and Red Hill.
Sources of supply in use, springs from chalk rising and overflowing ground.
Character of water, very good, clear and bright.
Filtration scheme and plans being prepared (1907) ; softening, none.
Annual supply of water, 2,882,051,185 gals.
Average daily consumption per head, 25 gals.
Number of meters, 1,156.
Length of mains, 217 miles.
Assessment charge, rateable annual value.
Price per 1,000 gals., 1s. 6d. to 8d.

Port Talbot, Wales (supplied by ABERAVON).

Pottenend supplied by GREAT BERKHAMPSTEAD).

Potter Street (supplied by HERTS AND ESSEX WATERWORKS Co.).

Poulton (supplied by WALLASEY).

Poulton-le-Fylde (supplied by FYLDE).

Poulton-with-Fearnhead (supplied by WARRINGTON).

Prenton, Cheshire (supplied by BIRKENHEAD).

Prescot, Lancs. (supplied by LIVERPOOL)

Prestbury, Gloucester (supplied by CHELTENHAM).

Prestbury, Cheshire (supplied by MACCLESFIELD).

Prestolee (supplied by BURY).

Preston, Kent (supplied by FAVERSHAM).

Preston, Sussex (supplied by BRIGHTON).

Preston, Lancs. Railways, L.N.W. and L. & Y. Distance from London, 210 miles.
Authority, Corporation.
Chairman, Ald. J. C. Hamilton.
Secretary, H. Hamer, Town Clerk.
Engineer and Manager, Thos. Cookson.
Office, Town Hall.
Loan capital, £455,740.
Interest on loan, £11,154.
Works established, 1831. Special Acts, 1853 and 1869.
Total population supplied, 125,000.
Average death rate, 17·74 per 1,000.

PRESTON—*continued.*

> Towns and villages in the area supplied—county borough of Preston, urban
> district of Longridge, also Penwortham, Loughton, Hutton and Howick, Hoole,
> Tarleton, Hesketh-with-Becconsall, parishes within Preston rural district.
> Sources of supply, Whitewell and Longridge Fells.
> Character of water, excellent.
> System of filtration, screened through copper gauge, 5,000 holes to square inch.
> Storage capacity, 430,000,000 gals.
> Annual supply of water, 1,700,000,000 gals.
> Daily consumption per head—domestic, 25 gals. ; trade, 12 gals.
> Scale of charges—
>   Assessment charge, 1s. in the £ on rateable value.
>   Price per 1,000 gals., trade and municipal purposes, sliding scale.
> Number of meters, 850.
> Length of mains, about 100 miles.
> Total water rent received, £22,342.

Prestwich (supplied by MANCHESTER).

Prestwick (supplied by NEWCASTLE-ON-TYNE)

Prestwold (supplied by LOUGHBOROUGH).

Pudsey, Yorks. Railway, G.N. Distance from London, 189 miles,
> Authority, Pudsey Corporation.
> Town Clerk, B. Dufton.
> Inspector, James Booth.
> Office, Municipal Offices, Pudsey.
> Area supplied, 2,409 acres.
> Purchased by Local Authority April 1st, 1893.
> Total population supplied, 15,000.
> Daily consumption per head, 11 gals.
> Sources of supply, water purchased in bulk from Bradford Corporation at 9d.
>   per 1,000 gals.
> Character of water, soft moorland.
> Death rate, 15·4 per 1,000 (1902).
> Number of meters, 80.
> Length of mains, about 16 miles.
> Scale of charges—assessment charge on mains, £455; price per 1,000 gals., 4s. 6d.
>   minimum per quarter, or on a consumption of 3.000 lowest charge 1s.
> Total water rent received, £4,432. March 31st, 1902. (The charge for baths and
>   w.c's has been abolished.)

Purbrook (supplied by PORTSMOUTH).

Purleigh and District Water Supply, Essex.
> Authority, Rural District Council of Maldon.
> Clerk, A. W. Freeman.
> Works at Woodham Walter.

Purley, Surrey (supplied by EAST SURREY WATERWORKS).

Purton (supplied by CRICKLADE).

Puttenham (supplied by WEY VALLEY).

Pwllheli, Carnarvon. Railway, L.N.W. Distance from London, 270 miles
> Authority, Limited Company.
> Population supplied, 3,675.
> No returns supplied.

Pyecombe, Sussex (supplied by BRIGHTON).

Pyrford (supplied by WOKING).

Quakers Yard, Glam. (supplied by MERTHYR TYDVIL).

Quarrington (supplied by SLEAFORD).

Quarrybank (supplied by SOUTH STAFFS. WATERWORKS Co.).

Queenborough, Kent.
  Authority, The Queenborough Council Water Board, Queenborough. This undertaking has just started.

Queensbury, Yorks. (supplied by BRADFORD).

Queensferry, Flint. (supplied by HAWARDEN).

Queensville, Staffs. (supplied by STAFFORD).

Quinton (supplied by SOUTH STAFFS. WATERWORKS Co.).

Quorn (supplied by LEICESTER).

Rachub (supplied by BETHESDA).

Radcliffe, Lancs. (supplied by BURY).

Radcliffe-on-Trent (supplied by NOTTINGHAM).

Radford, Notts. (supplied by NOTTINGHAM).

Radford, Staffs. (supplied by STAFFORD).

Radyr, Glam. (supplied by CARDIFF).

Rainford (supplied by ST. HELEN'S).

Rainham, Kent. Railways, S.E. & C. Distance from London, 39 miles.
  Authority, Rainham Waterworks Co., Ltd.
  Office, 76, High Street, Sittingbourne.
  Share capital paid up, £20,000.
  Towns and villages in the area supplied, Rainham, Upchurch, Hartlip, Newington, Lower Halstow.
  Source of supply, lower green sand.
  Storage capacity, 400,000 gals. Character of water, very soft.
  Scale of charges, payable quarterly in advance—
  Annual value not exceeding

£5 ...	3s. 3d. per quarter, and 3d. extra on every £ up to £9 per quarter.
£11 ...	4s.	„	„	6d.	„	£2	„ £17	„
£20 ...	7s.	„
£21 ...	7s. 3d.	„	„	3d.	„	£1	„ £29	„
£30 ...	10s.	„
£35 ...	11s. 6d.	„
£40 ...	12s. 6d. per quarter.
£45 ...	13s. 3d.	„
£50 ...	14s.	„
£55 ...	15s.	„
£60 ...	16s.	„

  Butchers, bakers and beer retailers 25 per cent. extra on above charges.
  Horses, 1s. 6d.; cows, 1s. 3d.; carriage, four-wheel, 2s.; two-wheel, 1s. 6d. each per quarter.

18   (273)

RAINHAM—*continued.*

Price per 1,000 gals., as follows, with intermediate charges—

							£	s.	d.
6,000 gals. per quarter	...	...	...	...	...	...	0	15	0
10,000 „	„	...	...	...	...	...	1	5	0
20,000 „	„	...	...	...	...	...	2	7	11
50,000 „	„	...	...	...	...	...	4	16	3
100,000 „	„	...	...	...	...	...	8	1	3
150,000 „	„	...	...	...	...	...	10	18	9
Minimum charge per quarter	...	...	...	...	...	0	12	6

Rainhill, Lancs. (G. and W.)　Railway, L.N.W.　Distance from London, 193 miles.
　Authority, Rainhill Gas and Water Co.
　Chairman, Samuel Robinson.
　Manager, Joseph T. Broughton.
　Secretary, Frederick Pritchard.
　Office, Gas Works, Rainhill.
　Share capital paid up, £12,356 ; gas and water combined.
　Works established, 1870. Special Act, 1870. Total population of area supplied, 2,600.
　Area supplied, Rainhill only.
　Source of supply, boreholes.　Storage capacity, 30,000 gals.
　Character of water, hard.
　Annual supply of water, 15,360,000 gals.
　Scales of charges—assessment, 5 per cent. on gross rental above £10 per annum ;
　　8s. 8d. below £10.
　Price per 1,000 gals., trade, 9d.　Total water rent received, £575.
　Number of meters, 10.　Length of mains, 6 miles.

Ramsbottom, Lancs. (supplied by BURY).

Ramsey, Essex (supplied by TENDRING HUNDRED).

Ramsgate and District.　Railways, S.E. and L.C.D.　Distance from London, 79
miles.
　Authority, Ramsgate Corporation.
　Chairman, Alderman W. Coleman, J.P. (Mayor).
　Secretary, Geo. Cockburn, Boundary Road, Ramsgate.
　Engineer, T. N. Ritson, A.M.I.C.E.
　Office, Gas and Water Offices, Boundary Road, Ramsgate.
　Works established, 1835.　Purchased by local authority, 1877.
　Special Acts, Ramsgate Local Board Act, 1877 ; Provisional Orders, 1880, 1887,
　　1891, and 1899.
　Total capital invested, including loans, £148,164.
　Total population of area of control, 1891, 28,000 ; 1901, 35,000.
　Estimated population actually supplied, 70,000, holiday ; 35,000, normal.
　Annual profit, including capital charges, £6,024 9s.
　Average death rate, 15·7 per 1000.
　Towns and villages within the area of control, Ramsgate and St. Lawrence,
　　Haine, Manston, and Minster.
　Source of supply, deep wells and adits in the chalk, in the parishes of Ramsgate
　　and Minster.
　Maximum annual rainfall over drainage area, 30·60 in. (1903).
　Minimum　　„　　„　　„　　„　15·77　„　(1901).
　Average　　„　　„　　„　　„　21·13　„　(period 10 years).
　Authority have no control over drainage area ; population on same, very limited.
　Character of water, of great purity ; hardness, 27·7° (average)
　Filtration, none ; softening, none.
　Storage capacity, service reservoirs—high level, 750,000 gals. ; low level, 250,000
　　gals.
　Head on distributing mains—maximum, 200 ft. ; minimum, 50 ft.

RAMSGATE AND DISTRICT—*continued.*

    Annual supply of water (ending March, 1906)—
        For domestic purposes   ...   .   364,888,163 gals.
        „   trade   „   ...   .   33,102,412 „
        „   municipal „   ...   .   26,774,165 „
                                                     ————————
                                                       424,764,740
    Average daily supply per head—domestic, 28·56 ; trade, &c., 4·69 gals.
    Maximum day's consumption, 1,500,000 gals., in August.
    Assessment charge, 4·58 per cent. to 7½ per cent. on rental value.
    Price per 1,000 gals., trade 1s. and 1s. 3d. ; outside borough, 1s. 6d.
    Number of meters, 275.
    Total length of mains, 45 miles.

Ramsgrave (supplied by BLACKBURN).

Rastrick, Yorks. (supplied by BRIGHOUSE).

Rattray, part of (supplied by BLAIRGOWRIE).

Ravensthorpe, Yorks. (supplied by DEWSBURY).

Rawcliffe (supplied by GOOLE).

Rawmarsh (supplied by ROTHERHAM).

Rawdon, Yorks. (supplied by YEADON).

Rawtenstall, Lancs. (supplied by BURY).

Reading, Berks. Railways, G.W., S.E., and L.S.W. Distance from London, 36
miles.
    Authority, Corporation, 1868.
    Chairman, Alderman Felix B. Parfitt.
    Town Clerk, W. S. Clutterbuck.
    Resident Engineer and Manager, Leslie C. Walker.
    Office, Valpy Street, Reading.
    Waterworks Debt 31st March, 1907—   £   s. d.   £   s. d.
        Loans 20,000 0 0
        Less paid off 1,851 17 1
                                                            ————————   18,148 2 11
        Stock 209,041 19 11
        Less amount cancelled and amount standing
            to credit of Loans Fund for that purpose ... 41,030 17 0
                                                            ———————— 168,011 2 11
                                                                        ————————
                                        Net Debt £186,159 5 10

    Works established, 1629. Special Act, 1826.
    Total population supplied, 91,117.
    Average death rate, 12·76 per 1,000.
    Towns and villages in the area supplied—
        The parish of Reading, together with such parts of the following parishes of
        Sonning, Early, Whitley, Southcote and Tilehurst, in the county of Berks,

READING—*continued.*

and Caversham, in the county of Oxford, as are enclosed within a circle, the
the radius of which is 2 miles, measured in an horizontal plane from the
centre of the tower of St. Mary's Church, Reading.

Since the framing of the Act from which the definition of limit of area is
taken, the borough boundary has been extended so that in places the supply
extends beyond the circle.

Source of supply, River Kennet. Storage capacity, 13,000,000 gals.
Character of water, total hardness, 14°, permanent hardness, 3°.
System of filtration, polarite chamber and sand combined.
Head on distributing mains, maximum, 220 ft., minimum, 35ft.
Annual supply of water, 1,347,802,000 gals.
Daily consumption per head, domestic, 20 gals., trade, 20 gals.
Maximum day's supply, 4,617,000, August 8th, 1906.
Scale of charges—Assessment charge, 4 to 4½ per cent. on rateable value.
  Price per 1,000 gals., 6d. to 1s. 9d.
  Rural districts outside the defined limit are supplied with water in bulk at
    1s. 6d. per 1,000 gals.
  Charge for municipal purposes, street watering, £525 ; urinals, by meter.
Total water rent received, £23,404 ; surplus profit, £2,500, paid over to district
rate.
Number of meters, 433.

Reading Street (supplied by BROADSTAIRS).

Reculver, Kent (supplied by HERNE BAY).

Redcar, Yorks. Railways, G. N. and N. E. Distance from London, 247 miles.
  Authority, Redcar Urban District Council.
  Directors—Coatham Ward, Walter S. Hill ; Redcar Ward, William Baker.
  Secretary, Alfred H. Sill, Solicitor, Redcar.
  Engineer and Surveyor, James Howcroft, 5, Teresa Terrace, Chatham, Redcar.
  Estimated population actually supplied, 11,000 normal.
                    ”   ”   20,000 holiday season.
  Area of control—the town is divided into two wards, each having separate water
    supply, Redcar Ward and Coatham Ward.
  Source of supply—Upleatham Hill springs.
  Redcar is also supplied by the Cleveland Water Company.
  Character of water, average softness.
  Service reservoir—new reservoir, Upleatham, capacity, 10,000,000 gals., open.
  Maximum day's consumption, 150,000 gals. normal.
          ”   ”   200,000 ,, holiday season.
  Price per. 1,000 gals. domestic, 1s. 10½d.
  Length of distributing mains, 16 miles.
  Number of meters in use, 25.

Redditch (supplied by EAST WORCESTERSHIRE WATER Co.).

Redhill, Surrey (supplied by EAST SURREY WATERWORKS).

Red Hill, Hants. (supplied by PORTSMOUTH).

Redruth, Cornwall. Railway, G.W. Distance from London, 303¾ miles.
  Authority, Redruth Urban District Council.
  Chairman, S. H. Lanyon.

Redruth—*continued.*

Engineer and Manager, H. D. Strange.
Clerk to authority, Henry Paige.
Office, Council Office, Station Hill, Redruth.
Works established, 1895.
Total population of area supplied, 10,451.
Average death rate, 15·6 per 1,000.
Towns and villages in the area supplied, Redruth Town, Highway North Country, and South Downs.
Sources of supply, springs in granite and pumping from old mine.
Character of water, very good from springs and a little coppery from mine.
Filtration, none.
Storage capacity, 5,000,000 gals.
Pressure on distributing mains—maximum, 122 lbs. ; minimum, 32 lbs. per sq. in.
Total quantity of water pumped per annum, 5,674,500 gals.
Daily consumption per head, domestic, 20 gals.
Number of meters, 50.
Length of mains, 13 miles.
Scale of charges—assessment charge, 8d. in the £ on rateable value.
Price per 1,000 gals., trade 2s. to 1s. according to quantity.
　No charge for municipal purposes.
Total revenue received, about £1,000.

Reedley Hallows (supplied by Nelson).

Reigate (supplied by East Surrey Waterworks).

Renfrew (supplied by Glasgow).

Retford, East.   Railways, G.N. and G.C.   Distance from London, 138½ miles.
Authority, East Retford Corporation.
Chairman, Alderman J. W. Holmes, J.P.
Town Clerk, W. Percival Jones.
Engineer and Manager, J. B. Fenwick.
Office, Grove Street.
Share capital paid up, £27,224.
Loan capital, £21,500.
Annual profit, £407.
Works established, 1880.   Special Act, 1880.
Total population of area supplied, 16,500.
Death rate, 14 per 1,000.
Towns and villages in the area supplied—East, West, and North Retford, Ordsall, and Welham.
Sources of supply—deep wells and borings in New Red Sandstone.
Character of water, very good for domestic and manufacturing purposes.
Total hardness, 11° ; filtration, none.
Length of supply mains, 5 miles ; distributing mains, 16 miles.
Storage capacity, 100,000 gals.
Annual supply of water, 124,000,000 gals.
Daily consumption per head—domestic, 20 gals. ; trade, 10 gals.
Maximum day's supply, 330,000 gals. in August.
Scale of charges—assessment, £4 house, 1s. 3d. ; £6, 1s. 9d. ; £10, 2s. 2d. ; £20 3s. 6d. ; £40, 8s. ; £50, 12s. ; £100, 24s. per quarter; present charge, 10 per cent. off these prices.
Price per 1,000 gals., trade, 9d. to 5d., according to consumption.
Municipal purposes and baths, free.
Number of meters, 12.

Revesby (supplied by Boston).

Reydon (supplied by Southwold).

Rhiwderin, Mon. (supplied by Newport).

Rhos, Denbigh. (supplied by Ruabon).

Rhuddlan (supplied by Rhyl).

Rhondda. *See* Ystrad.

Rhondda Valley (supplied by Pontypridd).

Rhyl, Flint. Railway, L.N.W. Distance from London 209 miles.
Authority, Rhyl Urban District Council.
Chairman, Thomas Witley.
Secretary, Arthur Rowlands, Town Clerk.
Engineer and Manager, Leonard G. Hall, A.M.I.C.E.
Office, Paradise Street.
Loan, outstanding, £120,000; Interest 3 to 3½ per cent.
Works established, 1865; purchased by Council, 1893; Special Act, 1893.
Total population supplied, resident, 16,500; summer estimated, 36,000.
Average death rate, 16·5 per 1,000.
Towns and villages in the area supplied—Abergele, Pensarn, St. Asaph, Llan-
dullas, St. George, Towyn, Rhuddlan, Trefnant, Foryd and Bodelwyddau.
Sources of supply—impounding reservoirs at Llanefydd, auxiliary pumping-
station on river Elwy.
Character of water, soft.
System of filtration, sand.
Storage capacity—impounding reservoirs, 103,000,000 gals.; service reservoirs,
1,072,000 gals.
Annual supply of water—domestic, 145,000,000 gals.; trade, &c., 30,500,000 gals.
Maximum annual rainfall over drainage area, 38·95 in. (1903).
Minimum   „   „   „   „   26·46 in. (1905).
Average   „   „   „   „   29·05 in. (period 13 years).
Daily consumption per head—domestic, 17·7; trade, 3·2.
Maximum day's supply, 480,000 gals. in August.
Scale of charges—assessment charge, 1s. 6d.
Price per 1,000 gals., trade, 1s. 6d.; municipal purposes, 1s.
Number of meters, 88.
Length of mains, 50 miles.

Rhymney, Mon. (G. & W.) Railway, G.W. Distance from London, 173 miles.
Authority, Rhymney and Aber Valley Gas and Water Co., Ltd.
Chairman, H. Oakden Fisher.
Secretary, A. P. James.
Resident Engineer, Albert R. Cawley.
Office, Caerphilley.
Date of formation, 1867. Special Act, 1898.
Area of supply, Gelligaer, Rhymney, Bedwellty, Mynyddisllwyn, Dedwas, Llan-
fabon, Eglwysilan.
Population supplied, 7,914.
Source of supply—moorland drainage, and impounding reservoirs on Rhymney
River.

Rhymney—continued.

Character of water, soft.
Storage capacity—impounding reservoirs, 46,000,000 gals; service reservoir, 5,000,000 gals.
Assessment charges, 2d. per week to 10 per cent on R.V.; charge by meter 6d. to 1s. 6d. per 1,000 gals,
No. of meters, 150.

Riccarton, N.B. (supplied by Kilmarnock).

Richmond, Surrey. L.S.W., N.L., Met. and District. Distance from London, 9¾ miles.
Authority, Corporation of Richmond.
Chairman, Councillor W. J. Cook.
Town Clerk, F. B. Senior, Town Hall.
Engineer, W. G. Peirce, C.E., Waterworks Office, Richmond.
Office, Riverside, Richmond, Surrey.
Loans outstanding, less sinking fund, £63,000 at 3 per cent. to 4 per cent.
Works established, 1876.
Special Act, Public Health Act.
Total population of area of control (1901), 32,000.
Estimated population actually supplied, 34,358 (1907).
Average death rate, 11 per 1,000.
Towns and villages supplied—Richmond, fully ; and Kew, Petersham, and North Sheen with water for road watering and sewer flushing only.
Sources of supply—deep wells and borings, principally in the chalk.
Filtration, none.
Storage reservoir—capacity, 750,000 gals.
Annual supply of water (1906) 395,031,000 gals.
Daily consumption per head—domestic, 21·7; trade, 9·8 gals.
Assessment charge, 8d. in £ on rateable value.
Price per 1,000 gals., domestic, 1s., 8d., 6d. and 4d.
Number of meters in use, 279.
Length of distributing mains, 40 miles.

Richmond, Yorks. Railways, N.E., G.N. and M. Distance from London, 237 miles.
Authority, Corporation.
Chairman of Committee, S. W. Close.
Secretary, John Procter, Borough Accountant.
Water Inspector, Edward Walker.
Office, Borough Accountant's Office.
Works established, 1837.
Population supplied, 3,800.
Area supplied, Richmond only.
Sources of supply, springs at Coalsgarth.
Assessment charge, 5 per cent. on R.V.
Price by meter, 4d. to 1s. per 1,000 gals.

Rickmansworth and Uxbridge, Herts. Railways, L.N.W. and Met. Distance from London, 21¼ miles.
Authority, Rickmansworth and Uxbridge Valley Water Co.
Chairman, Sir Henry E. Knight.
Engineer, J. D. K. Restler.
Manager, J. D. Roper.
Secretary, L. B. Linnett.
Share capital paid up, £143,760.
Debentures, £19,000 ; Interest on loan, 4 per cent.

RICKMANSWORTH AND UXBRIDGE—*continued*.

Towns and villages in the area supplied—Rickmansworth, Harefield, Hillingdon, Hayes, Harlington, Cowley, Iver, West Drayton, King's Langley, Bovingdon, Sarratt, Northolt, Greenford, Perivale, Twyford Abbey, Yiewsley, Abbots Langley, Hunton Bridge, Leavesden, Garston, Horton. Denham, Chalfont St. Peters, Fulmer, Missenden.
Works established, 1887. Special Acts, 1884, 1885, 1900.
Source of supply, deep well.
Character of water, hard.
Storage capacity, 540,000 gals.
Scale of charges—assessment, 5 per cent. on R.V.
Price for 1,000 gals., 3s. to 1s. 6d.
Number of meters, 250.
Total water rent received, about £12,270.

Ringmore (supplied by TEIGNMOUTH).

Ripley, Derbyshire. Railway, M. Distance from London, 137 miles.
Authority, District Council.
Clerk, G. M. Capon.
Works established, 1867.
Total population supplied, 10,113.
Sources of supply—springs.
Scale of charges—assessment charge, A.
Price per 1,000 gals., 1s. 3d.

Ripley, Surrey (supplied by WOKING).

Ripon, Yorks. Railway, N.E. Distance from London, 214 miles.
Authority, Ripon Corporation.
Chairman, W. Harrison, J.P.
Secretary, M. Kirkley, Town Clerk.
Manager, J. W. Kirkley.
Office, Town Hall.
Loans outstanding, £29,328.
Annual profit, including capital charges (1906), £1,968 8s. 2d.
Works established, 1865. Special Acts, 1886.
Total population supplied, 9,000.
District of supply—Ripon, Aismunderby and Bondgate, Sharow, Copt Hewick, Bridge Hewick, Gwendale, Newsby, Skelton, Whitcliffe and Thorpe, Bishopston, Studley Roger, Lindrick and Studley Royal, Fountains, Hedfield, Granbey and North Stainley, Sleningford.
Average death rate, 15·1 per 1,000.
Daily consumption per head—domestic, 25 gals.
Sources of supply—springs and impounding reservoirs on Lumley Moor.
Character of water, soft, 6·1° hardness.
System of filtration, gravel and sand.
Storage capacity—impounding reservoirs, 92,000,000 gals. ; service reservoirs 750,000 gals.
Pressure on distributing mains—maximum, 92 lbs. ; minimum, 60 lbs. per sq. in.
Annual supply of water (1906), 86,440,000 gals.
Average daily supply for all purposes, 25 gals.
Maximum day's supply, 29·2 gals. in June.
Scale of charges—assessment charge, 1s. to 1s. 4½d. in £ on R.V.
    Price per 1,000 gals.—domestic, 10d. and 1s. 3d. ; trade, 1s.
Number of meters, 80.
Length of mains, 34 miles.

Risca and Pontymister, Mon. Railway, G.W. Distance from London, 157½ miles.
Authority, Western Valleys (Mon.) Water and Gas Co. ·
Population supplied, 9,661.
No returns supplied.

Rishton, Lancs. (supplied by Accrington and Blackburn).

Riverhead (supplied by Sevenoaks).

Rixton-with-Glazebrook (supplied by Warrington).

Roall (supplied by Pontefract).

Robertsbridge (supplied by Ticehurst)

Roborough, Devon. (supplied by Plymouth).

Rochdale, Lancs. Railway, L. & Y. Distance from London, 195¾ miles.
Authority, Corporation.
Secretary, Town Clerk.
Manager, W. Tomlinson.
Works established, 1809.
Total population of area supplied, about 100,000.
Daily consumption per head, 18 to 20 gals.
Source of supply, moorlands.
Storage capacity, about 600,000,000 gals.
Character of water, very soft and good.
System of filtration, sand.
Scale of charges, assessment, 7 to 10 per cent.
Price per 1,000 gals., sliding scale from 1s. to 6d.

Rochester, Kent. *See* Chatham.

Rock (supplied by Blackwood).

Rogerstone, Mon. (supplied by Newport).

Rolvenden (supplied by Cranbrook).

Romanby (supplied by Northallerton).

Romford, Essex (supplied by South Essex Water Co.).

Romsey, Hants. (supplied by South Hants Waterworks Co.).

Rosemont (supplied by Blairgowrie).

Rosiwell (supplied by Bonnyrigg).

Ross, Herefordshire. Railway, G.W. Distance from London, 133 miles.
Authority, Trustees of the late Thomas Blake.
Office, Broad Street, Ross.
Towns and villages in the area supplied—Ross, and surrounding district.
Works established, 1887 ; Special Acts, 1892.
Total population supplied, about 5,000.
Annual supply of water, 58,000,000 gals.
Daily consumption per head, domestic, 24 gals., trade, 8 gals.
Sources of supply—spring at Alton Court (domestic), and river water from Wye
    for trade purposes.
Storage capacity, 400,000 gals. ; System of filtration, none required.
Character of water, bright, pure.
Death rate, 12 per 1,000.
Number of meters, 21.
Length of mains, 11½ miles.
Scale of charges—assessment charge, 6 to 10 per cent. on rateable value.
Price per 1,000 gals., domestic, 2s. to 1s., trade by agreement, municipal purposes
    free for a term of years ending 1908.

Rothbury Northumberland. Railway, N.B. Distance from London, 314 miles.
Authority, Rothbury Waterworks Company.
Managing partner, Lionel Crawford Davy, Rothbury.
Office, Rothbury.
Total capital invested, £3,060.
Dividend, private company.
Works established, 1866. Purchased by present company, 1886.
Total population of area of control, 1891, 1,192; 1901, 1,340 (Urban District).
Total number of consumers, 250.
Estimated population actually supplied, 1,200.
Death rate per 1,000, 14·2 for 1906 ; average, 16·5.
Towns and villages supplied, Rothbury and Whitton.
Annual supply is not measured ; the supply is 100 gals. per minute.
Total quantity of water drawn per annum—from surface springs, 52,560,000 gals.
Sources of supply—surface springs situate at Simonside Hills, Northumberland.
Drainage area—uncultivated heather.
Water authority have no control of drainage area.
Strata or formation yielding springs—sandstone.
Nature of subsoil yielding water—mountain drift and peat.
Locality and extent of outcrop of same—sandstone down to mountain limestone.
Character of water—excellent, soft ; hardness before treatment, 6·3° ; no filtration.
Service reservoir, Whitton, capacity, 8,000 gals., covered. Another is being
    constructed to hold other 16,000 gals.
Price per 1,000 gals., 1s. 6d.
Number of meters in use, 1.
Length of distributing mains, 2 miles.

Rotherfield Grays and Rotherfield Peppard (supplied by South Oxfordshire).

Rotherham, Yorks. Railways, M., G.N., and G.C. Distance from London, 167
miles.
Authority, Rotherham Corporation.
Chairman, Alderman E. Hickmott, J.P.
Town Clerk, W. J. Board.
Engineer, G. Jennings, Borough Surveyor.
Office, Town Hall, Rotherham.
Loans outstanding, £107,976.
Loans on undertaking for 1905, £520.

ROTHERHAM—*continued*.

Works established, original company, 1854.
Purchased by Local Authority, 1871.
Special Acts, 1862, 1870, 1896, 1899.
Total population supplied, 91,000.
Average death rate, 19 per 1,000.
Sources of supply, springs, local gathering grounds and from Sheffield supply.
Towns and villages in the area supplied—Rotherham, Rawmarsh, Greasborough, parts of Whiston, Wentworth and Ecclesfield.
Character of water, good, slightly discoloured from peaty watershed, hardness 3·8°.
Filtration, none at present ; softening, none.
Storage, impounding reservoirs, Ulley, 150,000,000 gals.
     „   „   „   Langsett, 1,450,000,000 gals,
Langsett reservoir is jointly owned with Doncaster and Sheffield service reservoir, 1,500,000 gals.
Pressure on distributing mains—max., 120 lbs. ; min., 40 lbs. per sq. in.
Annual supply of water, 650,000,000 gals.
Daily consumption per head—domestic, 16 gals. ; trade, &c., 5 gals.
Maximum day's supply, 1,800,000 gals. in July and August.
Scale of charges—assessment charge, 10 per cent. on rateable value; cottages, 8s. per annum.
Price per 1,000 gals., trade purposes, 10d. to 1s. 3d. ; municipal purposes, some cases free, and other cases by meter, 3d. to 10d.
Number of meters, 200.
Length of mains—supply, 21 miles ; distributing, 80 miles.

Rothesay, Scotland. Railways, Cal., N.B., and G.W.S. Distance from London, 400 miles.
Authority, Burgh of Rothesay, Isle of Bute.
Chairman, Bailie D. Fred Dalziel.
Secretary, Town Clerk.
Engineer in charge, John Morrison, Burgh Surveyor, 31, High Street, Rothesay.
Office, Burgh Buildings, Rothesay.
Loans outstanding, £25,724.
Works established, 1860 and 1879. Special Acts, none.
Purchased by local authority, 1873.
Total population of area of control, 1881, 8,291 ; 1891, 9,034 ; 1901, 9,323.
Total number of consumers, 2,468 ; during summer months, 7,000.
Estimated population actually supplied, 10,500 ; during summer months, 50,000.
Average death rate, 13 per 1,000.
Towns and villages within the area of control, Rothesay, Kingarish and North Bute.
Source of supply, two lochs.
Character of water—soft, mostly rainfall, good.
Maximum annual rainfall over drainage area, 58 inches.
Minimum   „   „   „   „   „   38 „
Nature and surface formation of drainage areas, hill ground, moor, moss and rocks.
Storage—Loch Ascog   ...   . capacity, 180,000,000 gals.
       Dhu Loch ...   .   „   60,000,000 „
Filtering area provided, 1,164 square yards in sand filter beds and Reeve's system.
Length of supply mains, 12 miles ; distributing mains, 20 miles.
Pressure on distributing mains—maximum, 140 lbs. ; minimum, 120 lbs. per sq. in.
Annual supply of water—for domestic purposes, 200,000,000 gals.
Daily consumption per head, domestic, 30 gals.
Maximum day's consumption, 760,000 gals. in July.
Charge for municipal purposes, £703.
Assessment charge, 3¼ per cent. to 8½d. to 11d. on rental value.
Price per 1,000 gals., 6d.

Rothley (supplied by LEICESTER).

Rothwell, Northampton.
Authority, Urban District Council.
Clerk, Wm. Tozer.
Engineer and Surveyor, F. C. Betts.
Daily supply of water, 120,000 gals.
Sources of supply, the old Shotwell Mill about 33 acres in extent.
Storage capacity, 200,000 gals.

Rottingdean, Sussex (supplied by BRIGHTON).

Roundhay (supplied by LEEDS).

Rowley Regis (supplied by SOUTH STAFFS. WATERWORKS Co.).

Rowten (supplied by CHESTER).

Royston, Herts.　Railway, G.N.　Distance from London, 44¼ miles.
Chairman, John Phillips.
Manager and Secretary, W. T. Rowley.
Office, Baldock Street.
Share capital paid up, £7,500 ordinary and pref., £1,850 debentures.
Dividend (1906), 3¾ per cent. on original Ordinary shares; 2⅝ per cent. on additional Ordinary shares.
Total water rent received, £1,099 (1906).
Works established, 1859.　Special Act, Provisional Order 1897.
Total population supplied, 3,500,
Area supplied, Royston.
Source of supply, deep well.
Character of water, chalk water.
Storage capacity, 60,000 gals., new reservoir, 200,000 gals,
Daily consumption per head, 20 gals.
Assessment charge, 6 per cent. on net assessment.
Price per 1,000 gals., 1s. 3d. to 1s.
Number of meters, 12.

Royton (supplied by OLDHAM).

Ruabon, Denbigh.　Railway, G.W.　Distance from London, 197 miles.
Authority, Ruabon Water Company.
Chairman, Sir Watkin Williams Wynn, Bart.
Secretary, Geo. E. Woodford.
Engineers, Dennis & Sons.
Works Manager, J. H. Dean.
Office, Ruabon.
Share capital paid up, £12,000.
Loan　　　　　,,　　　£4,000.
Interest on loan, 3½ per cent.　Dividend, 8 per cent.
Works established, 1870.
Total population supplied, 18,000.

RUABON—*continued.*

Towns and villages in the area supplied—Rhos, Ruabon, Rhosmadoc, Ponkey. Street Issa, Pentre and Penycae, Plasbenion.
Source of supply, stream.
Storage capacity, 34,000,000 gals.

Rugby, Warwickshire. Railways, L.N.W., M. and G.C. Distance from London, 82½ miles.
Authority, Urban District Council.
Clerk to authority, T. M. Wratislaw.
Engineer, D. G. Macdonald.
Office, Urban District Council Offices, High Street.
Towns and villages in the area supplied, Rugby, Newbold, Vicarage Hill, Bilton, New Bilton, Brownsover and Newbold.
Loans outstanding, £26,957.
Works established, 1863. Special Acts, 1863, 1901.
Total population supplied, about 23,000.
Average death rate, 10·8 per 1,000.
Sources of supply—upland collecting ground on the south side of Rugby, and impounding reservoirs on the River Avon.
Character of water, very good; total hardness, 26°.
System of filtration, sand.
Storage capacity, about 2,000,000 gals.
Annual supply of water, about 226,000,000 gals.
Daily consumption per head—domestic, 20 gals.; trade, 7 gals.
Maximum day's supply, 1,000,000 gals. in August.
Scale of charges—assessment charge, 7d. in the £ per annum.
Price per 1,000 gals., 9d. by meter.
Length of mains, about 30 miles.
Number of meters, 20.

Rugely, Staffs., part of (supplied by SOUTH STAFFS. WATERWORKS CO.)

Rumney (supplied by CARDIFF).

Runcorn, Cheshire. Railway, L.N.W.
Authority, Runcorn Urban District Council.
Clerk, E. Marshall.
Engineer and Surveyor, James Wilding, Office, Town Hall, Runcorn.
Total capital invested, including loans, £71,250.
Towns and villages within the area of control, Runcorn, Weston, Weston Point, Halton.
Works purchased by local authority, September 30th, 1893.
Special Acts—Runcorn, Weston and Halton Waterworks Act, 1865, Runcorn Improvement Commissioners Act, 1893.
Total population of area of control—1881, 19,203; 1891, 25,422 (temporary increase during construction of ship canal); 1901, 20,000.
Annual supply of water—
      For all purposes   ...   .   146,000,000 gals.
Maximum day's consumption, 400,000 gals.
Total quantity of water drawn per annum—
    Deep well or borings ...   .   146,000,000 gals.
Estimated total quantity of water available per annum—
    Deep wells or borings   ...   ... possibly 100,000 gals. per day more.
Sources of supply in use—deep wells or borings situated at Runcorn, Cheshire.

Runcorn—*continued.*

Natural rest level of water below surface, 219 feet; practically stands at ordnance datum.

Level of water below surface (when pumping 400,000 gals. per day), 262 feet.

Strata tapped by wells or borings, new red sandstone.

Pumping stations, Runcorn ... ... 600,000 gals. per day.

Service reservoirs, ,, ... capacity, 1,000,000 ,, covered.

,, ,, Weston ... ... ,, 20,000 ,, ,,

,, ,, Halton ... ... ,, 35,000 ,, ,,

Number of meters in use, 30.

Length of distributing mains, between 10 and 11 miles.

Assessment charge, R.R. or value—

Not exceeding £20, 6 per cent. per annum, one w.c., 3s.

Over £20, and not exceeding £40, 5½ per cent. per annum, one w.c., 4s.

,, £40, ,, ,, £80, 5 ,, ,, ,, ,, 5s.

,, £80, ,, ,, £100, 4½ ,, ,, ,, ,, 5s.

Baths, 10s. per annum.

Runton (supplied by Cromer).

Rushall (supplied by South Staffs. Waterworks Co.

Rushden. *See* Higham Ferrers.

Rusholme (supplied by Manchester).

Ruswarp, Yorks. (supplied by Whitby).

Rutherglen (supplied by Glasgow).

Ruthin, Wales. Railway, L.N.W. Distance from London, 215 miles.

Authority, Ruthin Water Company.

Office, 38, Well Street.

Area supplied, Ruthin and neighbourhood.

Works established, 1868. Special Acts, 1868.

Total population supplied, about 4,000.

Daily consumption per head, 50,000 gals., including trade.

Source of supply, mountain stream.

Character of water, soft.

Death rate, 18·9 per 1,000.

Number of meters, 21.

Length of mains, 4½ miles.

Scale of charges—assessment charge, 1s. 6d. in the £.

Price per 1,000 gals., domestic and trade, 1s., with discounts according to consumption.

Ryde, Isle of Wight. Railways, L.S.W., L.B.S.C. and I. of W. Distance from London, 90 miles.

Authority, the Corporation of the Borough of Ryde.

Town Clerk, Charles G. Vincent, Town Hall, Ryde.

RYDE—*continued*.

Towns and villages within the area of control—Ryde, Binstead, Haylands, Ashey, St. Helens (including Sea View, Springvale and Carpenters).
Works established—Ashey, 1855 ; Knighton, 1861.
Special Acts, 1854 and 1861.
Total population of area of control—1891, 10,952 ; 1901, 11,043.
Total number of consumers, 20,000 holiday season.
         „   „   11,043 normal.
Annual supply of water—
      For domestic purposes ...   .   208,073,800 gals.
      In bulk to other authorities   ...   ...   12,356,000 „
Maximum day's consumption, 800,000 holiday season
      „   „   500,000 normal.
Total quantity of water drawn per annum—
      Surface springs ...   .   104,200,700 gals.
      Deep wells or borings ...   .   103,873,100 „
Estimated total quantity of water available per annum—
      From surface springs ...   .   104,200,700 gals.
      „   deep wells or borings ...   .   300,000,000 „

BOROUGH OF RYDE WATER-WORKS

GEOLOGICAL SECTION OF STRATA AT WORKS.

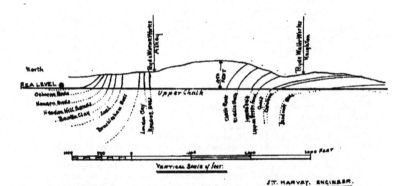

J.T. HARVEY, ENGINEER.

Sources of supply in use—
Surface springs, from lower chalk and upper green sand strata (Knighton).
Deep wells or borings situated at Ashey, upper chalk strata.
      „   „   Knighton, lower green sand strata.
Estimated maximum daily discharge at points of collection, 2,000,000 gals.
     „   average   „   „   285,000 „
Maximum annual rainfall over drainage area, 40·00 inches.
Minimum   „   „   25·00 „
Average   „   „   30·00 „   (period 10 years).
Nature of ditto, mainly grass land.
The Corporation are negotiating the purchase and control of land immediately adjoining works at Ashey and Knighton for protective purposes.
Natural rest level of water, artesian supply overflowing above Ordnance datum 53 feet.

RYDE—*continued.*

Level of water below surface (when pumping 500,000 gals. per day), 50 feet.
Surface formation of drainage areas—upper chalk at Ashey, lower chalk, upper and lower green sand at Knighton.
Strata or formation yielding springs—chorloritic marl, and carstone rock and sandrock beds.
Nature of subsoil yielding water—carstone rock and sandrock beds.
Locality and extent of outcrop of same—about 500 acres of chalk, 200 acres of upper green sand and 1,000 acres of lower green sand.
Storage reservoirs—2 reservoirs at Knighton, capacity, 10,000,000 gals.
Pumping stations—

Ashey ...	...	...	...	capacity,	80,000 gals. per day.
Knighton	...	...	...	,,	1,029,000　　,,

Service reservoirs—

Ashey ...	...	...	...	capacity,	500,000 gals., covered.
,, ...	...	...	...	,,	600,000　　,,

　　　　　　　　　　　　　　　　　　　　1,100,000

Death rate, 14·1 per 1,000.
*Analysis of water—

Total solids ...	...	...	. .	...	...	..	22·72
Organic carbon	...	...	...	...	...	...	·046
,, nitrogen	...	...	...	...	...	...	·007
Ammonia ...	...	...	...	..			·0
Nitrates as nitrates and nitrites	...		...	...	...	...	·124
Total combined nitrogen	...	...	...	...	...		·131
Chlorine ...	...	...	...	...	...	...	3·30

Hardness—

Temporary ...	...	...	...	...	...	...	11·0
Permanent ...	...	...	...	...	..	...	3·9

　　　　　　　　　　　　　　　　　　　　14·9

Remarks, clear.
Hardness before treatment, 14·9°; and after 10°.
Number of meters in use, 280.
Length of distributing mains, 40 miles.
Scale of charges—
Assessment charge, 1s. 3d. in £.
Price per 1,000 gals., 1s. in borough, 2s. outside.
The supply from the Ashey pumping station is pumped direct (from deep wells in the upper chalk) to the service reservoirs and is not treated. The supply from the Knighton pumping station, which is derived from the lower green sand formation, is first thoroughly broken up by perforated plates, etc., and thus oxidised and afterwards treated by adding milk of lime; this combines with the iron and is allowed to precipitate in one of the storage reservoirs. Good results are thus obtained, the temporary hardness being also reduced; 1lb. of lime per 1,000 gals. is found sufficient.

Rye, Sussex. Railway, S.E. Distance from London, 71¼ miles.
Authority, Corporation.
Clerk, Walter Dawes.
Engineer, J. Moore.
Population supplied, 3,871.
Source of supply, deep wells.
No returns supplied.

---

*This water possesses an extremely high degree of organic and bacteriological purity, and is of the most excellent quality for dietetic and all domestic purposes. The Ashey supply contained only fifteen microbes per centimetre, whilst any number not exceeding 100 per c.c. is considered satisfactory.

Ryhope (supplied by Sunderland).

Ryton, Durham. Railway, G.N. Distance from London, 274 miles.
Authority, Ryton Urban District Council.
Chairman, John B. Simpson, M.I.C.E.
Clerk to authority, Henry Dalton.
Engineer, John P. Dalton.
Office, U.D.C. Offices, Ryton.
Works established 1881-2, Special Act, 1881.
Total population supplied, 9,000 by Ryton U. D. C., and about 1,000 by the
  Newcastle and Gateshead Company direct.
District of supply, Ryton, Crawnook, Woodside,
Source of supply, the whole of the water distributed by the council is pur-
  chased in bulk from the Newcastle and Gateshead Water Co., the council's
  springs having been drained away by coalmining.
Pressure on distributing mains—average, 50 lbs. per sq. in.
Annual supply of water, 36,065,000 gals.
Average daily supply per head for all purposes, 10·98 gals.
Price per 1,000 gals., 1s. 2d.

Saffron Walden, Essex. Railway, G.E. Distance from London, 43½ miles.
Authority, Corporation 1878.
Chairman, Alderman S. Leverett.
Manager, Engineer and Secretary, A. H. Forbes.
Office, 3, Hill Street.
Loan capital, £9,900, repaid £7,410.
Interest on loans, 3¼, 3½ and 3¾ per cent.
Annual profit, including capital charges, £315.
Works established, 1862 ; purchased, 1878. Special Act, 1878.
Population supplied, 6,000.
Average death rate, 14·5 per 1,000.
District of supply, Saffron Walden only.
Sources of supply, deep well boring into the chalk, 350 feet deep.
Character of water, 28° hardness, softened by Adkin's process to 11°, quite pure.
Storage capacity, 220,000 gals.
Pressure on distributing mains, maximum, 65 lbs. ; minimum, 10 lbs. per sq. in.
Annual supply of water, about 43,000,000 gals.
Daily consumption per head, domestic, 14 ; trade, 9.
Maximum day's supply, 205,000 gals., in July.
Assessment charge, 5 per cent. on R.V.
Price per 1,000 gals., municipal purposes, 1s. 2d. ; domestic, 1s. 2d. ; trade, 1s. 2d.,
  less 10 per cent. over the first 50,000 gals. during the half year.
Number of meters, 78.
Length of mains, 9 miles.

St. Albans. Railways, M., L.N.W., and G.N. Distance from London, 20 miles.
Authority, St. Albans Waterworks Company.
Chairman, A. H. Baynes.
Secretary, C. Fox, F.C.A.
Engineer and Manager, A. F. Phillips, M.I.C.E.
Offices, 38, Parliament Street, London, S.W.
Share capital paid up, £42,331. Loan capital paid up, £8,000.
Interest, 4 per cent. ; Dividends, 10 and 7 per cent.
Works established, 1865. Special Acts, 1865, 1879, 1900.
Total population supplied, 22,000.
Area supplied, St. Albans and Park Street.
Sources of supply, wells in chalk.
Annual supply of water, 236,500,000 gals.
Average daily supply per head—domestic, 25 gals. ; trade, &c., 4·6 gals.

St. Albans—*continued*.

    Maximum week's supply, 5,898,000 gals. in August.
    Assessment charge, 5 per cent. on R.
    Price per 1,000 gals.—domestic, 7d. ; trade, 1s. 6d. to 9d.
    Total water rent received, £6,473.
    Number of meters, 38.
    Length of mains, 31 miles.

St. Andrews, Fife.　Railway, N.B.
    Authority, St. Andrews Town Council.
    Chairman, Provost George Murray.
    Town Clerk, Hugh Thomson.
    Engineer, William Watson.
    Office, Town Hall Buildings.
    Loans, outstanding £22,600.
    Works established, 1867 and 1885.
    Total population supplied, 8,000.
    Average death rate, 11·992 per 1,000.
    Sources of supply, upland springs and surface bores, 150 feet deep.
    Character of water, hardness 12°.
    System of filtration, gravel and sand ; softening, none.
    Storage capacity, 17,500,000 gals.
    Pressure on distributing mains—maximum, 56 lbs. ; minimum, 22 lbs. per sq. in.
    Annual supply of water, 127,500,000 gals.
    Daily consumption per head, all purposes, 43·5 gals.
    Maximum day's supply, 373,000 gals., in August.
    Assessment charge, 8$\frac{1}{16}$d. in the £.
    Price per 1,000 gals., trade, 9d.
    Total water rent received, £190.
    Number of meters, 12.
    Length of mains, 12·59 miles.

St. Annes, Lancs. (supplied by the Fylde Waterworks Co.).

St. Asaph, Flint. (supplied by Rhyl).

St. Aubin (supplied by Jersey New Waterworks Co., Ltd.).

St. Austell Cornwall.　Railway, G.W.
    Authority, Urban District Council.
    Population supplied, about 11,377.
    No returns supplied.

St. Budeaux, Devon. (supplied by Plymouth).

St. Columb, Major and Minor (supplied by Newquay)

St. Dogmaels (supplied by Cardigan).

St Fagans, Glam. (supplied by Cardiff).

St. George, Flint. (supplied by RHYL).

St. Helens, Lancashire.   Railway, L.N.W., and G. C. (goods only).   Distance from London, 192¾ miles.
Authority, St. Helens Corporation.
Chairman of Water Committee, F. R. Dixon-Nuttall, J.P.
Secretary, W. H. Andrew, Town Clerk.
Engineer in charge, J. J. Lackland, M.I.M.E., A.M.I.C.E.
Office, Town Hall, St. Helens.
Total capital invested, including loans, £283,384.
Works established, 1843.
Purchased by local authority, 1850.
Special Acts, St. Helens Water Act, 1843 ; St. Helens Improvement Act, 1869; St. Helens Water Acts, 1882, 1893, 1898.
Total population of area of control, 1881, 58,000 ; 1891, 75,000; 1901, 90,000.
Estimated population actually supplied, 97,000.
Average death rate, 17·2 per 1,000.
Towns and villages within the area of control, with population of each (1901 Census)—County Borough of St. Helens   84,500
            Parishes of Eccleston, Windle, Melling, Urban
                District Council of Rainford   5,500
Sources of supply in use—
Wells and boreholes in the new red sandstone, as shown on map—
1. Eccleston Hill pumping station. Depth of well, 210 feet. Bore hole, 178 feet, additional below bottom of well, capacity, 550,000 gals. per day.
2. Whiston pumping station. Depth of well, 225 feet. Bore hole, 240 feet, additional below bottom of well, 450,000 gals. per day.
3. Sutton Road pumping station is only used on emergency. Water is supplied from the Collins Green Colliery, from the sandstone above the coal beds, capacity, 600,000 gals. per day.
4. Knowsley pumping station. Depth of well, 173 feet. Bore hole, 526 feet, additional below bottom of well, capacity, 1,000,000 gals. per day.
5. Kirkby pumping station. Depth of well, 164 feet. Bore hole, 360 feet. additional below bottom of well, capacity, 1,400,000 gals. per day.
6. Melling pumping station. The full quantity of water here available has not yet been proved, but for the past three years 1,500,000 gals. per day have been obtained.
7. Water-softening Works and Brown Edge reservoir—3,000,000 gals. are softened here every 24 hours. It is received from the Knowsley, Kirkby and Melling pumping stations. The softening process is a modification of the original Clark process with the addition of cloth filters.
8. Two small catchment reservoirs for manufacturing purposes only, under 100,000 gals. per day.
Total quantity of water drawn per annum (1901)—
        From drainage areas ...   .   24,000,000 gals.
        „   deep wells or borings ...   .   1,325,880,000 „
Estimated total quantity available per annum—
    From drainage areas, 25,000,000 gals.
    „   deep wells or borings 2,007,500,000 gals.
Geological data—
    Drainage areas partly boulder clay, partly sandstone.
    Strata tapped by wells and borings, bunter beds, and new red sandstone.
Natural rest level of water not accurately known, as pumping is constant.
Level of water when pumping is generally at or near sea level.
Character of water—hardness before treatment, 22° ; after, 10°.
Number of meters in use, 340.
Length of distributing mains, 114 miles.
Storage reservoirs—
    Eccleston Dams (for manufacturing purposes only) capacity, 6,000,000 gals.

St. Helens, Lancs.—*continued.*

Service reservoirs—
 Eccleston Hill ... ... capacity, 500,000 gals., covered.
 Brown Edge, No. 1 ... ... „ 2,000 000 „ „
 Brown Edge New Reservoir, No. 2 „ 10,000,000 „ „
Head on distributing mains—max:, 115ft. ; min., 23ft.

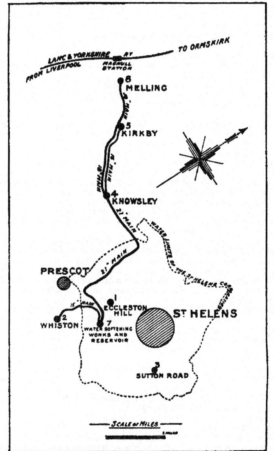

Annual supply of water (1906)—
 For domestic purposes (including trades, without
  meters) ... ... 759,505,000 gals.
 For trade purposes ... ... 575,375,000 „
 For municipal purposes—included in domestic
  purposes
 In bulk to other authorities .., ,... 15,000,000 „

St. Helens, Lancs.—*continued.*

Average daily supply per head—domestic, 23 gals. ; trade, &c., 17 gals.
Maximum day's consumption, 4,500,000 gals.
Scale of charges—
> For domestic purposes, at such rate per cent. per annum upon the gross annual value as shall be fixed for the time being ; present charge, 4⅘ per cent. on gross annual value.
> Water supplied by meter will be according to the quantity of water used, in addition to a fixed charge for the use of the meter, and will be at such a rate per 1,000 gals. as shall be fixed for the time being, and is now 5¾d. per 1,000 gals.
> Charge for the use of meters, from 1s. 9d, per quarter for a ⅜-inch to £1 5s. 10d. for a 5-inch meter.
> The water is supplied at cost price, no profit being allowed.

St. Helens, I. of W. (supplied by Ryde).

St. Heliers, Jersey (supplied by Jersey New Waterworks Co., Ltd.).

St. Ives, Cornwall.   Railway, G.W.   Distance from London, 319½ miles.
Authority, Corporation.
Treasurer, F. Jennings.
Clerk, Ed. Boase.
Population supplied, 6,697.
Total water rent received, £602.

St. Ives, Hunts.   Railways, G.E. & G.N., M.R.   Distance from London, 70½ miles.
Population, supplied, 2,910.
Authority, East Hunts Water Co.
Secretary and Engineer, Cyril Watts.
Office, Market Place, St. Ives.
Population supplied, about 5,000, including parishes on pipe line,
District of supply, Bourn, Longstowe, Knapwell, Connington, Fenstanton, and St. Ives.
Wells and borings from 117 ft. to 50 ft. O.D., into the low green sand.
Character of water, high degree of purity, rather hard, and contains iron.
Filtration sand for removal of oxide of iron.
Service reservoirs, 100,000 gals.
Head or distributing mains, max., 200 ft.
Annual supply of water, 18,000,000 to 20,000,000 gals.
Average daily supply, 10 gals.
Maximum day's supply, 70,000 gals., in July.
Assessment charge, five per cent. on R.V.
Average charge by meter, 1s. 6d. per 1,000 to small consumers, 6d. to borough.

St. James' End (supplied by Northampton).

St. Just, Cornwall.
Authority, Urban District Council.
Population, 5,600.

St. Lawrence (supplied by Ramsgate).

St. Leonards-on-Sea (supplied by Hastings).

St. Mary Church, Devon (supplied by Torquay).

St. Mellons (supplied by CARDIFF).

St. Michaels (supplied by CRANBROOK).

St. Neots. Company wound up, 1906; and the U.D.C. are seeking powers to buy the works.

St. Peters (supplied by BROADSTAIRS).

St. Thomas' (Exeter), Devon. These works were absorbed by the Exeter Corporation Works, November, 1900.

St. Woollas (supplied by NEWPORT, Mon.).

Sale, Cheshire (supplied by NORTH CHESHIRE WATER Co.).

Salehurst (supplied by TICEHURST).

Salford, Lancs.　Railways, L. and Y. and L.N.W.　Distance from London, 189 miles.
　　Authority, Corporation.
　　Treasurer, John Elliott.
　　Superintendent, F. J. Dunn.
　　Total population of area supplied, 221,587.
　　Source of supply, bought in bulk from Manchester Corporation as to Salford Township (having a population of 108,438), and distributed by Salford Corporation. The Townships of Pendleton and Broughton, within the Borough of Salford, are supplied direct by the Manchester Corporation.
　　Total water rent received, about £31,000.

Salisbury, Wilts.　Railway, L.S.W.　Distance from London, 83½ miles.
　　Authority, Corporation, 1853.
　　Chairman, The Mayor.
　　Town Clerk, F. Hodding.
　　Engineer, J. C. Bothams, M.I.C.E.
　　Office, Endless Street.
　　Original cost, £14,500.
　　Works established, 1853.　Area supplied, 598 acres.
　　Total population supplied, 22,000.
　　Annual supply of water, 220,000,000 gals.
　　Daily consumption per head, 35 gals. with constant supply.
　　Sources of supply, wells in chalk.
　　Storage capacity, 243,000 gals.
　　Character of water, 23° hardness.
　　Death rate, 17·6 per 1,000.
　　Number of meters, 80.
　　Scale of charges—assessment charge, 6d. in £.
　　Price for 1,000 gallons, 8d. to 3d.
　　Total water rent received, £2,876.

Saltash, Devon (supplied by PLYMOUTH).

Saltburn-by-the-Sea, Yorks.　Railways, G.N. and N.E.　Distance from London, 251 miles.
　　Authority, Cleveland Water Company.
　　Chairman, W. H. A. Wharton.
　　Engineer and Secretary, Wm. I'Anson, A.M.I.C.E.
　　Office, Saltburn-by-the-Sea.
　　Share capital paid up, £80,000.

Dividend, 10 per cent. on half the capital and 7 per cent. on the other half during the last six years, free of income-tax = 10 and 7 per cent. maximum dividend.

Towns and villages in the area supplied, Cleveland Ironstone District, viz., East Loftus, Loftus, Skinningrove, Carlinhow, Kilton Thorpe, Brotton, N. Skelton, Lingdale, Boosbeck, Magrapark, Skelton, New Marske, Warrenby. Seaside resorts, viz., Redcar, Marske, and Saltburn.

Works established, 1868.　Special Acts, 1869, 1871, 1876, 1889.

Total population supplied, about 29,800.

Daily consumption per head—domestic, 10·62 gals. ; trade, 14·49 gals.

Sources of supply, springs in freestone rock, half ; filtered water from reservoir on moorlands, half.

Storage capacity, 140,000,000 gals.　Character of water, 5° and 3° hardness.

Number of meters, 183.

Scale of charges—assessment charge, R.

Price for 1,000 gals.—domestic, 1s. 6d. and 1s. 3d. ; trade and municipal, 9d. to 7d.

Total water rent received, £10,231.

Saltcoats (supplied by Irvine).

Saltley and Washwood Heath (supplied by Birmingham).

Saltney (supplied by Chester).

Saltwood, Kent (supplied by Hythe).

Sandal (supplied by Wakefield).

Sandbach and District, Cheshire.　Railway, L.N.W.　Distance from London, 162¼ miles.

Authority, Sandbach Urban District Council.

Clerk, A. E. Stringer.

Population supplied, 5,556.

Source of supply—artesian tubes at Taxmere, two miles from Sandbach.　There is an abundant supply, and the water flows by gravitation to the waterworks, where it is treated by Clark's process, and afterwards pumped to a tank with a capacity of 58,413 gals.　The water supply to town is constant.

Water is supplied to Congleton Rural District Council for the townships of Bradwall, Elton, and Betchton.

Scale of charges—assessment charge, public rate.

Houses under £9 per annum, 2s. 2d. per quarter.

　　,,　　£9 and upwards per annum, 5 per cent. per annum.

Hotels, 7½ per cent. on rateable value. Beersellers, 6¼ per cent. on rateable value.

Horses, cows, and 2-wheeled carriage, 1s. each per quarter.

Price per 1,000 gals., 1s.　Meters hired out by the Board.

Sanderstead (supplied by East Surrey Waterworks).

Sandgate, Kent.　Railway, S.E. & C.　Distance from London, 68½ miles.

Authority, District Council.

Chairman, W. H. Jacob.

Clerk, J. Shera Atkinson.

Engineer, R. A. Skelton.

Works established, 1859.　Total population supplied, 2,400.

Sources of supply, rock and sand.　Character of water, very pure.

SANDGATE—*continued.*

> Death rate, 12·4 per 1,000.
> Annual supply of water—20,000,000 to 30,000,000 gals., by gravitation.
> Assessment charge—general district rate.
> Length of mains, about 5 miles.
> The town is also partly supplied by Folkestone Waterworks Company. Not included in above population.

Sandhurst (supplied by FRIMLEY).

Sandown, Isle of Wight. Railway, L.S.W. Distance from London, 86 miles.
> Authority, Company.
> Works established, 1861 ; Special Act, 1861.
> Population supplied, 5,000.
> No returns supplied.

Sandwich, Kent. Railway, S.E. Distance from London by road, 69 miles ; by rail, 84½ miles.
> Authority, Sandwich Corporation.
> Secretary, Town Clerk.
> Works established, 1895.
> Total population supplied, 5,348, Sandwich and neighbourhood.
> Source of supply, reservoirs.

Sandycroft, Flint. (supplied by HAWARDEN).

Sankey, Lancs. (supplied by WARRINGTON).

Sanquhar, Dumfriesshire, N.B.
> Authority, Sanquhar Water Co., Ltd.
> Chairman, F. R. Tweddel.
> Secretary, James R. Wilsden.
> Manager, David McKendrick.
> Office, High Street.
> Share capital paid up, £2,550 ; last dividend, 5 per cent.
> Population supplied, 1,315 in burgh, and 400 outside.

Sarratt (supplied by RICKMANSWORTH).

Sawbridgeworth (supplied by HERTS AND ESSEX WATERWORKS Co.).

Scalby, Yorks. Railway, N.E. Distance from London, 236 miles.
> Authority, Scalby Urban District Council by purchase, 1905.
> Area supplied, Scalby and Newby.
> Works established, 1870.
> Daily consumption, 24,000 gals.
> Source of supply, springs.
> Storage capacity, 100,000 gals.
> Filtration, none,
> Assessment charge, 9d. in the £ on rateable value of buildings without land.
> Price per 1,000 gals., 1s.

Scalthwaiterigg (supplied by KENDAL).

Scarborough. Railways, G.N. and N.E.   Distance from London, 230¼ miles.
Authority, Corporation of Scarborough.
Chairman, Alderman Wm. Chas. Land, J.P.
Secretary, Town Clerk.
Engineer in charge, William Millhouse. Office, Town Hall.
Total capital invested, including loans, £231,195.
Works established, 1845; purchased by local authority, 1878.
Special Acts, Scarborough Water Works Acts, 1845, 1856, 1863, and 1878 ;
  Scarborough Corporation Water Act, 1878.
Death rate average for the last 10 years, 16 61 per 1,000.
Towns and villages within the area of control :—

Scarborough (summer)	...	...	...	population	62,000
„ (winter)	...	...	...	„	40,670
Seamer, village	...	...	...	...	„	711
Cayton „	...	...	...	...	„	605
Irton „	...	...	...	...	„	148

                                                            42,134

Estimated total quantity of water available per annum—
        From deep wells or borings ...   . 1,000,000,000 gals.
Sources of supply in use—Wells situated at—
  Irton, 4 miles S.W. of Scarborough ; Osgodby, 3¼ miles S. of Scarborough.
  Cayton Bay, 3 miles S.E. of Scarborough.
Average annual rainfall over drainage area, 23·82 inches (period 7 years).
The water authority has no control of drainage area.
Natural rest level of water below surface, at Osgodby well, 68·80 feet.
Spring level, 100 feet above Ordnance Datum ; Autumn level, 93 feet above
  Ordnance Datum.

Osgodby Well—
        Ground level above O.D. ...   ...·   ...   ... 161·80
        Rest level of water above O,D. ...   . 97·45
        S.W. when pumping 980,000 gals. per day   .. 89·00

Irton Well—
        Ground levels above O.D. ...   . 96·00
        Natural rest level above surface 10ft., above O.D. 106·00
        Level of water below surface when pumping
          1,400,000 gals. per day, 6 ft.... ..   ... 90·00 O.D.
        „   „   „ when pumping 2,500,000
          gals. per day, 17 ft. ...   . 79·00 O.D.

The Irton well overflows at the ground level. The water-bearing strata lying
  under pressure between the Oxford and Kimmeridge clays.
The River Derwent crosses the outcrop of the strata in which the Irton well is
  sunk, and acts as a feeder by several million gallons per day.
Strata tapped by wells or borings, calcareous grit and limestones of the Coralline
  Oolite, resting on the Oxford clay.
Geological section is well shown on the geological maps and sections of the
  ordnance survey of Yorkshire.

Analysis of Water—

	Cayton Bay.	Osgodby.	Irton.	
Total solid residue	... 23·00	... 26·00	... 18·00	grains per gal.
Chlorine	... 2·25	... 2·60	... 1·60	„ „
Free ammonia	·0186 ...	·0200 ...	·0192	parts per 1,000,000
Albuminoid ammonia	·0200 ...	none ...	·0040	„ „
Temporary hardness	... 13·8	... 12·7	... 10·0	degrees (Clark)
Permanent „	... 1·1	... 2·3	... 1·4	„ „
Total hardness	... 14·9	... 15·0	... 11·4	„ „

The above analysis represents waters of a very high degree of purity, and well adapted for the
supply of a town. They are absolutely free from any trace of contamination, and are fairly soft.

Filtration, none.

Pumping stations—

Irton	...	...	...	max. capacity,	1,400,000 gals.
Osgodby	...	...	...	,, ,,	980,000 ,,
Cayton Bay	...	...	...	,, ,,	720,000 ,,

Service reservoirs—

Osgodby reservoir	...	...	capacity, 4,000,000 gals.,	open.
Lower ,, Oliver's Mount		,,	1,500,000 ,,	covered.
Upper ,, ,, ,,		,,	1,500,000 ,,	,,

Head on distributing mains—max., 200 ft.; min., 60 ft.

Annual supply of water, 1906,

Domestic	...	...	399,000,000 gals.
Trade ...	..	...	95,000,000 ,,
Municipal	...	...	6,000,000 ,,
Total ...	...	...	500,000,000 ,,

Maximum day's consumption, 1,890,000 gals., August (holiday season); 1,250,000 gals. (normal).

Average daily supply per head—domestic, 25 to 28 gals.; trade, &c., 10 gals.

General charges for water—

Dwelling-houses, with shops, hotels, inns, clubs, schools, taverns, &c., including baths and w.c., 1s. 2d. in the £ on rateable value per annum.

Lock-up shops, offices, warehouses, workshops, 4d. in the £ on rateable value; minimum, 5s. per annum.

Charges for water by meter :—

			£	s.	d.	
1,000 gallons	...		0	5	0	including rent of meter.
2,000 ,,	...		0	7	0	,,
5,000 ,,	...		0	13	0	,,
10,000 ,,	...		1	3	0	,,
25,000 ,,	...		2	7	0	,,
50,000 ,,	...		3	12	0	,,
75,000 ,,	...		4	7	0	,,
100,000 ,,	...		5	0	0	,,

For any quantity exceeding 100,000 gallons up to 200,000 gallons, 1s. per thousand gallons.

For any quantity exceeding 200,000 gallons up to 400,000 gallons, 1s. per thousand gallons for the first 200,000 gallons, and 6d. for every additional thousand gallons.

For any quantity above 400,000 gallons, 9d. per thousand gallons.

Quarterly minimum charge for water by meter—

½ inch meter supply, not less than				5/-	per quarter.	
¾ ,,	,,	,,	,,	6s.	,,	
1 ,,	,,	,,	,,	8s.	,,	
1¼ ,,	,,	,,	,,	10s.	,,	
2 ,,	,,	,,	,,	12s.	,,	
3 ,,	,,	,,	,,	14s.	,,	

Number of meters in use, 450.

Length of supply mains, 7½ miles; distributing mains, 45 miles.

Scarborough—*continued.*

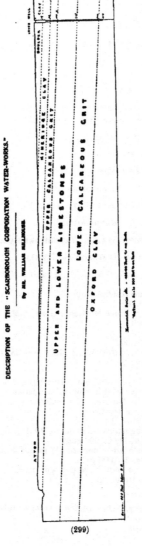

DESCRIPTION OF THE "SCARBOROUGH CORPORATION WATER-WORKS."

By Mr. William Belhouse.

The drawing from which this reduction is made is 16 inches long.

Scarcliffe (supplied by Bolsover).

Scarthill Nick (supplied by Matlock Bath).

Scone (supplied by Glasgow).

Scotby (supplied by Carlisle).

Scotstoun and Scotstounhill (supplied by Glasgow).

Scriven (supplied by Harrogate).

Scunthorpe, Lincoln.
    Authority, Urban District Council.
    Engineer, A. M. Cobban.
    Capital expenditure, £17,000.
    Source of supply, deep wells at Sawcliffe Hill.

Seacombe (supplied by Wallasey).

Seacroft (supplied by Leeds).

Seaford, Sussex. See Newhaven.

Seaham Harbour (supplied by Sunderland).

Seal (supplied by Sevenoaks and Wey Valley).

Seamer, Yorks. (supplied by Scarborough).

Sedgley (supplied by South Staffs. Waterworks Co.).

Seghill U.D.C. (supplied by Newcastle-on-Tyne).

Selby, Yorks. Railways, N.E., G.N., G.E., M., and L.N.W. Distance from London, 175¼ miles.
    Authority, Selby Urban District Council.
    Chairman, Mark Scott, J.P.
    Engineer and Manager, Bruce McGregor Gray, A.M.I.C.E.
    Secretary, J. H. Bantoft.
    Office, Council Offices.
    Loans outstanding, £35,000.
    Works established, 1851. New Works, 1907, Special Act, 1904.
    Total population supplied, 9,500.
    Average death rate, 13·3 per 1,000.
    Area supplied, Selby Urban, and Selby Rural District, if required.
    Source of supply, artesian well in new red sandstone.
    Character of water, total hardness 12° ; softening, none.
    System of filtration, none required.
    Storage capacity, 946,016 gals.
    Pressure on distributing mains—maximum, 70 lbs. ; minimum, 35 lbs. per sq. in.
    Annual supply of water, 71,000,000 gals.
    Daily consumption per head—domestic, 17 gals. ; trade, 3 gals.
    Maximum day's supply, 200,000 gals.
    Assessment charge, 8 per cent. to 20 per cent in £.
        Price per 1,000 gals., trade, 1s.
    Number of meters, 23.

Selkirk, Scotland. Railway, N.B. Distance from Edinburgh, 39¼ miles.
    Authority, Corporation.
    Population supplied, 5,700.
    No returns supplied.

Selly Oak (supplied by BIRMINGHAM).

Selsey. Water and Gas Bill before Parliament, 1907.

Send (supplied by WOKING).

Settle, Yorks. Railway, M. Distance from London, 236 miles.
Authority, Settle Rural District Council.
Clerk, T. E. Pearson.
Total population supplied, 2,500.

Sevenoaks, Kent. Railway, S.E. & C. Distance from London, 20 miles.
Authority, Sevenoaks Waterworks Company, Ltd.
Chairman, Sydney Thompson.
Secretary, Alfred Grainger.
Consulting Engineer, A. F. Bowker.
Office, Oak Lane.
Share capital paid up, £43,500. Loan capital paid up, £11,500.
Dividends—Ordinary, 10 and 7 per cent.; Preference, 4 per cent.; Debentures, 3½ per cent.
Works established, 1864. Special Acts, 1878, 1892, 1900.
Total population of area supplied, about 12,000.
Average death rate, 15 per 1,000.
Towns and villages in the area supplied—Sevenoaks, Seal, Riverhead, The Weald, and Seal Chart.
Sources of supply, wells and borings to lower green sand.
Character of water, excellent; total hardness, 16·6 and 20·2.
Filtration, none; softening, none.
Daily consumption per head—domestic, 15 gals.
Storage in service reservoirs, 1,000,000 gals.
Head on distributing mains—maximum, 300 ft.
Total quantity of water supplied per annum, 75,000,000 gals.
Assessment charge, 7½ per cent. on rateable value.
Price per 1,000 gals.—trade, 2s.
Number of meters, 102.
Length of mains, about 40 miles.

Shadwell (supplied by LEEDS).

Shaftesbury, Dorset. Railway, L.S.W. Distance from London, 104 miles.
Owner, Lord Stalbridge.
Works established, 1852.
Total population supplied, 2,027.
Sources of supply, well (140 ft. deep).
Storage capacity, 150,000 gals.
Character of water, rather hard.
Scale of charges—assessment charge, annual rental.

Shalford (supplied by GUILDFORD and GODALMING).

Shanklin, Isle of Wight. Railway, I.W. Distance from London, 87 miles.
Authority, Urban District Council.
Chairman, Francis Cooper.
Engineer, Ernest C. Cooper.
Office, Council Chambers, Victoria Avenue, Shanklin.
Works established, 1863.
Total population supplied, about 4,700; summer months about double.
Average death rate, 9·6 per 1,000 of the population.
Area supplied, parish of Shanklin only.
Sources of supply, wells and springs, upper green sand and chalk.
Character of water, high degree of purity, both chemical and bacteriological, temporary hardness.

SHANKLIN—*continued.*

Storage capacity, about 1,300,000 gals.
Head on distributing mains—maximum, 348 feet ; minimum, 50 feet.
Daily consumption per head—domestic, 20 gals. ; trade, 5 gals.
Maximum day's supply, 200,000 gals. in August and September.
Water rate, 6d. in £ on rateable value.
Price for 1,000 gals., trade 1s. 6d. by meter.
Number of meters, 24.
Length of supply mains, 5 miles ; distributing mains, 24 miles.
Total water rent received, £1,200 per annum.

Sharrow (supplied by RIPON).

Sheddens, N.B. (supplied by BUSBY).

Sheerness, Kent. Railway, S.E. Distance from London, 49 miles.
Authority, Urban District Council.
Manager, T. F. Berry.
Engineer in charge, L. Wornall.
Clerk to Council, Vincent H. Stallon.
Office, Trinity Road.
Area supplied, Sheerness District.
Works established, 1860.
Total population of area supplied, 18,179.
Daily supply of water, 230,000 gals.
Sources of supply, deep wells, artesian.
Storage capacity, 120,000 gals.
Character of water, very good.
Death rate, average 12·63 per 1,000.
Length of mains, 14 miles.

Sheffield, Yorks. Railways, G.C., M., and G.N. Distance from London, 158½ miles.
Authority, Corporation of the City of Sheffield.
Chairman, Alderman T. R. Gainsford, J.P.
General Manager, William Terrey.
Engineer in charge, L. S. M. Marsh.
Waterworks' Office, Town Hall, Sheffield.
Total capital invested, including loans, £3,354,843.
Works established, water company incorporated 1830.
Purchased by local authority, 1888.
Special Acts—Sheffield Waterworks Acts, 1853, 1860, 1864, 1866 ; (New Works)
  1867. (Amendment) ; 1867, 1873 and 1881 ; Sheffield Corporation (Water) Act,
  1887 ; Sheffield and Handsworth Provisional Order, 1889 ; Sheffield Corporation
  (Water) Acts, 1893 and 1896 ; Barnsley Corporation (Water) Act, 1896 ;
  Derwent Valley Water Act, 1899 ; Barnsley Corporation Act, 1900 ; Sheffield
  Corporation Acts, 1900 and 1901 ; Derwent Valley Water Act, 1901 ; Sheffield
  Corporation Act, 1903.
Total population of area of control, 1881, 324,160 ; 1891, 372,630 ; 1901, 447,109.
Estimated population actually supplied (1906), 477,448.
Average death rate, 16·7 per 1,000.
Towns and villages within the area of control, with population of each (1901
  Census)—

Sheffield	409,070
Ecclesfield	18,324
Bradfield	7,916
Tinsley	1,885
Norton	1,097
Dore	1,305
Totley	912
Beauchief	34
Stocksbridge	6,566

SHEFFIELD—*continued.*

Supplies in bulk furnished to Rotherham and Doncaster corporations, Handsworth Urban District Council, Wortley and Rotherham Rural District Councils and the Dearne Valley Water Company.

Sources of supply in use—drainage areas situated at Redmires (Rivelin Watershed), Bradfield (Loxley Watershed), and Langsett (Little Don Watershed).

Estimated average daily discharge, for town supply, at points of collection, 13,149,397 gals.

Maximum annual rainfall over drainage area, 59·835 inches (1872).

Minimum „ „ 24·780 „ (1887).

Average „ „ 40·456 „ (period 71 years).

Population on drainage area, very small.

Nature of ditto, principally moorland.

Storage reservoirs,	Redmires,	Upper	...	...	capacity,	343,000,000 gals.
„	„	„ Middle	...	...	„	187,500,000 „
„	„	„ Lower	...	...	„	139,500,000 „
„	„	Rivelin, Upper	...	...	„	48,500,000 „
„	„	„ Lower	...	...	„	175,000,000 „
„	„	„ depositing pond	...		„	8,000,000 „
„	„	Agden ...	...	...	„	629,000,000 „
„	„	Strines	...	...	„	513,000,000 „
„	„	Dale Dike	...	...	„	486,000,000 „
„	„	Damflask	...	...	„	1,158,000,000 „
„	„	Langsett	...	...	„	1,400,000,000 „
Service	„	Ringinglow	...	...	capacity,	300,000 gals., open.
„	„	Carsick Hill	...	...	„	20,000 „ „
„	„	Lydgate	...	...	„	500,000 „ „
„	„	Hadfield	...	...	„	21,000,000 „ „
„	„	Ralphs Dam	...	...	„	4,000,000 „ „
„	„	Misfortune	...	...	„	4,000,000 „ „
„	„	Godfrey	...	...	„	15,800,000 „ „
„	„	New Dam	...	...	„	10,500,000 „ „
„	„	Old Great Dam	...	...	„	21,000,000 „ „
„	„	Ecclesfield	...	...	„	75,000 „ „
„	„	Moonshine	...	...	„	5,000,000 „ „

Annual supply of water (1906)—

For domestic purposes ... ... 1,945,874,671 gals.

„ trade „ ... ... 1,478,794,015 „

„ municipal „ ... ... 193,257,600 „

In bulk to other authorities ... ... 1,092,247,310 „

Maximum day's consumption for town supply ... 15,078,573 „

Total quantity of water drawn per annum (1906) from drainage areas, excluding compensation water, 4,710,173,596 gals.

Estimated total quantity of water available per annum for town supply from drainage areas, 4,799,529,905 gals.

Total domestic and trade supplies, 173,492.

Character of water, very soft.

Filtration, none.

Assessment charge, R.

Price per 1,000 gals., 10d. to 6d.

Number of meters in use, 3,999.

Length of distributing mains, 452¾ miles.

Shelf, Yorks. Railways, G.N., M., L. & Y. Distance from London, 194 miles.

Authority, Shelf Waterworks Company, Ltd.

Office, Carr House Lane.

Share capital paid up, £1,500. Dividend, 10 per cent. (1906).

Works established, 1878.

Average death rate, 19·6 per 1,000.

SHELF—*continued*.

Area supplied, 1¼ miles circumference.
Sources of supply, Bradford Corporation gathering grounds.
Character of water, soft.
Annual supply of water, 5,000,000 gals.
Assessment charge, A.
Price per 1,000 gals., 2s. 6d. Total water rent received, £509.
Number of meters, 28.

Shenley (supplied by COLNE VALLEY WATER CO. and BARNET).

Shenstone (supplied by SOUTH STAFFS. WATERWORKS CO.).

Sheppy, Isle of. *See* SHEERNESS, MINSTER and QUEENBOROUGH.

Shepshed (supplied by LOUGHBOROUGH).

Shepton Mallet, Somerset. Railways, G.W. and L.S.W. Distance from London, 121 miles.
Authority, Shepton Mallet Waterworks Company.
Chairman, J. R. Allen.
Secretary, H. C. Budd, 12, Commercial Road.
Offices, 12, Commercial Road.
Share capital paid up, original   ...   £2,400.
    „   further capital,   ...   £2,400.
    „   5 per cent. Preference shares, £400.
4 per cent. Debentures   ...   .£1,300.
Dividends, original, 10 per cent.
    „   F.C.   7   „
Works established, 1859. Special Acts, 1859 and 1876.
Estimated population actually supplied, 5,000.
Source of supply—springs from the Mendip Hills.
Character of water, very good. Total hardness, 10°.
Filtration, none; softening, none.
Storage capacity, 130,000 gals.
Pressure on distributing mains—maximum, 80 lbs. minimum, 35 lbs. per sq. in.
Annual supply of water, about 40,000,000 gals.
Average daily supply—domestic, 55,000 gals.; trade, &c., 48,000 gals.
Maximum day's supply, 960,000 gals. in January and December, 1906.
Assessment charge, 7 per cent. on R.V.
Charge by meter, according to scale.
Number of meters, 15.

Sheringham, Norfolk. Railway, G.N. Distance from London, 161 miles.
Authority, Sheringham Gas and Water Co.
Managing Director, E. B. Read.
Manager, George H. Judd.
Office, Gas and Water Office, Gas Works, Sheringham.
Population supplied, about 3,000 in winter.
District of supply, Sheringham and Beeston Regis.
Source of supply, springs from Sheringham Woods.
Character of water, soft; of excellent analysis.
Filtration, shingle beds.
Storage in impounding reservoirs, 500,000 gals.
Average charge by meter, 2s., 1s. 6d., and 1s.

Shettlestone (supplied by GLASGOW).

Shifnal (supplied by MUCH WENLOCK).

Shildon (supplied by WEARDALE AND CONSETT WATER Co.)

Shinfield (partly supplied by READING).

Shipbourne (supplied by Tonbridge).

Shiplake (supplied by Henley).

Shipley, Yorks. Railway, M. Distance from London, 196 miles.
    Authority, Urban District Council.
    Total population of area supplied, 28,000.

Storage capacity—	Capacity.	Level above sea.
Eldwick reservoir (compensation) ...	27,398,250 gals. ...	689 feet.
Graincliffe reservoir (storage)... ...	95,530,000 ,, ...	845 ,,
Upper Bank Top reservoir (service) ...	4,517,625 ,, ...	612 ,,
Lower Bank Top reservoir (service) ..	10,198,173 ,, ...	592 ,,

The drainage area for the Eldwick reservoir is 1,248 acres, the water from which flows through a conduit to the Baildon Bank service reservoirs, being augmented in its course by the Glovershaw Beck from a drainage area of 352 acres. The supply was augmented in 1904-5-6 by spring water from Rombald's Moor, giving 350,000 gals. per day.

Scale of charges—

Houses from £4	to £20	per annum 7½ per cent. on rental.		
,, above £20	,, £40	,,	7	,, ,,
,, ,, £40	,, £60	,,	6½	,, ,,
,, ,, £60	,, £80	,,	6	,, ,,
,, ,, £80	,, £100	,,	5½	,, ,,
,, over £100		,,	5	,, ,,

No charge for first bath or w.c., 10s. for each extra bath or w.c. Shops, warehouses or offices connected to dwelling-houses are charged on two-thirds of entire rental. Cows, horses, carriages, &c., as per scale.

Shire Oak (supplied by South Staffs. Waterworks Co.).

Shoeburyness, Essex.
    Authority, Urban District Council.
    Works established, 1897.
    Total population of area supplied, about 6,000.
    Sources of supply, deep wells in Thanet sands, 475 feet deep.
    Storage capacity, service tank on tower, 43,000 gals.
    Character of water, soft and pure.

Sholto (supplied by Lanarkshire).

Shopwyke (supplied by Chichester).

Shoreham and District (supplied by the Brighton Corporation).

Shottermill (supplied by the Wey Valley).

Shotton Durham (supplied by Sunderland).

Shotton, Flint. (supplied by Hawarden).

Shorncliffe Camp, Kent (supplied by Folkestone).

Shortheath, Staffs. (supplied by Wolverhampton).

Shrewsbury, Salop. Railways, L.N.W. & G.W. Distance from London, 162¾ miles.
    Authority, Corporation.
    Chairman, Samuel Meeson Morris.
    Engineer, W. Chapple Eddowes, Borough Surveyor.
    Office, The Square.
    Total population of area supplied. 28,396.
    Sources of supply, River Severn, and for drinking, springs.
    Assessment charge, 5 per cent. on net rental.
    Price per 1,000 gals., trade, 1s., 9d. and 6d.

Shuttleworth (supplied by Bury).

Shuttington (supplied by Tamworth).

Sidley (supplied by Bexhill).

Sidmouth, Devon. Railway, L.S.W. Distance from London, 167 miles.
Authority, The Sidmouth Water Co.
Population supplied, 3,755.
No returns supplied.

Sileby (supplied by Leicester).

Silsdon, Yorks. (supplied by Bradford).

Silsey (supplied by Boston).

Silverdale (supplied by Staffordshire Potteries Water Co.).

Sinfin Moor (supplied by Derby).

Sissinghurst (supplied by Cranbrook).

Skegness. Railway, G.N. Distance from London, 131 miles.
Authority, Skegness Water Company.
Chairman, The Earl of Scarborough.
Manager, S. Coetmore Jones.
Secretary, S. Coetmore Jones.
Engineer, M. Robertshaw.
Consulting Engineer, Percy Griffiths.
Office, Skegness.
Works established, 1879. Company, 1905. New supply in course of construction
(1907).
Special Acts, 1905.
Average death rate, 12 per 1,000.
District of supply, Skegness and parts of Winthorpe, and part of Croft.
Source of supply, wells and borings in lower green sand.
Character of water, 3° hardness.
Filtration, none ; softening, none.
Service reservoirs, 400,000 gals.
Head on distributing mains—maximum, 200 feet.
Maximum day's supply, 240,000 gals. in August.
Charges authorised—(domestic), from 10 per cent. to 8 per cent. on gross
estimated rental.
Present charge, 5 per cent. on rack rental.
Charge by meter, 1s. 6d. per 1,000 gals.
Length of supply mains, 8 miles ; distributing mains, 4 miles.

Skellingthorpe (supplied by Lincoln).

Skelmanthorpe, Yorks. (supplied by Dewsbury).

Skelmersdale, Lancs. Railway, L. and Y. Distance from London, 200 miles.
Authority, Skelmersdale Urban District Council.
The Urban District Council have agreed to sell their undertaking to Southport, Birk-
dale and West Lancashire Water Board for £22,500, January, 1907.
Clerk, A. Dickinson.
Office, Town Hall, Sandy Lane.
Towns and villages in the area supplied—Skelmersdale, part of Bickerstaffe, and
part of Lathom.
Works established, 1876.
Source of supply, well.
System of filtration, sand rock.
Character of water—very good, soft.
Number of meters, 10.
Length of mains, 7 miles.
Price per 1,000 gals.—trade, 9d.

Skelton, Yorks. (supplied by CLEVELAND and RIPON).

Skinningrove, Yorks. (supplied by CLEVELAND).

Skipton, Yorks.
Authority, Urban District Council.
Population, 12,500, estimated.
Surveyor and Engineer, John Mallinson.
A new reservoir at Embsay and a pipe line to Skipton are now in progress of construction. Estimated cost, £72,000 (1907).

Skirbeck (supplied by BOSTON).

Slangham (supplied by CUCKFIELD).

Sleaford, Lincs. Railways, G.N. and G.E. Distance from London, 112 miles.
Authority, the Sleaford Water Co.
Chairman, H. K. Knight.
Secretary, H. A. Peake.
Manager, Alfred Bird.
Office, 25a, Jermyn Street, Sleaford.
Share capital paid up, £6,000. Dividend, 10 per cent. (1906).
Works established, 1879. Special Acts, 1879 and 1906.
Total population supplied, 6,000.
Average death rate, 15·7 per 1,000.
Area supplied, Sleaford Quarrington and Leasingham.
Source of supply, springs from oolite Limestone.
Analysis expressed in parts per 100,000 was found to be as under—

Chlorine	1·80
Sulphuric acid	5·80
Nitric acid	0·26
Free ammonia	0·0018
Albuminoid ammonia	0·0067
Oxygen absorbed from permanganate at	
o80 F. in 15 min.	0·0124
do. in 4 hrs.	0·0248
Total solids dried at 212o F.	40·00
Loss on ignition	3·28
Appearance of solids on heating	No visible change.
Total hardness	32·0
Colour and appearance	Faint blue ; clear.

Bacterioscopic results—

Number of organisms in each cubic centimetre...	5
Number growing at blood-heat in neutral agar ...	2
„ „ in phenolised acid agar ...	None

Of exceptional purity. No signs of animal or other pollution, either by chemical analysis or bacterioscopic examination. The supply is almost sterile. The somewhat considerable hardness is its only criticisable characteristic.
System of filtration, none.
Storage capacity, 375,000 gals.
Head on distributing mains—maximum, 55 feet ; minimum, 33 feet.
Annual supply of water, 46,000,000 gals.
Average daily consumption per head, 21 gals.
Scale of charges—assessment, 6 to 7 per cent. on gross rental.
Price for 1,000 gals., trade 1s. 3d.

Sleekburn (supplied by BEDLINGTON).

Sleningford (supplied by RIPON).

Slough, Bucks. Railway, G.W. Distance from London 18½ miles.
Authority, Slough Waterworks Company.
Chairman, E. O. Secker.

SLOUGH—*continued*.
    Manager, William Curr.
    Engineer, J. H. Secker.
    Secretary, R. G. Harrison.
    Office, High Street.
    Last dividends, 10 and 7 per cent.
    Works established, 1868. Special Acts, 1868, 1875, 1906.
    Total population of area supplied, 15,000.
    Average death rate, 10·2 per 1,000.
    Towns and villages in the area supplied, Slough, Chalvey, Stoke Poges, Langley,
        Datchet, part of Farnham Royal, Colnbrook and Wexham.
    Sources of supply, deep wells in chalk.
    Character of water, excellent.
    Storage capacity in service reservoirs, 1,200,000 gals.
    Annual supply of water, 121.349,000 gals.
    Daily consumption per head, about 23 gals.
    Scale of charges—assessment, 6 to 7½ per cent. on R.R.
    Price for 1,000 gals., 1s. 7d. to 6d.
    Number of meters, 69.
    Length of mains, 40 miles.

Smallthorne, Staffs. (supplied by STAFFORDSHIRE POTTERIES WATER Co.).

Smeaton (partly supplied by PONTEFRACT).

Smethwick (supplied by SOUTH STAFFS. WATERWORKS Co.).

Snaith (supplied by GOOLE).

Snarestone (supplied by HINCKLEY).

Snodland, see EAST KENT WATER CO.

Solihull (supplied by BIRMINGHAM).

Soothill-Nether (supplied by DEWSBURY).

Soothill-Upper (supplied by HALIFAX).

Southampton. Railway, L. & S.W. Distance from London, 79 miles.
    Authority, County Borough of Southampton.
    Chairman, Councillor H. J. Weston.
    Secretary, R. R. Linthorne, Town Clerk.
    Engineer, Wm. Matthews, M.I.C.E.
    Offices, 33 and 35, French Street.
    Total capital invested, including loans, £317,078; balance unredeemed, £171,498.
    Annual profit, including capital charges (1906), £745.
    Works established, 1290; presented to the Town by the Friars Minor, 1310.
    Special Acts, 1747, 1803, 1810, 1836, 1850 and 1885; Provisional Orders, 1891,
        1894, 1897, 1899 and 1902.
    Total population of area of control, 1881, 60,051; 1891, 65,325; 1901, 76,777.
    Total number of consumers, 15,100.
    Estimated population actually supplied, 80,000.
    Average death rate, 13·21 per 1,000.
    District of supply—Borough of Southampton as constituted prior to the Extension
        Order of 1895.
    Sources of supply—a group of 4 wells, each 100 feet deep and about ¼ a mile
        of heading at a depth of 60 feet, situated at Otterbourne, near Shawford, Hants.
    Drainage area, 24 square miles.
    Maximum annual rainfall over drainage area, 42·8 inches (1872).
    Minimum   „   „   22·4   „   (1905).
    Average   „   „   28·5   „   (period 35 years.)
    The water authority have secured control of drainage area by purchase of land
        contiguous to wells and headings.

SOUTHAMPTON—*continued.*

Natural rest level of water below surface, 17·5 feet; above Ordnance datum, 72·5 feet.

Level of water below surface (when pumping 4,000,000 gals. per day), 50·8 feet.

Geological data—upper chalk, bare at surface.

Locality and extent of outcrop of same—southern outcrop of chalk close to works; area comprises the larger portion of Hampshire.

Character of water—normal chalk water; hardness before treatment, 18°; and after, 6°; softened by the "Haines" system.

General analysis—

		Well water parts in 100,000.		Softened water parts in 100,000.
Total solid matters	... ...	31·69	...	14·07
Organic carbon ...	... ...	0·024	...	0·021
„ nitrogen ...	... ...	0·012	...	0·013
Ammonia	... ...	0·005	...	0·004
Nitrogen, as nitrates and nitrites	...	0·365	...	0·381
Total combined nitrogen	... ...	0·381	...	0·397
Chlorine	... .	1·6	...	1·6

Mineral analysis—

		Well water		Softened water
Silica (SiO_2)	... ...	1·02	...	0·94
Oxide of iron and alumina $\begin{Bmatrix} Fe_2 O_3 \\ Al_2 O_3 \end{Bmatrix}$		0·14	...	0·11
Lime (CaO)	... ...	14·53	...	4·42
Magnesia (MgO) ...	... ...	0·25	...	0·28
Soda (Na_2O) ...	... ...	1·21	...	1·12
Sulphuric acid (SO_3) ...	...	0·39	...	0·45
Nitric acid ($N_2 O_5$) ...	...	1·41	...	1·47
Chlorine (Cl.)	...	1·60	...	1·60
Carbonic acid (CO_2) from carbonates of lime and magnesia ...	... ...	10·64	...	2·64
		31·19		13·03
Less oxygen—equivalent of chlorine		0·36		0·36
Total solid residue ...	...	30·83	...	12·67
Carbonate of lime (Ca CO_3)	...	23·93		5·67
„ magnesia (Mg CO_3)	...	0·21		0·29

		Degrees.		Degrees.
Hardness $\{$ Temporary	... ...	16·10	...	3·92
Permanent	... ...	1·89	...	2·13
Total ...	... ...	17·99	...	6·02

Gals.

Estimated maximum daily discharge at point of collection ... 4,500,000

minimun „ „ „ „ ... 4,000,000

average „ „ „ „ ... 4,250,000

Total quantity of water drawn per annum (1906)—

From deep wells and headings ... 1,164,624,000 gals.

Estimated total quantity of water available per annum—

From deep wells and headings ... ... 1,550,000,000 gals. from existing works.

Pumping station, Otterbourne, capacity, 6,000,000 gals. per day.

Service reservoirs, Otterbourne Hill ... capacity, 1,000,000 gals., covered .

„ „ Southampton Common ... „ 5,000,000 „

Annual supply of water (1906)—

For domestic purposes ... . 751,131,000 gals.

„ trade „ ... ... 329,587,000 „

„ municipal „ 83,906,000

SOUTHAMPTON—*continued.*

　　Average daily supply per head, domestic, 25·73 gals.; trade, etc., 14·15 gals.
　　Maximum day's consumption, 4,026,000 gals. in June.
　　Meters in use, 1,230.
　　Length of distributing mains, 75·4 miles.
　　Scale of charges—5 per cent. in the £ on R.V. domestic supply ; 8d. and 6d. per
　　　1,000 for trade ; hose, 10s. 6d. per year.

South Blyth, Northumberland.
　　Authority, The Urban District Council is supplied with water by the Rt. Hon.
　　　Viscount Ridley.
　　Agent, J. Easton.
　　Total population supplied, 5,172.

Southborough, Kent. Railway, S.E.
　　Authority, Urban District Council.
　　Clerk, Philip Hanmer.
　　Surveyor and Engineer, William Harmer.
　　Office, Council Offices, London Road.
　　Works, constructed under Public Health Act, 1875, opened June, 1885.
　　Total population of area supplied, 7,000.
　　Daily consumption per head, domestic, 10½ gals.
　　Source of supply, springs at Modest Corner in district, well 150 feet deep, at
　　　Haysden outside district.
　　Storage capacity, two days' (daily pumping).
　　Character of water, very pure; total hardness, 5·9°; permanent, 2·8°.
　　Death rate, 12·4 per 1,000.
　　Scale of charges—assessment, rateable value for poor rate.
　　Water rent received, varies.

Southborne, Hants. (supplied by CHRISTCHURCH).

Southchurch, Essex (supplied by SOUTHEND).

South Church (supplied by BISHOP AUCKLAND).

Southend-on-Sea, Essex. Railways, L.T.S., G.E., M. Distance from London, 35¾
　　miles.
　　Authority, Southend Waterworks Company.
　　Chairman, H. L. C. Brassey.
　　Managing Director, E. M. Eton.
　　Secretary and Manager, C. S. Bilham.
　　Engineers, T. & C. Hawksley.
　　Office, 13, Cambridge Road.
　　Dividend, 5 per cent.
　　Works established, 1871. Special Acts, 1879, 1894, 1898, 1904.
　　Total population supplied, 50,000.
　　Towns and villages in the area supplied—Southend, Prittlewell, Southchurch, &c.

Southerndown, Glam.
　　Water supplied in bulk from Bridgend Waterworks through a local private
　　　company.

South Essex. Railways, G.E. and L.T.S. Distance from London, 12 miles.
Authority, South Essex Waterworks Company.
Chairman, Courtenay C. S. Fooks.
Engineer, Bernard W. Bryan, M.I.M.E., and C.E.
Secretary, C. J. Fox.
Office, Hornchurch Road, Romford.
Share capital paid up—10 per cent., £85,700 ; last dividend, £8 10s. per cent.
    „   „   „ — 7   „   £75,000 ;   „   £5 19s.   „
    „   „   „ — 5   „   £100,000 ;   „   £4 5s.   „
    „   „   5 per cent. Preference, £100,000 ;   „   £5 0s.   „
    4   „   Debentures, £75,350.
Works established, 1861. Special Acts, 1861, 1882, 1901.
Area supplied—Havering-atte-Bower, Shenfield, Brentwood, Romford, Barking,
    Hornchurch, Upminster, Dagenham. Gt. Ilford, Rainham, Wennington, Aveley,
    Purfleet, Ockendon (North and South), West Thurrock, Little Thurrock, Grays,
    Horndon-on-the-Hill, Stanford-le-Hope, Bulphan, and Orsett.
Total population of area supplied, 166,570.
Sources of supply, wells and borings to the chalk.
Character of water, moderately hard.
Storage capacity, 5,000,000 gals.
Annual supply of water, 1,352,000,000 gals.
Assessment charge, 6 and $6\frac{1}{4}$ per cent. on rateable value.
Price for 1,000 gals., trade and municipal purposes, 10d. to 8d.

Southall (supplied by South West Suburban).

South Hants District. Railway, L.S.W.
Authority, South Hants Water Works Co.
Chairman, W. E. Darwin, J.P.
Manager, G. Greenslade, 21, Shirley Road, Southampton.
Engineer, Baldwin Latham.
Secretary, E. G. Burnett.
Office, 2, High Street, Southampton.
Share capital paid up, ordinary, £233,997; preference, £10,100 ; Debenture
    Stock, £50,000.
Dividends, $9\frac{1}{2}$ per cent. on the 10 per cent. maximum, $6\frac{13}{16}$ per cent. on the
    7 per cent. maximum, $4\frac{3}{4}$ per cent. on the 5 per cent. maximum.
Works established, 1876. Special Acts, 1876, 1878, 1894, 1899.
Annual supply of water, 620,019,490 gals.
Daily consumption per head, 20·41 gals., including trade.
Source of supply, springs in chalk.
Storage capacity, 4,400,000 gals.
Character of water, 8° hardness.
Number of meters, 295.
Scale of charges—assessment, 6 per cent. on R.R.
Price per 1,000 gals., 1s. 6d. trade.

Southminster Water Supply, Essex.
Authority, Rural District Council of Maldon.
Clerk, A. W. Freeman
Works at Asheldham.

South Molton, Devon. Railway, G.W. Distance from London, 197 miles.
Authority, Corporation.
Secretary, Town Clerk.
Total population of area supplied, 3,100.

SOUTH MOLTON—*continued*.

Daily consumption per head, domestic and trade, 25 gals.
Sources of supply, spring and upland surface works from Exmoor.
Character of water, soft.
System of filtration, gravel.

Southowram (supplied by HALIFAX).

South Oxfordshire.

Authority, South Oxfordshire Water and Gas Company.
Chairman, H. J. Robus.
Secretary, F. C. Robus, F.C.I.S.
Resident Engineer, L. S. Geer.
Office, 2 and 3, Norfolk Street, Strand, London, W.C.
Share capital paid up on water undertaking (December 31st, 1906), £60,572 3s. 9d.
Last dividend, 2½ per cent.
Annual profit after paying interest and all charges for 1906, £1,882 18s. 1d.
Loan capital paid up, £2,600 ; rate of interest, 4, 4½, and 5 per cent.
Works established, 1888.   P.O. 1888, 1902 and 1903.   Special Act, 1905.
Parliamentary area of supply—

Baldwin	Eye	Pishill
Benson	Goring-on-Thames	Pyrton
Berrick Salome	Harpsden	Rotherfield
Bix	Ipsden	Rotherfield Greys
Brightwell	Kidmore	Shiplake
Britwell Prior	Mapledurham	Shirburn
Britwell Salome	Mongewell	Sonning
Checkendon	Nettlebed	South Stoke
Crowmarsh Giffard	Newington	Stonor
Cuxham	Newnham Murren	Streatley
Dorchester	North Stoke	Swyncombe
Drayton St. Leonard	Nuffield	Warborough
Dunsden	Whitchurch	Watlington
Ewelme	Peppard	

The Mains are laid, and supply afforded in—

Benson	Goring-on-Thames	Rotherfield Greys
Bix	Kidmore	Rotherfield Peppard
Checkendon	Mongewell	Stoke Row
Cray's Pond	Newnham	Streatley
Crowmarsh	Newnham Murren	Whitchurch
Gifford	North Stoke	Woodcote

Source of supply, wells.
Analysis of water—

Physical character- *istics—*	From Crowmarsh. Oct. 24th, 1906.	From Gravel Hill, Peppard. Nov. 3rd, 1906.	From High St., Streatley. Nov. 17th, 1906.
Colour when examined in a tube 2 ft. long ...	Pale blue, clear.	Pale yellowish, clear.	Pale yellow, clear.
Suspended matter ...	Nil.	Nil.	Nil.
Smell when heated to 100° F.　...　...	Nil.	Nil.	Nil.
Total hardness (Clark's Scale)　...　...	18°	18°	18°
Chemical Results—	Grains per gal.	Grains per gal.	Grains per gal.
Total solid matter ...	24·5	21·7	24·5
Chlorine...　...　...	·99	·99	·99
„ equal to chloride of sodium　...　...	1·64	1·64	1·64

SOUTH OXFORDSHIRE—*continued.*

Chemical Results.	Grains per gal.	Grains per gal.	Grains per gal.
Lead and copper ...	Nil.	Nil.	Nil.
Iron	Nil.	Nil.	Nil.
Phosphoric acid ...	—	—	Nil.
Nitrogen as ammonia ...	·0003	Nil.	·0005
„ albuminoid ammonia ...	·0005	·0005	·0025
„ nitrites ...	Nil.	Nil.	Nil.
„ nitrates ...	·4477	·4032	·2795
Oxygen absorbed by organic matter from solution of permanganate of potash, at 80° F. in 15 minutes	Nil.	·0028	·0028
Do. do. in 4 hours	·0084	·0084	·0168
Remarks	Free from pollution with animal organic matter, and good for drinking and domestic purposes.	There is no indication of contamination with animal organic matter. It is bright, clear, and an excellent supply for drinking and domestic purposes.	Free from animal contamination, and is an excellent supply for drinking and domestic purposes.

Storage capacity in service reservoirs, 3,000,000 gals.
Head on distributing mains—maximum, 460 feet.
Total quantity of water supplied per annum, about 25,000,000 gals.
Charges authorized (domestic)—Low Level, 6 to 8 per cent. on rental value.
                 High Level, 7½ to 10 per cent. on rental value.
    „   „   by meter, 1s. 6d. to 2s. 6d. per 1,000 gals.
Number of meters, about 125.
Length of supply mains, 50 miles.

Southport.
Authority, Southport, Birkdale and West Lancashire Joint Water Board.
Chairman, Thomas P. Griffith, J.P.
Clerk, Alleyne Brown.
Manager, A. Watchorn,
Resident Engineer, G. H. Abbott.
Consulting Engineer, H. Rofe, M.I.C.E.
Office, Portland Street, Southport.
Works established, 1854 ; purchased, 1902. Special Acts, 1901-1905.
Total population supplied, 92,000.
District of supply, Ainsdale, Aughton, Altcar, Banks, Bickerstaffe, Birkdale, Downholland, Formby, Halsall, Magbull, North Meols, Scarisbrick, Southport.
Source of supply, wells and borings at Aughton, Springfield, and Bickerstaffe.
Character of water, very pure, moderate hardness. No filtration, no softening.
Storage capacity, 6,000,000 gals.

South Shields. *See* SUNDERLAND.

South Staffordshire. Railways, L.N.W., M., G.W.
Authority, South Staffordshire Waterworks Company.
Chairman, Frank James, J.P., D.L.
Secretary, G. J. Sparrow. Office, Paradise Street, Birmingham.
Engineer-in-chief, H. Ashton Hill, M.I.C.E., 3, St. Augustine's Road, Birmingham.
Total capital invested, £1,415,191.
Current rate of dividend, 7 per cent.

SOUTH STAFFORDSHIRE—*continued.*

Works established, 1853.
Special Acts—
    The South Staffordshire Waterworks Act, 1853; the South Staffordshire
    Waterworks Amendment Acts, 1857 and 1864; the South Staffordshire
    Waterworks Acts, 1866, 1875, 1878, 1893, 1901, P.O. 1903; also the Dudley
    Waterworks Act, 1834; the Dudley Waterworks (Amendment) Act, 1852;
    the Burton-upon-Trent Water Act, 1861.
Total population of area of control, 1891, 546,258 ; 1901, 623,159.
Total number of consumers, 134,560.
Estimated population actually supplied, 655,285.
Towns and villages within area of control—
    Burton, Burton Extra, Horninglow, Stapenhill, Winshill, Branstone, Stretton,
    Barton-under-Needwood, Whittington, Shenstone, Hammerwich, Burnt-
    wood, Alrewas, Shire Oak, Lichfield St. Michael's, Rugeley (part of),
    Cannock, Huntington, Essington (part of), Walsall (including part of
    Rushall within the Parliamentary boundary), Rushall, Pelsall, Aldridge,
    Great Barr, Walsall Wood, Ogley Hay, Norton Canes, Darlaston, Wednes-
    bury, Sutton Coldfield, West Bromwich, Rowley, Tipton, Sedgley, Coseley,
    Brockmoor, Pensnett, Kingswinford, St Mary's, Brierley Hill, Quarry Bank,
    Dudley, Smethwick, Oldbury, Warley, Cradley, Quinton, Hasbury, Hawn,
    Cakemore, Hill, Halesowen.
Annual supply of water (1906)—
    For all purposes ...   .   4,900,728,714 gals.
Maximum day's consumption, 18,477,415 gals.
Pumping stations, 15.
Reservoirs, 14.
Number of meters in use, 3,503.
Length of distributing mains, 800 miles.

Southwark and Vauxhall Water Co. *See* METROPOLITAN WATER BOARD.

Southwell, Notts. (supplied by NEWARK).

South West Suburban. Railways, L.S.W. and G.W. Distance from London,
    Egham, 20 miles.
    Authority, South-West Suburban Water Company.
    Office, Egham, Surrey.
    Share capital paid up, £170,000.
    Loan, £24,600 4½ per cent. debenture stock.
    Towns and villages in the area supplied, Egham, Staines, Southall, Ascot, Sun-
      ninghill, Sunningdale, Cranford, Bedfont, Feltham, Thorpe, Old Windsor,
      Norwood, Hanworth, Stanmore, Ashford, Laleham.
    Works established, 1877, amalgamation, 1883.
    Total population of area supplied, 72,000.
    Annual consumption, about 290,000,000 gals.
    Sources of supply, artesian wells and Thames.
    Character of water, very good.
    Price for 1,000 gallons, varies.

Southwick, Sussex (supplied by BRIGHTON).

Southwick (supplied by SUNDERLAND).

Southwold, Suffolk. Railways, G.E. and S. Distance from London, 109½ miles.
    Authority, the Southwold Waterworks Co., Ld.
    Chairman, T. Cave.
    Secretary, Ernest R. Cooper.
    Superintendent, Engineer, and Collector, G. Frederick Lockyer.

SOUTHWOLD—*continued.*

Office, Southwold.
Share capital paid up, £3,290
Loan   „   „   £4,196
Dividend, 45 per cent. ordinary, 5 per cent. preference.
Works established, 1886.
Total number of consumers, 3,000 normal ; holiday season, over 6,000.
Average death rate, 10 3 per 1,000.
Area supplied, Southwold, Reydon, and Easton Bavento.
Source of supply in use, wells in craig and gravel.
Character of water, excellent, fairly soft.
System of filtration, none.
Service reservoir (one), capacity, 47,000 gals., covered.
Daily consumption per head, under 10 gals.
Pumping stations, Southwold, gas engine and 6-7 × 2 feet deep well pumps,
    „   „   Reydon, steam power.
Number of meters, 43.
Assessment charges, payable quarterly—
   Dwelling houses for domestic purposes only, and including one w.c. :
    Rateable value under £20 per annum, 7½ per cent. minimum, 8s. 8d. per annum.
    Over £20 per annum and under £40, 7   „
    „ £40   „   „   ., £60, 6½   „
    „ £60   „   6   „
   Hotels, public-houses, beer-houses, &c., where no brewing is done, same rate
    as above, with extra for horses, carriages, cows, &c.   Extra w.c, 10s. each
    per annum ; baths (not over 50 gals.), 10s. per annum.
Price per 1,000 gals., trade—
   Minimum charge   ...   12s. per quarter, exclusive of meter rent.
   Under 10,000 gals. per quarter   ...   .   12s.
    Over 10,000 gals. and under 60,000 gals. per quarter   1s. 2d.
    „ 60,000   „   „   100,000   „   „   1s. 1d.
    „ 100,000   „   „   200,000   „   „   1s. 0d.
    „ 200,000   „   „   400,000   „   „   0s. 11d.
    „ 400,000   „   „   600,000   „   „   0s. 10d.
    „ 600,000   „   „   1,000,000   „   „   0s. 9d.
   Meters to be provided and kept in repair by the consumers, or rented from the
    Company, who will maintain them at a charge of 15 per cent. per annum
    upon their cost and fitting to the main.

Southworth-with-Croft (supplied by WARRINGTON).

Sowerby Bridge, Yorks. Railway, L. and Y. Distance from London, 195 miles.

Authority, Urban District Council, 1863.
Chairman, Councillor John Bates.
Manager, John Hopkinson.
Office, Town Buildings.
Capital expended, £10,353. Loans outstanding, £349.
Works established, 1856. Special Acts, 1861, 1863, 1884.
Total population supplied, 11,900.
Average death rate, 9·28 per 1,000.
Area supplied, 670 acres
Source of supply, Halifax Corporation Works.
Character of water, pure, soft.
Storage capacity, 250,000 gals.
Head on distributing mains—maximum, 340 ft. ; minimum, 50 ft.
Annual supply of water (1906), 58,646,000 gals.
Daily consumption—through meter, 7¾ ; not by meter, 12¾ gals. per day ; trade,
   44,000 gals. per day.

SOWERBY BRIDGE—*continued*.

Maximum day's supply, 262,000 gals. in August, 1906.
Scale of charges.
Price per 1.000 gals., 10d. for manufacturing purposes, and 1s. for domestic
purposes, less discounts of 10, 15 and 20 per cent. on accounts under £1, £1 to
£4 and over £4 respectively, if paid within 28 days.
Number of meters, 581.
Length of mains, 15 miles.

Spalding, Lincs. Railways, G.N. and G.E. Distance from London, 93 miles.
Authority, Company.
Population supplied, 9,385.
No returns supplied.

Spannton (supplied by KIRKBY MOORSIDE).

Speldhurst (supplied by TUNBRIDGE WELLS).

Spennymoor (supplied by WEARDALE AND CONSETT WATER Co.).

Spetchley (supplied by WORCESTER).

Spettisley (supplied by BLANDFORD).

Spital, Cheshire (supplied by BIRKENHEAD).

Spittal.
Authority, Private Water Co.
Character of water, good, but quantity insufficient in dry seasons.

Spondon (supplied by DERBY).

Springfield and Great Baddow, Essex.
Authority, Rural District Council.
Total population of area supplied, about 6,000
Source of supply, spring.
Storage capacity, 40,000 in tank on tower, 96 ft. high.

Springhead (supplied by OLDHAM).

Stafford. Railways, L.N.W. Distance from London, 130 miles.
Authority, Corporation of Stafford.
Chairman, Alderman Lovatt, J.P.
Town Clerk, Richard Battle.
Borough Engineer and Surveyor, William Blackshaw, A.M.I.C.E.
Office, Borough Hall, Stafford.
Total capital invested, including loans, £46,600.
Towns and villages within the area of control, Milford, Brocton, Walton, Weeping
Cross, Radford, Queensville, Moss Pitt, Dean's Hill, Tillington, Tixall.
Works established, 1890.
Special Acts—Stafford Corporation Acts, 1876 and 1880. No Provisional Order.
Total population of area of control, 1901, 25,800.
Total number of consumers, 4,707 properties supplied.
Estimated population actually supplied, 25,800.
Annual supply of water (year ending March 31st, 1907), 215,234,200 gals.
For domestic purposes...   ...   .   170,256,200 ,,
,, trade and municipal purposes   ...   ...   44,978,000 ,,
Maximum day's consumption, 638,000 gals.

STAFFORD—*continued.*

Total quantity of water drawn per annum (year ending March 31st, 1907)—·
    From deep wells or borings ... ... 215,234,200 gals.
Source of supply in use—deep wells sunk in the Bunter pebble beds, new red
    sandstone formation at Milford.
Corporation has secured freehold of the well, pumping station, and service reser-
    · voir, but has no control over the drainage area.
Natural rest level of water below surface, 12·69 feet; above ordnance datum,
    234·69 feet.
Level of water below surface (when pumping 600,000 gals. per day), 23·10 feet.
Geological— · ·
    Surface formation of drainage areas, conglomerate pebble beds of the new red
        sandstone formation.
    Strata or formation yielding springs, ditto.
    Nature of subsoil yielding water, ditto.
    Strata tapped by wells or borings, ditto.
    Locality and extent of outcrop of same, Milford and Brocton, on the Trent Valley
        branch of the L. and N.W. Railway, at least 4 square miles.
Filtration, none.
Pumping station, Milford.
    The boilers, engines, and pumps are in duplicate, and each boiler, engine, and
        pump is capable of lifting about 41,000 gals. per hour. The well is 42 feet
        deep from the surface of the ground, but the pebble beds have been proved
        by boring to a depth of 197 feet.
Service reservoir, Stafford Plantation, capacity, 577,575 gals, covered.
Number of meters in use, 88.
Analysis of Milford well water—

	Grains per gallon.
Total solid matter dried at 212° Fah.	14·70.
Free and saline ammonia	0·000.
Albuminoid ammonia	0·000.
Nitric nitrogen	0·31.
Combined chlorine	1·19.
Oxygen absorbed in 4 hours at 80° Fah.	0·005.
Appearance...	Clear.
Colour through 2 feet	Very pale bluish tinge.
Hardness before boiling	9·63°.
„ after „	5·10°.
Temporary hardness	4·53.
Bacteriological exam. :—	
On gelatine at 20° C.	56.
On agar—agar at 37°	1.
„ „ acidified and phenolised	0.

Assessment charge, domestic, 5 per cent. on rateable value.
Price per 1,000 gals., trade, 1s. 6d. to 1s.
Death rate, 17·53 per 1,000.

Staffordshire Potteries. Railways, L.N.W. and North Stafford. Distance from
    London, 147 miles.
    Authority, Staffordshire Potteries Water Works Co.
    Chairman, James Maddock.
    Secretary, Horace J. Wildin.
    Manager and Engineer, G. B. H. Soame.
    Office, Albion Street, Hanley.
    Towns and villages in the area supplied, Longton, Fenton, Stoke-on-Trent,
        Hanley, Burslem, Tunstall, Newcastle-under-Lyme, Kidsgrove, Smallthorne,
        Silverdale, Chesterton, and other outlying districts.
    Works established, 1846. Special Act, 1847, 1853 to 1888.

STAFFORDSHIRE POTTERIES—*continued.*

Share capital, £325,285; last dividends, 10 and 7 per cent.
Loan   „   £104,950 at 4 and 3½ per cent.
Total population of area supplied, 310,000.
Annual supply of water, 2,810,000 gals.
Daily consumption per head, domestic, 20 gals.; trade, 5 gals.
Maximum day's supply, 8,200,000 gals. in July and August.
Sources of supply, wells and springs, new red sandstone.
Impounding reservoirs, capacity 330,000,000, for compensation only.
Service reservoir, capacity, 8,000,000 gals.
Character of water, excellent; total hardness, 11°.
Average death rate, 20 per 1,000.
Number of meters, about 950.
Head on distributing mains—maximum, 345 ft.; minimum, 23 ft.
Scale of charges—assessment, A. 5 to 4 per cent. on R.V.
Price for 1,000 gals., 8d. to 3d. per scale.
Total water rent received, about £59,500.

Staines, Middlesex (supplied by SOUTH-WEST SUBURBAN).

Stalybridge (supplied by ASHTON-UNDER-LYNE).

Stamford Waterworks, Lincolnshire.   Railways, G.N., M., L.N.W.   Distance
from London, 92½ miles.
Owner, the Most Hon. the Marquis of Exeter.
Manager, Engineer, and Secretary, Thomas Booth, Burghley Estate Office, Stamford.
Consulting engineer, J. Eunson, C.E., Northampton.
Total capital invested in undertaking, £35,288.
Annual profit, including capital charges, £1,165.
Works established, about 1768.
Special Acts, the Stamford Water Acts, 1837, 1877.
Total population of area of control, 1881, 8,000; 1891, 8,358; 1901, 9,000.
Estimated population actually supplied, 8,500.
Average death rate, 15·5 per 1,000.
Area of control, the Borough of Stamford, Wothorpe, St. Martin's Without, and
Whittering.
Sources of supply in use—surface springs, Charcoal Hollow, Whitewater.
Well at Wothorpe.   The well would at a depth of   yield 150,000 gals.
per day.
Maximum annual rainfall over drainage area, 25·49 inches (1892 to 1901).
Minimum   „   „   17·41   „
Average   „   „   21·44   „   (10 years).
Population on drainage area, 11·82.
Nature of cultivation of drainage area—well cultivated; about half is arable
land.
The proprietor of the works owns the entire drainage area.
Natural rest level of water... { below } ordnance datum { 237·3 feet Whitewater.
below surface   ...   ... { above }   „   „   { 176·3   „   Wothorpe
Strata or formation yielding springs, lime and iron stone.
No pumping done.
Water supplied has gradually improved in quality, as the management has
secured sources of supply nearer to the springs; no recent analysis.
Character of water—charcoal hollow, 16·5°; and Wothorpe, 18° hardness.
Filtration, none.
Head on distributing mains—maximum, 152 ft.; minimum, 95 ft.
Water is not softened.
Annual supply of water for all purposes—47,500,000 gals.

STAMFORD WATERWORKS—*continued.*

Total quantity of water drawn per annum—
    Surface springs (Whitewater) ... ... 15,330,000 gals.
    Shallow wells or subsoil (Wothorpe) ... 30,660,000 „
Estimated total quantity of water available per annum—
    Surface springs (Whitewater) ... ... 17,155,000 gals.
    Shallow wells or subsoil (Wothorpe) ... 37,396,440 „
Maximum day's consumption, 142,700 gals. in August, 1907.
Average daily supply, 14·5 to 15 gals. for all purposes, about one quarter of this
    is for trade purposes.
Assessment charge by house rental.
Authorised charge by meter, 1s. 6d. to 8d. per 1,000 gals.
Present   „   „   „   9d. to 10d. per 1,000 gals.
Number of meters in use, 52.
Length of supply mains, 18½ miles; distributing mains, 12½ miles.

Stanbury (supplied by KEIGHLEY).

Stanground (supplied by PETERBOROUGH).

Stanley (supplied by WEARDALE AND CONSETT WATER CO.).

Stanmore, Great and **Little** (supplied by COLNE VALLEY WATER CO.).

Stannington (supplied by NEWCASTLE-ON-TYNE).

Stanton-by-Dale (supplied by ILKESTON).

Stanway Rural District, part of (supplied by COLCHESTER).

Stanwell (supplied by SOUTH-WEST SUBURBAN).

Stansted Mountfitchet, Essex.
    Authority, Stansted Water Co.
    Source of supply, wells in the chalk.
    Population supplied, about 2,500.

Stapenhill (supplied by SOUTH STAFFS. WATERWORKS CO.)

Stapleton (supplied by HINCKLEY).

Staplefield (supplied by CUCKFIELD).

Starbeck (supplied by HARROGATE).

Starling (supplied by BURY).

Station Town, Co. Durham (supplied by WINGATE).

Stepps Road (supplied by GLASGOW).

Stevenage, Herts. Railway, G.N. Distance from London, 28½ miles.
    Authority, Urban District Council.
    Clerk, William Onslow Times.
    Office, Council Offices, Stevenage.
    Area supplied, Urban District of Stevenage, and a few cottages in the parish of
      Great Wymondley.
    Total population of area supplied, about 4,100.

Stevenage—_continued._

Source of supply, deep well in the chalk at Rooksnest, Stevenage; well, 200 feet; bore, 425 feet.
Scale of charges—assessment, rateable value.
Cottages of and under £8, for which rates are paid by owner, 6s. per annum; private house exceeding £8, 5 per cent. on rateable value for domestic purp)ses only; houses attached to and rated with shops, 7½ per cent. on rateable value; for trade purposes, butchers, fishmongers, blacksmiths, 5s. each; bakers and dairies, 10s. each; slaughter-houses, 15s.; baths, 10s.; horses, cows, and carriages, 5s.; stand pipes, 10s. No extra charge for gardens under 10 poles.
Price per 1,000 gals., 1s., minimum charge, £2, plus meter rent, 10s. per annum.

Stevenston (supplied by Irvine).

Stirling, Scotland.
Authority, Stirling Waterworks Commissioners.
Chairman, James Thomson.
Engineer, And. H. Goudie, Burgh Surveyor.
Secretary, D. B. Morris, Town Clerk.
Office, Burgh Buildings, Stirling.
Loans outstanding, £26,946.
Works established, 1848. Special Acts, 1848 to 1893.
Total population supplied, 24,746.
Average death rate, 16·52 per 1,000.
Towns and villages in the area supplied, Stirling, St. Ninians, Logie, Bannockburn, Whins-le-Milton, Causewayhead, etc.
Sources of supply, surface drainage. Impounding reservoirs on Touch Hills. Storage capacity, 195,000,000 gals.
Character of water, good potable water, 3·5° hardness.
System of filtration, sand.
Average daily consumption per head—domestic, 51·02; trade, 14·54.
Scale of charges—assessment charge, 8d. in the £ on rental value.
Charge for municipal purposes, £10. Price per 1,000 gals.—trade, 6·4d.
Length of supply mains, 5 miles; distributing mains, 31 miles.

Stockbridge (supplied by Sheffield).

Stockland Green (supplied by Tunbridge Wells).

Stockport, Cheshire. Railways, L.N.W., M., G.C. and Cheshire Lines. Distance from London, 177½ miles.
Authority, Stockport Corporation.
Chairman, Alderman Albert Johnson, J.P.
Engineer, Thomas Molyneux, A.M.I.C.E.
Office, St. Peter's Square, Stockport.
Works established, 1820; purchased by Corporation, 1899, by Act of Parliament.
Total population of area supplied, 160.000.
District of supply, County Borough of Stockport, Urban District of Alderley Edge, Bredbury and Romiley, Cheadle and Gatley, Handforth, Hazel Grove, Heaton Norris, Marple, New Mills, Wilmslow. Townships of Chorley, Disley, Lyme, Lyme Handley, Nether Alderley, Pownall Fee, Poynton, Woodford.
Sources of supply—watershed near Disley, borehole in New Red Sandstone, and Manchester Corporation Works.
Character of water—reservoir water, about 5° to 6° hardness.
              well   „   „   14°   „

Stockport—*continued.*

Filtration, sand; softening (well water), Archbutt Deeley; hardness after treatment, 6°.

Storage capacity, impounding reservoirs, .158,000,000 gals.; service reservoirs, 10,000,000 gals.

Pressure on distributing mains—maximum, 180 lbs.; minimum, 30 lbs. per sq. in

Annual supply of water, 1,312,000,000 gals.

Maximum day's supply, 4,100,000 gals., in July.

Daily consumption per head—domestic 18 ; trade, 5 gals.

Number of meters, about 1,200.

Price per 1,000 gals.—from 2s. to 9d., according to scale.

Stocksfield (supplied by Newcastle-on-Tyne).

Stockton and Middlesbrough. *See* Tees Valley Water Board.

Stockton Heath, Lancs. (supplied by Warrington).

Stoke (supplied by Nottingham).

Stoke, Surrey, part of (supplied by Guildford).

Stoke-on-Trent (supplied by Staffordshire Potteries Water Co.).

Stoke Poges, Bucks. (supplied by Slough).

Stoke Row (supplied by (South Oxfordshire).

Stoneferry (supplied by Hull).

Stonegrave, Yorks. (supplied by Kirkby Moorside).

Stonehaven, Kincardineshire, N.B. Railway, Caledonian. Distance from London, 512 miles.

Authority, Stonehaven Town Council.

Chairman, Provost Torry.

Secretary, D. C. Booth, Town Clerk.

Engineer in charge, Geo. Murdoch, Burgh Surveyor.

Office, 46, Barclay Street, Stonehaven.

Consulting Engineers, Jenkins & Marr, Aberdeen.

Total capital invested, including loans, £8,560.

Loans outstanding (1907), £5,848.

Works established, 1887—Public Health Act.

Total population of area of control—1891, 4,500; 1901, 4,577.

District of supply, part of Dunnottar and part of Fetteresso.

Estimated population actually supplied, 7,000 holiday season, 5,000 normal.

Average death rate, 16·2 per 1,000.

Average daily supply per head, 38 gals. at dryest season.

Service Reservoirs—

No. 1 Fetteresso	...	capacity, 164,000 gals., covered.
No. 2 „	...	„ 164,000 „ „
No. 1 Dunnottar	...	„ 7,000 „ „
No. 2 „	...	„ 82,000 „ „

Number of meters in use, 14.

Analysis of Fetteresso Water Supply by County Analyst, 3rd June, 1902.

One million parts of this water yield—

Free ammonia	...	...	...	...	·014
Albuminoid ammonia	...	...	...	...	·018
Carbonate of lime, etc.	...	...	...	...	39·69
Chlorine	...	...	...	...	12·00
Nitrogen as nitrates	...	...	...	...	None

STONEHAVEN—*continued.*

Nitrites	None
Hardness in Clark's degrees	2¼ degrees.
Lead or other metals	None

Annual supply of water—

For domestic purposes	99,000,000 gals.
„ trade „	1,825,000 „

Total quantity of water drawn per annum—

From surface springs, approximately ... 101,105,000 gals.

Estimated total quantity of water available, undetermined.

Source of supply in use—spring 6 miles to the west of town.

Maximum annual rainfall over drainage area, 30 inches.

Minimum   „   „   „   25   „

Average   „   „   „   26   „

Population on drainage area, none.

Nature of ditto—moor in Fetteresso ; arable in Dunnottar.

Strata or formation yielding springs—gneiss in Fetteresso, old red sandstone in Dunnottar.

Head on distributing mains—max., 120 ft., min., 75 ft.

Length of supply mains, 10 miles ; distributing mains, 10 miles.

Character of water, soft ; 2¼° hardness.

Scale of Charges—

Assessment, 6½d. per £ on rental ; trade, 6d, per 1,000 gals.

Stonehouse, Devon (supplied by PLYMOUTH).

Stonehouse, Scotland (supplied by DISTRICT OF THE MIDDLE WARD OF LANARKSHIRE).

Stones Green (supplied by TENDRING HUNDRED).

Stony Stratford, Bucks. Railway, L.N.W. Distance from London, 54 miles.

Authority, Rural District Council of Stratford and Wolverton.

Chairman of Council, G. M. Fitzsimmons, J.P.

Clerk to authority, W. R. Parrott.

Manager, Alfred E. Abbott, Engineer and Surveyor R.D.C.

Office, The Square, Wolverton.

Works first constructed, 1889.

Loans outstanding, £1,463.

Total population supplied, 4,500.

Average death rate, 11·47, period 8 years.

Source of supply, wells and borings to water-carrying seams of sand at bottom of the oolite.

Towns and villages in the area supplied, Stony Stratford East, Stony Stratford West, Wolverton, St. Mary's and Calverton.

Analysis of water, 9th May, 1902—

Description, the sample is clear and bright.

Odour, none.

Appearance in two-foot tube, pale bluish tint.

The results of the analysis are stated in grains per gallon.

	grains.
Total dissolved solid matter	38·92.
Chlorine in chlorides	2·0.
Ammonia, free and saline	·005.
ditto albuminoid	003.
Nitrogen in nitrates	·45.
ditto in nitrites	·0.
Oxygen required to oxidise organic matter (in 3 hours)	·012.

Remarks.—The total mineral constituents and the chlorides and nitrates have not changed in any important degree ; the proportion of organic matter remains very small.

Stony Stratford—*continued.*

The water is an unpolluted supply, and of good quality for drinking and domestic purposes, but rather hard.

Filtration, unnecessary.

Storage capacity, 37,000 gals.

Pressure on distributing mains—maximum, 65 lbs. ; minimum, 30 lbs. per sq. in.

Annual supply of water, about 20,000 000 gals.

Average daily supply per head—domestic, 10·8 gals. ; trade, &c., from 1·2 gals. to 1·7 gals. (say 1·4 average).

Maximum day's supply, 62,000 gals.

Assessment charge, domestic, 5 per cent on net rateable value.

Price, per 1,000 gals. per meter ... $\begin{cases} \text{under} & 50,000 \text{ gals, 1s. 6d.} \\ \text{,,} & 100,000 \text{ ,, 1s. 3d.} \\ \text{over} & 100,000 \text{ ,, 1s. 0d.} \end{cases}$

Number of meters, 5.

Length of mains, about 4 miles.

Storkingford, Warwick (supplied by Nuneaton).

Stourbridge. Railway, G.W. Distance from London, 121 miles.

Authority, Stourbridge Waterworks Company, Ltd.

Chairman, William Blow Collis.

Secretary, Harry Barratt.

Engineer and Managing Director, E. B. Marten.

Office, 10, Hagley Road, Stourbridge.

Total capital invested, including loans, £65,433 10s.

Dividend—Preference, 4 per cent. ; original (including B and C) 8 per cent. D. shares, 7 per cent.

Towns and villages within area of control, with population of each (1901 Census)—

Stourbridge...	
Oldswinford	16,299
Wollaston ...	
Amblecote ...	3,128
Pedmore ...	489
Lye ...	7,197
Wollescote ...	3,775
Wordsley, portion of Kingswinford	estimated 4,000
Hagley	1,399
Clent	978

Works established, 1854.

Special Acts, Stourbridge Waterworks Act, 1854; Stourbridge Water Orders, 1879 and 1899.

Total population of area of control, 1891, 36,519 ; 1901, 39,741.

Total number of consumers, 8,423.

Estimated population actually supplied, 35,000.

Annual supply of water (1906)—

For domestic purposes ...	522,197,975 gals.
,, trade ,, ...	37,350,000 ,,
,, municipal ,, ...	{ only water carts and flushing chambers.

Maximum day's consumption, 1,817,864 gals. Sept., 1906.

Total quantity of water drawn per annum (year 1906)—

Deep wells or borings ... 559,547,975 gals.

Estimated total quantity of water available per annum—

Deep wells ... 900,000,000 gals.

All the wells are lined, and the boreholes piped, so that the supply all comes from about the level of the sea.

Sources of supply in use—

Deep wells or borings situated at Mill Meadow, Coalbournbrook, and Tack. See sketch attached.

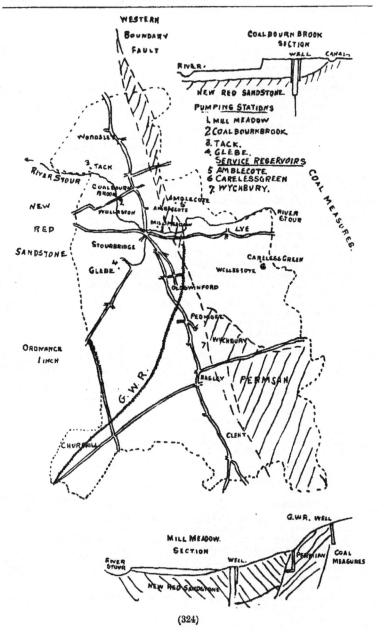

STOURBRIDGE—*continued.*

    Natural rest level of water below surface, 20 feet, 207 feet above Ordnance datum.
    Level of water below surface when pumping, 30 feet.
    Strata tapped by wells or borings, new red sandstone.
    Extent of outcrop, several square miles. See sketch.

Pumping stations,	Mill Meadow	...	...	capacity,	600,000	gals. per day.
„	Coalbournbrook	...	...	„	750,000	„
„	Tack	...	...	„	700,000	„
Service reservoirs,	Amblecote	...	...	„	300,000	„ covered.
„ „	Careless Green	...	...	„	90,000	„ „
„ „	Hagley	...	...	„	60,000	„ „

    Death rate, 16 per 1,000.
    Number of meters in use, 62.
    Analysis of water, August 3rd, 1904—

	Mill Meadow.	Coalbournbrook.
Total solid matter dried at 212° Fah. ...	47·6	42·0 gr. per gal.
Free and saline ammonia	0·000	0·000 „
Albuminoid ammonia	0·000	0·000 „
Nitric nitrogen	1·08	1·00 „
Combined chlorine	6·16	4·48 „
Oxygen absorbed in 4 hours, at 80° Fah.	0·003	0·001 „
Appearance	clear	clear
Colour through 2 feet	very pale blu-ish green tinge.	very pale blu-ish green tinge.
Hardness before boiling	26·34°	25·88° „
„ after „	15·48°	15·26° „
Temporary hardness	10·810°	10·62° „

Both these waters are exceedingly pure, organically, their worst feature for domestic purposes is their hardness.

	Tack.
Total solid matter dried at 212° Fah.	24·5 gr. per. gal.
Free and saline ammonia	0·000 „
Albuminoid ammonia	0·007 „
Nitric nitrogen	0·63 „
Combined chlorine	1·96 „
Oxygen absorbed in 4 hours at 80° Fah.	0·000 „
Appearance	clear „
Colour through two feet	very pale bluish green tinge.
Hardness, temporary	8·30° „
„ before boiling	15·30° „
„ after boiling	7·00° „

This water is exceedingly good, organically, and in all respects excellent for drinking and domestic use.

    Assessment charge, 8¼ per cent. on rateable value up to £42 10s., and six per cent. above that figure.
    Scale of charges—price per 1,000 gals., 1s. to 8d.

Stourport (supplied by KIDDERMINSTER).

Stowmarket, Suffolk.
    Owners, private.
    Source of supply, well.

Stranraer, Wigtownshire. Railways, Caledonian and G.S.W. Distance from London, 400 miles.
    Authority, Town Council.
    Engineer, John Douglas, 4, Academy Street.
    Works established, 1850.
    Total population supplied, 6,000.
    Daily consumption per head, domestic, 35 gals.
    Source of supply, gravitation.

Stranraer—*continued.*

Storage capacity, 35,000,000 gals.
System of filtration, gravel and sand.
Length of mains, about 14 miles.
Assessment charge, 1s. in the £.

Stratford-on-Avon, Warwick. Railways, G.W., L.N.W. Distance from London.
110¼ miles.
Authority, Corporation.
Population supplied, 8,318.
No returns supplied.

Strathblane (supplied by GLASGOW).

Street Issa (supplied by RUABON).

Streatley (supplied by (SOUTH OXFORDSHIRE).

Strensal Camp and **Village** (supplied by YORK).

Stretford (supplied by MANCHESTER).

Stretton (supplied by SOUTH STAFFS. WATERWORKS Co.).

Stretton (supplied by WARRINGTON).

Strood, Kent. Railways, L.C.D. & S.E. Distance from London, 31 miles.
Authority, Corporation of Rochester.
Chairman, Charles Willis, J.P.
Clerk to Authority, Apsley Kennette.
Inspector, William T. Patterson.
Consulting Engineer, Wm. Banks, A.M.I.C.E.
Office, Guildhall, Rochester.
Loans outstanding, £17,033 17s. 7d.
Annual profit, including "capital charges," £500.
Works established, 1849 ; taken over by Corporation, 1880.
Population supplied with water, 15,635.
Average death rate, 11·4.
District of supply, Strood and Frindsbury.
Source of supply, wells in the chalk.
Character of water, excellent ; total hardness, 16·3º.
Filtration, none ; softening, none.
Storage in service reservoirs, 368,000 gals.
Head on distributing mains—maximum, 265·76 ft. ; minimum, 46·22 ft.
Annual supply of water, 97,000,000 gals.
Average daily supply per head—domestic, 17·8 gals. ; trade, 3·75 gals.
Maximum day's supply, 302,000 gals. in July.
Assessment charge, 1·35 per cent. to 5 per cent on R.V.
Charge by meter, according to scale.
Number of meters, 84.
Length of supply mains, ½ mile ; distributing mains, 11½ miles.

Stroud, Glos. Railways, G.W. and M. Distance from London, 102¼ miles.
Owners Company.
Share capital paid up, £80,000. Loan, £20,000.
Works established, 1887.
Total population supplied, 42,000.
Daily consumption per head, about 20 gals.
Sources of supply, inferior oolite and Mitford sands.
Storage capacity, 1,750,000 gals.
Assessment charge, gross estimated rental.
Price per 1,000 gals., sliding scale.

Studley Roger and Studley Royal (supplied by Ripon).

Stubbins (supplied by Bury).

Stuntney Hamlet, Cambs. (supplied by Ely).

Sturry, Kent (supplied by Canterbury).

Sudbury, Suffolk. Railway, G.E. Distance from London, 58¾ miles.
　　Authority, Municipal Corporation.
　　Chairman, Alderman C. E. Mouldon, J.P.
　　Engineer and Manager, Wm. J. Tait.
　　Clerk to Authority, W. Bayly Ransom.
　　Office, Town Hall.
　　Loan outstanding, £777, March, 1906 ; interest, 3¼ per cent.
　　Works established, 1870.
　　Total population supplied, 8,000.
　　Average death rate, 16·4 for last seven years (12·6 in 1906).
　　Towns and villages in the area supplied, Sudbury, Ballingdon, and portions of
　　　　Cornard and Chilton.
　　Source of supply, well 80 ft., and deep boring, 375 feet into chalk.
　　Character of water, clear, colourless, saline residue, not affected by heat, great
　　　　organic purity.
　　Storage capacity, 300,000 gals. in service reservoir.
　　Annual supply of water, 60,000,000 to 70,000,000 gals.
　　Daily consumption per head, domestic, and trade, 17 gals.
　　Assessment charge, 4 per cent. on net annual rateable value ; double charge out-
　　　　side borough.
　　　　Price per 1,000 gals., domestic, 1s. to 9d. ; trade,
　　　　Municipal purposes, nil.
　　Total water rent received, £1,100.
　　Number of meters, 40.
　　Length of mains, about 11 miles.

Sunderland and South Shields, Durham. Railway, N.E. Distance from London,
　261 miles.
　　Authority, Sunderland and South Shields Water Co.
　　Chairman, Robt. H. Gayner, J.P.
　　Secretary, John W. Sutherland.
　　Manager and Resident Engineer, Alfred B. E. Blackburn, B.S.C., A.M.I.C.E.,
　　　　F.G.S.
　　Consulting Engineers, F. and C. Hawksley.
　　Office, John Street, Sunderland.
　　Works established, 1846.   Special acts, 1846, 1849, 1852, 1859, 1868, 1891.
　　Total population supplied, 420,000.
　　District of supply, Sunderland, South Shields, Jarrow, Hebburn, Southwick,
　　　　Hylton, Ryhope, Seaham Harbour, Murton, Easington, Shotton, &c.
　　Source of supply, wells, headings, and borings in the magnesian limestone and
　　　　underlying sand.
　　Character of water, extremely high degree of organic purity ; an excellent drink-
　　　　ing water ; about 24° hardness.
　　Average daily supply per head—domestic, 14 gals. ; special, 6 gals.
　　Total length of supply and distributing mains, 350 miles.

Sunningdale (supplied by South West Suburban).

Sunninghill (supplied by South West Suburban).

Sutton, Cheshire (supplied by Macclesfield).

Sutton, Surrey. Railway, L.B.S.C. Distance from London, 14½ miles.
　Authority, The Sutton District Water Company.
　Chairman, E. W. Martin.
　Manager and Resident Engineer, G. F. Derry.
　Secretary, E. F. Course, A.C.I.S.
　Office, Carshalton Road, Sutton.
　Consulting Engineer, W. Vaux Graham, M.I.C.E.
　Share capital paid up, £181,472; last dividend, 10 per cent.
　Loan capital paid up, £26,894, at 3¼ per cent.
　Annual profit, including "capital charges," £13,788.
　Towns and villages within the area of control, with population of each (1901

Census)—Banstead...							5,624
Beddington	...	...	...	...	...	...	3,844
Carshalton	...	...	...	...	...	..	6,746
Cheam ..	...	...	...	...	...	...	8,404
Cuddington	...	...	...	...	...	...	774
Ewell ...	...	...	...	...	..	...	3,338
Morden ...	...	...	...	...	...	...	960
Sutton ...	...	...	...	..	...	...	17,223
Wallington	...	...	...	...	...	...	5,152
Woodmansterne	...	...	...	...	...	...	534

47,599

　Works established, 1863.
　Special Acts, The Sutton District Waterworks Acts, 1871, 1887, 1903 and 1906.
　Total population of area of control, 1881 34,028, 1891 37,368, 1901 47,599.
　Estimated population actually supplied, 60,000 estimated.
　Annual supply of water, 1906, for all purposes, 641,178,358 gals.
　Maximum day's consumption, 2,225,394 gals., June, 1906.
　Total quantity of water drawn per annum from deep wells in chalk (1906),
　　641,178,358 gals.
　Sources of supply in use, deep wells or borings situated at Sutton and Wood-
　　mansterne.
　Pumping station, Sutton.
　Head on pumping main, 650 feet;
　Head on distributing mains, maximum, 340 feet; minimum, 100 feet.
　Storage capacity in service reservoirs, 7,737,000 gals.
　Number of meters in use, 1,079.
　Length of supply and distributing mains, 156 miles.
　Character of water, chalk water, 19° hardness, softened by Clarke's process and
　　Haine's softening apparatus. Hardness after treatment, 9°.
　Assessment charge, 5 and 7½ per cent. on rack rental value; price per 1,000 gals.,
　　varies; average 1s.

Sutton, Yorks. (supplied by HULL).

Sutton Coldfield (supplied by SOUTH STAFFS WATERWORKS Co.).

Sutton-in-Ashfield, Notts. Railways, M. and G.N. Distance from London,
　138¾ miles.
　Owners, District Council.
　Population supplied, 13,596.
　No returns supplied.

Sutton-in-Craven, Yorks. Railway, M.
　Authority, Sutton-in-Craven Water Co., Ld.
　Chairman, James Bairstow, J.P.
　Manager, John Widdup, Sutton Mill.
　Secretary, Walter Thornton.

SUTTON-IN-CRAVEN—*continued.*

Office, Sutton, near Keighley.
Share capital paid up (Dec. 31st 1906) ... £1,700.
3½ per cent. Debenture Stock „ ... £1,180.
Last dividend, 5 per cent. (Dec. 1906).
Works established, 1882.
Population within area of control (1901 Census)—Sutton, 892 ; Sutton Mill 1,074. Total, 1,966.
Total number of consumers, 340.
Estimated population actually supplied, 1,360.
There is one reservoir at Lane Top, Sutton, with a capacity of 258,000 gal., supplied from springs in the neighbourhood, with about 2½ miles of distributing mains.
Character of water, soft and good.
Daily consumption per head, about 10 gals.
Scale of charges—

When rent or annual value is under			£4	0	0	... 1s. 6d.	per quarter.	
„	„	„	£5	0	0	... 1s. 8d.	„	„
„	„	„	£10	0	0	... 2s. 6d.	„	„
„	„	„	£15	0	0	... 3s. 9d.	„	„
„	„	„	£20	0	0	... 4s. 6d.	„	„
„	„	„	£30	0	0	... 5s. 6d.	„	„
„	„	„	£50	0	0	... 8s. 0d.	„	„

and 6d. per quarter extra for every £5 rent or annual value.
Water closets, 2s. each per quarter. Baths, 2s. each per quarter.
Horses and ponies, 1s. each per quarter.
Cows, 9d. each per quarter.
Carriages (2 wheels), 1s. ; (4 wheels), 1s. 6d. each per quarter.

Swadlincote (supplied by ASHBY-DE-LA-ZOUCH).

Swaffham, Norfolk. Railway, G.E. Distance from London, 111 miles
Authority, Swaffham Water Co.
Chairman, Fred Everett.
Engineer and Manager, J. G. Culling.
Secretary, S. Matthews.
Office, Swaffham.
Share capital paid up, £3,000.
Last dividend, 6 per cent.
Works established, 1865. Special Act, 1901.
Total population of area supplied, 3,371.
Average death rate, 11·5 per 1,000.
Area supplied, Swaffham only.
Source of supply, deep well.
Character of water, hard.
Filtration, none.
Storage capacity, 16,000 gals.
Daily consumption per head, domestic, 15 gals.
Total quantity of water raised, 60,000 gals. per day.
Pressure on distributing mains—max., 30lbs.; min., 15lbs. per sq. in.
Assessment charge, 6 to 8 per cent.
Price per 1,000 gals., for all purposes, 1s. 6d.
Total water rent received, £700.
Number of meters, 12.
Length of mains, 4 miles.

Swainswick (supplied by BATH).

Swallowfield (partly supplied by READING).

Swanage, Dorset. (G. & W.) Railway, L.S.W. Distance from London, 131¾ miles.
Authority, Swanage Gas and Water Company.
Chairman. Sir John Mowlem Burd, J.P.
Manager, W. G. Perrin.
Secretary, A. G. Such.
Office, 19, Grosvenor Road, Westminster, and Swanage, Dorset.
Town and villages in the area supplied, Swanage, Herston, Langton and Ulwell.
Source of supply, direct from chalk formation.
Length of mains, about 20 miles.

Swansea, Wales. Railways, G.W., M., L.N.W., Rhondda and Swansea Bay, Swansea
and Mumbles. Distance from London, 206 miles.
Authority, Corporation.
Chairman, Roger Thomas.
Engineer and Manager, R. H. Wyrill, M.I.C.E.
Town Clerk, John Thomas.
Office, Guildhall.
Loans outstanding, £1,024,374 19s. 5d.
Annual loss, including "capital charges," £18,000.
Total water rent received, £28,892.
Works established—Lliw Works, 1860 to 1888; Cray Works, 1895 to 1907.
Special Acts, 1860, 1873, 1884, 1892, 1902, and 1905.
Total population supplied, 120,000.
Average death rate, 18·5 per 1,000, period 16 years.
District of supply, Swansea Rural District Council, Pontardawe D.C., and all
districts, within one mile of the Cray pipe lines.
Sources of supply, gravitation works on the Lliw, Blaenant Ddu, and Cray
streams.
Character of water, soft moorland water. Filtration, none; softening, none.
Hardness, Velindee water, 1½°; Cray water, 3°.
Storage capacity in impounding reservoirs, 1,512,544,000 gals.
Head on distributing mains—maximum, 430 ft.; minimum, 50 ft.
Annual supply of water, 1,825,000,000 gals.
Daily consumption per head—domestic, 34 gals.; trade, 7 gals.
Assessment charge, up to £5 rateable value, 7s. 2d. per annum.
      „   „   £5   „   £7   „   „   9s. 4d.   „
      „   „   £7   „ £10   „   „   11s. 0d.   „
      „   „   above £10   „   „   5½ per cent. per annum.
Price per 1,000 gals., 1s. 2¾d. to 6d.
Number of meters, 332.

Swarthmoor (supplied by Ulverston).

Swepstone (supplied by Hinckley).

Swindon and District, Wilts. Railways, G.W., and M.S.W. Joint. Distance from
London, 77¼ miles.
Authority, Corporation of Swindon.
Chairman, Alderman A. W. Deacon.
Town Clerk, R. Hilton.
Manager, E. R. Bowering.
Engineer, H. J. Hamp.
Office, Town Hall.
Capital Expenditure, £169,000; loans outstanding, £153,700.
Estimated net profit, 1906-7, £569.
Total revenue received, £13,359.
Works established, 1867, bought by Corporation, January 1st, 1895. Special Act,
Swindon Water Act, 1894.

SWINDON AND DISTRICT—*continued.*

　　Total population of area supplied, 56,000.
　　Death rate, New Swindon, 12·4 per 1,000 ; Old Swindon, 12·3 per 1,000.
　　Area supplied, Swindon, Stratton, St. Margaret, Rodbourne, Cheney, and part of Wroughton.
　　Sources of supply—wells in chalk, springs from upper greensand.
　　Character of water, 20° hardness.
　　System of filtration, sand and polarite.
　　Storage capacity, impounding reservoirs, 12,000,000 gals. ; service reservoirs, 2,000,000.
　　Pressure on distributing mains, maximum 90 lbs ; minimum, 10 lb. per sq. in.
　　Total quantity of water raised per annum, 182,000,000 gals.
　　Daily consumption per head, domestic and trade, 11 gals.
　　Maximum day's supply, 700,000 gals., in July.
　　Assessment charge, 8½ to 5 per cent. on rateable value.
　　Price per 1,000 gals., domestic and trade, 2s. 6d. to 1s. 6d.
　　Number of meters, 800.
　　Length of mains, 50 miles.
　　Swindon is also partly supplied by Cheltenham.

Swindon, Glos. (supplied by CHELTENHAM).

Swinton, (supplied by MANCHESTER).

Syston (supplied by LEICESTER).

Tadcaster, Yorks.　Railways, G.N. and M.　Distance from London, 189 miles.
　　Authority, Rural District Council.
　　Partly supplied by Wakefield.
　　Population supplied, 3,552.

Taffs Well (supplied by PONTYPRIDD).

Tamerton Foliot, Devon (supplied by PLYMOUTH).

Tamworth, Stafford.　Railways, L.N.W. and M.　Distance from London, 110 miles.
　　Authority, Tamworth District Waterworks Joint Committee of Tamworth Urban and Rural District Councils.
　　Engineer and Manager, H. J. Clarson.
　　Clerk to the Joint Committee, John Matthews.
　　Office, 22, Church Street.
　　Towns and villages in the area supplied—borough of Tamworth, parishes of Fazeley, Wiggington, Two Gates, Wilnecote, Bolehall, Glascote, Amington, Stonydelph, Hopwas, Dorthill, and Shuttington outside area.
　　Works established, 1880.　Special Act, 1875, Public Health Act.
　　Total population supplied, 20,000.
　　Annual supply of water, 159,000,000 gals.
　　Daily consumption per head—domestic, 18 gals. ; trade, 22 gals.
　　Sources of supply—red sandstone (deep well).
　　Storage capacity, 750,000 gals.
　　Character of water—fairly hard ; temporary, 11·97°, permanent, 9·71°.
　　Death rate, 13·9 per 1,000.
　　Length of mains, 33 miles.

Tanners (supplied by BURY).

Tanshelf, for Pontefract, Yorks.　Railways, M. and N.E., G.N., and L. and Y. Distance from London, 175 miles.
　　Authority, Pontefract Corporation.
　　Source of supply—wells only used for baths now ; Roall Waterworks supply has superseded Tanshelf.

Taplow, part of (supplied by MAIDENHEAD).

Tarbock (supplied by WIDNES).

Tarleton (supplied by PRESTON).

Taunton, Somerset. Railway, G.W. Distance from London, 163 miles.
Authority, Corporation, 1877.
Office, Municipal Buildings.
Works established, 1858. Purchased by Local Authority, 1877. Special Act, 1858.
Total population of area supplied, 21,078.
Daily consumption per head, all purposes, 20 gals.
Source of supply, green sand.
Storage capacity, 40,000,000 gals.
Character of water, very soft and pure,
Scale of charges—assessment A, nearly 5 per cent.
Price for 1,000 gals., 2s., 1s. 9d., 1s. 6d., 1s. 3d., 1s., and 10d.

Tavistock, Devon. Railways, L.S.W. and G.W. Distance from London, 213¼ miles.
Owner, the Duke of Bedford.
Office, Estate Offices, Tavistock.
Total population of area supplied, 4,728.

Tees Valley.
Tees Valley Water Board.
Chairman, Sir Hugh Bell, Bart.
Manager and Clerk to authority, D. D. Wilson.
Consulting Engineers, Mansergh & Sons.
Office, Municipal Buildings, Middlesbrough.
Loans outstanding (March 31st, 1906), £2,515,488 17s. 4d.
Annual loss (last year 1906), £17,712.
Works established, 1851. Company formed in 1851; purchased by the Corporation of Stockton and Middlesbrough in 1878, under the Stockton and Middlesbrough Water Act, 1876.
Special Acts, 1851, 1854, 1858, 1864, 1876, 1884, 1888, 1890, 1899, 1901, 1905.
Total population supplied, 245,000.
Average death rate, about 20 per 1,000.
Area of supply, the Boroughs of Middlesbrough, Stockton and Thornaby, and about 30 parishes outside, all supplied.
Sources of supply—water pumped from the River Tees, 2,941,079,000 gals.
            impounding reservoirs   2,419,287,000 „
Character of water, soft.
Analysis—
Physical examination—turbidity, nil; colour, brown; odour, normal.

Chemical examination— Determinations.	Results in	
	Grains per gal.	Parts per 100,000.
Total solid matter dried at 180° C. ...	8·2	11·7
Chlorine	0·7	1·0
Equivalent to Chlorides (60 per cent. Cl.)	1·16	1·65
Nitric Nitrogen	0·047	0·067
Equivalent to Nitrates (17 per cent. N.)	0·282	0·40
Nitrates	absent.	
Hardness: permanent 4·5, temporary 0·5, total 5·0		
Lead, copper, zinc, and iron	absent.	
Free ammonia	0·00098	0·0014
Organic ammonia	0·0012	0·0017
Oxygen absorbed at 98° F. in 3 hours ...	0·248	3·354

Tees Valley—*continued.*

Report on the bacteriological examination—
Number of organisms per cubic centimetre capable of growing on alkaline nutrient jelly at 20° C. in 4 days, counted by aid of pocket lens—364.
Smallest quantity of water in which growth occurred, with production of acid and gas in bile-salt glucose broth (1, 5, 10, or 20 c.c.)—5 c.c.
Nature of organisms found in this growth.
　　　　　　　　　　　Not Bac: Coli. Communis.
Spores of the bacillus enteritidis sporogones in 150 c.c.—absent.
　　　　　　　　　　　in 350 c.c.　　,,
　　　　　　　　　　　in 500 c.c.　　,,
This water gives excellent results upon chemical examination, there being no trace of organic matter save that derived from peat.
The bacteriological results are also entirely satisfactory, the number of bacteria is not excessive, and even using considerable quantities of the water no organisms indicative of sewage or manurial contamination could be discovered.
The water is therefore admirably adapted for all the purposes of a public supply.
Filtration, sand ; softening, none.
Storage capacity—impounding reservoirs, 1,322,137,000 gals.; service reservoirs, 275,464,000 gals.
Annual supply of water (1906), 5,360,366,000 gals.
Average daily supply per head—domestic, 15 gals.; trade, &c., 45 gals.
Maximum day's supply, 11,750,000 gals. in September, 1906.
Charges authorised—domestic 7½ per cent. to 6 per cent. on rental value.
　　　,,　　　,,　by meter, 1s. 6d. to 3¼d. per 1,000 gals.
Present average charge by meter, 4¼d. per 1,000 gals.
Number of meters, 774.

Tealby, Lincoln (supplied by Market Rasen).

Teignmouth, Devon.　Railway, G.W.　Distance from London, 204¼ miles.
Authority, Urban District Council.
Engineer and Surveyor, C. F. Gettings.
Clerk, A. Percival Dell.
Office, Town Hall.
Towns and villages in the area supplied, East and West Teignmouth, Shaldon and Ringmore.
Special Act, 1836.
Total population supplied, 9,000. normal, summer, 12,000.
Annual supply of water, 52,678,700 gals.
Daily consumption per head, domestic, about 15 gals.
Sources of supply—Coombe Brook, and well in red sandstone, 83 feet deep ; 12 in. borehole, 250 feet ; spring out of green sand.
Storage capacity, Hazledown reservoir, 2,000,000 gals, Landscare reservoir, 600,000 gals.
Character of water, very pure.
System of filtration, Coombe Brook, filtered through polarite.
Death rate, 13·73 per 1000 (1902).
Number of meters, 60.
Length of mains, 20 miles.
Assessment charge, 2s. in £.
Price per 1,000 gals. trade purposes, 3s.
The Paignton Urban District Council have entered into an agreement to supply Teignmouth with water (1907).

Tenby, Wales. Railway, G.W. Distance from London, 263 miles.
Authority, Corporation.
Town Clerk, G. Lort Stokes.
Office, St. Mary's Street.
Area supplied, the Borough of Tenby.
Total population of area supplied, 4,400.
Annual supply of water, 80,000,000 gals.
Daily consumption per head, domestic and trade, 40 to 45 gals.
Sources of supply, springs, gathering grounds, and pumping from rivulet.
Storage capacity, 6,000,000 gals.
Character of water, 5° to 12° of hardness, according to source of supply.
System of filtration, none.
Death rate, 14·5 per 1,000
Length of mains, about 8 miles.
Scale of charges—assessment, 1s. 7d. in £ for all purposes.
Price for 1,000 gallons, trade, 2s. 6d.
Owing to legal difficulties, the St. Florence Valley scheme has been abandoned,
and the Council contemplate getting water from Precelly Mountain, 22 miles
away, by gravitation, at a rough estimated cost of £25,000, and are now corre-
sponding with Mr. J. Mansergh, C.E., of London, in reference to a report on the
scheme. The water has been analysed and proved to be pure.

Tendring Hundred, Essex. Railway, G.E.
Authority, Tendring Hundred Waterworks Company.
Chairman, Wm. R. Dockrell, Frinton-on-Sea.
Secretary, Norman W. Jackson.
Office, Waterworks, Mistley, Essex.
Total capital invested, including loans, £130,354 6s. 5d.
Dividend, 4½ per cent.
Works established, 1884.
Special Acts—Tendring Hundred Waterworks Co., 1884, 1886, and 1901 ; Walton-
on-Naze and Frinton-on-Sea Gas Order, 1878.
Total number of houses supplied, 3,820.
Estimated population actually supplied, 450,000 (holiday season).
    ,,   ,,   ,,   ,, 153,000 (normal).
Towns and villages within the area of control—Lawford, Manningtree, Mistley,
Ardleigh, Bradfield, Wix, Stones Green, Beaumont, Kirby-le-Soken, Thorpe-le-
Soken, Little Clacton, Great Holland, Weeley, Walton-on-Naze, Frinton-on-Sea,
Wrabness, Ramsey, Dovercourt, Parkeston, Harwich.
Total quantity of water drawn per annum—from deep well, 124,000,000 gals.
Sources of supply in use—deep wells, Mistley and Lawford.
Pumping station, Mistley and Lawford.
Service reservoirs, Laurel Grove, Dovercourt   ...   250,000 gals., covered.
  ,,   ,,   ,,   ,, ...   75,000 ,,   ,,
  ,,   ,,   Frinton-on-Sea   ...   ...   50,000 ,,   ,,
Annual supply of water—for all purposes, 160,000,000 gals.
Maximum day's consumption, 600,000 gals.
Number of meters in use, 207.
Length of distributing mains, about 76 miles.

Tenterden (supplied by Cranbrook).

Tetbury, Glos. Railway, G.W. Distance from London, 98 miles.
Authority, Tetbury Urban District Council.
Clerk, A. P. Kitcat.
Loan capital, £3,450.
Works established, 1894.
Total population supplied, 2,000.

TETBURY—*continued*.

> Sources of supply, deep well.
> Death rate, 16·8 per 1,000.
> Scale of charges—domestic purposes, 5 per cent. on rateable value.
> Trade purposes by special arrangement, free to public hydrants.

Tettenhall, Staffs. (supplied by WOLVERHAMPTON).

Tewkesbury, Glos. (*See* CHELTENHAM).

Thames Valley Water Works.
> Resident Engineer, C. E. Oxbrow.
> Office, Woodcote, nr. Reading.

The Tors (supplied by LYNMOUTH).

Thelwall Lancs. (supplied by WARRINGTON).

Thetford, Norfolk. Railway, G.E. Distance from London, 91 miles.
> Authority, Corporation, 1877.
> Superintendent, E. S. Greenwood.
> Town Clerk, John Houchen.
> Works established, 1877. Special Act, Public Health Act, 1875.
> Total population supplied, 4,613.
> Annual supply of water, 28,000,000 gals.
> Source of supply—well.
> Storage capacity, 250,000 gals.
> Assessment charge, A.

Theydon Bois (supplied by HERTS AND ESSEX WATERWORKS Co.).

Theydon Garnon (supplied by HERTS AND ESSEX WATERWORKS Co.).

Thimbleby, Yorks. (supplied by NORTHALLERTON).

Thirsk, Yorks. Railways, N.E., G.N., M. Distance from London, 210½ miles.
> Chairman, Reginald Bell.
> Secretary and Manager, Thomas Stokes.
> Office, Westgate, Thirsk.
> Share capital paid up, £24,000. Loan, £8,000.
> Dividend, 4 per cent.
> Works established, 1878. Special Acts, 1878, 1879.
> Total population of area supplied, 5,342.
> Sources of supply—springs and watershed.
> Storage capacity, 45,000,000 gals.
> Character of water, 4° hardness.
> Death rate, 20 per 1,000.
> Number of meters, 7.
> Assessment charge, R.R.
> Price per 1,000 gals., 1s.

Thornaby-on-Tees. See STOCKTON-ON-TEES.

Thornhill (supplied by HALIFAX).

Thornton (supplied by BRADFORD, Yorks.).

Thornton Hough, Cheshire (supplied by BIRKENHEAD).

Thornliebank (supplied by GLASGOW).

Thornwood (supplied by HERTS AND ESSEX WATERWORKS Co.).

Thorpe (supplied by SOUTH-WEST SUBURBAN).

Thorpe, Yorks. (supplied by RIPON).

Thorpe-le-Soken (Supplied by Tendring Hundred).

Thurmaston (supplied by Leicester).

Ticehurst, Sussex. Distance from London, 44 miles.
　　Authority, Ticehurst and District Water and Gas Company.
　　Office, 99, Cannon Street.
　　Works established, 1902 (New Company, 1904) ; special Acts, 1902 and 1904.
　　Capital, ordinary, £37,610 ; 5 per cent. preference, £9,145 ; debentures, £18,200.
　　Dividends, 4 per cent.
　　District of supply, Ticehurst, Burwash, Hurst Green, Etchingham, Salehurst,
　　　　Robertsbridge, Heathfield=60 square miles ; rateable value of district, £52,000.
　　Population supplied, 10,000.
　　Source of supply, well in the Ashdown Forest sands, pumped to reservoir situate
　　　　on Burwash Common, 600 feet above O.D. Capacity 150,000 gals.

Tidenham, Mon. Railway, G.W. Distance from London, 141¾ miles.
　　Authority, Tidenham Waterworks Company, Ltd.
　　Secretary, A. H. Rowe.
　　Office, 16, Welsh Street, Chepstow.
　　Works established, 1886.
　　Total population supplied, 300.
　　Source of supply, spring.

Tillington (supplied by Stafford).

Tinsley (supplied by Sheffield).

Tipton (supplied by South Staffs. Waterworks Co.).
　　Population, 30,543.

Tirphil (supplied by New Tredegar).

Tiverton, Devon. Railway, G.W. Distance from London, 179 miles.
　　Authority, Corporation.
　　Chairman, J. Cotterell.
　　Engineer, J. Siddalls, Borough Surveyor.
　　Office, Town Hall.
　　Loans outstanding, £1,410.
　　Total population of area supplied, 10,382.
　　Average death rate, 13·56.
　　Sources of supply, springs.
　　Character of water, soft.
　　System of filtration, sand.
　　Storage capacity, in service reservoir, 350,000 cubic feet.
　　Daily consumption per head—domestic, 30 gals.
　　There is no charge for water for domestic purposes, the cost being defrayed out
　　　　of the General District Rate ; a charge is made for water used for business
　　　　purposes.
　　Total water rent received, about £40 for water used for trade purposes.

Todmorden, Lancs. Railways, G.N., L.N.W., and M. Distance from London, 203
miles.
　　Authority, Todmorden Corporation.
　　Chairman, Alderman Edward Lord.

TODMORDEN—*continued.*

Manager and Resident Engineer, John H. Parkin, A.M.I.C.E.
Clerk to authority, D. Sutcliffe.
Consulting Engineer, G. F. Deacon, C.E.
Office, Waterworks Office, Todmorden.
Loans outstanding, £86,500.
Works established; Gorpley Reservoir Works completed, 1905.
Special Act, 1898.
Total population of area supplied, 25,418.
Average death rate, 17 per 1,000.
Source of supply, impounding reservoir on Gorpley Clough.
Character of water, organically pure, very soft; total hardness, 2·9°.
System of filtration, slow sand filtration, through grit and limestone sand.
Storage capacity, impounding reservoirs. 130,000,000 gals.; service reservoirs, 200,000 gals.
Head on distributing mains—max., 415 ft.; min., 93 ft.
Annual supply of water, 90,000,000 gals., exclusive of compensation and flood water.
Average daily supply per head—domestic, 24 gals.; trade, 5 gals.
Maximum day's supply, 648,000 gals., in July.
Charges authorised, 7¼ per cent. to 6 per cent. on R.V.; minimum, 2d. per week.
" " by meter, 2s. to 8d. per 1,000 gals.
No. of meters, 130.
Length of supply mains, 12⅜ miles; distributing mains, 7½ miles.

Tolcarne (supplied by MADRON).

Tollcross (supplied by GLASGOW).

Ton (supplied by YSTRAD).

Tonbridge, Kent. Railways, S.E. and C. Distance from London, 29¾ miles.
Authority, Tonbridge Waterworks Company, Ltd.
Chairman, John Fagg.
Engineer, Manager, and Secretary, James Lees.
Office, 4, The Terrace, Tonbridge.
Share capital paid up, £40,059; loan capital paid up, £6,200 at 3½ per cent. and 4 per cent.
Dividend, 9 per cent. and 6⅛ per cent., two classes of shares.
Annual profit, £2,979.
Works established, 1852. Provisional Orders, 1886 and 1900.
Total population of area of control, 1881, 12,370; 1891, 15,560; 1901, 23,300.
Total number of services, 3,663.
Estimated population actually supplied, 21,300.
Average death rate, 11·1 per 1,000.
Towns and villages within the area of control, with population of each—

Tonbridge	16,000
Hildenborough	3,200
Shipbourne	1,300
Leigh	2,800

Sources of supply in use—
Shallow wells, close to town, situated at the pumping station, New Wharf, Tonbridge.
Nature of drainage area, grass land. Water authority purchased 53 acres in 1900.
Natural rest level of water below surface, 17 feet, above Ordnance datum 58·5 feet.
Level of water below surface (when pumping 485,000 gals. per day), 20 feet.
Strata tapped by wells or borings, alluvium and gravel.

22 (337)

TONBRIDGE—*continued*.

Total quantity of water drawn per annum—
 From shallow wells or subsoil ... ... 171,039,000 gals.
Estimated total quantity of water available per annum—
 From shallow wells or subsoil ... ... 250,000,000 gals.
Pumping stations, New Wharf ... ... capacity, 960,000 gals per day.
Service reservoirs at Bloodshot, covered ... „ 500,000 „ „
 „ „ Hangman's Hill, covered „ 110,000 „ „
Head on distributing mains—maximum, 230 feet; minimum, 185 feet.
Analysis of water—
 Physical character, clear and bright; no smell, and no sediment.
 Free ammonia ... ... ·00 per 100,000 parts.
 Albuminoid ammonia ... ... ·006 „ „
 Oxygen absorbed in 4 hours at 80° Fah. ·019 „ „
 Total solids... ... ... 32 „ „
 Loss on ignition ... ... 5 „ „
 Hardness total ... ... 17·38 „ „
 „ permanent ... ... 3·25 „ „
 Chlorine ... ... 3·7 „ „
 Nitrogen as nitrites ... ... nil.
 „ as nitrates ... ... ·237 „ „
 Poisonous metals ... ... nil.
 Alkalinity as Ca Co 3 ... ... 15·5 „ „
 The condition of the water is highly satisfactory, and the tabulated results of
 the medical officer's periodical examinations have shown the water, both
 chemically and bacteriologically, to be absolutely pure.
Filtration, 4 Bell's patent high-pressure filters, very satisfactory.
Annual supply of water (1907)—
 For domestic purposes ... ... 165,039,000 gals.
 „ trade „ ... ... 4,500,000 „
 „ municipal „ ... ... 1,500,000 „
Average daily supply per head, domestic, 22 gals.
Maximum day's consumption, 485,000 gals. in July.
Assessment charge, 7½ per cent. to 5 per cent. on rateable value; price per
 1,000 gals., trade, 1s. 6d. to 1s. 1d.; municipal purposes, 1s.
Total water rent received, about £5,500.
Number of meters in use, 52.
Length of mains, 60 miles.
These works are only small, and not important, but are being brought up to
 modern lines, and as the town is increasing rapidly, new plant is being
 installed. There is plenty of water.

Tong (supplied by BRADFORD, Yorks.).

Tongwynlais (supplied by CARDIFF).

Tonypandy (supplied by YSTRAD).

Torpoint, Devon. Distance from London, 340 miles.
 Authority, St. Germans District Council.
 Office, 64, Fore Street, Torpoint, Devonport.
 Towns and villages in the area supplied, Torpoint, Trevor H.M. Drill Field, and
 Park View.
 Works established, 1887.
 Total population of area supplied, about 5,000.

TORPOINT—*continued.*

Daily consumption per head, about 20 gals.

Source of supply, springs supplying about 150 gals. per minute.

Storage capacity, 7,000,000 gals.

Character of water, medium.

System of filtration, sand filter beds.

Length of mains, about 20 miles.

Price for 1,000 gals., 9d. to 6d.; urinals and flush tanks for sewers and schools free.

Total water rent received, about £600.

Torquay. Railway, G.W. Distance from London, 215¼ miles.

Authority, Torquay Corporation.

Chairman, Councillor, F. J. Crocker, J.P.

Town Clerk, F. S. Hex.

Engineer in charge, Samuel C. Chapman, A.M.I.C.E.

Office, Town Hall Chambers, Torquay.

Total capital invested, including loans, about £330,000.

Purchased by local authority, 1856.

Special Acts, 1856, 1897, and 1903.

Total population of area of control, 1891, 43,483 ; 1901, 46,393.

Total number of consumers, 11,199.

Estimated population actually supplied, 53,000.

Average death rate, 15 per 1,000.

Towns and villages within the area of control, Torquay, Newton Abbot, Cockington, Kingskerswell. Chudleigh Knighton, Abbotskerswell, supplied in bulk.

Sources of supply in use.—drainage areas situated at Tottiford and Trenchford, 2 miles E.S.E. of Moretonhampstead, and 11 miles S.W. of Exeter.

Surface springs, in Torquay.

Deep wells in the borough of Torquay.

Geological data—

Surface formation of drainage areas, sandy and peaty soils, and decomposed granite.

Strata or formation yielding springs, granite.

Population on drainage area, 115 in 1896, but now not a single inhabitant.

Nature and extent of cultivation of ditto in acres, 250, roots and oats, remainder grazing and moorland and larch plantations.

Water authority purchased watershed at £67,000, and removed all inhabitants and dwelling houses by Act of Parliament, 1897.

Delivery of streams, 60 per cent. of rainfall.

Evaporation from water surface, 20·97 inches ; average of 5 years, 830 feet above Ordnance Datum.

4 rain gauges and one evaporation gauge.

Water is not softened, 2 to 3° hardness (varies according to amount of water in stream when analysis is made).

Filtering, none.

Water aerated by passing over 2 umbrella jets and running down ¼ mile of conduit, with steps for breaking up the water.

Storage reservoirs, Kennick   ..   ...   capacity, 194,000,000 gals.

„   „   Tottiford   ...   ...   „   103,000,000   „

„   „   Trenchford, under construction
and nearly completed   „   200,000,000   „

Pumping station, Barton, for high levels only   „   150,000   „   per day.

Campbell's oil engine used with 3-throw pumps.

Torquay—*continued.*

			Above Ord. Datum.
Service reservoirs, Warberry (open) ...	capacity,	2,000,000 gals.	... 409·00
,, ,, ,, (covered)	,,	500,000 ,,	... 398·76
,, ,, Chapel Hill (open)	,,	1,500,000 ,,	... 247·00
,, ,, Cockington ,,	,,	50,000 ,,	... 280·00
,, ,, Barton ,,	,,	70,000 ,,	... 480·00
,, ,, Newton Abbot ,,	,,	500,000 ,,	... 298·00
,, ,, Kingskerswell ,,	,,	60,000 ,,	... 335.00

Pressure on distributing mains—maximum, 120 lbs.; minimum, 10 lbs. per sq. in.
Trunk mains scraped annually, and delivery increased by 23 to 28 per cent.

Maximum annual rainfall over drainage area ...	52·18 inches (1882)
Minimum ,, ,, ...	28·04 ,, (1887)
Average ,, ,, ...	40·76 ,, (period, 29 yrs.)

Estimated maximum daily discharge at points of collection ... 37,500,000 gals.
,, minimum ,, ,, ... 152,000 ,,
Estimated average daily discharge at point of collection ... 2,350,000 ,,
Total quantity of water drawn per annum (1906) from drainage areas (2,241 acres) ... ... 621,609,000 gals.
From surface springs ... ... 2,000,000 ,, used for Cary Green fountain only, and street watering.
Estimated total quantity of water available per annum—
  From drainage areas—858,863,000 gals.
  From surface springs, 16,000,000 gals., Ellacombe, Torquay.
Annual supply of water (1906)—

For domestic purposes	...	...	...	502,389,000 gals.
,, trade ,,	...	...	...	74,771,000 ,,
,, municipal ,,	...	...	...	39,948,000 ,,
In bulk to other authorities	...	...	...	4,500,000 ,,
Average day's consumption—domestic	...	...		1,348,320 ,,
trade	...	...		354,680 ,,

Maximum day's consumption, 1,967,000 gals. in July.
Number of meters in use, 500.
Length of supply mains, 28 miles; distributing mains, 105 miles.
Assessment charge—domestic, 6 to 6¾ per cent. on rateable value.
Price per 1,000 gals.—1s. 4d., inside borough: 1s. 8d., outside.

Torrington, Devon. Railways, L.S.W. and G.W. Distance from London, 225 miles.
Authority, Limited Company.
Population supplied, 3,436.
No returns supplied.

Totland, Isle of Wight. Railway, L.S.W. Distance from London, 102 miles.
Authority, Totland Water Company.
Office, Clayton House, Queen's Road, Freshwater.
Works established, 1883.
Special Act, Totland Water Works Act, 1899.

Totley (supplied by Sheffield)

Totnes, Devon. Railway, G.W. Distance from London, 218¼ miles.
Authority, Corporation.
Population supplied, 4,034.
No returns supplied.

Tottenham. *See* Metropolitan Water Board.

Tottington (supplied by BURY).

Towcester, Northants.　Railway, L.N.W.　Distance from London, 67 miles.
　　Authority, Rural District Council.
　　Chairman, Wm. Geo. Stops.
　　Clerk, W. K. Higham.
　　Consulting Engineer, John Eunson, C.E.
　　Office, Town Hall, Towcester.
　　Loan capital, £2,200.　The repayment of the loan is spread over a term of 30 years from 1883.
　　Additional loan, £1,400.　The repayment of this loan is spread over a term of 27 years from 1901.　This was obtained for erection of a pumping station and auxiliary supply.
　　Works established, 1883.　Special Acts, 1875, 1878.
　　Total population of area supplied, 2,371.
　　Total number of consumers, 450.
　　Death rate, 13 per 1,000.
　　Area supplied, Towcester parish.
　　Source of supply, a spring called Dockle Mill.
　　Character of water, good, rather hard.
　　System of filtration, nil.
　　Reservoir storage capacity, 50,000 gals.
　　Daily consumption per head, 12 gals.
　　Scale of water rents payable quarterly on the first days of March, June, September, and December:—

	s.	d.
Houses at and under £8, gross estimated rental (payable by owner)	2	0
Houses exceeding £8 and not exceeding £15	3	0
,, ,, 15 ,, ,, 20	4	0

　　　　And 1s. extra for every extra £5 up to £120, 24s.
　　　Water closets 1s. each, pan closets, 6d. each per quarter extra.
　　The above charges do not include water used for engines, brewery, other trade purposes, or for fountains.
　　Water by meter at the rate of 1s. per 1,000 gals., the minimum charge being 9s. per quarter.
　　Number of meters, 12.
　　Length of mains, 5,390 yards.
　　Total water rent received, £400.

Towlaw (supplied by WEARDALE AND CONSETT WATER Co.)

Townend, Derbyshire.
　　Authority, Townend Water Co., Ltd.
　　Office, Chapel-en-le-Frith.
　　No returns supplied.

Towyn, Flint. (supplied by RHYL).

Tranmere (supplied by BIRKENHEAD).

Trealaw (supplied by YSTRAD).

Tredegar, Mon. (G. & W.) Railway, L.N.W. Distance from London, 173 miles.
　Authority, Tredegar Urban District Council.
　Clerk to Authority, H. J. C. Shepard (solicitor).
　Resident Engineer, D. Walter Davies.
　Office, Gas Works, Tredegar.
　Capital, gas, £36,178; water undertaking, £23,703, equals £59,881.
　Works established, 1882; special Acts, 1882 and 1892.
　District of supply, Tredegar and part of Bedwellty.
　Total population supplied, 18,574.

Treeton (supplied by SHEFFIELD).

Trefnant, Flint. (supplied by RHYL).

Treharris, Glam. (supplied by MERTHYR TYDVIL).

Treherbert (supplied by YSTRAD).

Trelewis, Wales (supplied by MERTHYR TYDVIL).

Trevichy (supplied by YSTRAD).

Trevor (supplied by TORPOINT).

Tring, Bucks. *See* AYLESBURY.

Troedyrhiw, Wales (supplied by MERTHYR TYDVIL).

Trowbridge, Wilts. Railway, G.W. Distance from London, 96¾ miles.
　Secretary, H. Saunders French.
　Share capital, £60,223. Loan capital, £12,500.
　Works established, 1873. Special Acts, 1873 and 1878.
　Total population supplied, 30,000.
　Sources of supply—spring from chalk, and well and boring to greensand.
　Assessment charge, annual value.
　Price per 1,000 gals., 2s. to 7d.

Trumpington (supplied by CAMBRIDGE).

Truro. Railway, G.W. Distance from London, 294¾ miles.
　Authority, Truro Water Company.
　Office, 31, Lemon Street.
　Consulting Engineers, Henderson and Sons, Truro.
　Works established, 1875. Special Act, 1875.
　Total population of area supplied, 11,562.
　Total number of consumers, 10,000 approximately.
　Annual supply of water, 80,000,000 gals.
　Daily consumption per head, domestic, 21·8 for all purposes.
　Source of supply, Stairfoot stream.
　Character of water, soft.
　System of filtration, sand.

TRURO—*continued.*

Service reservoirs, one.
Number of meters, 79.
Length of mains, about 12 miles.
Scale of charges—assessment, under £6, 2d. per week ; 7 per cent. on annual
  value up to £30, 6 per cent. over £30.
Price for 1,000 gals. 2s. to 1s.

Tunbridge Wells. Railways, S.E. & C., L.B.S.C. Distance from London, 34½
miles.
Authority, Tunbridge Wells Corporation.
Chairman, Alderman Putland.
Secretary, W. C. Cripps.
Waterworks Engineer, W. H. Maxwell, A.M.I.C.E.
Office, Town Hall.
Total capital invested, including loans, £242,285.
The waterworks undertaking was transferred to the Improvement Commissioners
  under the Tunbridge Wells Water Act, 1865.
Special Acts, 1865 and 1890.
Estimated population actually supplied, 36,000. Increased considerably during
  the summer months.
Population, Tunbridge Wells Borough, 35,000.
Average death rate, 11·68 per 1,000.
Towns and villages within the area of control—Tunbridge Wells, Pembury,
  Frant, Langton, Speldhurst, Stockland Green, Southborough, &c.
The supply is obtained from a number of springs and deep wells in the neigh-
  bourhood of Pembury (Kent).
Average rainfall for 22 years ending 1897, 27 inches.
Total quantity of water drawn per annum (1906)—springs, 253,366,624 gals. ;
  deep wells or borings, 113,510,862 gals.
The supply is soft, of about 2° to 3° hardness only, and is of the highest degree
  of purity.
Storage reservoir of Pembury, 45,000,000 gals. capacity.
Filtering area provided, 1 acre, 4 filter beds.
Service reservoirs, at Blackhurst, about 900,000 gals.
Annual supply of water for all purposes, 300,000,000 gals.
Maximum day's consumption, 1,100,000 gals.
Number of meters in use, about 110.
Assessment charges, 25 per cent. below scale fixed by 1865 Act.
Price per 1,000 gals., trade, 2s.
Total water rent received, £21,732, year ending March, 1906.

Tunstall (supplied by STAFFORDSHIRE POTTERIES WATER Co.).

Turton (supplied by BOLTON).

Turriff, Aberdeenshire, N.B.
Authority, Town Council.
Chairman, Provost Hutcheon.
Secretary, W. F. Stewart.
Manager and Engineer, William Johnstone.
Office, Surveyor's Office, Turriff.
Loans outstanding, £600.
Works established, 1861.
Total population of area supplied, 2,273.
Average death rate, 19·797 per 1,000.
District of supply, Turriff only.

TURRIFF—*continued.*

Sources of supply—springs in gravel on land four miles from town, which the
Town Council have recently purchased for £6,000, thus securing a perpetual
hold of the water and the gathering grounds.

There is a very large supply of water, the supply main is only 5 in. diameter, and
carries 88,000 gals. per day, leaving on an average an overflow of 90,000 gals.
per day at the cistern on the gathering grounds.

Character of water, very pure.
System of filtration, none needed.
Storage capacity, 75,000 gals.
Daily supply of water, 78,000 gals. every 24 hours.
Daily consumption per head, 40 gals.
Annual supply of water, 32,032,000 gals.
Scale of charges—water assessment, owner and occupier, each 4½d. in the £.
Total valuation of Burgh, £8,237 1s.
Price, trade purposes, masons and builders, 1s. per rood of building.
Hiring establishments, horses, carriages or machines, 2s. 6d. each per year. Other
business premises, the quantity used is considered and a price is then agreed
upon. About £40 per year is collected from the trade supply.
Length of supply mains, 4 miles; distributing mains, 3¼ miles.

Tweedmouth, Northumberland. Railway, G.N. Distance from London, 337 miles
Source of supply, part private company, and part private well.
Character of water, unsatisfactory, and quite insufficient in dry weather.
Population supplied, 3,409.

Twerton, Som. (supplied by BATH).

Twyford Abbey (supplied by RICKMANSWORTH).

Tyldesley-with-Shakerley, Lancs.
Authority, Urban District Council.
Population, 14,900.
Source of supply, the Manchester Corporation mains from Thirlmere.
Engineer, R. H. Ginman.

Tynemouth and **North Shields.** Railway, G.N. Distance from London, 278
miles.
Authority, Tynemouth Corporation.
Chairman of Committee, Aldermam J. P. Spencer.
Secretary and Manager, Henry Clarke.
Engineer in charge at Font, F. R. Hall, M.I.C.E.
Office, Town Hall, Tynemouth.
Consulting Engineers, James Mansergh & Sons, 5, Victoria Street, London, S.W.
Daily consumption per head, 19·20 gals.
Total capital invested, including loans, £425,000.
Works established, 1849; purchased by local authority, 1897, 1899.
Special Acts, 1897, 1898.
Total population of area of control, 1881, 46,360; 1891, 49,900; 1901, 59,219.
Estimated population actually supplied, 59,000.
District of supply, Municipal Borough of Tynemouth with Whitley and Monk-
seaton.
Source of supply, Font River at Evesley, near Rothbury, Northumberland,
The Font Reservoir Works were started in 1901, but since 1904 a temporary
supply has been sent to Tynemouth, the amount in 1906 being 220,000,000 gals.
The works will be completed in 1907, and then Tynemouth will have an avail-
able supply from the Font of over 5,000,000 gals. per day.

Tynemouth and North Shields—*continued.*

Estimated maximum daily discharge at points of collection, 235,000,000 gals.
　　　" 　　　minimum 　　 " 　　　 " 　　　 " 　　　 " 　　　500,000 　"
　　　" 　　　average 　　 " 　　　 " 　　　 " 　　　 " 　　　7,600,000 　"
Maximum annual rainfall over drainage area, 44·53 ins. (in 1900).
Minimum 　　" 　　　" 　　　" 　　　" 　　　" 　38·44 ins. (in 1904).
Average 　　" 　　　" 　　　" 　　　" 　　　" 　35·26 ins. (period 9 years).
Population of drainage area, 22.
Nature of drainage area, moorland.
Control over drainage area, Rivers Pollution Prevention Act, 1876.
Surface formation of drainage area, glacial or boulder drift.
Character of water, soft; about 5° hardness.
Filtration, slow sand filtration.　Total area, 1¼ acres.
Softening, none.
Storage reservoirs—Font Reservoir, capacity, 730,000,000 gals.
　　　　　　　　Whitley 　　" 　　　" 　　35,000,000 　"
　　　　　　　　Ridges 　　" 　　　" 　　14,000,000 　"
Filtering area provided, 6,430 sq. yds. in 5 filter beds.
Service reservoirs, Moorhouses—capacity 3,215,000 gals.
　" 　　　　" 　　Billy Mill 　　" 　2,200,000 　"
　" 　　　　" 　　Brock Farm 　" 　8,820,000 　"
Pumping stations—Whitley, capacity per day, 250,000 gals.
　　　　　　　　Ridges 　　" 　　" 　" 　150,000 　"
Head on distributing mains—High Town, average 120 ft.
　　　　　　　　　　Low Town 　　" 　40 ft.
Annual supply of water, 462,000,000 gals.
Average daily supply for all purposes, 19·78 gals.
Number of meters, 138.
Scale of charges—
　Assessment charge, 6 per cent. to 7½ per cent. in the £ on rental value.
　Price per 1,000 gals., 1s.
Total water rent received, £17,000.
Length of supply mains from Font, 24½ miles, distributing mains

Tynemouth Rural Sanitary Authority (supplied by Newcastle-on-Tyne).

Tywyn (supplied by Conway).

Uckington (supplied by Tewkesbury).

Uddingston Scotland (supplied by District of the Middle Ward of Lanarkshire).

Ulverston. Lancs. (G. & W.)　Railways, L.N.W. and Furness.　Distance from London, 256 miles.
　Authority, Urban District Council.
　Chairman, A. E. Sadler, J.P.
　Engineer and Manager, John Swan.
　Clerk, John Poole.
　Office, Gasworks, Ulverston.
　Loans outstanding, £15,758.
　Annual profit, including capital charges, £1,661 2s. 7d.
　Works established, 1851; purchased, 1871.　Special Act, 1852.
　Total population supplied, 12,060.
　Average death rate, 14·5 per 1,000.
　Towns and villages in the area supplied—Ulverston, Swarthmoor, Bardsea, Urswick, Osmotherley, and Pennington.
　Source of supply, impounding reservoir of moors and pasture land.

ULVERSTON—*continued.*

Character of water, soft, principally surface drainage.
System of filtration, sand.
Storage capacity, 2,000,000 gals.
Head on distributing mains—maximum, 370 ft.; minimum, 185 ft.
Annual supply of water, 146,000,000 gals.
Average daily consumption per head—domestic, 30 gals.; trade, 5 gals.
Maximum day's supply, 400,000 gals. in January.
Authorised charge, not to exceed 7 per cent. of rack rent.
Present charge, 1½ per cent. to 7 per cent.
Price per 1,000 gals., trade, 1s. to 6d.
Number of meters, 34.
Length of mains—supply, 2 miles; distributing, 21 miles.

Ulwell (supplied by SWANAGE).

Unsworth (supplied by BURY).

Upchurch (supplied by RAINHAM).

Uphill, Som. (supplied by WESTON-SUPER-MARE).

Upper Bebington, Cheshire (supplied by BIRKENHEAD).

Upperby (supplied by CARLISLE).

Upper Inglesham, Wilts. (supplied by HIGHWORTH).

Uppingham, Rutland.　Railway, L.N.W.　Distance from London, 98 miles.
Authority, Uppingham Waterworks Company.
Chairman, T. E. Monckton.
Secretary, F. E. Hodgkinson, Solicitor, Uppingham.
Engineer and Manager, B. Burn, Waterworks Cottage, Uppingham.
Office, The Water Tower.
Consulting Engineers, G. and F. W. Hodson, Loughborough.
Share capital paid up, £6,000; last dividend, 2½ per cent.
Debentures, £1,300 at 4 per cent.
Annual profit, including "capital charges," £250.
Works established, 1876.　Special Act, 39 & 40 Vict., session 1876.
Estimated population actually supplied, 2,500.
Area of control, Uppingham only.
Source of supply, wells and headings—10 wells at old works, 1 well at new
　works; springs from blue rock and ironstone at old works, and gravel bed
　at new works.
The new works were completed, April, 1904, at a cost of £17,500.
Character of water, very hard, 25°, softened by Dr. Clark's process, Archbrett and
　Deely's patent; hardness after treatment, 8·5°.
Filtration, none.
Storage capacity, impounding reservoirs, 200,000 gals.; service reservoirs, 300,000
　gals.
Head on distributing mains—maximum, 30 lbs.; minimum, 22 lbs. per sq. in.
Annual supply of water, 20,000,000 gals.
Total quantity of water drawn, 15 wells, 30,000 gals. per day.
Maximum day's supply, 50,000 gals. in July.
Water rates charged on rateable value, scale fixed by Act.
Length of supply mains, 5 miles; distributing mains, 2½ miles.

Upton, Cheshire (supplied by MACCLESFIELD).

Upton (supplied by CHESTER).

Upton, Oxford. *See* BURFORD.

Upton, Notts. (supplied by NEWARK).

Urmston (supplied by MANCHESTER).

Urswick (supplied by ULVERSTON).

Uxbridge. *See* RICKMANSWORTH.

Ventnor, Isle of Wight. (G. & W.) Railways, L.S.W., L.B.S.C., I. of W. Distance from London, 92 miles.
    Authority, Ventnor Gas and Water Company.
    Engineer Manager and Secretary, J. S. Ineson.
    Office, Victoria Street and 39, High Street.
    Share Capital paid up, £40,140 ⎱ gas and water.
    Loan Capital paid up, £9,150 ⎰ gas and water.
    Interest, 4 and 5 per cent. Dividends, 5½, 5, and £3 17s. per cent.
    Towns and villages in the area supplied, Ventnor, Bonchurch and St. Lawrence.
    Works established, 1866. Special Acts, 1866 and 1879.
    Total population supplied, 7,000.
    Daily consumption per head, 60 gals.
    Sources of supply, deep springs.
    Storage capacity, about two days' supply.
    Character of water, excellent.
    Death rate, 14 per 1,000, including visitors.
    Number of meters, 36.
    Length of mains, about 9½ miles.
    Price per 1,000 gals., trade purposes, 1s. 6d. to 6d., municipal purposes, 7½d.

Vicarage Hill (supplied by RUGBY).

Waddesdon, Bucks. *See* AYLESBURY.

Wakefield (City of). Railways G.N. and N.Y. Distance from London 175½ miles.
    Water Authority, City of Wakefield.
    Chairman, Alderman W. H. Milnes, J.P.
    Engineer, C. Clemesha Smith, M.I.C.E.
    Town Clerk, W. W. Greenhalgh.
    Office, Town Hall.
    Total capital invested, £860,000.
    Works established, 1837.
    Purchased by Local Authority, 1877.
    Special Acts—Wakefield Waterworks (Co.), 1837, 1842, 1862, 1873, 1874, 1876; following Corporation Acts, Wakefield Improvement Act, 1877; Wakefield Corporation Waterworks Act, 1880; Wakefield Corporation Act, 1887, 1894, 1897, 1899.
    Estimated population actually supplied, 138,000.
    Total quantity of water drawn per annum—
      From drainage areas ... ... (1906) 950,000,000 gals.
    Estimated total quantity of water available per annum—
      From drainage areas, 930,000,000 gals., exclusive of compensation water.
    Drainage areas situated at Rushworth, near Halifax, portions of Moss Moor and Rushworth Moor.

WAKEFIELD—*continued*.

Maximum annual rainfall over drainage area, 57·02 inches (1886).
Minimum　　　　　　„　　　　　　„　　　30·24　„　(1887).
Average　　　　　　„　　　　　　„　　　45·36　„　(period 21 years).
Town and villages within the area of control, with the population of each (1901) Census).

City of Wakefield	41,413
Altofts	4,024
Castleford	17,386
Featherstone	12,093
Methley	4,271
Normanton	12,352
Whitwood	4,873
Stanley	12,290
Sandal	6,843

(All Urban Districts.)
Portion of Wakefield Rural District Council ... 10,500 (approximate.)
　　„　　Tadcaster　　　　„　　　9,000　　　„
　　„　　Pontefract　　　　„　　　3,000　　　„
Average annual death rate 14·4 per 1,000 in city only.
Population on drainage area, 6 (gamekeeper's family).
Nature and extent of cultivation of ditto, about 150 acres grass, rest moorland.
The water authority have no control of drainage area.
Surface formation of drainage areas, millstone grit.
Storage reservoirs—
　　Ardsley　　...　...　...　...　capacity, 334,000,000 gals.
　　Ringstone　　...　...　...　...　　„　　244,000,000　„
　　Green Withens　　...　...　...　　„　　242,000,000　„
Filtering area, 10,000 square yards in 5 filter beds.
Service reservoirs—
　　Lindale Hill ...　...　...　...　capacity, 1,250,000 gals.
　　(Service reservoirs and tanks are also owned by several of the authorities taking water in bulk).

Analysis of water before filtration—　　　　　　　　　Grains per gal.

Chlorides equal to common salt	1·6
Nitrogen as nitrates and nitrites, equal to nitric acid ...	none.
Poisonous metals	none.
Free ammonia...	0·06
Albuminoid ammonia	0·01
Oxygen absorbed by organic and other oxidizable matter	0·11
Degrees of hardness (each degree representing a soap-destroying power equivalent to one grain of chalk per gallon)	2·7
Total dissolved solid matter...	4·62

Suspended matter, small, containing animaculæ.
Colour of column two feet in depth, brown, distinctly turbid.
Smell when warmed to 100° Fahrenheit, peaty.

Analysis of water after filtration and treatment to prevent action upon lead—
　　　　　　　　　　　　　　　　　　　　　Grains per gal

Chlorides equal to common salt	1·6
Nitrogen as nitrates and nitrites, equal to nitric acid ...	0·07
Poisonous metals	none.
Free ammonia	0·001
Albuminoid ammonia	0·002
Oxygen absorbed by organic and other oxidizable matter	0·02
Degrees of hardness (each degree representing a soap-destroying power equivalent to one grain of chalk per gallon)	3·8
Total dissolved solid matter...	6·27

WAKEFIELD—*continued.*

Suspended matter, practically none.

Colour of column two feet in depth, very slight.

Smell when warmed to 100° Fahrenheit, very slight.

Annual supply of water (year 1906), for domestic purposes, including all unmetered supplies for trade, street watering, etc.—262,268,000 gals. within city only.

For trade purposes, including public institutions, 225,634,000 gals., within city only.

For municipal purposes, included partly in domestic and partly in trade.

In bulk to other authorities, 460,746,000 gals.

Maximum day's consumption (Dec. 21st, 1906), 3,287,000 gals.

Scale of charges—

					£	s.	d.
Not exceeding £6 annual rent or value	...	...	...		0	7	6
„ £7 „ „	...	...	...		0	8	9
„ £8 „ „	...	...	...		0	10	0
„ £9 „ „	...	...	...		0	11	3
„ £10 „ „	...	...	...		0	12	6

Payable by the owner.

All dwelling-houses and dwelling-houses with shops, for domestic purposes only—

					£	s.	d.
Not exceeding £11 annual rent or value	...	...	...		0	13	9
, £20 „ „	...	...	...		1	4	0
„ £30 „ „	...	...	...		1	15	0
„ £40 „ „	...	...	...		2	5	0
„ £50 „ „	...	...	...		2	15	0
„ £60 „ „	...	...	...		3	0	0

and intermediate charges.

Above £60, Five pounds per centum per annum on rent or value.

Charges by meter, from 9d. per thousand for 50,000 gals. per quarter to 7d. per thousand for 6,000,000 gals. and upwards per quarter.

Number of meters in use, 400.

Length of distributing mains, 80 miles.

Wallasey, Cheshire. Railways, L.N.W., and G.W. Joint, and G.C. Distance from London, 200 miles.

Authority, Wallasey Urban District Council.

Chairman, Walter Eastwood.

Clerk and Solicitor to authority, H. W. Cook.

Engineer and Manager, J. H. Crowther.

Office, Dock Road, Seacombe, Cheshire.

Total capital expenditure, December, 1906, £177,932. Loans outstanding, £104,033 (mortgage debt, 31st March, 1906).

Works established, 1858.

Purchased by Local Authority, 1863.

Special Acts, 1861, 1863, 1872.

Total population of area of control—1881, 21,192 ; 1891, 33,227 ; 1901, 53,579.

Estimated population actually supplied, normal 62,000 ; holiday season, 72,000 to 100,000.

Average death rate, 16·53 per 1,000.

Towns and villages within area of control, Poulton, Seacombe, Egremont, Liscard, New Brighton and Wallasey.

Sources of supply in use, deep wells or borings in the Red Sandstone situated at Liscard, in the parish of Wallasey.

WALLASEY—*continued.*

Supplementary supply from Lake Vyrnwy (Liverpool Corporation).
Pumping stations, Liscard No. 1 ...   „   2,250,000 gals. (stand-by) per day.
    „   „   Liscard No. 2 ...   „   2,250,000   „   „
Service reservoir, Gorsehill, No. 1 ...   „   2,000,000   „   covered.
    „   „   „   No. 2 ...   „   4,300,000   „   „
Estimated total quantity of water available per annum, 1,733,750,000 gals.
Character of water, excellent for domestic purposes ; total hardness, 10°.
Analysis of water taken from No. 1 Station, Liscard, November, 1897.

Results expressed in parts per 100,000.

Mark and denomination of sample   ...   . Well at Liscard.
Total solid matter in solution   ...   .   28·0
Organic carbon, organic nitrogen   ...   .   traces only
Ammonia ...   .   0·003
Ammonia from organic matter by distillation with
    alkaline permanganate...   ...   .   0·007
Nitrogen as nitrates   ...   .   0·188
Combined chlorine   ...   .   4·30
Hardness ...   .   12·6deg.
Oxygen consumed in 15 minutes   ...   .   0·0025
    „   „   „   3 hours ...   .   0·0025
Very few organisms.
This is good water.
Analysis of water taken from No. 2 Station, Liscard, May, 1902.

Results expressed in parts per 100,000.

	Borehole 810ft.		Borehole 903ft.
Mark and denomination of sample	No. 1	...	No. 2.
Total solid matter in solution	29·6	...	31·1
Organic carbon	0·086	...	0·083
Organic nitrogen	0·029	...	0·023
Ammonia	0 004	...	0·005
Ammonia from organic matter by distillation with alkaline permanganate ...	0·008	...	0·002
Nitrogen as nitrates and nitrites ...	0·137	...	0·091
Total combined nitrogen	0·167	...	0·118
Combined chlorine	4·2	...	3·2
Hardness, temporary	1·34deg.	...	1·5deg.
„ permanent	9·71deg.	...	9·7deg.
„ total	11·05deg.	...	11·2deg.
Oxygen required to oxidise—			
In 15 minutes	0·005	...	0·000
In 3 hours	0·011	...	0·011

No 1 contains no organisms and is clear.
No. 2 contains no organisms and is clear.
The water is excellent.
Head on distributing mains—maximum, 176 feet ; minimum, 77 feet.
Annual supply of water (1906)—
        For domestic purposes   ...   .   548,704,594 gals.
        „   trade   „   153,449,459   „
        „   municipal   „   16,494,869   „
Total quantity of water drawn from deep wells, etc. (1906), 523,982,922 gals.
    „   „   „   „   „   „   Liverpool supply, 194,666,000 gals.
Natural rest level of water below surface 145 feet ; below O.D., 35 feet 6 inches.
Level below surface when pumping 2,250,000 gals. per day, 175 feet.
Average daily supply of water per head—
        For domestic purposes ...   .   25·49 gals. per head.
        „   trade   „   ...   .   7·12   „   „
        „   municipal   „   ...   .   ·76   „   „
Maximum day's supply, 2,520,998 gals. in July, 1906.

WALLASEY—*continued*.

    Assessment charge authorized, 10 per cent. on R.V.; present charge, 7½ per cent. on R.V.
    Authorised charge by meter   ...   . 2s. 6d. per 1,000 gals.
    Present   ,,   ,, ,, trade   ...   ... 1s. 2d.   ,,   ,,
    ,,   ,,   ,, ,, hotels, &c.   ... 2s. 3d.   ,,   ,,
    Number of meters, 460.
    Length of mains, 70 miles.

Wallingford Berks. Railway, G.W. Distance from London, 51 miles.
    Authority, Urban District Council.
    Secretary, Town Clerk.
    Works established, 1884.
    Total population of area supplied, 3,500.
    Annual supply of water, 14,600,000 gals.
    Daily consumption per head, domestic and trade, 13 gals.
    Source of supply, artesian well from below green rock.
    Character of water, very good.
    Death rate, 10·2 per 1,000.
    Number of meters, 4.
    Length of mains, about 4 miles.
    Scale of charges, domestic purposes free.
    Price for 1,000 gals., gardens, factories, stables, buildings, &c., 1s.
    Total water rent received, about £70.

Wallington (supplied by SUTTON).

Wallsend (supplied by NEWCASTLE-ON-TYNE).

Walmer, Kent. *See* DEAL.

Walsall, Staffs., population, 71,784 (supplied by SOUTH STAFFS. WATERWORKS Co.

Walsall Wood (supplied by SOUTH STAFFS. WATERWORKS Co.).

Walshaw (supplied by BURY).

Waltham Abbey (supplied by EAST LONDON WATERWORKS Co.).

Waltham St. Lawrence (supplied by MAIDENHEAD).

Walthamstow (supplied by METROPOLITAN WATER BOARD).

Walton, Staffs. (supplied by STAFFORD).

Walton-on-Thames, Surrey (supplied by WEST SURREY WATER Co.).

Walton-on-the-Naze (supplied by TENDRING HUNDRED).

Walton, Superior and **Inferior,** Lancs. (supplied by WARRINGTON).

Wanstead (supplied by EAST LONDON WATER Co.).

Wantage, Berks. Railway, G.W. (Wantage Road). Distance from London, 60¼ miles.
  Authority, Wantage Water Company, Ld.
  Chairman, E. Ormonde.
  Hon. Secretary, E. Ormond.
  Manager, F. J. Pegler.
  Office, Market Place.
  Share capital, £1,410; last dividend, 10 per cent. Loan capital, £2,000 at 4½ per cent.
  Works established, Provisional Order, 1876.
  Total population supplied, 4,648.
  Towns and villages in the area supplied—Wantage, Grove and Charlton.
  Average death rate, 15·9 per 1,000.
  Source of supply, chalk hills by gravitation.
  System of filtration, charcoal and gravel.
  Supply unlimited ; charges range from 5s. to 21s. per house.

Warblington (supplied by PORTSMOUTH).

Ware, Herts. Railway, G.E. Distance from London, 22 miles.
  Authority, Urban District Council.
  Engineer, R. Boyd.
  Clerk to Council, G. H. Gisby.
  Office, Ware.
  Total population of area supplied, 6,000.
  Sources of supply, deep wells.
  Character of water, good.

Warfield, Berks (supplied by WOKINGHAM).

Wargrave (supplied by WOKINGHAM).

Warley (supplied by SOUTH STAFFS. WATERWORKS Co.).

Warlingham (supplied by EAST SURREY WATERWORKS Co.).

Warminglid (supplied by CUCKFIELD).

Warminster, Wilts. Railway, G.W. Distance from London, 100¼ miles.
  Authority, Urban District Council of Warminster.
  Chairman, E. J. Bradfield.
  Secretary, Herbert J. Wakeman.
  Office, 32, Market Place.
  Engineer and Surveyor, Charles Henry Lawton.
  Loans outstanding, £8,600.
  Towns and villages in the area supplied, Warminster and parish of Bishopstrow.
  Works established, 1885.
  Total population of area supplied, 5,800.
  Total number of consumers, 1,360.
  Maximum day's consumption, 146,000 gals. in July.
  Total quantity of water supplied per annum, 44,254,000 gals.
  Estimated total quantity of water available per annum, 60,000,000 gals.
  Source of supply in use, springs in the upper green sand.

WARMINSTER—*continued.*

Filtration, none required.
Character of water, soft, pure.
Analysis of Water—

Solid matter, 100·000	...	8·60	Hardness	before boiling..	6·00°
Chlorine ...	... ...	2·90		after boiling. ...	5·8°
Sulphuric acid	... ...	3·12	Am. in 1,000,000	Saline	·02
Nitric acid ...	... ...	0·38		Organic	·04
Lime	... ...	3·52	Nitrogen as nitrates, etc. ...		0·100
Magnesia ...	... ...	1·03			

Death rate, 13·5 per 1,000.
Pumping station, Crockerton.
Plant, one Worthington triple expansion condensing engine, and two turbine driven pumps.
Service reservoirs, capacity, 300,000 gals., and one new covered collecting reservoir at pumping station, capacity 50,000 gals.
Number of meters in use, 96.
Length of distributing mains, 8 miles.
Pressure on distributing mains — maximum, about 90 lbs. ; minimum, 25 lbs. per sq. in.
Scale of charges—assessment, net annual rateable value. Houses under £3, 1s. 6d. per quarter ; houses over £3 and under £8, 2s. 2d. per quarter ; houses £8 and upwards at the rate of 1s. 3d. in the £ per annum.
Consumers requiring water for both domestic and trade purposes can be supplied by meter, provided that the quarterly payments are at least equal to what would be paid if water were taken at the *full rateable value.*
Water closets, the foregoing charges include the supply to closets as under—
In every case, 1 W.C. free.
Where the rateable value of the whole premises exceeds £20, 2 W.C.s free.

			£30, 3	”
”	”	”	£50, 4	”

Additional water closets, 1s. per quarter.
Fixed baths, each, 1s. per quarter.
Dwelling-houses partly used as retail shops, or for other business purposes not requiring an abnormal supply, the charge will be made on three-fourths of the rateable value when exceeding £16, except where the following businesses are carried on, when the charge will be made on the full rateable value or by meter, at the option of the council—bakers, butchers, pork butchers, hairdressers, hotels, inns, temperance hotels, restaurants, printers, fishmongers, laundry keepers.
Price per 1,000 gals. as follows with intermediate charges—

						£	s.	d.
2,000 gals. per quarter	...	...	...	...		0	3	0
10,000 ”		...	...	...	...	0	12	6
20,000 ”		...	...	...	...	1	5	0
50,000 ”		...	...	...	...	2	10	0
100,000 ”		...	...	...	...	4	3	4
200,000 ”		...	...	...	...	7	1	8
400,000 ”		...	...	...	...	10	16	8
500,000 ”		...	...	...	...	12	10	0

Meters to be provided and kept in repair by the consumers, or they can be hired from the Council on the following terms—

For ½-inch meter	...	...	...	...	1s. 6d. per quarter.
” ¾ ”	...	...	...	...	2s. 6d. ”
” 1 ”	...	...	...	...,	3s. 6d. ”

Warmsworth (supplied by DONCASTER).

Warrenby, Yorks (supplied by CLEVELAND).

Warrington, Lancs.   Railways, L. & N.W. and G.C.   Distance from London, 182¼ miles.

Authority, Warrington Corporation.
Chairman, Alderman R. W. Francomb, C.C.
Engineer in charge, James Deas, A.M.I.C.E., M.I.M.E.
Office, Municipal Offices Town Hall.
Total capital invested, including loans, £448,998.
Towns and villages within the area of control, with population of each (1901 Census)—

Warrington	64,702
Burtonwood	2,187
Winwick-with-Hulme	1,253
Houghton-with-Middleton	214
Southworth-with-Croft	970
Kenyon	329
Rixton-with-Glazebrook	998
Culcheth	2,294
Woolston-with-Martinscroft	484
Grappenhall	987
Poulton-with-Fearnhead	1,428
Thelwall	481
Appleton	3,885
Stretton	310
Hatton	319
Daresbury	153
Great Sank y	1,034
Keckwick	65
Moore	408
Acton Grange	145
Penketh	1,735
Walton Superior	215
„ Inferior	719

Works established, 1846.
Purchased by local authority, 1891.
Special Acts, Warrington Waterworks Acts, 1846, 1849, 1855, 1868, 1878, Warrington Corporation Acts, 1890, 1899.
Total population of area of control, 1891, 73,556 ; 1901, 85,325.
Total number of consumers, 19,475.
Estimated population actually supplied, 97,375.
Annual supply of water (1906)—

For domestic purposes	501,351,000 gals.
„ trade „	241,933,000 „
„ municipal „	43,890,000 „

Normal day's consumption, 2,462,000 gals.
Total quantity of water drawn per annum (1906)—

From drainage areas	about 179,898,000 gals.
„ deep wells or borings	607,276,000 „

Estimated total quantity of water available per day—
From drainage areas, about 375,000 gals. (minimum yield, 3 dry years' basis).
  „   From deep wells or borings—
    (a) Winwick, estimated minimum yield, about 1,400,000 gals.
    (b) Myddleton   „   „   „   1,350,000 „
Sources of supply in use—drainage areas situated at N.E. of village of Hatton on Dennow and Bog Rough Brooks (S. of Warrington).
Deep wells or borings—(a) Winwick, and (b) Myddleton, N. of Warrington.
Estimated maximum daily discharge at points of collection, 40,000,000 gals. (very exceptional flood, supposititious only).
Estimated minimum daily discharge at points of collection, 180,000 gals.
  „   average   „   „   „   „   800,000 „
Maximum annual rainfall over drainage area, 49 inches (supposititious only).

Minimum	„	„	„	23 „ „
Average	„	„	„	35 „ „

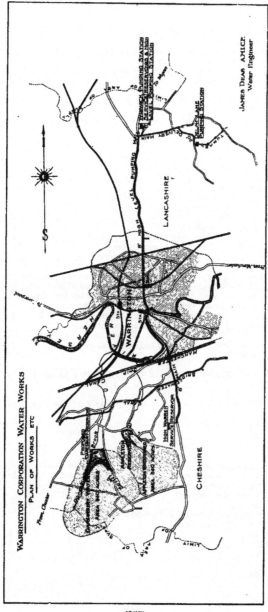

WARRINGTON—*continued.*

Population on drainage area, about 300 persons.

Nature, mostly highly cultivated.

Corporation has contributed to the carrying of the sewage of about 200 of above population out of the drainage area.

Winwick works—natural rest level of water, about ordnance datum level, but not properly ascertainable, as continuous pumping has been going on for a few years.

Level of water below surface (when pumping 1,400,000 gals. per day), 30 feet below ordnance datum.

Myddleton Works—natural rest level, 36 feet above ordnance datum.

Geological data—

Surface formation of drainage areas, red marl and keuper sandstone of the Triassic.

Strata tapped by wells or borings, pebble beds of the Triassic (new red sandstone, Bunter).

Locality and extent of outcrop of same, between Warrington and Leigh, about 6 square miles.

Level of surface, about 110 feet above ordnance datum.

Well, 127' 5" deep, diameter, 9' 0".

Depth in feet.		Thickness feet. inches.	
30' 0"	Moss...	2	0
	Fine white sand	28	0
127' 5"	Fine grained sandstone	97	5
172' 6"	Coarse compact sandstone, millet seed grains, and band of red marl ...	45	1

Storage reservoir, Appleton reservoir, original capacity, 62,000,000 gals., now silted up till effective capacity does not probably exceed 50,000,000 gals.

Filtering area provided, 1,370 square yards in 3 filter beds (one being a spare).

Details and dimensions, wells, borings, headings, &c.—

Winwick—3 wells, about 9' diameter; connected to adit, 5' × 3½', about 1,300 yards long; invert, 38' below ordnance datum.

Myddleton—well, 12' 6" diameter, 160 feet deep, with adit, 6' × 4', about 1,200 yards long; invert, 90' below ordnance datum at well, and rising 1 in 1,200 from well.

Pumping stations—

  (a) Winwick, estimated minimum yield, 1,400,000 gals. per day.

  (b) Myddleton   ,,   ,,   1,350,000   ,,

Service reservoirs—

Winwick (1) ...	...	...	capacity 2,000,000 gals., covered.	
,, (2) ...	...	...	,, 4,500,000	,, ,,
High Warren ...	...	...	,, 1,200,000	,, ,
Appleton ...	...	...	,, 700,000	,, ,,

Number of meters in use, 353.

Length of distributing mains, about 148 miles.

Result of analysis expressed in parts per 100,000—Winwick.

				Winwick		Appleton.
Total solid matters	...	...	...	30·68	...	34·48
Organic carbon	...	...	...	·031	...	·364
Organic nitrogen	...	...	...	·007	...	·036
Ammonia	...	...	...	0	...	·005
Nitrogen as nitrates and nitrites	...			·451	...	·304
Total combined nitrogen	...	...		·458	...	·344
Chlorine	...	...	...	2·0	...	2·3
Hardness—temporary	...	...		12·1	...	8·2
Permanent	...	...	...	9·1	...	13·3
					...	
Total	...	...	...	...	21·2	...	21·5
					...	
Remarks	...	...	...	slightly turbid.		turbid.

WARRINGTON—*continued.*

All water drawn from drainage areas is used for trade supply, the domestic
supply and part of the trade supply being from underground sources.
Scale of charges :
Domestic purposes—
    Six per cent. per annum on the rateable value, but no domestic tenement is
    charged less than 5s. each per annum.
    The domestic rate on cottages assessed at £10 and under is charged to the
    owner, who is allowed a composition of 10 per cent. if paid within the time
    specified on the demand note.
Terms and conditions of supply per meter, trade purposes—
    For any quantity up to 200,000 gals. per quarter, at 1s. per 1,000, but not less
    than 10s. per quarter.
    For any quantity exceeding 200,000 gals., and up to 5,000,000 gals. per quarter,
    at 1s. per 1,000 for the first 200,000 gals., and 9d. for every additional
    1,000 gals.
    For any quantity exceeding 5,000,000 gals. per quarter, at 1s. per 1,000 for the
    first 200,000 gals., and 8d. for every additional 1,000 gals., but not less than
    £190 per quarter.
    Together with meter rents at the following rates, ½ inch, 3s. ; ¾ inch, 4s. ;
    1 inch, 5s. ; 1¼ inch, 7s. ; 2 inch, 9s. ; 3 inch, 15s. ; 6 inch, 45s. per
    quarter.
    The Corporation will clean, keep in repair, and renew all meters when such
    repairs are necessary owing to ordinary wear.
    Building and temporary supplies per meter will be charged at the rate of 2s.
    per 1,000 gals., but not less than £1 per quarter.
Charges for supplies other than domestic, or per meter, per annum—
    Offices, lock-up shops, &c., 3 per cent. on rateable value.
    Baths in dwelling houses, houses assessed at £10 or under, 5s. ; over £10, 10s.,
    and 5s. for each additional one.
    Blacksmiths, 10s. for the first hearth, and 5s. each additional one.
    Beerhouses and hotels, ¼ of domestic rate extra for business purposes, with a
    maximum of £1.
    Cattle troughs, 20s. each.
    Churches and chapels, 7s. 6d. to 20s. ; two w.c's. allowed ; over two, 5s. each.
    Water for organs extra.
    Cows, 2s. 6d. each.
    Gardens, 10s. for the first 1,000 square yards and under, and 7s. 6d. for each
    additional 1,000.
    Horses, 5s. each.
    Hydrants for fire protection, 20s. each.
    Water-closets in works, warehouses, &c., 15s. each.

Warton (supplied by CARNFORTH).

Warwick. Railways, G.W. and L.N.W. Distance from London, 107¼ miles.
    Authority, Town Council.
    Chairman, T. Kemp, Mayor.
    Secretary, B. Campbell, Town Clerk.
    Resident Engineer, Fred. Stanyer.
    Works first constructed, 1874.
    Total population supplied, about 12,000.
    District of supply, Warwick, Haseley, Beausall, Budbrooke, Hatton, St. Mary's,
    St. Nicholas.
    Average death rate, 12·2 per 1,000.
    Source of supply—one well lined with cast iron cylinders sunk down to the rock ;
    the other source is by gravitation from some highlands four miles from town. The
    water is obtained by driving adits into water-bearing strata, and allowing it
    to percolate into pipes.

WARWICK—*continued.*

The supply is constant, but not abundant in dry seasons; when the supply is short the outside villages are not supplied, but the barracks, which are outside the borough, are allowed to draw from the main which passes near them.
Character of water, hard.
Filtration, none; softening, none.
Storage capacity in service reservoirs, 500,000 gals.
Head on distributing mains—maximum, 130 ft.; minimum, 60 ft.
Annual supply of water, 107,508,000 gals.
Average daily supply per head for all purposes, 24·48 gals.
Maximum day's supply, 364,000 gals. in July.
Scale of charges, domestic rate, 6d. in £ on R.V.
Price per 1,000 gals., 9d.
No. of meters, 130.

Waterfoot (supplied by BURY).

Waterloo (supplied by PORTSMOUTH).

Waterloo with Seaforth (supplied by LIVERPOOL).

Water Orton (supplied by BIRMINGHAM).

Watford, Herts. Railway, L.N.W. Distance from London, 17½ miles.
Authority, Urban District Council.
Secretary, H. Morton Turner.
Engineer, D. Waterhouse.
Offices, Council Offices, High Street, Watford.
Loan outstanding, £20,379 4s. 1d.
Works established, 1854.
Total population supplied, 33,924.
Average death rate, 10 per 1,000.
A small part of the Rural District is supplied by the Colne Valley Water Co.
Source of supply, wells and borings to the chalk.
　　　　Well and 12-inch boring, total depth 117 feet.
　　　　,,　　9-inch　,,　　,,　　,,　150　,,
　　　　,,　　24-inch　,,　　,,　　,,　140　,,
Analysis of water—
　　Particulars of source, chalk well.
　　Physical examination—
　　Colour, greenish tint; odour, none.
　　Turbidity, clear and bright; no deposit.
　　Chemical examination—

	Results in Grains per gallon.		Parts per 100,000.
Total solid matter dried at 180° C.			
Chlorine	1·8	...	2·6
Equivalent to chlorides	3·0	...	4·3
(60% Cl.)			
Nitric nitrogen	0·53	...	0·76
Equivalents to nitrates	3·18	...	4·56
(17% N.)			
Nitrites	absent.		
Hardness, permanent 5°; temporary, 13°; total　18°	...		26°
Lead, copper, zinc, iron	absent.		
Free ammonia	0·0015	...	0·0022
Organic ammonia	0·0020	...	0·0028
Oxygen absorbed at 98 F. in 3 hours ...	0·0112	...	0·0160

WATFORD—continued.

Bacteriological examination—
Number of organisms per cubic centimetre capable of growing
on alkaline nutrient jelly at 20° C. in four days. Counted by
aid of pocket lens. ... ...   56 only.
Smallest quantity of water in which growth occurred with
production of acid and gas in bile-salt glucose broth. (1,   No acid or
5, 10, or 20 c.c.) ... ...   gas in 36c.c
Nature of organisms found in this growth. ... ...   No objection-
   able bacteris
   of any kind.
Spores of the bacillus enteritidis sporogones—in 150 cc., absent; in 350 c.c.,
absent; in 500 c.c., absent.
Both the chemical and bacteriological results are eminently satisfactory.
The water is of a very high standard of purity, and is well adapted for all the
purposes of a public supply.
Storage in service reservoirs, 1,000,000 gals.
Head on distributing mains, maximum, 90 lbs.; minimum, 10 lbs. per sq. in.
Annual supply of water, 388,199,873 gals.
Average daily supply per head—domestic, 27·98 gals.; trade, 3·37 gals.
Maximum day's supply, 35,702,719 gals., August, 1906.
Assessment charge, 5 per cent. on R.V.
Price by meter, 1s. per 1,000 gals.
Number of meters, 8.
Total length of supply and distributing mains, 40 miles.

Wath-upon-Dearne, Yorks. Railways, M., G.C., and Hull and Barnsley. Distance
from London, 165 miles.
Authority, Wath-upon-Dearne Urban District Council.
Chairman, J. H. Kelly, C.C.
Clerk to authority, Nicholson & Co.
Engineer and Manager, H. Cecil Poole.
Office, Town Hall.
Loans outstanding, £19,000.
Works established, 1858. Special Act, 1898 (for compulsory purchase).
Total population of area supplied, 12,122.
Daily consumption per head—domestic, 11 gals.; trade, practically nil.
Average death rate, 14 per 1,000.
Towns and villages in the area supplied, Wath-upon-Dearne, West Melton,
Brampton, Bierlow and Ardwick-upon-Dearne.
Sources of supply, watershed (160 acres); well, 200 feet deep; one, 16 in.-driven
tube well; and arrangement with Dearne Valley Water Company.
Character of water, no organic impurity; total hardness, 24°; hardness after
treatment, 15°; softening, aeration and lime. System of filtration, sand.
Storage capacity, 5,000,000 gals.; service reservoirs, 1,500,000 gals.
Head on distributing mains—maximum, 250 feet; minimum, 50 feet.
Annual supply, 60,000,000 gals.
Average daily supply per head—domestic, 11½ gals.; trade, about 2 gals.
Maximum day's supply, 170,000 gals., in August.
Charge authorised, 1s. 1½d. in the £ on gross R.V.
Present rate of charge, 1s. 1½d. in the £ on net. R.V.
Authorised charge by meter, 1s. 6d. per 1,000.
Present average, 1s. to 1s. 6d. per 1,000.
Number of meters, 80. Length of mains—supply, 5 miles; distributing, 25 miles.

Weald, The (supplied by SEVENOAKS).

Weardale and Consett, Railways, G.N. and N.E. Distance from London, 250 miles.
    Authority, Weardale and Consett Water Company.
    Chairman, John Brownlees,
    Secretary, W. Harding.
    Engineer, R. Askwith, M.I.C.E.
    Head Office, Darlington. Engineer's Office, Bishop Auckland. Branches at Durham and Consett.
    Share capital, ordinary, £865,000; preference, 4 per cent., £105,615. Loan capital, £109,445.
    Dividend, 5¾ per cent.
    Total water rent received, £77,050 (1906).
    Works established, 1866. Special Acts, 1866, 1869, 1875, 1879, 1894, 1902.
    Total population supplied, 320,280.
    Towns and villages in the area supplied, City of Durham, Consett, Stanley, Chester-le-Street, Towlaw, Crook, Spennymoor, Shildon, West Auckland, etc.
    Sources of supply, Wear and Derwent watersheds, millstone grit.
    Character of water, soft.
    System of filtration, sand.
    Storage capacity, 1,381,000,000 gals.
    Total annual supply of water, 2,317,086,600 gals.
    Daily consumption per head, domestic, 10·45 gals.; trade, 9·61 gals.
    Number of meters, 1,480.
    Length of mains, 527 miles.
    Assessment charge varies.
    Price per 1,000 gals., trade, varies.
    NOTE.—The Consett Company has been amalgamated with the Weardale and Shildon Waterworks Company by Act, 1902, and is now known as Weardale and Consett Water Company.

Weaverham, Northwich, Cheshire.
    Authority, Company.
    Population supplied, 1,761.
    No returns supplied.

Wednesbury (supplied by the SOUTH STAFFS. WATERWORKS Co.).

Wednesfield (supplied by WOLVERHAMPTON).

Weekley (supplied by KETTERING).

Weeley, Essex (supplied by TENDRING HUNDRED).

Weeping Cross (supplied by STAFFORD).

Welham (supplied by RETFORD).

Wellingborough, Northants. Railways, M. and L.N.W. Distance from London 63½ miles.
    Authority, Urban District Council.
    Clerk to Council, J. T. Parker.
    Surveyor and Engineer, E. Y. Harrison, A.M.I.C.E.
    Office, 29, Church Street.
    Works established, 1871.
    Annual supply of water, 56,304,112 gals.
    Daily consumption per head, 8·33 gals.
    Source of supply, two wells.

WELLINGBOROUGH—*continued.*

Storage capacity, 650,000 gals.
Character of water, 35° of hardness, softened by Atkins' process.
System of filtration, disc filters, Atkins' type,
Number of meters, 300.
Scale of charges—assessment, 4 per cent. on rental.
Price per 1,000 gals., domestic and trade, 1s. 6d. to 1s., sliding scale.
Total water rent received, about £3,940.

Wellington, Salop. Railways, L.N.W. and G.W. Distance from London, 144 miles,
Authority, Urban District Council.
Secretary, Clerk to Urban District Council, Bank Chambers.
Area supplied, 5 miles.
Works established, 1851. Special Acts, 1860.
Total population supplied, 12,700.
Daily consumption per head, 24½ gals.
Source of supply, surface.
Storage capacity, 23,000,000 gals.
Character of water, medium, hard and soft.
Death rate, 17·2 per 1,000.
Assessment charge, net rateable value, £36,158.
Price per 1,000 gals, charged by percentage, 1s.

Wellington, Somerset.
Authority, Urban District Council.
Population, 7,400.

Wells, Somerset. Railways, G.W. and L.S.W. Distance from London, 125 miles.
Authority, Corporation.
Clerk, E. P. Foster.
Area supplied, in and out parishes of St. Cuthbert, Wells, Somerset.
Works established, 1870. Purchased by Local Authority 24th June, 1902, for
£19,176. Special Acts, 1870, 1901.
Total population of area supplied, about, 5,000.
Sources of supply, springs from limestone beds on the Mendip Hills.
Storage capacity, 350,000 gals.
Character of water, excellent.
Service reservoirs, 2.
Scale of charges—assessment charge, 1s. in the £ on rental.

Welshpool, Montgomery. Railways, L.N.W., G.W. and Cambrian. Distance from
London, 182 miles.
Authority, Corporation.
Secretary, Town Clerk.
Works established, 1863.
Total population of area supplied, 6,114.
Daily consumption per head, domestic and trade, 12 gals.
Source of supply, watershed on Lord Powis' property.
Character of water, soft.
System of filtration, sand and gravel.
Death rate, 13 per 1,000
Price for 1,000 gals., trade, 9d.
Total water rent received, about £600.

Wemyss, Scotland.
 Authority, District Council.
 Population, about 8,000.
 Date of formation, 1878.　Special Act, 1878.
 Source of supply, gathering grounds.

Wenlock. *See* MUCH WENLOCK.

Wentbridge (supplied by PONTEFRACT).

Wentworth (supplied by ROTHERHAM).

Werrington (supplied by PETERBOROUGH).

West Auckland (supplied by WEARDALE AND CONSETT WATER Co.).

Westbere, Kent (supplied by CANTERBURY).

West Blandon (supplied by WOKING).

West Blatchington, Sussex (supplied by BRIGHTON).

West Bradford, Lancs. (supplied by CLITHEROE).

West Bromwich (supplied by SOUTH STAFFS. WATERWORKS Co.).

Westbury, Wilts.　Railway, G.W.　Distance from London, 101 miles.
 Authority, Westbury and Dillon Marsh Joint Water Committee.
 Clerk to Authority, John Callaway.
 Manager, T. Harley Rushton.
 Office, Laverton Institute, Westbury, Wilts.
 No returns supplied.

West Cheshire Water Company. Railways, L.N.W. and G.W. joint. Distance from
London, 200 miles.
 Authority, West Cheshire Water Company.
 Chairman, John Holt.
 Secretary and Resident Engineer, Philip Howard Bettle.
 Office, 9, Hamilton Square, Birkenhead.
 Consulting Engineer, Isaac Carr, M.I.C.E.
 Share capital paid up, £80,000 ; last dividend, 6 per cent.
 Works established, 1884.
 Special Acts, West Cheshire Water Company, 1884, 47 and 48 Vict., cap. 52, and
  Provisional Order, 1892.
 Total population of area supplied, 32,835.
 Towns and villages in the area supplied—the Urban Districts of Higher
  Bebington, Lower Bebington, Bromborough, Ellesmere Port, and part of Rural
  Districts of Wirral and Chester.
 Sources of supply, wells and boreholes in red sandstone at Prenton and Hooton,
  Cheshire.
 Character of water, hard.
 Filtration, Candy's patent.
 Annual supply of water, about 321,783,000 gals.
 Daily consumption per head—domestic, about 35 gals.
 Assessment, 6 to 7 per cent.
 Price per 1,000 gals., 9d. to 1s. 6d., trade.
 Number of meters, 73.
 Length of mains, 150 miles.

West Clandon (supplied by WOKING).

West Drayton, Middlesex (supplied by RICKMANSWORTH).

Westergate, Sussex (supplied by BOGNOR).

Western Valleys Water and Gas Co., Mon. *See* RISCA.

West Gorton (supplied by MANCHESTER).

West Farley (supplied by MAIDSTONE).

Westgate and Birchington, Kent. Railway, L.C.D. Distance from London, 72 miles.
    Authority, Company.
    Population supplied, 2,670.
    No returns supplied.

West Gloucestershire Water Co.
    Offices, Kingswood Hill, near Bristol.
    No returns supplied.

West Ham, Essex (supplied by METROPOLITAN WATER BOARD).

West Hampshire Water Co. *See* CHRISTCHURCH.

West Hartlepool. *See* HARTLEPOOL.

West Horsley (supplied by WOKING).

Westhoughton, Lancs. (supplied by BOLTON).

West Kirby, Cheshire. *See* HOYLAKE.

West Lancashire. *See* SOUTHPORT.

West Melton, Yorks. Purchased by Wath-upon-Dearne Urban District Council, October 1st, 1898.

West Middlesex. *See* METROPOLITAN WATER BOARD.

Weston. *See* RUNCORN.

Weston-super-Mare, Som. Railway, G.W. Distance from London, 137½ miles.
  Authority, Urban District Council.
  Engineer in charge, Hugh Nettleton, A.M.I.C.E.
  Clerk, S. C. Smith.
  Office, Town Hall.
  Towns and villages in the area supplied, Weston, Uphill, and Milton.
  Works established, 1853. Special Act, 1878.
  Total population of area supplied, about 21,000.
  Annual supply of water, 240,000,000 gals.
  Source of supply, wells. The Council own 40 acres of land, adjoining the wells.
    The supply is practically inexhaustible.
  Storage capacity, 3 days' supply.
  Character of water, 30° hardness. System of filtration, none.
  Death rate, 13·33 per 1,000.
  Length of mains, about 35 miles. Number of meters, 150.
  Assessment charge, 6 per cent. on rateable value below £20, and 5 per cent. above
    £20.
  Price for 1,000 gals., trade, 10s. up to 5,000; 1s. 6d. for each 1,000 up to
    30,000 ; 1s. 3d. up to 50,000 ; above 50,000, 1s.

West Pennard (supplied by GLASTONBURY).

West Surrey Water Company. Railway, L.S.W.
  Chairman, A. T. Simpson, J.P., M.I.C.E.
  Engineer, J. K. Hill, M.I.M.E,
  Secretary, W. Colnbrook, F.C.I.S.
  Office, 38, Parliament Street, Westminster, S.W.
  Share capital, £109,280.
  Loan capital, £30,900.
  Dividend—ordinary, 7 and 9 per cent.; preference, 5 and 6 per cent.
  Works established, 1869 ; Special Acts, 1869, 1877, 1888, and 1901.
  Total population supplied, 28,000.
  Towns and villages in the area supplied—Walton, Oatlands, Hersham, Weybridge,
    Chertsey, Addlestone, and Byfleet, in the County of Surrey ; and Shepperton,
    Littleton, in the county of Middlesex.
  Source of supply, Thames.
  Character of water, excellent.
  Assessment charge—R.R. value.
  Price for 1,000 gals., 9d.

West Tarring (supplied by WORTHING).

Westwood (supplied by BROADSTAIRS).

West Worthing, Sussex (supplied by WORTHING).

Wetherby District Water Co. *See* LINTON.

Wexford.
  Authority, Corporation.
  Total expenditure, £27,000.
  Source of supply, gravitation.
  Storage capacity, 20,000,000 gals., three months' supply.
  Assessment charge, 2s. in the £.

Wexham (supplied by SLOUGH).

Weybridge, Surrey (supplied by WEST SURREY WATER Co.).

Weymouth, Dorset. Railways, L.S.W. and G.W.
    Distance from London, 142¼ miles.
    Owners, private company.
    Population supplied, 25,000.
    No returns supplied.

Wey Valley.
    Authority, Wey Valley Water Co., Farnham, Surrey.
    Chairman, G. F. Roumein, J.P.
    Secretary, F. C. Potter.
    Waterworks Manager, Arthur H. Cooper, Farnham District.
        ,,   ,,   H. C. Mitchell, Hindhead District.
    Office, South Street, Farnham.
    Consulting Engineer, A. C. Pain, M.I.C.E., 17, Victoria Street, Westminster.
    Total capital raised—
        Ordinary 10 per cent. share capital under Act of 1898, £30,000.
        Irredeemable 3½ per cent. debenture capital and rent charge under Act of 1898,
        £7,500.
        Additional ordinary 7 per cent. share capital under order of 1905, producing
        £3,594 7s. 6d.—£3,000.
        Irredeemable 3½ per cent. debenture capital under order of 1905, £890.
    Dividend, 4 per cent.
    Works established, 1898.
    Special Act, Wey Valley, Frimley, and Farnham Water Act, 1898, 1905.
    Total number of consumers, about 8,900. Number of houses connected, 1,666.
    Number of meters in use, 183.
    Area of control—the parishes of Farnham Rural, Frensham, Dockenfield, Shotter-
        mill, Seale, Puttenham, Wanborough, and part of the Parish of Farnham, in
        the county of Surrey ; the parishes of Bentley, Binstead, Kingsley, Greyshott,
        Headley, and Bramshott, in the county of Hants ; and the parishes of Fern-
        hurst, Linchmere, and North Ambersham, in the county of West Sussex ; there
        being, however, a restriction on the exercise of the company's powers in the
        Hampshire parishes entailing the consent of the District Council for the
        district within which the parishes are respectively situate. Pursuant to
        the consent of the Alton Rural District Council, the parish of Grayshott and
        part of the parish of Binstead are now included in the company's area of suppy.
    Source of supply, four Wells, 250 ft. deep to the upper green sand (at Hindbead).
        The greater portion of this district is supplied by the Frimley and Farnborough
        District Water Co., Itchell Pumping Station, Crondall, Hants.
    Pumping station, Hindhead.
    Analysis taken March, 1906. Bacteriological examination :—
        Number of organisms per cubic centimetre capable of growing on alkaline
        nutrient jelly at 20° C. in 14 days, counted by aid of pocket lens—68.
        Smallest quantity of water in which growth occurred, with production of acid
        and gas in bile-salt glucose broth (1, 5, 10, or 20 c.c.)—No acid or gas in any.
        Nature of organisms found in this growth—No objectionable bacteria.
        Spores of the bacillus enteritidis sporogones, in 150 c.c.—Absent.
                                 in 350 c.c.—Absent.
                                  in 500 c.c.—Absent.
    Water is of most exceptional purity, admirably adapted in every respect for
        all the purposes of a public supply.
    Turbidity, none. Colour, normal. Odour, none.

WEY VALLEY—*continued.*

Determinations.	Results in Grains per gal.	Parts per 100,000
Total solid matter dried at 180° C	13·7	19·6
Chlorine	1·1	1·6
Equivalent to chlorides (60 per cent. Cl.)...	1·83	2·66
Nitric nitrogen	·25	·36
Equivalent to nitrates (17 per cent N.) ...	1·5	2·16
Nitrites	Absent	Absent
Hardness: Permanent, 5·5° ; temporary, 3.5° ; total	9·0°	
Lead, copper, zinc, iron	Absent	Absent
Free ammonia	·00168	.0024
Organic ammonia	·0011	.0016
Oxygen absorbed at 80° F. in 3 hours ...	·0050	.0171

Service reservoir, Hindhead, capacity, 200,000 gals., covered.
Maximum day's consumption, 73,000 gals., holiday ; 65,000 gals., normal.
Scale of charges on annual rateable value—
From 2s. 3d. per quarter on houses not over £5 per annum.
To 31s. 10d.   „   „   £100   „
Over £100, 1½ per cent per quarter.
The above charges include 1 w.c.
No meter allowed for domestic supply.
Water by meter—
Minimum charge, 20s. per quarter.

Exceeding	10,000 gals., and not exceeding	15,000	2s.	per 1,000
„	15,000 „ „ „	30,000	1s. 9d.	„
„	30,000 „ „ „	60,000	1s. 6d.	„
„	60,000 „ „ „	120,000	1s. 3d.	„
„	120,000		1s. 0d.	„

Meter rents from ¼″ at 3s. to 2″ at 15s. per quarter.
Length of distributing mains, 60 miles.

Wheatley (supplied by DONCASTER).

Whickham (supplied by NEWCASTLE).

Whins-le-Milton (supplied by STIRLING).

Whipton (supplied by EXETER).

Whiston (supplied by ROTHERHAM).

Whitby, Yorks. Railways, G. N. and N. E. Distance from London, 244¾ miles.
Authority, Whitby Waterworks Company.
Chairman, Robert Elliott Pannett, J.P.
Secretary, Henry Sinclair.
Office, Baxtergate, Whitby.
Consulting Engineer, Henry Tobey, Malton.

Share capital paid up—Ordinary	...	...	...	... £20,000	0	0
Mortgage Loans	...	...	...	5,000	0	0
3½ per cent. Preference Stock, 1895	...			8,000	0	0
Premiums	...	...	...	432	0	0
New Shares, 1897	...	...	...	7,700	0	0
Premiums	...	...	...	2,278	1	0
				£43,410	1	0

Dividends—Preference, 3½ per cent.; original, 8½ per cent.; new shares, £5 19s.
per cent.

WHITBY—*continued.*

Works established, about 1860.
Special Acts—Whitby Waterworks Act, 1864; Whitby Water Act, 1895.
Total population of area of control, 1891, 13,300; 1901, 12,048.
Total number of consumers, 3,054.
Estimated population actually supplied—18,000 (holiday).
　　　　　　　　　　　　　　　12,000 (normal).
　　　,,　　　　,,　　　　　,,　　　　,,
Towns and villages within the area of control, with population of each (1901
　　Census)—Whitby　　　...　　...　　...　　...　　...　　...　　11,748
　　　　　　　Sleights　　...　　...　　...　　...　　...　　...　　300
　　　　　　　Ruswarp—included in Whitby.
Sources of supply in use—drainage areas situated at Egton High Moor, North
　　Riding, Yorks.; surface springs situated at Egton High Moor, Hazel Head,
　　North Riding, Yorks.
Nature of drainage area, moorland.
The Water Authority have no control of drainage area.
Surface formation of drainage areas, moorland.
Nature of subsoil yielding water, sandstone.
Character of water, 9° hardness.
Filtration, none; softening, none.
Total quantity of water drawn per annum—
　　　　　　From drainage areas　　...　　...　　...　　...　　20,000,000 gals.
　　　　　　　,,　　surface springs　...　　...　　...　　...　100,000,000　,,
Estimated total quantity of water available per annum—
　　From drainage areas and surface springs, 200,000,000 gals.
Storage reservoir, Randymere, 13,000,000 gals.
Service reservoir, Sneaton Castle, Whitby, 288,000 gals., covered.
Annual supply of water (1906)—
　　　　　　For domestic purposes, not ascertained.
　　　　　　For trade purposes　　　　,,
　　　　　　　,, municipal purposes　　,,
Maximum day's consumption—410,000 gals. (August holiday).
　　　　　　　,,　　　,,　　　,,　　250,000　,,　(normal).
Authorised rate—7 per cent. per annum on rack rent, minimum 9s. per house;
　　w.c.'s, 5s. each; baths, 10s. each.
Present charge not exceeding　　£4, gross annual rental,　9s. 0d. per annum.
　　　　　　　　　　　　　　　　£7,　　　,,　　　,,　　9s. 9d.　　　,,
　　　　　　　　　　　　　　　　£10,　　　,,　　　,,　　14s. 0d.　　　,,
　　　　　　　　　　　　　　　　£20,　　　,,　　　,,　　27s. 0d.　　　,,
　　　　　　　　　　　　　　　　£30,　　　,,　　　,,　　35s. 0d.　　　,,
　　　　　　　　　　　　　　　　£40,　　　,,　　　,,　　45s. 0d.　　　,,
　　　　　　　　　　　　　　　　£50,　　　,,　　　,,　　55s. 0d.　　　,,
　　　　　　　　　　　　　　　　£100,　　　,,　　　,,　　90s. 0d.　　　,,
　　　　　　　　　　and intermediate charges.
Meter charge—
　　Quantity used per Quarter.　　　　　　　Price per 1,000 gals.
　　Under 10,000 gallons　　...　　...　　...　　2s.　6d.
　　10,000 gallons and under 15,000 gallons　　2s.　0d.
　　15,000　　　,,　　　,,　　　25,000　　,,　　1s.　9d.
　　25,000　　　,,　　　,,　　　50,000　　,,　　1s.　8d.
　　50,000　　　,,　　　,,　　　75,000　　,,　　1s.　7d.
　　75,000　　　,,　　　,,　　100,000　　,,　　1s.　6d.
　　100,000　　　,,　　　,,　　250,000　　,,　　1s.　3d.
　　250,000　　　,,　　　,,　　500,000　　,,　　1s.　0d.
　　500,000　　　,,　　　,,　1,000,000　　,,　　0s.　10d.
　　　　　　　Over 1,000,000 gals., special prices.
　　Municipal purposes, 9d.
　　Minimum charge, 10s. per quarter.
Number of meters in use, 37.
Length of supply mains, 7½ miles; distributing mains, 16 miles.

Whitchurch (supplied by SOUTH OXFORDSHIRE).

Whitchurch (supplied by CARDIFF).

Whitcliffe (supplied by RIPON).

Whiteabbey (supplied by DUBLIN).

Whitefield (supplied by BURY).

Whitehaven, Cumberland. Railway L.N.W. Distance from London, 303½ miles.
Authority, Corporation.
Chairman, Alderman J. R. Musgrave.
Town Clerk, Thomas Brown.
Resident Engineer, Ernest E. Stiven.
Office, Town Hall.
Loans outstanding, £57,709.
Annual profit including capital charges, £127.
Works established, 1849. Special Acts, 1849, 1864, 1878, 1885, 1899.
Total population of area supplied, 24,000.
Average death rate per 1,000—within borough, 18·46 ; outside, 12·38.
Towns and villages in the area supplied, Whitehaven, Hensingham, Preston
Quarter, Parton, Sandwith, Rothington, Ennerdale and Kinniside, Keltern,
Salter, and Eskett Lamplough.
Source of supply, Ennerdale Lake, overflow level of which is 369 O.D. ; area of
watershed, 10,000 acres ; area of surface of lake, 740 acres.
Under the Act of 1899 the Council have power to draw 2,000,000 gals. per day
from the lake ; at present only 1,500,000 gals. are being drawn, and all that
can be got through the supply mains.
Analysis of Ennerdale water—

	Grains per gallon.
Total solid matter in solution dried at 220° Fahr. ...	1·901
Chlorine existing as chlorides	0·602
Ammonia	None
Albuminoid ammonia	0·003
Nitrogen existing as nitrates	0·017
Oxygen absorbed in 15 minutes at 80° Fahr.	0·009
Oxygen absorbed in 4 hours at 80° Fahr.	0·018
Lead and other poisonous metals	None
Hardness before boiling (Clark's degrees)	0·4
Hardness after boiling (Clark's degrees)	0·3
Appearance in two-foot tube	Faint green
Smell when heated to 100° Fahr.	None
Microscopical examination	Vegetable débris, sand, diatoms.

Inorganic constituents.—Analytical results :—

Carbonic acid (combined)	0·067	grain per gallon
Sulphuric acid ,, ...	0·238	,, ,,
Nitric acid ,, ...	0·066	,, ,,
Chlorine	0·602	,, ,,
Silica	0·119	,, ,,
Alumina	0·014	,, ,,
Magnesia	0·095	,, ,,
Lime	0·189	,, ,,
Potash	0·051	,, ,,
Soda	0·453	,, ,,

Constituents expressed in combination :—

Sodium chloride	0·855	,, ,,
Potassium sulphate	0·094	,, ,,
Calcium chloride	0·130	,, ,,
Calcium nitrate	0·100	,, ,,
Calcium sulphate	0·216	,, ,,

WHITEHAVEN—*continued.*

Magnesium sulphate	...	...	...	0·102 grain per gallon.
Magnesium carbonate	...	...	...	0·128 ,, ,,
Alumina ...	...	...	...	0·014 ,, ,,
Silica ...	...	...	...	0·119 ,, ,,
Organic matter and water		...	...	0·143 ,, ,,

Total solid matter ... 1·901 ,, ,,

The source of supply is one of the purest in the kingdom.

System of filtration, none.

Storage in lake (minimum), 500,000,000 gals.; in service reservoir, 1,200,000 gals.

Head on distributing mains—maximum, 250 ft.; minimum, 30 ft.

Annual supply of water, 547,500,000 gals.

Average daily supply per head—public and sanitary, 34 gals : trade, 20 gals. This includes the supply to the Corporation Electricity Works for condensing purposes.

Average daily supply, 1,500,000 gals.

Charges authorised, domestic supply not to exceed, 6 per cent. on R.V.

Present charge   ,,   ,,   5 per cent. on R.V.

Supplies by meter—

Average about 6d. per 1,000 gals.; minimum charge, 7s. 6d. per quarter.

					Per 1,000 gals. per Quarter.
For the first 50,000 gallons at the rate of			...	8d.
,,	next 100,000	,,	,,	...	7d.
,,	,, 100,000	,,	,,	...	6½d.
,,	,, 200,000	,,	,,	...	6d.
,,	,, 400,000	,,	,,	...	5½d.
,,	,, 800,000	,,	,,	...	5d.

1,650,000

For any quantity over

1,650,000   do.   ... 4d.

Shipping and maritime purposes—

For a supply not exceeding 100 gallons ... ... 1s. 0d.

And for every additional 100 gals., or the fractional part of 100 gallons ... ... 0s. 6d.

Note.—The foregoing scale does not in any case preclude the Corporation from affording the supply of water by agreement, either with or without meter; and either by quarterly payments or otherwise.

Number of meters, 104.

Length of mains—supply, 16 miles; distributing, 34 miles.

Whitkirk (supplied by LEEDS).

Whitland, Carmarthen. Railway, G.W.

Authority, Whitland and District Water and Gas Co., Ltd.

Chairman, Evan Evans.

Secretary, H. Percy Davies.

Resident Engineer, Rex Vivian.

Consulting Engineer, Frank G. Vivian, F.C.I.S.

Office, Whitland Registered Offices, Bres Chambers, Llanelly.

Share capital, £25,000; paid up, £6,000.

Company formed, November, 1906. Special acts, Companies' Acts, 1862 to 1900.

Works in course of construction, (May, 1907).

Whitley (supplied by TYNEMOUTH).

Whitstable Kent. Railways, L.C.D. and S.E. Distance from London, 58 miles.
Authority, Whitstable Water Co., Ltd.
Chairman, J. W. Hayward.
Secretary, Robt. B. Reeves.
Manager, Wm. Wyner.
Office, Horsebridge Road, Whitstable.
Area supplied, Whitstable town and village of Church Street.
Total population supplied, about 7,100.
Source of supply—artesian wells into chalk formation, 400 feet deep. The supply is continuous.
Assessment charge, annual value—

    Not exceeding £9   ...   4s. 4d. (payable quarterly); 4d. extra per £ up to £12.
     ,,   ,,   £13   ...   5s. 3d.   ,,   ,,   3d.   ,,   £   ,, £20.
     ,,   ,,   £21 ..   7s. 2d.   ,,   ,,   2d.   ,,   £ upwards.

Houses rated at £8 and under paid for by landlord as follows—£6 and under, 2s. 6d. per quarter; above £6 and not exceeding £8, 2s 9d. per quarter, whether tenanted or not.
The above charges include one w.c. Extra w.c., 1s. 3d. each; bath, 1s. 6d.; horses, cows, and two-wheeled carriages, 1s. each.
Price for trade and special purposes—

        10,000 gals. and under   ...   ...   1s. 6d. per 1,000 gals.
        10,000 ,, to 25,000 gals.   ...   ...   1s. 5d. ,,   ,,
        25,000 ,, ,, 50,000 ,, ...   1s. 4d. ,,   ,,
        50,000 ,, ,, 75,000 ,, ...   1s. 3d. ,,   ,,
        75,000 ,, ,, 100,000 ,, ...   1s. 2d. ,,   ,,
    Minimum charge, 9s. per quarter.

Whittington (supplied by SOUTH STAFFS. WATERWORKS Co.).

Whittington (supplied by WORCESTER).

Whitton (supplied by ROTHBURY),

Whitwood (supplied by WAKEFIELD).

Wickhamford, Worcester (supplied by EVESHAM).

Wicklow, Ireland.
Authority, Wicklow Urban District Council.
Chairman, S. V. Delahunt.
Town Clerk, S. William MacPhail.
Resident Engineer, J. Pansing, A.M.I.C.E.
Office, Town Hall, Wicklow.
Loan outstanding, £1,000.
Works established 1882, Act Public Health (Ireland) 1878.
Total population supplied, 3,288.
Average death rate, 20 per 1,000.
District of supply, Urban District only, comprising part of the parishes of Rathnew and Kilpoole.
Source of supply, impounding reservoirs on about 4 acres, townlands of Ashtown and Hawkestown, Lower.
Character of Water, fairly good, with a rather large number of micro-organisms, total hardness, 7°.
Filtration, sand filter in a cellular concrete wall forming part of the embankment.
   Storage in impounding reservoirs, 9,000,000; service reservoir, 75,000 gals.
Head on distributing mains—maximum 230 ft.; minimum, 140 ft.
Annual supply of water, 18,359,500 gals.
Average daily supply per head, domestic and trade, 15½ gals
Maximum day's supply, 50,300 gals. in March, 1907.

WICKLOW—*continued*.

Charges authorised, domestic free, trade 6d. per 1,000 gals.
Present rate, 8d. in the £ on valuation of district, to pay off loan.
No. of Meters, 25.
Length of supply mains 1¾ miles, distributing mains 4½ miles.

Widford (supplied by CHELMSFORD).

Widnes, Lancs. Railway, L.N.W., G.N., M. and M.S.L. Distance from London, 188½ miles.
Authority, Widnes Corporation.
Chairman, H. S. Timmis, J.P.
Engineer in charge, Isaac Carr, M.I.C.E
Office, Gas and Water Works.
Waterworks Loan to date, £178,575 5s. 7d.
Works purchased by Local Authority, 1867.
Special Acts, Widnes Improvement Act, 1867.
Estimated population actually supplied, 35,000.
Towns and villages within the area of control—Widnes, Cuerdley, Bold, Cronton, Ditton, part of Rainhill, Hale, Halebank, Halewood and Tarbock.
　Sources of supply in use—
　　Deep wells or borings situated at Netherley, near Gateacre.
　　　　　　　　　　　　　　　Stocks Well, Hough Green.
　Maximum annual rainfall over drainage area 33·7 inches (1900).
　Minimum　　　　,,　　　　　,,　　20·4　　,,　　(1893).
　Average　　　　,,　　　　　,,　　28·8　　,,　　(period 14 years).
　Level of water below surface (when pumping 3,000,000 gals. per day) 70 feet.
　Strata tapped by wells or borings, red sandstone.
　Pumping stations—Netherley　...　...　capacity　2,500,000 gals. per day
　　　　　　　　Stocks Well　...　...　　,,　　1,500,000　　,,
　　　　　　　　Belle Vale (undeveloped)　,,　　2,500,000　　,,
　Service reservoirs—Pex Hill, No. 1　...　,,　　1,500,000　,,　covered
　　　　　　　　,,　　No. 2　...　,,　10,500,000　　,,
　Character of water, hardness, 6·0°.
　Annual supply of water—
　　　For domestic purposes　　...　...　...　288,542,497 gals.
　　　,,　trade　　,,　　...　...　...　689,872,652　,,
　Maximum day's consumption, 3,000,000 gals.
　Total quantity of water drawn per annum—
　　　Deep wells or borings ...　...　...　...　978,415,149 gals.
　Estimated total quantity of water available per annum—
　　　Deep wells or borings ...　...　...　2,372,500,000 gals.
　*Water analysis by Dr. Campbell Brown, April 23rd, 1902—

	Stocks Well.	Netherley.
Total solid matter in solution	22·0 ...	14·4
Oxygen required to oxidise, in 15 minutes	·006 ...	·002
,, ,, 3 hours...	·011 ...	·011
Ammonia	·009 ...	·011
Ammonia from organic matter, by distillation with alkaline, permanganate ...	·01 ...	·004
Nitrogen as nitrates	·284 ...	·306
Combined chlorine	1·9 ...	1·9
Hardness, temporary	·00 ...	1·00
,, permanent	5·86 ...	5·50
,, Total	5·86 ...	6·50
	clear ...	clear
Water is not filtered.	No organisms ...	No organisms.

*These samples are both satisfactory for domestic use.

WIDNES—*continued.*

Number of meters in use, 150.
Length of distributing mains, 50 miles.
Scale of charges—
　Assessment charge, domestic, from 1s. 4d. per quarter for house poor rate
　　valuation, £5 per annum., to £1 6s. 3d. per quarter for house poor rate
　　valuation, £100 per annum.
　Where yearly value does not exceed £100, £5 5s. per cent. per annum.
　　　　　 ,,　　　　　　 ,,　　　 £150,　　　 ,,　　　　 ,,　　 up to
　　£100, and £5 per cent. on all above £100.
　Where yearly value exceeds £150 at above rates up to £150, and £1 5s. per
　　cent. on all above £150 ; 10 per cent. allowed if paid within one month.
　Lock up shops charged on one-third of yearly value.
　Dwellings occupied in part as retail shops exceeding £12 and under £50 on
　　three-fourths yearly value, over £50 on two-thirds of the rate of domestic
　　supply only.
　Charges for meters, 4¾d. per 1,000 gals. with rebate of ½d. per 1,000 gals. if paid
　　within one month ; over 40,000,000 gals. per annum and under 50,000,000 gals.
　　a further rebate of 1d. per 1,000 gals.; over 50,000,000 gals., 2d. for each
　　1,000 gals. nett cash.
　Meter rents from 2s. 2d. per quarter for ⅜-inch meter to 18s. 9d. per quarter for
　　6-inch meter.

Wigan, Lancs. Railways, L.N.W., G.C., and L. & Y. Distance from London, 194
miles.
　Authority, Corporation.
　Surveyor, W. Bolton.
　Town Clerk, Harold Jevons.
　Office, Chapel Lane.
　Area supplied, Wigan only, 2,188 statute acres.
　Works established, 1853.　Special Acts, 1853, 1860, 1874, 1880, and 1897.
　Total population supplied, 83,000.
　Annual supply of water, 422,276,488 gals.
　Daily consumption per head—domestic, 12 gals. ; trade, 4¾ gals.
　Sources of supply, gathering grounds.
　Storage capacity, 330,000,000 gals.
　Character of water, 8° of hardness.
　System of filtration, sand.
　Death rate, 20·25 per 1,000.
　Number of meters, 246.
　Length of mains, 36¾ miles.
　Assessment charge, 5 per cent. rateable value.
　Price per 1,000 gals., municipal purposes, 3d. ; trade and domestic, 1s.

Wigston (supplied by LEICESTER).

Wigton, Cumberland.　Railways, L.N.W., M., and M.C.　Distance from London
311 miles.
　Authority, Urban District Council.
　Office, U.D.C. Offices.
　Loan capital, £9,000.
　Area supplied, 1,000 acres.
　Works established, 1868.
　Total population of area supplied, 3,691.
　Annual supply of water, 28.270,000 gals.
　Daily consumption per head, domestic, and trade, 28 gals.
　Source of supply, springs.
　Storage capacity, 132,000 gals,

WIGTON—*continued.*

> Character of water, 4° hardness.
> Death rate, 17·40 per 1,000.
> Number of meters, 6.
> Scale of charges—assessment, 6d. on R.V.
> Price for 1,000 gals., 9d. to 6d.

Willenhall, Staffs. (supplied by WOLVERHAMPTON).

Willerby, Yorks. (supplied by HULL).

Wilpshire (supplied by BLACKBURN).

Wilsden, Yorks. (supplied by BRADFORD).

Wilton, Wilts.　Railway, L.S.W. and G.W.　Distance from London, 86 miles.
> Authority, Corporation.
> Total population supplied, 2,120.
> No returns supplied.

Winchester.　Railways, L.S.W. and G.W.　Distance from London, 66½ miles.
> Authority, Winchester Water and Gas Company.
> Chairman, J. C. Warner.
> Secretary, Charles Wooldridge.
> Engineer and General Manager, H. C. Head, A.M.I.C.E., A.M.I.M.E.
> Office, 19, Staple Garden, Winchester.
> Share capital, £186,350 ⎱ Gas and Water.
> Loan capital, £40,500 ⎰
> Last dividend, 4 per cent.　Rate of interest 3½ per cent.
> Works established, 1847.　Special Acts, 1865, 1888, and 1903.
> Total population of area supplied, 21,000.
> Average death rate, 11·6 per 1,000.
> District of supply, City of Winchester, Headbourne Worthy, Kingsworthy Martyr Worthy, Itchen Abbas, and Avington.
> Source of supply, wells and borings in hard chalk.
> Character of water, 15·4° hardness.
> Filtration, none; softening, none.
> Annual supply of water, 253,727,000 gals.
> Storage capacity in service reservoir, 931,000 gals.
> Daily consumption per head, domestic and trade, 31·1 gals.
> Maximum day's supply, 800,000 gals. in July, 1906.
> Number of meters, 106.
> Scale of charges, assessment, 6 per cent to 4½ per cent., R.V.
> Price for 1,000 gals., 1s.; present average, 11d.

Winchfield (supplied by FRIMLEY).

Windermere.　Railway, L.N.W.　Distance from London, 259½ miles.
> Authority, Windermere District Gas and Water Company.
> Chairman, James Wirgley, J.P.
> Manager, John Duxbury.
> Secretary, J. T. Borman.
> Office, Gasworks, Brantfell Road.
> Share capital paid up, £18,690.
> Last dividend, 8 per cent.
> Works established, 1869; Special Acts, 1869, 1889.

WINDERMERE—*continued*.

    Total population of area supplied, 5,500.
    Average death rate, 10·5 per 1,000.
    Sources of supply, gathering grounds.
    Character of water, very soft.
    Storage capacity, 24,000,000 gals.
    Daily consumption per head, 41 gals.
    Scale of charges, assessment, 4 to 5¼ per cent. annual value.
    Price per 1,000 gals., 1s. to 8d.

Windle, Lancs. (supplied by ST. HELENS).

Windsor, Berks. Railways, G.W. and L.S.W. Distance from London, 21¼ miles.
    Authority, Windsor Corporation.
    Chairman, The Mayor.
    Town Clerk, Edward Cecil Durant.
    Engineer and Manager, Christopher Sainty, M.I Mech.E.
    Office, Tangier Island, Eton.
    Total capital invested, £164,000 (stock).
    Current rate of interest, 3 per cent.
    Towns and villages within the area of control, Windsor, Eton and Clewer.
    Works purchased by Local Authority, 1888.
    Special Act, Windsor and Eton Water Works Act, 1883.
    Total number of consumers, 20,000.
    Annual supply of water
        For all purposes ... ... 32,000,000 gals.
    Maximum day's consumption, 1,100,000 gals.
    Maximum annual rainfall, 22·47 inches (1899).
    Source of supply, wells.
    Natural rest level of water below surface, 20 feet, below ordnance datum ·67
      feet.
    Level of water below surface (when pumping), 24 feet.
    Nature of subsoil yielding water, chalk.
    Strata tapped by wells or borings, gravel and chalk, 135 feet.
    Locality and extent of outcrop of same, Thames Valley.
    Pumping station, Tangier Island, Eton.
    No reservoirs, direct pumping into mains.
    Character of water, excellent.
    Number of meters in use, 110.
    Length of distributing mains, 25 miles.
    Assessment charge, 4¼, 3¼ and 5 per cent.
    Price per 1,000 gals., from 9d. to 1s. 6d., according to scale.

Wingate, Co. Durham. Railway, N.E, Distance irom London, 230 miles.
    Authority, Wingate and District Water Company, Ltd.
    Office, Gatenby House.
    Share capital, £5,000.
    Dividend, 5 per cent.
    Towns and villages in the area supplied, Wingate and Station Town, part of
      township of Castle Eden and Monk Hesleden.
    Works Established, 1895. Special Acts, Companies Acts 1862 to 1890.
    Total population of area supplied, 6,000.
    Daily consumption per head, domestic and trade, 10 gals.
    Sources of supply, magnesia limestone.
    Storage capacity, 230,000 gals.
    Character of water, hard, free from all organic matter.

WINGATE—*continued.*

Death rate, 18·23 per 1,000.
Number of meters, 20.
Length of mains, about 1 mile.
Price for 1,000 gals., 2s. 6d. to 7d., according to quantity.

Winlaton (Parish of) Durham (supplied by NEWCASTLE-ON-TYNE).

Winsford, Cheshire.
Authority, Urban District Council.
Population, 10,400.

Winshill (supplied by SOUTH STAFFS. WATERWORKS Co.).

Winthorpe. *See* SKEGNESS.

Winthorpe, Notts. (supplied by NEWARK).

Winwick-with-Hulme (supplied by WARRINGTON).

Wirksworth, Derbyshire. Railways, M. and L.N.W. Distance from London, 141 miles.
Authority, Urban District Council of Wirksworth.
Chairman, Wm. J. Harrison, J.P.
Clerk, J. Gratton, solicitor.
Engineer in charge and Consulting Engineer, F. E. Wintle, C.E.
Office, Town Hall.
Loans outstanding, £851 (now being paid off).
Annual profit, about £140, after charging all expenses except instalments of loan and interest.
Works established, prior to 1802, and confirmed by old Enclosure Act, 1802.
Taken over by Local Authority from Water Commissioners on establishment of district in 1877.
Special Acts—42 Geo. III., c. 110, Provisional Order, 10th May, 1880.
Total number of consumers, about 3,500.
Average death rate, 15·69 per 1,000 (period 10 years).
District of supply, parish of Wirksworth, but certain parts are not supplied.
Sources of supply, deep springs in millstone grit.
Geological; cap of millstone grit overlying shales and limestone.
System of filtration, none required.
Character of water, sparkling, soft, very pure.
Analysis of water—

	Grains per gal.			Grains per gal.
Sulphate of lime ...	0·6500	Silica	0·0080
Bicarbonate of lime ...	2·4480	Carbonate of potass. ...	Traces.
„ magnesia...	·1370	Organic matter... ...	1·1210
„ iron ...	0·0090	Free carbonic acid ...	7·2160
Carbonate of soda ...	Traces.	Specific gravity... ...	1·00014
Chloride of sodium ...	0·0258		

Storage capacity, 40,000 gals.
Pressure on distributing mains—maximum, 128 lbs. ; minimum, 90 lbs. per sq. in.
Total quantity of water drawn per annum from springs, 36,000,000 gals.
Estimated total quantity of water available per annum, 50,000,000 gals.
Daily consumption (domestic), about 30 gals. per head.

WIRKSWORTH—*continued*.

 Maximum day's supply, 295,584 gals. in March.
 Pumping stations, none.
 Number of meters in use, 1.
 Length of distributing mains, about 6 miles.
 Scale of charges—
  Assessment charge, 6d. in the £ on rateable value of premises supplied, with extra charges for trades in some cases.

Wirral, Cheshire. Railways, L.N.W. and G.W. joint. Distance from London, 200 miles.
 Authority, Wirral Waterworks Co.
 Chairman, John Holt.
 Manager and Secretary, Phillip H. Bettle.
 Consulting Engineer, Isaac Carr, M.I.C.E.
 Office, 9, Hamilton Square, Birkenhead.
 Share capital paid up, £50,000. Dividend, 8 per cent.
 Works established, 1859.
 Special Act, Wirral Water Works, 1859, 22 and 23 Vict., cap. 58.
 Total population of area supplied, 7,935.
 Towns and villages in the area supplied—parts of the borough of Birkenhead.
 Sources of supply—wells in red sandstone. Character of water, rather hard.
 Annual supply of water, about 265,570,000 gals.
 Assessment charge, average 6¼ per cent. on R.V.
 Price per 1,000 gals., trade, 1s. 6d. to 9d., municipal purposes, 9d.

Wisbech, Cambridgeshire. Railways, G.E., G.N., M. Distance from London, 93¾ miles.
 Authority, Wisbech Waterworks Company.
 Engineer and Manager, J. G. Hawkins.
 Consulting Engineer, Edward Easton.
 Secretary, Robert Dawbarn.
 Office, Chase Street.
 Share capital paid, £66,000. Loan capital, £14,800 debentures.
 Dividend, 4½ and 6 per cent.
 Works established, 1864. Special Acts, 1864, Provisional Orders, 1876 and 1884.
 Total population of area supplied, 55,000.
 Source of supply, springs in chalk.
 Number of meters, 50.
 Assessment charge, annual value.
 Price for 1,000 gals., 2s. to 1s. 3d.

Wishaw, Scotland.
 Authority, Town Council of the Burgh of Wishaw.
 Chairman, William B. Thomson, Provost.
 Clerk to Authority, John L. Jack, Town Clerk.
 Resident Engineer, Wm. Rodger.
 Office, Burgh Chambers, Wishaw.
 Loans outstanding, £137,334.
 Works established, 1870 ; special Acts, 1862, 1898, 1904.
 Population supplied, 28,000.
 Average death rate, 16 per 1,000.
 District of supply, parishes of Cambusnethan and Dalzell.
 Source of supply, impounding reservoirs ¦and weirs on Pedea, Potrenick and Potrail Burns.
 Filtration, sand filters.
 Storage capacity—impounding reservoirs, 72,000,000 gals. ; service reservoirs, 3,000,000 gals.

Wishaw—*continued.*

Pressure on distributing mains—maximum, 140 lbs.; minimum, 36 lbs. per sq. in.
Annual supply of water, 800,000,000 gals.
Average daily supply per head for all purposes, 33 to 36 gals.
Assessment charge, 2s. 6d. in £ on R.V.
Charge by meter, 6d. per 1,000 gals.
No. of meters, 44.
Length of supply mains, 55 miles; distributing mains, 15 miles.

Wisley (supplied by Woking).

Witham, Essex.
Authority, Witham Urban District Council.
Chairman, Philip Huntley, J.P.
Secretary, W. Bindon Blood.
Resident Engineer, W. P. Perkins.
Office, Collingwood Road, Witham.
Loans outstanding, £11,810.
Works established, 1869. New works, 1902-3.
Total population supplied, 3,500.
Average death rate, 13·4 per 1,000.
Area of supply, Witham only.
Two borings, 600 ft. deep.
Character of water, good; total hardness, 14o.
Storage in service tanks, 45,000 gals.
Annual supply of water, 24,965,380 gals.
Average daily supply per head, 19·59 for all purposes.
Maximum day's supply, 92,210 gals. in July.
Present charge, 1s. in £ for half-year on R.V.
    "   " by meter, per 1,000 gals., 1s.
No. of meters, 7.
Length of supply mains, 2 miles; distributing mains, 4 miles.

Withington (supplied by Manchester).

Withycombe (supplied by Exmouth).

Witley, Surrey (supplied by Godalming).

Witney, Oxon.
Authority, Urban District Council.
Population, 3,600.

Witton, Warwick (supplied by Birmingham).

Wivelsfield, Sussex (supplied by Cuckfield).

Wix, Essex (supplied by Tendring Hundred Water Co.).

Woking and District, Surrey. Railway, L.S.W. Distance from London, 24¼ miles.
Authority, Woking Water and Gas Co.
Chairman, Sir John Baker, M.P.
Manager, H. J. Crane.
Secretary, B. D. Holroyd.
Consulting Engineers, J. Quick & Son.
London Office, 5 and 6, Great Winchester Street, E.C.
Share capital paid up, £168,514. Loan capital paid up, £38,312.

Woking and District—_continued._

Dividend, 4½ per cent.   Int. on loan capital, 4 per cent.
Annual profit, £9,354.
Works established, 1882.   Special Acts, 1881, 1885, 1887, 1899.
Total population supplied, 35,000.
Average death rate, 10·8 per 1,000.
Towns and villages in the area supplied—Woking, Send, Ripley, E. and W.
    Clandon, E. and W. Horsley, Merrow, Horsell, Pirbright, Worplesdon, Bisley,
    Pyrford, Wisley, and Ockham.
Sources of supply—wells in the chalk at Clandon, Horsley, and Stoke; springs
    from gravel beds at Guildford and Chertsey, and impounding reservoirs on the
    Thames at Chertsey.
Character of water, very pure.   Filtration, sand; softening, none.
Storage capacity in impounding reservoirs, 2,000,000 gals.; service reservoirs,
    1,000,000 gals.
Annual supply of water, 261,500,000 gals.
Assessment charge, 7½ to 5 per cent. on gross estimated annual rental.
Price per 1,000 gals., according to agreement.
Total water rent received, £15,237.
Number of meters, 513.
Length of mains, 124 miles.
The company does not supply gas, having disposed of nearly all its powers.

Wokingham, Berks. Railway, L.S.W. Distance from London, 36½ miles.
Authority, Wokingham District Water Company, Ltd.
Office, Finchhampstead Road.
Share capital paid up, £20,000.
Loan capital paid up, £5,000.
Towns and villages in the area supplied, Wokingham, Bracknell, Binfield,
    Warfield, Emmbrook, Bullbrook, Wargrave.
Works established, 1877. Special Act, 1878.
Total population of area supplied, 10,000.
Annual supply of water, 55,000,000 gals.
Daily consumption per head, domestic and trade, 15 gals.
Source of supply, deep well in the chalk.
Storage capacity, 150,000 gals.
Character of water, 10° hardness; excellent quality.
System of filtration, none.
Number of meters, 40.
Length of mains, 20 miles.
Scale of charges—assessment, 6 per cent. on gross value.
Price for 1,000 gals., 1s. 6d. to 1s.
Total water rent received, about £2,200.

Wollaston (supplied by Stourbridge).

Wollescote (supplied by Stourbridge).

Wolverhampton, Stafford. Railways, L.N.W., M., G.W. Distance from London,
    124¾ miles.
Authority, Corporation.
Engineer and Manager, E. A. B. Woodward, A.M.I.C.E.
The Wolverhampton works are leased to the Corporation on a fixed rental
    per cent. on ordinary, and 5 per cent. on preference shares.
Office, Town Hall.
Area of water limits, 64 square miles.
Towns and villages supplied, Wolverhampton, Willenhall, Tettenhall, Heath
    Town, Wednesfield, Short Heath, Penn, Oaken, Albrighton, and Bushbury.

WOLVERHAMPTON—*continued.*

　　Works established, 1845.　Special Act, 1869.
　　Total population of area supplied, 152,000.
　　Annual supply of water, about 1,200,000,000 gals.
　　Daily consumption per head, domestic, 16·02 gals.　Trade, 5·58 gals.
　　Source of supply, wells in new red sandstone.
　　Storage capacity, 16,000,000 gals.
　　Character of water, 10° to 12° hardness.
　　Average death rate, 15 per 1,000.
　　Number of meters, about 740.
　　Length of mains, 150 miles.
　　Scale of charges, assessment, 1s. 3d. in £.
　　Price for 1,000 gals., 1s. 4d. to 6d. (including rent of one meter).

Wolverton. *See* STONY STRATFORD.

Wolverton St. Marys (supplied by STONY STRATFORD).

Wombwell, Yorks.　Railways, G.C. and M.　Distance from London, 168 miles.
　　Authority, Urban District Council.
　　Clerk, Percy M. Walker.
　　Office, Council Offices, Wombwell.
　　Loan capital, £12,000.
　　Works established, 1878.
　　Total population of area supplied, 14,000.
　　Source of supply, water bought from the Dearne Valley Waterworks Company in
　　　bulk.
　　Storage capacity, 3,000,000 gals.
　　Character of water, deep well water.
　　Death rate, 15·9 per 1,000.
　　Number of meters, 18.
　　Length of mains, about 10 miles.
　　Assessment—rateable value, £256.
　　Price for 1,000 gals., trade, 1s. and 10½d. ; municipal purposes, free.
　　Total water rent received, about £2,240, including meters.

Wonford (supplied by EXETER).

Wooburn (supplied by GREAT MARLOW).

Woodcote (supplied by SOUTH OXFORDSHIRE).

Woodford, Essex (supplied by EAST LONDON WATER Co.).

Woodford Halse, Northants.　Railway, G.C.　Distance from London, 72 miles.
　　Authority, Woodford Halse Water Co., Ltd.
　　Chairman, H. Phipps.
　　Secretary, S. Stubbs.
　　Engineer in charge, J. B. Williams.
　　Office, Woodford Halse, Byfield, R. S. O.
　　Share capital paid up, £1,822.
　　Dividend, 5 per cent. generally.
　　Area supplied, Woodford Halse only.
　　Works established, 1870.
　　Total population of area supplied, 1,214.
　　Sources of supply, sand beds and limestone rock near village.
　　Storage capacity, 30,000 gals., likely to be increased.
　　Character of water, chiefly hard.
　　System of filtration, none.
　　Total water rent received, upwards of £100.

Wood Green (supplied by Metropolitan Water Board.)

Woodhall Spa, Lincoln. (G. & W.) Railway, G.N. Distance from London 124¼ miles.
　Authority, Woodland Spa Gas and Water Company.
　Office, Woodhall Spa.
　Area supplied, Woodhall Spa only.
　Works established, 1889. Special Acts, 52 & 53 Vict.
　Total population supplied, 1,000.
　Daily consumption per head, about 10 gals.
　Source of supply, Cawkwell-on-the-Wolds, 9 miles beyond Horncastle.
　Storage capacity, 120,000 gals.
　Character of water, very good.
　Length of mains, from source of supply at Horncastle to reservoir 5 miles ; about
　　3 miles supply mains.

Woodhead (supplied by Cheadle).

Woodmansterne (supplied by Sutton).

Woodstock, Oxon. Railway, G.W. Distance from London, 72 miles.
　Population supplied, 1,684.
　Water is supplied from the Blenheim estate.

Woodstone (supplied by Peterborough).

Woolaton (supplied by Nottingham).

Woolstone-with-Martinscroft (supplied by Warrington).

Wootton Bassett, Wilts. Railway, G.W. Distance from London 84 miles.
　Authority, Rural District Council.
　Engineer, F. Redman, Wood Street, Swindon.
　Clerk to Council, H. Bevir.
　Office, Wootton Bassett.
　Works constructed, 1891.
　Total population of area supplied, about 2,000.
　Source of supply, upper green sand, gravitation.
　Character of water, pure, but rather hard.
　　Storage　{ Service reservoir, 10,000 gallons at source.
　　capacity　{ 　Do.　in town, 5,000 gallons.

Worcester, City of. Railways, G.W. and M. Distance from London, 120¼ miles.
　Authority, Corporation of City of Worcester.
　Chairman, Chris. I. Whitehead.
　Clerk, Samuel Southall, Town Clerk.
　Engineer, Thomas Caink, A.M.I.C.E., City Engineer.
　Office, Guildhall.
　Total capital invested, £18,308 ; 3¼ per cent. redeemable stock.
　Works established, 1857.
　Total population of area of control, 1881, 41,385 ; 1891, 43,937 ; 1901, 46,623 ;
　　1906, estimated at 48,000.
　Total number of consumers, 11,411.
　Estimated population actually supplied, 48,000.
　Death rate, 19·2 per 1,000.
　Towns and villages within the area of control—
　　City of Worcester, part of villages of Hallow, Whittington and Spetchley ;
　　　also Norton Barracks.
　Total quantity of water drawn per annum—
　　From River Severn　　…　　…　　…　　…　　550,000,000 gals.

WORCESTER—*continued.*

Estimated minimum daily discharge at points of collection   100,000,000 gals.
   ,,   average   ,,   ,,   ,,   ...   1,000,000,000 ,,
Average annual rainfall over drainage area ...   .   44·9, 30 years.
Subsiding tanks (3)   ...   .   capacity, 1,003,000 gals.
Filtering area provided, 6,401 square yards in 9 filter-beds.
Pumping stations at Worcester Waterworks—
   No. 1 engine, low level   ...   .   capacity, 550,000 gals.
   ,, 2   ,,   ,, ...   ,,   550,000 ,,
   ,, 3   ,,   ,, ...   ,,   750,000 ,,
   ,, 4   ,,   ,, ...   ,,   750,000 ,,
   ,, 5   ,,   { (all low level, or 1,200,000 low level, and 600,000 high level) ...   ... } ,,   1,800,000 ,,
   Two electric motor pumps   ...   ...   ,,   480,000 ,,
Service reservoirs, Rainbow Hill, low level ...   ,,   800,000, covered.
   ,,   Elbury Hill, high level   ...   ,,   250,000   ,,
Hardness, 6° to 8°.
Number of meters in use, 490.
Length of mains, about 55 miles.
Analysis—

	River in full flood.	River Water.		Pure Water.
	Grains per gallon.	Grains per gallon.	Parts per 100,000 gallons.	Grains per gallon.
Solids in suspension	10·444	Trace.	—	None.
,, solution	12·6	19·88	28·4	16·1
Appearance of solids	Yellow.	Dirty white.	—	Yellow.
Solids after ignition	9·1	13·65	19·5	12·6
Behaviour of solids on ignition	Blackening and bad odour.	Blackening and bad odour.		Slight blackening.
Phosphates	Nil.	Nil.	—	None.
Chlorine as common salt ...	2·452	6·132	8·76	4·5
Free and saline ammonia ...	0·0098	0·01036	0·0148	0·0005
Albuminoid ammonia ...	0·0341	0·01876	0·0268	0·0044
Oxygen absorbed in 3 hours...	0·288	0·098	0·14	0·07
Nitrogen in nitrates and nitrites	Nil.	Trace.	—·	None.
Colour	Brown.	Yellow.	—	Slightly yellow.
Deposit...	Moderate brown.	Moderate brown.	—	None.
Smell	Nil.	Nil.	—	None.
Hardness, permanent... ...	4·5° Clark.	3·2° Clark.	—	3·6° Clark.
,, temporary	4·5° ,,	5·9° ,,	—	6·4° ,,
Total ...	9·0°	9·1°		10·0°
Poisonous metals	Nil.	—		None.

Sample of water for bacteriological examination—

Date. 1902	Water.	Period of Cultivation.	Number.
15 July ...	Pure water tank	2 days... ...	30
22 ,, ...	Do.	Do.	3
31 ,, ...	Do.	Do.	5
5 Aug. ...	Do.	Do.	11
18 ,, ...	River water	Do.	2,126
18 ,, ...	Pure water tank	Do.	29

WORCESTER—*continued.*

Annual supply of water—

For domestic purposes	...	...	...	...	397,000,000 gals.
„ trade „	...	...	...	...	120,000,000 „
„ municipal „	...	...	...	...	30,000,000 „
In bulk to other authorities	...	...	...	3,000,000 „

Maximum day's consumption, 2,300,000 gals.

Assessment charge on net annual poor rate. Owners of houses or tenements under £10 are liable.

Price per 1,000 gals., 7d., with a minimum of 2s. 6d. per quarter ; meter rents from 1s. 6d. per quarter for ¼ inch to 20s. for 4 inch meter.

Wordsley (supplied by STOURBRIDGE).

Workington. Railway, L.N.W. Distance from London, 312 miles.
Authority, Corporation of Workington.
Chairman, Mayor of Workington.
Clerk to authority, John Warwick, Town Clerk.
Engineer and Manager, W. L. Eaglesfield. Chief Assistant Engineer, H. B. Williams.
Office, Town Hall, Workington.
Loans outstanding, £90,894.
Works established, 1878. Cockermouth and Workington Water Act, 1878, and Workington Corporation Act, 1899.
New main, 21 in. diameter, and Intake Works completed, 1902.
Total population supplied with water, 41,000.
Average death rate, 16·8 per 1,000.
District of supply—Borough of Workington, Cockermouth, Brigham, Great Broughton, Wyndham Row, Camerton, Great Clifton, Little Clifton, Grey-southern, Seaton, Stainburn, and Harrington.
Source of supply—Crummock Lake, Watershed 25 sq. miles, comprising three lakes, viz.—Buttermere, Loweswater and Crummock Water. Height of supply above O.D., 322·75ft. Area of Lake, 644 acres.
Analysis of water—

Smell when heated to 100° Fahr.	...	...	...	none
Chlorine, in chlorides	...	...	...	...	0·56
Phosphoric Acid in phosphates	...	...	...	none
Nitrogen in nitrates	...	...	...	...	0·007
Ammonia	...	...	...	...	...	none
Albuminoid ammonia	...	...	...	...	0·0008
Oxygen absorbed in 15 minutes	...	...	...	0·0252
„ „ „ 4 hours	...	...	...	0·0495
Hardness in degrees before boiling	...	...	...	0·4
„ „ „ after boiling	...	...	...	0·4
Total solid matter dried at 200° Fahr.	...	...	1·96

Microscopical examination, very satisfactory.
Filtration, none ; water passes through copper screen at intake.
Storage in impounding reservoirs, 505,000,000 gals. ; in service reservoirs, 1,013,500 gals.
Annual supply of water, 547,368,000 gals.
Average daily supply per head—domestic, 32 gals.
Maximum day's supply, 35·70 gals. per head in March.
Charges authorised, not exceeding 10 per cent. on rateable value.
Actual charges—
On all properties with a rateable value of under £15—2s. in the £ or minimum charge.

WORKINGTON—_continued._

On all properties with a rateable value of £15 and under £25—1s. 11d. in the £.

"	"	"	£25	"	£35—1s. 10d.	"
"	"	"	£35	"	£45—1s. 9d.	"
"	"	"	£45	"	£55—1s. 8d.	"
"	"	"	£55	"	£65—1s. 7d.	"
"	"	"	£65 and over		1s. 6d.	"

Lock-up shops, one-half the domestic rate, with a minimum of 10s. per annum.
Quarterly scale for water supplied for trade purposes by meter—
Under 15,000 gals., 10s. per quarter.
Above 15,000 gals. and under 30,000 gals., 9d. per 1,000 gals.

"	30,000	"	"	50,000	"	8d.	"	"
"	50,000	"	"	100,000	"	7½d.	"	"
"	100,000	"	"	150,000	"	7d.	"	"
"	150,000	"	"	200,000	"	6½d.	"	"
"	200,000	"	"	400,000	"	6d.	"	"
"	400,000	"	"	700,000	"	5½d.	"	"
"	700,000	"	"	1,000,000	"	5d.	"	"
"	1,000,000	"	"	2,000,000	"	4½d.	"	"
"	2,000,000	"	"	"		4d.	"	"

Trunk mains, two side by side, each 15 miles long, one varies in diameter from 15in. to 13in., and the new one laid under 1899 Act is 21in. diameter; primary distributing mains, 30 miles.
Workington has another supply of water for WORKS PURPOSES ONLY from the River Derwent.
Authority, officials, &c., same as above.
Loans outstanding, £16,200. Annual profit, £1,121. Works established, 1885, under Workington Local Board Act, 1883.
Annual supply of water, mostly to iron and steel works, 661,000,000 gals.
Source of supply, the River Derwent.
Length of mains, 3¼ miles.

Worksop, Notts. Railways, M.S.L., G.N., and M. Distance from London, 146¼ miles.
Authority, Worksop Waterworks Company.
Office, 5, Eastgate, Worksop.
Share capital paid up, £17,000. Loan capital, £3,000. Interest on loan, 4 per cent. debentures, 4½ per cent. pref. stock. Dividend, 8 per cent.
Works established, 1871. Special Act, 1875.
Total population supplied, 16,000.
Annual supply of water, 88,000,000 gals.
Source of supply, well in red sandstone, 356 feet deep.
Storage capacity, 3,000,000 gals.
Scale of charges—assessment charge; rack rental, municipal purposes, by meter on scale.
Price per 1,000 gals., trade, 1s. to 6d.

Worplesdon (supplied by WOKING).

Worsley, Higher Division, Lancs. (supplied by BOLTON).

Worsley (supplied by MANCHESTER).

Worsborough, Yorks. (supplied by BARNSLEY).

Worthing, Sussex. Railway, L.B.S.C. Distance from London, 61 miles.
Authority, Corporation.
Borough Engineer, Frank Roberts, A.M.I.C.E.

Worthing—*continued.*

Office, Municipal Offices, Liverpool Road.
Capital expended, £24,590.
Towns and villages in the area supplied, Worthing Broadwater, West Tarring, Durrington, and Salvington.
Total population of area supplied, 26,000.
Annual supply of water, 320,000,000 gals.
Daily consumption per head, all purposes, 34 gals.
Source of supply, wells and boreholes in the chalk.
Storage capacity, 2,500,000 gals.
Character of water, chemically and bacteriologically of very high quality.
Death rate, 14·9 per 1,000 in 1906.
Number of meters, about 450.
Length of mains, 38 miles.
Scale of charges, assessment, 10d. in £ on rateable value.
Price for 1,000 gals., 1s. for first 100,000, 10d. for second, and 9d. for third.

Wrabness (supplied by Tendring Hundred Waterworks Co.).

Wrexham, Wales. Railways, G.W., G.C. & C. Distance from London, 201¾ miles.
Authority, Wrexham and East Denbighshire Water Company.
Chairman, J. Allington Hughes.
Engineer and Secretary, Frederick Storr.
Office, Egerton Street.
Share capital, £189,000.
Loan capital, £50,750.
Dividend, 4 per cent., £4 11s. per cent., and 6¼ per cent.
Total revenue received, £10,479.
Towns and villages in the area supplied, Wrexham, and 55 townships in the counties of Denbigh, Flint and Cheshire.
Works established, 1864.
Special Acts, 1864, 1874, 1880, 1902. Provisional Order, 1898.
Total population supplied, 31,300.
Annual supply of water, 246,000,000 gals.
Daily consumption per head, 21·6 gals.
Sources of supply, Upland surface water, streams and springs, and deep boreholes in millstone grit.
Storage capacity, 170,000,000 gals.
Character of water, 7·4° hardness.
System of filtration, sand.
Number of meters, 150.
Length of mains, 105 miles.
Assessment charge, 6 per cent. on gross value.
Price per 1,000 gals., 1s. 6d. to 6d. ; street watering, 9d.

Wroughton, part of (supplied by Swindon).

Wyberton (supplied by Boston).

Wyches, The (supplied by Malvern).

Wyke (supplied by Bradford, Yorks).

Wylam (supplied by Newcastle-on-Tyne).

Wymering (supplied by Portsmouth).

Wymington (supplied by Rushden)

Wynnstay (supplied by Ruabon).

Yardley (supplied by Birmingham).

Yarmouth, Norfolk. *See* Great Yarmouth.

Yeadon, Yorks. Railways, G.N. and M. Distance from London, 205¾ miles.
  Authority, Yeadon Waterworks Co.
  Chairman, Joseph Peel.
  Manager and Secretary, Wm. Parsons.
  Office, High Street.
  Share capital paid up, £44,991. Loan capital paid up, £8,760.
  Interest, 3½ per cent. Dividend, £7 and £4 18s.
  Works established, 1862. Special Acts, 1870 to 1889.
  Total population of area supplied, 15,000.
  Sources of supply, gathering grounds.
  Towns and villages in the area supplied, Yeadon, Rawdon, and Guiseley.
  Character of water, soft.
  Storage capacity, 100,000,000 gals.
  Assessment charge, 7½ per cent. to 10 per cent. on rateable value.
  Price per 1,000 gals., trade, 6d.
  Number of meters, 34.

Yelverton, Devon (supplied by Plymouth).

Yeovil, Somerset. Railways, G.W. & L.S.W. Distance from London, 133 miles.
  Authority, Corporation, 1874.
  Town Clerk, H. B. Batten.
  Manager, A. Oddy.
  Office, Municipal Offices.
  Area supplied, 800 acres.
  Works established, 1874. Special Acts, 1874, 1896, 1898.
  Total population of area supplied, 12,000.
  Daily consumption per head, 28 gals.
  Sources of supply, springs at Melbury, Bubb and Stockwood.
  Storage capacity, 1,267,798 gals.
  Character of water, 19° hardness.
  Death rate, 12·19 per 1,000.
  Number of meters, 90.
  Assessment charge, rateable value.
  Price per 1,000 gals., trade, sliding scale, 2s. 6d. to 4d.

Yiewsley (supplied by Rickmansworth).

Yoker (supplied by Glasgow).

York. Railways, N.E., G.N., L.N.W., M., G.E., L.Y. and G.C. Distance from
  London, 188½ miles.
  Authority, the York Waterworks Company.
  Chairman, Sir Joseph Sykes Rymer, J.P.
  Manager, Engineer and Secretary, W. H. Humphreys, A.M.I.C.E.
  Office, Lendal Bridge, York.
  Share capital paid up, £180,000.
  Loan   „   „   £25,000.
  Dividend, pref., 5 and 3½ per cent. ; ordinary, 10 and 7 per cent.
  Interest on loans, 3½ per cent.

YORK—*continued*.

Works first constructed, 1677.
Formation of present company, 1846.
Special Acts, York Waterworks Acts, 1846, 1876, 1895.
Total population of area of control, 1901, 90,000.
Estimated population actually supplied (1906), 93,000.
Average death rate, 14·63 per 1,000.
Towns and villages within the area of control—City of York, Acomb, Bishop-
thorpe, Clifton, Dringhouses, Fulford, Haxby, Heworth, Huntington, Middle-
thorpe, New Earswick, Strensall, Towthorpe, and Wigginton.
Source of supply, impounding reservoirs on River Ouse.
Character of water — excellent for potable and manufacturing purposes;
temporary hardness, 9·8°; permanent, 1·7°; total, 11·5°.
System of filtration, double filtration through sand after settlement in three
subsidiary reservoirs.
Filtering area provided, 15,100 square yards in 8 filter-beds.
Storage capacity, 3 reservoirs, 6,800,000 gals.
Service reservoir, Severus Hill, capacity, 2,000,000 gals., open.
Annual supply of water, 1,058,890,000 gals.
Average daily supply per head—
　For domestic and municipal purposes　...　...　2,363,500 gals.
　　„　trade purposes　...　...　...　...　...　811,500　„
Maximum day's consumption...　...　...　...　3,721,000　„　in August.
Total quantity of water drawn per annum, 1,135,304,000 gals.
Assessment charge, 5 per cent. to 3 per cent. on annual value.
Price per 1,000 gals.—meter supplies, 6d. to 1s. 6d.; for municipal purposes
free.
Number of meters in use, 984.
Length of supply and distributing mains, 92 miles.

Yorktown, Hants. (supplied by FRIMLEY).

Ystrad, Pentre, R.S.O., Glam. (G. and W.). Railway, Taff Vale. Distance from
London, 178 miles.
Authority, Rhondda Urban District Council.
Chairman, W. D. Wight.
Clerk to Authority, W. P. Nicholas.
Manager, Octavius Thomas.
Office, Pentre, R.S.O., Glam.
Loans, outstanding £116,000.
Works established, 1868. Purchased 1898. Special Acts, 1868, 1890, 1896, 1899.
Total population of area supplied, 70,000.
Towns and villages in the area supplied, Ystrad, Treherbert, Treorchy, Ton,
Trealaw, Llwynypia, Tonypandy, Penygraig, and Pentre.
Source of supply, springs and streams.
Character of water, 2° hardness. Filtration sand.
Daily consumption per head, domestic 16 gals., trade ½ gal.
Scale of charges—assessment, 5⅝ to 9¾ per cent.
Price for 1,000 gals., 1s. 6d. to 6d.
Total length of mains, 50 miles.
Number of meters, 70.

Zukella, Yorks. (supplied by HULL).

DIRECTORY AND STATISTICS

OF

FOREIGN WATER WORKS

WITH OFFICES IN LONDON.

II.—DIRECTORY AND STATISTICS

OF

FOREIGN WATER WORKS

WITH OFFICES IN LONDON.

Alexandria, Egypt.
Authority, Alexandria Water Co., Ltd.
Chairman, J. E. Cornish, M.I.C.E.
Secretary, J. Euston Cornish, Jun.
Manager and Resident Engineer, H. R. C. Blagden, M.I.M.E.
Office, Alexandria, Egypt.
Share capital paid up, £500,000 ; last dividend, 10½ per cent.
Works established 1859, company formed 1879.
Total population supplied, 400,000.
Area supplied, Alexandria and Ramleh-Mex.
Source of supply, from the River Nile by canal about 45 miles.
Character of water, soft.   Hardness after filtration. 58 Cª C.O.² per litre.
System of filtration, Jewell Rapid Filtration gravity system.
Storage capacity—impounding reservoirs, 7,000,000 gals. ; service reservoirs, 1,500,000 gals.
Head on distributing mains—max., 110 ft. ; min., 10 ft.
Annual supply of water, 3,300,000,000 gals.
Maximum day's supply, 7,500,000 gals. in August.
Length of mains, about 150 miles.
Price per 1,000 gals., 10d.

Anglo-Portuguese. (G. & W.)
Owner of the Gas and Water Works, Figuiera da Foz.
Chairman, R. Laidlaw.
Secretary, W. A. Laurie.
Engineer, A. F. Phillips, C.E.
Manager, W. B. Jones, A.M.I.C.E.
London Office, 38, Parliament Street, S.W.
Works established, 1887.
Total population supplied, 7,000.

Antwerp.
Chairman, Easton Devonshire.
Secretary, J. M. Hamilton.
Manager, Ad. Kemna.
London Office, Suffolk House, 5, Laurence Pountney Hill, E.C.
Share capital, £300,000.
Loan capital, £96,200.
Dividend, 8½ per cent. (to 31st Dec., 1906).
Works established, 1880.
Total population supplied, 150,000.
Source of supply—River Nethe, Anderson's revolving purifier used.
Character of water, soft.

Beaconsfield, South Africa. *See* KIMBERLEY.

Beyrouth.
　　Authority, Beyrouth Waterworks Company, Ltd.
　　Chairman, Edward Easton, C.E.
　　Manager and Engineer, Percy Martindale.
　　Secretary, A. C. B. Douglas.
　　London Office, 13, Throgmorton Avenue, E.C.
　　Works established, 1873.
　　Source of supply, springs in limestone mountain.
　　Character of water, 10° hardness.

Bulawayo, S. Africa. Rhodesian Railway. Distance from London, 7,400 miles.
　　Authority, Bulawayo Waterworks Co.
　　Chairman, Colonel the Rt. Hon. A. R. M. Lockwood, M.P.
　　Secretary, Geo. R. Saunders.
　　Engineer, F. L. Lister.
　　Managers, Willoughby's Consolidated Co., Ld.
　　Offices, Bulawayo, Rhodesia, and 5, London Wall Buildings, London, E.C.
　　Share capital paid up, £206,000; last dividend, 2 per cent.
　　Loan　　,,　　,,　　£60,000 at 6 per cent.
　　Works established 1895, completed 1898. Special Acts, Agreement under
　　　　British South Africa Co.
　　Total population supplied, about 5,000.
　　Towns and villages in the area supplied, Bulawayo and suburbs.
　　Impounding reservoir (capacity, 42,000,000) gals. four miles south of Buluwayo.
　　Character of water, excellent.
　　Annual supply of water, 11,256,700 gals.
　　Price per 100 gals.—Sliding scale up to 3,000 gals. 1s. 3d. per 100 gals.
　　　　　　　　　　　From 3,000 to 10,000 gals. ... 1s. 0d.　　,,　　,,
　　　　　　　　　　　,, 10,000 ,, 20,000 ,, ... 0s. 11d.　　,,　　,,
　　　　　　　　　　　Over 20,000 gals.　...　... 0s. 9d.　　,,　　,,

Cagliari. (G. and W.)
　　Authority, Cagliari Gas and Water Co., Ltd.
　　Chairman, Sir John Aird, Bart.
　　Secretary, Wm. B. Peat.
　　Manager, Sophus Simmelkjor.
　　London Office, 11, Ironmonger Lane, E.C.
　　Area supplied, with villages, equal to 7 square miles.
　　Works established 1862 to 1865. Special Act, 1861 (for water), August 2nd,
　　　　1863 Italian Parliament. Company formed 1866.
　　Total population supplied, 65,000.
　　Source of supply—impounding reservoir on mountain stream; water collected
　　　　during winter.

CAGLIARI—*continued.*

Character of water, very soft.

Analysis						
				Na	Cl	0·119,311
				Ca	Cl2	0·043,209
				Ca	S.O.4	0·005,977
				Mg	S.O.4	0·016,488
				Mg	C.O.3	0·025,145
				K2	C.O.3	0·022,990
Organic matters	...	...	...	...	...	0·014·875

Total per 1,000 grains 0·248,530

Or, shortly, ¼ gramme impurities in 1,000 grammes of water.

System of filtration, sand, no softening.

Storage capacity—impounding reservoirs, 1,250,000 C.M., service reservoirs, 10,00 C.M.

Pressure on distributing mains—max., 120 lbs. ; min., 20 lbs. per square inch.

Annual supply of water, 1,355,389 C.M.

Average daily supply per head, 64 litres.

Maximum day's supply, 4,871 C.M. in August.

Charges, 25 to 40 centimes per cubic metre.

Number of meters, 1,390.

Length of supply mains, 18,600 metres ; distributing mains, 18,000 metres.

Galatz Waterworks Co., Ltd.
London Offices, Caxton House, Westminster, S.W.

Imperial Continental Waterworks Co.
London Offices, 35, New Broad Street, E.C.
No returns supplied.

Johannesburg Waterworks Estate and Exploration Company, Ltd.
Sold to the Rand Water Board in 1905.

Kimberley and Beaconsfield.
Owners, Kimberley Waterworks Co., Ltd.
Date of formation, 1880.
Source of supply, the Vaal River.
Area supplied, Kimberley and Beaconsfield.
Office, 20-21, Laurence Pountney Lane, E.C.

Menzies Waterworks, Ld.
Authority, Menzies Waterworks, Ld.
Manager at Menzies, R. Gouinon.
Secretary, C. J. Cooke.
London Office, 24, St. Mary Axe, E.C.
Share capital, £50,007.
Dividend, 5 per cent.

MENZIES WATERWORKS, LD.—*continued.*

Works established, August 15th, 1895.
Owing to the introduction by the West Australian Government of a system of
water supply which directly competes with the system of the company, the
directors have been empowered to dispose of the company's plant with a view
to winding up.

Monte Video.
Authority, The Monte Video Waterworks Co., Ltd.
Chairman, James Anderson.
Secretary, George Proctor.
Resident Engineer, William Gawley.
Consulting Engineer, Hon. R. C. Parsons.
London Office, 52, Moorgate Street, E.C.
Share capital paid up, £500,000 ; last dividend 7 per cent.
Loan   „   £200,000 first debenture stock at 5 per cent.
  „   „   „   £150,000 second debenture stock at 5 per cent
Works established, 1879.
Total population supplied, 200,000.
Source of supply, River St. Lucia.
Character of water, very good.

Naples Waterworks Co., Ltd.
London Office, 5, Laurence Pountney Hill, E.C.

Prietas Water Co., Ltd.
Secretary, James Wright.
London Office, 3 and 4 Great Winchester Street, E.C.
Share capital paid up £20,000.   Last dividend, 20 per cent.
Works established, 1899.
District of supply, Mining Camp at Sonora, Mexico.
Source of supply, springs.

Rosario.
Authority, Consolidated Waterworks Company of Rosario, Ltd.
Chairman, W. T. Western.
Secretary, G. Proctor.
Resident Engineer, W. J. Martin.
Consulting Engineer, Hon. R. C. Parsons.
London Office, 52, Moorgate Street, E.C.
Works established, 1886.
Share capital paid up, ordinary shares, £149,625 ; 6 per cent. preference shares,
£140,000.   Debenture stock at 4 per cent., £190,000.   Dividends (1907),
ordinary, 7 per cent. ; preference, 6 per cent.
Number of services, 1904, 10,374 ; 1905, 11,255 ; 1906, 12,009.
Total population supplied, 150,000.
Source of supply, River Paraná.
Character of water, good.

St. Petersburg (City of) New Waterworks Co., Ltd.
The works are now the property of the Municipality of St. Petersburg, Aug.
1901

San Nicolas, Argentine Republic. Railways, Buenos Ayres and Pacific.
Authority, San Nicolas Waterworks Co., Ltd.
Chairman, A. F. H. Darby.
Secretary, G. Carnaby Harrower, C.A.
Manager, G. R. W. Tucker.
London Office, College Hill Chambers, E.C.
Share capital, £120,000.
Dividend, 1, 1¾, and 2 per cent.; pref., 2 per cent.
Works established, 1892. Concession dated 24th Sept., 1887.
Total population supplied, about 19,000.
Source of supply, River Paraná.
Storage capacity, 480,000 gals. (can supply 720,000 gals. in 24 hours).
Price per 1,000 gals., 2s. 8d. to 2s. 4d. Free to public fountains and prisons.

Santos.
Authority, City of Santos Improvements Co.
Chairman, D. M. Fox, M.I.C.E.
Secretary, J. E. Rimmer.
London Office, 174, Gresham House, E.C.
Consulting Engineer in London, H. K. Heyland
Area supplied, Santos only.
Total population supplied, 45,000.
Daily supply of water, 6,500,000 gals.
Daily consumption, 2,500,000 gals.
Sources of supply, gravitation, 100 miles of main.
Number of meters, 1,900.
Length of mains, 130 miles.
Price per 1,000 gals., domestic and trade, 9d.

Seville.
Chairman, C. Lambert.
Secretary, J. M. Hamilton.
Engineer and Manager, C. A. Friend, M.I.C.E.
London Office, Suffolk House, 5, Laurence Pountney Hill, E.C.
Share capital, £271,120.
Loan capital, £160,480.
Dividend, 1 per cent. (31st March, 1906).
Works established, 1883.
Sources of supply, springs in the Guadaira Valley.
Character of water, soft.
Scale of charges—assessment charge, special.

Shanghai, China.
Authority, Shanghai Waterworks Co., Ltd.
Chairman, A. McLeod, Shanghai.
Secretaries, A. P. Wood, Shanghai ; W. G. Howells, London.
Engineer, A. P. Woods, M.I.C.E.
Office, Shanghai.
London Office, 60, Gracechurch Street, E.C.
Total capital invested, £410,000. Last dividend, 13 per cent.
Interest on loans, 5 per cent. and 6 per cent.
Works established, 1880.
Total population supplied, 1881, 250,000 ; 1891, 325,000 ; 1907, 450,000.
Source of supply, Wangpu river, an affluent of the river Yang-Tze-Kiang. Shang-
hai is situated on the Wangpu.
Character of water, soft.

SHANGHAI—*continued.*

    Annual supply of water, 1,781,114,573 gals.
    Maximum month's supply, 191,601,708 gals.
    Area supplied, 3 square miles.
    Towns and villages in the area supplied—the foreign settlements of Shanghai,
       which embrace a large native population.
    Scale of charges—
       Assessment, 5 per cent. on rentals.
       Price per 1,000 gals., municipal purposes, 1 tael for 5,000 gals.

Tarapaca.
    Owners, Tarapaca Waterworks Co., Ltd.
    Formed, 1888.
    Share capital paid up, £400,000.
    Office, 55 and 56, Bishopsgate Street Within, E.C.

"Meldrum"
Furnaces.

(IMPROVED LOW GRATE TYPE).

We have fitted scores of Boilers at Water Works, and secured

Minimum Fuel Cost, Smoke Reduction, Ample Steam Supply.

If you require these advantages, please write us.

MELDRUM BROS., Ltd., TIMPERLEY, MANCHESTER.

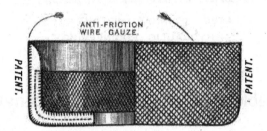

26

E. TIMMINS & SONS,

LTD.,

Bridgewater Foundry,

———— RUNCORN.

General and Artesian Well Engineers, Pumpmakers, and Ironfounders.

Contractors for

WATERWORKS,

ARTESIAN WELLS,

DUG WELLS,

BORINGS for WATER and MINERALS,

TRIAL SHAFTS, &c.

Gas, Soap, and Chemical Works Plant.

PUMPING, DIVING, AND VARIOUS PLANTS FOR HIRE.

ESTABLISHED 1827.

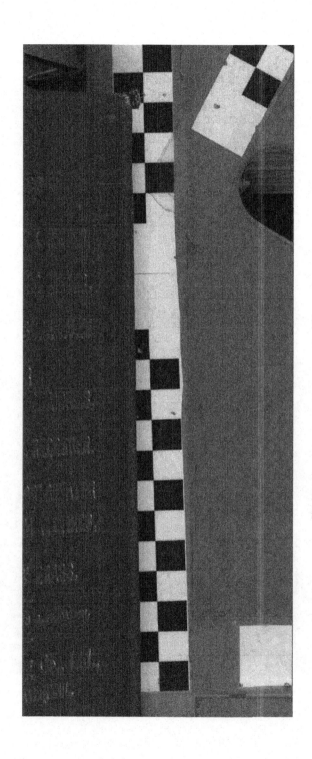

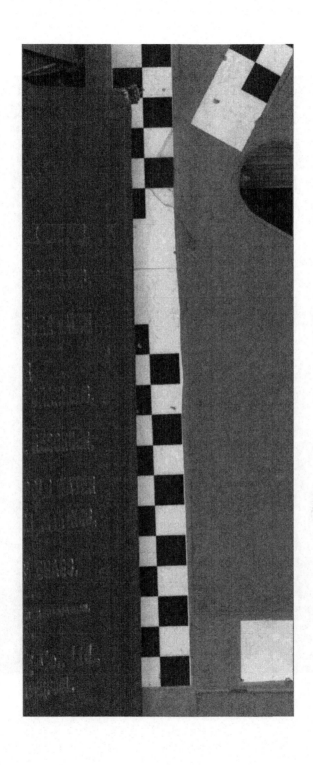

CPSIA information can be obtained
at www.ICGtesting.com
Printed in the USA
BVOW06*0942031217

501731BV00008B/15/P

9 781347 030462